ALL 4 volumes of
The Palace of Nestor
are OP, 1992

28 ⁵⁰

Ⓐ 001828

for This
volume

D0161472

ALL 4 volumes of
The Palace of Nestor
are OP, 1992

THE PALACE OF NESTOR
AT PYLOS
IN WESTERN MESSENIA

THE PALACE OF NESTOR
AT PYLOS
IN WESTERN MESSENIA

Excavations Conducted by
the University of Cincinnati
1939, 1952-1965

Edited by
Carl W. Blegen and Marion Rawson

❖

Published with a Grant from
The Classics Fund
of the University of Cincinnati,
a Gift of Louise Taft Semple
in Memory of Charles Phelps Taft

THE PALACE OF NESTOR AT PYLOS IN WESTERN MESSENIA

VOLUME III

ACROPOLIS AND LOWER TOWN
THOLOI, GRAVE CIRCLE, AND
CHAMBER TOMBS
DISCOVERIES OUTSIDE THE CITADEL

BY CARL W. BLEGEN, MARION RAWSON,
LORD WILLIAM TAYLOUR, WILLIAM P. DONOVAN

1973
PUBLISHED FOR THE UNIVERSITY OF CINCINNATI
BY PRINCETON UNIVERSITY PRESS

L.C. Card: 65-17131
ISBN 0-691-03529-6

Printed in the United States of America
by Princeton University Press, Princeton, New Jersey
Illustrations Printed by the Meriden Gravure Company
Meriden, Connecticut

TO THE MEMORY OF

ELIZABETH PIERCE BLEGEN

FOREWORD

ACKNOWLEDGMENTS

THE Cincinnati Archaeological Expedition for nearly twenty seasons has been carrying on excavation in Western Messenia (Figs. 299, 300) at the site we have called the Palace of Nestor. We are now reaching the end of our enterprise and are glad to have another opportunity to express our warm thanks to all those who bountifully helped in various ways, and also to those who have generously taken part in conducting, supervising, and recording the work itself.

Professor and Mrs. William T. Semple founded and supported the re-excavation of Troy from 1932 to 1938; and later provided for the Cincinnati Expedition in Western Messenia in 1939 before the war and from 1952 to 1969. In her will Mrs. Semple presented to the University of Cincinnati the Classics Fund, "a gift of Louise Taft Semple in memory of Charles Phelps Taft." We thank the Trustees of the Fund, which has made it possible to complete the work of uncovering the capital of King Nestor and to publish the results. We remember gratefully our benefactors, Mr. and Mrs. Semple.

Dr. Konstantinos Kourouniotis, who invited us to join him in Messenia to explore that province in search of Mycenaean settlements and tombs, will always be remembered. He came with us to Englianos in 1938 and 1939, but his death in 1945 denied us the benefit of his continued collaboration. His memory is honored in the foreword and dedication of Volume I.

Elizabeth Pierce Blegen, who died September 21, 1966, left an emptiness in our staff at Chora. She was a member from the very beginning in 1939 when she took over the responsibility for the excavation of Tholos III; the account of the tomb in this Volume is drawn largely from her notebook. During many later campaigns she uncovered part of the southwestern unit of the palace and much of the steep scarp on the southwest and around the southern corner of the hilltop.

Piet de Jong died April 20, 1967. His training as an architect, his admirable drawings, watercolors, and sketches, his thoughtful and always helpful advice, and his ingenuity in overcoming problems and difficulties, all these qualities made him a wonderful archaeologist, and a congenial companion. His death was a calamity for our expedition and will be long mourned. Our remembrance of Piet de Jong will live by his works. Volume II is dedicated to his memory.

To the Greek Archaeological Service and to its earlier leaders and its present Inspector General, Professor Spyridon Marinatos, our colleague here in Messenia, we extend our warmest thanks for friendly help always shown us during the eighteen seasons of excavating in and about the palace. We are deeply indebted to the Service for rebuilding the dome of Tholos IV and especially for erecting a metal roof over the Main Building of the palace so that visitors may walk about in the rooms and halls whatever the weather may be. We also felicitate the Service for the handsome Museum built in Chora, which has already nearly filled its *vitrines* with gold objects, Mycenaean jewelry, bronzes, frescoes, abundant pottery, all from Western Messenia from the work of Dr. Marinatos and from that of the Cincinnati Expedition.

Dr. Nikolaos Yalouris, during his service as Ephor at Olympia, also had charge of Messenia and was unfailingly ready to aid us. He and Mrs. Yalouris and students from the College Year in Athens set up the new Museum. Mr. George Papathanasopoulos later took over the ephorate and often visited us, having worked with us through three campaigns at Pylos.

We were especially grateful that the Tsakonas family of Chora, who owned the olive grove on the Englianos hilltop and part of the deep hollow below, graciously transferred to the Greek Archaeological Service the land on which stand the remains of the Palace of Nestor.

We were greatly impressed by the friendly willingness with which the owners of the fields, threshing floors, olive orchards, etc., allowed us to dig soundings in exploring both higher and lower ground encircling the Englianos hill. In Volume I we thanked all those who gave such permission. Since many of these widespread areas were touched in our search for a circuit wall, the lower town, and tombs, we would like to thank the owners once again by name: George Petropoulos, Nikos Antonopoulos, Andreas Anastasopoulos, Mr. and Mrs. P. Kanakaris, Evstathis Vayenas, Nikolaos Gliatas, and in wider areas Demos Paraskevopoulos, Evstathis Deriziotis, Panagiotis Tsakalis, Aristomenos Kontos, Nikos Charalambopoulos, and the Kokkevis family, all of Chora.

A good many objects from the Palace of Nestor were sent to the National Museum; some are now on exhibition, others are in storage. Most of them were taken there in the early years of our excavations when no museum was close to Chora, and those nearest were already full of archaeological objects. We were very grateful to Dr. Karouzos, who gave us table space in a room opening from the Mycenaean Hall, and also space for storage in the basement of the National Museum. The same generous hospitality was shown us by Dr. B. Kallipolitis when he succeeded Dr. Karouzos. It was a great help to us also to have the expert workmanship of the Museum's trained menders and cleaners. All the Linear B tablets from Pylos are stored in the National Museum, some examples exhibited, and others in safe storage. Objects from Tholos III and Tholos IV are also on exhibition or stored in the National Museum.

Grateful acknowledgment is made to all who shared in the preparation of the drawings that appear in this volume: maps, plans, and sections—Hero Athanasiades, William B. Dinsmoor, Jr., William P. Donovan, Angela C. Evans, Jesse E. Fant, Lewey T. Lands, George Papathanasopoulos, Joseph W. Shaw, H. A. Shelley, William D. Taylour, Demetrios R. Theocharis, John Travlos, and Wilma E. Wolfley; miscellaneous objects—E. Gillieron (Figs. 169, 170), Piet de Jong (Figs. 108, 192, 193, 231), A. C. Evans (Figs. 227:8-11, 291) and H. A. Shelley (Figs. 191, 195, 226, 227:1-7, 273, 279) based on sketches by W. D. Taylour; pots—Piet de Jong (watercolors, Figs. 235, 236, 244; reconstruction of a hunting scene on a krater, Fig. 289).

The Cincinnati Expedition has been very fortunate in its photographers, who have given so much of their knowledge and skill. We are greatly indebted to Miss Alison Frantz, who came to Pylos in five seasons, ranging from 1952 to 1960, before the roof of the main unit was built. Some of her photographs of the Northeast Gateway, the Belvedere area, and Tholos IV appear in this volume (Figs. 4, 186-189). We owe particular thanks to Professor Mabel Lang, who took hundreds of pictures of pots and of innumerable potsherds and miscellaneous objects recovered from soundings, trenches, and tombs. These comprise a large part of the illustrations.

Professor John L. Caskey in 1962 photographed nearly all the pots in the Chora Museum from our excavations in Messenia, many singly, some in groups, on nearly 300 negatives. This was an arduous task, but indispensable for the completion of our records. Emile Saraphis of Athens in 1963 came to the Chora Museum and took many pictures of room- and tomb-groups and of pots from the palace and from tombs for Volume III. Lord William Taylour, a photographer in his own right, supplied us with most of the illustrations for the areas under his supervision: Tholos IV (Figs. 175, 178, 180-185), the grave circle (Figs. 197-224), Chamber Tomb K-1 (Figs. 266-272), the Deriziotis property (Figs. 275-278), Chamber Tomb K-2 (Figs. 280-290), and the Protogeometric Tholos (Figs. 294-297). Kosta Konstantopoulos, the photographer of the National Museum in Athens, took pictures for us of the many miscellaneous objects from Tholos III and Tholos IV and of the pots put together from sherds found in Tholos III.

It is eminently proper to offer our warmest thanks to all the members of the Cincinnati Expedition who worked in the trenches and the tombs at the excavations, and in the workrooms and museum, some through numerous seasons and others for shorter periods, all deserving to be mentioned by name: Marion Rawson (14 seasons), Elizabeth Blegen (13), Mabel Lang (11), Piet de Jong (9), Lord William Taylour (6, and several shorter visits), Demetrios R. Theocharis (4), George Papathanasopoulos (3), William P. Donovan (3 and short visits), William A. McDonald (2); others for one season: George E. Mylonas (1952), Eugene Vanderpool (1952), Rosemary Hope (1953), Watson Smith (1954), Emmett L. Bennett, Jr. (1954), Robert J. Buck (1954), Rolf Hubbe (1955), Patricia Donovan (1957), David French (1958), Caryl F. and William G. Kittredge (1962), Peter Smith (1963), John Pedley (1964), John Camp, II (1968), Eiler Hendrickson, Jr. (1969). Mrs. Kittredge, Mrs. Donovan, Mr. P. Smith assisted Miss Rawson with the pottery inventory. Miss Anne H. Blegen typed long sections of manuscripts and assisted in describing manifold small objects from Tholos III for the catalogue. Miss Lang did the typing needed in Chora. To all these workers we extend our deep gratitude for their help in completing our undertaking.

As mentioned in the Forewords of Volumes I and II, Dionysios Androutsakis was an admirable foreman through all the campaigns from 1952 to the end. He became at once an indispensable organizer, ingenious and improvising, who faced and overcame all difficulties. He also quickly learned to understand antiquities and to take the greatest care to protect all objects uncovered. We owe him a great debt.

The American School of Classical Studies at Athens from the beginning to the end of our work has generously come to the rescue whenever we were in need. We extend our warmest thanks to three Directors, Professor John L. Caskey, Professor Henry S. Robinson, and his successor, Professor James McCredie, and to all the members of the staff of the School.

Through nineteen seasons of archaeological activity the people of Chora have been very kind and friendly, doing everything they could to help us. At the suggestion of Dr. Charalambos Panagopoulos in 1954, when he was the President of the Village Council, that body agreed to turn over to our expedition a small empty clinic, equipped with beds, attached to the chapel of the Assumption. With some additional rooms, a kitchen, and plumbing, a home-like, comfortable center was made for our headquarters. From 1954 to 1969 Mrs. Antonia Theo. Matzaka ruled the kitchen, and when we were many, with her daughters, kept the house neat and in good order, and provided the table daily with the best food that could be found, a necessity to archaeologists working in the open air all day. Our deep-felt thanks to Madame Antonia.

In the western hemisphere, likewise, we are indebted to friends who have aided us in various ways. At our headquarters in Cincinnati numerous assistants have given us a welcome hand. We thank most cordially the President of the University of Cincinnati, Dr. Walter Langsam and Mrs. Langsam, who together ventured on a long journey to give us the deep pleasure of their visit at the excavation. To the other administrative officers of the University, who always encouraged us and did what they could to make our efforts easy, we express our gratitude.

Mrs. Cedric G. Boulter offered valiant aid in reading manuscript, in judging, choosing, and arranging innumerable illustrations, and in coping with all manner of difficulties. She and Professor Boulter and Mr. and Mrs. Edward L. Wolfley, Jr., supplied the extra energy needed to bring the work to completion.

Miss Jeannette Woodward and Miss Grace Rowe helped in the final preparation of the manuscript and plates. Mrs. Wolfley trimmed the photographic prints, and placed them to their best advantage on the plates. She also made finished plans and sections of the chamber tombs excavated, measured, and drawn by Mr. Donovan. Mrs. Donald W. Bradeen typed the final manuscripts and was very skillful in reading difficult handwriting.

PLAN OF PUBLICATIONS

The publication of Volume I in December 1966 described the palace along with its many rooms and their contents of innumerable kinds, including more than 7,000 pots, cups, and other vessels of 80 different shapes. Volume II appeared early in 1969, the work of Professor Lang, who through seven annual campaigns cleaned, sorted, and joined thousands of fragments of frescoes fallen from the walls or thrown out, and in three added seasons completed her book.

Volume III presents the discoveries made under and outside the palace, clustered about the royal capital, some near and some rather far away. The ruins brought to light and the objects recovered are of considerable diversity, and we have divided our work into three different sections.

The first section, compiled by Miss Rawson and me from the notes and reports of the excavators, deals with remains from the hilltop, from under the palace, and from the lower town where the inhabitants lived. The second section presents the tombs—the sepulchers of the rulers, the lords of the domain and their families, written by the excavators: Tholos III by Mrs. Blegen and me; Tholos IV and a grave circle enclosing numerous pit-graves, by Lord William Taylour. The second section also offers accounts of the chamber tombs used for burial by the ordinary citizens and households along with the objects that were placed in the graves—Tombs E-3, E-4, E-6, E-8, E-10, all excavated and recorded by Mr. Donovan; and an undisturbed tomb, K-1, which was excavated, drawn, and described by Lord William Taylour. The third section, discoveries outside the citadel, excavated and described in detail by Lord William Taylour, deals with Early Helladic walls and pottery under a modern *aloni* approximately 400 m. southwest of the hill to the east of the road; a chamber tomb, K-2, about 2 km. distant southward from Englianos, and close by, above the plain, at the inner side of the highroad, a small tholos tomb of Protogeometric date.

Cincinnati 1970   C. W. B.

Carl Blegen died in Athens on the twenty-fourth of August, 1971. He had seen and verified all the manuscripts which make up the text of this book and had reviewed all the illustrations. The volume comes directly from his hand: another task finished, like many before. It is being seen through the press by Marion Rawson, in collaboration with Harriet Anderson at Princeton and John Peckham at Meriden. Miss Rawson has had continuing assistance from Cedric and Patricia Boulter and other members of the Department of Classics in the University of Cincinnati.

Cincinnati, February 1972   J. L. Caskey

CONTENTS

FOREWORD   vii-xii

ABBREVIATIONS   xv-xvii

ACROPOLIS AND LOWER TOWN   3-68
  Northeastern Gateway and Wall   4-8
  The Circuit Wall   8-18
  Belvedere Area (W 38)   18-24
  Trenches Southeast of Palace and Aqueduct   24-27
  Trenches Northwest of Aqueduct   27-29
  Area Northeast and Southeast of Wine Magazine   29-31
  Remains Found under the Palace of Mycenaean III B   32-40
      Underneath the Wine Magazine, 32. Underneath Corridor 26, 32.
      Corridor 25: Pit under Pavement to *Stereo*, 33. Pit outside Room
      24, 33. Underneath Rooms 18, 20, 21, and 22, 34. Underneath
      Rooms 55, 56, 57, and Archives Room 7, 35. Under Hall 65, 36.
      Under Stairway 69, 37. Under Room 74, 38. Trench 64-6, 38. Com-
      plex of walls under southwestern side of Court 63, 39. Trench 64-
      17, 40.
  Building X   40-41
  Southern Corner   41-42
  Exploration of Stratification Northwest of Main Building   43-47
  The Lower Town   47-68
      The Northwestern Scarp, 48. The Southwestern Scarp, 50. The
      South Corner (W 21), 51. The Southwestern Quarter: Trench LT I,
      52; Trench LT II, 57; Trench LT III, 57; Trench LT IV, 59;
      Trench LT V, 60. The Southeastern Quarter, 61. The Northern
      Quarter, 63. The Northeastern Quarter, 64.

THOLOI, GRAVE CIRCLE, AND CHAMBER TOMBS   71-215
  Tholos Tomb III   73-95
  Tholos Tomb IV   95-134
  Grave Circle   134-176
  Chamber Tombs   176-215
      Grave E-3, 176. Trial Trenches, 178. Dromos E-1, 179. Dromos
      E-2, 180. Tomb E-4, 180. Tomb E-6, 184. Tomb E-8, 192. Tomb
      E-9, 201. Tomb E-10, 207. Tomb K-1, 208.

DISCOVERIES OUTSIDE THE CITADEL   219-242
  An Early Helladic Site   219-224
  Chamber Tomb K-2   224-237
  Protogeometric Tholos   237-242

INDEX OF REFERENCES TO ILLUSTRATIONS   243-257
GENERAL INDEX   259-269
ILLUSTRATIONS

ABBREVIATIONS

AAA	*Athens Annals of Archaeology*
AJA	*American Journal of Archaeology*
AM	*Mitteilungen des deutschen archäologischen Instituts, athenische Abteilung (Athens)*
Annuario	*Annuario della R. Scuola Archeologica di Atene*
AR	*Archaeological Reports published by the Council of the Society for the Promotion of Hellenic Studies and the Managing Committee of the British School at Athens*
Asea	Holmberg, E. J., *The Swedish Excavations at Asea in Arcadia* (Göteberg, 1944)
Asine	Frödin, O., and A. W. Persson, *Asine: Results of the Swedish Excavations 1922-1930* (Stockholm, 1938)
Athenaion	’Αθήναιον (Athens, 1872-1881)
BCH	*Bulletin de correspondance hellénique.* École française d’Athènes (Paris)
BSA	*The Annual of the British School at Athens* (London)
ChT	Wace, A. J. B., *Chamber Tombs at Mycenae (Archaeologia 82.* Oxford, 1932)
CM	Inventory number, Chora Museum
CMS I	Sakellariou, A., *Die minoischen und mykenischen Siegel des Nationalmuseums in Athen (Corpus der minoischen und mykenischen Siegel* I, eds. F. Matz, H. Biesantz, 1964)
Crete and Mycenae	Marinatos, S. N., and H. Hirmer, *Crete and Mycenae* (London, 1960)
Deltion	’Αρχαιολογικὸν Δελτίον
Eleusis	Mylonas, G. E., Προϊστορικὴ ’Ελευσίς (Athens, 1932)
EphArch	’Εφημερὶς ’Αρχαιολογική
Ergon	Τὸ ’Έργον τῆς ἀρχαιολογικῆς ’Εταιρείας
Eutresis	Goldman, H., *Excavations at Eutresis in Boeotia* (Cambridge, Mass., 1931)
Gournia	Hawes, H. B., *et al., Gournia, Vasiliki and Other Prehistoric Sites on the Isthmus of Hierapetra* (Philadelphia, 1908)
Hesperia	*Hesperia. Journal of the American School of Classical Studies at Athens*
KG	Lolling, H. G., *Das Kuppelgrab bei Menidi* (Athens, 1880)
Korakou	Blegen, C. W., *Korakou: A Prehistoric Settlement near Corinth* (Boston and New York, 1921)
Mallia Maisons	*Fouilles exécutées à Mallia. Exploration des maison et quartiers d’habitation:* I: Demargne, P., and H. G. de Santerre (Paris, 1953); II: Deshayes, A., and A. Dessenne (Paris, 1959)
MMS	*Metropolitan Museum Studies* (New York)

Mochlos	Seager, R. B., *Explorations on the Island of Mochlos* (Boston and New York, 1912)
MonAnt	*Monumenti Antichi pubblicati per cura della Reale Accademia dei Lincei* (Rome)
MP	Furumark, A., *The Mycenaean Pottery: Analysis and Classification* (Stockholm, 1941)
MPChron.	Furumark, A., *The Chronology of Mycenaean Pottery* (Stockholm, 1941)
MV	Furtwaengler, A., and G. Loeschcke, *Mykenische Vasen* (Berlin, 1886)
NM	Inventory number, National Museum, Athens
NT,Dendra	Persson, A. W., *New Tombs at Dendra near Midea* (Lund, 1942)
Pachyammos	Seager, R. B., *The Cemetery of Pachyammos, Crete* (University of Pennsylvania Anthropological Publications, Vol. VII, no. 1, 1916)
Palaikastro	British School at Athens Supplementary Paper No. 1, *The Unpublished Objects from the Palaikastro Excavations, 1902-1906,* Part I (London 1923)
PM	Evans, A., *The Palace of Minos* (London, 1921-1936)
PN	*The Palace of Nestor at Pylos in Western Messenia.* I: Blegen, C. W., and M. Rawson, *The Buildings and Their Contents* (Princeton, 1966); II: Lang, M. L., *The Frescoes* (Princeton, 1969)
Phylakopi	*Excavations at Phylakopi in Melos Conducted by the British School at Athens. Society for the Promotion of Hellenic Studies, Supplementary Paper No. 4* (London, 1904)
Praktika	Πρακτικὰ τῆς ἐν Ἀθήναις Ἀρχαιολογικῆς Ἑταιρείας
ProcPS	*Proceedings of the Prehistoric Society*
Prosymna	Blegen, C. W., *Prosymna: The Helladic Settlement Preceding the Argive Heraeum* (Cambridge, 1937)
Pseira	Seager, R. B., *Excavations of the Island of Pseira* (University of Pennsylvania, the Museum, Anthropological Publications, III, 1. Philadelphia, 1910)
RT,Dendra	Persson, A. W., *The Royal Tombs at Dendra near Midea* (Lund, 1931)
SCE	*The Swedish Cyprus Expedition: Finds and Results of the Excavations in Cyprus, 1927-1931).*
Schachtgräber	Karo, G., *Die Schachtgräber von Mykenai* (Munich, 1930-1933)
SME	Valmin, M. N., *The Swedish Messenia Expedition* (Lund, 1938)
Sphoungaras	Hall, E. H., *Excavations in Eastern Crete: Sphoungaras* (University of Pennsylvania Anthropological Publications, Vol. III, no. 2, 1912)
TI	Dörpfeld, W., *Troja und Ilion: Ergebnisse der Ausgrabungen in den vorhistorischen und historischen Schichten von Ilion* (Athens, 1902)
Wace, *Mycenae*	Wace, A. J. B., *Mycenae: An Archaeological History and Guide* (Princeton, 1949)

Zygouries   Blegen, C. W., *Zygouries: A Prehistoric Settlement in the Valley of Cleonae* (Cambridge, Mass., 1928)

[   ]   Bracketed numbers in the text indicate the position of pots on plans of various tombs.

Miscellaneous small objects, described in the catalogues but not included in the inventories of the National Museum in Athens or of the Chora Museum, may be found in labeled containers in the storerooms of the Chora Museum.

ACROPOLIS
AND
LOWER TOWN

ACROPOLIS AND LOWER TOWN

Readers of this chapter should be warned that it deals with innumerable trenches that usually produced only small and meager prizes. We have tried not to offer too severe a test. It all arose from the advice of a kindly and distinguished archaeologist who some 15 or more years ago suggested to me, and urged me to follow, this council: "in the excavation of Nestor's citadel (if this site is really the abode of Nestor) every square meter of earth deserves to be dug, thoroughly examined, and sifted, both on the hilltop and in the lower town." That is why we have taken pains to probe wherever our eyes fell on any and all tempting ground that might cover treasures.

We sounded in many places on the hilltop, under the palace, along the slopes of the steep scarp of the hill, and in the lower town, all together at least 99 trenches; but we did not venture to turn over every patch of earth.

We did, however, discover that the hill in the Middle Helladic period was occupied by a settlement that had an inclination to spread to the lower ground. The town apparently continued into the early Mycenaean period (Late Helladic I and II) without upheaval. If there was a mansion of a ruler, the remains of it might be safely buried underneath the Palace of Nestor. Traces of a circuit defensive wall existed from the earliest period and a fortified gateway at the northeast end of the hill.

In the era of Mycenaean III A some houses seem to have stood on the hill and also in the town below, but the defensive works around the hillock appear to have been dismantled altogether. Scanty indications suggest that there may have been a palace of Mycenaean III A regime: a short section of a substantial stone wall built of large squared blocks underneath the floor of Room 7 (*PN* 1, 44, 94, 227) survives just inside the southeast exterior wall of the main front façade of the later palace.

In the final era, Mycenaean III B, considerable changes appear to have been made. All the small and large earlier buildings were evidently razed to the ground by fire, not only to provide for the palace itself, but to clear the whole acropolis, presumably for the exclusive use of the king and his family and household. The strangest circumstance at a site like Englianos Hill is the lack of a circuit wall of defense. Almost all the Mycenaean strongholds of importance were well protected. Was the Lord of Pylos confident that he could protect his hilltop without a defensive wall? The trenches have given us no answer. Reading about the trenches is much easier than supervising the digging, but the latter is a great deal livelier.

NORTHEASTERN GATEWAY AND WALL

The northeastern end of the Englianos ridge forms a broad convexly rounded curve (Fig. 302). The elevation rises in an abrupt acclivity from a hollow in a lower-lying olive grove to the level of the plateau some 4 m. and more high. On the northeast and southeast the steep slope curves more sharply and continues somewhat irregularly toward the southwest. The southeastern edge of the high plateau divides into two banks, separated by a somewhat narrow intervening terrace that descends toward the eastward and southeastward. The total breadth of the hill at this end is about 95 m., but the higher ground is only 60 m. wide.

Some 20 m. southeast of the northeastern bend of the hill a stone-paved road-way was exposed,[1] descending northeastward in a cutting through the sloping bank (Fig. 1). It was bordered on either side by remnants of stone walls to a length of 5 m. or more (W 1 on the plan, Fig. 302).

In its course through the sharp decline the roadway heads straight toward Tholos IV (Fig. 4) on the far side of the depression mentioned above. Whether this direction was a mere coincidence or was planned is not clear, but the road is surely a continuation of the street which was traced mainly by the accompanying aqueduct[2] from the area outside the northeast portal of the Main Building of the palace to the end of the hill. In the late phases of the palace the connection of the portal with the street seems to have been blocked by the closing of Court 42.

The road through the gateway is 3.60 m. wide (Figs. 2, 304). At the upper end the bordering walls are in a badly damaged state and the exact length of the gate is not determinable. In the roadway near its northwestern side and apparently inside the gateway, lies a squared block of poros, possibly of the palace period. On the southeastern side near the top, and almost opposite the poros stone, is a large block which looks as if it may have been part of a threshold or the support of one (Fig. 2). To the northeast and lower down is a pavement of several irregular steplike sloping slabs of limestone—seven can be counted. Whether they were laid as steps and were later depressed by erosion or wear to form a descending floor is not clear. The northwestern side of the roadway retains in place some ten low steps still recognizable, extending down to the line of the outer face of the gateway. The middle of the roadway with *stereo* exposed is almost bare of flat stones: this space seems to have been disturbed in a late period when a channel or drain for carrying off water was installed. It was

---

[1] By Mr. McDonald in 1953 and Miss Rawson in 1958 and 1959; *AJA* 58 (1954), 30; 63 (1959), 124; 64 (1960), 155f.

[2] *PN* I, 332ff., fig. 416.

roughly cut in an irregular course along the road (Figs. 2, 304). In one place near the southeastern side it runs over a step; elsewhere the steps had evidently been removed. The channel, ranging from 0.20 m. to 0.40 m. wide, was bordered by thin flattish stones set on edge in the manner of the channels leading from the aqueduct to the complex of buildings in Area 103 (*PN* 1, fig. 248). This drain in the roadway may have provided water from the aqueduct for use down in the hollow, or perhaps it merely disposed of the overflow at the junction of the wooden bridge that must have carried the water across the hollow to the citadel. The northeast gateway was no doubt in use for a considerable time during which the paving slabs might often have had to be repaired or readjusted.

The wall bordering the southeast side of the road in the gateway (Fig. 1), built of rough unworked limestone, stands to a maximum height of four courses, ca. 0.60 m. The outer corner is in a bad state of preservation but it was evidently aligned with its counterpart on the northwest. The inner south corner is no longer certainly determinable but the total length of the passage is ca. 5 m. The thickness of the wall can only be conjectured. The outside northeastern face, also standing to a maximum height of 0.60 m. in three or four courses, can be followed some 3 m. southeastward. Beyond that point there may have been a southerly bend, but real evidence is lacking. In any event a mass of stones behind the northeast and southeast faces implies that a substantial structure stood here, perhaps a tower of some kind.

To the southeast of the gateway nine trenches at relatively short intervals were dug down the slope (W 39 to W 47, Fig. 302). In this stretch of nearly 50 m. no trace of any continuation of the wall was found (W 45, Fig. 39). Erosion in the course of many centuries has certainly worn away the steep banks on all sides of the acropolis. Apparently it is for the most part only in the few places where later buildings were superposed on early remains in the edges of the hill that remnants of those more ancient structures were thus covered and protected.

The wall on the northwestern side of the road, though built of the same material as that opposite, is not so well preserved. The inner line is nonetheless recognizable near its upper end, in the outer corner (Figs. 2, 304), and in the foundations. At the lower end it forms a sharp corner as the wall turns northwestward (Fig. 1). How thick it was beside the gateway cannot be determined, but it must have been as substantial as that on the other side of the road. One may conjecture that the gateway was flanked by a tower on each side and it is possible that the passage was roofed.

In any event there can be no doubt that this was a gateway and as such it must surely have opened through a barrier or a wall of some kind. A considerable stretch of the actual wall is preserved to the northwest of the gateway (Fig. 3). The first section, standing to a height of four courses, extends some 4 m. northwestward to an angle bending slightly westward. In this new direction it continues to a point ca. 6 m. farther, beyond which there is a stoneless gap. In its preserved part the wall has a minimum thickness of 1.40 m. and it seems to have been laid on a flattish cutting in *stereo*. Outside the wall *stereo* continues to slope downward, but much more gently than in the bank.

The northeastern slope had suffered much from erosion and the deposit covering the gateway yielded very little evidence of orderly stratification. In the approach from the top of the plateau a thin layer of plowed earth, from 0.10 m. to 0.20 m. thick, rested on yellowish *stereo* and covered a remnant of a wall some 3 m. long, ca. 0.50 m. thick, in a single course of rough unshaped stones. About 1.10 m. to the north are remains of a similar parallel wall. Neither retains sufficient evidence to interpret its purpose.

Somewhat farther down the slope the brown topsoil is considerably deeper, 0.60 m. to 0.70 m., under which lay scattered about many unworked stones and traces of a much dilapidated water channel leading to its continuation, running through the gateway. The deposit filling the gateway itself showed no clear-cut succession of layers, though the upper part of the fill contained a considerable mixture of pottery, including glass and glazed ware of medieval times, a stray Hellenistic or classical black-glazed sherd, a few pieces of Geometric ware, and a good many kylix stems of the palace period; and especially in the lower part, on and among and under the stones of the pavement and steps, earlier Mycenaean pottery, mainly of Late Helladic I, with some fragments of Mattpainted Ware (e.g., Figs. 119, 120).

To the northwest of the gateway and encroaching on the latter was a fairly extensive intrusion of the eleventh and twelfth centuries A.D. Alongside the gateway a small building had been erected in a cutting into the bank; it had evidently been roofed by curved tiles and the floor seems to have been fashioned of medieval flat tiles along with stone slabs (Fig. 5), which had presumably been taken from the earlier roadway.

This latest occupation was marked by an abundance of plain ribbed pottery (Fig. 121, Nos. 1-7) and finer vessels with patterns finished in green and yellow lead glaze (Fig. 121, Nos. 8-18). Many bits of glass were also found.[3] The Geometric sherds probably belonged to the eighth or seventh century B.C. when an olive oil press seems to have existed on the hill. The stems and fragments of

[3] The glazed pottery was identified and dated by   cott, to whom we are greatly indebted.
Miss Alison Frantz and the glass by Miss Lucy Tal-

kylikes and a good many other shapes assignable to the period of the palace no doubt found their place here in connection with the installation of the water channel. So far as could be determined, however, the Early Mycenaean ware, principally of Late Helladic I, with a few pieces that might belong to Late Helladic II (e.g., Figs. 119, 120), must mark the period when the gateway had been built and was in use. No evidence was found to indicate that it continued to exist in Late Helladic III B. The ruins at that time must surely have been covered over and were no longer visible.

Directly outside the gateway the low stone steps were found to continue northeastward, descending into the hollow. Some four or five steps can be recognized but they may have gone on farther down into an area filled by a mass of disordered stones (Fig. 1). The steps also extended at least 2 m. northwestward beyond the opening of the gate; perhaps the gateway originally was much broader in some earlier time, or may have been shifted farther southeastward in a later phase. The pottery found here was similar to that from the gateway itself, especially in the presence of Early Mycenaean sherds, chiefly of Late Helladic I.

Resting on the steps to the northwest of the gate was a segment of a circle, some 3 m. over-all, built of fairly large rough stones (Figs. 6, 305) which obviously supported a small structure of some kind. Was it possibly an exedra on the right-hand side of the gateway as one approached, or a guard's post, where distinguished visitors could be properly greeted? Underneath this foundation is a line of fairly regularly laid stones almost parallel to the wall. Perhaps it was the support for a predecessor of the conjectural exedra, or it may mark an earlier phase of the wall. The pottery recovered here, though not at all distinguished, is obviously of a period antedating the palace.

OBJECTS FOUND[4]
(Figs. 104:11-20 and 105:4)

BRONZE

Pin, fragment (No. 16): l. 0.057 m., d. 0.002 m. Bent, twisted, apparently broken at both ends.

Flat strip (No. 17): 0.004 m. to 0.005 m. wide. Broken, four pieces. Badly bent, not measurable.

STONE

Arrowhead, fragment, gray flint or obsidian (No. 14): l. pres. 0.012 m., max. w. 0.012 m., th. 0.003 m. Point missing.

Blade, light gray flint (No. 19): l. 0.035 m., w. 0.014 m., th. 0.004 m.

Pestle, gray stone (No. 20): l. 0.042 m., d. of convex end 0.025 m., d. of flattened end 0.025 m., d. waist 0.021 m. Neatly worked.

Arrowhead, obsidian (No. 11): l. 0.04 m., max. w. 0.017 m., th. 0.003 m. Barbed type, large, intact.

[4] The miscellaneous objects found in this area were deposited in labeled containers in the storeroom of the Chora Museum but have not been given museum numbers.

[7]

Disk, fragment (No. 12): d. ca. 0.048 m., th. 0.006 m. Well cut, smooth surface, sandy stone.

SHELL
Small pierced whelk shell (No. 15): l. 0.063 m., d. 0.01 m.

TERRACOTTA
Shanked button (No. 13): h. 0.015 m., d. 0.023 m. Crude, worn, gray clay.

Disk, pierced with two holes (No. 18): d. 0.06 m., th. 0.01 m., d. perforation 0.005 m. Made from coarse sherd, reddish-brown on outside, black on inside. Polished.

Loomweight (Fig. 105:4): h. 0.11 m., top almost rounded off, max. w. 0.07 m. Surface lumpy, uneven. Trace of groove at top. Bottom flattened. Brick-red clay.

POTTERY
In course of excavation of gateway in 1958 and 1959 27 baskets or more, many overflowing, others partly filled with potsherds collected. Material had fallen casually into roadway and no pots could be put together. Deposit of tilled soil yielded nondescript fragments of no significance. Next deeper layer contained numerous kylix stems of type found in palace, presumably thrown away at time late water channel laid. Still deeper accumulation produced examples of earlier Mycenaean ware, mainly Late Helladic I, a few II (Figs. 119, 120). All these remnants mentioned above need no further comment. No whole pots recovered.

THE CIRCUIT WALL

In an effort to ascertain what, if any, remains of a circuit wall still exist elsewhere throughout the periphery of the acropolis, some 47 or more probings, soundings, and trenches were dug into the steep bank. In this survey we begin to the northwest of the Northeast Gateway and proceed around the northwestern, southwestern, southeastern, and northeastern borders of the hill. These tests at irregularly spaced intervals were carried out in many seasons and by many members of the staff. In this concluding survey we have renumbered the areas investigated in numerical order as we work our way around the full periphery (trench plan, Fig. 302).

Under the supervision of Miss Rawson to the west of the Northeast Gateway (W 1), five soundings were made in 1959 in an arc of about 25 m. from the truncated end of the wall described above (W 2-W 6). Trench W 2 disclosed a mass of biggish fallen stones at the foot of the bank (Fig. 7). Trench W 3 was bare of stones. Trench W 4 revealed, about in the middle of the slope, a line of wall standing to a height of 0.55 m. in three irregular courses with fallen stones to the north of it (Fig. 8). Trench W 5 also contained abundant stones, possibly the back filling of a wall the outer face of which is missing. Some fine fragments of Mycenaean pottery in the style of Late Helladic I were found among the fallen stones (Fig. 122). Trench W 6 crossed a wall running almost from east to west high in the bank (Fig. 9). It stands in eight irregular courses to a height of 1.10 m. and is 1.40 m. thick (Fig. 10) with a fall of stones below to the northwest. It might well be a remnant of a defensive wall. Its foundations were laid in a slot cut in *stereo* and behind it, to the southeast between Trenches CK 8 and CK 19, lies an extensive deep deposit containing abundant Mattpainted, incised, and coarse sherds of Middle Helladic date (e.g., Fig. 123:17-27) (p. 27). Among the stones and in the earth outside the stones and wall in Trench W 6 were recovered a good many sherds, all apparently of Early Mycenaean and Middle Helladic types (e.g., Fig. 123:1-16).

Farther southwestward four similar probings into the steep bank (W 7, W 8, W 10, W 11, Fig. 302) had been made by Mr. McDonald in 1953. These tests were variously spaced through a stretch of some 70 m. extending to a point behind the north corner of Room 27. Sounding W 7, about 12 m. southwest of Trench W 6, disclosed a wall of three or four courses of small field stones. There was nothing to show whether this was the foundation of a house or part of a circuit wall. The potsherds collected here were scanty and of nondescript character.

Approximately 8 m. father southwestward Trench W 8 exposed in the middle of the sloping bank a mass of stones, large and small, and, near the bottom of the heap, some remnants of at least two courses, one containing two large stones (Fig. 11). No proper face appeared. These remains might have been part of a circuit wall but no positive confirmation could be recognized. A few fragments of plaster with traces of painted decoration and some potsherds of mixed character were recovered.

Trench W 9, 12 m. wide, excavated in 1963 by Mr. P. Smith, opened a broad area across the brow of the bank about 2.50 m. northeast of the Wine Magazine. Masses of fallen stones (Fig. 12), the line of a drain running northwestward, and remnants of a wall parallel to the bank but lacking its outer northwestern face were brought to light, all in a bad state of dilapidation. A good deal of pottery, including Middle Helladic Mattpainted Ware and sherds of Late Helladic I and II (e.g., Fig. 125), and some other miscellaneous objects, e.g., two obsidian arrowheads and a button were recovered (Fig. 106:3, 4, 5). Though no certain vestiges of a fortification wall were recognized, the fallen stones might have come from such a structure.

In anticipation of laying a line of drain pipes to carry rain water from the metal roof that covers the Main Building of the palace and in order to prevent its flooding the currant vineyard below, Mr. Smith cleared the vegetation through a stretch extending northeastward about 45 m. along the bottom of the northwestern scarp. While it disclosed no traces of a circuit wall, this work yielded a few miscellaneous objects (e.g., a bronze javelin point, Fig. 106:1), and the potsherds recovered shed some light on the stratification of the deposit on the hill (e.g., Fig. 126:1-4, 7, 8).

Just outside the northwestern wall of the Wine Magazine Trench W 10, 3 m. wide, first opened by Mr. McDonald, was further investigated and broadened by Mr. Smith. A wall built in 9 or 10 courses, 1.50 m. high and running from east to west, was uncovered. Its eastern end was in a demolished state but it apparently turned a corner continuing southeastward. This angle probably belongs to a house rather than to a fortification wall. Several fragments of painted plaster were collected along with a mixed lot of potsherds ranging from Middle Helladic to Late Mycenaean (e.g., Fig. 126:5, 6, 9-12).

In a southwestern extension of W 10 along the foot of the scarp Mr. Smith discovered a substantial wall, 1 m. thick and 11 m. long. It was built up against a vertical cut in *stereo* and at its southwestern end it formed a corner turning at right angles to the northwest. This wall is evidently part of a house that stood in the lower town under the acropolis. A layer of dissolved red brick and debris covered the top of the wall and from that point downward was a deposit of yellow-brown earth. The potsherds collected from both strata are mainly nondescript and worn, representing a mixture of Middle Helladic and Mycenaean. The Mycenaean fragments seem to be earlier than Late Helladic III B.

Outside the northwest wall of Room 27 another sounding, W 11 (Fig. 302), was made by Mr. McDonald, and renewed digging in the same place was undertaken in 1958 by Mr. Papathanasopoulos. Two parallel walls running approximately east and west were brought to light but they were judged rather to be terrace walls than a wall around the acropolis.

Behind the central part of the Main Building intensive exploration was carried out near the bottom of the steep bank in 1961 by Miss Rawson in Trench W 13 (Figs. 13, 302) and in 1962 by Mrs. Kittredge in Trench W 12 (Fig. 14). These investigations were made on each side of the great cache of painted plaster discarded from the palace. The material, comprising some 3,000 fragments, was systematically extricated from its heap by Miss Rawson in 1961; in the following years these disconnected pieces were cleaned, joined together, studied, and published by Miss Lang (*PN* I, 22; *PN* II, 5ff.). Though in this area nothing that looked convincingly like a defensive circuit was found, several substantial walls were seen; all, however, appeared to belong to buildings outside, those in the lowest layer clearly attributable to Middle Helladic times. A good deal of broken pottery came to light, most of it evidently from the wreckage of the houses in the lower town. The deepest level that was reached yielded three Middle Helladic pots that could be partly restored (p. 49).

In 1962 Mr. Kittredge, starting from the top of the acropolis, carried out a thorough stratigraphic investigation behind the Main Building and farther to the southwest (W 14, Figs. 302, 311). In this area, some 25 m. long from northeast to southwest and 15 m. wide, he dug through a deposit more than 3 m. deep to *stereo*. He discovered a sequence of walls, evidently of houses superposed one above another, in which at least eight building periods could be recorded,[5] but at the outer edge of the hill no certain remains of an enclosing wall were recognizable.

Not more than 6 m. or 8 m. distant from the large excavation (W 14), a further sounding (W 15, Fig. 302) was made by Miss Rawson in 1961 near the bottom of the bank (Fig. 15). Remnants of two or three walls at different levels were noted, all belonging to buildings and not to a fortification. Much pottery was found in stratified order, Late Mycenaean sherds of the palace period at the top, earlier Mycenaean underneath, evidently Late Helladic III A, and still deeper typical wares of Late Helladic I with an admixture of Middle Helladic.

Two years later, in 1963, Mr. Smith also probed along the foot of the steep bank (W 16, Fig. 302), examining the whole stretch to the westernmost angle of the hill, where he encountered a vast accumulation of fragmentary pots that had obviously been thrown away. Everywhere much shattered pottery of mixed character was collected, comprising not only Mycenaean III B but Early Mycenaean (Fig. 127:1-11, 13, 14) and also Middle Helladic (Fig. 127:12, 15, 16). Nowhere, however, did we find unmistakable traces of a circuit wall.

The southwestern slope of the citadel was likewise thoroughly examined in a search for the possible surrounding wall. Near the western corner of the site Mr. McDonald in 1953 (Fig. 302, W 17a) and Mr. Papathanasopoulos in 1960 (W 17b), in almost contiguous areas, uncovered several walls, some apparently of houses which had been partly demolished at the time when the foundations of the western tower of the Southwestern Building were being built (Fig. 16). Farther southeastward in 1953 two additional small trenches were dug by Mr. McDonald; they revealed no evidence bearing on the problem of a circuit wall.

From 1958 to 1963, mainly under the supervision of Mrs. Blegen with the cooperation of Mr. Papathanasopoulos, the entire southwest end of the hill (W 18 and W 19, Fig. 302) was cleared of the overlying earth. The outer wall of the Southwestern Building was traced and partly exposed through almost the whole of its extent (*PN* I, 281ff.); but this, though a substantial wall, was not a fortification.

In further explorations under the supervision of Mr. Pedley in 1964, an Early Mycenaean wall was brought to light just outside the foot of the scarp that marks the southwestern end of the acropolis. Five trenches and soundings were dug to expose the face and the foundations of the wall and to permit a study of the

---

[5] See pp. 43-46.

stratification of the deposit lying against it (e.g., Trench 64-1, Fig. 140). Three supplementary probings of the same kind were made in 1965.

Beginning just west of the right-angled corner formed by Sections 5 and 6 of the exterior wall of the Southwestern Building, about 12 m. southeast of Hall 65, this early structure could be traced in a fairly regular line running from west to east approximately 27 m. to the west corner of Building X (east end of Area W 19, Figs. 302, 306). The first section of the wall, about 5.50 m. long, was built of flattish field stones, standing in some places as high as 1 m. in five or more courses (Fig. 17). The next section, 3 m. long, could not be examined because of a pavement made of flattish stones that we were reluctant to destroy (Fig. 18). At 8.50 m. from our starting point the line of the wall reappeared, continuing unchanged a further distance of 4 m.; in this stretch it was observed here and there that smallish squared blocks of poros were used in the construction. From 12.50 m. to 15.50 m. no part of the wall was visible. In the ensuing section (Fig. 19) from 15.50 m. to 18.50 m. it reappears in a line containing some worked blocks, though the principal drain tunnel that carried off water from the palace of Mycenaean III B was cut diagonally through it. Beyond this point to 23.50 m. from the westernmost truncated end, the wall is wholly concealed by a stucco pavement of Late Mycenaean date (Fig. 20). From 23.50 m. to 27.05 m. the wall becomes visible once more (Fig. 21), here constructed of field stones in the manner that characterized Section 1. In this short segment 11 courses of relatively thin slablike stones were preserved *in situ,* reaching a maximum height of 1.09 m., with a thickness of ca. 0.95 m. Wherever it was possible to probe beneath the foundations they were found to rest not on *stereo* but on a thinnish layer of dark earth, containing potsherds (Fig. 128). No trace of a bedding trench or *baugrube* was found, and it is likely that most of the earth outside the wall had accumulated after the latter was built.

At 27.05 m. to the eastward of our starting point the field stones had been superposed upon a large, roughly dressed, squared block projecting from the substructure that supported the western corner of Building X (Fig. 22). The latter might therefore have existed in a phase preceding the erection of the wall, unless the wall at this point had been repaired or adjusted.

In the light (or darkness) of this uncertainty we could not definitely settle the problem of the date of Building X in relation to that of the wall built of flattish field stones. Building X, described on pages 40-41, now appears, however, to be older than Mycenaean III A, to which we once conjecturally ventured to attribute it (*PN* 1, 283); and it may well have been contemporary with, if not indeed older than, the circuit wall and may have been incorporated in it.

In the section marked W 20 on the plan (Fig. 302), three small test probings were dug—two by Mr. Pedley in 1964 and one by Mr. Blegen in 1965—at intervals along and against the southerly foundation of Building X (e.g., Fig. 23). They show some patching and also the use of thinnish flat field stones to serve as the substructure for the large squared blocks above. Whether the flattish slabs were surviving remnants of the early circuit wall or were first laid for Building X could not be determined.

In most of the sections of the wall as differentiated above, where smallish squared blocks were used along with rubble it was noted that they generally also lay on a bedding of one or two courses of flattish field stones. The blocks of poros had not been carefully squared nor had they been so smoothly worked as the elegantly dressed blocks that formed the veneer of the exterior walls of the palace of Mycenaean III B (*PN* I, 35f.). The elements of poros that had been built into the earlier structures differ in character from the material that was employed in the later building. In the period of Mycenaean III B the contractors presumably obtained their blocks from a different quarry that produced stone of a more finely grained and more easily worked type.

The small transverse trenches, opened at intervals across the line of the circuit wall in Sections W 19 and W 20 (Fig. 306), revealed a fairly consistent pattern of the stratification in the deposit that had accumulated against the face of the wall (Fig. 24). These soundings varied in depth from 0.50 m. to a maximum of 1.25 m. At the top the first cut produced a mixed bag of potsherds, ranging from Late Helladic III B to Late Helladic I. Digging deeper we found pottery fragments of Late Helladic II and I (Figs. 129, 130), and at the very bottom of the soundings on *stereo* many sherds of coarse domestic vessels decorated with bands and patterns in mat paint or in incision of Middle Helladic type (Fig. 128) along with some pieces of Minyan Ware. The miscellaneous items and broken pottery recovered presumably belonged mainly to the area outside the citadel. We have therefore placed our brief catalogues in the chapter dealing with the Lower Town (p. 51).

So far as we could determine, the wall itself seems to have been built in the period of Late Helladic I, if not earlier. The appearance of small simply worked blocks of poros in some sections and not in others suggests that the wall had been repaired or strengthened from time to time.

Eastward beyond Building X and what we have called its annex (p. 51), in the area labeled W 21 on the plan (Fig. 302), excavations were carried out in 1963-1965. Nothing was discovered monumental enough to be certainly recognized as part of a defensive circuit. Two parallel walls were, however, brought to light, both badly dilapidated, continuing in the same general easterly direction (Fig. 25). Each has been shaken out of the perpendicular, presumably by earthquakes, and now leans over sharply following the attraction of the southern slope. The two walls stand close together, not precisely parallel, the space between them ranging from 0.70 m. to 0.90 m. and narrowing from west to east (Fig. 26). Loosely constructed, they were built of field stones laid in irregular courses. No dressed blocks were noted in either wall. The northerly wall, built of somewhat larger stones than the other, had a thickness of ca. 1.30 m. and could be traced to a length of nearly 11 m., terminating at the east end in a right-angled junction with a narrower wall running northward (Fig. 27). A short stub of a branch wall extended southward 1 m. short of the corner. The southern wall, which stood with a maximum thickness of 1.60 m. to a height of about 1.50 m. (Fig. 28), could be traced only to a length of 6 m. The purpose of these walls could not be determined, since no clue to the original ground level and no floors were found. We wondered if the upper wall might possibly be a continuation of the early Mycenaean defensive circuit, while the lower wall perhaps belonged to a house of the town below the acropolis. We were not convinced.

The southeastern flank of the hill has also at intervals been subjected to a series of soundings. In Section W 22 (Fig. 302) Mr. Smith in 1963 opened two transverse tests across the steep bank close to the southern extremity of the hill. Here erosion had carried away all walls, if there ever had been any, and only a relatively thin deposit covered bare *stereo* in which ruts of a not very ancient bridle path contained a few iron horseshoe nails.

Farther northeastward two trenches about 30 m. apart were dug in 1953 by Mr. McDonald, one in area W 23 and a small sounding called W 26. These probes disclosed no signs of fortification walls and yielded almost no pottery.

In the closing days of the campaign of 1957 two short trenches (W 24 and W 25, Fig. 302) were opened just above the brow of the steep scarp along the southeastern slope. Trench W 24 was aligned almost exactly with the outer face of the northeastern exterior wall of the Main Building of the palace. Ca. 6 m. long and 1 m. wide, W 24 revealed a stone wall running parallel to the edge of the hill, but it was not judged to be thick enough for a defensive work. Trench W 25, ca. 5 m. farther to the northeast, contained many fallen stones, though no real wall, and it produced only a small lot of mixed pottery.

Somewhat farther toward the northeast three exploratory trenches (W 27, W 28, and W 29, Fig. 302) were dug in 1959 by Miss Rawson, all near the outer edge of the lower terrace which descends eastward toward the modern highway. The southwesternmost (W 27) disclosed a corner of two walls, one running from east to west, the other from north to south. The former was found standing to a height of four courses, the other to only two. These walls, 0.60 m. thick, must surely be remains of a small building or house. Very little pottery was found and that in a miserable state, all, so far as determinable, Mycenaean III B of the period in which the palace existed.

Some 7 m. to the eastward beyond Trench W 27 in a sounding (W 28), a much more substantial wall, 1.30 m. thick, was uncovered. Running across the trench from east to west and founded on *stereo,* it was preserved to a height of 1.15 m. in nine irregular courses (Fig. 29). The deposit to northwest and southeast of it yielded a great deal of debris of crude brick and much pottery of Mycenaean III B style. Sherds bearing traces of decoration had suffered from the action of the lime in the earth, which in some instances had detached most of the paint of the patterns, an admirable anticipation of modern decalcomania (Fig. 143: 15 a-b, 16 a-b). The wall itself is probably not part of a fortification but it surely indicates that a building of considerable size stood in this area. Whether it belonged to the acropolis or to the lower town is not clear.

About 5 m. farther eastward a small probe, W 29, exposed a mass of fallen stones. In one place, where deeper digging was possible, a deposit exactly like that in W 28 appeared; and it is probable that the large building conjectured to be there extended into and perhaps beyond this area.

On the northwestern side of the modern driveway, which provides access to the site (probably following the course of the original entrance in Mycenaean times), and almost directly opposite W 29, some stones attracted attention. A small test (W 30) was dug in 1962 by Mrs. Kittredge, who uncovered some scattered flat slabs including one circular in shape, with a diameter of ca. 0.50 m. (Fig. 30). It may perhaps have been a column base, but no trace of a wall came to light. *Stereo* was reached at 0.25 m. to 0.50 m. below the surface of the ground. The associated pottery included fragments of kylikes and of other vessels apparently of Mycenaean III B.

About 29 m. to the west of W 30, ruins of a structure, which must have been of impressive size, were found. In three trenches close together (W 31, W 32, and W 33, Fig. 302) Mrs. Kittredge laid bare a great mass of stones, large and small, covering a widespread area. The northerly face of a wall, running diagonally across W 32 (Fig. 31) and appearing also in W 31 (Fig. 32), was cleared. It was not possible to ascertain the thickness of the wall for the southerly face was nowhere preserved. Toward the south in all three trenches, however, stones lay scattered about in heaps (e.g., in W 33, Fig. 33). No plan of any building was indicated. Among the stones were collected, in addition to the usual bits of bronze, flint, obsidian, crumbling plaster bearing color, whorls or buttons of terracotta and one of steatite, as well as abundant potsherds, predominantly fragments of kylikes of the palace period but with some pieces slightly earlier.

In a few places where it was possible to dig deeper, pre-palace pottery was found, including a few Middle Helladic sherds. In the western edge of Trench W 31, 0.27 m. below the modern surface, Mrs. Kittredge discovered three joining fragments of a gold band or diadem.

OBJECTS FOUND

GOLD

Diadem CM. 2527 (Fig. 108 a-d), from W 31. L. 0.17 m., max. w. 0.04 m., lessening to 0.034 m. near preserved end, which has perforation for fastening. Fairly thick sheet gold, put together from three joining fragments. Decoration in punctated technique, covering whole surface of diadem, divided into several small compartments. Moving from right to left, first panel bears pair of dotted half circles arranged convexly back to back, one at preserved end made of two lines of dots, other of three. Two transverse lines of dots separate first from second panel, which contains mushroom-like figure, perhaps intended as papyrus blossom. Next comes triply divided panel, each unit enclosing zigzag line with ten angles. Beyond, longer panel framing odd arrangement difficult to interpret—possibly suggesting plow or chariot with shaft. In remaining space large circle formed by triple rows of dots with eight spokes radiating from central dotted circle. Circle may have been centerpiece, in which case diadem must have had total length of 0.31 m. or more.

No close Mycenaean parallel to this diadem hitherto known to us. Technique and general appearance recall silver band found by Tsountas at Chalandriane in Syros.[6] That diadem has always been recognized as belonging to Early Bronze Age. But comparable diadem was found in 1957 by Lord William Taylour, decorated in similar manner (Fig. 225:1).

STONE

Disk (Fig. 107:8): d. ca. 0.05 m., th. 0.005 m. Light gray stone. Fragment carefully worked, central perforation. From W 31.

Flint arrowhead (Fig. 107:1): l. 0.023 m., w. 0.016 m., th. 0.005 m. Flat on one side, plump on other. Barbs, if once existed, broken off. From W 33.

TERRACOTTA (FIG. 105)

Loomweight (No. 1): h. 0.094 m., w. top 0.036 m., max. w. 0.06 m., th. 0.022 m., d. perforation 0.006 m. Soft light brick-red clay, irregular in shape. From W 32.

Loomweight (No. 2): h. 0.077 m., max. w. 0.057 m., th. 0.022 m., d. perforation 0.007 m. Light brick-red clay. Neatly shaped, flattened piriform. From W 31.

Loomweight (No. 3): h. 0.09 m., w. top 0.043 m., max. w. 0.06 m., th. 0.003 m., d. perforation 0.011 m. Carelessly made, surface uneven. From W 31.

Continuing her exploration, Mrs. Kittredge supervised three parallel trenches at intervals in the upper bank, which rises from the terrace to the plateau (W 34, W 35, W 36, Fig. 302). W 34 (Fig. 34), almost directly to the northwest of W 31, ran up the steep slope. Toward each end *stereo* was reached at depths varying from 0.30 m. to 1 m. below ground level. An irregular spread of unworked stones ran across the middle of the trench in a deposit of black earth.

[6] *EphArch*, 1899, 123f., pl. 10:1.

No signs of a wall are preserved. The stones appear to have fallen from above. The sherds collected both in the bare areas and among the stones were judged to be of Mycenaean III B.

W 35 (Fig. 35), some 10 m. farther to the northeastward in the same steep bank, was excavated to *stereo* at a depth of 0.25 m. to 0.55 m. Very few stones and no walls came to light. At the lower end of the trench a rough rocky surface, ca. 1.40 m. wide, might conceivably mark the bedding of a transverse wall. The pottery recovered was assignable to Mycenaean III B.

W 36 (Fig. 36), 7.50 m. beyond W 35, reached *stereo* at 0.15 m. to 0.65 m. below the surface of the slope. Nothing was found here except the usual potsherds of Mycenaean III B and a whetstone (Fig. 107:11).

Parallel to W 36 and 4 m. to the east, a small sounding 2 m. long, W 37, was made by Miss Rawson in 1959. It crossed the brow of the slope, reached *stereo* at 0.20 m. to 0.50 m. below the surface, yielded no trace of a wall, and produced little or no pottery worth recording.

Some 2 m. beyond this sounding is W 38, which was begun by Mr. McDonald in 1953 (Fig. 302). He found here a complex of walls, water channels, and drains, which in 1959 were further investigated by Miss Rawson, who extended the excavation northward across the plateau ca. 35 m. (Figs. 37, 307). At the southern edge no certain traces of a fortification wall were brought to light. The remains found in this large area are described in detail on pages 18-24.

Completing the circuit of the entire acropolis we come now to the final sector, which curves around the eastern end of the hill from W 38 to the Northeast Gateway (W 1), a total distance of approximately 60 m. The bank is very steep in the easterly part in two successive slopes separated by a terrace. In this arc nine exploratory trenches were dug in the declivitous edge (Fig. 302): three by Mr. McDonald in 1953, two running down the upper bank (W 42, W 44), and the third not far from the Northeast Gateway at the bottom of the lower bank (W 47); three by Miss Rawson in 1959, one (W 39) extending from the top, across the terrace and down the lower bank (Fig. 38), and two (W 45, W 46) farther northwestward, which descended from the terrace to the olive grove below (Figs. 39, 40); and three by Mrs. Kittredge in 1962, two in the upper bank (W 40, W 41) and one (W 43) in the lower. All these trenches yielded the same, namely nothing; *stereo* without walls, very few stones, and only a little nondescript pottery. It is clear that in this sector no remains of a circuit wall have survived.

Altogether in the course of many seasons nearly 50 investigations were made in the outer edge of the hill. Some were minor probings, others were broader trenches, and a few were extensive excavations, such as those of the Northeast

Gateway (W 1), the northwest bank behind the Main Building (W 14), and the entire southwestern slope (W 18, W 19, W 20, and W 21). Many of these tests produced little or no information, but the Northeast Gateway, flanked on each side by a tower-like structure, and a segment of a contiguous substantial wall running 10 m. northwestward from it and, at the opposite end of the citadel, remnants of a comparable wall, traceable to a length of more than 25 m., clearly demonstrate that there once was a circuit wall. It can be dated by ceramic evidence to Late Helladic I or earlier. Four of the trenches on the northwestern side gave some corroborative evidence in an abundance of fallen material, though the wall itself was not fully preserved. Conglomerations of fallen stones along the southeastern side may have come from a similar wall.

Nowhere in the entire circumference of the hill could we discover even the slightest trace of a fortification wall attributable to the period of the palace of Mycenaean III B. We are thus obliged to conclude that no defensive works existed on the acropolis in the period when the Palace of Nestor stood. It is true that our investigations were limited mainly to the steep banks of the Englianos hill and relatively little exploration was carried out within a much wider periphery. Consequently the possibility cannot yet be wholly excluded that a wall ran around much farther down, enclosing both the lower town and the acropolis in the palace period.

BELVEDERE AREA (W 38)

We turn now to survey remains, chiefly of a pre-palatial era, that have been exposed on the hill itself as well as underneath the various buildings of the palace. Beginning at the northeasterly end of the acropolis we proceed southwestward.

Near the northeastern scarp of the upper plateau scanty visible remnants of stone walls, uncovered by Mr. McDonald in 1953, invited examination (p. 17). Finding a foundation made in part of large blocks, and enjoying from the spot a magnificent prospect of the Bay of Navarino, he very appositely christened his trench Belvedere (Fig. 41). This was adopted by all the members of the staff. Ultimately, starting from the steep edge of the hill and extending northward some 37 m., an area under the supervision of Miss Rawson was opened to view Fig. 42). It varied from 4 m. to 13 m. in width as was required to follow the branching walls that were encountered (Figs. 302 W 38, 307). These walls occupy a relatively narrow strip of ground lying in a slight hollow that crosses the plateau roughly from north to south and slopes downward in that direction. Most of the walls exposed run in the same orientation. It looks as if these crumbling remains are those of houses with stone foundations standing on each side of a narrow street or lane with accompanying drains and water channels (Fig. 43). The wear of traffic through a long period presumably had deepened the little road below the level of the plateau.

At the northern end of the area examined, a few meters beyond the surviving walls and channels, were uncovered remains of a small kiln (Figs. 44, 45, 307), the lower part of which had been sunk into *stereo*. Almost oval, it was oriented with its opening pointing 20 degrees east of north. The fire box was lined on the inside by crude bricks set on edge (Fig. 44) and in the center a tongue-like supporting foundation, also built of bricks, extends out from the back toward the opening, stopping 0.40 m. short of the latter. Since all the bricks used are straight and rectangular, the oval is consequently somewhat irregular (Fig. 308). Examples of the bricks that could be measured in the partition were 0.52 m. and 0.54 m. long, 0.30 m. wide, and 0.10 m. thick. Three courses of bricks were preserved in the base and it is likely that it rose considerably higher in order to give adequate room for the fuel and fire underneath. The central support must have held up the floor of the kiln on which were placed the pots or other objects that were to be fired. The floor was no doubt perforated so that the heat could rise into the firing chamber. Several fragments of clay, 0.02 m. to 0.03 m. thick, smooth on both sides, perhaps came from such a floor, though none of the pieces recovered bears signs of holes. Other thick chunks of clay, however, presumably from the dome, have traces of flues or holes, ca. 0.08 m. in diameter. The fire box below could be fed with fuel through the opening mentioned.

On its western side the doorway was lined with crude brick as indicated by a remnant, 0.36 m. long. Between the last brick set on edge in the chamber and the lining of the passage is a sharp empty angle (Fig. 308) forming a vertical slot. Traces of a similar angle and slot can be recognized on the opposite side of the opening though the brick lining of the passage is for the most part missing. The distance across the inner end of the doorway from the last brick on the western side of the chamber to the corresponding brick on the east is 0.58 m. If the corner of the eastern jamb in the doorway corresponded to the opposite corner on the west, the actual width of the door must have been 0.48 m. The depth of the doorway from front to back is not preserved.

The two upright slots, which seem not to have been filled with clay, might conceivably have served as vertical grooves in which a sliding door could have been moved up and down.

The upper part of the structure is altogether missing but it was presumably a dome made of crude bricks and clay. Although no rejected failures or trial pieces were found immediately around it, there is no reason to doubt that it was a potter's kiln.[7]

Some 100 sherds, split and damaged by fire, coated with lime accretion and thus difficult to date, were collected from the interior of the kiln. In a preliminary survey it was thought that some pieces resembled types of Mycenaean III B but later a more careful scrutiny made it clear that the potsherds are of Early Mycenaean date. It was noted also that the plowed earth covering the kiln contained sherds exclusively of pre-palace times.

This kiln is the only one that has yet been found on the site or in its neighborhood. Somewhere in the vicinity, however, there must have been pottery works of considerable size, for the thousands of pots stored on the shelves in the palace pantries, all in unused condition, were unquestionably of local manufacture. Indeed as suggested (*PN* I, 352) the variations from pantry to pantry in material, character, and types of wares definitely imply that two or three, if not more, potteries were at work in the era of the palace.

About 3 m. to the south-southeast of the kiln are remnants of a water channel (L, Fig. 307) with small flat slabs set on edge forming the sides (Fig. 43). Though dilapidated, it can be traced in a meandering course southward to a length of 7 m. Its ultimate source was not discovered but it seems to have started at its north end at a kind of platform, 1.55 m. long by 0.90 m. wide, built of large stones (Fig. 46). Neither the size of the original structure nor its purpose could be determined but it evidently required water or needed drainage. At its lower end the channel (L) seems to have emptied through a gap in Wall K and must presumably be of later date than the wall.

To the west and south of Water Channel L are remains of a stone wall (K, Fig. 307) running from northwest to southeast then bending in a more easterly direction. Based on loose earth which rests on *stereo*, it stands to a height of only a single course (Fig. 47). A little beyond the bend is the gap for the water channel (L). The wall has no proper beginning nor end, broken off at the northwest and southeast. Loosely built of unworked stones, it could not support more than another course or two.

Farther to the east Walls M and N form a right angle, evidently the corner of a building (Fig. 47); both walls have been cut off and the original lengths are unknown. Founded on or in *stereo*, Wall M consists of a single course of field

[7] Dimensions: l. north-south 1.48 m.; w. east-west 1.35 m.; l. central partition 1.13 m.; w. central partition 0.30 m.; l. of bricks in lining, mostly 0.36 m., others 0.17 m., 0.32 m., 0.43 m.; w. opening 0.58 m.; h. pres. 0.27 m.-0.34 m.; depth below modern surface 0.15 m. to 0.20 m.

Cf. G. M. A. Richter, *The Craft of Athenian Pottery* (1923), figs. 72-80.

stones, the corner formed by a fairly large roughly squared block. Beyond, Wall N for 1 m. stands to a height of two courses, then only one.

These remains resemble foundations of a rectangular house, though the walls are rather thin (0.37 m. to 0.41 m.) to support a superstructure of any considerable height. Along the inner side of Wall N at the corner of the building are six flattish slabs laid on earth, possibly a remnant of a stone floor or a platform or a threshold inside the doorway.

Within the house only a few miserable sherds were found, nothing that looked as late as the period of the palace.

To the south of Wall K and Building MN two long walls extend in a southerly direction, apparently bordering the sides of a street or road (Fig. 48). Wall J, on the west, is preserved in an unbroken stretch of 12 m. maintaining a width of 0.60 m. with good straight edges (Fig. 47). It stands in one, two, or three courses, to a maximum height of 0.35 m. Although largely founded on *stereo*, in the northerly end some earth was apparently laid to form a smoother bed than that offered by the underlying rough pitted rock. Wall J terminates at the south in a finished end (Fig. 49) but at the north it has been broken off abruptly. No trace of a branch wall running westward was found, but on that side of Wall J is a line of flat stones carelessly laid, ca. 3 m. long and 0.25 m. to 0.60 m. distant from the wall (Fig. 47). These stones look as if they form one side of a water channel or drain that ran between them and the wall. After a gap of ca. 5 m. in which no stones are left in place, this water channel continues in a more southerly direction.

Wall H on the eastern side of the street is preserved to a length of 9.40 m. with a finished end at the south opposite that of Wall J (Fig. 49). About 0.45 m. to 0.50 m. thick and standing in one or two courses to a maximum height of 0.35 m., Wall H was founded in part on *stereo* and in part on a layer of earth like that observed in Wall J. Wall H runs in a slight though definite curve bulging out toward the east (Fig. 47). It seems, however, to be a house wall, for a few stones are preserved of a branch wall running eastward. Some 4.15 m. farther to the north are remnants of another approximately parallel crosswall R, 0.70 m. thick, extending 1.80 m. to the east. The wall, lying on earth that provided a level bedding on *stereo*, was built of fairly large blocks forming each face, with rubble between. No corresponding perpendicular wall is recognizable farther north.

The street between Walls H and J is 1.30 m. wide at each end and 1.70 m. at the widest point of the curve (Figs. 47, 49). The stratification showed plowed earth at the top and below an apparently homogeneous deposit of gray earth changing to yellowish at the bottom on *stereo*. It contained vast quantities of small potsherds, all of Early Mycenaean types (e.g., Figs. 131, 132), many bones and small stones and miscellaneous discarded objects, altogether the typical debris often found in streets. It looks as if Water Channel L, passing through Wall K, emptied its flow into the sloping street.

At its southern end the street opens into an apparently rectangular area (Figs. 49, 50), bordered on the south by Wall F and on the west by Wall I, which at its northern end overlaps the outer face of Wall J.

Forming an approximate right angle with Wall I, Wall F rises to a maximum height of 0.50 m. in four courses, extending eastward 4.80 m. Here it apparently once formed a corner with Wall E, which runs southward. Both Walls I and F appear to have been founded directly on the uneven *stereo*.

Crossing the open area is a drain or water channel (Figs. 50, 307, G). It was built of rough stones in two lines enclosing between them a channel, 0.20 m. wide. Several unworked flattish slabs of limestone were found in place covering the drain. The channel was filled to the top with earth which contained little or nothing except a few nondescript undatable potsherds. At its western end the channel had been carried through Wall I (Fig. 50) outside which it appears to have emptied into the drain that descends along the western side of Walls J and I.

South of the open area is a maze of walls and it is difficult — not to say impossible — to determine exactly which walls belong together (Figs. 37, 307). The remnants are short fragments in the sloping ground and at least 14 walls could be separated. In a crowded space three habitation levels could be distinguished. The latest, we conclude, is represented by remains of two truncated walls running from north to south (Fig. 307 D 1 and D 2), which were exposed just below the modern surface of the ground. These two walls gave no clue to their purpose but obviously belong to the late period of the palace. To the west of Wall D 1 a limelike stratum, possibly a floor, was observed only a few centimeters below the modern surface. On it lay a large mass of pottery, almost exclusively plain undecorated ware of Mycenaean III.

To the same era may with probability be assigned the Drain A-B, which runs from north to south (Fig. 51), preserved to a length of ca. 4.50 m. It probably served to carry the water brought down by the channel from the area of the aqueduct. Innumerable fragments of pottery, for the most part plain with the kylix predominantly represented, belonged to the thirteenth century B.C.

To a next earlier stage belongs Wall C (Fig. 307) with its two southward projecting wings, one at each end. Between the wings, in front of Wall C, are two worked blocks of poros, and near the western end a third block jutting out southward. One large block of poros, running from north to south, lies at the other end of Wall C. The eastern part of this structure was disrupted by the drain, A-B. The monumental structure looks somewhat like a rectangular exedra high on the bank above the modern entrance to the site, but this is pure conjecture. Whatever its character, it must be attributed to the period of the palace in which squared poros blocks were used.

Assignable to the earliest period is the system comprising Walls I, F, E, and a remnant, Wall U, invisible underneath Wall C, all founded on *stereo* (Fig. 307). They enclose an area approximately 4.80 m. long from east to west by 3.90 m. wide. Vestiges of an earth floor were noted, and in the middle area an irregular flat slab fitted in *stereo,* which might have supported a post or column, though no marks of a circle or a setting place of any other shape could be recognized.

Above the floor and *stereo* lay a quantity of animal bones, many bits of flint, obsidian, and other stone, much broken pottery, for the most part miserable little pieces, but identifiable as of early Mycenaean times. The total absence of kylix fragments was the most noteworthy observation in the collection of sherds.

Remnants of walls to the west, south, and east show that there once were buildings in the area but the ruins are too scanty to allow any conclusion concerning their date and purpose. Only Drain W (Figs. 37, 307) needs a brief description: it slopes down in a southwestward line, built with walls of thinnish flat stones on each side and covered with fairly large slabs spanning the channel. At the upper end a later wall blocks the drain. The channel, filled with earth, contained 30 fragments of pottery, including two bits from the leg of a tripod vessel, and some animal bones. Not one sherd was distinctive enough to be dated, but the drain must have belonged to an earlier installation.

The survival of these early walls lying in the hollow, worn or sunk in *stereo,* extending across the plateau of the acropolis, gives ground to conclude that the hill in Late Helladic I was occupied by houses. In any event it is clear that the walls once had branches extending out; only truncated stubs are left. The missing parts were evidently founded on *stereo* at a higher level than that of the hollow, and must have been razed and removed in a considerable transformation of the hilltop in a later period, presumably the time when the palace of Mycenaean III B was being constructed.

OBJECTS FOUND [8]
(Fig. 109)

BRONZE

Arrowhead (No. 4): l. pres. 0.022 m., max. w. 0.014 m. Two joining fragments, point and barbs missing.

LEAD

Fragment (No. 12): l. 0.058 m., max. w. 0.02 m. Thin, flat, and bent.

Another piece (No. 13): l. 0.038 m., max. w. 0.024 m. Flat with one rounded end.

STONE

Bead (No. 3): h. 0.005 m., d. 0.006 m. Almost spherical, perforated. Carnelian.

Remnants of rhyton (Nos. 1 and 2): larger piece l. 0.10 m., max. w. 0.058 m., max. th. 0.025 m., min. th. 0.005 m.; smaller piece 0.014 m. by 0.017 m., th. 0.004 m. to 0.005 m. Two fragments of greenish Lacedemonian stone. Chief piece skillfully carved, apparently rhyton in form of lion's head, but no clue to exact shape of vessel. Cf. rhyton of gold from Fourth Shaft Grave at Mycenae (*Schachtgräber*, 77f., pls. CXVII and CXVIII).

Point (No. 5): l. pres. 0.022 m., w. 0.013 m. Tip missing. Petal-shaped, brownish flint.

Arrowhead (No. 6): l. pres. 0.018 m., w. across barbs 0.012 m., th. 0.003 m. Barbed type; point, tips of barbs missing. Brownish flint.

Arrowhead (No. 7): l. 0.034 m., w. 0.025 m., th. 0.006 m. Greenish and reddish mottled flint.

Blade (No. 11): l. 0.026 m., w. 0.022 m., th. 0.005 m. One serrated edge. Flint or sandstone.

Disk (No. 9): d. 0.056 m., th. 0.008 m., d. perforation 0.007 m. Only half preserved. Smoothly worked. Sandstone or other gritty stone.

Fragment (No. 10): l. 0.031 m., w. 0.028 m. Smoothly rounded on one side, straight on other. Opaque stone.

Large button (No. 8): h. 0.02 m., d. 0.033 m., d. small end 0.007 m., d. perforation 0.005 m. Shanked conoid type. Brownish stone, perhaps steatite.

BONE

Awl (No. 15): l. pres. 0.048 m., w. 0.015 m., th. 0.008 m. Fragment, neatly pointed.

Awl (No. 16): l. pres. 0.07 m., w. 0.01 m., th. 0.006 m. Tip lacking.

CLAY

Miniature bowl? (No. 14): h. 0.02 m., d. 0.035 m., d. of hollow 0.02 m. Small hemispherical object of coarse clay, red on outside, black inside. Very crude and rough.

TERRACOTTA

Whorl (No. 17): h. 0.015 m., d. 0.021 m., d. perforation 0.006 m. Small, rounded, conical. Made of red clay containing mica.

Whorl (No. 18): h. 0.027 m., d. 0.027 m. Large, biconical.

POTTERY

Everywhere in area broken pottery was collected in abundance but no pots could be put together. Most of sherds are Early Mycenaean wares. Fragments found in street between Walls H and J shown in Figs. 131, 132.

TRENCHES SOUTHEAST OF PALACE AND AQUEDUCT

The aqueduct that brought water to the Main Building of the palace, running from northeast to southwest along the top of the Englianos hill (*PN* I, 332ff., fig. 416), divides the northeasterly half of the plateau into two areas, southeastern and northwestern. For convenience we take advantage of this division in deal-

[8] Objects recorded were scattered throughout whole Belvedere area.

ing with the many trial soundings that were opened on the hilltop (Fig. 302). We begin with the southeastern slope in front of the Main Building of the palace and proceed northeastward to the northeasterly end of the hill and then return southwestward on the northwestern side of the water channel.

To the southeast of the Main Building and the Workshop nine trenches were excavated descending the gradual slope toward the lower terrace, which has often been mentioned. Those numbered S 3, S 5, S 7, S 9, and S 11 (Fig. 302) were parallel explorations carried out in 1952, some 8 m. to 10 m. apart, in an attempt to ascertain the limits of the palace structures on this side. Trenches S 3, S 5, and S 7 crossed into what was later found to be the Main Building; S 9 ascended into Ramp 91, and S 11 reached the middle of the Northeastern Building. Trenches S 6, S 8, S 10, and S 12 were dug in 1962 under the supervision of Mrs. Kittredge. Three of the soundings, S 6, S 8, and S 10, did not encroach on the palace structures since they were laid out lower down the slope, S 10 lying at the level of the terrace below (Fig. 52). Here, near the lower end of the latter trench, *stereo* seemed to have been cut in a diagonal slot crossing the trench; to the southeast of the cutting, which probably marked the line of a missing wall, a deposit of debris reached a depth of 1.56 m. It contained fallen stones, mixed pottery, kylix stems of the palace period, Early Mycenaean, and sherds of Minyan Ware.

In one respect all these nine trenches were generally alike: on the actual slope *stereo* appeared at a depth of only 0.15 m. to 0.30 m.; no walls, no stones, and only a few nondescript sherds were found. Once the crest of the ascent was passed, or the lower terrace reached, however, the accumulation was much deeper and many stones were exposed.

Trench S 12 (Fig. 53), laid out below the Palace Workshop, was later extended northwestward 2 m. across the southeastern limit of Room 100. In this upper section the deposit had a maximum depth of 1.12 m., the lower part of which appeared to be an undisturbed Middle Helladic layer, 0.62 m. deep. Though containing much coarse pottery, some fragments bearing incised decoration, it also yielded sherds of Gray Minyan and Mattpainted Wares. A flint blade recovered in the deposit is illustrated in Figure 107 No. 2.

Near the northeastern end of the Englianos hill, about 15 m. from the steep edge, a trial trench (MY 2, Fig. 302) was dug in 1958 by Miss Rawson. Running from north to south, it was 1 m. wide and 29 m. long. At a depth of 0.15 m. to 0.30 m., *stereo* was reached. No walls, no stones, and only a few nondescript potsherds, but no kylix stems, were recovered along with a piece of flint and a fragment of an arrowhead.

This unproductive sounding crossed at right angles the eastern end of Trench

IV (Fig. 302), which had been opened in 1939 by Mr. McDonald in a test of the northeasterly part of the hill. Running from west to east to a length of 50 m., with a breadth of 2 m., it was a handsome trench but, except for the walls encountered in the Belvedere area (Fig. 54), only a smooth, bare stretch of *stereo* was brought to view with virtually no objects. The evidence provided by this single trench in 1939 did not lead us to the conclusion, which we reached after many later campaigns, that almost everything rising above *stereo* in that quarter had been destroyed and carried away, and it was only in natural or artificial hollows that remains earlier than Mycenaean III B were preserved.

The line of Trench IV was shifted a short distance southward from the alignment of Trench III in 1939 in order to avoid destroying a large fine olive tree. Trench III (Fig. 55) was stretched out to a length of 60 m. with a width of 2 m., starting eastward from the north corner of Room 32 in the Main Building. Some 10 m. distant from the exterior wall of the palace the trench in a diagonal line crossed the rubble foundations of a small structure (later when fully uncovered it was found to be a house of four rooms, 103 on Fig. 309; *PN* I, 336) and continuing 25 or 30 m., passed over the aqueduct that runs from Court 42 to the far end of the hill (*PN* I, 332ff.). In the spaces between the buildings mentioned, bare *stereo* was exposed and nothing of any consequence was brought to light.

About 20 m. northeast of the Palace Workshop a trial trench, E 3 (Fig. 302), running from southeast to northwest, was first dug in 1952, and in 1965 enlarged and extended. Through the greater part of its course *stereo* was quickly reached, as in the other trenches in the neighborhood. In one section, however, a transverse wall, built of rubble, 0.60 m. thick and more than 8 m. long, was uncovered (Fig. 56). It rested in part on a very black carbonized deposit, which was probed to a depth of 2.20 m. A good deal of shattered, nondescript, and lime-coated pottery was recovered. The sherds were of types belonging to Mycenaean III B. If not an incinerator of primitive design, this hollow filled with burnt matter might perhaps have been a rubbish pit where trash, debris, and discarded crockery were thrown away.

Opened in 1958 by Miss Rawson, Trench MY 1, beginning just outside the corner of Room 98, extended 22.50 m. northeastward (Figs. 57, 302), ultimately intersecting Trench E 3 mentioned above. Close beside the wall of the Workshop lay a mass of stones, small below and large above, along with debris of crude brick, evidently fallen when the building was destroyed. In the next stretch, 7 m. long, there was a complete change in the earth: here it was black and greasy, containing an abundance of stones and a good deal of pottery occupying a hollow in *stereo*. All was discolored as in the similar deposits noted in Courts 3, 42, and 88 of the palace;[9] here too Geometric sherds revealed the date of the dark intrusion. Farther northeastward the *stereo* rises considerably, and in the continuing course of the trench no walls were found and almost no remnants of pottery below the cultivated soil. A few other soundings in this area produced the same general negative result, the finding of *stereo* some 0.20 m. to 0.30 m. below the surface of the ground.

O B J E C T S   F O U N D
(Fig. 104)

STONE

Fragment of vessel (No. 9): h. pres. 0.042 m., max. d. 0.049 m., d. waist 0.032 m., d. lower part 0.04 m. Remnant of pedestaled cup. Carefully worked. Surface scratched but no trace of decoration. Gray soapy stone.

Button (No. 10): h. 0.007 m., d. 0.041 m., d. perforation 0.003 m. Very small conoid. Light greenish stone.

TRENCHES NORTHWEST OF AQUEDUCT

On the northwestern side of the aqueduct, 18 m. to 34 m. southwest of the Northeast Gateway, three exploratory trenches (CK 8 Ext. III, CK 18, CK 19, Fig. 302) were dug by Mrs. Kittredge in 1962. They disclosed a fairly deep hollow, cut or worn in *stereo*, spreading over an area at least 17 m. from northeast to southwest and more than 16 m. wide, probably extending to the northwestern edge of the hill as indicated by observation in the upper end of Trench W 6 (pp. 8-9). No proper walls appeared though there were a few scattered stones. The space was found filled with a thick deposit reaching a maximum depth of 1.35 m. and containing great quantities of potsherds, for the most part coarse and evidently belonging to the Middle Helladic period (Fig. 134). The pottery was accompanied by quantities of animal bones, much obsidian and a few pieces of flint, a bronze nail, and half a terracotta whorl. The meaning of this accumulation has eluded us: perhaps here too was a repository where broken dishes and other rubbish had been thrown away by the inhabitants of the Middle Helladic settlement.

O B J E C T S   F O U N D
(Fig. 107)

STONE

Arrowhead (No. 5): l. 0.017 m., w. 0.013 m., th. 0.003 m. Barbed type, obsidian.
Blade (No. 6): l. 0.017 m., w. 0.009 m., th. 0.002 m. Obsidian.
Blade (No. 3): l. 0.025 m., w. 0.017 m., th.

0.003 m. One serrated edge. Red-brown flint.
Blade (No. 4): l. 0.035 m., w. 0.012 m., th. 0.004 m. Similar to foregoing; one serrated edge. Red-brown flint.
Blade (No. 7): l. 0.03 m., w. 0.018 m., th.

[9] *PN* I, 64, 184, 294.

0.007 m. One serrated edge, gray flint.

POTTERY

One- or two-handled squat jug (CM. 2669, Fig. 133): h. top rim 0.188 m., h. top handle 0.238 m., h. neck 0.055 m., d. bottom 0.07 m., w. handle ranging from 0.03 m. to 0.06 m. at lower end. Barely half of vessel preserved. Flat bottom, plump ovoid body; wide neck, slightly concave rising to splaying plain rim. One thick flattened handle springs upward from rim and loops down to greatest diameter of pot. Incised decoration beginning on shoulder continues nearly down to bottom. Motive consists of irregular multiple parallel incisions slanting down from right to left, ending in clusters of chevrons. Starting on flattened surface of handle, groups of parallel chevrons open broadly toward base, four incised lines on left and six carelessly drawn on right; widening space between filled with many horizontal lines, far from exactly parallel. Despite negligent execution and poor state of preservation, clearly evident that this was once fine pot. Coarse brown clay, mottled with red and black.

Such thick household vessels in comparable shapes and bearing incised patterns have been found at many sites in Neolithic, Early Helladic, and Middle Helladic levels in south, central, and north Greece. Though the two earlier cultures mentioned no doubt in turn bequeathed some if not many of their methods and inventions to the succeeding way of life, it will be enough to give references to some heavy domestic household crockery of Middle Helladic times: e.g., Olympia, Weege, *AM* 36 (1911), 169f., figs. 12-16, 18; northern Messenia, Valmin, *SME*, 256ff., 286ff., pls. I, II, XVI, XXI; Boeotia, Goldman, *Eutresis*, 180, fig. 250; near Corinth, *MMS* III (1930-1931), 75ff.; Arcadia, Holmberg, *Asea*, 106-110, figs. 105-107; Argos, Vollgraff. *BCH* XXX (1906), 17f., 30, figs. 56-57.

Parallel to the northwest edge of the site Mr. Buck in 1954 extended a trench, continuing the line (but skipping some 20 m.) of an exploration begun by Mr. Mylonas in 1952. The new test (Fig. 302 BB), 25.50 m. long, with two transverse branches, throughout its course discovered no trace of walls. The depth to *stereo* was only 0.50 m.; the earth which had been disturbed, contained a few potsherds, badly worn, including some kylix stems.

In a small area, 10 m. to 22 m. northeast of the Wine Magazine, Mr. Pedley in 1964 uncovered part of the foundations of a rectangular building, 6.73 m. long from east to west (P 13, Fig. 302), the walls varying from 0.73 m. to 0.78 m. in thickness (Fig. 58). Covered by an ashy gray layer, the walls were laid on a yellowish subsoil with sandy patches; no floor could be found nor was there any sign of a doorway in the area exposed. In the western angle a corner of another wall was discovered. Since no floor deposits had survived there was little or no evidence for the character and date of the buildings. It was conjectured that the walls were foundations for a superstructure that had been razed and swept away.[10] The sherds recovered were almost entirely coarse and seemed to be of

[10] In the disturbed deposit was found a barbed arrowhead of light brown flint (Fig. 110 No. 12).

Middle Helladic wares, but there were also some fine pieces of Late Helladic I.

Passing through the same area is a water channel, apparently laid at a time when the above-mentioned walls already existed. The channel was built with two lines of flattish stones set on edge (Fig. 59), but a floor of stones was lacking and no cover slabs appeared. The channel follows close beside the southerly and westerly walls of the rectangular building, then cuts westward through the corner of the second structure, showing that the channel is later than the walls. The deposit lying in the channel contained a good many kylix stems of Mycenaean III B, along with earlier sherds. The conduit was installed in the period of the palace, no doubt carrying water from the aqueduct to the channel descending the steep bank discovered by Miss Rawson in 1958 and exposed a few meters farther by Mr. Smith in 1963 (p. 9).

AREA NORTHEAST AND SOUTHEAST OF WINE MAGAZINE [11]

To the northeast of the Wine Magazine, as well as between the latter and the Palace Workshop, ruins of many walls forming a complex maze indicate that a broad area in this part of the citadel had been occupied by houses before the palace of Mycenaean III B was built (Figs. 303, 309). The surviving evidence shows that all these earlier structures were demolished practically to ground level and deeper in some places. The houses seem to have been built in a neat and orderly manner and most of the rooms, courts, and corridors were provided with good stucco floors as indicated by the patches that have somehow been preserved (Fig. 60). The stucco contains many small pebbles and numerous bits of plaster retaining traces of paint. On the floors and the ground level outside, abundant masses of pottery were found, most of which, so far as we could determine, were of characteristic Mycenaean III B types. Many fragments, however, possibly the majority, displayed no evidence of having passed through a fire; perhaps these were broken kylikes and other pots which had been discarded during a long period before the disaster. All of this layer as well as the walls and a barracks-like structure, belonging to the final phase of the palace, were covered by the burned wreckage of the palace. The earlier buildings were demolished before or when the Wine Magazine was being built, as shown by the evidence of the cutting through of older walls. Similar activity can also be seen at the southeastern limit of the area where earlier walls were truncated during the erection of the Palace Workshop. The destruction of this pre-palatial settlement was certainly very thorough and what has survived is not adequate for a

---

[11] *PN* I, 336-341, figs. 249-252, 410.

reconstruction on paper of the plan and the extent of the buildings, though enough is left to illustrate some striking details of construction. The latest element in the complex, Building 103, has already been dealt with (*PN* 1, 336ff.).

Just to the northwest of that building is a quarter that was apparently occupied by a broad open court paved with good stucco from which one could enter a fairly spacious portico 4 m. wide and 5 m. deep (Figs. 61, 309). It seems to have had a single column in its façade facing southwestward, and a properly made stucco floor (Fig. 62). At its northern corner it opened into a long dog-leg corridor, which exhibits no fewer than five turnings proceeding northeastward and northwestward to a total length of ca. 12 m. It was lined on both sides by stone walls, the opposite sides, however, not being exactly parallel. The corridor thus varies considerably in width from angle to angle. A final stretch, 8.50 m. long with a maximum breadth of 2 m., ends apparently against a wall just short of the steep northwestern edge of the hill. Evidence for an opening in the southwestern wall not far from the northwestern end implies that a doorway gave access into a room or rooms which were surely razed when the Wine Magazine was built (Fig. 63). No other doorway was certainly indicated in the whole extent of the corridor.

In an area between the structures that have been briefly dealt with and the Main Building of the later palace are patches of stucco pavement extending some 10 m. southeastward, one or two stubs of walls, and a circular flat stone, surrounded by smaller stones, probably a column base. All these remnants are too badly damaged or too scanty to be interpreted. There can be no doubt, however, that this area was occupied by houses of the settlement before the palace was built.

The absence of undisturbed floor deposits has left us without adequate evidence for the dating of these houses. The debris covering the area contained innumerable fragments of kylikes, which seem to have been discarded helter-skelter so that no cup could be put together. Among this collection of rubbish were noticed some very fine pieces that might have come from pottery of Mycenaean III A (Fig. 144). This evidence is not wholly adequate to demonstrate that the settlement surely belonged to Mycenaean III A.

Near the northwestern end of the corridor described above, Mr. Smith in 1963 dug a deep sounding to test the stratification under the stucco paving. In a series of arbitrary cuts, the pit was excavated to *stereo* at a depth of 1.25 m. The earth did not change markedly, though it became darker in the deeper strata. Each cut produced a small quantity of animal bones. The pottery directly under the pavement included some pieces of Mycenaean III A with a few elements that look earlier. From a depth of 0.65 m. downward the painted pieces are attributable to Late Helladic I (Fig. 124); from 1 m. Mattpainted Ware becomes much more abundant (Fig. 125), though Mycenaean pieces of Late Helladic I continue scantily to *stereo*.[12]

In our preliminary report of 1958 (*AJA* 63 [1959], 123) we ventured to conjecture that the houses in this area might belong to the early part of Mycenaean III B. We are now inclined to suggest that they may rather have been built in the later phases of Mycenaean III A. It seems highly unlikely that the king installed in the Main Building would have tolerated such houses so close to the palace.

OBJECTS FOUND
(Fig. 112)

LEAD

Disk (No. 6): d. 0.025 m., th. ca. 0.004 m., 18 grams. Irregular in shape and thickness, perhaps weight.

Disk (No. 7): d. 0.024 m., th. ca. 0.004 m., 14 grams. Irregular in shape and thickness.

STONE

Flint arrowhead (No. 1): l. 0.015 m., max. w. across barbs 0.015 m., th. 0.003 m. Barbed type, point missing.

Flint blade (No. 2): l. 0.035 m., max. w. 0.02 m., th. 0.006 m. One serrated edge, grayish.

Obsidian blade (No. 3): l. 0.043 m., max. w. 0.028 m., th. 0.003 m. Flattened oval, serrated edge.

Steatite button (No. 4): h. 0.011 m., d. 0.018 m., d. base 0.004 m. Shanked conoid type, top slightly hollow, perforation off center. Dark bluish.

Celt (No. 13): l. 0.065 m., w. 0.041 m., th. 0.02 m. Edge chipped. Greenish stone.

Whetstone (No. 14): l. 0.084 m., max. w. 0.024 m., th. 0.02 m.-0.027 m. On each side a hollow (d. ca. 0.01 m.), perhaps useful for fastening handle. Gray sandy stone, worn, cracked.

TERRACOTTA

Animal figurine (No. 8): h. 0.044 m., l. pres. 0.048 m., d. body 0.019 m. Hind quarters with only one leg preserved. Short bobbed tail projecting about 0.009 m. Scant traces of paint between legs. Brick-red clay.

Button (No. 5): h. 0.016 m., d. 0.022 m., d. bottom 0.008 m. Broad end hollowed, small perforation (d. 0.003 m.). Shape almost shanked. Dark grayish-brown clay.

Whorl (No. 9): h. 0.02 m., d. 0.029 m., d. perforation 0.005 m. Rounded bicone, light buff clay.

Whorl (No. 10): h. 0.02 m., d. 0.03 m., d. perforation 0.005 m. Rounded bicone, dark brown clay.

Large whorl (No. 11): h. 0.035 m., d. 0.035 m., d. perforation 0.008 m. Bicone with flat band around middle. Coarse gritty brown clay.

Large whorl (No. 12): h. 0.036 m., h. of cylindrical part 0.02 m., d. 0.027 m., d. of perforation 0.007 m. Odd shape, conical, superposed on cylinder. Gritty, sandy brown and blackish clay; notably heavy.

[12] Beyond the northeastern wall of the corridor deep digging produced pottery of the same early kinds in sequence: wares of Late Helladic I and near the bottom almost exclusively Mattpainted Ware.

REMAINS FOUND UNDER THE PALACE OF MYCENAEAN III B

Underneath the Wine Magazine

Under the floor of the vestibule of the Wine Magazine (Fig. 303 Room 104) a sounding made in 1958, begun by Miss Rawson and continued by Mr. French, revealed at a depth of 0.82 m. a substantial wall, 1.45 m. thick (Fig. 64). For the greater part it was built of flattish stones, standing to a height of 0.40 m. to 0.55 m. in six courses. Running from southwest to northeast, it was covered with yellowish earth resembling *stereo* which lay beneath a loose deposit of small stones and mixed earth that contained quantities of potsherds. In the deeper part of the trench the earth alongside the wall yielded an arrowhead and some bits of flint, many animal bones, and sherds of Middle Helladic wares. *Stereo* was reached at 1.60 m. below the floor of the vestibule.

Too little of the wall was seen to shed light on its character and purpose. It is thick enough to be part of a substantial circuit wall or the foundation of a large building, and it must probably be assigned to the Middle Helladic period. The yellow layer above the wall contained a good deal of pottery of mixed Early and Late Mycenaean ware. As noted by Mr. French, the whole deposit looked as if it had been heaped up at the time of the construction of the Wine Magazine or the palace of Mycenaean III B.

In the same year, 1958, Mr. Papathanasopoulos dug a small trial pit between the southwest wall of the Wine Magazine and the northeastern wall of the Main Building alongside Room 27. Here a deposit like that described above was discovered and an abundance of broken pottery was brought to light. These sherds, which closely resemble those produced by the sounding in the vestibule (104), ranged in date from Mycenaean III A to earlier fabrics going back to the Middle Bronze Age.

Underneath Corridor 26

Corridor 26 (Fig. 303), 1.63 m. wide, was not paved with stucco but had an earth floor. It therefore offered an opportunity to examine the deposit underneath this quarter of the palace. Accordingly in 1960 Miss Rawson carried out a thorough investigation which revealed some interesting items. Barely 0.40 m. below the floor of the corridor were found remnants of the bottom parts of three large jars or pithoi, clear evidence of an earlier period of occupation (Fig. 65). Still deeper was uncovered a substantial wall, running from southeast to northwest, above which were superposed the northwestern wall of Room 32 as well as the southeastern wall of Room 27 (Fig. 66). This earlier structure, 1.25 m. thick and standing to a height of 1.85 m., was based on *stereo*. It was built largely of rough field stones, though these were reinforced in some courses by roughly squared blocks of poros of various sizes. This style of masonry using a mixture of field stones and dressed stones has been observed in some walls of Early Mycenaean date, going back at least as far as Late Helladic I. In the earth that had accumulated against the southwestern face of the wall, a considerable amount of pottery was recovered. It seemed to lie in stratified order, with a very few Late Mycenaean sherds just under the floor of the corridor, a good many Early Mycenaean fragments, Late Helladic I, in the next lower level, and in the greatest depths almost exclusively fragments of Middle Helladic wares, comprising Mattpainted, coarse incised, Argive and Gray Minyan types (Fig. 135).

Corridor 25: Pit under Pavement to *Stereo*

In 1957 the Department of Restoration and Conservation in the Greek Archaeological Service proposed to build a protective roof over the Main Building of the palace. Soundings were made for the foundations of concrete piers to hold up the superstructure that had been planned. The work was postponed later when the Service changed the design, and the erection of the roof was delayed to allow the Expedition more time to study the details of the building and to take more photographs. Not far from the northwestern end of Corridor 25 (Fig. 303) a hole for a pier had been dug to a depth of 0.75 m. below the floor without finding *stereo*. In the following season, 1958, we were glad to have a chance to deepen this pit to study the stratification under the palace. The area was broadened considerably without finding walls on any side. The deposit, consisting of light brown clay, showed no visible layers or strata; a good many animal bones and potsherds were recovered down to the very bottom on *stereo*. In the upper 0.75 m. Mycenaean pottery antedating the palace was found (Fig. 136). A few early Mycenaean sherds accompanied by Middle Helladic pieces continued to appear in the middle layer to a depth of 1.15 m. (Fig. 137). Beyond that point to *stereo* we reached what seemed to be almost a pure Middle Helladic deposit in which Gray Minyan, Mattpainted, and coarse wares were all represented (Fig. 138). A study of the fragments shows a considerable mixture of wares especially in the upper strata, although the general evolution from Middle Helladic to late Mycenaean III B is recognizable. As in other parts of the hill, beneath and behind the palace, much evidence of disturbance of the underlying layers is unmistakable, a condition we attribute to the large-scale preparation of the site for the erection of the palace.

Pit outside Room 24

In 1955 Mr. Hubbe made a deep sounding outside the northwest wall of Room 24, extending the line of a trial trench that was dug in 1952 by Mr. Vanderpool (Fig. 67; *PN* I, fig. 403). The pit reached a depth, on *stereo*, of 3.30 m. but shed little light on the stratification of the deposit under the palace. Beneath surface soil, 0.30 m. deep, lay hard black earth covering the top of the wall. A bedding trench had been dug for the laying of the foundations of the palace leaving some traces of the *baugrube* on the outside. It was cut through a fairly thin ashy gray stratum and continued on into a much deeper light gray deposit. The wall stopped at 1.77 m. below the surface, 1.53 m. above *stereo*. Unfortunately no distinctive sherds were recovered from the black earth or the ashy gray stratum nor was there any evidential material in the earth filling the *baugrube*. The deep light gray layer provided abundant sherds including characteristic pieces of Late Helladic I in its upper levels, and in the lower reaches many fragments of Matt-painted as well as Gray and Black Minyan Wares (Fig. 145). Fragments of painted plaster were found to a depth of 1.42 m. and from this point to the bottom animal bones appeared in quantities.

The stratigraphic evidence indicates that much of the deposit above the lowest Middle Helladic layers had been disturbed. One might conjecture that in preliminary grading operations when the project for the Palace of Nestor was laid out, it was found necessary to raise the level of the ground toward the northwestern edge of the hill.

Underneath Rooms 18, 20, 21, and 22

Brief mention was made (*PN* I, 120f., 127, 133f.) of patches of stucco pavement which were found here and there some 0.20 m. to 0.30 m. below the earth floors of Rooms 18, 20, 21, and 22. These remains pointed to an earlier phase of occupation. The entire western corner of the Main Building also indicates that the whole angle had at some time been seriously damaged or destroyed by a catastrophe of some magnitude—probably by fire or earthquakes—and had been subsequently rebuilt without the framework of great vertical and horizontal timbers, which were used throughout the palace in the original construction. Exactly when this event occurred could not be determined, but it was almost surely in one of the very late phases of Mycenaean III B. The underlying stuccoed floors mentioned above, however, evidently belong to an earlier period.

Three short sections of walls clearly associated with the pavements were exposed to view (Fig. 303). Two segments appeared, one running from northeast to southwest (Fig. 68), the other from northwest to southeast, under the floor of Room 21, the two obviously having once joined to form a corner. At the northwestern end of Room 22, another stretch of wall was revealed, aligned with the remnant oriented from northeast to southwest in Room 21.

Underneath the northwestern part of Room 18 no earlier wall has survived, but below the latest earthen floor an area of stuccoed pavement is preserved:

it has a straight finished edge, running from northwest to southeast and turning upward toward the northeast. The rising edge once made contact with a plastered wall along the northeastern side. Similar evidence of two upturned edges of stucco flooring, one rising to the southeast and the other to the northwest, revealed between them a gap, 0.86 m. broad, running from northeast to southwest, which had been covered by the earth floor of Room 18. A wall must once have stood in the empty strip, bordered on each side by a stucco paving.

In the northwestern part of Room 20—and seen only in a break of the floor that we enlarged—another patch of the earlier pavement was recognized. It had a straight worked edge toward the southwest, turning upward in the usual manner of adjusting stucco floors to walls. The alignment here agrees with the parallel orientation followed by the traces of the wall, running from northeast to southwest, that was uncovered in Room 21.

The stucco floors, despite the damage they had suffered, contribute a little evidence to suggest that the older building contained rectangular rooms, though the remains are too scanty to permit a reconstruction.

No distinctive pottery was recovered from the stucco pavements to give a decisive chronological clue. In any event, it was obvious that the underlying structure must certainly be earlier than the palace. We were led to conclude that the house or building to which the skimpy stucco floors and crumbling walls belonged was a structure of Mycenaean III A.

Underneath Rooms 55, 56, 57, and Archives Room 7

As recorded (*PN* I, 225-227), several earlier walls were discovered below the level of the palace of Mycenaean III B just to the northeast of the Propylon (Fig. 303). Beneath Room 56 are ruins of two walls running from southeast to northwest and two others oriented from northeast to southwest. One of the latter (m, Fig. 310) is broad enough to have supported an exterior wall. Remnants of two floors made of stucco (s) and a third paved with pebbles evidently mark three successive phases of occupation. Three hollow cuttings into *stereo*, two of which still retained considerable remains of large pithoi (p), clearly belong to this complex of buildings. Underlying Room 57 another more substantial foundation (Wall y), possibly 2.20 m. wide, was certainly at some time the substructure of an outside wall. Before our excavations began, this area had been subjected to illicit digging by persons unknown and a deep pit filled with loose earth and small stones showed that the original deposit had been badly disturbed to its very bottom on *stereo*. A part of one jar, below Room 55, still contained five or more small plain conical cups (*PN* I, fig. 337). Although they are unfortunately not decorated with painted patterns of distinctive types to fix the chronology and although the other scattered potsherds left by the marauders provided no decisive clue, we felt that we were dealing with wares of Mycenaean III A.

Underneath Archives Room 7, on the southwest side of the Propylon (Fig. 303), a surviving segment of a well-built wall was exposed in 1952 (*PN* I, 94, figs. 15-17). This short fragment was obviously part of the front wall of an earlier palace building and it must surely have been associated with one or the other of the two outside walls northeast of the Propylon. The ashlar blocks likewise belong to a structure that antedates the surviving palace or to an earlier phase of Mycenaean III B. The orientation of the walls in question leads us to conclude that the older palace too had its main entrance approximately where the later Propylon now stands. If this conjecture is correct, it follows that the front of the older building also had an outward jog in its northeastward course beyond the gateway. The early wall beneath Room 7 was covered over with debris ranging from 0.18 m. to 0.30 m. thick, upon which was laid the earthen floor of Room 7. The filling material contained many fragments of horizontally ribbed pithoi, the rope-bands bearing irregular transverse gashes made by fingernails or hard implements. The clay of these jars was thickly permeated with particles of mica. Along with this coarse ware were numerous nondescript sherds of thinner fabrics, some of III B, the majority probably of Mycenaean III A, and a few possibly still earlier.

Under Hall 65

In 1956 Mrs. Blegen opened an exploratory sounding in the middle of Hall 65 (Fig. 303) to ascertain whether there was a hearth like that in the Throne Room of the Main Building. Two years later she enlarged the cutting into a trench, 2 m. broad and 3.25 m. long, running transversely from southeast to northwest (B 58, Fig. 302). After removing the surface soil, 0.20 m. deep—which already lay beneath the level of the eroded floor of the hall—she reached a deposit of ashy gray earth, 0.30 m. thick and resting just above yellowish *stereo*. This stratum contained great quantities of shattered pottery which may possibly have been packed into the area to form a bedding for a hearth within the rectangle marked out by one stone column base and remains of the foundations of three others (*PN* I, 256f.). No certain vestiges of a hearth could be recognized. A study of the pottery from the gray earth disclosed that it consisted almost exclusively of wares assignable to Mycenaean III A (e.g., Figs. 139, 141). Some sherds from the plowed ground exhibit the style of Mycenaean III B, and a few from the lowest stratum on *stereo* are distinctive of Late Helladic II and I.

Probings here and there in the southwestern parts of Hall 65, far below the level of the missing floor, produced only Early Mycenaean pottery. Worthy of special mention is a small sealstone of jasper, found just after a heavy rain in 1963 on the eroded slope. It was discovered by Mrs. Charles S. Lamy of St. Louis, who was visiting the site in a group under the guidance of Professor G. E. Mylonas. She kindly turned the gem over to the archaeological authorities and it is now displayed in the museum at Chora.

OBJECTS FOUND

Already published (*PN* I, 258f., fig. 300 nos. 6, 8, 12, 14, 15): ring of thin silver wire (12), flat bronze strip (14), small cylinder of lead perhaps for mending pottery (15), stone bead, steatite button (6), and arrowhead of flint (8).

Sealstone (CM. 2532, Fig. 111:a, b): l. 0.019 m., w. 0.017 m., th. 0.0065 m. Jasper. Almost amygdaloid in shape. Pierced longitudinally. Decorated face, carefully carved, bears a cuttlefish: body ending below in round swelling, narrows somewhat, then broadens upward to top; from latter on each side long arm swings outward, then downward to terminate in spiral coil on right and almost a circle on left. Near right and left edges of seal (crossing over perforation) apparently two arms, probably extensions of two or three branching out and upward to right and left from mouth. Well designed, sparing in detail. Only six arms can be counted instead of ten possessed by *Sepia*. In National Museum at Athens are several comparable seals from Crete, all illustrated in *CMS* I, nos. 450-454.

Under Stairway 69

In 1962 a small probe was undertaken, supervised by Miss Rawson, in the narrow space that once contained Stairway 69 (Fig. 303). The latter, leading to the upper story of the Southwestern Building, was flanked on the northwest by Corridor 70 and Room 74 and on the southeast by the walls of Halls 64 and 65 (*PN* I, 263f.). Only insignificant remnants of two actual steps had survived *in situ* in the otherwise empty area to explain its original function. Below the level of the vanished stairs a transverse pit (R 62, Fig. 302) was dug to investigate the underlying deposit and the substructures of the lateral walls, especially of that belonging to Hall 65. This foundation was seen to be remarkably thick (Fig. 69), having a width of 1.55 m. in its lower southwestern section, which was reduced by 0.60 m. at the northeastern end, where contact with the northwestern wall of Hall 64 was made (*PN* I, 255). We failed to determine why this fine wall changed its thickness before reaching its end. The builders may have thought it necessary that support for the wall should be appreciably thickened in its course running down the steep edge of the acropolis where it was laid on *stereo* nearly 2 m. deeper than in the northeastern section. The probe yielded its quota of potsherds, for the greater part nondescript, many fragments of coarse ware from large storage jars, and all apparently earlier than the stage of Mycenaean III B.

Under Room 74

Under the supervision of Mr. Pedley in 1964 a trial trench was dug beneath the floor level of Room 74 in the Southwestern Building (Fig. 303). The cutting was later extended southwesterly across the exterior wall of the palace. The digging was carried out in eight arbitrary cuts and the total depth to *stereo* was nearly 1 m. Since the underlying deposit in this place had apparently been disturbed, perhaps by the foundation trenches for the construction of the Southwestern Building, no clear stratification could be recognized, though a thin layer of ashes and burnt matter was noted at a depth of ca. 0.50 m. The space in the trench was much restricted by an earlier wall of substantial thickness (1.10 m.) which was uncovered below the floor of Room 74; it had been found and traced by Mr. Papathanasopoulos in 1960 to a length of 16 m., and it must have belonged to a large older structure (Fig. 70) which was apparently demolished when Room 65 was built.

A good many animal bones were recoved from the trench along with a relative abundance of potsherds. Fragmentary remnants of wares attributable to Mycenaean III B were found in all levels down to *stereo,* accompanied by an admixture of earlier material.

O B J E C T S   F O U N D
(Fig. 110)

BRONZE

Fragment of pin (No. 14): l. pres. 0.058 m., d. 0.002 m. Broken at one end.

STONE

Button (No. 11): h. 0.008 m., d. 0.014 m., d. perforation 0.003 m. Conoid. Steatite.

TERRACOTTA

Upper part of figurine (No. 13): h. pres. 0.028 m., w. head 0.012 m., w. across shoulders 0.024 m. Pinkish-buff clay. Birdlike face, large blobs for eyes, one breast preserved.

Trench 64-6

Outside the corner once formed by Sections 6 and 7 of the exterior southwestern wall of the Southwestern Building in its early phases (*PN* 1, 279) but underneath a room belonging to Mycenaean III B, Mr. Pedley in 1964 dug a small trench to test the underlying deposit (Fig. 306). The sounding was 2.40 m. long and 1.40 m. wide. The angle was found to contain many large worked blocks of poros (Fig. 71) that had been tumbled together in a disorderly heap. Most of the stones had been badly damaged by fire and the area was filled with ashy burnt matter and black earth that contained many animal bones and an impressive collection of pottery. In the upper levels—comprising much more than half of the total depth of the sounding—pottery of Mycenaean III B was abundantly, if not exclusively, represented; toward the bottom of the trench wares of Mycenaean III A and earlier (including six conical cups)[13] began to appear (Fig. 142), but even at the very lowest point reached, at 1.55 m. below the ground, some fragments in the style of Mycenaean III B were still being found.

Complex of walls under southwestern side of Court 63

Jutting out from underneath the ragged edges of the stucco pavement that still survives along the southwestern flank of Court 63 is a complex of stone walls, obviously belonging to an earlier building in this area (Fig. 306). It has already been briefly described (*PN* I, 282), but some further mention should be made of these remains of habitation found beneath the palace of Mycenaean III B.

The principal wall, 0.85 m. thick, running from northwest to southeast, was traced to a total length of 15 m. without reaching a finished beginning or end. Five somewhat thinner walls branch off at right angles toward the southwest, all but one merely short truncated stubs. Two of these were found to continue also northeastward beyond the main wall, but it was not possible to ascertain how many more extended in that direction and how far they proceeded underneath the well-preserved stucco floor of Court 63. The evidence is in any event adequate to show that there were five or more rooms of no great size in the southwesterly row, and at least three or more in the northeasterly.

All these walls were trimly built of field stones of no great size, along with a good many small blocks of poros, squared and rather neatly dressed. This is a style that seems to have been favored in Late Helladic I and II and probably also in the ceramic period of Mycenaean III A but not observed in Phase III B.

The main wall mentioned above appears to have been cut off when Sections 9 and 10 of the exterior wall of the Southwestern Building were erected (Fig. 306). Some 2 m. to the north of the long wall, underneath Corridor 61, a segment of a similar wall was uncovered (Fig. 72); and beneath the floor of Room 62 another substantial wall of the same kind, with a spur to the southwest, was brought to light. Whether these various walls, unconnected in their present state, originally belonged to one large building or to separate structures, we were unable to determine.

No floor of stucco and none clearly marked by tamped earth or clay could be recognized; we thus lacked floor deposits altogether to help fix the date of this complex of walls. The ground level contemporary with the buildings had presumably been dug away for the Late Mycenaean palace, or had been eroded by rain and wind. Based on very little factual evidence, we think that the wall complex was a work of the fourteenth century B.C. or earlier.

[13] CM. 1988-CM. 1994. Cf. *PN* I, Shape 11, 359f., figs. 353, 354.

Trench 64-17

Outside the southwestern face of Section 10 of the exterior wall and underneath the ruined rooms of the latest phase of the palace, a pit was opened by Mr. Pedley in 1964 (Fig. 306). The wall was found to be supported on three or four courses of field stones, 0.60 m. high, resting on yellowish-gray clay (Fig. 73). The earth lying alongside the wall contained burnt matter, especially intensified at the bottom of the substructure. The upper stratum yielded a few sherds of Mycenaean III B but the deeper deposit produced only early Mycenaean fabrics, as well as a fragment or two of Middle Helladic wares.

BUILDING X

Building X (p. 12 and Fig. 306) may indeed have formed an integral part of the defensive wall that has been traced, perhaps the substructure of a tower in the circuit and possibly standing beside a gateway. The foundations are massive, built in part of large roughly dressed blocks, and in part repaired or reinforced by patches of rubble. The southerly wall of the building is 1.70 m. thick and 10.45 m. long on its outer face (Fig. 74). The big blocks were laid on smaller flattish slabs in the foundation. The opposite parallel wall on the north, also 1.70 m. broad, is only 10.10 m. long. The western and eastern end walls, approximately 6 m. long, varied in thickness, 1.40 m. on the west, 1.50 m. on the east. Both had been laid intentionally along slightly inward tapering lines running northward. This curious plan of building recalls the similar taper that was observed by Dörpfeld in several of the large houses of Troy VI, which in some instances were bordered by streets that ascended toward the summit of the hill (*TI*, 158f., 162). Evidence of a street on either side of Building X is lacking.

The western end of the building was in part covered over by an extensive structure clearly contemporary with the palace of Mycenaean III B. Although scanty, the ruins may be the substructure of a projecting colonnade along the southwesterly side of Court 58 (Fig. 303).

The sole clue is a long column base with a diameter of 0.64 m. (*PN* I, 228, fig. 175), surviving about 4 m. toward the northeast of Building X, almost in line with the northeastern wall of Room 60 (Fig. 306). The hypothetical colonnade would have had to stand at a much higher level than the remains of Building X.

In 1964 Mr. Pedley sank two exploratory shafts (64-5 W and 64-5 N, Fig. 306) to investigate the foundations of the northern corner of Building X. The substructure on the west was seen to be built mainly of irregular smallish stones along with one large squared block (Fig. 75). On the northern side the supporting wall has been badly dismantled; it had been constructed chiefly of rubble.

No traces of a floor had survived in Building X: all had been carried away by erosion and we have no potsherds to provide evidence for dating the use and period of construction.

Immediately beyond the easterly end of Building X a massive foundation was exposed (Fig. 306). It looks as if it was either an annex or a remnant of a similar earlier structure that had for the greater part been demolished in order to make way for Building X. Only a small part of the eastern end has survived, having a breadth of 6.75 m. and jutting out some 3 m. from the eastern wall of Building X. The foundation walls are remarkably broad, those on the side having a thickness of 1.80 m. and that on the eastern end 1.40 m. No floor and no deposits of pottery were found to give chronological clues.

SOUTHERN CORNER

The greater part of the southern corner of the site, containing the ruined walls described on pages 13-14ff., was excavated during the seasons of 1961-1965 by Mr. and Mrs. Blegen and in 1963 also by Mr. Smith. The entire area (W 21, Fig. 302) was found to be a repository for masses of wreckage and debris of buildings, evidently dumped from the higher ground. One might reasonably conjecture that this large task of shifting earth and stone away from the top of the acropolis was necessary in preparation for clearing space for the construction of the palace of Mycenaean III B.

The dump lay as if it had been brought in successive waves: a deep layer of pebbles and small stones was followed and partly covered by a thick stratum of grayish clay, consisting chiefly of dissolved crude brick; behind and overlapping the latter is a formidable heap of much coarser rubble and smallish stones (Fig. 76). The whole mass filled and rolled over some artificial pits or hollows that had been gouged out in *stereo,* then flowed on across the ruined parallel walls, ultimately to bury some burned and blackened houses of Mycenaean III A in the upper edge of the lower town.

The layer of gravelly bits of broken stone and that of the coarser material yielded almost no potsherds, but on the top of the intervening gray deposit of disintegrated brick were recovered a basin and 17 small pots of various shapes, almost all in shattered state with surface badly weathered and worn away (Fig. 77). Most of these vessels were undecorated; they seemed to be attributable to Mycenaean III A and III B.

OBJECTS FOUND
(Fig. 106)

STONE

Arrowhead (No. 16): l. 0.02 m., max. w. 0.014 m., th. 0.003 m. Barbed type, tips of barbs missing. Red flint.

Arrowhead (No. 17): l. pres. 0.016 m., max. w. 0.01 m. Barbed type, point missing; long, narrow shape, very thin. Gray flint.

Petal-shaped point (No. 7): l. 0.03 m., w. 0.01 m., th. 0.004 m. Flint.

TERRACOTTA

Head of figurine (No. 15): h. pres. 0.012 m., w. head 0.013 m., w. neck 0.01 m. Seen in profile has a decided notch to indicate mouth. Buff clay, no paint preserved.

POTTERY

Conical cups (CM. 2675, CM. 2676, CM. 2677, CM. 2678, Fig. 143:1-4; CM. 2687, Fig. 143:7): cf. Shape 11, *PN* I, 359f., figs. 353, 354; *MP*, Type 204. H. ranging from 0.055 m. to 0.087 m., d. from 0.06 m. to 0.155 m.

Small pithoid jars (CM. 2679, CM. 2681, CM. 2682, CM. 2683, Fig. 143:8, 9, 10, 12): cf. Shape 51, *PN* I, 386, figs. 375, 376; *MP*, Type 28. H. ranging from 0.104 m. to 0.115 m., d. from 0.087 m. to 0.097 m.

Narrow-necked spouted jug (CM. 2684, Fig. 143:13): no exact parallel. Cf. CM. 1556 from Chamber Tomb E-6 (p. 187 and Fig. 244:21; and *MP*, Type 144, p. 30, fig. 5). H. 0.273 m., d. neck 0.035 m., d. body 0.197 m., d. foot 0.063 m., d. base 0.068 m., w. handle 0.028 m. Two-thirds of neck, all of spout, some pieces of body missing. Surface practically gone, leaving faint traces of curving vertical bands on shoulder (cf. *PN* I, fig. 391 no. 595). Rather elegant shape. Narrow neck, slightly concave. Probably had high spout. Raised ridge at junction of neck and body, ovoid body tapering to pedestal base or foot with ring base, hollow underneath. Ridged handle terminating in elongated knob.

Fragment of shallow spouted bowl (CM. 2680, Fig. 143:11): resembles Shape 7, *PN* I, 357f., figs. 351, 352; *MP*, Type 253, but has open trough spout. H. 0.043 m., d. 0.126 m., l. of spout ca. 0.015 m. About one-fourth of rim and side missing, as well as handle. Flattened bottom, no real base. Slightly offset rim sloping inward.

Shallow rounded bowl (CM. 2685, Fig. 143:5): H. 0.051 m., d. 0.113 m., d. base 0.05 m. Rounded side curving to plain rim. Flat bottom with string marks. Tiny spout where rim is pulled out slightly. Handle not preserved; chips of rim missing. Coarse red-brown fabric with gritty surface.

Very shallow rounded bowl (CM. 2686, Fig. 143:6). Shape 66, *PN* I, 411, figs. 395, 396; *MP*, Type 311, but shallower. H. 0.028 m., d. 0.105 m., d. flattened bottom 0.035 m. Traces of handle-attachment on rim (illustrated handle does not join). Red-brown mottled with black. Surface worn away.

Basin with two small horizontal handles (CM. 2688, Fig. 143:14). H. 0.14 m., d. rim 0.345 m., w. rim 0.014 m., d. base 0.145 m. From slightly raised base rounded side rises to rim flat on top and offset on outside. One handle and almost one-half rim and side missing. Surviving handle small, round not flattened or pinched out but comes off rim horizontally. Comparable to Shape 1 (*PN* I, 355f., figs. 349, 350; *MP*, Type 295) except for handles.

EXPLORATION OF STRATIFICATION NORTHWEST OF MAIN BUILDING

The most extensive investigation of the habitation debris that had accumulated on the hill behind the palace was begun during the season of 1958, resumed in 1959 and 1963 under the supervision of Mr. Papathanasopoulos, and was widely extended in 1962 under the direction of Mr. Kittredge. This area with a maximum length of 35 m. from northeast to southwest and a breadth from 6 m. at the northeast to 25 m. at the southwest, lies immediately outside the rear of the Main Building of the palace and stretches from the latter to the abrupt slope that here forms the edge of the acropolis. No certain remains of a fortification wall were brought to light in this sector (Fig. 302 W 14 and p. 11), but the deep deposit of ruins and rubbish from human occupation yielded some information about the history of the settlement.

The excavations of Mr. Papathanasopoulos were conducted outside the exterior northwestern wall of the palace (Rooms 21, 22, 23, 24, and Corridor 25), broadening southwestward from 6 m. to 15 m. (Fig. 78). Here directly underneath the plowed earth were exposed in 1958 stone foundations of several small buildings which represented the latest phases of the palace (Rooms 83, 84, 85, 86, 87; *PN* I, 291-293, figs. 218, 219) and were destroyed by the fire that devastated the entire palatial establishment. The northwesternmost remnant of this complex is a crumbling truncated corner of two walls, shown unlabeled on key plan northwest of Room 82 (Fig. 303) to indicate that buildings once extended farther northwestward.

In the space between the rear wall of the palace and the group of Rooms 83-87, Mr. Papathanasopoulos opened several soundings, some of which reached *stereo* at a depth of 3 m. or more below the ground level of the palace. These probes yielded quantities of animal bones and potsherds. The latter were observed by Mr. Papathanasopoulos to show a regular sequence from Minyan and Mattpainted Wares of the Middle Helladic Period at the bottom depths through Late Helladic I, II, III A, and finally III B just below and in the stratum associated with the last elements in Rooms 83 to 86. Some distinctive fragments of the various periods mentioned are illustrated in Figures 146, 147.

In the course of a long season in 1962, Mr. Kittredge completed the arduous task of broadening substantially the investigation to the northwest behind the palace. The work was conducted in a series of 10 trenches, laid out in various sizes, shapes, and depths, as the topography dictated; most of them were eventually joined together. In all but one probe, stone walls appeared and it became obvious that many periods of building and rebuilding were represented (Fig. 79). In the end Mr. Kittredge differentiated and recorded on his plan (Fig. 311) 40 walls and five underground water channels or drains built of stones. These structures finally covered so much space that they occupied almost three-fourths of the total expanse under excavation. Since they were not removed by our expedition, digging to the bottom depths became more and more difficult as the scanty room available for examination grew steadily more restricted.[14] The walls and substructures revealed successive chronological stages, one above another; they are shown on the plan in different kinds of hatching.

In the area northwest of the latest Mycenaean buildings 83, 84, 85, 86, 87, only the scantiest remnants of walls and pottery had been left by erosion. As digging proceeded, many walls contemporary with and connected with Room 82 (*PN* I, 289-291) came to light; they are shown in simple hatching sloping down from right to left (Fig. 311 D, E, F, G, I, K, S, X, Y). The buildings were oriented more or less as was the palace of Mycenaean III B.

Nothing more needs to be said about Room 82 (*PN* I, 289-291), but we take the opportunity to correct a minor error in the measurement of the interior width of the added chamber. It should have been 5.10 m. instead of 5.25 m.[15]

At a deeper level five or six additional walls were exposed. Designated on the plan with simple hatching sloping down from left to right (A, B, J, H, M, and Drains a, b) they are obviously earlier than the foregoing group.

Next below was discovered a long wall (U) oriented from north to south (indicated in solid black on the plan). Two branch walls (T and Z) seem to run westward, as if they once formed partitions or rooms. On the east, ca. 3.60 m. distant, the long wall is paralleled by another, V. It is tempting to identify the passage between the two as a narrow road or street. But no street paving was found.

At the lowest level, ca. 3 m. under the ground of the palace, on or just above *stereo*, numerous remnants of disintegrating walls appeared, for the greater part short, broken segments, many laid out from north to south or east to west. At least 17 of these fragments were recognized (C, L, N, O, P, W, AB, AC, AD, AE, AF, AG, AI, AK, AL, AM, AN), marked with small-stone edging on each side. A scrutiny suggested that the earliest settlement consisted of small houses crowded together.

The five drains mentioned above were also dismantled, in ruined state. At

---

[14] The walls have all been left *in situ* covered by earth.

[15] The latter dimension was taped on the upper part of the wall where it had bulged considerably out of the perpendicular.

different levels, they were presumably used for draining and conveying unwanted water to flow out over the steep bank to the lower ground.

A strange phenomenon encountered in the deposit puzzled us greatly, namely that not one proper floor of any kind was recognizable at any level (except in one of the latest Mycenaean strata). A further peculiarity in this maze of walls stirred our curiosity: few if any recognizable complete or partial rooms could be distinguished; and even more remarkable no signs of doorways or other openings were discernible in the walls of any stratum. Without pavements and flooring, and lacking entrances and communicating passages, these barren walls provided little evidence from which deductions could safely be made regarding the character and purpose of the buildings. The bare remains were probably substructures that supported walls of crude brick.

In the deposit that buried so many walls and had a depth of more than 3 m., Mr. Kittredge recorded the changes of earth through which he was digging. It was made up of successive irregular superposed strata, differing in color, texture, and thickness. His interpretation was based on the stratigraphy and on the study of the material recovered in its sequence, broken pottery, and other objects as well as animal bones. Altogether he was able to distinguish seven strata, especially in the southwestern scarp of his Trench 7 (Fig. 80).

In a large area crowded with walls that had to be excavated by innumerable separate probings, it was very difficult to coordinate the pottery from sounding with sounding, but Mr. Kittredge managed successfully to keep abreast with one another the sherds recovered from the scattered pits. The first and second groups from an old rubbish heap and from plowed earth gave little chronological information. The third lot yielded mainly wares of Mycenaean III B along with some admixtures of Mycenaean III A and a few earlier pieces (Fig. 149, Group III). The fourth group produced still a good deal of pottery of Mycenaean III B but a marked increase of III A was noted (Fig. 149, Group IV).

The fifth assemblage of fragments was composed of an abundance of Mycenaean III A fabrics, accompanied by a good many pieces assignable to Late Helladic II and Late Helladic I (Fig. 149, Group V) along with parts of coarse jars and jugs. The sixth group came from a dark stratum with a mixture of Mycenaean III A, II, and I (Fig. 149, Group VI), in association with Middle Helladic Mattpainted, Argive Minyan and coarse ware. From the seventh and deepest stratum was brought up much Middle Helladic Mattpainted pottery and some abundance of Late Helladic I. At the bottom of one trench fragments of an alabastron of Late Helladic II appeared; and on *stereo* itself was found a sherd of Mycenaean III B (Fig. 150, bottom row, second from left), a startling intruder from the higher strata, where it once probably formed part of the rim of a krater-bowl.

Perhaps it had fallen from a top level into the pit, or been dislodged from the side of the upper part of the trench.

In his study of the pottery, Mr. Kittredge had to sort out an immense quantity of material dealing with more than 350 lots of broken pots and potsherds recovered from all 10 trenches in which corresponding strata could be identified. In general there can be no doubt that this series presents the full normal sequence of ceramic phases ranging from late Middle Helladic through Late Helladic I, II, III A, and III B. But it is obvious that there had been considerable disturbance penetrating deeply into the deposit almost everywhere throughout the whole area, and thereby to a substantial degree contaminating the purity of the stratification. Much of this damage must have been unwittingly caused by the great activity in building and rebuilding that has already been mentioned, and the laying of some of the drains. In any event, the deepest strata, the sixth and seventh, though by no means free from intrusions, were preponderantly characteristic of the transition from Middle to Late Helladic I. The indications of disorder seem to have increased markedly in the higher strata, where the soil had evidently been more frequently stirred up by wall-builders.

The absence of floors and even of tramped-down surface patches made it impossible to associate with certainty any of the datable potsherds with any of the specific walls.

The area dug by Mr. Papathanasopoulos in 1963, close behind the Main Building of the palace, in some way had the good fortune (from the point of view of the archaeologist) to escape such intensive disturbance as was visited upon the crowded warren of constructions farther to the northwestward.

OBJECTS FOUND[16]

BRONZE (FIG. 114)

Part of flat handle (No. 1): w. 0.014 m., th. ca. 0.003 m. Projects from remnant of side of vessel.

Handle (No. 2): d. 0.01 m. Round in section, misshapen by fire.

Point of awl or other implement (No. 3): l. pres. 0.045 m., max. th. 0.005 m. Square in section.

STONE (FIG. 114)

Tiny obsidian arrowhead (No. 4): l. 0.018 m.,

max. w. across barbs 0.01 m., th. 0.03 m. Barbed type.

Flint arrowhead (No. 5): l. 0.024 m., max. w. 0.013 m., max. th. 0.004 m. Barbed type, red.

Steatite button (No. 6): h. 0.006 m., d. 0.013 m., d. perforation 0.002 m. Tiny conical shape, brownish.

Button (No. 7): h. 0.012 m., d. 0.021 m., d. perforation 0.004 m. Green stone, conical, chipped.

Seal, unfinished (No. 8): d. 0.017 m., max. th.

[16] The miscellaneous objects found in this area were deposited in labeled containers in the storeroom of the Chora Museum but have not been given museum numbers. All the pots that could be put together bear the inventory numbers of the museum.

0.01 m. Grayish stone, perhaps not worked but looks as if start had been made in representing goddess with raised arms. Not pierced.

Obsidian blade (No. 9): l. 0.031 m., w. 0.01 m., th. 0.003 m.

Obsidian blade (No. 10): l. 0.021 m., w. 0.01 m., th. 0.003 m.

Flint blade (No. 11): l. 0.033 m., w. 0.019 m., th. 0.009 m. Serrated, tan.

Flint blade (No. 12): l. 0.036 m., w. 0.015 m., th. 0.007 m. Red-brown, serrated.

Celt (No. 15): l. 0.06 m., max. w. 0.037 m., w. of blade end 0.027 m., max. th. 0.02 m. Greenish stone.

TERRACOTTA (FIG. 114)

Fragment of animal figurine (No. 16): h. 0.04 m. to top of head, l. pres. 0.025 m. Forepart of animal. Legs, half of body, and nose missing.

Fragment of whorl, weight, or stamp (No. 13): h. 0.02 m., oval bottom 0.022 m. by 0.027 m. Has transverse perforation. Coarse clay.

Whorl (no. 14): h. 0.021 m., d. 0.022 m., d. perforation 0.005 m. Biconical.

POTTERY (FIG. 148)

Shallow bowl with two pinched-out handles (CM. 1933, not illustrated): cf. Shape 4, *PN* I, 356, figs. 349, 350; *MP*, Type 295, p. 53 fig. 15. H. 0.058 m., d. rim 0.155 m., d. base 0.047 m., w. handle 0.014 m., capacity 0.45 liter. Stratum 6.

Conical cups: 11 examples (CM. 1921-CM. 1931, Fig. 148:1-11) restored from fragments recovered from Strata 2, 3, 4, 5, and 6: cf. Shape 11, *PN* I, 359f., figs. 353, 354; *MP*, Type 204, p. 53 fig. 15. Dimensions vary: h. 0.036 m.-0.052 m., d. 0.092 m.-0.113 m., d. base 0.038 m.-0.052 m., capacity 0.09 liter-0.20 liter.

Shallow one-handled cup (CM. 1934, Fig. 148:13): cf. Shape 12, *PN* I, 360, figs. 353, 354; *MP*, Type 220, p. 48 fig. 13. H. 0.052 m., d. 0.123 m., d. base 0.038 m., w. handle 0.014 m., capacity 0.24 liter. Stratum 4.

Bell-shaped cup (CM. 1920, Fig. 148:12): cf. Shape 17, *PN* I, 362, figs. 355, 356; *MP*, Type 231, p. 53 fig. 15. H. 0.07 m., d. rim 0.107 m., d. base 0.039 m., capacity 0.24 liter. Stratum 5.

One-handled angular kylix (CM. 1936, Fig. 148:14): cf. Shape 27, *PN* I, 366f., figs. 359, 360; *MP*, Type 267, p. 61 fig. 17. H. 0.096 m., d. 0.125 m., d. stem 0.02 m., d. base 0.051 m., capacity 0.25 liter. Stratum 4.

Very small kylix, two high handles (CM. 1935, Fig. 148:15): h. 0.071 m., h. top restored handles 0.106 m., d. 0.09 m., d. base 0.05 m., capacity 0.075 liter. Part of rim missing. Stratum 5. Cf. *Prosymna*, fig. 438:183.

Large one-handled narrow-necked jug (CM. 1897, Fig. 148:16): h. 0.368 m., h. neck 0.072 m., d. rim 0.12 m., d. neck 0.091 m., d. 0.28 m., d. base 0.10 m. Stratum 4. No exact parallel known to us.

THE LOWER TOWN

Below the acropolis on which the palace stands, remnants of a fairly extensive settlement have been observed. Almost all our information about the houses that formed the lower town has been obtained from exploratory trenches in many areas: beneath the northerly end of the citadel in an *aloni* owned by the George Petropoulos family; along the foot of the steep, lengthy northwestern bank of the hill; in the olive orchard of Nikos Antonopoulos below the southwestern limit of the elevation; and in a field belonging to the Andreas Anastasopoulos family between the southeastern scarp and the modern highway. No real excavation on a large scale has yet been conducted outside the citadel but, pending further investigation of that kind, a modest array of factual knowledge has been gleaned from these many widely separated soundings, sufficient to allow some relatively safe general conclusions.

It is clear in any event that the community clustering about the acropolis (the latter evidently wholly reserved for the royal family), was of considerable size, large enough, as compared with other contemporary sites that have hitherto been discovered in southwestern Peloponnesos, to be ranked as a capital center.

The Northwestern Scarp

Beneath the abrupt northwestern edge of the Englianos hilltop is an extensive currant vineyard belonging to George Petropoulos of Chora. It slopes somewhat sharply downward across an upland that soon drops more precipitously into the valley of a little stream called Bouga. Much earth and many stones from the acropolis have been carried down into the vineyard and beyond by heavy rains that have long been eroding the steep bank as well as the plantation itself. In the cultivated earth among the vines, numerous Mycenaean potsherds and sometimes bits of plaster with traces of painted decoration, along with stones and other debris, may be seen. It looks as if this slope was once occupied by the lower town. The Cincinnati Expedition refrained from excavating here and destroying the flourishing currant vines.

Through the course of several seasons, however, a long stretch of the steep northwestern scarp of the citadel was investigated: by Mr. McDonald in 1953, Mr. Papathanasopoulos in 1958, Miss Rawson in 1961 and 1962, Mrs. Kittredge in 1962, and Mr. P. Smith in 1963. In all these probings, remains were brought to light indicating that houses of the lower town had been built up to and against the almost vertical escarpment of the hill. Under the plowed ground abundant accumulations of discarded broken pottery and other rubbish were spread along the entire periphery, evidently a convenient place into which to throw them down from above. A few remnants of Mycenaean walls were recognized and in the deeper levels several substantial foundations of buildings were exposed. This lowest stratum contained a good deal of Middle Helladic pottery that may be taken to date the beginning of the settlement. Since these walls have been mentioned in the account of the search for a circuit wall (W 5, W 6, W 7, W 9, W 10, W 12, W 13, W 14, W 15, W 16, Fig. 302 and pp. 8-11), they need not be described again here. The ruins are too scanty to provide enough evidence for the reconstruction of the plans of any houses, but the miscellaneous objects and pots recovered that were judged to be worth publishing are recorded in the following catalogues, trench by trench.

Trench W 9 (Fig. 106)

BRONZE

Point with pyramidal head (No. 1): l. as bent 0.054 m., l. head 0.014 m., w. base head 0.006 m. Pin tapers, becoming rounded, d. at end 0.002 m.

STONE

Tiny flint arrowhead (No. 3): l. 0.013 m., max. w. 0.009 m., th. 0.002 m. Barbed type, dark brown.

Small flint arrowhead (No. 4): l. 0.016 m., max. w. 0.011 m., th. 0.003 m. Barbed type, mottled gray. Tips of barbs broken away.

Small steatite button (No. 5): h. 0.008 m., d. 0.015 m., d. perforation 0.004 m.

CLAY

Disk (No. 2): d. 0.034 m., d. raised part 0.026 m., th. 0.005 m., d. perforation 0.004 m. Apparently made from bottom of little pot with low pedestal base. Neatly perforated. Light red clay.

Trench W 10 (Fig. 106)

CLAY

Disk (No. 6): d. 0.04 m., th. 0.011 m. Apparently made from bottom of base of small pot. Crudely cut, small perforation.

Trench W 12

POTTERY

Wide-mouthed jar with two horizontal handles (CM. 1642, Fig. 148:21): h. 0.285 m., d. rim 0.254 m., d. 0.276 m., d. base 0.131 m., w. handle 0.021 m. Parts of rim, body, one handle lacking, more than half missing. No decoration. Though they have no knobs, this jar and CM. 1644 (below) resemble in general two coarse household pots that were found in the Middle Helladic layer at Eutresis (*Eutresis,* 176, fig. 244).

Wide-mouthed jar with two horizontal handles (CM. 1644, Fig. 148:20): h. 0.337 m., d. rim 0.292 m., d. 0.353 m., d. base 0.141 m., w. handle 0.021 m. One handle, parts of rim, body, base missing. No decoration.

Tall jug with three handles (CM. 1643, Fig. 148:19): h. 0.388 m., d. neck 0.106 m., d. rim 0.13 m., greatest d. 0.288 m., d. base 0.133 m. A few pieces missing from rim, body, base. Decoration in rusty black with broad bands along rim and bottom of neck. Two irregular horizontal bands in shoulder zone, crossed by broad vertical stripe running down from top of vertical handle. Middle Helladic Mattpainted Ware. Two vessels of comparable shape and decoration (Nos. 597, 598, Shape 50, *PN* I, 385f., figs. 373, 374) were found in Room 38 of palace. Cf. also *Korakou,* 23, fig. 32.

Trench W 16

BRONZE

Pin with crooked head (Fig. 106 No. 9): l. 0.049 m., d. 0.003 m., w. across head 0.008 m. In two pieces, badly corroded.

LEAD

Small rivet with circular head (Fig. 106 No. 14): d. 0.01 m. Used to mend broken pot and still held in red potsherd.

STONE

Flint arrowhead (Fig. 106 No. 13): l. pres. 0.017 m., max. w. 0.011 m., th. 0.003 m. Barbed type, tip missing. Brown.

Flint blade (Fig. 106 No. 11): l. 0.034 m., w. 0.015 m., w. tang 0.01 m., l. tang 0.013 m.-0.017 m., th. 0.006 m. Unusual shape with tang. Sharp edges, gray.

Disk (Fig. 106 No. 10): d. 0.041 m., th. 0.004 m., d. perforation 0.003 m. Fragment, about one-third of edge chipped away. One surface flat, other slightly convex, sloping down to thin edge. Perforation neatly cut. Greenish sandy stone.

Tool, pounder or pestle (Fig. 113 No. 6): l. 0.117 m., max. d. 0.04 m. Oval in section, both ends worn, flattened from use. Greenish gritty stone.

IVORY

Large chunk (Fig. 113 No. 5): l. pres. 0.08 m., w. 0.055 m., max. th. 0.015 m. Unworked fragment illustrating how ivory separates into layers.

BONE (FIG. 106)

Pendant? (No. 8): l. 0.044 m., original width nowhere preserved, th. ca. 0.004 m. In two pieces, part of edge missing. Perhaps originally oval in shape with blunt ends. Remnants of three perforations.

Needle (No. 12): l. 0.046 m., w. at top 0.008 m., th. 0.004 m. Made from large bone. Sharp point. Perforated near top, split through perforation. Highly polished.

TERRACOTTA (FIG. 113)

Whorl (No. 1): h. 0.019 m., d. 0.03 m., d. top 0.017 m., d. bottom 0.014 m., d. perforation 0.006 m. Biconical with beveled ends. Dark brown clay, fairly solid.

Small whorl (No. 2): h. 0.017 m., d. 0.023 m., d. top 0.012 m., d. perforation 0.006 m. Biconical with beveled top. Part of bottom missing. Light brown clay with gray core.

Large whorl (No. 4): h. 0.036 m., d. 0.043 m., d. bottom 0.015 m., d. perforation 0.008 m. Crudely made. Blackish clay, red around bottom.

Spool-like whorl (No. 3): h. 0.033 m., d. large end 0.025 m., d. middle 0.015 m., d. small end 0.014 m., d. perforation 0.006 m. Top beveled, slightly hollow. Brownish clay.

The Southwestern Scarp

Along the southwestern flank of the acropolis also, habitations of the lower town seem to have been crowded as close as possible to the border of the palace grounds. Throughout this entire sector great quantities of potsherds and not a few other objects were recovered—much flotsam and jetsam thrown out from the plateau above. Outside the exterior wall of the Southwestern Building, alongside Rooms 74 and 65, as well as beyond (W 19, W 20, Fig. 302), truncated stubs of walls projecting southwestward were brought to view under the supervision of Mrs. Blegen and Mr. Papathanasopoulos in the seasons of 1959, 1960, and 1961. Still farther southeastward, similar remnants were exposed outside the southerly foundation of Building X (pp. 13f. and Figs. 81, 306) and the ruins of another structure beyond.

Erosion and the looting of stone had taken a generous toll at this end of the hill, and too little was left to determine exactly just when these structures were built and what purpose they served. All of them seem to have been destroyed by fire and later to have been covered over with wreckage and trash, containing much broken pottery in some places (Fig. 82). In one area a floor that was ultimately reached was found to be strewn with many fine potsherds of Mycenaean III A.

Section W 19 (Fig. 110)

STONE

Flint arrowhead (No. 1): l. pres. 0.024 m., w. 0.011 m., th. 0.002 m. Fragment, narrow barbed type, point missing. Tan.

Flint arrowhead (No. 3): l. pres. 0.023 m., w. 0.011 m., th. 0.002 m. Barbed type, point and one barb missing. Brown.

Flint arrowhead with stem (No. 4): l. 0.023 m., w. 0.01 m., l. stem 0.004 m., th. 0.002 m. No barbs. Tan.

Obsidian arrowhead (No. 2): l. pres. 0.014 m., w. 0.01 m., th. 0.0015 m. Barbed type, fragment, point missing.

Blade (No. 6): l. 0.039 m., w. 0.017 m., th. 0.004 m. One serrated edge. Gray stone, not much like flint.

Fragment of marble (No. 5): l. pres. 0.029 m., w. 0.018 m., th. 0.008 m. Worked piece, possibly part of handle. One face flat, one convex.

TERRACOTTA

Whorl (No. 15): h. 0.023 m., d. flat top 0.016 m., d. 0.03 m., d. perforation 0.006 m. Biconical with beveled top. Red-brown clay.

FRESCOES

Small fragments of plaster bearing painted decoration. On one remnant are depicted two heads wearing boar's tusk helmets (*PN* II, 75f., 32Hsw, pl. 24, c).

POTTERY

Conical cups (CM. 1983, CM. 1984, CM. 1985, CM. 1986, CM. 1987, CM. 1995, CM. 1996): cf. Shape 11, *PN* I, 359f., figs. 353, 354; *MP*, Type 204. H. ranging from 0.032 m. to 0.042 m., d. 0.10 m. to 0.118 m.

Section W 20 (Fig. 110)

STONE

Flint arrowhead (No. 8): l. pres. 0.017 m., w. 0.01 m., th. 0.003 m. Barbed type, point missing. Brown.

Obsidian arrowhead (No. 9): l. 0.02 m., max. w. 0.011 m., th. 0.004 m. Barbed type, tip of one barb broken.

Blade (No. 10): l. 0.024 m., max. w. 0.016 m., th. 0.006 m. One serrated edge. Gray flint or obsidian.

The South Corner (W 21)

The southern corner of the acropolis has been dealt with (pp. 41ff.) in its northerly part occupying the slope of the hill inside the limits of the circuit wall. The excavation, however, was extended farther southward into the lower town. Here also masses of discarded wreckage and debris, obviously brought down from the plateau above, had been deposited in a thick heap, revealing the same three layers that had been seen inside the palace ground (p. 41). The middle stratum yielded many small pots like those found within the circuit. Underneath that accumulation some dilapidated stone walls and patches of floors were reached; on them were collected a good many sherds in the style of Mycenaean III A (e.g., Figs. 151, 152) and others from which several vessels were put together. The architectural remains, destroyed by fire and plunderers, were inadequate to help determine the plans of the buildings.

POTTERY

Basin with two pinched-out handles (CM. 1641, Fig. 155:6): cf. Shape 1, *PN* 1, 355, figs. 349, 350. H. 0.134 m., d. 0.34 m., w. of flattened rim on top 0.012 m., d. base 0.132 m. Pieces of rim, bowl, and base missing. No decoration.

Handleless, conical cups (CM. 1787, CM. 1914 [Fig. 155:4], CM. 1916 [Fig. 155:5], CM. 1981, CM. 1982, CM. 2671, CM. 2672, CM. 2673, CM. 2674): cf. Shape 11, *PN* 1, 359f., figs. 353, 354; *MP*, Type 204. H. ranging from 0.022 m. to 0.052 m., min. d. 0.049 m., max. d. 0.115 m.

Diminutive one-handled cup (CM. 1915, Fig. 155:3): h. including restored handle, 0.059 m., h. of bowl 0.019 m., d. rim 0.066 m., d. base 0.027 m., capacity 0.020 liter.

Shallow cup with one high handle (CM. 1917, Fig. 155:2): h. with handle 0.052 m., d. 0.082 m., d. base 0.03 m., w. handle 0.011 m., capacity 0.060 liter. Some bits missing.

Shallow cup with one high handle (CM. 1918, Fig. 155:1): h. bowl 0.033 m., d. rim 0.088 m., d. base 0.035 m., capacity 0.080 liter. Handle missing, restored.

Pedestal cup with one handle (CM. 1640, Fig. 155:8): h. 0.10 m., d. 0.11 m., d. base 0.051 m., w. handle 0.017 m. Some pieces lack-ing. Coated with blackish paint all over.

Two-handled pedestal cup (CM. 1908, Fig. 155:7): h. 0.136 m., d. rim 0.145 m., max. d. 0.149 m., d. foot 0.068 m., w. flat handles 0.022 m., capacity 1.150 liter.

Stemmed krater with two handles (CM. 1637, Fig. 155:10): cf. Shape 63, *PN* 1, 400ff., figs. 387, 388; *MP*, Type 8. H. pres. (lower part of stem and foot missing) 0.28 m., d. rim across handles 0.28 m., perpendicular to handle 0.322 m., w. handle 0.04 m. Broad band along rim inside and out, just below greatest diameter three broad horizontal stripes, two similar bands at upper part of pedestal. In shoulder zone two narrow bands running around vessel and framing multiple parallel transverse lunate lines close together. Bands along each edge of handle, continuing down and joining in broad circle below. Decoration done in brownish paint. Mycenaean III A.

Small two-handled spouted jug (CM. 1789, Fig. 155:9): cf. *MP*, Types 150, 151. H. with spout 0.244 m., d. neck 0.026 m., max. d. body 0.15 m., d. base 0.055 m. Two somewhat rounded vertical handles set at right angles to spout: d. handles 0.016 m. Base hollowed underneath. Gray-buff clay with pink patches.

The Southwestern Quarter

In 1959 five trenches were laid out in the olive grove mentioned above, the kind permission of the owner, Mr. Antonopoulos, having been granted. Trenches LT I and II, nearest the citadel, were supervised by Mr. Papathanasopoulos; the other three were dug under the observation of Mr. Blegen with the assistance of Miss Rawson when he was obliged to be absent.

Trench LT I

Beginning just outside the fifth sharp angle (i.e., the south corner of Room 65, Figs. 303, 312) of the southwestern exterior wall of the palace, Mr. Papathanasopoulos laid out Trench LT I (Fig. 83). It was 1.50 m. wide, ranging in depth from 1.20 m. to 1.65 m., nearly 30 m. long and aimed approximately toward a storeroom built in the orchard. In the cultivated soil, worked over by the plow, varying from 0.20 m. to ca. 0.40 m. deep, many Mycenaean potsherds came to light as well as 27 fragments of tablets, bearing Linear B writing.[17] All these and various other objects were scattered about in the disturbed earth where they had somehow found a lodging during the holocaust that destroyed the palace and the lower town, and the area was later left as a very good plundering ground through many centuries.

Underneath the tilled soil Mr. Papathanasopoulos observed superposed three layers, clearly differentiated: the uppermost and the next, each accompanied by remains of fire; still deeper a more ancient deposit containing wreckage of stone buildings resting on *stereo,* obviously the first settlement built on this ground.

In the narrow breadth of the exploratory trench many stone walls were exposed to view at different levels and running in various directions. It was not easy in some instances to determine certainly to what layer a specific wall belonged. More than a few, as they are drawn on the plans (Figs. 313, 314) provided by Mr. Papathanasopoulos, are as accurately identified as could be done without opening a large area in the olive grove and causing damage. Altogether 18 or 19 walls were noted and studied.

First Settlement, Mycenaean I-II

The lowest layer of the deposit varied from 0.35 m. to 0.60 m. in thickness, resting on *stereo,* at a maximum of ca. 1.65 m. below the modern surface. Almost all the walls had been laid on hardpan (Nos. 2, 11, 12, 14, 15, Figs. 313, 314). No. 10, though not standing on *stereo,* was considered a structure of the early Mycenaean period, although very little of it had survived. Possibly Walls 6 and 7 were a solid part of an old building too substantial to be destroyed and good enough to be renovated for further useful purposes in the intermediate era of Mycenaean III A.

In the spaces on and between the walls Nos. 10, 11, and 12, as well as Nos. 14 and 15, were found here and there some fragments of Minyan and a good many of Mattpainted Wares, along with early Mycenaean fabrics. It is clear that the southwestern slope below the citadel was already occupied at a time before the Middle Helladic period had ended. Much more abundant was the early and later Mycenaean pottery, and Mr. Papathanasopoulos noticed especially the numerous kylikes and cups. Perhaps some of the sherds had become mixed in the disturbed areas.

Farther southwestward in the trench the two additional walls (Nos. 14 and 15, Fig. 314) with substantial foundations laid on *stereo* joined together at a right

[17] Mabel Lang, *AJA,* 64 (1960), 160-164, pls. 44-47.

angle (Fig. 84). The two branches, each with a thickness of ca. 0.55 m., survived to a height of not more than 0.50 m.

In this area a good deal of pottery was collected, mainly recognized as of early Mycenaean types. Ashes in considerable quantity at this level suggested that the first establishment of a lower town was not altogether free from fire. The walls in general were neatly constructed with the use of smallish flat stones well fitted.

Second Settlement

The accumulation left by the intervening settlement was not leveled flat but had an undulating course, with a depth ranging from 0.35 m. to 0.65 m. Here many signs of burning certainly pointed to a catastrophe that drove out the occupants and ruined the lower town. Several stone walls, Nos. 3, 6, 7, 9 (Fig. 314) and possibly a few more, were judged to belong to Mycenaean III A.

A substantial corner of a large room was formed by Walls 6 and 7; each had a thickness of ca. 0.60 m., and both were solidly laid in *stereo* from which they still rose to a height of ca. 1.15 m., protruding into the space of the upper layer. In the triangle of the structure Mr. Papathanasopoulos noted a floor of clay and small pebbles. In the space of the angle between Walls 6 and 7 much pottery came to light, a considerable mixture of Mycenaean III A and Mycenaean III B. The well-built structure may have been reused for some purpose in the period of Mycenaean III B.

Another long triangle was formed by two walls, labeled 17 and 18, near the southwestern end of the trench. Each of the two foundations was laid near the top of the middle layer, and so must belong to Mycenaean III B.

Much broken pottery was collected from which we were able to put together 37 vessels in the style of Mycenaean III A. The greater part of this heap of fragments came from Section E, the next to the last in the southwesterly end of the trench. Just beyond the shattered potsherds were found the remnants of a table of offerings in poor condition (Fig. 85); two legs were recognized but the third was missing. One leg is ca. 0.30 m. high. The diameter of the table could not be accurately measured. The offering table seems clearly to belong with the pottery hoard of eight different shapes that could have been used for ceremonies in Mycenaean III A.

OBJECTS FOUND

POTTERY

Handleless, conical cup (6 examples: CM. 1708, CM. 1709, CM. 1710, CM. 1718 [Fig. 155:14], CM. 1719, CM. 1720). Cf.

Shape 11, *PN* I, 359f., figs. 353, 354; *MP*, Type 204, p. 53 fig. 15. Considerable variation in profile and size.

size:	largest	smallest	average
h.	0.054	0.04	0.043
d.	0.125	0.102	0.114
d. base	0.048	0.041	0.045

Shallow cup with one low handle (7 examples: CM. 1721-CM. 1724 [Fig. 155:13], CM. 1725-CM. 1727). Shape essentially same as Shape 12 "teacup" found in the palace (*PN* I, 360 figs. 353, 354) but with raised base and more refined. Cf. also *MP*, Type 219, p. 48 fig. 13 (II B-III A:1).

size:	largest	smallest	average
h.	0.052	0.043	0.047
d.	0.135	0.126	0.13
d. base	0.035	0.033	0.034
w. handle	0.017	0.015	0.016

Painted bands on lip, base, and above, and on handle. Allover thrush's-egg or stipple pattern on body of cup (*MP*, Motive 77, p. 422 fig. 73:2, II B-III A:2e). Flaring, bell-shaped cups (7 restored: CM. 1711, CM. 1712 [Fig. 155:18], CM. 1713-CM. 1717); cf. Shape 17, *PN* I, 362, figs. 355, 356; *MP*, Type 230 (III A:2), Type 231 (III B), p. 53 fig. 15. Considerable variation in size and profile.

size:	largest	smallest	average
h.	0.067	0.059	0.063
d.	0.11	0.108	0.107
d. base	0.034	0.032	0.033
w. handle	0.015	0.016	0.016

Painted bands below rim, on base and above base on side, and on handle. Allover thrush's-egg or stipple pattern on body of cup (*MP*, Motive 77, p. 422 fig. 73:2).
High-handled cup (CM. 1744, Fig. 155:12): cf. Shape 19, *PN* I, 363, figs. 355, 356; *MP*, Type 241, p. 48 fig. 13 (III A:2). Ring-base, flaring lower side, convex shoulder, rounded lip; two high broad flattened handles rise vertically from rim and descend in wide loop to side just below shoulder. H. with handles 0.124 m., h. 0.068 m., d. rim 0.161 m., d. base 0.048 m., w. handles 0.025 m.

Painted band on lip and base, narrow band above base on which rests an argonaut on each side filling space between handles. Argonaut has two large spirals and one smaller but no shell (*MP*, Motive 22:15 curtailed argonaut, III A:1, p. 307 fig. 50).
Kylix, small, high stemmed (5 examples: CM. 1732-CM. 1736 [Fig. 155:11]). Two wide flat ribbon handles attached horizontally just below rim and pinched out slightly; base flat with vertical edge, hollow in center underneath stem; stem varies slightly in height, thickness, and profile— cylindrical, slightly tapering or with a bulge; shallow conical bowl with rounded shoulder and spreading lip.

No parallels found with similar horizontal band handles. *MP*, Type 295 (III A-III C:1), p. 53 fig. 15, nearest to shape of bowl and handles; cf. also *MP*, Type 266 (III A:1-III A:2l), pp. 60, 61 figs. 16, 17, although the diameter of ours is greater than the height, and ours is smaller.

size:	largest	smallest	average
h.	0.153	0.129	0.144
d. rim	0.16	0.15	0.157
d. base	0.063	0.055	0.059
d. stem	0.02	0.02	0.02
h. stem	0.065	0.052	0.063
w. handles	0.014	0.017	0.015

Stem and foot probably entirely coated with paint although much worn; bands on lower and middle of body and lip; variety of patterns in zone of decoration:

CM. 1732, wavy line *MP*, Motive 53:20 (III C:1l), p. 373 fig. 65.
CM. 1733, intersecting diagonal lines like beaker CM. 1729. Nothing comparable in *MP*.
CM. 1734, sacral ivy *MP*, Motive 12:27 (III A:1), p. 271 fig. 36.
CM. 1735, multiple stem and tongue *MP*, Motive 19:1, p. 299 fig. 47. Like beaker CM. 1730.
CM. 1736, papyrus-like blossoms with curving stem *MP*, Motive 11:54 (II B), p. 265 fig. 34.

Kylix with two low handles (5 examples: CM. 1737-CM. 1741 [Fig. 155:16]). Almost the size of the smaller of the medium size kylikes from the palace but with relatively higher stem; base flat on top and bottom with central hollow underneath and vertical edge; conical bowl closing slightly at top; pronounced rounded lip. Flattened handles extending in wide loop from rim to just below shoulder.

size:	largest	smallest	average
h.	0.16	0.155	0.158
d.	0.18	0.169	0.173
d. stem	0.022	0.021	0.021
h. foot	0.053	0.053	0.054
d. base	0.076	0.073	0.072
w. handles	0.022	0.019	0.02

Cf. Shape 29c, *PN* I, 369, figs. 361, 362; *MP*, Type 259 (III A:2l), p. 61 fig. 17. Ours undecorated and the bowl is more conical and less convex.

Kylix with two high handles (2 examples: CM. 1742, CM. 1743 [Fig. 155:15]). Medium size, deep bowl, fairly high stem.

size:	CM. 1742	CM. 1743
h.	0.161	0.152
h. with handles	0.23	0.215
d. rim	0.18	0.173
d. base	0.079	0.077
d. stem	0.022	0.021
h. stem	0.04	0.04
w. handles	0.024	?

Cf. Shape 30c, *PN* I, 373, figs. 365, 366; *MP*, Type 272 (III A:1), p. 60 fig. 16. In ours, bowl not so deep, foot not so high.

Beaker (4 examples: CM. 1728-CM. 1731 [Fig. 155:17]). Side only slightly concave with a raised rib around middle or slightly above. Plain rim, flattened bottom. All handles (if any) missing. Zone between rib and rim decorated with a variety of patterns. Bands in groups of three and two around lower part and concentric circles

on bottom. Proportions and dimensions uncertain as pots fragmentary:

CM. 1728: h. 0.155 m. Zigzag and pendant rock pattern (*MP*, Motive 61, p. 383 fig. 67).

CM. 1729: h. 0.153 m., d. rim 0.149 m., d. base 0.144 m. Diagonal intersecting lines, cf. CM. 1733 (p. 55).

CM. 1730: h. 0.156 m., d. base 0.147 m. Multiple stem and tongue, *MP*, Motive 19:1, p. 299 fig. 47. Cf. CM. 1734, CM. 1735 (p. 55).

CM. 1731: (Fig. 155:17): h. 0.149 m., d. rim 0.16 m., d. base 0.14 m. Running spiral, *MP*, Motive 46:54, p. 357 fig. 60 (III A:2-C:1e).

Cf. *MP*, Type 225 (III A:1-2), p. 53 fig. 15. *RT, Dendra*, 31:1, 54; fig. 31, pl. viii (h. 0.17, d. 0.155): wooden vessel or stoop (stoup) with bronze mountings. Wace, *Mycenae*, fig. 48 c, Treasury of Atreus, pottery from rock cleft. Cf. mug, Late Helladic II. Slightly taller than ours, has rib around middle, side like ours, less concave than those from palace.

Conical rhyton? (Fig. 153). Fragment (h. pres. 0.23 m.) comprising small piece of rim and possibly one quarter of side of tall tapering vessel with steeply rising side, rounding in slightly to offset, splaying rim. Cf. *MP*, Type 199, p. 67 fig. 20. In part preserved, one hole (ca. 0.01 m. in diameter) and a trace of another 0.014 m. distant high up near shoulder (ca. 0.035 m. below rim); tops of two other holes in the lower edge. Holes unmistakable.

Decoration in dark brown, streaky, crackled paint on creamy white: band extending over rim and lip; half way down side as preserved, ghosts of two narrow bands; between upper of these and rim band parts of two grass or reed motives (*MP*, Motive 16, p. 281 fig. 40, I-II B). The better preserved surrounds the upper hole which is lined with paint, as are the other holes; so it could not have been intended to receive a handle but must have been open.

Farther down side, three bands of irregular thickness, and above lower holes two narrow bands.

Third Settlement

The uppermost stratum, ranging from 0.30 m. to ca. 0.60 m. in depth, clearly represents the era of the late palace. Throughout this deposit the whole length of the trench yielded an abundance of broken pottery exactly like that which was recovered from the floors of the palace halls, courts, and pantries. Traces of burning on all sides show that the latest town was razed along with the royal abode on the hilltop.

In the topmost layer, contemporary with the palace, we believe that we have located the walls (Nos. 1, 3, 4, 5, 6, [7], 8, 13, 17, and 18: Figs. 313, 314) in use during the latest period. These structures are evidently parts of ruined houses that were wrecked in the destruction of the final lower town. As in earlier eras the population built their homes as near as possible to the royal residence on the hill. Some of the foundations of the houses are solidly built and at least two rooms are substantial and spacious.

O B J E C T S   F O U N D

S T O N E
Carnelian bead (Fig. 115 No. 16): d. 0.008 m., d. perforation 0.003 m. Almost spherical.

Found in sifting earth from connecting trench at intersection of W 19 with upper end of Trench LT I.

Trench LT II

Only a few steps southwestward from the first sounding, Trench LT II (Figs. 312, 315) was laid out by Mr. Papathanasopoulos from northeast to southwest; it was nearly 10 m. long and 1.50 m. wide. Two substantial transverse stone walls were exposed and two others, badly dilapidated, at right angles to the others (Fig. 86). They certainly belonged to houses in the lower town, and at least to two periods of occupation, presumably to Mycenaean III A and III B. Fragments of pottery collected from the trench range from Early Mycenaean through Mycenaean III A and III B.

Trench LT III

Trench LT III, 13 m. long from north to south and 1.50 m. broad, ran parallel to, and only 16 m. distant from Trench LT I (Figs. 312, 316). Here too several stone walls were exposed (Fig. 87) and evidence for three successive layers was noted, though the stratification was not so sharply marked off as in Trench LT I. *Stereo* was reached throughout the trench at a depth ranging from 1.60 m. to 2 m. and more. Beneath the top soil the upper layer, ca. 0.25 m. to 0.75 m. thick, obviously represents the period of Mycenaean III B, contemporary with the palace, as indicated by a multitude of parts and stems of distinctive kylikes and other pots of various shapes.

The next lower stratum, roughly 0.75 m. to 1.10 m. or more below the surface, produced a good many sherds in the style of Mycenaean III A (Fig. 154). Fragments of the same kind came from deeper pockets along with the upper part of a terracotta figurine of the disk-shaped type. Still deeper, remnants of earlier Mycenaean wares, Late Helladic II and Late Helladic I, appeared (Fig. 156) and at the very bottom on *stereo* were recovered a few relatively coarse pieces decorated in Mattpainted style (Fig. 157).

No plans of houses could be determined in this narrow trench and only a few vestiges of earth floors had survived. Evidence of burning was noted in the upper (III B) and the middle (III A) layers, no doubt reflecting the manner of destruction of those two settlements.

A few special items recovered in Trench III deserve brief mention.

OBJECTS FOUND

BRONZE

Fragment of tang of knife or other weapon (Fig. 116:11) with remains of rivet hole: l. pres. 0.025 m., w. 0.017 m. to 0.02 m., th. 0.006 m. Heavy solid piece.

Shapeless chunk (Fig. 116:17): l. 0.03 m., max. w. 0.028 m.

LEAD

Flat fragment (Fig. 116:16): l. 0.042 m., w. 0.024 m.

Small disk (Fig. 116:12): d. 0.019 m., th. 0.003 m. Split and cracked.

STONE

Flint flake (Fig. 116:2): l. 0.029 m., max. w. 0.013 m., th. 0.003 m. Serrated edge.

Marble pommel (Fig. 116:8): h. 0.03 m., d. 0.053 m., d. hole for shaft 0.017 m., h. rim of socket 0.028 m., over-all d. socket 0.03 m. Edges chipped, almost half rim of socket missing. Top convexly rounded. Probably from sword, dagger, or scepter.

Three-sided steatite seal (CM. 2512, Fig. 117: a, b, c): l. 0.018 m., w. of faces 0.01 m., 0.011 m., 0.009 m., d. perforation 0.004 m. Dark greenish stone. Each face roughly ellipsoid, with both ends cut off nearly straight. Decoration difficult to interpret.

Side *a* (Fig. 117) probably gives misleading suggestion of human face or caricature with two eyes under heavy brows, long nose, and large mouth indicated by two nearly parallel lines. May have been meant to represent something totally different.

Side *b* (Fig. 117) bears three circles in diagonal row at left; in middle, parallel diagonal stroke possibly sword (?), at upper right, circle enclosing dot; traces of other circles.

Side *c* (Fig. 117) occupied by lozenge or diamond-shaped figure, carelessly drawn by four lines, making two V-shaped angles, arranged open side to open side, but not touching. Within lozenge at least one circle enclosing dot. Outside diamond five parallel short strokes branching toward right edge; traces of similar lines at left.

Buttons

Large truncated bicone (Fig. 116:3): h. 0.015 m., d. 0.026 m., d. perforation 0.006 m. Dark gray.

Small conoid (Fig. 116:4): h. 0.009 m., d. 0.018 m., d. perforation 0.004 m. Dark purplish-blue, neatly shaped. Top slightly convex.

Small (Fig. 116:13): h. 0.01 m., d. 0.016 m., d. perforation 0.008 m. Dark bluish.

IVORY

Lentoid seal (CM. 2513, Fig. 118): d. 0.019 m., th. 0.0035 m.-0.006 m., d. perforation 0.003 m. One part of edge perpendicular to perforation broken away. Design neatly carved in fairly high relief. In foreground powerful bull facing right, head raised high, large nose and eye indicated, forward-curving horns, four legs visible, full body, lifted tail swinging up along left edge of seal. To right of this animal appears what looks like forequarter of another similar smaller bovine, going or facing left. Composition relatively good, recalling scenes on Vapheio cups, though somewhat short of those masterpieces.

PASTE

Flat dark black strip (Fig. 116:15): l. 0.044 m.; broken at both ends, w. at one end 0.019 m., at other 0.018 m., th. 0.004 m. Edges rounded; hard, gritty material with smooth surface.

TERRACOTTA (FIG. 116)

Upper part of figurine (No. 1): h. 0.068 m., w. across stumps of arms 0.045 m., w. head 0.02 m., w. neck 0.013 m., d. stem 0.02 m. Lower part of stem missing. Pinched-out nose and ears, hollows for eyes, lumps for hands resting on sides of body; both arms missing. Traces of paint: necklace, longitudinal stripes, solid color on top of head. This type, with molded arms bent to reach body, probably assignable to Mycenaean III A.

Stem of figurine (No. 9): h. pres. 0.053 m., d. disk 0.03 m., d. stem 0.013 m., w. spread at broken top 0.027 m. Yellowish clay. Traces of stripes in red paint. Stem cylindrical, splaying slightly at top and base; latter hollow underneath.

Large whorl (No. 14): h. 0.028 m., d. broader end 0.048 m., d. other end 0.029 m., d. perforation 0.012 m. Mushroom-like shape. Soft pinkish-buff clay. Tapering conoid stem with beveled top spreading widely. Perhaps forerunner of shanked type whorls.

Whorl, bicone, truncated at one end (No. 5): h. 0.02 m., d. 0.028 m., d. perforation 0.005 m. Brown clay.

Small button (No. 6): h. 0.012 m., d. 0.016 m., d. perforation 0.0015 m. Light tan clay. Hollowed neatly at broader end.

Small button (No. 7): h. 0.011 m., d. 0.014 m., d. broad end 0.01 m., d. stem 0.005 m., d. perforation 0.0025 m. Odd shape, flat top, convex side projecting above cylindrical stem.

Small button or whorl (No. 10): h. 0.016 m., d. 0.023 m., d. broader end 0.015 m., d. perforation 0.004 m. Bicone, beveled, top slightly hollowed. Brownish sandy clay.

Trench LT IV

About 60 m. to the westward of Trench LT III an uncultivated strip of ground between two parts of a vineyard offered us an opportunity for another test, 15 m. long and 1.50 m. wide (Figs. 88, 317). At its northern eroded end *stereo* was reached just below the plowed surface soil. In the middle and southern sections, however, the deposit had a maximum depth of 1.20 m. Stone walls of buildings were uncovered and at least two habitation levels could be differentiated.

The middle section was found to contain two fairly large pithoi, both badly crushed, though one still retained its flat stone cover (Fig. 89). No clear evidence survived to explain what had been stored in these jars. Numerous high kylix stems and fragments of other vessels, distinctive of Mycenaean III B, showed that this level of occupation was contemporary with the palace. Evidence of a destructive fire was noted as in the other trenches in the southwestern area.

The lower layer produced potsherds assignable to Mycenaean III A in association with a stone wall of a house that lay underneath the remains of Mycenaean III B. No undisturbed floor deposit was preserved. From the deeper levels down to *stereo* at 1.25 m. below the surface of the ground came a few fragments of still earlier Mycenaean pottery.

OBJECTS FOUND
(Fig. 115)

BRONZE

Flat fragment (No. 6): l. pres. 0.043 m., w. 0.019 m., tapering to 0.014 m. Fairly solid despite its thinness. Longitudinal edges finished, ends broken.

Fragment (No. 7), possibly belonging to No. 6: l. pres. 0.026 m., w. 0.019 m. Thin flat piece folded over.

Fragment of wire (No. 8): l. (when straightened) 0.057 m., d. 0.003 m. Both ends flattened.

STONE

Flint arrowhead (No. 4): l. 0.023 m., max. w. 0.004 m., th. 0.004 m. Apparently unfinished; barbed type. Opaque yellowish-white.

Steatite button (No. 5): h. 0.015 m., d. 0.029 m., d. perforation 0.006 m. Slightly beveled at broad end. Dark blue.

Steatite button (No. 11): h. 0.01 m., d. 0.021 m., d. perforation 0.005 m. Slightly beveled at smaller end. Dark bluish.

IVORY

Fragment (No. 12): l. 0.04 m., w. 0.032 m., th. 0.015 m. Two sides meeting at right angle preserved, curving side broken. No trace of decoration.

TERRACOTTA

Head of figurine (No. 9): h. pres. 0.03 m., w. head 0.023 m., th. front to back 0.025 m., d. neck 0.014 m. Light reddish clay. Surface worn, badly incrusted with lime. No trace of paint.

Whorl, very large (No. 1): h. 0.028 m., max. d. 0.049 m., small end 0.03 m., at wider end 0.034 m., d. perforation 0.011 m. Bicone, truncated; coarse red clay containing particles of stone. Surface chipped, carelessly shaped.

Large whorl (No. 2): h. 0.034 m., d. 0.04 m., d. perforation 0.01 m. Bicone, truncated. Dark red-brown clay. Surface worn, once had smooth finish.

Whorl (No. 10): h. 0.023 m., d. 0.033 m., d. perforation 0.004 m. Rounded bicone. Pinkish-buff clay.

Small button (No. 3): h. 0.012 m., d. 0.02 m., d. small end 0.015 m., d. perforation 0.003 m. Conical, beveled, slightly hollowed around perforation.

Trench LT V

In a bare patch of ground some 85 m. to the southwest of the region of Trenches LT I, II, and III, another exploratory test was carried out by Miss

Rawson. Trench LT V, running from southwest to northeast, was 15 m. long and in part 2 m. wide (Figs. 90, 318). At its upper and lower ends *stereo* appeared just below the plowed soil; in the middle section, however, a greater accumulation of earth was found to cover two stone walls which had been laid on or just above *stereo* and which probably once formed the corner of a house, though the actual angle is missing. There were no traces of a floor or a floor deposit, but the fragmentary pottery recovered within the area that had apparently been enclosed in the building is typical of Mycenaean III B. One or two pieces found close to *stereo* could be attributed to Mycenaean III A and a single fragment might be of Late Helladic II.

O B J E C T S   F O U N D
(Fig. 115)

STONE

Celt (No. 14): l. 0.052 m., w. 0.037 m. Plump type, beveled from both sides.

TERRACOTTA

Whorl (No. 13): h. 0.033 m., d. 0.04 m.
Button (No. 15): h. pres. 0.011 m., d. 0.025 m. Broken at bottom.

The Southeastern Quarter

Below the abrupt southeastern edge of the hill, between the latter and the modern highway, is a small cultivated field belonging to the Andreas Anastasopoulos family of Chora. Across this sloping terrace, with the friendly permission of the owner, two trenches, both running from northwest to southeast (Fig. 301), were dug by Miss Rawson in 1960.

Trench AA I, on the southwest, 7.50 m. long, 1 m. wide, was excavated to a depth of 3.27 m. at the northwestern end where a stucco floor was found (Fig. 91). Parallel to and projecting slightly from the southwestern scarp of the trench was a wall built with a socle of stone and a superstructure of crude brick. Traces of a horizontal beam slot were seen at 0.56 m. above the floor, and much plaster was preserved to a height of 0.75 m. to 1 m. This wall formed the southwestern side of three small rooms connected by doorways which were exposed within the narrow limits of the trench. Each room had a good stucco floor. No stone thresholds were found: perhaps there had been wooden sills. The middle room had a length of 3.35 m. from northwest to southeast; the other rooms were not cleared to their outer ends and could not be fully measured. The stratified deposit covering the house revealed a thick surface layer presumably washed down from the acropolis; next was a stratum of very black earth, stones, and chunks of crude brick, accompanied by some associated Geometric potsherds. This deposit rested in part on a whitish fill, no doubt eroded or thrown out from the citadel. Under this lay a deep mass of reddish dissolved crude brick and stone along with a few sherds of pottery and six fragments of ivory bearing carved decoration, apparently representing wings or feathers. Lying on the stucco floor was a thin black stratum which contained sherds for the greatest part Mycenaean, accompanied by some pieces resembling Argive Minyan (Fig. 158).

O B J E C T S   F O U N D

POTTERY

One-handled Geometric cup (CM. 1788, *PN* I, 21, fig. 347:982): h. 0.085 m., d. rim 0.075 m., d. body 0.095 m., d. base 0.052 m. Assembled from fragments; some missing from rim, body, and base. Handle flat-tened, w. 0.016 m. Flat bottom. Coated inside and out with brownish-black paint. Three incised parallel horizontal lines between shoulder and rim. Buff-gray clay. Found in black layer high above Mycenaean level.

Trench AA II, 8.60 m. long, 1 m. wide, was dug to *stereo* at a maximum depth of 2.10 m. (Fig. 92). In this area also transverse stone walls divided the trench into three compartments or rooms. At the northwestern end in a space only 1.15 m. long a floor was reached on *stereo* at 0.50 m. below the modern surface; on this floor lay part of a large crushed pot. Beyond the first cross wall, 0.65 m. thick and standing to a height of 1.65 m. in nine courses, *stereo* lay much deeper, at 2.10 m. A lateral wall on the northeast, running parallel to the trench, rises in 19 courses to a height of 2.10 m. Flat stones in part of the area seem to mark a floor level at 0.40 m. above *stereo*. This compartment is 1.50 m. long from northwest to southeast. The next room appears to have been somewhat more than 4 m. long, probably ending at a bench or shelf 0.62 m. high, cut in *stereo*-like earth but resting on a black stratum.

Below the topsoil, 0.25 m. thick, the accumulation filling these rooms was a homogeneous deposit of yellowish-whitish earth resembling *stereo*. In Room 3 red burned plaster was preserved on the northwestern and northeastern walls to a height of 0.75 m. The northwestern part of the room contained a very black deposit 0.40 m. thick covering the floor, while the southeastern end was filled with red disintegrated crude brick. Lying on the floor were found layer upon layer of thin plaster in various shades of blue-gray, similar to that on the walls. The sherds recovered in the burned deposit above the floor include many fragments of kylikes of Late Helladic III B types. A few pieces of earlier Mycenaean Ware were collected here and there in the deep fill which had apparently been washed down from the higher ground of the citadel (Fig. 158).

The houses brought to light in these two trenches demonstrate that the settlement of the palace period extended down the southeastern slope below the Englianos hill. Two houses do not make a lower town, but a brief survey of the steep descent toward the little river far down into the ravine disclosed a great many building stones and a considerable amount of broken pottery.

The Northern Quarter

In our quest for possible remains of a lower town we observed below the steep northwestern scarp, near the northeasterly end of the acropolis, a fairly large *aloni* belonging to George Petropoulos. With his kind permission Miss Rawson in 1959 opened an exploratory sounding, 23 m. long and 1.50 m. wide, running across the terrace from north to south (Figs. 93, 301).

Underneath the surface soil in a thick disturbed stratum, 0.65 m. deep, Mycenaean potsherds were found, for the greatest part stems and fragments of kylikes. About 5 m. distant from the southern end of the trench lay a deposit of very black earth filling a hollow in this disturbed layer; it contained stones, chunks of crude brick, and potsherds coated with a black accretion, resembling the accumulations noted in several parts of the palace and in its vicinity (*PN* I, 294, 296, 300, 303; and above, pp. 26-27). This pottery was predominantly Mycenaean with an admixture of black-glazed ware, apparently Geometric, some tile fragments, and a bronze coin.

The mixed layer and the late intrusion had been superposed on a stratum as much as 1 m. deep of yellowish *stereo*-like earth containing only a few potsherds and lying on rough unworked native rock or yellow *stereo*. At this depth were collected many fragments of pottery of Middle Helladic types well-known at Lerna in Period 5 (Fig. 159).

No walls of any kind were discovered in the three southernmost sections of the trench, 15 m. long, but in the northernmost section, 8 m. long, three walls at different levels were exposed to view (Fig. 94). The uppermost and latest system at 0.55 m. below the modern surface formed a right-angled corner of a house or room substantially built in a tidy, orderly manner of field stones. A reddish stratum marked by an associated floor yielded 85 potsherds, mainly nondescript but of Middle Helladic date.

The next earlier system, found at 1 m. below ground level, is represented by a wall running from northwest to southeast. It is 0.70 m. thick, standing in four courses 0.47 m. high; the stones were laid with care forming a regular face along each side, but were not founded on *stereo*. No floor and no floor deposit could be recognized. The pottery recovered alongside the wall is exclusively of Middle Helladic date.

The deepest and earliest structure, at 1.25 m. below ground, is a short stretch of wall at the extreme northern end of the trench. There survives only a single course of smallish stones based on *stereo*. Its depth and character indicate that it belongs to an older system of building. The accompanying potsherds are all of early Middle Helladic wares.

This trench thus offers evidence that the lower town existed around the northeasterly end of the acropolis, going back, so far as can be determined, to the very beginning of the settlement. The absence of Mycenaean buildings under the modern *aloni* may be due to chance or erosion. A test pit was dug only some 15 m. to the eastward at the boundary between the property of Mr. Petropoulos and the olive orchard of the Tsakonas family. It revealed below the surface soil a proper Mycenaean stratum of the palace period, which was superposed over a layer at least 1 m. deep that yielded Middle Helladic pottery.

O B J E C T S   F O U N D
(Fig. 104)

LEAD

Fragment (No. 8): l. 0.052 m., max. w. 0.025 m., th. 0.004 m. Flattened, roughly rectangular.

BONE

Fragmentary pin (No. 1): l. pres. 0.072 m., w. 0.005 m.-0.007 m., th. 0.004 m. Three pieces, ends missing. Bird bone. Probably polished.

Tip of pin (No. 2): l. pres. 0.029 m., d. 0.004 m. Nicely polished and pointed. Bone or ivory.

TERRACOTTA

Miniature bowl (No. 3): h. 0.019 m., d. 0.025 m.-0.029 m. Has no proper base and cannot stand. Thick walled, crudely fashioned.

Whorl (No. 5): h. 0.012 m., d. 0.042 m., d. perforation 0.005 m. Flattened, spherical, chipped and worn. Soft, light pinkish-red.

Disk (No. 4): h. 0.012 m., d. 0.03 m., d. perforation 0.005 m. Made from raised base of small pot and pierced. Surface polished. Crudely cut and uneven. Soft pinkish-buff clay.

Large disk (No. 6): h. 0.011 m., d. 0.047 m. Made from raised base of pot and pierced. Broken around perforation. Soft reddish clay.

Large disk (No. 7): max. h. 0.01 m., d. 0.046 m. In five fragments, chips missing. Like the two foregoing. Broken around perforation. Base hollow underneath. Soft buff clay.

The Northeastern Quarter

In our explorations to ascertain how far the lower town extended around the acropolis, the area lying to the northeast of the Englianos hill (Fig. 301) between the latter and Tholos Tomb IV was the last to be investigated. During the late summer of 1968 an opportunity was offered Mr. Blegen and his colleague, John Camp, II, to make a sounding in this quarter, which was occupied by a widely spaced venerable olive orchard.

A trench, 1.50 m. wide, was laid out, running from southeast to northwest, first crossing a deep hollow, ca. 45 m. broad, then ascending westward over a ridge and beyond, stretching out some 50 m. or more (Fig. 95). Sections 5 m. long were measured and numbered, but the northwesterly part of the trench, passing over the divide exposed *stereo* at a depth of little more than 0.25 m. and yielded nothing of interest.

Through the hollow, however, deep digging was necessary, striking bottom at the lowest point which measured 4.25 m. below present ground level (Fig. 97). In the depression beneath the cultivated soil, which rarely appears to be more than 0.25 m. to 0.30 m. thick, we encountered a heavy, clammy, leathery earth, manifestly mixed with clay, extremely hard to cut with a pickax or a mattock. This kind of earth continued with little or no alternation to the very bottom of the trench, lying in a roughly horizontal, stratified formation, showing numerous, minor, thin striations with frequent changes of color: white, gray, yellow, red-brown, and blackish (Fig. 96). It looked like accumulation deposited from time to time.

As we proceeded to dig deeper, we uncovered at different levels a few smallish areas spread with stones, for the most part only in a single layer, some fairly large but the majority of no great size (Fig. 98). They looked as if they might have been unloaded from carts. No proper stone walls came to light in the hollow, at any level. Indeed, in the whole deep accumulation of various stratified kinds of earth neither ground-surface nor a floor of any sort to support a wall could be recognized.

From top to bottom, however, the filling material of the hollow contained a great many potsherds, all in miserable condition, weather-worn, soggy, coated with lime and clay. At a depth of ca. 3 m. and deeper we observed a notable increase in the abundance of pottery, and it was in a somewhat better state of preservation in comparison with the rubbed remnants from the upper levels. We also thought that the yield of ceramic material from the depths included many more sherds bearing painted decoration. All fragments recovered through the entire range of the 4 m. of the deposit, so far as we could distinguish, were Mycenaean of a late period belonging mainly to III B with some fragments from III A.

On the very bottom of a part of the trench we noticed that the *stereo* had obviously been worked over by human effort. Two cuttings in hardpan sloped one from east and one from west, meeting in an area descending southward in a direction aiming at the Englianos hill. Their purpose was not clear to us; perhaps a path to the center of the hollow, whatever that held, or possibly the bedding for the walls of some kind of structure.

With Eilert Henrickson, Jr., as a colleague in 1969 in place of Mr. Camp, who was unable to come, a small campaign from August 14 through September 11 was carried out. A new trench was laid out, running roughly from north to southwest at a right angle to the sounding of 1968. Like the latter it was 1.50 m. wide and had a total length of 31 m. measured off into three sections, each ca. 10 m. long, labeled A, B, and C, reading from north to south (Figs. 99, 100). The deepest points, ranging from 5.50 m. to 5.60 m., were reached in some parts of all three sections.

Section A, beginning ca. 2 m. south of the trench of 1968, was dug to a depth of ca. 2.50 m. without finding much pottery, but displaying five striations in the deposit. At this level lay a long spread of smallish stones, for the most part only in a single layer, but continuing through the greater length of Section B, where there was a thicker heap of stones (Figs. 100, 101). In Section A beneath the stone-spread more and more potsherds came to light and at the bottom on *stereo* several little pots of various shapes were recovered (Figs. 102, 103). From this section we collected 33 large baskets filled with potsherds, and underneath the stones three or four strata could be distinguished. Section B produced an additional 26 baskets full of fragments.

O B J E C T S   F O U N D

T E R R A C O T T A

Female figurine (CM. 2921, Fig. 103:1). Head missing. H. cylindrical stem to neck 0.109 m.; d. bottom 0.035 m. to 0.037 m., hollow 0.011 m. deep underneath. Right arm bends downward to abdomen; left arm swings down above right. Decoration: broad band around bottom; higher, widely spaced, two or three slender horizontal bands around cylinder. Above arms garment badly damaged; still higher, close to neck, two circular lumps indicating mammary glands. On back of figurine above horizontal bands six or more parallel wavy streamers. Section A, 5.10 m. below surface.

P O T T E R Y

Small angular kylix (CM. 2913, Fig. 103:2): cf. Shape 27, *PN* I, 366f., figs. 359, 360; *MP*, Type 267, p. 61 fig. 17. Handle and part of rim and side missing. H. 0.116 m.; d. rim 0.117 m., th. stem 0.024 m.; d. foot 0.074 m. Light clay. No decoration. Section B, 1.50 m. from north end, 4.60 m. below surface.

Miniature bowl (CM. 2914, Fig. 103:3). H. 0.033 m.; d. rim 0.051 m.; d. bottom (unsymmetrical) 0.015 m. Loop-handle on one side broken away. Brownish clay. Section B with CM. 2913.

One-handled cup (CM. 2915, Fig. 103:7): cf. Shape 12, *PN* I, 360, figs. 353, 354; *MP*, Type 220, p. 48 fig. 13, Type 222, p. 53 fig. 15. H. 0.045 m.; d. 0.101 m., d. flat bottom 0.043 m. Lightish clay. Section A, 4.65 m. below surface.

Diminutive kylix (CM. 2916, Fig. 103:8): cf. Shape 26, *PN* I, 366, figs. 359, 360. One handle broken away and missing above place of attachment. H. to rim 0.065 m., to top of handle 0.098 m.; d. rim 0.075 m., d. stem 0.019 m.; d. foot 0.047 m.; th. handle 0.012 m. Brownish clay. Section A with CM. 2915.

One-handled shallow cup (CM. 2917, Fig. 103:9): cf. Shape 12, *PN* I, 360, figs. 353, 354; *MP*, Type 220, p. 48 fig. 13, Type 222, p. 53 fig. 15. One side of rim missing. H. rim 0.04 m.-0.043 m.; d. rim 0.113 m.; d. bottom 0.044 m.; w. flattened handle 0.013 m. Section A with CM. 2916.

Two-handled kylix (fragment, foot missing) (CM. 2918, Fig. 103:4): cf. Shape 29c, *PN* I, 369, figs. 361, 362. H. of bowl 0.084 m.; d. rim 0.193 m.; w. handles 0.013 m. Fine light smooth clay with pinkish patches. Section A, 4.80 m. below surface.

Amphoriskos (CM. 2919, Fig. 103:5): cf. Shape 47, *PN* I, 383, figs. 371, 372. Top missing and both handles broken off. H. pres. 0.095 m.; d. body 0.066 m.; d. stem 0.021 m., d. flat bottom 0.046 m. Fine light smooth whitish clay. Section A, 4.90 m. below surface.

Krater-bowl (CM. 2920, Fig. 103:6): cf. Shape 60 small, *PN* I, 397f., figs. 385, 386; *MP*, Type 284, pp. 48, 49 figs. 13, 14. H. 0.101 m.-0.104 m.; d. rim 0.13 m.; d. raised base 0.05 m.-0.06 m.; th. loop handles ca. 0.01 m. Smooth whitish clay. Decoration in brownish color: broad band around foot; two parallel bands just below handles; band on each handle and ring around attachment to vessel. On each panel between handles flower with large bulb in center and leaves to each side. Section A, 4.55 m. below surface.

At a depth of 3 m. the southern part of Section C was covered by a spread of loose stones, and for lack of time we excavated only the northern end barely 4 m. long. *Stereo* was reached at 5.50 m. below ground level, as in Sections A and B. Below 3 m. the pottery was similar to that found in the other sections at the same depth, but since only a short part of the deep area of Section C was excavated, we gathered barely 13 baskets of potsherds.

The deposit above the stones in the southern part of Section C gave us a startling surprise, presenting us a small collection of thick and some thin sherds that look like Hellenistic wares, or earlier. This kind of pottery was found only in the southerly part of Section C. Nowhere on the hilltop of Englianos or below it had we hitherto seen any signs of early or late classical ceramics in the neighborhood.

Except for the few fragments of late classical pots found in a small spot, all the copious sherds recovered in the hollow are clearly Mycenaean. We believe that the refilling of the huge "basin-like" hollow was not done by man power but rather by erosion from a lofty tumulus piled upon Tholos IV (pp. 95ff.). No indication of a barrow can now be seen, but the whole top of the stone-built tomb had been razed away, destroyed to the lintel-level, and smoothed with clay and earth to serve as a flattish bed for drying currants in the sun. Many a damaged and ruined tholos tomb in Messenia has been converted into modern use as an *aloni,* and several tholoi in the Peloponnesos have retained remnants demonstrating that they were once covered by a tumulus.

Libations to the gods and farewell toasts to the dead were certainly carried out abundantly in tombs and dromoi; the cups and vessels were often thrown to the floor and shattered. Surely the same sepulchral rites, services, and customs prevailed on mounds and barrows over the graves of kings and princes and other great and perhaps some not so great.

Tholos IV, a large tomb, was undoubtedly built for a king and presumably for a large family. As so many others, it had been plundered of most of its treasures but some remnants of pottery remained, suggesting that it had been in use through a good many generations. Numerous services were surely held on the tumulus and perhaps in the dromos, and great numbers of kylikes in fragments were strewn about.

The tomb stands, what is left of it, on a hillock only some 50 m. distant from the center of the deep hollow. The winds and the rains often blow and sweep from the north and a heavy downpour from that direction could easily carry along a slide of earth full of potsherds to spread over the depression. A scrutiny of the masses of pottery that came to rest in the hollow discloses that the wine cup, the kylix, is represented vastly more often than all other shapes.

After all this deep digging in our exploration, aimed to discover whether the lower town had spread around the northeastern end of Englianos, we have found no trace of any houses or other buildings in the hollow so far examined.

C. W. B.

THOLOI,
GRAVE CIRCLE,
AND
CHAMBER TOMBS

THOLOI, GRAVE CIRCLE,
AND CHAMBER TOMBS

BEFORE archaeological excavations began on and in the vicinity of the hill called Englianos, superficial indications of three tholos tombs had been noted and known to many. One was recognizable, proclaiming its presence by a surviving lintel block near the highway approximately 1 km. to the southwest of the acropolis in a region known as Kato Englianos. Another, some 80 m. to the northeast of the palace site, had been identified from some large broken blocks of a massive lintel stone. The existence of a third tomb, some 140 m. to the southwest of the citadel, was suggested by the arc of a curving stone wall barely exposed to view at the surface of a threshing floor. These were known to our senior colleague, Dr. Kourouniotis, in 1938. In the course of our many seasons of excavations all three were ultimately opened and thoroughly explored, one in 1939 by Mrs. Blegen, the others in 1953 and 1957 by Lord William Taylour. Since their uncovering followed the excavation of the two tholoi in 1912 and 1926 by Dr. Kourouniotis,[1] the additional sepulchers were duly numbered III, IV, and V, in the chronological order of their excavation.

Usually circular, these underground chambers, dome-shaped, constructed of stone, and often called "beehive tombs," are generally regarded as the distinctive funeral monuments of Mycenaean kings and princes and their families. They have a widespread distribution from Thessaly to Southern Peloponnesos, as well as in Crete, and are relatively numerous in Messenia and the region of the western coast. Few, if any, have ever been found intact and undisturbed, but sometimes valuable treasures have been recovered from grave pits under the floor which have eluded the attention of professional tomb robbers. In several instances grave circles without a dome over them have also been used for the high and mighty.

Tomb V, south of the palace hill, was represented by a curving wall, almost a half circle, in the *aloni* of E. Vayenas; we were led to name the arc Tholos V. It proved to give a rich yield of pit graves containing gold, jewelry, bronze weapons, and much pottery of early Mycenaean style. But when the excavation had been completed and we had time to study what had been exposed, we recognized not one sign of a tholos: no underground chamber, no entrance passage covered with lintel blocks, no doorway, and no dromos. The only structure revealed was a thin wall built at ancient ground level of small stones, preserved

---

[1] *EphArch* 1914, 99ff., *Praktika* 1925-1926, 140f.; *Hesperia* XXIII (1954), 158-162.

only in one or two courses, enclosing at least seven grave pits. This cemetery is strikingly similar to the grave circle that Dr. Yalouris discovered near Samikon, just south of the Alpheios River,[2] and comparable with the more majestic Grave Circles A and B at Mycenae.

Citizens of lesser rank, many of them also prosperous, built family burial vaults of a different kind. They were usually hollowed out in an underlying layer of hard clay beneath a ledge or shelf of conglomerate or other rock that formed the roof. A dromos led inward and downward to a doorway that opened into a chamber of varied shape, circular, rectangular, oval or irregular. Such tombs in many instances served through numerous generations and were no doubt maintained for two or three centuries by long-lived families.

A somewhat extensive ridge descends westward from the citadel of Englianos, sloping down to a deep ravine through which flows a small stream of water that comes in part from the Kephalovrysi above Chora. On the southern flank of this declivity the formation of rock and earth, with its layers of limestone lying over hard white clay, was recognized by the Mycenaeans as very suitable for their chamber tombs. Here the inhabitants of the lower town surrounding the acropolis in Mycenaean times established a cemetery of such sepulchers (Fig. 301). Soundings carried out during the seasons of 1956, 1957, and 1966 by Mr. Donovan exposed a dozen or more dromoi presumably leading to chambers under the ledge. Six have been excavated by Mr. Donovan and one by Lord William Taylour, yielding gold jewelry as well as bronzes, terracottas, and some very good pots ranging in date from early Mycenaean to the stage of III B. Traces of additional tombs which have not been systematically investigated were expected on the western and northwestern flanks of the ridge.

In another area, some two or more kilometers south of the palace, generally called Mavroudia but sometimes loosely referred to as Kato Englianos, further explorations by Lord William Taylour revealed a chamber tomb, which was excavated in 1958 and 1959, as well as the remaining one-third of a small tholos tomb of the Protogeometric period.

The following pages present descriptions by the excavators of all the tombs that were examined and also provide detailed catalogues of the objects recovered in each. The report on Tholos III has been compiled mainly from Mrs. Blegen's notebook. The tholos tombs and grave circle take precedence in the order of their excavation, and are followed by the chamber tombs. The Hellenic-American Archaeological Expedition extends its warmest thanks to the late Nikolaos Gliatas, Mr. and Mrs. P. Kanakaris, and Mr. Evstathis Vayenas, who generously

[2] *Deltion* 20 (1965), 6-40.

gave us permission to excavate in their threshing floors and vineyards as we exposed Tombs III and IV and the grave circle. We thank also those who allowed us to explore and dig in their properties in the search for chamber tombs: Demetrios Paraskevopoulos, Evstathis Deriziotis, Panagiotes Tsakalis, Aristomenos Kontos, Nikolaos Charalambropoulos, Ioannis Kokkevis and family.

C. W. B.

THOLOS TOMB III
(Plan and Section, Figs. 319-320)

This tholos lies some 35 m. northwestward of the highway at a point about one kilometer southwest of the acropolis of Englianos (Fig. 301). Here Nikolaos Gliatas of Chora, owner of the land, had built directly over the tomb a stone storehouse for his tools and his currants (Fig. 160), as well as a deep cistern, and just below had made a threshing floor or drying bed for currants. In order to excavate the tomb the storeroom had first to be demolished and rebuilt outside the area of the tomb (Fig. 161); we were then free to dig.

Mrs. Blegen, with assistance from Mrs. Hill, supervised the excavation and recorded all the objects found. This work was carried out from April 14 to May 7, 1939, with a small group of workmen, varying as needed from four to ten in number. The plan of the tomb (Fig. 319), comprising a dromos, doorway, and chamber, was drawn up by Lewey Lands from the detailed measurements and sketches and notes recorded in Mrs. Blegen's field notebook.

The dromos, oriented almost precisely from southwest to northeast, is 8.10 m. long, 2.35 m. wide at the outer end, narrowing a trifle to 2.25 m. at the inner end. The passage, descending toward the tomb, had been cut into a rising slope formed by a firm undisturbed bed of yellowish clay. The sides of the cutting, approximately vertical, as was customary in similar tombs in Argolis, were not lined with stone walls.

The dromos was found to be full of earth to the level of the modern surface. The right half of this deposit was first excavated, leaving on the left side a vertical scarp following the longitudinal axis of the dromos and showing the stratification of the remaining fill. As viewed in section (Fig. 320) four layers were clearly distinguishable, separated in each instance one from another by a thin stratum of dark carbonized matter. This sequence led us to conclude that the tomb after its first use for burial had been reopened and reclosed in at least three subsequent periods to receive later interments. On each successive occasion less earth was evidently removed than had been taken out the time before. The final ingress was made by means of a short and somewhat steep descent not far from the doorway itself. The potsherds recovered from the four layers, one above the other, were kept in separate containers for each level in the hope that some evidence for the chronology might be recognized. Unfortunately, however, the nondescript fragments collected shed no convincing light on the exact dating of the phases represented by the four striations.

In addition to a relatively scanty quantity of shattered bits of pottery, the dromos yielded a few small remnants of gold jewelry and inlays, fragments of bronze, a bead of carnelian, bits of flint and obsidian, and some much damaged beads of glass paste. All lay scattered about helter-skelter, no doubt because the whole area had been repeatedly disturbed by the frequent reopening of the passage for the later burials. No trace of a pit, such as often appears in the dromoi of tholoi in Argolis, was found in the entranceway to Tomb III, and no certain human bones were noted.

The doorway leading from the dromos to the chamber is 3 m. deep from the outer to the inner face, 1.65 m. wide, and it has a height of 3.10 m. from the floor to the soffit of the lintel. The lateral walls, about 1 m. thick, were sturdily built of somewhat irregular, flat or flattish slabs of no great size, little if at all worked, but well put together in the structure. No stone threshold seems to have been judged necessary, a flooring of earth running through the opening. Originally three or four large flat stones were apparently used to form the lintel over the doorway. Part of the innermost slab still survives on the top of the southeastern jamb and a much larger fragment of it had fallen into the doorway, evidently after the last burials were made (Fig. 162). Lodging diagonally against the southeastern jamb the slab protected a human skull, perhaps belonging to the final period of interments. The fallen fragment of the lintel was left by us in the doorway leaning against the jamb but no longer blocking the entrance (Fig. 163).[3] The second block (Fig. 162) was found in its place across the doorway: it is 2.25 m. long, 0.85 m. wide, and 0.31 m. thick.[4] How the rest of the doorway was covered is uncertain since no stones survive. The unfilled space extending beyond to the façade is about 1.55 m. broad, and it is possible that one substantial single block could have served to cover that width. Alternatively two narrower stones may have been preferred by the builders. The jambs forming the sides of the doorway taper appreciably inward; in some places, where measuring was possible, it seems to follow a batter of 0.10 m. in 1 m., but the walls on both sides have buckled too much to permit accurate measurement.

The outer façade of the doorway seems to have presented a simple architec-

---

[3] Dimensions of fallen and broken block: l. 1.50 m., w. 1.02 m., th. 0.21 m.

[4] An earthquake in 1968 dislodged the block.

tural refinement—perhaps a little aesthetic touch. It is a rabbet along the exterior corner of the jamb on each side of the entrance passage, approximately 0.20 m. deep and, on the southwestern face, 0.25 m. long. The rebate presumably may also have been carried across the front of the lintel.

At the outer end of the doorway some remains of the blocking wall were preserved. Indeed two separate structures offered evidence that there were two successive barriers to close the doorway. The upper and later one, resting on earth high above the floor of the dromos and projecting outside the façade of the doorway, consisted of loose stones, two irregular rows wide and two carelessly disjointed courses high (Fig. 164). Behind and below these lines of loose stones was an earlier and much better constructed wall made of bigger blocks; it had been broken down in the middle but was still found to rise to four or five courses at the sides of the doorway (Fig. 165).

The doorway was found encumbered with masses of stones over which lay the fallen lintel slab that had presumably brought them down. Underneath the flat stone and almost in the middle of the entrance lay the skull mentioned above (A, Fig. 319). A second skull (B), badly crushed, was found farther to the southeast, about 0.60 m. above the floor and near the southeastern jamb. Two human leg bones were uncovered more or less in the same stratum farther to the northwest. We concluded that these crania must have belonged to the last Mycenaeans who were buried in this tomb at a high level in a place at the front of the grave where there was space. Of course, it would be far more tempting to conjecture that the skulls might have belonged to marauders who had entered the tomb for plunder and were caught there in an earthquake and in that way paid for their trespassing.

Relatively few objects were recovered from the debris filling the doorway. Among items worthy of special mention are several fragments of gold leaf and rosettes, as well as a bead; a fragment of a bronze pin, a piece of an arrowhead, a terracotta whorl, and a basket of potsherds, including some pieces of early Mycenaean style. No understandable stratification could be discerned: the whole deposit was jumbled together in complete disorder, except perhaps at the very bottom where fragments of Mycenaean pottery, apparently of Late Helladic II, were recovered.

The tomb chamber was laid out in an almost exact, but not quite perfect, circle (Fig. 319). Measured approximately along the extension of the axis of the dromos, it has a diameter of 7.66 m., which increases to 7.71 m. in the transverse axis. The wall surrounding the chamber was constructed of relatively smallish unworked stones, many flat but others irregular in shape. The lowest one or two courses were strengthened by the use of larger and more substantial blocklike stones (Fig. 166). The exact thickness of the wall was difficult to determine but it appears to vary from ca. 0.70 m. to 1 m. or more. The enclosing wall rises vertically from the floor to a height of ca. 1 m. before the curvature of the vault begins. This is a feature observed by Lord William Taylour in our Tholos IV (p. 97) and by Valmin at Malthi in several tombs.[5] Through the greater part of the circumference the wall is preserved to a height ranging from 2.50 m. to 3 m., not quite so high as the level of the lintel of the doorway. The inner corner of the doorway, on the left as one enters, had crumbled away either as the result of an earthquake or some other calamity; and a large section of the upper courses in the southeastern quarter was at some time precipitated into the tomb. At the rear of the chamber, slightly to the southeast of the middle, is the modern cistern that had been built by Mr. Gliatas, cutting away part of the wall of the tholos. Since the whole deposit in the area of the cistern had been removed and since the water for spraying the currant vineyard was precious to the owner, we let his structure remain undisturbed where it was and still is.

It is clear that the circular space for the chamber had been hewn out through the rather loose and not very cohesive limestone rock overlying the clay layer beneath. The cutting did, in any event, form the shape of the chamber, and the stone wall was laid against the rock that formed a natural buttress; thus the variation in the thickness of the stone wall, ranging from 0.70 m. to 1 m. and more, depended on the breadth to which the rock had been cut back.

Like the dromos the chamber was filled from top to bottom with earth, an immense quantity of stones from the collapsed dome, and other debris. Among the latter were innumerable small fragments of thick, coarse ware, obviously coming from two or more large pithoi. The remnants include bits of handles representing two types, as well as broken rims of differing profiles. Some crumbling human bones were also recognized in this debris and it is possible that these huge jars had been used as burial urns in Late Mycenaean times. As digging approached the floor through the final meter of deposit, a scene of great disorder and confusion was exposed to view. Small splinters and fragments of human bones lay strewn about, along with occasional isolated larger pieces. The forequarters and the skull of a bull, one horn surviving, were uncovered in reasonably good order in the inner left section of the chamber; and to the right of the central area parts of the backbone, ribs, and jaws of a goat or sheep came to light. Tiny bits of gold and bronze, remnants of ivory, beads and ornaments of stone and glass paste, were found. Single sherds of pottery in considerable abun-

---

[5] *SME*, 213; *Bulletin de la société royale des lettres de Lund*, 1926-27, 53ff.

dance appeared here and there and were duly salvaged but no whole pots were recognizable. On the floor itself the same evidence of wanton destruction was to be seen on all sides. In a dozen different places on the floor fragments of human skulls and other distinctive bones were noted and recorded, all indicated on the plan by capital letters ranging from C to P (Fig. 319). In small letters, ranging from a to h, bones of animals not further identified are similarly marked.

In a preliminary report on the first season of excavation at Englianos in 1939,[6] we were led to wonder if Tomb III had for some unknown reason been sacked, plundered, and ruthlessly destroyed by enemies, for we had never seen in eastern Peloponnesos the utter annihilation displayed at Kato Englianos. In the long interval since 1939, however, two or three other tholoi have been excavated in Messenia which seem to have suffered a similar grim fate, apparently in late Mycenaean times.[7] Was it an affliction visited on the Mycenaean inhabitants at the end of the Neleid period?

Two pits—presumably graves—were discovered cut into the floor of Tomb III, one near the center of the tholos, the other far to the right. The first-mentioned, 1.27 m. long and ranging from 0.43 m. to 0.55 m. in width, was 0.45 m. deep (Fig. 319). It contained three fragments of skulls, a few other scattered bones, a great many stones of various sizes (Fig. 167), beads of glass paste, and potsherds lying in total disorder. The pit had obviously been ransacked and all objects of value had been taken away. Whether this was an original shaft grave or was made to be used for a secondary burial when space in the tomb was becoming scarce is uncertain.

The other pit, near the southeastern wall of the chamber, had been hewn out in an irregular oblong shape, ca. 1.30 m. wide, with a maximum length of 2.70 m. (Fig. 168). It had been cut down into *stereo* to a depth of 1.30 m. where a more or less level bottom was made. Masses of stones along with a good many human bones comprised the greater part of the debris filling the shaft. This pit too must surely have held one or more burials but its contents, like those of the smaller grave, had been thoroughly looted and what was left lay scattered in confusion. At a depth of 1 m. a narrow shelf or bench, 0.15 m. wide, had been left along the whole southeasterly side. At 1.10 m. to 1.12 m. a stratum of red and black earth or clay looked as if the discoloration had been caused by fire, perhaps a burnt offering of some kind.

In the shaft grave lay two blocks of poros, neatly squared and properly dressed. Approximately a dozen such pieces were noted resting on the floor

---

[6] *AJA* XLIII (1939), 573.
[7] Tholos II, Kourouniotis, *Praktika*, 1925-1926,

140f.; *Hesperia* XXIII (1954), 158-162. See also Tholos IV in this volume (pp. 108f.).

of the chamber all the way around the circle close to the enclosing wall, but not arranged in any semblance of intentional order. Most of these stones were observed to be somewhat wedge-shaped and it seemed obvious that they could have had their place in the dome. Our conjecture is that this material may have formed a ring of blocks running around the vault, possibly comparable to the well-known zone at the level of the lintel in the so-called "Tomb of Clytemnestra" at Mycenae.[8] Some stones, even many, of the same kind could well have been shattered when they fell from above; but it would take vastly more than twelve blocks to build such a ring at the height of the lintel, even in our relatively diminutive Tholos III. A possible theory, however, is that an encircling band could have been laid much higher in the dome.

Some scattered traces of fire were noticed here and there when the floor of the chamber was cleaned and scraped. No evidence whatever was seen by us to suggest that cremation may have been practiced. These small spots where something had been consumed by fire might merely mark places where little offerings could have been made; or, if torches were used during burial services in the tomb, accidents might have occurred.

Drilled into the floor in the inner left quarter of the chamber, two rather odd-looking holes, roughly circular in shape, attracted our attention; another appeared in the inner right quarter, not far from the north corner of the large pit. Each had a diameter of ca. 0.30 m. and was 0.25 m. deep. One was close beside the wall of the tomb, the other two at about 1.40 m. and 3 m. distant from the wall. Their purpose was not clear but it occurred to us that they might have been useful as setting places for upright timbers to give temporary support during the construction of the dome.

In its thoroughly wrecked and shattered state this tomb poses some difficult problems of interpretation. At the outset one is naturally inclined to inquire how and why so barbarous a treatment was visited on this resting place of the dead. Ordinary looters and professional grave robbers could surely have collected and carried away the objects of greatest intrinsic value—gold, silver, bronze, jewelry, gems, ivory, etc.—without turning the whole tomb topsy-turvy and crushing the human bones into scattered fragments and splinters. Vandals might have been able to create so impressive a ruin, and even to shatter into small bits the skeletons in the grave pits, as well as all the pots that were put in the tomb. A severe earthquake, toppling the stones of the dome to the floor and smashing what lay upon it, would hardly have produced so detailed a picture of annihilation and surely could not have treated the grave pits so severely. No

---

[8] *BSA* xxv (1921-23), 361ff. and pl. LVIII.

satisfactory answer to the question is obvious and it is unlikely that any adequate explanation can be established from the actual evidence available.

A good many fragments of human skulls were duly recognized and recorded in various parts of the doorway and the chamber, but exactly how many persons were buried in the tomb cannot be surely determined. At least 16 fragments of crania are indicated on the plan by capital letters, as mentioned above (pp. 75-77 and Fig. 319). Although some of these scattered pieces may perhaps have belonged to one and the same skull, the great majority no doubt came from different skulls. Indeed it is not unlikely that the number of interments in the tomb may have reached a greater total than 16.

The presence of animal bones in the tomb has been observed at many other places. A large part, perhaps one side, of the carcass of a bull or an ox and the side of a sheep or goat might have been placed in the grave to provide a supply of food for the journey into the beyond. Other items of food and drink were certainly provided in pots of various shapes and kinds. Many fragments of large pithoi, mentioned above (p. 76), beginning to appear high up in the deposit that filled the chamber and continuing downward, were also noted on the floor of the tomb.

The date of Tholos III can be approximately determined. On the floor and in the dromos were recovered a few fragments of pots assignable to the "Palace Style" of pottery decoration and perhaps to Late Helladic II; this would mean that if these pots were not long-cherished heirlooms the vault must have been built and used for burials at least as early as the middle of the fifteenth century B.C., if not before. Other scattered sherds bearing painted decoration point to a considerably later period, Mycenaean III A and III B. It is therefore evident that the tholos served for burials beginning between 1500 and 1450 and continuing down to the middle or the end of the thirteenth century. The ceramic evidence thus indicates that the use of the tomb lasted into the time of the Palace of Nestor in Mycenaean III B.

As abundantly demonstrated by the surviving remainders left behind by the looters, it is obvious that this royal sepulcher, Tomb III, though not very large, once contained relatively rich funeral gear. In spite of the severe pillaging that had made away with almost all objects of intrinsic value, remnants of gold, silver jewelry, and bronze weapons, a gem and beads of various stones, fragments of carved ivory, as well as innumerable beads and plaques of faience or glass paste, suffice to testify to the original wealth deposited here. These leavings were scattered about in all areas of the dromos, the doorway, and the chamber. Only the partial skeletons of an ox and a wild goat were left untouched. Items that were large enough to be seen were duly recorded by Mrs. Blegen as to their place of finding. Many beads, however, were so small that they could be recovered only by sifting the earth removed. Since they had been overlooked, carelessly dropped, or thrown aside by the ancient plunderers, their find-spots were of little or no value. In the following catalogue we have therefore presented the material in three groups, coming respectively from the dromos, the doorway, and the chamber. But even this does not certify that the finding place of objects marked the original point of deposit, for some of the pots were made up of joining fragments from all three areas.

In concluding the description of Tomb III we may add that some attempts were made in 1939, with the help of a professional mason, to preserve what was left of the structure. It was a practical temporary measure, though lacking somewhat aesthetically as compared with Mycenaean workmanship. On each side of the façade of the doorway a substantial wall made of stone and cement was built to support the one slab of the lintel surviving in place. At the inner end of the entrance both angles with the vault, to right and left, were in a perilous state; here too reinforcement in cement gave strength to assure maintenance of the corners for some time. Several cracks and gaps in the wall of the chamber were also mended as well as the encroaching side of the cistern which jutted out southwestward into the tomb. Through 29 years since the tholos was excavated the precautions taken continued to hold firm, but in 1968 an earthquake shook the upper part of the doorway to the ground.

When the exploratory excavations of 1939 came to their end on June 9, all the small objects and the shattered pottery collected from Tomb III along with the valuable items found in the palace were transported to Athens and deposited in the National Museum. This was necessary since no repository for archaeological material was at that time available in western Messenia. Moreover, in the preliminary testing campaign we had no technician at the site to deal with the problem of washing and putting together what was found.

In Athens Andreas Mavraganis, who had been trained in the excavations of the Athenian Agora conducted by the American School of Classical Studies, undertook not only to clean and conserve the tablets from the palace but also the pottery from Tomb III. This work, which was regularly supervised by Mr. Hill, was carried out in the autumn of 1939 and the winter and spring of 1940. Mavraganis, a skillful mender, preserved all the numerous bits of tablets, joined them together and prepared them for photographing by Miss Alison Frantz. We are greatly indebted to him for that work and also for cleaning and salvaging the pottery collected from the tomb. The yield, as recorded in the field notebook, comprised 75 separate lots, 16 coming from the dromos, six from the doorway, and 53 from the chamber, along with 35 baskets of human and animal bones.

The ceramic material at first glance looked extremely discouraging: multitudes of small bits, giving little indication of shapes represented and for the most part consisting of plain ware, largely coarse, and with only a few rare pieces bearing painted decoration. Not a single intact vessel had survived. The patience and perseverance of our mender ultimately succeeded in reconstructing more than 20 pots of many different shapes.

With the coming of World War II to Greece the reconstructed vessels and the bulk of the sherds suffered considerable damage. All the contents of the National Museum were speedily stowed away underground in order to be protected from bombs and shells. No bombs were actually exploded in the Museum, but it is recorded that 76 mortar shells landed on the roof and some penetrated it. In the rebuilding of the Museum after the war, an operation requiring many years, all the material that had been buried was dug up and subsequently several times shifted from place to place. More recently a flood in the basement also ruined many of the sherd baskets and all of the mended pots were broken again and some of their constituent parts lost.

In 1966, however, through the kind cooperation of Mr. Kallipolites, Director of the Museum, Mrs. Touloupa, Curator of the Mycenaean Collection, and her competent assistants, Mrs. Konsola, Mrs. Kypraiou, Miss Boudouroglou, and Miss Lempese, managed to find the material from Tomb III and bring it back to the light of day. Mr. Yalouris also lent a helping hand and Mr. Papathanasopoulos likewise found some of the missing fragments. With the help of Andreas Mavraganis and Triandaphyllos Kontogeorges all the pots have now once again been restored.

C. W. B.

O B J E C T S   F O U N D

Dromos

GOLD

Rosette (NM. 7865,[9] Fig. 169:6): d. ca. 0.02 m.; fragments of others. Thin gold leaf with 12 petals radiating from central circle.

Bead (NM. 7866, Fig. 169:5): l. 0.015 m., w. 0.01 m. Another similar (Fig. 169:4): l. ca. 0.01 m., w. 0.005 m. Amygdaloid with longitudinal grooves; pierced lengthwise for stringing.

Circular disk (NM. 7865): d. 0.008 m. Two small holes opposite each other near edge for stringing. No decoration.

Scraps of gold leaf and small bits of wire, perhaps from inlays in bronze.

[9] These are numbers of National Museum where objects are housed.

BRONZE

Two small shapeless chunks (NM. 7844); fragment of pin or awl.

Thin fragment, l. 0.026 m., w. 0.023 m., broken on all sides.

Fragment of pin or dart.

LEAD

Small flattish circular disk, d. 0.016 m.-0.017 m., th. 0.005 m. Slight projection in edge. Pierced for stringing.

STONE

Carnelian, amygdaloid bead (NM. 7865, Fig. 169:18): l. 0.016 m., w. 0.008 m., th. 0.004 m.; longitudinal groove on each flat side.

Flint, shapeless pieces: three gray, one reddish-brown, three small fragments. Three larger pieces, each with one toothed edge.

Obsidian flake and three shapeless fragments.

BONE

Small bits, apparently worked, but purpose not certain.

GLASS PASTE

Beads

Fragment bearing pattern of leaf with four lobes; one radially-grooved pale blue; five small and fragments of others, "grain of wheat"; half of spherical with stripes.

POTTERY

Eight lots of sherds nearly all from undecorated vessels. A few fragments bear painted motives assignable to Mycenaean III B. Kylix commonest shape, parts of at least seven counted. Remnants of two stirrup-vases found just outside wall blocking doorway, both belonging to Mycenaean III B. Two scoops in relatively coarse ware, put together from sherds.

Scoop (NM. 9136, Fig. 173:9): Shape 66 (*PN* I, 411f., figs. 395, 396); *MP*, Type 311, p. 75 fig. 21, comparable, but not exactly identical. H. 0.055 m., transverse d. on lip 0.124 m., l. handle 0.115 m., w. handle 0.035 m., large hole for suspension near outer end of handle. At rim opposite handle scanty remnants of pour channel recognizable.

Scoop (NM. 9137, Fig. 173:10, similar to foregoing): h. 0.063 m., transverse d. 0.126 m.; slightly raised flat base, d. 0.053 m., l. handle 0.11 m., w. handle 0.035 m. Big suspension hole near outer end of handle. Opposite handle pour channel formed by turning rim outward.

Doorway

GOLD

Beads (NM. 7870): eight diminutive spherical (Fig. 169:7).

Rosettes (NM. 7867, 7869, Fig. 169:10). 12 eight-petaled rosettes of thin gold leaf, many fragmentary, some with d. 0.02 m., others 0.019 m., and 0.017 m. Each has three small holes in symmetrical triangular formation for attachment to background.

Two pieces of rectangular shape (Fig. 169:8, 9): (a) l. 0.02 m., w. 0.017 m.; (b) l. 0.019 m., w. 0.017 m. Three holes for attachment as in rosettes.

Several small plain disks, one d. 0.009 m.; many bits of gold leaf. A few small studs.

BRONZE

Rivet heads (NM. 7870): one gilded, d. 0.012 m., and one without gilding, d. 0.01 m., perhaps from weapons. Fragments too badly corroded to indicate from what objects they came.

STONE

Amethyst bead (NM. 7869, Fig. 169:19): d. 0.013 m.; spherical, dark purple.

Carnelian bead (NM. 7871, Fig. 169:15): d. 0.014 m.; spherical, decorated with shallow fluting.

Obsidian arrowhead (NM. 7870): l. 0.015 m., w. 0.0075 m.

GLASS PASTE

Fragments of leaf-shaped ornament.

TERRACOTTA

Fragment of whorl or button.

POTTERY

Five lots of sherds. No pots could be reconstructed. Much coarse ware; in finer fabrics plain undecorated vessels predominate. Shapes noted: small bowls, angular kylix of Mycenaean III B, conical cup, and from floor a few pieces with remains of decoration in style of Late Helladic II.

Chamber

GOLD

Pendant or ornament (NM. 7871, Fig. 169:1): cluster of three heart-shaped leaves or sacral ivy. Max. w. group 0.022 m., w. leaves varies from 0.009 m. to 0.011 m. From one leaf, evidently forming bottom of triad, two lines in fine granulated technique swing upward to upper two leaves; each of latter bordered around edge by similar granulation that also forms decorative spray or flower within leaf.[10] Lower leaf has no flower, lacks dotted border. When pendant found, some attached bluish matter seen; may have been an inlay of paste of some kind. No exact parallel known to us.

Pendant in form of one-handled jug or ewer (NM. 7855, Fig. 169:2a-c): h. 0.018 m., max. w. 0.013 m. Relatively small high base, somewhat squat body, broad high neck splaying out to wide rim. Pendant decorated with lines of granulation, one around base, pair circling body just above greatest diameter, single row along edge of rim, continuing down edge of handle. In broad lower zone two wavy lines meander up and down. Larger ornament of gold also in form of spouted pitcher came from Vestibule of Palace of Nestor, having evidently fallen from upper story (*PN* I, 75, fig. 273:20). Two somewhat similar gold beads were recovered in tholos tomb near Menidi (*KG*, taf. v:10).

Bead (NM. 7855, Fig. 169:3) in form of shield shaped like figure eight: l. 0.011 m.,

w. 0.004 m.-0.0055 m. Decorated with granulated border running around edge of bead. Larger ornament of same general shape, also in gold, found in Tholos IV (p. 114). Similar small gold shield recovered by Wace in Tomb 518 at Mycenae (*ChT*, 87, pl. XXXVIII:77); two comparable diminutive beads of same kind yielded by Tomb III at Heraeum (*Prosymna*, 271, figs. 460:6, 578). Examples in ivory or glass paste found in tholos at Menidi (*KG* pl. VI:13, 14).

Bead (NM. 7867, Fig. 169:7 bottom bead): d. 0.004 m. Very small, decorated in relief with central knob, six smaller knobs or petals as on a rosette. Comparable bead found by Tsountas in tomb at Vapheio (*EphArch* 1889, pl. 7:11).

Bead (NM. 7868, Fig. 169:7 next to bottom): l. ca. 0.003 m., d. 0.002 m. Cylindrical, exterior surface decorated with four longitudinal rows of granulations.

Fragment of upper part of bead with coiled wire attached.

Rosettes (NM. 7869, Fig. 169:10): sizes vary, d. ranging from 0.02 m. to 0.015 m. and smaller. Thin gold leaf similar to example found in doorway (Fig. 169:6). Ten counted, in most instances not intact. Stamped in low relief with eight petals radiating from small dotted circle at center. Many fragments of similar examples.

Rosettes of gold and ivory have been found in chamber tombs at Mycenae by Tsountas,[11] by Wace;[12] they appeared also at Argive Heraeum;[13] especially at Midea where Swedish Expedition recovered magnificent necklace of 36 beads.[14] Comparable gold rosettes of two sizes came to light in chamber tombs at Asine,[15] and at Spata.[16]

Disks (NM. 7871, cf. Fig. 169:10): dimen-

---

[10] For Sir Arthur Evans' discussion of the sacral ivy and its development see *PM* II ii, 478-493.

[11] *EphArch* 1887, pl. 13:8; 1888, 140, Tomb 10, 37 gold and 35 glass paste.

[12] Tomb 515, *ChT*, pl. XXXII:72b, 80c.

[13] *Prosymna* 304:12; fig. 362:2, 14.

[14] *RT, Dendra*, 13f., 40f., pl. XVIII.

[15] *Asine*, 372, fig. 241; 387, fig. 251; 399, fig. 262; 406, fig. 266.

[16] *Athenaion* VI (1877), 171, pl. B:24.

sions vary: d. ca. 0.01 m. to 0.016 m. Small, circular, of thin plain gold leaf; five counted. Fragments of many broken pieces. All disks pierced for attachment with two small holes on opposite sides of circumference.

Gold leaf: more than 50 shapeless fragments.

Strips of heavier gold leaf: l. 0.016 m. and w. 0.005 m. ranging to l. 0.021 m., w. 0.009 m. Each strip has perforation near each end.

Fragments of straight, curved, or bent pin-like bits of wire. More than 55 pieces counted: probably used for inlays in bronze weapons or jewelry.

SILVER

Small bits giving no indication of objects to which they belonged.

BRONZE

Sword or dagger (NM. 7844, NM. 7853, Fig. 169:11): four fragments, aggregate total length 0.167 m., max. w. 0.025 m. Strong longitudinal midrib.

Flanged tang (NM. 7849, Fig. 169:11): l. 0.038 m., w. 0.023 m. Fragment, perhaps from same weapon recorded in preceding paragraph.

Rivet heads (NM. 7869, 7870): two, one gilded.

Fragments of pin, not restorable.

Shapeless chunks, may small fragments and scraps.

LEAD

Two small bits of wire such as have been found in chamber tombs in Attica, Argolis, and elsewhere.[17]

STONE

Carnelian beads (NM. 7869, Fig. 169:12, 13, 14): three small spherical, one broken; average d. ca. 0.0045 m. (NM. 7867, Fig. 169:16, 17): two somewhat flattened, almost annular; d. ca. 0.004 m.

Crystal: three fragments of clear quartz;

nothing to show from what kind of objects they came.

Flint: 11 shapeless fragments.

Gypsum plaque (NM. 7847): l. 0.075 m., w. 0.048 m., th. 0.0065 m.; flat, rectangular. Finished along one edge, broken on other sides. Grooves or scratches on both faces but no decoration, no indication of purpose.

Jasper trifacial seal (NM. 7856, Fig. 169:20a-c = *CMS* I No. 287): on face *a,* lion to right,[18] head hanging down in frontal view, with two large circular eyes; body curved over unrecognizable object perhaps an animal being devoured. Face *b* bears wild goat running to left[19] with head turned back to right in strange contortion; two long pointed ears; behind back rises branch of tree or shrub. Faces *a* and *b* with scenes ca. 0.0145 m. in diameter; face *c,* 0.015 m. by 0.013 m., empty of decoration.

Steatite: shank of button, two fragments.

Limestone grinders (NM. 7863): h. 0.071 m., d. 0.04 m. to 0.05 m.; irregularly conical. Worn away below on grinding surface.

Another piece of harder limestone: h. 0.081 m., d. bottom 0.06 m. Bottom badly worn.

Whetstone (NM. 7848): l. 0.048 m., w. 0.017 m., th. 0.006 m. Three joining fragments. Fine-grained reddish-gray limestone, rectangular in section, tapering slightly toward one end.

IVORY

Plaque (NM. 7890, Fig. 170:3): fairly large flat; l. 0.097 m., w. 0.047 m., th. 0.003 m., broken on three sides, put together from several smaller fragments. Decorated on one face with rows of double nautiluses. In upper row, as photographed, three shells: each a curious double creature emitting both to left and right usual three spiraliform tentacles. In next lower row five double shells have in part survived, each, like those above, provided with triple ten-

---

[17] *EphArch* 1888, 142; 1895, 208f.; *Prosymna,* 255.

[18] To left in impression.

[19] To right in impression.

tacles on each side, and these are some-what better preserved. Traces of third row, if not more, and whole plaque must originally have been at least 0.165 m. wide.

Carving done by a delicate, skillful hand that neatly delineated curving corrugations of shells. Even diminutive suckers on many of tentacles carefully indicated by tiny dots.

Panel may have belonged to one side of small jewel chest or toilet box, but not enough left to confirm suggestion. Eight small fragments, some decorated with nautiluses, look as if they might belong to same receptacle, but no actual joins have been discovered.

Fragment (NM. 7846, Fig. 170:7): another piece obviously from same container; l. 0.076 m.; w. 0.025 m., broken on three sides. Remnants of five nautiluses, exactly like those on NM. 7890, probably from bottom of panel.

This curious double argonaut clearly a favorite motive in decoration of beads and plaques, as indicated by many examples found in widespread distribution. The Chieftain's Grave and Tomb 7 in Zafer Papoura cemetery near Knossos yielded gold plaques with decoration of this type (Evans, "The Prehistoric Tombs of Knossos," *Archaeologia* 59 [1905], figs. 60, 119:36k; "The Tomb of the Double Axes," *Archaeologia* 65 [1914], fig. 59:21; *PM* IV ii, 862, fig. 845; *Crete and Mycenae*, pl. 120 left). Sir Arthur Evans suggested that ornaments in gold were in general earlier than those of glass paste. The cemetery at Phaistos also produced comparable gold pieces (*MonAnt* XIV [1904], 595, figs. 58, 59, pl. XXXIX; *Crete and Mycenae*, pl. 120 right). From Argolis similar plaques are known (Tsountas, Mycenae, Tomb 8, *EphArch* 1888, pl. 9:4; Tomb of Clytemnestra, Wace, *Mycenae*, 36, fig. 57a; *Crete and Mycenae*, pl. 200; Argos, chamber tomb, Vollgraff, *BCH* XXVIII [1904], 383f., figs. 11, 15) as well as from Attica (Menidi, *KG*, pl. IV:21, 24); from Thessaly (Iolkos, Kourouniotis, *EphArch* 1906, 228, pl. XIV), and

from Ialysos in Rhodes (*BM,* Catalogue of Jewelry, 59, Nos. 793-94, pl. VIII).

Corresponding ornaments in gold and glass paste have been found in Crete ("The Prehistoric Tombs of Knossos," *Archaeologia* 59 [1905], fig. 20), in Attica (Menidi, *KG,* taf. iv:21, 24), in Argolis (Mycenae, Tsountas's Tomb 8: *EphArch* 1888, 139, pl. 9:4; Argos, *BCH* XXVIII [1904], 383, figs. 11, 15; *Asine,* Tomb 1:2, 389, fig. 252; *RT, Dendra* 102, pl. XXXIII:6; *Prosymna,* 306, fig. 379). Of much interest is mold (acquired in Smyrna and in 1880 presented to Berlin Museum) for making three different glass ornaments, one decorated with double argonauts, published in 1886 by Furtwaengler and Loeschcke (*MV,* 34, fig. 22). Single nautiluses were also much favored in Crete and on Greek mainland on beads and plaques of glass paste (e.g., found by Tsountas in house at Mycenae, *EphArch* 1887, pl. 13:2, 3; from Attica, Spata, *BCH* II [1878], 201, pl. XV:12, 14). Argonauts carved in ivory appear more rare than gold and paste.

Leg of pyxis or casket (NM. 7854, Fig. 170:9a-b): h. 0.054 m., w. 0.026 m., th. 0.027 m. Nearly square in section. Decorated on each of two contiguous faces, meeting at corner with three nautiluses, each in small rectangular, almost square panel, latter bordered by beading of tiny dots; whole exquisitely carved (cf. *EphArch* 1887, pl. 13:18 and 18a). These are single nautiluses and not double. Decorated area bordered on each side by plain half-round molding, and two similar moldings of smaller size separate little panels.

Technique almost identical with that on NM. 7890 and leg may well have belonged to same box.

Fragment of leg (?) of box or inlay decorating leg (NM. 7845, Fig. 170:2a-b): l. or h. 0.079 m., w. 0.024 m., th. 0.01 m. Long sides and one end preserved, other end broken. Daintily carved with motive of half rosettes, back to back, separated by small panel bearing three spirals. At least two such groups, with minimum length or height of 0.086 m.; if a third group, dimension would be 0.129 m. Fragmentary edges of leg and remnants of half-rosettes as well as panels of spirals all bordered by lines of tiny round beading, probably do not come from pyxis NM. 7890, but from different box. Still another fragment in miserable condition, l. 0.056 m., retains remnants of additional pair of half-rosettes.

Motif of paired half-rosettes familiar at other sites in Crete and in mainland Greece, often in stone (Knossos, *PM* II, ii, 591, fig. 368; Mycenae, *PM* IV, i, 222ff.). Comparable strip of ivory, bearing similar design, found by Tsountas in Tomb 27 at Mycenae (*EphArch* 1888, pl. 8:11), and similar piece recovered by Wace in House of Shields (*BSA* L [1955], 183, pl. 26), as well as in glass paste (Menidi, *KG*, 32, taf. III:24) and in fresco painting (cf. *BSA* xxv [1921-23], pl. xxxv).

Narrow strip (NM. 7846, Fig. 170:1a, b): l. 0.065 m., w. 0.018 m., th. ca. 0.01 m. Long sides and one end preserved, other end broken; carved surface worn. May have decorated handle of dagger or some other weapon, or served as inlay, possibly back of comb. Worked in shallow relief. At left, moving to right, hindquarters of lion with long curling tail; in center, head of sphinx facing left. Apparently contorted representation with head turned backward as animals often portrayed by Mycenaean gem-cutters. Face of sphinx clearly carved with long nose, deep eye. On head flattish hat or headgear with tassel or mop of hair streaming back to right. In background beyond lion's tail outstretched wing, presumably belonging to sphinx. Some elements at right may be taken as other wing, but in worn and incomplete condition of ivory interpretation partly conjectural. On ivory comb found in tomb at Spata similar sphinx in same attitude appears at left in upper row of carved decoration (B. Haussoullier, *BCH* II [1878], 203f., pl. xvii).

Two flat disk-shaped fragments of circular containers of some kind (NM. 7853, Fig. 170:5, 6): Larger (5) is 0.125 m. long, 0.06 m. wide, and 0.0014 m. thick; original diameter, as indicated by arc, must have been ca. 0.136 m. Very badly crushed and split, but patched together by the mender, Andreas Mavraganis. Traces on surface indicate that it was once polished. A rebate along outer curving edge, 0.006 m. wide, 0.0025 m. deep, obviously a groove into which side was fitted and fastened. Piece evidently from lid or from bottom of cylindrical vessel, presumably not meant to hold liquid.

Smaller piece (6), l. 0.051 m., w. 0.025 m., th. 0.005 m.; remnant of arc points to original diameter of ca. 0.097 m. This fragment too has slot cut in upper surface, running parallel to outer curving edge and 0.0045 m. inside the circumference. Rebate is 0.011 m. wide, 0.002 m. deep. Whether it formed top or bottom of larger vessel or belonged to another container uncertain.

Fragment (NM. 7858, Fig. 170:8): l. 0.039 m., w. 0.009 m. at broader end, th. 0.006 m., tapering irregularly toward narrow end; put together from several small pieces, with carved decoration on two adjoining sides. Decoration: longitudinal grooves and ridges, framed on each side by row of dots not very neatly rounded. Purpose uncertain.

Disk (NM. 7845, Fig. 170:4): d. 0.014 m., th. 0.0015 m. Small; decorated with eight petals as in rosette, each petal divided from its neighbor by fine shallow incised line on each side. At outer edge of disk lines terminate with deep triangular cutting from which shallow line curves to next one, indicating outer end of petal. Similar disks found at Mycenae in Tomb 523 (*ChT*, 37, pl. xx:15).

Fragment of pin (NM. 7891): l. 0.034 m., d. at widest 0.0075 m., at smaller end 0.003 m. Tapering toward point, broken at both ends.

BOAR'S TUSKS

More than a dozen thinnish slices cut from boar's tusks (NM. 7852). None finished to fit into helmet but many pieces smoothly polished. Most of pieces badly damaged, broken, worn.

AMBER

Only a few crumbling remnants of beads. No shapes recognized.

FAIENCE AND GLASS PASTE

Greater part of material in this category found in very bad state of preservation, most of beads and ornaments fragmentary and crumbling. Some of larger pieces white and show traces of having been smoothly finished if not polished when cleaned of black coating that covers most remnants; probably discolored because they lay a long time in deposit of charred matter on floor. Made of faience or frit of some kind. Larger pieces seem to have no string holes for suspension or attachment and just how they were securely displayed not clear. In any event, presumably ornaments rather than beads. Latter were regularly pierced for stringing and no doubt served for necklaces, armlets, and bracelets.

Ornaments

   Items of same general kind but differ in their decorative motives.

Plaques (NM. 7879, Fig. 171:1): small thin flat, resembling a not very natural leaf; 15 pieces whole or nearly whole, more than 100 fragments. Dimensions vary considerably: e.g., 0.019 m. by 0.025 m., and 0.018 m. by 0.019 m. Irregular five-lobed outline. From lowest lobe a carelessly marked stem, in most instances, rises through middle of leaf, sometimes dividing into two or three. On each side two lobes. No sign of any means of attachment. Nearly all white or yellowish-white, a few blackened by fire. No exact parallel to this type

of decoration has come to our attention.

Plaques (NM. 7872, Fig. 171:2): h. 0.028 m., w. 0.023 m.; another, h. 0.022 m., w. 0.026 m. Flat; upper face decorated by fairly large feather pattern or spray of grass or foliage in slender leaves. Four examples almost intact, four more considerably damaged, a good many additional small fragments. Some blackened by contact with burnt matter, one yellowish, others white. Nothing to show how it was attached to anything else. Same decorative motive appears on two gold plaques found in Tholos IV (pp. 114f.). Similar ornaments of glass paste bearing comparable motive came from Tsountas's Tomb 69 at Mycenae [20] and from Chamber Tomb 2 at Dendra (*RT, Dendra,* 104f., no. 22, fig. 80, pl. xxxv).

Plaques (NM. 7876, Fig. 171:6): flat with decoration of four cockleshells in high relief on upper surface; 14 examples more or less nearly whole and many small fragments. Sizes vary greatly: largest 0.027 m. by 0.028 m.; medium group 0.022 m. by 0.022 m.; another 0.019 m. by 0.023 m.; smallest 0.012 m. by 0.014 m. Design quartered by two deep crossing grooves; in each quadrant a cockleshell. Most of these thick ornaments badly blackened. No indication of how attached. Perhaps inlay. Tsountas recovered single cockle beads at Mycenae in Chamber Tomb 8 (*EphArch* 1888, 139) as well as in Tombs 14 and 17; [21] others of ivory, also single, found by Wace in House of Sphinxes outside Mycenaean acropolis (*BSA* L [1955], 189, pl. 30:d). Chamber tombs at Spata also yielded gold or gilded examples (*Athenaion* VI [1877], pls. B:19, 20) and others came from tholos tomb at Menidi (*KG,* pls. IV:8, V:6).

Plaque (NM. 7873, Fig. 171:4): flat almost rectangular, decorated with argonaut in relatively low relief. One example well preserved, l. 0.028 m., w. 0.022 m.; 22 frag-

---

[20] On display in National Museum, Mycenaean Room, Case 1.

[21] On display in National Museum, Mycenaean Room, Case 26.

ments counted, nearly all very thin. Nautilus neatly pictured moving to left with three tentacles spiraling above shell. Some fragments blackened but most are white with tan tinge. Comparable plaques have appeared in Attica from chamber tombs at Spata (*BCH* II [1878], 201, pl. xv:12) as well as in Argolis, where on citadel of Mycenae Schliemann discovered a mold for making ornaments of many kinds, one a single argonaut (H. Schliemann, *Mycenae*, 108, fig. 162); Vollgraff found similar ornaments in chamber tombs at Argos (*BCH* XXVIII [1904], 383, fig. 11). Tsountas and Wace discovered plaques decorated with argonauts at Mycenae (*EphArch* 1887, pl. xiii:2-3; and from Tomb 8 came double argonauts, six of gold and eight of glass paste: *EphArch* 1888, 139, pl. 9:4; and *BSA* xxv [1921-23], 383, fig. 89a, f). It seemed curious that our Tholos III contained not a single plaque decorated with double argonauts molded in glass paste as compared with the abundance in ivory.

Plaque (NM. 7885, Fig. 171:3): one example intact; l. 0.026 m., w. 0.017 m. Flat, decorated in high relief. Pattern represents projecting shield, shaped like figure eight. Small gold example found in same tomb (p. 83) and larger similar shield in gold came from our Tholos IV (p. 114, Fig. 190:20). Beads of this kind seem to have been made more often in gold than in glass paste.

Rosettes (NM. 7861, Fig. 171:7): six examples intact, many fragments; largest, d. 0.032 m., smallest, d. 0.022 m. High relief, all have eight petals. Parallel transverse string-holes, one in each of two adjoining petals. In larger examples petals radiate outward from plain circular raised centerpiece bordered by line of small delicate granules. Smaller pieces similar except that they have no granules. Many examples blackened by their environment, but some still white.

Rosettes of gold and paste, much like those from our Tholos III, familiar from other Mycenaean sites in Argolis and elsewhere: e.g., from house on acropolis of Mycenae Tsountas recovered many specimens (*EphArch* 1887, pl. 13:7, 8, 9, 10); and in Tomb 10 collected 37 of gold and 35 of paste[22] (*EphArch* 1888). Gold and ivory rosettes were later found at Mycenae by British School (*ChT*, Tomb 502, pl. xiii:28; Tomb 523, pl. xx:15, ivory; Tomb 15, pl. xxxii:72b, 80c). Other examples recorded: from cemetery at Argive Heraeum (*Prosymna*, 304, figs. 359; 362:2, 14 [paste] 542:18); from Thebes, gold and paste (*Deltion* 3 [1917], Tomb 4, 133f., fig. 98); from Argos (*BCH* xxviii [1904], 383, fig. 12 gold); from tholos near Volo (*EphArch* 1906, pl. 15:16 gold). Cf. royal necklace from Dendra (p. 83). Rosettes were among most favored of Mycenaean ornaments.

Plaques (NM. 7881, Fig. 171:5): l. 0.044 m., w. 0.022 m. Thin lozenge-shaped with pointed ends; fragments of another. In high relief, two murex shells, head to head, in middle of ornament; two tentacles from each murex curve out to meet on one side. On other side small but delicately delineated rosette. Shells themselves shown with realistic corrugations and generous use of granulations. No string-holes. Ivory white, somewhat blackened. A comparable single murex found by Tsountas in tomb at Mycenae (*EphArch* 1888, pl. 9:7; it had lost its label with number of tomb).

Plaque (NM. 7887, Fig. 171:8): l. 0.03 m., w. 0.022 m. Thin rectangular; two joining fragments. One corner broken off; each of other three corners preserved has hole running through plaque from front to back, obviously for stringing or being attached to backing of some kind. Design badly damaged, not easy to interpret, but may have borne floral motive, perhaps representing liliaceous plant. Ivory white. No parallel has come to our attention.

---

[22] On display in National Museum, Mycenaean Room, Case 26.

Ornament (NM. 7882, Fig. 171:10): fragment, l. 0.02 m., w. 0.015 m. Upper and right edges preserved, left side broken. Spiraliform motive much like volute; perhaps part of inlay, possibly delineating capital of column. Closely resembles gold ornament found by Tsountas in chamber tomb at Mycenae (*EphArch* 1888, pl. 9:5, label lost). Ivory white blackened by fire or carbon.

Strip (NM. 7880, Fig. 171:11): six fragments of narrow strip, bearing spiral motive; longitudinal edges preserved, all ends (except one) broken. Total length of six pieces illustrated, plus six smaller bits: 0.162 m., w. 0.0075 m. to 0.009 m. Apparently inlay forming a border. Decorated in high relief with unconnected spirals, each having a fairly large centerpiece. Spirals somewhat resemble snail-shells but not really depicted as such in this border. No sign of string-holes. Ivory white. Comparable strips decorated with spirals came from Spata (*BCH* II [1878], 193, pl. XIII:5) and from tholos near Menidi (*KG,* pl. VI:4).

Bead (NM. 7887, Fig. 172:1): large, of bi-pyramidal shape; l. 0.032 m., w. at middle 0.016 m., th. 0.013 m. Tapers at each end to width of 0.005 m. Coated heavily with adhesive black matter as are many remnants that lay in burned stratum. Longitudinal string-hole from end to end. Very light in weight. No decoration. No exact parallel known to us.

Beads

In general we have classified as beads small pieces provided with perforations for stringing many together. Some of these too seem to have been molded in faience but most of them are probably made of frit or some kind of paste.

Floral plaque (NM. 7886). Fragment perhaps representing a flower; very much soiled and blackened from association with burnt matter: h. 0.014 m., w. 0.026 m. Generously pierced for stringing, one hole down center from top; two small holes close together, running from front to back at left; one tiny hole near end of point, and yet two others. They are difficult to explain, but perhaps some small trimmings were suspended from them. Not well enough preserved to recognize any parallels.

Twin pendants (NM. 7884, Fig. 172:5): two complete flat, h. 0.019 m., w. 0.02 m.; fragments of several others. Shaped to resemble "twin peaks" but almost certainly rather represent twin pointed pendants hanging downward as is demonstrated by string-hole that in some instances runs transversely through broad top. If design is interpreted other way up, string-hole would be running along bottom of plaque. Horizontal upper part decorated with parallel longitudinal ridges and grooves. Same motive runs up and down in pendants. One white, one yellowish-white. Similar ornaments have been found in chamber tombs at Spata (*BCH* II [1878], 201, pl. XVI:1, 2) and at Mycenae in Tomb 73 by Tsountas.[23]

Altar-shaped (NM. 7884, Fig. 172:6): two, completely preserved, h. 0.014 m., w. 0.018 m.; fragments of other examples. Flat bottom; molded base has horizontal concave groove, bordered below and above by raised molding formed of tiny dots in a row. Relatively narrow concave stem broadens out to upper part, which has same profile as bottom with same two rows of granulations. Horizontal string-holes run through upper section as well as lower. Yellowish-white, one blackened. Beads of this shape are recorded from many other sites: e.g., from Phaistos in Crete, glass (*MonAnt* XIV [1904], 633, fig. 105); from Menidi, in gold (*KG,* pl. V:9, 24); from Spata (*Athenaion* VI [1877], pl. B:27 and *BCH* II [1878], pl. XIII:3); from Mycenae (Tsountas, *Eph-*

---

[23] On display in National Museum, Mycenaean Room.

Arch 1888, 143, glass paste,[24] and from Tomb 75, NM. 2601).[25]

Flower (NM. 7884, Fig. 172:3): diminutive, h. 0.011 m., w. 0.0095 m. Slender, short stem from which on each side rises a spiral petal to right and left; in center relatively large cluster or bundle of small flowers(?) indicated by transverse row of six tiny granulations across top. Detail has suffered considerable wear of surface and interpretation may be erroneous. Four small beads of gold from tholos tomb at Dendra (*RT, Dendra*, 29, pl. XXVII, third row from top) almost exactly like our glass example help to identify the latter. No other parallel known to us.

Soutache (NM. 7884, Figs. 171:9, 172:7): l. 0.01 m., w. 0.008 m.; flattish, ivory white, badly worn. Mrs. Blegen suggested that decorative motive might have been taken from handiwork in trimming or embroidery braid applied on background of wool or silk. No parallel has come to our attention. Women of Mycenaean Age, surely skillful in dressmaking and embroidering, may have contributed motives of their own design for beads.

Papyrus blossom (NM. 7878, Fig. 172:13): two, the larger, h. 0.016 m., max. w. 0.02 m. Decorated with horizontal grooves and ridges. Upper edge of flower bordered by granulations. Second bead is from different mold, smaller and has only one raised band around calyx and row of dots along upper edge. Gold ornaments in this form are familiar from Crete, e.g., from Phaistos (*MonAnt* XIV [1904], 596-598, figs. 60, 61), and Zafer Papoura cemetery of Knossos (*Crete and Mycenae*, pl. 120); from Argolis, Tsountas' tomb 75 at Mycenae;[26] from Asine (*Asine*, color plate 3); from Argive Heraeum (*Prosymna*, 269, fig. 362:1). Mold found by Schliemann on citadel of Mycenae has two matrices for papyrus blossoms

(Schliemann, *Mycenae*, 107f., fig. 162). Gold or gilt examples also came from chamber tombs at Spata (*BCH* II [1878], 210, pl. XV:4).

Tubular (NM. 7878, Fig. 172:13): 11 examples; l. ca. 0.01 m., d. ca. 0.003 m. Some transversely fluted, others plain; pierced longitudinally for stringing. At Argive Heraeum five or six slender tubular beads found, somewhat like, but not precisely parallel to examples from our Tholos III (*Prosymna*, 302, group 4; 310, group 9, in glass and faience).

Cylindrical (NM. 7878, Fig. 172:14): six short, l. 0.01 m., d. 0.008 m. Band around middle part of cylinder demarcated by two deep incised lines, within which zigzag pattern of punctated dots. Longitudinal string hole. No real parallel has come to our attention.

Fluted cylindrical (NM. 7888, Fig. 172:8): five fragments, thickish; longest ca. 0.015 m.; d. 0.004 m. to 0.005 m. Fluted diagonally; longitudinal string-hole. Three tan in color, two white. No close parallels yet found.

Bracket-shaped (NM. 7860, Fig. 171:12): sometimes called "curled leaf" or, alternatively because of its shape "bracket bead." Four examples nearly whole and fragments of 20 additional. Sizes vary, largest h. 0.022 m., w. 0.011 m. Horizontal roll at top, terminating in volute at each end. String-hole runs transversely through roll from side to side. Row of tiny dots crosses lower part of bead; in space below, in two instances, two string-holes, one above other, running through from front to back, perhaps for hanging delicate ornaments. All partially preserved beads and many fragments blackened by fire or by lying in contact with carbonized matter. Bracket-like beads have come to light at many Minoan and Mycenaean sites; there

---

[24] On display, National Museum, Mycenaean Room, Case 26.

[25] On display, National Museum, Mycenaean Room, Case 2.

[26] On display in Case 2 in Mycenaean Room of National Museum.

has been much discussion about which way up they were worn (Wace, *BSA* xxv [1921-23], 397 ff. pl. lxi; Evans, *JHS* xlv [1925], 1; Maiuri, *Annuario* vi-vii [1926], 101, fig. 19; Holland, *AJA* 33 [1929], 173 ff.; Persson, *RT, Dendra* 16, 36, 63, fig. 41, pl. xxv:1). Beads of same general shape found at Mycenae by Wace in Tomb 15 (*BSA ibid.*), as did Tsountas in his Tombs 71 and 93;[27] he also recovered fine example from house on citadel of Mycenae (*EphArch* 1887, pl. 13:18, 18a). Other sites have yielded bracket beads in abundance (e.g., *Prosymna*, 305, fig. 121; *Asine*, 389, fig. 252; tholos tomb at Dendra, *RT, Dendra*, pl. xxv:1; Spata, *BCH* II [1878], pl. xiv:5; good mold of this type found on Mycenaean acropolis: *EphArch* 1897, 97 ff. pl. 7:1).

Disk-shaped (NM. 7884, Fig. 172:2): three flat; largest, d. 0.012 m.; smallest, d. 0.007 m. Disks very thin; one has one small hole for stringing; one two holes opposite each other; third one hole but opposite side broken away. One white, two blackened.

Small disks of glass relatively rare in chamber tombs: only one was found by Wace at Mycenae in Tomb 518 (*ChT*, 205, pl. viii:71d). A few flat pieces found at Asine may be of this type (*Asine*, 389, fig. 252). Chamber Tomb 2 at Midea yielded at least four disk-shaped beads (*RT, Dendra*, 105, Nos. 41, 42, fig. 80). Glass paste not strong enough to assure lasting use for thin washer-like type. In a few instances ornaments of glass paste gilded to make them resemble gold; probably manufactured for burial offerings to the dead like so many objects found in tombs.

Some disk-like beads found also at Phaistos (*MonAnt* xiv [1904], 633f.); and in Tomb 8 in Katsamba cemetery (St. Alexiou, Ὑστερομινωϊκοὶ τάφοι λιμένος Κνωσοῦ (Κατσαμβᾶ) [Athens, 1967], 57f., no. 37B, 7205, pl. 37) near harbor of Knossos, Mr. Alexiou recently found string of beads

including 28 small disks, white and gray.

Ivy leaf (NM. 7874, Fig. 172:10): sizes vary — largest, l. 0.0095 m., w. 0.01 m. Nine examples, three have lost part of lobe. Thin, flat; string hole running from stem notch to point of leaf. No applied decoration. Nearly all blackened, but some reddish. Comparable beads of glass paste found by Tsountas at Mycenae in Chamber Tombs 8, 11, and 71.[28] Ivy leaves of different design, three ivory inlays recovered by Wace in House of Shields (*BSA* xlix [1954], 236, pl. 33a).

Annular (NM. 7877, Fig. 172:12): tiny; some 95 can be counted on string. Beads vary considerably in size as well as in color. Annular beads appear familiarly in Mycenaean chamber tombs almost everywhere, though they are sometimes exceedingly small and not always found in great numbers: e.g., at Mycenae (Tomb 520, *ChT*, 26, fig. 12:41d; at Argive Heraeum (*Prosymna*, 301f.), and at Asine (*Asine*, 389, fig. 252, Tomb 1, 2).

"Grain of wheat" (NM. 7878, Fig. 172:14): String of 44 beads varying from little less than 0.01 m. to 0.017 m. in length and from 0.0035 m. to 0.0075 m. in width. Decorated with longitudinal grooves, apparently imitating wheat grains, though not very accurately. Many other scattered similar types in badly worn condition. Shape known from tombs in Crete (*MonAnt* xiv [1904], 632, fig. 101c) and in mainland Greece (e.g., *BSA* xxv [1921-23], 380 no. 4537a, fig. 88o, 382 no. 4539, fig. 88a from Tomb of Genii; *ChT*, 37, pl. xx:10, 11 examples; *Prosymna*, 311, group 11; *Asine*, 389, fig. 252; *RT, Dendra*, pls. xv, at bottom, xxxv, at top).

Spherical (NM. 7874 and 7878, Fig. 172:13): heterogeneous collection of 20 items varying considerably in size and color. Largest, d. ca. 0.01 m. Some have flutings, most are plain. Similar beads found in Mycenaean

---

[27] On display, National Museum, Mycenaean Room, Case 1.

[28] On display in National Museum, Mycenaean Room, Cases 2 and 26.

tombs in all parts of Greece, as well as Crete. Spherical beads have made their appearance in most, if not all, tholoi and chamber tombs. At Mycenae they came to light in hundreds in faience and glass (Wace, *ChT*, 205, pl. VIII:71 and pl. IX:7), also at Heraeum (*Prosymna*, 298-300, 307f.).

Flattened spherical (NM. 7878, Fig. 172:13): six intact; d. ca. 0.007 m., th. 0.0035 m. At widest dimension of bead, decoration of short parallel transverse grooves. This shape also familiar but not so well represented as truly spherical. Some good examples in glass and faience salvaged from chamber tombs at Mycenae (*ChT*, pl. IX:7d) and 119 beads from tombs at Argive Heraeum (*Prosymna*, 300f., 308).

Short ovoid (NM. 7878, Fig. 172:13): one longish ovoid, or perhaps more exactly ellipsoid—l. 0.016 m., d. ca. 0.013 m. Decorated by two broad grooves running transversely around bead. Comparable type, but not close parallel, found in chamber tomb at Heraeum (*Prosymna*, fig. 599:11).

Amygdaloid (NM. 7875, Fig. 172:11): 16 examples, some variations in size, but most have length of ca. 0.017 m. and maximum width of ca. 0.01 m. Many grayish-white, others bluish-gray. Nearly all have one or two grooves running longitudinally on each face. This type resembles closely "grain of wheat" (p. 91) except that it is far too big to have any connection with wheat grains. It may very likely be an offshoot from amygdaloid group of beads and seals.

Lentoid (NM. 7874, Fig. 172:9): three examples, d. ca. 0.008 m. Variegated grayish in present state. Lentoid beads of faience and glass paste seem to be rare. At Prosymna lentoid seal of this material found in Chamber Tomb 3; plain bead came from Chamber Tomb 13 (*Prosymna*, 279, fig. 503:4; 303, fig. 464:2). Tomb of Genii at Mycenae yielded one such lentoid bead (*BSA* xxv [1921-23], 383, fig. 89h). Other lentoids found by Wace in chamber tombs at Mycenae (*ChT*, Tomb 502, no. 29m, two

examples, pl. XIII; Tomb 517, no. 34h, one example, pl. XXXV).

Gadroon (NM. 7876, Fig. 172:13): l. 0.026 m., d. 0.009 m. Decorated with grooves and ridges spiraling diagonally from one end to other.

TERRACOTTA

Whorls or buttons (NM. 7862). Three diminutive, truncated biconical: h. 0.008 m., w. 0.014 m.-0.017 m. Pierced vertically along axis.

POTTERY

Comparable in shape to pots found in palace

Shallow angular bowl, two horizontal loop-handles (NM. 9132, Fig. 173:1): cf. Shape 4, *PN* I, 356, figs. 349, 350; *MP*, Type 295, p. 53 fig. 15. H. 0.043 m., d. across axis of handles 0.153 m., transverse d. 0.149 m., d. base 0.051 m. Light buff plain ware. Many pieces missing.

Conical cup (NM. 9129, Fig. 173:2): cf. Shape 11, *PN* I, 359f., figs. 353, 354; *MP*, Type 204, p. 53 fig. 15. H. 0.04 m.-0.045 m., d. 0.12 m., d. bottom 0.052 m. Eight fragments, good deal lacking. Thickish walls, slightly convexly curving profile. Plain ware; pinkish-buff clay.

Shallow one-handled cup (NM. 9127, Fig. 173:3): cf. Shape 12, *PN* I, 360, figs. 353, 354; *MP*, Type 220, III B, p. 48 fig. 13. H. 0.04 m., d. 0.113 m.-0.115 m., d. base 0.032 m. Plain ware; pinkish-buff clay. Put together from many small pieces.

One-handled angular kylix (NM. 9121, Fig. 173:4): cf. Shape 27, *PN* I, 366f., figs. 359, 360; *MP*, Type 267, p. 61 fig. 17. H. 0.114 m., d. along handle axis 0.145 m., d. transverse axis 0.117 m., d. base 0.066 m. Plain ware; gray clay with slightly greenish tinge. Put together from many fragments.

One-handled angular kylix (NM. 9122, not illustrated): cf. Shape 27, *PN* I, 366f., figs. 359, 360; *MP*, Type 267, p. 61 fig. 17. H. 0.105 m., d. rim 0.11 m., d. base 0.067 m., large hollow in bottom. Plain ware; pale buff clay. Handle, large part of rim missing.

Two-handled kylix (NM. 9120, Fig. 173:5):

cf. Shape 29b, *PN* I, 368f., figs. 361, 362; *MP*, Type 259, p. 61 fig. 17. H. 0.179 m., d. 0.145 m., d. base 0.087 m. Plain ware; greenish-gray clay. Handles, many pieces missing.

Two-handled kylix (NM. 9123, not illustrated): cf. Shape 29b, *PN* I, 368f., figs. 361, 362; *MP*, Type 274, III B, p. 61 fig. 17. H. 0.163 m.-0.17 m., d. 0.182 m., d. base 0.083 m. Plain ware; light grayish-tan clay. One handle, part of other, and much of rim lacking.

Two-handled kylix (NM. 9119, Fig. 173:6): cf. Shape 29c, *PN* I, 368f., figs. 361, 362; *MP*, Type 259, p. 61 fig. 17. H. 0.187 m., d. 0.174 m., d. base 0.088 m. Plain ware; pinkish-buff clay. Put together from many fragments, much missing.

Two-handled kylix (NM. 9124, Fig. 173:7): cf. Shape 29c, *PN* I, 368f., figs. 361, 362; *MP*, Type 259, p. 61 fig. 17. H. 0.173 m., d. 0.155 m.-0.16 m., d. base 0.08 m. Plain ware; pinkish-buff clay. Large part of side and rim missing.

Fragments of large two-handled kylix (NM. 9125, not illustrated): h. 0.201 m. Plain ware, pinkish-buff clay. Not restorable.

Three-handled pithoid jar (NM. 9134, Fig. 173:11): has features of Shape 52, *PN* I, 386f., figs. 375, 376, also of Shape 53, *PN* I, 388f., figs. 377, 378. Cf. also *MP*, Type 37, p. 23 fig. 4. H. 0.335 m., d. 0.238 m., d. base ca. 0.10 m. Put together from many pieces, most of rim missing. Grayish clay, surface badly worn. Slightly raised ring between neck and shoulder. Rim slopes outward and downward. Traces of linear patterns: horizontal bands above base; three or four parallel horizontal bands below shoulder zone; two similar bands below neck, two or three on neck. Decorative motives in shoulder panels not certainly recognizable.

Three-handled pithoid jar on pedestal (NM. 9133, Fig. 173:13): cf. Shape 53, *PN* I, 388f., figs. 377, 378; *MP*, Type 35, p. 23 fig. 4. H. 0.383 m., d. rim ca. 0.138 m., d. 0.295 m., d. base 0.111 m. Handles flat-tened with slight groove in middle, set vertically on shoulder in small loop. At bottom of handle fairly large circular cavity. Gray clay, slightly pinkish tinge. Decoration in dark brownish paint. Pedestal coated over-all, horizontal bands above; group of two, three, or four horizontal bands just below handles. One or more bands below neck. In panels between handles, zigzag patterns of parallel lines. In one panel traces of multiple zigzags, at least seven parallel lines. Comparable pattern in another panel; third chiefly plaster. Patterns look like Mycenaean III B, if not even as late as beginning of III C.

Krater-bowl (NM. 9130, Fig. 173:12): cf. Shape 60, *PN* I, 397f., figs. 385, 386; *MP*, Type 284, pp. 48, 49 figs. 13, 14. H. 0.096 m., d. 0.131 m.-0.148 m., d. raised base ca. 0.052 m. Both handles, many fragments missing. Pinkish clay; thin fabric. Decorated in brick-red paint: ring inside lip and on top of rim; five parallel horizontal lines neatly drawn about one-third from bottom; from this group on each side between handles four upright dividers, approximately evenly spaced, framing three plain panels; uprights made of four lines; central space, broader than lateral spaces, carries zigzag patterns; handles decorated with blobs where attached to side. Obviously Mycenaean III B.

Scoop (NM. 9135, Fig. 173:8): cf. Shape 66, *PN* I, 411f., figs. 395, 396; *MP*, Type 311, p. 75 fig. 21. H. 0.063 m., d. 0.123 m.-0.13 m.; long thick handle projects 0.105 m. with slight downward curve; d. slightly raised flat bottom ca. 0.054 m. Near end of handle large, roughly circular suspension hole, d. 0.012 m. Coarse ware, reddish-brown clay. Pour channel opposite handle broken away; many pieces missing.

Shapes not identified in palace

Chalice or handleless goblet (NM. 9118, Fig. 174:1): restored h. 0.218 m., d. rim 0.104 m., d. base 0.071 m.; h. stem ca. 0.10 m., but part of stem missing, restoration may be too high; cup ca. 0.105 m. deep. Impressed horizontal line, separating lower and upper zone, runs around exterior of cup ca. 0.07 m. above angle. Put together from many small fragments, considerable part missing. Pinkish-tan clay. Decoration: in lower zone wavy, curving, parallel, bristled lines running up and down in reddish-brown paint. Motives in upper panel difficult to interpret. Surface badly worn. No real ceramic parallel has come to our attention, but comparable chalices of alabaster from Fourth and Fifth Shaft Graves at Mycenae (*Schachtgräber*, 118, 148, pl. CXXXVIII:600, 854), from Cyclades (NM. 3964, on display in Mycenaean Room of National Museum), and especially from palace at Kato Zakro (*Ergon* 1963, 170f., fig. 182) are related forms of vessels.

Urnlike cup (NM. 9126, Fig. 174:2): h. 0.108 m., d. rim ca. 0.106 m., d. bottom ca. 0.037 m. Made up of many pieces. Two arched handles, rounded in section, rising vertically from rim. Creamy-buff clay; thin-walled. Small round hole in bottom. Surface worn; no traces of decoration. No exact ceramic parallel known to us.

Small stirrup-vase with pedestal base (NM. 9128, Fig. 174:3): h. 0.14 m., d. ca. 0.106 m., d. base 0.056 m., d. disk 0.03 m. No exact parallel known to us but slightly resembles *MP*, Type 182, p. 44 fig. 12. Made up of numerous fragments, large part of side lacking. Creamy-gray clay; brownish-black paint. Pedestal coated solidly over-all. At about one-third of height two horizontal bands. Just above shoulder two fairly broad bands, enclosing two narrower bands, mark off shoulder zone. Wide band on false neck. Band on each edge of handles, framing diagonal stripes. Spiral on center of disk.

Large high alabastron with three arched handles (NM. 9131, Fig. 174:6): cf. *MP*, Type 85, p. 41 fig. 11. H. 0.185 m. to 0.188 m., d. rim 0.123 m., max. d. 0.245 m. Put together from many pieces. Surface badly worn. Clay varies from gray to pinkish.

Faint traces of decoration: apparently parallel horizontal bands (three or four or five) around greatest diameter. In panels above, traces of linear pattern, but nothing certainly recognizable.

Large part of small two-handled pithos (NM. 9138, Fig. 174:4a, b): cf. *MP*, Type 13a, p. 75 fig. 21. H. pres. 0.385 m., max. d. 0.293 m., d. lowest part preserved 0.155 m. Pointed bottom missing as well as rim and most of neck. Put together from many small fragments. Plain ware; no decoration. One of category of similar pots, sometimes called Egypto-Syrian, found at Mycenae, Argos, Menidi, Tsaritsane, and now Pylos, altogether a dozen or more from mainland Greece (*MP*, Type 13a, pp. 74, 75 fig. 21 and p. 587). These pointed pithoi apparently had their origin rather in Syria, where at Minet el Beida 80 such jars found standing on floor of one room; many others recovered at other Syrian sites. A few such pithoi found in Greece bear incised signs on handles, thought by some to be Minoan characters. High up on one side in middle between handles, example from our Tholos III has single character (Fig. 174:4b) that has no exact parallel in Linear A and Linear B. Sign clearly incised in soft clay before pot fired.

Fragments of alabastron (NM. 9139, Fig. 174:5a, b): d. rim ca. 0.125 m., d. calculated ca. 0.31 m. Many pieces but not enough to restore whole pot. Relatively thin walls. Creamy clay; pattern in brownish-black ranging to red paint. Bottom decorated with wheel pattern, having apparently six wavy spokes (*MP*, Motive 68:1, p. 403 fig. 70). Two horizontal bands at junction with body; wave pattern above, forming lower frame of panels between handles. In shoulder panels series of double axes of Cretan type, bordered with dots (cf. *MP*, Motive 35:4, p. 327 fig. 55).

Fragments of "animal pot" (NM. 9140, Fig. 174:7a-d). From right grave pit in tholos. Shape not reconstructable. Light tan clay; fairly coarse ware, painted in reddish-brown. Ovoid base (a) with angle jutting out. Upper part of vessel decorated with molded head of deer with two horns of four or six points: two ears and one projecting eye preserved (b-d). Comparable "animal pot" recovered by Professor Mari-

natos from Chamber Tomb A 6, at Volimidia, just above Chora (*Ergon* [1954], 42, fig. 54; *Crete and Mycenae*, pl. 235. On display in Chora Museum).

C. W. B.

THOLOS TOMB IV
(Plans and Sections, Figs. 321-326)

Description

This tomb lies about 145 m. to the northeast of the Palace of Nestor and ca. 70 m. from the edge of the hill (Fig. 301).[29] Here there was an *aloni* which with the surrounding vineyard was the property of Mr. and Mrs. Panayotis Kanakaris. Near its southwestern edge and overgrown with vegetation was a great, weathered lintel block, broken into four pieces. It measured ca. 3 m. by 2.30 m. and was ca. 0.45 m. thick (Fig. 175). The *aloni* had been laid out on top of the tomb.

Dromos

The dromos with its axis running from southwest to northeast is ca. 10.50 m. long and 4.40 m. wide. Its sides are cut in *stereo* and lean slightly outward.[30] The floor slopes down some 0.70 m. in the outer part, leveling out towards the doorway. The character of the *stereo* varies in the two parts of the dromos, the southwest being dry and flaky, the northeast end sticky and compact, and varying from yellow to greenish-brown in color.

Doorway

The doorway (Fig. 176) ca. 4.55 m. high, 2.26 m. wide at the outer face and 2.22 m. at the inner, with a depth from front to back of 4.62 m. on the southeastern side and 4.64 m. on the northwestern side, presents an imposing entrance. Its floor slopes down slightly towards the tomb. The great broken block, referred to above, was all that remained of a lintel that covered the rear part of the entrance. At least two other lintel blocks must have roofed the front part. The surviving lintel did not lie evenly balanced on its masonry support; one end of it barely rested on the southeast door jamb, while the other overlapped the

[29] I wish to take this opportunity of expressing my deep gratitude to Professor Blegen for allowing me to take part over a number of years in the excavations under his direction. And I wish to thank most sincerely those who helped me at different times both during and after the excavation: Miss Marion Rawson, Professor William McDonald, University of Minnesota, and Dr. Karouzos,

Director of the National Museum at Athens, where I was given every facility to study the finds. Finally, I should like to express my deep appreciation of the unfailing help I received from our excellent foreman, Dionysios Androutsakis.

[30] Today the outward inclination of the sides is very much greater because of the erosive action of the winter rains on the soft rock.

northwest jamb to a greater extent (Fig. 321). It is not certain that there was a relieving triangle. The inner faces of the doorway are constructed of well-dressed, flattish stones; so also in the main is the façade, but where this adjoins the natural rock the work is more casual. The jambs are approximately symmetrical, but the southeast one is slightly narrower. The width of each one at the top is ca. 1.50 m.; it is slightly less at the bottom. Good-sized stones have been used in the façade, headers and stretchers alternating. The top courses of the jambs, especially the southeast one, show the loss of many a stone (Fig. 177). At the tholos end of the doorway the jambs are very much strengthened, much greater blocks being used. As an example: the face of two of these measure 0.40 m. x 1.50 m. and 0.35 m. x 1.55 m. respectively. The masonry of the northwest jamb seems to lean very slightly toward the center of the tomb and the beginnings of the curve of the ruined vault are plainly visible in the uppermost courses (Fig. 178).

Filling the central part of the doorway a wall, 2 m. thick, had been built to close the entrance to the tomb (Figs. 176, 322). Its height originally, it is to be presumed, was the same as that of the doorway but, when excavated, there was a gap of ca. 1 m. between the top of the surviving wall and the lintel soffit on the southwestern side and ca. 0.60 m. in the central part. Although the gap was not great, it was sufficient to allow access to the tomb and indeed the top part of the wall had been pulled out by looters in antiquity for that very purpose. The upper courses were of loose construction but the middle section was built very differently. Here some well-squared blocks of considerable size were used.[31] There were two and a half courses of such blocks. Below, the construction was much as before, crude but strongly built. On the inner face of the wall (Fig. 179), fronting the tomb, there were also large, oblong, well-squared blocks but they were laid at a lower level than those on the outer face and continued down almost to the base of the wall (Fig. 176).

Chamber

The inner diameter of the tholos is 9.35 m. and its height was roughly the same.[32] The few tholoi that have survived intact have indicated that the height is approximately equal to the diameter. The vault of Tholos IV was preserved only to a height of 4.90 m. in the northwest part of it. The opposite side of the vault was about 0.50 m. lower. Its upper courses were coming apart and had

---

[31] The face of one block was 0.25 m. high and 0.90 m. long; another, 0.20 m. by 1.10 m. (Fig. 176). The stones used in the building of the wall were probably gathered wherever available. The material appears to have come from various sources and different quarries.

[32] The measurement was made by D. Androutsakis and helpers in 1968.

to be strengthened. The construction throughout is of smallish, flat stones of varying sizes. On an average the dimensions are ca. 0.35 m. by 0.16 m.; the thickness ranges from 0.05 m. to 0.25 m. The longer type predominates; the smaller stones are often roughly square in plan. There are also much larger blocks. Two examples can be given: (a) ca. 0.55 m. by 0.17 m., (b) ca. 0.38 m. by 0.28 m. They are usually thicker than the others. The only common denominator of these stones is that their major surfaces are flat above and below. From this unpromising material the vault (what is left of it) is constructed and yet the work is neat and solid. The stones are laid with skill in courses that overlap one another slightly in accordance with the corbel principle. At ca. 1.50 m. above *stereo* a course of larger stones is laid. It is at that level that the vault proper starts. Below that height the walls of the tomb are perpendicular. The thickness of the tholos wall at the point where excavation was started (4.90 m. above *stereo*) is ca. 1 m. Its thickness at the base is not known. The floor of the tomb slopes down from northwest to southeast to the extent of 0.50 m. in 9 m. or a gradient of 1 in 18; but this figure may be exaggerated as it is possible that more *stereo* than necessary was removed at the southeast end of the tomb. The floor is several centimeters lower in front of the threshold of the doorway. This is the true floor of the tholos but at an earlier stage in the excavation it was thought to have been reached at a level ca. 0.30 m. higher. It was then uneven and contained shallow pits of irregular shape that varied very much in extent. Some were small, others were long and sprawling. They had nothing to do with any burial. But one pit of a different character was exposed: a curving trench parallel to and 0.35 m. to 0.50 m. distant from the northwestern wall of the tomb, extending from near the doorway ca. 9 m. (Figs. 180, 188, 323). This pit was ca. 1.40 m. deep and ca. 1 m. wide. It had evidently been intended for primary burials or the disposal of earlier remains, which had to be removed to provide space for later interments. Very few bones were found in the trench. As elsewhere in the tomb there had been systematic and thorough spoliation, and no bone or object was ever found in its original position.

Against the southeastern wall of the vault is a stone cist (Figs. 181, 186, 187). One block was found on its face on the floor of the cist. It had at one time closed the northeast end of the grave. There was no sign of any covering slabs. The walls of the cist are of large dressed stones set up as orthostats on the *stereo*. Two of them are nearly 1 m. long and ca. 0.18 m. thick. Present dimensions of the grave (exterior measurements) are: length 2.24 m.; width 1.06 m.; height of blocks 0.47 m. The floor during excavation was found to be uneven, being ca. 0.20 m. higher on the southeast side where *stereo* is found up against the vault. It is also higher at the southwest end. As elsewhere in the tholos this cist had not escaped the attention of the tomb robbers.

The tomb today presents a different aspect from what it did when the excavation was completed (Fig. 188). As mentioned previously the sides of the dromos are no longer vertical but have a distinct slope, the surviving lintel has been repaired and placed in its original position, the doorway has been restored to its former height, and a new dome crowns the ruined vault (Fig. 189). There have also been changes within the tomb. The most noticeable of these is that the great semicircular trench has been filled in (to avoid standing water) and the poros block that closed one end of the stone cist is no longer there (it was removed during the course of excavation).

Excavation

Excavation began on May 25, 1953, and lasted until July 23, a total of fifty and one-half days. During the first few days, only four men were employed but very soon it was found necessary to increase the numbers and these at one time reached 18, but the average figure was 15. Only a limited number were employed in actual digging with the small pick. Owing to conditions imposed on us by circumstances in the early stages of the dig, a great deal of manual labor was used in transporting the soil; and at a later stage, when objects of value started to appear, many men were put on to sifting the earth.

Excavation was started in front of (to the southwest of) the blocking wall. At a depth of ca. 2.70 m. from the top of the doorway there was a layer of scattered stones extending up to the wall, and underneath this layer two further ones which filled the whole trench. These in turn were lying on earth. Among the stones was found a marble lamp of Minoan style. The removal of these stones revealed the change of construction in the blocking wall referred to above. The large, well-squared blocks of the middle section of the wall corresponded roughly with these three layers of stones to the southwest of it. It might be said that the latter represented tumble from the blocking wall but it is more likely that they were stones left over from the rebuilding of the wall after it had been partly dismantled to admit later burials, and the section in the dromos, which was excavated at a later stage, seemed to bear this out (Fig. 324). As the lowest course of large blocks in the wall corresponds with the third and lowest layer of stones in front of it, it is probable that this construction was effected on the conclusion of the funeral of one of the later burials; for, when the time came for us to dismantle the wall, it was found that this section of it was so firmly built that it was almost impossible to lever the blocks apart. It is doubtful therefore whether it was intended that that part of the wall should be demolished for any subsequent burials, and the pile of stones would provide an indication of the depth to which it was necessary to excavate the dromos to have re-access to the tomb.

In order to investigate the entrance doorway further, it was necessary to move the lintel away from its original position. This was no mean operation for, although the block had conveniently disintegrated into four pieces, the transport of the smallest of these taxed our limited resources. Our primitive equipment, consisting of wooden rollers of cypress, wooden stakes, and iron crowbars, and the use of stones as fulcra, cannot have been very different from that employed in ancient times. Two of the lumps were moved in this manner but the third, the largest, would not respond to this treatment. A monster jack (used for lifting cars) had to be hired. Even with its cooperation and with ten men pulling on ropes, it took four hours to move this enormous boulder a distance of 5 m. What it must have cost in ingenuity and labor not only to transport the original quarried block to the site but to place it in position!

Excavation was then transferred to the inner side of the blocking wall. Here a trench was dug lengthwise through half of the doorway to allow for a section. There was a considerable quantity of stones found in this area in the upper levels but a large number of them appear to have drifted in from the tomb with rain water after progressive collapses of the vault, and this seems to be borne out by the drift lines visible in the section (Fig. 325). Some of the stones may have fallen from the blocking wall and others at least from the doorway; such were the well-dressed blocks. Two of these had the following dimensions: (a) 0.35 m. x 0.78 m. x 0.26 m., (b) 0.43 m. x 0.43 m. x 0.20 m. But from ca. 3.65 m. down and thereafter to *stereo* (a depth of about 0.90 m.) there was one layer of stones after another in the inner doorway and these must have come from the blocking wall when the upper part of it was being dismantled for the admission of a burial (Fig. 325). This accumulation of stones is in marked contrast to what is found on the other (outer) side of the blocking wall, where the concentration is ca. 1 m. above *stereo,* very few stones being found on that side at ground level. This seems to provide further confirmation that the dromos was seldom if ever completely cleared to its original, excavated level.

The stage was now set for demolishing the wall itself. It took ten men two whole days to accomplish this. The stones from the upper courses were dislodged with comparative ease. All stones were carefully cleaned and the soil from the wall was sifted. Under one of these from the higher courses was found a mass of ivory fragments, unfortunately in too ruined a state to permit recognition of the object. The middle section of the wall, which contained the well-built masonry of long blocks (Figs. 182, 183), gave us infinite trouble in the dismantling of it. On the removal of the blocks from the outer (southwest) face of the wall, it was found that they rested on 0.10 m. to 0.20 m. of earth (visible in Fig. 184). This break in the construction of the wall would indicate the level at which the tomb was entered for a later burial, as was mentioned above.

In cleaning one of these outsize blocks a 12-petaled rosette of gold leaf was found. The only other find in the wall was a bronze arrowhead, the barbed ends of which had been bent right over. This was found at a height of 0.80 m. above *stereo*. Sifting produced a gold leaf rosette with eight petals punctured with holes, a disk of yellow glass paste, some bone fragments, bits of carbon, and some small pieces of gold leaf and bronze. On reaching the ground level on which the wall had been built a special investigation was made to discover whether any cist had been dug beneath it but everywhere *stereo* was found.

In excavating a tholos tomb, it is usual either to dig the dromos first and the chamber afterwards or to treat the two as one unit. Neither of these alternatives was open to us. The area occupied by the dromos was a vineyard of choice table grapes and very naturally the owner was most reluctant that they should be destroyed. Negotiations followed as to compensation. Until agreement was reached, operations had to be confined to the entrance and blocking wall, and to the tholos itself. Work on the dromos started only on the 25th day of the excavation or roughly at half time. It was, however, fortunate that we had to dig down in the chamber without demolishing the stone wall that closed the tomb. This gave us an opportunity to have an unrivaled view of the blocking wall from the inside (Fig. 179), an aspect that has seldom if ever been vouchsafed in the excavation of other tholoi.

The dromos was dug in two operations, the southeast half being taken first. The undug northwest half provided a section for the length of the dromos and a transverse balk was left at the northeast end to give a cross section. At a height of ca. 1.50 m. above *stereo* (measured at the northeast end) a few fragments of gold leaf were found. This height corresponds roughly with the large blocks found in the outer face of the blocking wall and the find would be related to the reopening of the tomb at this level, postulated earlier, when gilt objects were brought into the chamber — or brought out! An occasional tiny fragment of gold leaf was found at lower levels (at 1.45 m., 1.30 m., 1.20 m., 0.80 m., 0.20 m., above *stereo* — measurements from the northeast end of the dromos). At ca. 0.15 m. above *stereo* and ca. 1.70 m. distant from the doorway, there was a red patch of earth measuring ca. 0.30 m. x 0.55 m. Some fire may have been kindled here for an unknown purpose (purificatory?). When it was cleared away, nothing was found underneath except a few fragments of pottery. It contained no bones. The long section in the dromos gave some indication of its reuse at the level of ca. 1 m. above *stereo* (Fig. 324). Other reopenings of the dromos were less clearly defined. The information from the cross section was largely negative.

The tholos was excavated more or less concurrently with the doorway and the blocking wall. A trench 9.85 m. x 1 m. and roughly parallel to the lintel was laid across what was presumed to be the center of the tomb. The other side of the vault was soon found at the northwest end of the trench. When a depth of just over 1 m. had been obtained the trench was extended to cover about half the area of the tholos. In this way a section would be provided. Not many stones were found in the first meter of digging. They were, of course, part of the collapsed vault.

Owing to the fact that the obvious exit, the dromos, was not available to us during the greater part of the excavation, all the soil from the tholos had to be laboriously transported from the lower levels to the top of the *aloni* and thence to the dump. It was like ladling from a soup bowl. To facilitate exit from the tomb, steps were created as the excavation proceeded downwards (Fig. 177). In the end there were 19 of them and they reached to a depth of ca. 4.20 m.[33] Thus the greater part of the tomb had been excavated before the dromos was opened on the 36th day of the campaign.

After a depth of ca. 3.50 m. had been reached, a start was made of excavating the other half of the tholos, the southwest half. The balk that was left between the two sectors of the tomb was the staircase. Nothing outstanding was discovered in the upper levels. This was to be expected as we were digging through the fill brought in by centuries of winter rains as well as the earth that had formerly covered the dome. What was a little disconcerting was that the quantity of fallen stones retrieved seemed insufficient to account for the missing upper structure.[34] At a depth of ca. 1.85 m. there was a roughly circular patch of earth burnt red with a blackened upper surface. It measured ca. 0.50 m. by 0.60 m. and was about 0.20 m. thick. It was thought at the time to be part of the outer packing of the vault which had collapsed with it. A few tiny fragments of bronze were found at a depth of ca. 1.75 m.

At ca. 2.35 m., measuring from the top of the northwest side of the vault, a dark patch of earth appeared in the southwest sector of the tomb and up against

---

[33] Measuring from the lower edge of the southeast side of the vault, which is ca. 0.50 m. lower than the opposite edge.

[34] However, when the *aloni* was laid out many stones may have been carried away (see p. 95).

the central part of the staircase.[35] As we descended the extent of the area spread, radiating from the center of the tomb, up to a distance of 2.10 m. in a south-westerly direction. At this same level it stretched from step 7 to step 14, or ca. 3.75 m. (Fig. 326). The dark earth was mostly black in color with patches of brown earth and dotted with small lumps of chalk. (Bits of chalk were quite common in all the fill of the tomb.) The same black earth did not show up in the northeast half of the chamber (henceforth called northeast sector—see Fig. 322) until 0.65 m. lower than this level and then only desultorily. It continued to be observed in the northeast sector as low down as ca. 3.90 m., a depth that was roughly the equivalent of 1 m. above the floor of the tomb. In section it could be seen as a black stratum that stretched from step 7 to step 15. Another black layer showed higher up from step 4 to step 9. The digging of this dark earth did not reveal anything noticeably different from what had previously been found in the surrounding lighter colored deposit, but it can be stated that not so long after its appearance the finds became slightly more interesting, though these were by no means confined to the darker layers. The fragments of bronze increased in size and number. There were bits of bone, mostly splinters, and pieces of carbon. At a depth ca. 3.50 m. (1.40 m. above *stereo*) a few fragments of gold leaf were found and bronze occurred more frequently. At about the same level a stone celt was uncovered and some 0.10 m. lower two arrowheads (one flint and one obsidian) and two amber beads.

On the appearance of the gold leaf, preparations were made for gridding the whole chamber into squares, 2 m. x 2 m. Thereafter the position of all small finds was plotted by measurement within the square, each square having its own letter and number. Excavation proceeded by squares using arbitrary levels of 0.10 m. at a time, but where there was darker soil, that was plotted and dug first.

At a depth of 3.70 m. (1.20 m. above *stereo*) different objects started to appear in increasing numbers: a rosette in gold leaf, the sword pommel of alabaster, flint and obsidian arrowheads, an ivory leg (of a casket?), a bronze rivet, a fragment of a skull, and a quantity of beads of glass paste, amethyst, and amber. The skull fragment was the first of many to be found but not of course in its original position. Altogether there were about 40 fragments of skull discovered in the excavation of the tomb. Like the human bones—and there were but few of them—they were dispersed throughout the lower layers of deposit from approximately this level downwards. The sword pommel was found near the vault

---

[35] The southwest sector, having been started later, was always several levels behind the north-east sector, so the account given here does not follow in chronological order.

in clean soil that looked as if it was waterborne, being light in color and not dissimilar to *stereo*. This lighter earth was quite a feature of the section. It generally appeared against the vault and alternated from time to time with darker soils that did not, however, as a rule penetrate as far as the vault (Fig. 326). Its purer quality suggests that it was filtered through that part of the dome which had not yet collapsed.

The finds, briefly listed above, all came from the southwest sector. At the same level in the northeast sector nothing was found other than some fragments of bronze. Gold leaf only began to appear ca. 0.20 m. lower down and there were then three amethyst beads. Even at that level the finds remained few. They started to increase at the next level and were plentiful in the one below that (about 0.60 m. above *stereo*), in which the complete skull of a sheep or goat was uncovered; there was no sign of the rest of the skeleton. A little higher up, but in a different part of the sector there was a small burnt area ca. 0.40 m. by 0.30 m. and only a few millimeters thick. A great deal of carbonized wood was removed from it. Underneath, the soil was red and the surface of stones in the vicinity also showed traces of fire. This was ca. 0.70 m. above the floor of the tholos.

The distribution of miscellaneous objects over the tomb varied from level to level in both sectors. Sometimes they would be concentrated in the northwest and central parts of the tomb and objects at the opposite end would be rare or nonexistent. This was the case in the southwest sector in the upper levels when nothing other than bronze was being found in the northeast sector. Sometimes the objects were distributed in a rough arc parallel to the vault. At another time the concentration was along the northwest-southeast axis of the tomb. Apart from the more interesting small objects, of which mention has been made, a steadily increasing amount of gold leaf and bronze came to light as well as bone fragments, human and animal, and a quantity of carbon scattered over the area. The bronze was only fragmentary but it included quite a considerable amount of wire, some of it gilded. A few of the bones were stained green, showing that they had come in direct contact with bronze; some of them were burnt. The carbon was of two kinds: a black, rather friable variety; the other, dark brown, very light in weight and liable to disintegrate easily.

When miscellaneous objects started to appear in some abundance in the southwest half of the tholos, it was noted that there was an apparent concentration of gold leaf in the area opposite the doorway. A great deal of it was found at first but it began to fade out before the *stereo* in the doorway was reached. Furthermore, the area was now encumbered with stones previously referred to on page 99. The upper levels contained two attractive objects: a gold rosette suspended on a gold hook and a gold earring. When a depth of ca. 4.55 m. had been reached in the northeast sector and there was no sign of *stereo* (which according to that found in the tomb entrance should have been at that level, the height of the doorway), a trial cutting 0.60 m. wide was made in the northeast sector (which was further advanced than the southwest sector) in the axis of the doorway to reach it. A few beads, a broken flint arrowhead, and a gold rosette pierced for attachment were recovered. The rosette was found on *stereo* at a depth of ca. 4.90 m. From this information it was clear that the floor of the tomb was lower than the threshold of the entrance.

The number of finds that were uncovered in the lowest levels of the tholos was legion. Certain items kept on recurring; bronze rivets, flint and obsidian arrowheads, and quantities of beads, among which amber predominated. As *stereo* was reached in the northeast sector it was noticed that the floor was not level. Certain areas permitted excavation to a greater depth. They turned out to be pits or hollows of amorphous contour and varying depth. The outline of one of them was observed in the section of the trial cutting made to discover *stereo*. Most of these pits (three of them in this half of the tomb) were shallow but one of them turned out to be deep. This was the curved burial trench referred to above (see p. 97). It was the source of many interesting, varied, and even valuable finds. In this pit there were a fair number of stones and but few bones; everything was helter-skelter as in the rest of the tomb. One of these stones was of unusual size and had a semicircle cut out on one of its sides. Another large stone of similar shape was found in the tomb. It appears to have been broken but, if complete, the cut-out piece would have been square instead of semicircular. These two stones placed opposite one another would have left a roughly oval aperture which would be closed by the crowning slab or keystone of the vault (Fig. 185).

On the large stone found in the pit were green stains from disintegrated bronze. One of these looked like the outline of a dagger blade. There was a corresponding discoloration in the soil where it had lain but the weapon itself had perished. Low down in the pit, or rather trench, several large blocks of *poros* (soft limestone) were found. Among the more interesting finds from the pit were four gold drum beads, two gold leaf-shaped pendants belonging to the drum beads, a bead seal (of lapis lazuli)—one of five found in the excavation—a bronze ring, two bronze arrowheads, a large glass spacer bead of rare design. But the most important finds of all, not only from this pit but from the whole excavation, were discovered on almost the last day of the dig. These were the gold figure-of-eight shield, used as a pendant, the gold bead seal engraved with the royal griffin, and lastly, aesthetically not comparable but more important, an amber spacer bead. The importance of the last-named lies in the fact that it is almost the exact replica of one found in England in a Wessex cemetery.

The shallow pits also contained miscellaneous objects which, however, were fortuitous. The deepest was ca. 0.50 m. The others varied much in size and none of them had any recognizable shape (Fig. 323). It is very doubtful whether they had a funerary purpose. It is more likely that they were made by tomb robbers searching for treasure. One of them (Pit C), the deepest, was uncovered near the wall on the side opposite to the semicircular trench or pit (Pit A). Perhaps, after the successful and rewarding discovery of the latter, another mine of treasure was being sought at the other side of the tholos. Pit B was a long, meandering, and in places very broad trench. At one point it coalesces with Pit A. It looks as if it was the trench that led to the discovery of the latter. Pit D was near the center of the tomb, Pit E close to the east side of the tholos.

At the level where the pits started to appear, the upper part of the stone cist that was built against the southeast wall of the vault was uncovered (see p. 97 and Fig. 181). This cist was excavated in two operations, the northwest part being dug first. Thus a longitudinal section was created. No skeletal remains came to light other than a femur bone and this was obviously not in position. Scattered through the earth or fill were a variety of objects: a gold leaf-shaped pendant similar to the one found in Pit A, a bronze dagger or knife hilt, a bead seal of haematite, a bronze rivet, arrowheads, and beads; one of the amber beads of flattened spherical form was of exceptional size, having a diameter of 0.033 m. But the most precious find, and perhaps the only one of these objects that may have belonged originally to the grave, was a gold signet ring engraved with a religious scene. It was found near *stereo* at the northeast end of the cist.

On reaching *stereo* in the southwest part of the tomb a complete pot, but in fragments, was uncovered near the southeast jamb of the doorway, just inside the chamber and close to the wall. It was a large bellied amphora with linear decoration in slightly lustrous paint that would appear to be transitional between Middle and Late Helladic (Fig. 196:1). It was one of four vases found in this excavation and the only one that was complete. Of the other three one was a Palace Style jar, some of the fragments of which were found in the dromos and others in the tomb (Fig. 196:2); it could not be made up. The third was a jug(?) with tortoiseshell decoration, datable to Late Helladic I or II; it could be partly restored (Fig. 196:4). The fourth was the upper part of a small monochrome jug (Fig. 196:3 lower left corner). This scarcity of pottery in the tomb remains a mystery. There were certainly plenty of sherds, but the majority of them were of coarse fabric and a good percentage of pre-Mycenaean wares was often present. Late Helladic III fragments were found but they were usually undecorated. In the lower levels few, if any, sherds can have escaped the sieve. It may be that we were discouraged by finding so much coarse and nondescript ware and perhaps some of the Minyan style sherds could have been made up into vases which belonged to the tomb.

At a depth of ca. 4.70 m. the floor of the tholos appeared to have been reached. Only the pits and the stone cist were left to be excavated. The floor of the chamber indeed was uneven and there was a slight mound in the central part of the tomb, but everywhere, apart from the pits, the soil was yellowish, hard, and cut up like *stereo*. But an investigation of an extension of Pit B towards the northeast showed that there was a thin layer of dark earth under ca. 0.30 m. of "*stereo*." This dark layer proved to be prolific in gold leaf. The explanation could only be that what we had thought was *stereo* was waterlaid soil and because it was comparatively clean and unadulterated, it would seem to have filtered into the tomb from the dome before it had crashed. All of this "*stereo*" was now removed. It varied from 0.20 m. to 0.35 m. in thickness. It was completely sterile but the true floor of the tholos was reached underneath. It was littered with miscellaneous objects of which the following are noteworthy: three gold drum beads with leaf-shaped pendants, two gold foil ornaments in repoussé work but cut out in the shape of an owl (two other complete examples had previously been found at higher levels), two gold spacer beads, each with a different repoussé design, five oblong pieces of gold foil shredded to make a fringe, 31 rosettes of various sizes in gold leaf, some of them pierced for attachment, and a large number of the usual beads. More than half the rosettes were concentrated in one square. There was one human bone.

But the amount of gold leaf collected from the floor was quite staggering. It filled eight cigarette boxes (of 20-cigarette size) from the southwest sector alone. The average daily quota for the four or five previous prolific days had been one to one and a half boxes. Much of the gold leaf was found adhering to the *stereo*. Many pieces were of rectangular form. The largest of them measured 0.065 m. by 0.095 m. The next largest piece, 0.043 m. by 0.088 m., had a design of running spirals impressed on it. The central part of the tomb at least must have been carpeted with gold.

Most of the miscellaneous objects were distributed across the tomb in the axis of the doorway with a particular concentration in the center and again in the area in front of the entrance. But if one allows for those found in the shallow pits, the distribution is more homogeneous. There were a few objects in the neighborhood of the stone cist but not close to it, and a small part of the eastern sector of the tholos was sterile except for one amber bead. The *stereo* had so often proved to be deceptive that we proceeded to shave off the surface of the floor two centimeters at a time. A few pockets yielded up a little gold leaf. As a further precaution a trench 2 m. wide and in the axis of the dromos was dug across the tomb to a depth of ca. 1 m. Nothing was found.

Discussion

The use of small stones in the construction of the tholos, and the dromos cut in *stereo* without supporting masonry would place this tomb in the first and earliest group of tholoi at Mycenae, but it is unsafe to transfer such a criterion to this distant part of the Peloponnesos. A safer guide is the pottery which suggests a date of Middle Helladic—Late Helladic I for the building of the tomb. Though such a date may appear unduly high, it should be remembered that the tholos tomb at Koryphasion, which is ca. 5 miles from Tholos IV, contained much early pottery, of which a goodly proportion could be put together into Middle Helladic pots.[36]

If the tomb was built in the sixteenth century B.C., it was certainly in use for at least two and a half centuries after that, if not longer. About 40 skull fragments were retrieved from the tomb. Dr. Lawrence Angel of the Smithsonian Institution, Washington, D.C. has examined them and in his opinion they belong to at least 17 different individuals (10 males, six females, and a child). They would presumably all, or most of them, have been buried at different times. During the use of the tomb it is unlikely that any organized tomb-robbing took place and the evidence seems to bear this out, if I interpret it correctly. I think that the scattering of the small objects over the floor of the tholos (the true *stereo*) occurred on the occasion of subsequent reopenings of the tholos. At such times the remains of the last burial laid out in the center of the tomb would be disposed of and placed with his or her belongings in the semicircular trench[37] dug for that purpose. More solid objects—such as the vessels of gold, silver, and bronze, and the weapons—could easily be transported, but articles of personal adornment would have become detached, particularly in the case of necklaces. The string would have disintegrated, the beads dispersed. It would be difficult to gather up all the ornaments; some would remain where they were, others would be dropped in transport. The possibility of a certain amount of pilfering at times is not to be excluded. The concentration of objects immediately in front of the southeast half of the exit may indicate the place where a burial was laid

[36] C. W. Blegen, "An early tholos tomb in Western Messenia," *Hesperia* XXIII (1954), 158-162, pls. 37-38.

[37] The trench would be extended as the reburials increased.

out; the space immediately to the northeast was bare of finds. This concentration also suggests that the blocking wall was not dismantled to its full width on such occasions; this would be only sensible.

Reference has been made earlier to the gold leaf covering the floor of the tomb. This would not have stood up very well under the heavy traffic arising from the circumstances of each reburial. If it took place during a wet winter, there would be a lot of mire and the "carpet" would suffer even more. Some of the small bits of gold leaf found in the dromos at different levels may be explained in that way, fragments carried there on muddy sandals.

How long the tholos remained a royal mausoleum in constant use cannot be known with certainty. Perhaps there were no more burials after the first half of Late Helladic III. There followed a long period during which the tholos remainted intact, but the old fabric started to show weaknesses. Water began to percolate into the tomb, dripping minute grains of soil that slowly built up a layer of silt over the remains and debris of the last burial. When this tomb excited the cupidity of tomb robbers, probably in late Mycenaean times, their easiest means of access was through the blocked-up entrance. No doubt with long experience of these ventures they removed sufficient of the upper courses of the wall to allow entry. They found the floor of the tomb covered with "*stereo*" and not a scrap of loot in sight. Undismayed they set themselves to trenching the earth. No doubt the stone cist (which was built above ground) aroused their interest first. If there were slabs over the cist, it could have been rifled with little expenditure of energy. It was a different matter when it came to clear the great semicircular pit. From the fact that the outline of the pit was not, it would seem, apparent and that they had to dig at least two trenches before it was found, it is evident that the pit was filled in each time there was a reinterment of bones from a previous burial. Every bit of earth would have to be dug out of the semicircular pit before they could be sure of laying their hands on all the treasure it could yield. Their enterprise was richly rewarded and, when one considers the number and quality of the objects that have survived to be retrieved in the present excavation, the original contents of the tomb must have been of unparalleled wealth and value.

After the plunderers had left, the tomb presented a scene of chaos. Everywhere there were mounds of dug-up soil, for one cannot suppose they would "replace the divot." And in that state it remained until the next catastrophe. The passage of time continued to weaken the fabric of the building. Stones in the vault were loosened by rain (and earthquakes?) and finally the dome collapsed into the tomb. One of the great capping stones crashed into the now open semicircular pit. The "open" tholos must have invited the interest of other tomb robbers, but they would be disappointed and their harvest would be small. There is evidence, however, that they tried. Reference has already been made to the dark earth that was found at a high level in the southwest sector of the tomb and continued to some depth before it started to appear in the northeast sector. It will also be remembered that the first miscellaneous objects related to the tomb were in the higher levels of the southwest sector whereas the corresponding levels in the northeast sector were devoid of them (see p. 103). Now an entirely different prospect would present itself to the new plunderers. They would gaze upon all the debris of the crashed vault. Presumably the periphery of the tomb would be less encumbered. They would see the despoiled stone cist, and the outline of the semicircular pit could still be discerned. They must have realized that someone had been there before them, but undaunted they carried on a further excavation. The indications are that they chose the northeast sector for their operations. The earth that they excavated appears to have been piled up in the southwest sector; this was always the richest sector of the two. It is probable that in this manner small objects in the excavated soil of the previous tomb robbers were transferred to a higher level and they could change their position again if they dribbled or drifted down the slope of the dump. It was perhaps in this way that the gold leaf-shaped pendant found its way into the stone cist. It belonged to a necklace of which we recovered no fewer than 14 drum beads and six of the pendants. They were found in all parts of the tomb: on the floor (true *stereo*), in the great pit (where they were probably deposited), and in the upper levels. They must originally have formed part of a large necklace, or perhaps there were more than one of this kind.

However unsystematically the plunderers may have gone about their work, the creation of this pile of earth in the southwest sector seems to be vouched for. The evidence for it is borne out by the section in the tholos (Fig. 326). This shows that the filtered soil deposited close to the vault suffers an incursion every now and again from the dark earth. This would come about whenever the dump became top-heavy either from the deposition of soil that drifted in through the gap in the dome or because of a further collapse of the vault. One feature that remains unexplained is the small burnt patch referred to on page 103. It was found at ca. 0.60 m. above *stereo* in the northeast sector. This is at a height at which the tomb showed every evidence of having been thoroughly despoiled. It is presumably to be associated with the new plunderers.

There are three enigmas to which it is difficult to give a satisfactory answer: the scarcity of stones, of pottery, and of bones. Only tentative suggestions can be made. Although a considerable amount of stones were found in the excavation there did not seem to be a sufficient number of them to complete the collapsed vault; but it is possible that near the top the thickness of this particular dome was very much less; or the vault may have been higher at the time the area was adapted for use as an *aloni* and such stones as were found in the leveling process would have supplied material for building a terrace wall. As regards the pottery it may be that the preponderance of vessels were gold, silver, and bronze, and that they were supplemented by pots of crude fabric and by plain un-decorated vases. A similar scarcity of pottery was noted in the tholos tomb at Dendra where gold and silver vessels predominated (*RT, Dendra*, 66). Although a great deal of bone fragments were gathered up in the excavation, there were not sufficient to account for all the skeletons posited by skull fragments. Perhaps the latter provide a clue. There *were* only fragments. No complete skull was ever found. Both skulls and bones suffered from the depredations of the tomb robbers. They must have got broken many times [38] and in that state were less able to resist destructive elements in the soil. In that respect it may be noted that from stains observed in the soil some of the bronze seems to have disintegrated completely. A few of the bones were badly burnt but as they were so fragmentary it was impossible to say whether they were animal or human. The presence of so much carbon in the tomb would suggest that fires were quite common, but much of the carbon appeared to be wood (of furniture?) that had disintegrated in that manner; as mentioned on page 103, the carbon was of two kinds.

A lot of the attempted reconstruction of the history of the tholos may appear to be rash and unnecessary, for only one thing is certain and that is that the tomb was thoroughly ransacked; not one single object was in its original place, not one burial undisturbed. Nevertheless, I have thought it worthwhile to offer some explanation, however tentative, of how this state of affairs came about. In that connection I think that the section in the tholos and the relationship between the southwest and northeast sectors are significant, though I may have interpreted them wrongly.

W. D. T.

OBJECTS FOUND

Dromos

GOLD

Several minute fragments of gold leaf at various levels.

BRONZE

Several small fragments.

IVORY

Leg of small chest? (NM. 7976, Fig. 194:40): h. pres. 0.0865 m.; w. (of leg) ca. 0.011 m. In good condition. Inner surface broken and another break at back of molded part of leg higher up. Leg of rectangular sec-

[38] Nearly all the bones were fragmentary, often only splinters. One of the few complete bones was the femur from the stone cist.

tion beveled toward top. Some resemblance to rounded leg(?) from Menidi tholos (*KG*, pl. VIII:8, 9).

TERRACOTTA

Disk: d. 0.0145 m.-0.0155 m.; th. 0.002 m. Surface level. Plain; irregular circumference. Perhaps used as inlay.

POTTERY

About 25 trayfuls of potsherds (e.g., Fig. 196:5), 60 percent coarse ware, 30 percent to 35 percent semi-coarse—only ca. 5 percent fine Mycenaean ware. In upper levels percentage of coarse ware reached 75 percent. Among semi-coarse ware Middle Helladic well represented, including Minyan, Mattpainted, and many fragments of a Palace Style jar, insufficient for restoration of vase (Fig. 196:2). Very little painted Mycenaean pottery found. Kylix most common shape but impossible to date any piece closely. Some looked like Late Helladic III B; nothing later.

Doorway

GOLD FOIL

Rosette (NM. 7911?): Cf. Fig. 190:3, left. D. 0.018 m. Near *stereo*. Two fragments; circular, impressed with design of 12-petal rosette. Three holes irregularly spaced near circumference, for attaching to some material.

Butterfly (NM. 7913, Figs. 190:2, 191:1): h. 0.021 m.; w. 0.0385 m. Near *stereo*. Upper part pierced symmetrically with seven holes for attachment. Lower half (thorax), found separately, may or may not belong. Similar to butterfly engraved on bronze double axe from Phaestos (A. B. Cook, *Zeus* II, 644, fig. 560). Cf. also example from Shaft Grave III (*Schachtgräber*, pl. XXVII:49). Gold foil butterflies occur frequently in tholos tombs usually cut out in profile (*BSA* XXV [1921-23], 365, fig.

79:k, l and references p. 373, note 1. See also *AR* 1965-66, cover picture).
Several bits of foil from the lower levels.

BRONZE

Coil (NM. 7944): l. pres. 0.0185 m.; d. 0.0075 m. Shaped like tapering spring ending in point. Poor condition. Purpose unknown. Cf. coil from Tomb XXVI, *Prosymna*, 271:3; fig. 214:3; also *EphArch* 1889, pl. 8:3 from Vapheio tholos.

Blade of dagger or rapier: l. ca. 0.18 m.; w. 0.025 m.-0.04 m. Very much corroded.

Several small fragments: laminae, one with button-shaped boss; bits of wire.

STONE

Lamp (NM. 7958, Fig. 195:14): h. ca. 0.10 m.; d. 0.16 m.; d. base 0.11 m. Complete. Surface much worn and chipped. White marble.[39] From broad base body expands toward lip. Central part of upper surface hollowed out to depth of ca. 0.02 m. leaving margin or rim ca. 0.03 m. broad. On upper surface of rim, traces of two lips for wicks. Shape like *Gournia*, pl. V:14, described as small offering stand. Cf. *Mallia Maisons* II, pl. XLIX:4, with carved decoration and one from Troy (*ProcPS* N.S. XXXIII 1967, pl. VII, N29).

AMBER

Bead: d. ca. 0.01 m.; th. 0.003 m. In three fragments about half preserved.

Bead, fragment. Not measurable. Both found on or near *stereo*.

PASTE

Button? (NM. 7979, Fig. 195:20): h. 0.006 m.; d. 0.018 m. Complete. Convex upper surface with encircling groove just below the "dome." Many similar objects found by Tsountas at Mycenae mostly in Chamber Tomb 15. These are displayed in show case of National Museum. One illustrated in *EphArch* 1888, pl. 9:8 (15). Cf. also *Schachtgräber*, 213, fig. 93 left. Chamber Tomb I:2

---

[39] At my request Dr. Peter Warren examined some of the stone material from this tomb and his comments are incorporated in the text. I am deeply grateful for his help.

at Asine yielded seven bone buttons "with a shallow groove along the edge" of same type (*Asine*, 388, No. 5; 389, fig. 252:left, middle).

POTTERY

Jug, small, upper half only (Fig. 196:3): h. pres. 0.045 m.; d. pres. 0.08 m. Shape appears to be small spherical jug (*MP*, Type 126, p. 34 fig. 7 Late Helladic II). Narrow neck splays to missing lip. Handle round in section. Clay, greenish-yellow on inside, pink on outside. Traces of red paint, particularly on inside of neck, Late Helladic III A? For shape cf. *Deltion* 3 (1917), 147, fig. 109:2.

Seven trays of potsherds comprised much coarse ware: from the upper levels 62 percent of the total and from the lower 70 percent. In deeper strata Mycenaean was better represented. Most of pottery was undecorated but none attributable to later than Late Helladic III B. About 20 sherds that were extracted from crevices in door jambs, though nondescript, were judged to be predominantly Middle Helladic. No Mycenaean recognized among them.

The Blocking Wall [40]

GOLD LEAF

Rosettes (NM. 7921, NM. 7918) of three different sizes and form:

(a) (Fig. 190.3, top) d. 0.02 m. Twelve petals. Nearly every petal pierced with hole.

(b) (cf. small rosettes, Fig. 190.3) d. 0.01 m. Eight petals pierced with holes.

(c) d. 0.054 m. In poor condition. Just over half: eight of 12 petals preserved; central part missing. Differs from (a) and (b) in size and form: (a) and (b) have design impressed within a circle, (c) keeps outline of tips of petals, and within each petal is engraved outline of

a smaller and narrower petal (cf. Fig. 191:8). No holes for attachment; rosette was presumably glued to some article as decoration.

Several bits.

BRONZE

Arrowhead (NM. 7943, Fig. 194:1): l. pres. 0.0535 m.; w. 0.014 m.; th. 0.002 m. In crevice in wall ca. 0.80 m. above *stereo*. Lower half bent over. Elongated triangular shape with barbs but no stem. A well-known type (cf. *EphArch* 1888, pl. 9:22 (33) from Mycenae; *BSA* xxv [1921-23], 335, fig. 68:m from Heraion Tholos Tomb; *Prosymna*, figs. 440:3; 443:1). Several examples of the earlier version are illustrated in *Prosymna*, 341, fig. 216:1. Specimen from Tholos IV is half way between the earlier and later type.

Two pieces of twisted wire. Larger piece: l. pres. 0.03 m. Several fragments of laminae.

STONE

Lamp? fragment of rim (NM. 7959, Fig. 195:15): h. pres. ca. 0.06 m.; w. 0.055 m.; w. rim 0.05 m.; depth rim 0.033 m. Serpentine (Cretan).[41] Very poor condition; crust cracked, surface liable to peel off. Upper surface has shallow, rectangular recess or cutting on outer circumference. Vertical part of rim decorated with perpendicular grooves. Form of rim reminiscent of marble lamp from doorway (NM. 7958, p. 111). Reconstruction hypothetical. Shape probably like that illustrated in C. Tsountas and J. I. Manatt, *The Mycenaean Age* (London 1897) 80, fig. 31 (excluding stand). For grooves on rim see *Gournia*, p. 30, pl. II, S.76; lamp from Pseira has vertical grooves (P. Warren, "Minoan stone vases as evidence for Minoan foreign connections in Aegean Late Bronze Age," *ProcPS* N.S. xxxiii

---

[40] All of the following objects were retrieved from within or on face of blocking wall with exception of two gold rosettes which were found at

its base.

[41] See footnote 39, p. 111.

[1967], 37-56; pl. v:N. Pseira). Both this and the other lamp (p. 111) from Tholos IV are very probably Minoan imports. See Warren, *op.cit.,* 37-53. For rectangular recess compare *NT,Dendra,* 57(7), fig. 64 "three cavettos."

Steatite whorl or button: h. pres. 0.005 m.; d. 0.0165 m.; d. hole 0.003 m. Found high on face of wall. Fragment; most of shank missing. Furumark, Type C:2 (*MPChron,* 89, fig. 2). Late Helladic III A-B. Compare *Asine,* 375, fig. 246: second from right in bottom row, and *Prosymna,* fig. 602:5.

Flint arrowhead (NM. 7900, Figs. 194:10, 226 Type III): l. 0.02 m.; w. 0.015 m.; th. 0.004 m. Intact; dark brown, barbed. Convex cutting edges. Both faces cambered. Stubby but pointed barbs. No stem (i.e., four-sided figure). Both surfaces worked over. This is rare type (see p. 127).

Obsidian flake (fragment).

IVORY

A mass of fragments found under one stone, colored green. Original form unknown.

BONE

Part of bone pin (NM. 7950). Many bone fragments stained green from bronze found in wall.

PASTE

Disk (NM. 7931): d. 0.023 m.; th. ca. 0.005 m. Very friable condition. Like amber in texture but of yellowish color inside. Pierced vertically with two holes 0.0175 m. apart. Similar disks found by Tsountas in Tomb 24 (d. ca. 0.03 m.) and Tomb 88 (d. ca. 0.02 m.) at Mycenae can be seen in the National Museum, Cases 26 and 1.[42]

POTTERY

Sherds from dismantling blocking wall filled a tray. About 60 percent coarse ware, 5 percent semi-coarse, 35 percent Mycenaean, representing all periods from Middle Helladic to Late Helladic III B. Very few sherds of Middle Helladic, one with incised decoration. Recognizable Mycenaean shapes were Vapheio cup, alabastron, and kylix (several).

Tholos

GOLD

Personal Adornment

Signet ring with oval bezel [43] (NM. 7985, Fig. 192:9a, b = *CMS* I, No. 292): bezel, l. 0.0175 m.; w. 0.009 m.; th. 0.0015 m. Ring, d. 0.015 m.-0.016 m.; th. 0.002 m. Shape of ring slightly distorted. Bezel, set at right angles to axis of ring, bears engraved cult scene. In center shrine on hill or mountain peak? Two projections above shrine may represent horns of consecration. To left of shrine, goat rampant; to right, a divintiy in mid air (?) and a man with arm raised in adoration. Between figures a plant or tree.

Ring with heart-shaped bezel (NM. 7967, Figs. 190:7, 191:2): bezel, l. 0.015 m.; w. 0.0125 m.; th. 0.0015 m. Ring, outer d. 0.0165 m.; inner d. 0.0155 m. Ring soldered at right angles to bezel just below maximum width of latter; channeled on inside. Outside of ring convex, bordered by series of engraved notches along both edges. Bezel has raised rim with granular decoration. Must have served as setting for semiprecious stone or colored paste. Shape of bezel rare, if not unique. Compare gold heart-shaped beads from Shaft Grave III (*Schachtgräber,* pl. xx:80), which resemble frequently recurring motive of ivy-leaf.

Signet bead (NM. 7986, Fig. 192:8a-c = *CMS* I, No. 293): l. 0.027 m.; w. 0.021 m.; th. 0.006 m. Flattened cylinder bead, apparently made of single plate of yellow gold folded over and soldered together along

---

[42] I owe this information to Mrs. Helen Hughes-Brock.

[43] See B. Rutkowski, "The decline of the Minoan peak sanctuaries." In *Atti e Memorie del 1° Congresso Internazionale di Micenologia, Part I, Rome, 1967* (Incunabula Graeca, Vol. xxv, 1), 159.

long edge. Intervening space filled with some black substance (jet?). This has oozed out through break in surface of one side, spoiling the design. Section: flattened, lenticular shape. Ends covered by gold plates of this shape soldered on separately; one of them rather badly damaged. Bead was pierced longitudinally but melting of black substance no longer allows free passage for a thread.

Main face of seal, almost undamaged, engraved in intaglio of low depth and very fine workmanship representing couchant griffin with head turned back. Wings spread out to each side, and between lines that indicate feathers are rows of dots emphasizing their form and perhaps suggesting their variegated coloring. Head of griffin crowned with spreading plumes (ostrich feathers?). From neck hang two coils taking form of stylized ivy leaves, other coils decorate upper part of wing shoulders. Shading of underpart of belly and of hindquarters (here disfigured by oozing of black substance) shown by row of dots. Tail curved over in sinuous line. Griffin lies on dais decorated with frieze of well-known triglyph and half-rosette pattern made up of four and three quarters elements plus a half element (*MP*, "Triglyph and half rosette," p. 183, Motive 74, p. 414 fig. 72). The "triglyph" is represented by vertical groove with horizontal bars across it; the half-rosettes shown as series of dots confined within a semicircle, with central dot by side of triglyph. Above and below frieze two parallel grooved lines, that bordering the frieze in each case bearing row of dots.

Other face of bead rather badly damaged in one corner. Decorated with network pattern in fairly high relief,[44] creating diamond-shaped spaces intended to be filled with glass paste or some semiprecious stone. One inlay of black-blue paste survives. Where lines of network cross, is a raised boss; lines themselves striated with three or four incisions. Narrow ends (of network pattern) bordered by raised strip, ca. 0.001 m. wide, decorated with row of small bosses. This royal signet in workmanship vies with highest standards of Mycenaean toreutics.

Pendant in the form of figure-of-eight shield (NM. 7987, Fig. 190:20): l. 0.04 m.; w. upper lobe 0.0225 m., lower lobe 0.025 m., waist 0.0155 m.; th. 0.011 m. Slightly battered on back and along one side. Pendant made of two pieces of yellow gold plate soldered together along edges leaving hollow space between. Lower plate concave, upper markedly convex. Pinched together at waist; on each side of this constriction two holes for suspension, ca. 0.013 m. apart. Contour of pendant emphasized by ledge ca. 0.001 m. high and ca. 0.001 m. broad. Surface decorated in filigree work with groups of granular beads in rectangular formation following outline of "shield." Six beads to a group except near waist where they are three in line directed toward string-holes: five groups of six and two groups of three on upper lobe; seven groups of six and two groups of three on lower lobe. Unique example of its kind but very miniature replicas, without granulation, are known (*Prosymna*, fig. 578; *ChT*, pl. xxxviii:77). Cf. also miniature bead with granulated border from Tholos III (NM. 7855, p. 83) and from an Enkomi tomb ten gold figure-of-eight shields used as beads, three-quarters the size of our pendant. No granulation though outline decorated with two rows of dots.[45]

Spacer bead (NM. 7922, Fig. 190:6): l. 0.0285 m.; w. 0.0135 m.; th. 0.0035 m. Shape slightly distorted; a rent in back plate. Bead made up of two plates of yellow gold, each shaped like a rectangular lid,

---

[44] For use of this pattern compare *Schachtgräber*, pl. xxxii:61, earrings from Shaft Grave iii, and *RT,Dendra*, pl. xxi, hilt and pommel decoration.
[45] *SCE* i, pl. cxlvii:8.

soldered together along flanges leaving hollow space between. Long sides each pierced with two holes, 0.017 m. apart for two strings of beads. Top plate bears repoussé work with raised, notched ledge on long sides and rib decorated with bosses down middle. On each side of rib parallel curving lines giving effect of leaves, corresponding to pattern well-known in Mycenaean pottery (*MP*, Foliate band, Motive 64:23, p. 397 fig. 69). Similar pattern decorates plaques of paste from chamber tomb No. 2 at Dendra (*Rt,Dendra*, 105, fig. 80, top left and right, middle — pl. XXXV, fifth row). Cf. same kind of plaques from our Tholos III (NM. 7872, p. 87).

Spacer bead (NM. 7922, Figs. 190:8, 191:3): l. 0.0235 m.; w. 0.013 m.; th. 0.0035 m.- 0.0045 m. Crushed and distorted, badly so in one corner. Same construction as spacer bead above, but lower plate has very narrow flange and four string holes are pierced in flange of upper plate only. Latter has five transverse ribs of equal size, decorated in repousse work with diagonal lines, the direction alternating on each successive rib. String-holes pierced through each rib, except the central one.

Tubular bead with triple spirals (NM. 7901, Figs. 190:10, 191:4): l. 0.0185 m.; w. 0.0145 m.; d. tube 0.001 m. Three spirals of gold wire attached by soldering to tube; matching set attached to other side in same axis. Each set made of one piece of wire bent in two in middle and the two resulting strands made to revolve round center to form middle spiral. Each strand then parted company to form its own spiral, but rotating in opposite direction. Similar beads apparently of same technique found in Shaft Grave III (*Schachtgräber*, pl. XXI:59).

Tubular bead with double spirals (NM.

7901, Figs. 190:12, 191:5): l. 0.011 m.; w. 0.011 m.; d. tube 0.0015 m. Design similar to foregoing tubular bead but technique differs: ends of wire have been coiled over to make two spirals that meet and touch each other. Central (straight) part of wire was soldered on the tube. Matching pair on other side of tube. In parallels from Shaft Grave III (*Schachtgräber*, pl. XXI:56, 57) spirals seem to have been soldered on individually. This kind of bead is early, appearing to have an Anatolian origin, in tombs of Alaca Höyük[46] said to be 4,000 years old.[47] Also occurs later in the Palace of Mari (sometime in second millennium B.C.)[48] and again toward end of second millennium in a tomb at Lakkithra, Kephallenia (*EphArch* 1932, pl. 18:b). In last-mentioned example the spirals are formed differently and resemble pince-nez.

Fourteen drum beads and six pendants (NM. 7903, Figs. 190:16, 191:6a-c): some found badly crushed and true dimensions could not be established; average measurements d. 0.01 m.; w. 0.005 m. Drum bead made of two interlocking halves, each half shaped like a cup with vertical sides. One half slightly bigger than other to fit over it to form drum. Faces of bead are usually concave. Beads pierced transversally through sides (string-hole not always visible). They also have small loop or ring soldered onto side at right angles to axis of string-holes. In one instance two loops almost opposite one another and no sign of string-holes; possibly the thread passed through the loops. In another case two loops are at right angles to each other as if to provide suspension for two ornaments. Two incomplete examples, only half bead surviving.

Four of the six pendants found attached to drum beads. Pendants uniform in size and shape. Average dimensions: l. 0.03 m.;

---

[46] H. S. Koşay, "Allgemeines über die Schmucksachen der älteren Bronzeperiode." *The Aegean and the Near East. Studies presented to Hetty Gold-man*, pl. II:8, facing p. 39.

[47] *Ibid.*, 38.

[48] *Syria* 18 (1937), 82, pl. 15:2.

w. 0.014 m. Form is that of broad leaf with notch cut out at tip. Other end tapers to a wire twisted into loop for suspension. Both drum bead and pendant vary in color: gold in some instances is yellow, in others it has reddish streaks.

The combination of gold drum bead and pendant has not before been found, so far as I know. An elaborate and larger form of what appears to be a drum bead is illustrated in *RT,Dendra,* pl. xxvii (text, p. 39 no. 3). Cf. also half a locket bead (?) from Peristeria, Messenia (*Deltion* 21, B1 [1966], pl. 170:δ, right). Object on left of "spacer" tubes may also be part of one. No exact parallel to the pendant. Many decorated and more sophisticated specimens from an earlier age (*Mochlos,* 32, figs. 10, 11; 48, fig. 20; 72, figs. 41, 43) and contemporary but elaborate examples from Shaft Grave III (*Schachtgräber,* pl. xxv:121).

Eight biconical beads (NM. 7902, Figs. 190:5, 191:7): d. 0.008 m.; th. 0.007 m. Two hemispherical halves soldered together, with string-holes at right angles to carination. Two badly dented, one slightly so. Plain, hemispherical gold beads do not appear to be so common as the decorated kind in rich tombs. Higgins in *BSA* 52 (1957), 53, footnote 100 has given a number of examples of plain type. I can only add *NT,Dendra,* pl. v:1(8), p. 78; *BSA* xxv (1921-23), 334 (3), 354 (77:e). These are all round beads, however, whereas those from Tholos IV are biconical.

Earring in form of rosette (NM. 7901, Figs. 190:4, 191:8): d. 0.025 m. Repoussé work in thin gold plate, cracked in center; lower petals slightly bent. Sixteen-petal rosette. Smaller rosette with same number of petals contained within the larger. In center circle of dots with diameter of 0.007 m. one dot at base of each petal. One petal pierced near top, through which passes gold wire in form of hook. Compare rosette worn as an earring in *NT,Dendra,* 76, fig. 89 (and pl. III); our example is closer to fourteen-petal rosette illustrated *ibid.,* 84, fig. 93.

Earring with cylinder and coils (NM. 7901, Figs. 190:11, 191:12): l. 0.018 m.; d. cylinder ca. 0.005 m.; w. cylinder 0.0095 m. Ornament consists of two gold wires and a cylinder balanced horizontally. Upper wire coiled at both ends above and below cylinder; top end presumably pierced lobe of ear. Apparently all of one piece passing through cylinder, which is badly crushed. Above cylinder wire (max. w. 0.0015 m.) grooved on back; below round in section. Second wire, suspended from first, is bent into a loop with ends twisted into coils (two and a half twists to each). The cylinder may originally have held some ornament at either end. I know of no parallel to this earring.

Bead mounting (NM. 7901, Figs. 190:15, 191:13): d. 0.01 m.; d. hole 0.002 m. Cup-shaped disk with central hole. Convex side decorated along rim with beading in filigree work. Around perforation are soldered vertically six tiny rings or circular bands in star formation. Bands are only 0.002 m. broad (d. 0.003 m.) and are slightly channeled. Probably a twin to this mounting would enclose a large spherical bead. Such gold bead mountings are not uncommon. Elaborate examples are known from Mycenae (*ChT,* pl. xxix:24), Prosymna (*Prosymna* 1, frontispiece), and Vapheio (*EphArch,* 1889, pl. 7:7).

Pin mounting (NM. 7901, Figs. 190:13, 191:14): h. 0.011 m.; d. 0.0135 m.; d. stem 0.004 m. Concave disk, rim of which cut in shape of an eight-petaled flower. Originally held a jewel of amber (in fragments and shapeless when found). In center of concave side a small raised circle, the terminus of the pin which was either of silver or bronze covered with gold foil. Only the upper part of stem (0.008 m. long) survives, decorated with a circle of granulation ca. 0.006 m. below bottom of the flower-disk. Also two rows of granulation on convex side of the flower disk at its base where it joins the stem. A pin, said to be silver-gilt, with gold mounting and cap in granulated work to take a spherical bead, was found in the Vapheio tholos tomb (*EphArch,* 1889, pl. 7:4). There are many points of similarity. Cf. also gold pin decorated with six-petaled flower from Mallia (*PM* IV, 75, fig. 47).

Four owls (NM. 7907, Fig. 192:1-4).

Repoussé work on reddish-gold plate. Feathers indicated (in all four examples) by ridges alternating with channels. Circular depressions usually decorate the latter and notches the former, but sometimes depressions are on ridges and channels are left bare. As a rule a line of depressions across upper part of body. Claw shown tucked up under body, tail square. All examples pierced with holes for attachment and the most likely material for this purpose is clothing, though of course there is no evidence for this.

1 (Fig. 192): max. h. 0.0395 m.; max. w. 0.0175 m.; w. head 0.015 m. Tail almost torn away from body. Pierced with six holes: one in forehead, group of three to left, one on right, one in tail. The need for three holes in close proximity might mean that this owl was sewn onto stiff material, perhaps a headdress.

2 (Fig. 192): diagonal h. 0.036 m.; max. w. 0.019 m. One of best preserved.

3 (Fig. 192): h. 0.03 m.; max. w. 0.032 m.; w. head 0.015 m. Tail partly missing. Circular depressions made in channels, notching on ridges. Pierced with four holes: one between eyes, one on left side, and two on right.

4a, b (Fig. 192): max. h. 0.039 m.; central w. 0.022 m. Executed in yellow-gold plate. A rent to right of head and another in tail. Pierced with six holes: one over left eye, two together on left side, one on right, one near claw, one in tail.

A gold owl very similar to ours was found in Tholos A at Kakovatos (*AM* XXXIV [1909], pl. XIII:28 — *Crete and Mycenae,*

pl. 203:b) and at Peristeria, Messenia (*Praktika* 1965, pl. 140:3, middle).

Two pieces (NM. 7908, Fig. 192:5, 7) in gold foil (as opposed to gold plate) bear fragmentary representations of an owl, but I think they belong to a different category. Dimensions: (5) max. h. 0.0255 m.; max. w. 0.0255 m. (7) max. h. 0.0165 m.; max. w. 0.024 m. In (5) sketchy outline of owl's head appears in middle of fragment. It has not been cut out in profile like owls described above. On (7) only eyes of owl shown; no suggestion of modeling of head or wing. No holes for attachment could be recognized. Possibly these two pieces used for gilding furniture.

Bird? (NM. 7907, Figs. 191:11, 192:6): max. h. 0.035 m.; max. w. 0.0245 m. Repoussé work on yellow-gold plate cut out in roughly elliptical shape, apparently not a broken fragment as five holes for attachment pierced with fair regularity around edges. Object shows obvious workmanship but lineaments have suffered damage and it is very difficult to make out design. It might be interpreted as standing eagle with body facing to right and head turned back to left; [49] but other solutions are possible.[50]

Twelve small fragments of thin gold plate (NM. 7964), perhaps belonging to objects similar to those described above.

Butterfly (NM. 7913, Fig. 190:1): l. pres. of body 0.0105 m.; max. h. of wing 0.0205 m.; w. wings 0.0395 m. Outline of butterfly with spread wings cut out in gold leaf (reddish-yellow) and impressed with its main lineaments. Slightly better-preserved example than NM. 7913 (p. 111). Pierced with eight holes for attachment: four in left wing, three in right wing, and one hole below head. "Thorax" found separately, may or may not belong.

Fragments (NM. 7967): two of butterflies and three doubtful specimens too small to

---

[49] Compare *Schachtgräber,* pl. XXVI:44 and 60 from Grave III and pl. LXVI:689 from Grave V

(*Crete and Mycenae,* pl. 205:a).
[50] *Schachtgräber,* pl. XXI:43.

qualify for other than mention. One pierced with a hole. Also three "thorakes."

Nine rosettes pierced for attachment (NM. 7912, Fig. 190:3): Seven small with eight petals (average d. 0.01 m.); two larger (d. 0.019 m.). One of these, about three-quarters preserved, has 12 petals; the other, eight. All nine pierced with three or four holes. Some are of yellow gold leaf, others of red. Gold rosettes, pierced or unpierced, as mountings of rings or bracelets, used in necklaces, earrings or as decoration of vases, etc. are commonly found in Mycenaean tombs.

Sequins, 176 (NM. 7912, NM. 7962, NM. 7973, e.g., Fig. 190:21). Little roundels of all sizes and pierced with one or more holes for attachment. Diameters vary from 0.007 m. to 0.023 m., but majority 0.01 m. Included is a roundel engraved with what appears to be running spirals. In addition eleven fragmentary roundels. The color of gold varies as noted in previous examples.

Furniture Decoration

Two studs, very like drawing pins (NM. 7905, Fig. 190:14): d. head 0.01 m.; l. pin 0.01 m. Pin square in section. One pin, bent, ends in point, the other blunt. Both have ledge, ca. 0.001 m. thick and 0.001 m. broad, soldered onto rim of disk providing a mounting for an inlay. Pin passes through center of disk; projecting head has then been flattened out. Somewhat similar stud, illustrated in *BSA* xxv (1921-23), 335, fig. 68:i, comes from the Heraion tholos. Cf. also gold disks edged with filigree to hold inlay (*Asine*, 387, No. 7). These studs must have been used on some soft material, because of malleability of gold.

Stud with hemispherical head (NM. 7909-10): h. 0.014 m.; d. 0.009 m. Shaft, square in section, expands slightly toward cap end. Blunt tip. Stud similar to preceding, has

convex disk, probably served a like purpose. Compare numerous examples from Shaft Grave v (*Schachtgräber*, pl. CXLVI: 803-806). Cf. also *BSA* xxv (1921-23), 303, fig. 57:e, f, from the Tomb of Aegisthus, and *AM* XXXIV (1909), pl. XIII:32, 33 from Kakovatos, the last-named of gilded bronze. Staïs held that these studs were used on coffins (*EphArch* 1907, 47).

Two rosette studs (NM. 7906, 7947a). Shaft, round in section, expands gradually to attain diameter of disk. H. 0.011 m. Studs of bronze, disks plated with gold. Disk cut to shape of eight-petaled rosette. (a) d. 0.0115 m. has circle with d. 0.005 m. engraved in center and lines radiate from it to form the petals.[51] (b) Fig. 195:2: d. 0.01 m. has smaller circle with d. 0.002 m. and no lines to define petals. These studs could be used for tougher material. Gilding presumably was added later.

Two rivets (NM. 7909-10, Fig. 190:18): l. 0.012 m.; w. shaft 0.001 m. to 0.0015 m.; w. head 0.002 m. One twisted, may be slightly longer. Shaft square in section. These rivets seem ill-suited for securing hafts of weapons and a waste of this valuable metal; possibly used in some translucent material where gold would show.

Tiny disk (NM. 7909-10): d. 0.006 m. Slightly concave. Possibly used as inlay but more probably cap of small bronze rivet.

Inlay (NM. 7915, Figs. 190:19, 191:10): l. 0.0155 m.; w. 0.004 m.; th. 0.005 m. Minute piece of gold plate, beautifully incised with scale pattern.[52] Design almost identical with that used on lower part of the silver rhyton from Shaft Grave IV (*Schachtgräber*, pl. CXXII:481 and p. 108, fig. 39). On ours, however, the arc has dot punctuation. Cf. also *PM* II, ii, 731, fig. 457:b, the fresco pattern on the robes of the "Ladies in blue," where rows of dots are shown above the arc.

Tiny fragment of gold, a narrow strip with a

---

[51] Cf. *ChT,* pl. XXXVIII:74. A similar rosette decorating a ring.

[52] Cf. *MP*, Motive 62:10, p. 391 fig. 68.

slight undulation, possibly part of an inlay: l. 0.012 m.; w. 0.0025 m.; th. 0.0005 m.

Inlay in ivory (NM. 7915, Fig. 191:9): l. 0.02 m.; w. 0.0035 m.; th. ivory 0.0045 m.-0.008 m. Thin piece of ivory, with one convex edge. On opposite narrow edge remnants of gold inlay. Very little survives. Design apparently stylized leaves.[53]

Inlay? (NM. 7909-10, Figs. 190:17, 191:16): l. 0.0485 m.; w. 0.006 m.; th. 0.0005 m. Fairly solid piece of gold plate cut in a shape suggesting stylized feather or petal of flower. The object is curved. One end rounded, the other finishes in point. Possibly used in inlay work. Nearest parallel to shape is fresco fragment from Mycenae (*EphArch* 1887, pl. 12 —bottom left), painted in red. Form also that of foliate band in shoulder decoration of stirrup jar from Zafer Papoura (*PM* IV, i, 300, fig. 234a; Evans, "The Prehistoric Tombs of Knossos," *Archaeologia* 59 [1905], fig. 83). The headdress of the "Priest-King" may have consisted of feathers of this form (*PM* II, ii, frontispiece).

Rosettes (NM. 7911-2, NM. 7918-9, NM. 7921, NM. 7972, not illustrated, e.g., Fig. 190:22) ca. 52 of varying sizes, many very fragmentary. Largest, ca. 16, have diameter of ca. 0.07 m. Eight of these apparently had as many as 16 petals. One large rosette exceptionally contains second series of petals within larger ones (cf. earring CM. 7901 on p. 116). Twenty-four rosettes of medium size (average d. 0.035 m.) have 12 petals. Smallest, ca. 12 (d. 0.02 m.), have only eight petals. Profile of tips of petals cut out in all cases, usually rounded, although nearly a third of total are ogival. No rosettes had any holes for attachment and they could have been used for adornment of furniture. The gold color of many dullish red.

Roundels (NM. 7961, cf. Fig. 190:22), 115

varying from 0.009 m. to 0.024 m. in diameter (40 measure 0.017 m. and 0.018 m.). Included are five rosette roundels and one decorated with parallel ribs (average d. 0.012 m.). None is pierced for attachment and I assume that they were used for other decorative purposes than apparel. They could be glued to dress material but it would be more practical to sew them on.

Six pieces of foil with impressed designs (NM. 7971, NM. 7914):

(a) 0.025 m. by 0.0235 m. Design uncertain, possibly floral pattern (Fig. 191:15a).

(b) 0.047 m. by 0.05 m. Decorated with rhomboid impressions. Design uncertain (Fig. 191:15b).

(c) 0.045 m. by 0.088 m. Oblong piece of foil decorated with running spirals. Only one row clear (Fig. 191:15c).

(d) 0.014 m. by 0.024 m. Fragment with one impressed spiral.

(e) 0.021 m. by 0.034 m. Fragment with one impressed spiral, outline of another.

(f) 0.021 m. by 0.023 m. Fragment with outline of spiral.

Gold foil with impressed designs are usually pierced for attachment to some material, but some have no holes and were obviously intended for overlay of some less valuable substance or for decorating flat surfaces of boxes, furniture, etc. Compare *Schachtgräber*, pl. XXXIII:108; *BSA* XXV (1921-23), 353, fig. 74:d, f, g (Treasury of Atreus); *NT,Dendra*, 84, fig. 94.

Pieces of foil, 36 (NM. 7963, Fig. 191:17a-d) cut into various shapes. Most of these very fragmentary and many cannot be related to any known Mycenaean design. However, one pattern that recurs eight times is stylized papyrus (a). Upper part of stylized palm (b) as represented on cup from Vapheio[54] occurs once. Four examples of

---

[53] Cf. *MP*, Foliate Band, Motive 64:25, p. 397 fig. 69.

[54] *EphArch* 1889, pl. 9 — *Crete and Mycenae*, pl. 178:b. Cf. also *Schachtgräber*, pl. XXXIII:119, 120, silhouette of stylized palm on left.

segment of circle (c) with some attachment above or below.[55] Another fragment resembles upper part of handle of mirror (cf. *RT,Dendra*, 99, fig. 72; *MonAnt* XIV [1904], 550, fig. 34; Tsountas and Manatt, *The Mycenaean Age*, 188, fig. 84). Two specimens show volutes of lilies (d). There were fragments of cut-out gold leaf in tholos near Volos (*EphArch* 1906, pl. 15:13).

Oblong strips, 244 (NM. 7966): great variety of sizes, but none of them very large. Average dimensions:

> 0.045 m. x 0.011 m.
> 0.04 m. x 0.01 m.
> 0.037 m. x 0.008 m.
> 0.037 m. x 0.007 m.

One example is 0.028 m. x 0.016 m. Several pieces cut into narrow strips with tapering ends, e.g., 0.05 m. x 0.004 m. tapering to 0.003 m. and sometimes to 0.0015 m. These strips and the cut-up pieces of foil referred to above would be well adapted to embellish furniture, caskets, etc.

Fringe (NM. 7904, Fig. 190:9), eight pieces. Made from oblong strips of foil. Different sizes; largest piece: l. ca. 0.08 m.; w. ca. 0.02 m. Greater part of the laminae cut longitudinally into very thin parallel strips; 115 individual twisted strands (NM. 7965) that had become detached from the laminae. These fringes could have been used to decorate the frames of royal furniture or any object used on a state occasion. Compare the same type of gold fringe from Tholos 2, Peristeria (*Praktika* 1964, pl. 97:2 and 1965, pl. 141:3).[56]

Eleven pieces of gold-plated bronze wire (NM. 7916). Fragments only. One curved. In two cases gold foil was not only wrapped around the wire but part of it was free: one piece of bronze wire had strip of gold foil

(0.025 m. x 0.03 m.) adhering to it. These gilded bronze wires may in some instances have been pins, but more probably they played some functional part in reinforcement of furniture or gold metal work.

Ten large oblong pieces of foil (NM. 7923, NM. 7969, NM. 7970). Largest piece 0.095 m. x 0.065 m., another 0.045 m. x 0.035 m. Cut into rectangles, most from floor of tholos, comparatively undamaged. Hence suggestion that part of tomb was carpeted with gold.

Gold leaf and foil (not registered) collected from Tomb IV filled 41 boxes of 20-cigarette size. Anything which had shape such as roundels, oblongs, etc., described above have been extracted from these boxes. Color of gold varied from bright yellow to dull reddish.

SILVER

Ring (NM. 7949): d. 0.017 m.-0.024 m.; l. bezel 0.023 m.; w. 0.017 m. Very poor condition. Bezel detached from ring, of which whole circle not preserved. No design can be recognized on bezel. Form that illustrated in *RT,Dendra*, 56, fig. 35, but width of our ring narrower.

Jug? Fragment only: l. 0.048 m.; w. 0.031 m. Part of vessel with lipped spout, but shape not ascertainable as fragment flattened out. Apparently a raised ledge at right angles to, and below, rim.

Fragments (NM. 7949) found in earth in a row, ca. 0.05 m. long by 0.01 m. wide. Purpose unknown.

Many fragments of metal of blue color that appear to be silver (but bronze also takes on this color sometimes). One fragment had gold adhering.

BRONZE

Ring (not registered, Fig. 195:1): d. 0.023 m.; w. 0.008 m.; th. 0.002 m. Circular band.

---

[55] *Schachtgräber*, pl. XLIV:355, 357 are rather similar.

[56] At Peristeria these fringes were found in a heap together with bits of bronze wire, many of them bent, and in neighborhood some gold caps

or studs (*Praktika* 1965, 119). Hence there is the possibility that the wire was used for fixing the fringes. Note the pieces of gilt bronze wire described in next paragraph under NM. 7916.

Heavily encrusted. Circle not full; ends taper, leaving open space. Hole in one end and probably another in other end will show up after cleaning. Holes would be for mounting of bezel which has not survived. Badly preserved finger-ring of bronze of same form but slightly smaller found in chamber tomb No. 1 (*RT,Dendra*, 84f., fig. 58).

Pins, fragments of three. Very corroded.

(a) NM. 7953: l. pres. 0.119 m.; d. 0.004 m. End of long pin tapering to point.

(b) l. pres. 0.043 m.; d. 0.004 m. Shaft only.

(c) NM. 7944: l. pres. 0.032 m.; d. 0.0015 m. Tapering end. Perhaps silver.

Two beads (NM. 7927): (a) d. 0.011 m.; th. 0.003 m., half preserved (b) d. 0.0095 m.; th. 0.0065 m. Cf. *ChT*, pl. ix:6. Mrs. Hughes-Brock suggests possibly imported from Italy.

Three decorated studs (NM. 7947). Very corroded. All of different form:

(a) Similar to gold-plated rosette stud (b) described on p. 118. Dimensions practically identical. Length of present example including stem, 0.012 m.

(b) l. 0.0145 m.; d. 0.017 m.; d. stem 0.0035 m. Possibly four-petaled rosette. Disk more square than round.

(c) d. 0.02 m. Stem missing. Differs from others in having raised ledge, ca. 0.005 m. wide, along rim allowing for an inlay or jewel(?) in center. Form similar to highly decorated gold ring from Vapheio (*EphArch* 1889, pl. 7:8). Instead of stud therefore possibly bezel of ring.

Six studs (NM. 7947), two badly corroded, all slightly different. Purpose more decorative than functional. Presumably used on furniture.

(a, NM. 7945): h. 0.006 m.; d. 0.011 m. Head roughly conical (h. 0.0055 m.) and hollow, possibly silver-plated (blue coloring). Small part of pin survives. Cf. gold stud with convex head (p. 118).

(b) h. 0.014 m.; d. head 0.012 m.; w. stem 0.004 m. Head convex. Stem, square in section, tapers to blunt end.

(c, Fig. 195:3): h. 0.013 m.; d. head 0.01 m.-0.012 m.; min. w. stem 0.003 m. Slightly convex head. Stem, rectangular in section, expands nearly to full diameter of cap. Point missing.

(d) h. 0.011 m.; d. head 0.009 m.; min. w. stem 0.0035 m. Very similar to (c). Shaft, square in section, does not expand quite to full diameter of cap. Blunt tip or point missing (very corroded).

(e) h. 0.012 m.; d. head 0.0105 m.; max. w. stem 0.007 m. Flat top. Traces of silver on top or bronze corrosion; convex cap missing. Shaft rounded oblong in section and slightly askew. Does not quite expand to diameter of cap. Blunt tip.

(f) h. 0.012 m.; d. head 0.0095 m.; th. stem 0.004 m. Heavily corroded. More like (b) than others but stem rounded and off axis. Blunt tip slightly bent.

Leg of bronze vessel? (NM. 7945, Fig. 194:6): h. pres. 0.0565 m.; w. 0.015 m.; w. stem 0.004 m. Fair condition. Shaft of leg square in section; end bent over into scroll or spiral.

Three laminae with stump of handle, belonging to small vessels (NM. 7944, NM. 7945). Largest fragment 0.022 m. wide. Stump of round handle (d. ca. 0.005 m.) on each fragment. Piece of gold foil adhering to back of one lamina.

Loop-handle (NM. 7944, Fig. 195:4): h. 0.017 m.; w. at bottom 0.018 m.; th. han. 0.0025 m. Small part of body preserved. Handle distorted; impossible to determine whether attached vertically or at an angle. Probably handle of small bowl like that found in Grave Circle (see Figs. 227:3, 228:2).

What may have been similar handle found in another part of tomb: five fragments of curved bronze in a line. Too badly preserved for restoration or accurate measurement.

Three scroll handles, fragments only (NM. 7946, Fig. 195:5). Best example: l. pres. 0.023 m.; d. loop 0.012 m.; th. 0.001 m. Thin wire with end bent over to form loop. If a handle, it is of type illustrated in *EphArch* 1889, pl. 8:3 from Vapheio and *Gournia*, pl. IV:68 but it may not be a handle at all. Shape close to bronze spiral fragment found at Kakovatos (*AM* XXXIV [1909], pl. XIII:43).

Rim of small vessel? H. 0.006 m.; w. 0.018 m. Small lamina with overhanging rounded lip, ca. 0.002 m. thick; two similar fragments.

Base of vessel? Fragment only. L. 0.034 m.; w. 0.021 m.; h. 0.009 m.; th. 0.0015 m. Fragment has raised flat surface with rounded edge. Rest of piece is at an obtuse angle (not pronounced) to the flat ledge. Whole fragment possibly part of bronze vessel with raised base like that on silver cup from Dendra (*RT,Dendra*, 50, fig. 29). Curved lamina, ca. 0.04 m. x 0.03 m. possibly silver-plated, found elsewhere may be part of this object.

Two coils (NM. 7944) like that found in doorway (see p. 111). Best example: l. 0.0145 m.; d. 0.006 m.

Gilt laminae? (NM. 7925?). Two bronze pieces stuck together with gold foil between. Dimensions: ca. 0.021 m. x 0.018 m. The gold may have been imprisoned there fortuitously.

Very numerous fragments of bronze wire: 12 markedly bent; four curved; longest piece (chord measurement) 0.055 m. Some possibly silver-plated (blue surface). It is doubtful whether many of these straight wire fragments were parts of pins: they are consistently of the same diameter and the two obvious pins recorded above have tapering stems. Exact purpose of so much "wiring" is difficult to determine, but in the Grave Circle it was used for reinforcing silver metal work (see p. 156). It would also serve in cabinet making in the form of dowel pins.

Sword laminae? Four fragments, two fairly large: (a) 0.062 m. x 0.037 m., (b) 0.045 m. x 0.025 m. Possibly from swords and daggers.

Sword or dagger blade. Crushed fragment, folded over lengthwise and heavily corroded.

Rivets, 16 large (NM. 7925). No sword or dagger found in tomb, only an occasional fragment that may have belonged to one or other; but great number of rivets recovered. Length varies between 0.02 m. to 0.025 m. (three of 0.02 m., two of 0.021 m., one of 0.022 m., three of 0.023 m., one of 0.024 m., four of 0.025 m., two fragmentary). Diameter of head averages 0.012 m. In three examples both ends of rivet have gold caps. One loose gold cap, one perhaps silver-plated (NM. 7909-10); three plain bronze (NM. 7945). One rivet exceptionally has domed caps (NM. 7944). A single domed cap (d. 0.0185 m.) too large for average rivet. Shafts, usually narrower than head, round in section but four rectangular.

Rivets, 24 small (NM. 7924). Nearly all badly distorted, length varying from 0.007 m. to 0.012 m. (eight of 0.009 m., seven of 0.01 m., three of 0.011 m., four of 0.012 m.). One exceptionally small (0.006 m.); another exceptionally long and thin (l. 0.019 m.; w. 0.003 m.) is one of best preserved. D. of head averages 0.006 m. Six rivets with gilt heads or gold adhering, one possibly had silver-plated caps. Shafts round in section, usually with about same diameter as head. Many of these rivets belong to daggers but some must have supplemented the riveting of swords and rapiers. Very small rivet probably from knife or tool. Total number of average size rivets would account for at least eight weapons.

Knife or dagger hilt, flanged (NM. 7948): l. pres. 0.058 m.; w. 0.017 m.; d. 0.012 m. Heavily corroded. Flanges folded over to hold hilt pieces (cf. *Schachtgräber*, pl. XCVII: 450). This type hilt fairly common; several examples found in nearby Grave Circle. For straight-sided flange cf. *BSA* XXV (1921-23),

290-91, fig. 51, from the Cyclopean Tomb; and *Schachtgräber,* 140, fig. 57:738 from Shaft Grave v. Because of its small size this fragment presumably belonged to knife rather than dagger.

Spearhead? (NM. 7954, Figs. 194:7, 195:11): l. pres. 0.09 m.; w. 0.0185 m.; d. shaft 0.012 m. Fragment. Very corroded. Solid midrib. Only part of blade preserved, shape uncertain, but probably point of a spearhead of kind often found in Minoan and Mycenaean contexts (*PM* iv, ii, 844, fig. 825 and *ChT,* pl. vii from Mycenae acropolis). Although its core is solid, spearhead from Prosymna is also solid at pointed end (*Prosymna,* fig. 608, below) and other spearheads may have been made in this way (*Schachtgräber,* pl. xcvi:902, 903, 910, 933 from Shaft Grave vi).

Spearhead base ring? (NM. 7960): d. estimated 0.035 m.; th. ca. 0.005 m. Very corroded condition. Two curved fragments of ring of semicircular section. Flat inner surface preserves small part of tubular plate. Not therefore a finger-ring but more likely a securing ring at butt of spearhead of type referred to above (cf. *Schachtgräber,* pl. xcvii:449). Several other curved bits of laminae possibly belonging to this object.

Arrowheads, 12 (NM. 7943, Fig. 194:2-5), nearly all in very bad state of preservation and much corroded. At least four different types recognizable:

(a) One example (Fig. 194:2) like that from blocking wall (see p. 112): l. 0.05 m.; w. ca. 0.013 m. Point broken, now separate. Tips of barbs missing. Well-known type (see *Prosymna,* 340-42).

(b) Two examples:

(i) (Fig. 194:3) L. pres. 0.044 m.; d. 0.005 m.; d. butt 0.0045 m. Round section with slight expansion in diameter nearer point. Apparently

javelin point (see *Prosymna,* 340 and fig. 361:3)[57] but only head preserved with strong resemblance to object that Sir Arthur Evans identified as a locking-pin (*PM* iii, 12, fig. 6 and *PM* iv, ii, 995, fig. 946).

(ii) L. pres. 0.031 m.; w. 0.0075 m.; th. 0.005 m. Same type but even worse preserved.

(c) One example (Fig. 195:12c): l. pres. 0.021 m.; w. 0.016 m.; th. ca. 0.006 m. Point missing. Midrib on each face with blades of uncertain profile. Butt appears to be socketed. This type may be related to one found in the Palace of Nestor (*PN* i, 240, fig. 292); cf. also *Annuario* vi-vii (1926), 220, fig. 142 (4787) and *Deltion* 3 (1917), p. 188, fig. 134:6.

(d) Three examples

(i) (Fig. 195:12d) L. 0.053 m.; w. 0.017 m. In three fragments but shape preserved: isosceles triangle with slight re-entrant in the narrow butt. Upper and lower faces are coming apart, giving the impression that arrowhead has slots on each side. Broad midrib, not very pronounced, down center.

(ii) (Fig. 194:5) L. 0.031 m.; w. 0.008 m. Profile preserved. Smaller than preceding with hold near butt for hafting. No midrib.

(iii) (Fig. 194:4) L. pres. 0.0285 m.; w. 0.0125 m.; w. of break 0.0055 m.; th. 0.002 m. Point and part of butt missing. Part of hole near butt preserved. If complete, it would be midway in size between (i) and (ii). No midrib apparent.[58]

(e) Five examples, either fragments of type (a) or variants of (d):

(i) L. pres. 0.033 m.; w. 0.015 m.; th. ca. 0.007 m. Butt missing. Upper and lower faces breaking apart. If this

---

[57] Cf. also *Asine,* 390, 2.C (389, fig. 252) "solid, squarely hammered bronze rod with a swelling at one end hammered into a point."

[58] This fragmentary arrowhead, however, may be of type (a) as it very much resembles fragment illustrated in *Prosymna,* fig. 440:3 (last on right).

arrowhead had been preserved in its entirety, it would probably compare with (d:i) in length but butt would be broader. An alternative possibility is that it is a large version of *Prosymna*, fig. 512:1 (described as a javelin-point, *ibid.,* 340). It is notably thick. Cf. also *PN* I, 218, fig. 291:22.

(ii) L. estimated 0.026 m.; w. 0.012 m. Two nonjoining fragments: point and part of body. Appears to be triangular but shape uncertain.

(iii) and (iv) Two arrowheads of isosceles triangular shape. Better preserved in four pieces (l. ca. 0.033 m.; w. butt perhaps 0.01 m.); the other in two fragments, not properly measurable.

(v) L. pres. 0.0185 m.; w. 0.008 m.; th. 0.003 m. profile completely gone; possibly not an arrowhead.

Fragment of stem, square in section (l. 0.04 m.; w. 0.005 m.), possibly tang of javelin-point like that illustrated in *Prosymna,* fig. 361:4. Compare *KG,* pl. IX:9.

Of the classes of arrowheads listed above only (a) is a familiar type. The javelin-point (b) is not common. I have not come across any record or illustration of the type referred to under (d), the shape of which seems to be based on a rare form of flint arrowhead (see p. 127).

Great quantities of bronze fragments, mostly small strips, filled 125 boxes of 20-cigarette size.

STONE

Amethyst bead seal (NM. 7983, Fig. 193:1a-c = *CMS* I, No. 290): l. 0.0285 m.; w. 0.018 m.; th. 0.009 m. Amygdaloid shape. Back carved with five longitudinal ribs, curved and graduated to shape of seal, central rib wider than others and rounded. Perforation along long axis. Impression shows vivid scene of man attacking a lioness standing on hind legs. With one arm man thrusts

sword down its throat and with other hand holds it by the neck.[59] Scabbard hanging from belt flung backwards by violence of action, adding considerably to strong sense of movement in the design. Man, apparently bearded, wears a kilt.

Amethyst bead seal (NM. 7984, Fig. 193:3a, b = *CMS* I, No. 291): l. 0.021 m.; w. 0.015 m. Amygdaloid shape, shorter than preceding. Back plain. Obverse side presents fine carving of cow with calf. Head of cow turned to rear; shown in profile but horns are depicted full face. Calf apparently behind forelegs of cow, its stance similar but head faces the other way. Only one of its horns is shown. Not clear what the object is to right of cow's nose, or what is happening at her rear; it looks as if a third animal, perhaps another calf, is climbing onto her back.

Lentoid seal, lapis lazuli (NM. 7982, Fig. 193:4a, b = *CMS* I No. 289): d. 0.018 m.; th. 0.007 m. Poor quality. Lentoid shape but sides with string-holes cut vertically. Perforation made from one side only. Design of shaggy wild goat?, male, standing in grass with head turned back towards tail which is erect. Only one horn in profile indicated. A javelin, shown diagonally, pierces back just behind shoulders.

Bead seal, lapis lazuli[60] (NM. 7981, Fig. 193:2a, b = *CMS* I, No. 288): l. 0.0155 m.; w. 0.01 m.; th. 0.004 m. Poor quality, burnt. Shape pseudo-pentagonal in section; two of the five sides, broader than others, slightly curved combined to produce single convex surface. Seal impression of walking lioness with head turned back toward tail, which is erect and curled over in direction of head to balance composition. Tail ends in a tuft. Claws clearly delineated.

Amethyst beads (NM. 7892-3), 246 nearly all in good condition. Color mostly "amethyst" blue, some very dark, a few very light blue. Perforations usually made from both ends to meet in middle, rarely miscalculated. If

[59] Cf. interpretation of scene expressed in *CMS*.

[60] See footnote 39, p. 111.

worked from one end only, bore hole tapers.

177 spherical (Fig. 194:36, 39) (*Prosymna*, fig. 599:1) with diameters ranging from 0.0045 m. to 0.0135 m.

4	d. 0.005 m.	13	d. 0.011 m.
16	d. 0.007 m.	12	d. 0.012 m.
54	d. 0.008 m.	3	d. 0.013 m.
49	d. 0.009 m.	4	d. 0.014 m.
22	d. 0.010 m.		

The other 69 can be divided into the following categories:

(a) 27 flattened spherical[61] (NM. 7895, Fig. 194:35):

1	d. 0.006 m.	2	d. 0.01 m.
4	d. 0.007 m.	2	d. 0.011 m.
11	d. 0.008 m.	1	d. 0.012 m.
5	d. 0.009 m.	1	d. 0.013 m.

(b) 9 carinated (NM. 7897, Fig. 194:14): one with d. 0.008 m.; four 0.009 m., four 0.01 m.

(c) 9 pear-shaped[62] (NM. 7897, Fig. 194: 15), one with l. 0.011 m., two 0.012 m., one 0.014 m., two 0.016 m., one 0.017 m., one 0.018 m., one 0.023 m. Longest bead ribbed, unlike others (Fig. 195:6). Maximum d. 0.0095 m. Ratio of length to maximum diameter usually two to one.

(d) 7 oval (NM. 7896?, Fig. 194:38): three with l. 0.007 m., one 0.008 m., two 0.01 m., one 0.011 m. Diameter usually one millimeter less than length.

(e) 5 lozenge[63] (NM. 7899?, Fig. 194:38): one with l. 0.009 m., two 0.013 m., one 0.014 m., one 0.019 m. Ratio of length to diameter just under two to one.

(f) 5 with two string-holes (NM. 7893?, Fig. 194:37): These beads bored along different axes to one another. All spherical (one flattened spherical). Four have d. of 0.009 m.; one with d. 0.01 m. of interest because one bore has gold lining (Fig. 195:7). Bead badly cracked around its circumference; apparently it broke into two halves and was repaired with gold rivet, a new bore being made for the purpose. An amethyst bead with gold lining was found in tholos near Menidi (*KG*, pl. III:6) and one with two string-holes is mentioned as coming from a tomb in Thebes (*EphArch* 1910, 219, No. 2). Latter type may have been used as spacer bead. Compare the bead arrangement in a fresco (*Pseira*, pl. v).

(g) 7 beads of various forms (NM. 7898?):

(i) Tubular (Fig. 194:21; a shorter version of *ChT*, pl. IX:4c): l. 0.013 m.; d. 0.0095 m. Markedly tapering bore-hole.

(ii) Drum (Fig. 194:22): l. 0.006 m.; d. 0.0085 m. Beveled edges.

(iii) Cod-faced (Fig. 195:9): l. 0.0095 m.; h. 0.012 m.; th. 0.007 m. Elliptical shape in plan, but with transverse string-hole. Sides with perforation flattened. Bore-hole slightly asymmetrical.

(iv) Scarab (Figs. 194:25, 195:8): l. 0.0115 m.; w. 0.0085 m.; th. 0.006 m. String-hole passes through long axis. Underside plain; slightly domed upper surface engraved at broader end with equilateral triangle, of which the lines do not join. Apex directed toward end of bead. Stylistic rendering of head of beetle. Compare *ChT*, pl. IX:1.

(v) Flat-sided lozenge (Fig. 194:23): l. 0.0135 m.; w. 0.0025 m.-0.008 m.; th. 0.005 m. Shape that of an ordinary lozenge bead, but a third of it has been cut off along long axis giving it a flat undersurface.

(vi) Pentagonal (NM. 7896, Fig. 194: 19): l. 0.0185 m.; w. 0.006 m.-0.0135 m.; th. 0.008 m. String-hole in long axis. Three faces equal sided, other

---

[61] *Prosymna*, fig. 599:2.

[62] *ChT*, pl. VIII:36b.

[63] *Prosymna*, fig. 599:5.

two broader and slightly curved. The latter would be the visible faces. Very light blue, practically quartz color.

(vii) Pear-shaped pendant (Fig. 194: 24): l. 0.0135 m.; w. 0.01 m. Lower end pointed. Perforation at broad end.

Three carnelian beads (NM. 7927, Fig. 194: 59-61). Two spherical, d. 0.0075 m. and 0.004 m. Third (w. 0.006 m.; th. 0.0035 m.) a quatrefoil of four tiny spheres joined together in same plane. Bore-hole common to all four. This type of bead quite common in gold but rare in stone.[64] For examples in gold see *AM* xxxiv (1909), pl. xiii:38, 39 from Kakovatos; *RT,Dendra,* pl. xxvii; *KG,* pl. v:29; *BSA* xxv (1921-23), 381, fig. 88:q from Tomb of Genii.

Four flattened spherical beads (NM. 7926-27) two probably steatite, two unknown:

(a) d. ca. 0.015 m.; th. 0.009 m. Broken. Mottled black and dirty yellow. Steatite?

(b) d. 0.006 m.; th. 0.0035 m. Steatite?

(c) (Fig. 194:54) d. 0.011 m.; th. 0.007 m. Pink with dirty yellow veins.

(d) d. 0.085 m. Dirty gray.

Cylindrical bead, steatite? (NM. 7927, Fig. 194:52): l. 0.017 m.; d. 0.0055 m., irregular in section. Top surface worn away at both ends. Mottled blue in color.

Two drum-shaped beads. One (NM. 7927) blue steatite (d. 0.0075 m.; w. 0.0045 m.), one (NM. 7930) quartz (d. 0.007 m.; w. 0.004 m.).

Bead of irregular shape (NM. 7927, Fig. 194:57): l. 0.0145 m.; w. 0.0135 m.; th. 0.005 m.; d. hole 0.004 m. Stone classification unknown. Roughly circular in plan with slight protuberance. Dark brown. Polished surface on one side.

Two fossilized? beads (NM. 7928):

(a) shape of snail or spiral: d. 0.017 m.; d. hole 0.0025 m.; th. 0.013 m. String-hole passes through "eye" of spiral. Yellowish-brown and gritty, red in one spot. Fossilized snail?

(b) tubular (Fig. 194:52), remains broken at both ends: l. 0.016 m.; d. 0.004 m. Corroded, yellow outer surface. Breaks show up as black. Fossilized twig?

Fragment of bead (NM. 7927). Not measurable. Brown pebble, polished.

Four black steatite disks (NM. 7978). Two have d. of 0.009 m., two of 0.0085 m. Thickness of all 0.0015 m. Black glass-like surface. Very decorative, probably used as inlays.

Whorl of schist[65] (NM. 7952, Fig. 194:18): d. 0.049 m.; d. hole 0.007 m.-0.009 m.; th. 0.006 m. Greenish-gray. Edges beveled to rounded. Central hole has been bored from both sides, hence it has an hourglass section.

Whorl or button (NM. 7942, Fig. 194:34): h. 0.0265 m.; d. 0.012 m.-0.0335 m. Piece broken off edge. Soft limestone. Very powdery surface. Carinated, convex above carination, conical below. Pierced vertically with central bore, 0.004 m. in diameter. This seems to be a stone version of the well-known Late Helladic I and II whorls (or buttons) in clay.

Pommel of dagger (NM. 7977, Fig. 195:10): h. 0.042 m.; w. 0.05 m.; w. base 0.036 m. Limestone. In very poor condition; surface crumbly as if burnt. Roughly spherical with flattened bottom. Hole (d. 0.022 m., ca. 0.02 m. deep) bored in underside for tang of dagger, tapers to point. Another hole (d. 0.01 m.) bored ca. 0.004 m. from base at right angles to first for locking pin, extends right through to the other side. Beyond tang hole, channel slightly wider and smoother. This can be observed because part of the base that at one time obscured it has given way. Apparently this was original part of bore-hole; when it

---

[64] I owe this information to Mrs. Hughes-Brock and I should like to express my appreciation for all the help she has given, particularly in regard to the paste beads.

[65] See footnote 39, p. 111.

broke another perforation made from other side in same axis. Shape of pommel similar to *Schachtgräber,* 98, fig. 30, also 140, fig. 57: 778b and c and *PM* IV, ii, 931, fig. 902.

Pommel of sword (NM. 7955, Figs. 194:33, 195:13): h. pres. 0.029 m.; d. 0.064 m. Alabaster, probably Egyptian.[66] Upper surface white polished in fair condition, though pitted. Under surface much worn; much of base missing. Pommel roughly lentoid in section. Under part convex turning downward at almost right angles to form upper part of hilt. Tubular socket bored in center of base to depth of ca. 0.015 m. for tang. Transverse perforation for locking pin no longer exists, but outline of groove preserved in damaged part of base. Slight ridge on underside of pommel just below carination. For shape cf. *Schachtgräber,* pl. LXXVI:484. This also ridged on undersurface (*ibid.,* 108).

Celt (NM. 7956, Fig. 194:17): l. 0.09 m.; w. ca. 0.015 m.-0.03 m.; th. 0.0295 m. Hard, dark, metamorphic rock, purplish-black with brown patches. Serpentine.[67] Neolithic type. Shape in plan roughly that of tall truncated cone. In section biconical (one short, one narrow cone). Butt and sides rounded. Ca. 0.018 m. from functional end, the two faces ground down to meet in cutting edge. Beveled faces very worn near cutting edge. A hoard of apparently similar type of celt found at Lerna (*Hesperia* XXVI [1957], pl. 49:b).

Flint arrowheads, 42 of miter form (NM. 7900, Fig. 194:8-13). Variations in form; six different types noted (Fig. 226). Not intended to suggest any typological progression in the series—probably all contemporary—but they are useful for purposes of classification. (Karo distinguishes four types—*Schachtgräber,* 113.) Many arrowheads incomplete, many lacking tip or barbs particularly, but enough preserved to say that estimate of 42 is conservative.

Arrowheads have been made up, or partly made up, from fragments found in different parts of the tholos and in at least one case joining pieces were not only separated by several meters but also by many levels. Seventeen complete, or almost complete: lengths 0.018 m. to 0.04 m. (one 0.018 m., two 0.02 m., two 0.025 m., one 0.026 m., one 0.028 m., two 0.03 m., one 0.031 m., one 0.032 m., one 0.033 m., one 0.038 m., two 0.039 m., two 0.04 m.). Subdivision into types (Fig. 226): Type I one, Type II two, Type III one, Type IV two, Type V three, Type VI twenty-seven, six indeterminate (barbs not preserved).

Type VI predominates in flint arrowheads, but not in case of obsidian. Both faces of arrowheads show secondary working. Color usually dark brown; several examples of banded flint, i.e., dark brown combined with yellow.

Obsidian arrowheads, 24 of miter form (NM. 7900). Ten well-preserved, varying in length (one 0.02 m., two 0.022 m., one 0.023 m., one 0.024 m., one 0.025 m., one 0.031 m., one 0.033 m., one 0.034 m., one 0.038 m.). In general, obsidian arrowhead smaller than its counterpart in flint. Joining pieces from widely dispersed parts of tomb contribute two to total of 10 well-preserved specimens. Types (cf. Fig. 226): Type IV ten, Type V three, Type VI nine, two indeterminate.

Types IV and VI are here about equally represented. Types differentiated from one another by degree of angle at butt: Type I, very obtuse; Type III, right angle; Types IV and V, acute; Type VI, semicircular notch (Fig. 194:13). Type IV is midway between Types III and V. Types II and III are thicker than others. Type I in class by itself, but bronze arrowheads described under paragraph (d) on p. 124 seem to be copied from it.

Type I represented by one example each at Mycenae (*Schachtgräber,* pl. CI, last

---

[66] See footnote 39, p. 111.

[67] See footnote 39, p. 111.

in top row) and Kakovatos (*AM* xxxiv [1909], pl. xv:7). Two similar specimens from Dendra (*NT,Dendra* 46, fig. 51) but small notch in butt allies them with Type vi. Possibly Type i is an unfinished form of Type vi. Types v and vi are represented on most sites. Type vi is more popular at Dendra (*ibid.*). Type iv (or iii) predominates at Kephalovrison, Messenia (*Praktika* 1964, pl. 88:4).

The obsidian from Tholos iv not uniform in color, though predominantly black: three are light gray, one light blue, and two translucent. Same high standard of workmanship maintained as with flint. Obsidian flake: l. pres. 0.019 m.; w. 0.0125 m.; th. 0.0025 m. Broken blade. Two facets on upper surface, bulb of percussion below. No secondary working. Shiny surface, slightly translucent.

AMBER

Spacer bead (NM. 7940, Figs. 194:46, 195: 18): h. 0.0245 m.; w. 0.014 m.-0.036 m.; th. 0.005 m. In very poor condition but complete. Shape trapezoidal. Pierced longitudinally with five string-holes, three starting from top of trapezoid and one from each side, all five finishing at broad base. Bore-holes at different angles to conform with shape of bead.

Fragments of four or five similar spacer beads, from Shaft Grave iv (*Schachtgräber*, pl. lvii:513), have five string-holes but square or oblong shape. Of four amber spacers from Grave Omicron in the new Grave Circle[68] three, with complex V-borings, resemble well-known illustrated example from Tholos A at Kakovatos (*AM* xxxiv [1909], 280, fig. 4) but no such type

has been found in tholoi near Palace of Nestor. On other hand, Tholos iv example finds its replica at Kakovatos—though latter has nine string-holes—(*ibid.*, fig. 3) and appears to be identical with two examples from a burial in Lake, Wiltshire (*ProcPS*, N.S. iv [1938], pl. x, the two terminal plates[69]). The connection between Kakovatos beads and those in Central Europe and in England has long been recognized, although emphasis has naturally been on very unusual beads with complex V-borings.[70] Milojcic suggests that on account of finer quality of Kakovatos and Mycenae specimens they were made in Greece from imported amber and re-exported to England and Central Europe (*Germania* xxxiii [1955], 319). R. Hachmann (*Bayerische Vorgeschichtsblätter* 22, p. 20) points out that Greek examples have greater similarity with British than Central European products and he is of opinion that they were most probably imported from Wessex. In so far as Tholos iv spacer is concerned, which is a terminal plate and not complicated spacer bead under discussion, there is every indication that it was made in England; in any event connections, direct or indirect, between the two areas are undoubted.

Spacer bead (NM. 7939). Fragments only. Largest fragment: l. pres. 0.017 m.; w. 0.013 m. Two holes preserved. Shape seems same as that described above.

Flattened spherical beads, 355 (NM. 7936-8, NM. 7941, Fig. 194:48, 49) in various states of preservation: 267 measurable, many only partly preserved. The balance, though recognized as beads at time of finding, have largely disintegrated. Their sizes

---

[68] V. Milojcic, "Bernsteinschieber aus Griechenland," *Germania* xxxiii (1955), 317, fig. 1. See also G. E. Mylonas, *Mycenae and the Mycenaean Age* (Princeton, 1966), fig. 102.

[69] Other examples from Lake are illustrated in *Bayerische Vorgeschichtsblätter* 22 (1957), p. 31, fig. 12. The following offer parallels to the Tholos iv spacer bead: Nos. 16, 19, 20, 25, 26.

[70] S. Piggott, "The Early Bronze Age in Wessex," *ProcPS* N.S. iv (1938), 52-106. For recent discussion see R. Hachmann, "Bronzezeitliche Bernsteinschieber," *Bayerische Vorgeschichtsblätter* 22 (1957), 1-36 and N. K. Sandars, "Amber spacer-beads again," *Antiquity* xxxiii, iv (1959), 292-95. See also G. V. Merhart "Die Bernsteinschieber von Kakovatos," *Germania* xxiv (1940), 99-102.

vary enormously and a breakdown of diameters is given hereunder:

beads	diameter	beads	diameter
8	0.005 m.	4	0.016 m.
15	0.006 m.	4	0.017 m.
28	0.007 m.	3	0.018 m.
44	0.008 m.	2	0.019 m.
50	0.009 m.	2	0.020 m.
38	0.010 m.	1	0.021 m.
22	0.011 m.	3	0.022 m.
16	0.012 m.	1	0.024 m.
9	0.013 m.	1	0.029 m.[71]
7	0.014 m.	1	0.030 m.
7	0.015 m.	1	0.034 m.

Greater part of beads ranged between diameters of 0.006 m. and 0.012 m. (213). Largest bead (Fig. 194:45) d. 0.034 m., th. 0.022, well-preserved though slightly damaged.

Amber was imported throughout whole of Mycenaean period (*Prosymna*, 286) but greatest quantity found in tombs of Late Helladic I and II, notably in Shaft Graves and at Kakovatos where about 500 beads recovered (*AM* XXXIV [1909], 278). Amber is generally supposed to have been imported from Baltic through intermediaries who specialized in this trade[72] and undoubtedly most of it came from that quarter, but a limited test, carried out recently by Prof. Curt W. Beck of Vassar College, on four fragments of amber from nearby Grave Circle (see p. 162) showed that two of them were not of Baltic origin, although alternative source of origin could not be identified.[73] It is only fair to add, however, that the non-Baltic specimens are not beads but probably talismans.

Three carinated beads (NM. 7937). All of large size and comparatively well-preserved:

(a) (Figs. 194:44, 195:22): d. 0.022 m.-0.031 m.; th. 0.010 m.

(b) d. 0.014 m.-0.023 m.; th. 0.011 m.

(c) d. 0.0165 m.; th. 0.0085 m.

Lozenge bead? (NM. 7937): l. pres. ca. 0.018 m.; w. ca. 0.013 m. Fragmentary, and only partly preserved.

Cylindrical bead (NM. 7937): l. ca. 0.023 m.; d. ca. 0.018 m. Fragile; half preserved (the long axis).

Six unclassified (NM. 7939): lumps of amber of irregular shapes, probably talismans. Only one perforated. Mostly in fair state of preservation.

(a) Square: l. 0.013 m.; w. 0.014 m.; th. 0.005 m.

(b) Square: l. 0.009 m.; w. 0.009 m.; th. 0.006 m.

(c) Irregular oblong (Fig. 194:47): l. 0.0255 m.; w. 0.017 m.; th. 0.013 m. Powdery surface.

(d) Quadrant of circle: l. 0.026 m.; w. 0.02 m.; th. 0.018 m. If bead, d. estimated ca. 0.045 m.

(e) Cylindrical (NM. 7937): l. ca. 0.016 m.; d. 0.009 m. "Cylinder" slightly cambered.

(f) Shapeless: l. 0.016 m.; w. 0.010 m.; th. 0.005 m. Only lump with part of perforation. Possibly worn as pendant.

All amber in the tomb has weathered to dark brown, crumbly surface; sometimes color light brown on outside. Larger beads, when broken, show glasslike texture of original substance.

IVORY

Figure-of-eight shield (NM. 7934?, Figs. 194:42, 195:16): l. pres. 0.062 m.; w. waist pres. 0.02 m.; w. upper lobe 0.031 m.; w. lower lobe 0.041 m.; th. with handle 0.018 m.; th. without handle 0.014 m.; min. th.

---

[71] Fig. 194:43.

[72] J. M. de Navarro, "Prehistoric routes between Northern Europe and Italy defined by the Amber Trade," *Geographical Journal* LXVI (1925), 481-507.

[73] Information kindly supplied by Prof. Beck in a letter. A discussion of the whole problem, but not dealing specifically with the amber from the Grave Circle, is contained in *Archaeometry* 8 (1965), 96-109. C. Beck, E. Wilbur, S. Meret, D. Kossove and K. Kermani, "The infrared spectra of amber and the identification of Baltic amber."

0.0025 m. About four-fifths preserved. Pieces missing. Repaired. Back flat; from it projects "strap" handle parallel to back and 0.004 m. distant. Shield of usual type with convex upper surface rising from the extremities to reach its highest point at waist. Rim (w. 0.002 m.) square-cut and offset, thickness varying from 0.0025 m. at extremities to 0.0035 m. at waist. Several large ivory shields from Mycenae chamber tombs are displayed in National Museum. One example (7102) is about same size as Pylos specimen. Similar shield of ivory from Menidi (*KG,* pl. VI:13) has same type of handle or buckle but shield pierced with two holes for suspension. Cf. also one about same size from Mycenae, but underside of shield is different (*BSA* 52 [1957], pl. 40:b).

Cylindrical bead (NM. 7930): l. unknown; d. 0.008 m.; d. perforation 0.0045 m. Fragmentary. Not certain that it is ivory.

Finial of chair arm? (NM. 7935, Figs. 194:41, 195:17): d. 0.065 m.; th. 0.019 m.-0.0225 m.; Mortice: l. 0.03 m.; w. 0.0275 m.; depth ca. 0.017 m. D. locking pin bore 0.006 m. to 0.008 m. (elliptical). Restored from many pieces. Almost complete. Thick disk of slightly uneven depth. One side shaved off to take a thin, rectangular sliver of ivory. Although under surface of sliver worn, apparently not a break. On underside of disk (Fig. 194:41) a square mortice (one side broken) has been sunk with tiny recesses in each corner, possibly drilled holes to facilitate insertion of saw. Hole bored transversely for locking pin which passes through mortice area to the other side. A much smaller bore-hole drilled diagonally from circumference to under surface quite close to flattened side of disk.

The smooth outer surface shows the elliptical graining of the ivory and presumably this side faced the beholder. Flattened side of disk would then be fitted on a wooden upright of the chair and the arm-rest would be morticed into the disk. An alternative arrangement is unlikely because the armrest, being subjected to greater pressure than the upright, would need the stronger support of the mortice joint.[74] Purpose of smaller locking pin not clear; at angle of hole the pin can supply very little reinforcement to the armrest. Smaller locking-pin presumably made of bronze. Whatever other interpretation one chooses to put on the use of this object, one has to admire the high degree of excellence in the workmanship, which implies an advanced knowledge of joinery.

Plaque (NM. 7976): l. 0.053 m.; w. 0.013 m.; th. 0.002 m. No decoration visible.

Five tapering cylindrical fragments, perhaps parts of legs of some small chest? None complete. Dimensions of three best preserved:

(a) l. pres. 0.055 m.; d. 0.009 m.-0.017 m.
(b) l. pres. 0.027 m.; d. 0.006 m.-0.013 m.
(c) l. pres. 0.023 m.; d. 0.011 m.-0.0135 m.

Several curved fragments possibly belong to these legs. Largest piece remarkably like an ivory fragment from the Palace of Nestor described as a handle (*PN* I, 155, fig. 285:21). These fragments may also be parts of handles.

Several amorphous groups of ivory found but nothing could be made of them. Many other small fragments, though conserved, are not worth recording. Only fragment that showed some working is small piece with beveled edge (l. 0.0155 m.; w. 0.0145 m.; th. 0.004 m.).

BOAR'S TUSKS

Three examples (NM. 7951, Fig. 194:27-32), two complete. Best preserved (Fig. 194:31) cut to oblong shape (l. 0.0455 m.; w. 0.0215 m.; th. 0.004 m.) has two pairs of bore-holes, drilled from each of long edges of tusk and directed diagonally to under surface so they would not show. The pairs are not opposite one another but staggered.

[74] I have to thank Mr. James Coulton for useful suggestions on the technical aspects.

Cf. *ChT*, pl. xxx:46d which shows one pair of such drill holes.

Numerous fragments (NM. 7951), many apparently unworked or at least uncut. Four pieces have bore-holes like that described above; in two pieces, holes pass through material from front to back. One specimen has two holes in back; a break in crust shows that perforation was made in a loop to come out on same side without touching the front, i.e., a V-perforation. Surviving remnants suggest that at least one boar's-tusk helmet was in this tomb.

BONE

Bone spacer? fragment: l. 0.0205 m.; w. 0.0055 m.; th. 0.0045 m. Roughly semicircular in section. Possibly segment of a spacer of the kind published by Wace (*ChT*, 66, fig. 25:5b). Many beads of this type in glass were found in the tholos (see below).

Three pins? (NM. 7950). Fragments only. All tapering but, with exception of one, seem too large for pins.

(a) l. pres. 0.0125 m.; d. 0.0035 m.-0.0055 m.

(b) l. pres. 0.0245 m.; d. 0.0055 m.-0.0095 m.

(c) l. pres. 0.026 m.; d. 0.0055 m.-0.0115 m. Ellipsoidal in section.

Pins, 18 additional fragments.

FAIENCE[75]

Eleven beads (NM. 7926), with one exception in fairly good condition. Blue in color.

(a) Six spherical (four d. 0.009 m.; two d. 0.003 m.).

(b) Three flattened spherical: one (NM. 7979?) very large and well-preserved, d. 0.019 m., th. 0.014 m., d. hole 0.0035 m.; one, d. 0.009 m.; one, d. 0.006 m.

(c) One oval (l. 0.006 m.; d. 0.006 m.). Irregular outline. Light blue.

(d) Fragment only of very large bead (Fig. 194:55) shape uncertain (l. pres. 0.0105 m.; w. 0.011 m.; th. 0.008 m.). Appar-

ently painted with some sign (Fig. 195:21), although this may be fortuitous. Glaze has gone completely and only white frit remains.

Fragments of faience or glass paste:

(a) Two pieces of about same thickness (i) l. 0.013 m.; w. 0.016 m.; th. 0.0035 m. (ii) l. 0.0155 m.; w. 0.0235 m.; th. 0.003 m. White. Powdery surface.

(b) One fragment with traces of black-brown glaze: l. 0.0135 m.; w. 0.006 m.; th. 0.006 m. White, powdery texture.

PASTE

Two fluted spacer beads. Each consists of two vertically fluted oval beads set side by side with rounded ridge between and plain border above and below following their contour and that of the ridge. Each bead pierced with string-hole in axis. Back of the spacer flat. Type almost exactly that found at Mycenae (*ChT*, 66, fig. 25:5c).

(a) NM. 7933 (Fig. 194:20), complete, in very fragile state: l. 0.03 m.-0.0385 m.; w. 0.0265 m.; th. 0.0055 m.-0.0115 m. Bluish-white core with patina of yellowish-brown.

(b) NM. 7931 Half only, condition fair: l. 0.0135 m.-0.023 m.; w. 0.026 m.; th. 0.0065 m.-0.013 m. Blue glass. The complete fluted bead has string-hole preserved. Several fragments (NM. 7930) possibly belonging to other half found in three different places, widely dispersed.

This is a rare type. I know of no other example except the one found at Mycenae, but fragments of another such bead were found in nearby Grave Circle (see p. 170).

Eight multitubular spacer beads (NM. 7929, NM. 7931, NM. 7932) consisting of four cylindrical or tubular beads laid side by side in a row. Back of spacer flat. Two string-holes usually placed below junctions of first two and last two beads respectively (see *ChT*, 66, fig. 25:5b).

[75] It is not certain that all these objects are faience.

The spacer beads from Tholos IV are all in pieces. Complete, or almost complete, specimens were observed in five different places. Fragmentary examples of same type were recovered from eight other different find spots; they would have made up into at least three spacer beads. Dimensions of best-preserved bead: l. 0.023 m.; w. 0.021 m.; th. 0.006 m. Measurements possible in three others (max. l. 0.025 m.; max. th. 0.009 m.). All dimensions obtainable show that these beads are slightly smaller than example from Mycenae. The disintegrated glass shows up in various colors, sometimes in same bead: pale blue, white, dirty green, and brown. The glass has a vesicular texture.

In many instances this type of spacer bead has been found at Mycenae and Prosymna. Cf. *Schachtgräber,* pl. CL:209 (four examples, p. 69) *ChT,* 66, fig. 25:5b (two examples); Tomb of the Genii, *BSA* XXV (1921-23), 383, fig. 89:0 (but of three instead of four tubes and with three perforations, eight examples, p. 384); *Prosymna,* fig. 464:1 and fig. 284:7 (three examples, p. 303. For diagram see fig. 599:16). All these tombs date from Late Helladic I or II with exception of the Tomb of Genii, which is a little later, and the type of spacer bead found there differs from the others. Apart from Mycenae and the Heraeum, I have come across no other published record of this style of bead. It is of some importance therefore that no fewer than eight specimens should have been found at ancient Pylos. Of even greater interest is it that several examples of this kind of bead, but in bone, were unearthed in a fairly

recent excavation of the dromos of the Matarrubilla Dolmen in southern Spain.[76]

Mrs. Hughes-Brock, who is producing a thesis on Mycenaean beads, has seen the Pylos examples as well as some of the other beads referred to above. The distinctive quality about certain of them, as she points out, is that the outside surface has gone white and plastery but the core is almost perfectly preserved—bright blue and entirely glassy.[77] She suspects that they are imports from the Near East and gives me the following references for multitubular beads found in that area: Nuzi[78]; Megiddo —all Late Bronze Age levels; Lachish[79]; *Gezer* (Macalister, Vol. II, 107-108 and Vol. III, pl. 137b); *Alalakh* (Woolley, p. 270, no. 14). The aforementioned beads are usually found in association with objects that are clearly Mesopotamian and there is therefore a strong possibility that their ultimate source is Mesopotamia.

Beads (NM. 7927-28, NM. 7930-31): 17 of various shapes. Many have disintegrated completely and can no longer be measured.

(a) One spherical: d. 0.015 m. White paste.

(b) Two flattened spherical: (i) d. 0.0185 m.; th. 0.012 m. Yellowish-brown inside, white outside. (ii) d. 0.01 m. White paste.

(c) One oval: l. 0.065 m.; d. 0.009 m. Yellowish-white.

(d) One lozenge (Fig. 194:51): l. 0.028 m.; d. 0.007 m.-0.01 m. Broken. Brilliant blue core. White, powdery surface (see last paragraph on multitubular beads above).

(e) Five cylindrical:
(i) l. 0.015 m.; d. 0.01 m. Practically

---

[76] I saw these beads on a visit to the site in 1960 and Senor F. Callentes de Teran of the Museum of Archaeology at Seville very kindly allowed me to publish this information in my book, *The Mycenaeans,* 152-53.

[77] A unique specimen consisted of a brownish-black solid mass with blue-green particles embedded in it.

[78] R. F. S. Starr, *Nuzi* (1939), Vol. I, 453. Spacer

beads with three to seven ribs but mostly four. All have two string-holes except those with three ribs, which have three. For illustration see Vol. II, pl. 130:E, F.

[79] O. Tufnell, *Lachish IV, The Bronze Age* (1958), 83 and pls. 27:3; 28:23, 27. Pl. 28:23, a multitubular bead with four ribs, is a good deal larger than our example and has a curved profile.

square in section; hole near edge and hence eccentric. Most of surface worn off; inside powdery white.

(ii) l. 0.028 m.? Disintegrated completely on finding. Yellowish-white.

(iii) (Fig. 194:50) l. 0.0165 m.; d. 0.0045 m. Perforation eccentric. Light blue. Vesicular texture.

(iv) l. 0.0165 m.; d. 0.0045 m. Half of long axis missing. Color: blue and white.

(v) l. 0.016 m.; d. 0.005 m. Slightly oblong in section. One end broken. Tough material, perhaps composite glass.

(f) Amygdaloid, fragment (Fig. 195:19): l. pres. 0.014 m.; w. 0.0095 m.; th. pres. 0.004 m. White paste in bad state of preservation only partly preserved. Ridged, convex surface consisting of broad central and rounded rib with two narrow ribs on each side. String-hole eccentric, immediately under central rib. Type very common. Cf. amber bead illustrated in *ChT*, 86, fig. 33 closest in profile, also pl. XIII:29, and paste bead from Kakovatos (*AM* XXXIV [1909], 295, fig. 12:9).

(g) Talisman (bead?): l. 0.017 m.; w. 0.013 m. In fair state of preservation. Shape roughly trapezoidal with rounded corners. Light blue powdery surface, greenish-white inside. String-hole passes diagonally from wider to narrower side.

(h) Six indeterminate. All disintegrated on finding and shape could not be determined. On a few string-hole seen. One blue, two deep blue, and two glistened like mother-of-pearl.

Jewel?: h. ca. 0.013 m.; w. bottom ca. 0.013 m. White to yellowish paste. Shaped like a carbuncle; disintegrated completely on measuring. Side view looked like section of a tholos tomb with sides bulging out at bottom. Shape not dissimilar to crystal mount of a bronze pin from Shaft Grave III (*Schachtgräber*, pl. XXXI:102). It could have

been mounted as a jewel or possibly used as an inlay.

TERRACOTTA

Whorl or loomweight? (NM. 7957, Fig. 194: 16): h. pres. 0.052 m.; w. 0.023 m.; d. hole estimated 0.015 m. About one-third preserved. Biconical. Fired red on outside and black on inside. Outer surface has fine, dark brown burnish. Early Helladic? For shape cf. *Eutresis*, 194, fig. 266:1 and *SME*, 379, fig. 77 (pl. XXV:2).

UNKNOWN SUBSTANCE

Two hemispherical objects with bosses, stained green by contact with disintegrated bronze.

(i) h. ca. 0.01 m.; d. ca. 0.0225 m. Two projections like warts at bottom, roughly at right angles to one another.

(ii) h. ca. 0.01 m.; d. ca. 0.0155 m. Very irregular shape. One projection only.

POTTERY

Amphora (CM. 1137, Fig. 196:1): h. 0.398 m.; d. rim 0.12 m.; d. body 0.32 m.; d. base 0.148 m. Restored. About three-quarters complete; pieces of neck, body, part of one handle, parts of body and base missing. Ovoid shape. Two round loop-handles, uptilted, set at maximum girth of vessel. Flaring rim with flat lip, beveled slightly outward and downward. Slightly conical neck. Flat base. Pink to brown clay fired soft to medium and containing many small pot grits. Red, slightly lustrous paint. Broad band decoration only: on rim, on neck, at bottom of neck, and evenly spaced over body down to base. Middle Helladic-Late Helladic I. Found by the doorway. Slightly larger ovoid jar from nearby tholos tomb near Koryphasion not unlike this jar in shape but it has no neck. Band decoration almost identical (*Hesperia* XXIII [1954], pl. 38:6).

Jug (Fig. 196:4), parts of upper section made up of fragments coming from all parts of tomb. H. pres. without handle 0.094 m.; w. pres. 0.226 m. Shape spherical in upper half of vase (cf. *MP*, Type 103?, p. 30 fig. 5). Round vertical handle. Coarse pink clay with many pottery grits. Slightly lustrous, black paint. Decoration: Ripple Pattern (*MP*, Motive 78:1, p. 422 fig. 73) executed in registers separated by broad bands. Only two registers preserved. Small part of rim preserved painted on inside; handle painted all over. Late Helladic I. Shape perhaps that of *ChT*, pl. iv, bridge-spouted jug.

Throughout the whole excavation of the chamber coarse wares predominated except in the lowest levels. In the upper strata the percentage was as high as 75 percent and there were then about 23 percent semi-coarse and only 2 percent finer wares. Middle Helladic, including Minyan, Matt-painted and incised pottery, were well represented. It would appear that the packing of the vault of the tomb came from an earlier settlement nearby, perhaps on the very mound in which the chamber was excavated; it is difficult otherwise to account for such a large percentage of earlier

pottery in the tomb. But even in the lower levels, when the excavation had been gridded and the pottery was dealt with by squares (very often not more than ten sherds to a square), coarse ware was still well in evidence. The percentages worked out at 39 percent coarse, 35 percent semi-coarse, and 26 percent Mycenaean or finer wares (e.g., Fig. 196:3, 6). A considerable quantity of the semi-coarse would also contain Mycenaean, as Palace Style jar fabric would certainly qualify under that heading as also some Late Helladic I pottery. Among the finer wares kylikes were the most conspicuous, including the angular type. There were bowl fragments but the shape could not easily be determined. At least one amphora or hydria was represented and there was the base of a tankard or mug. Fragments of two or three Vapheio cups were found as well as part of ordinary cups including one with thrush-egg pattern. Decorated pieces were few. About the only design was the spiral. A few fragments had band decoration or were monochrome.

W. D. T.

GRAVE CIRCLE

(Plans and Sections, Figs. 327-335)

Description

The grave circle is situated about 145 m. to the south of Englianos hill (Fig. 301) and commands a superb view of the Bay of Navarino and the island of Sphakteria. It occupied a very much smaller space than Tholos IV and the excavation of it presented few problems. In the first place, there was no superstructure to excavate although this was not immediately apparent. Secondly, the burials were all found as they had been left at the time of their deposition and such disturbance as had taken place was the unpremeditated result of modern agricultural activity.

Of the circle itself a little less than half the circumference of the foundations survived. These consisted of two courses in a short arc and mostly of only one. The diameter was calculated to be ca. 5.50 m.; thus it was not a large grave circle (Fig. 327). Very small slabs were used in the construction of the wall and this was borne out not only by the foundations themselves but by the fallen stones—

and these were not many—that were recovered in excavating the area. Two examples can be given of their small size: (a) 0.23 m. x 0.17 m., (b) 0.33 m. x 0.24 m.; thickness ca. 0.08 m. The foundations, which were bedded on *stereo,* were only one stone's width, but it is possible that the upper courses were two stones' width. In any event it is unlikely that the thickness of the wall was more than 0.60 m. The circle contained a number of burial pits but these were all situated in the northern half of the area. Some of the pits contained pithos burials accompanied by weapons; these seem to have been the oldest interments. Three of these pithos burials were concentrated together in the eastern part and adjoining them was a shallow pit filled with bones of other interments. The whole complex is called Pit 3. The fourth pithos burial was in the west sector (Pit 1). A second bone pit, but this time a deeper one, was situated in the north sector. It contained the remains of at least five skeletons and is called Pit 4. Finally, in the very center of the tomb an extended burial had been laid out in a shallow pit, known as Pit 2. This was undoubtedly the last interment. According to Dr. Angel, who examined the skulls and bones, there were at least 27 people buried in this circle—all of them adult (20 males and 7 females).

Excavation

The campaign lasted from May 25 to July 13, 1957. The total working days were 43 and during most of that time four workmen were employed. Nearly every bit of soil was sifted and the work went forward slowly and steadily.[80] The site was an *aloni* (threshing floor)[81] on which, just visible, was a row of five flat stones, laid neatly in a line that had a slight but perceptible curve. A trench, 6 m. x 1 m. and with a west-east axis, was laid athwart the line of stones. A number of loose, small flat stones that were obviously fallen or disturbed were uncovered. Shortly after that six well-preserved flint arrowheads and a small bead of blue glass paste were revealed in the soil. The trench was only 0.30 m. deep at that time and a second course of stones had been uncovered under the line of small slabs that had originally been visible, but we were somewhat perplexed to find that no further courses lay beneath them. Investigation to the east of these two courses revealed only *stereo* and no further masonry to buttress them. They stood alone just one stone's width (Fig. 197). The original trench was then extended a further 3 m. to the west but it failed to reveal the other part of the circle. In its place *stereo* was encountered. But at ca. 2 m. from the west end of the extended trench and at a depth of ca. 0.50 m. a bronze cauldron, of shallow

---

[80] Once more I had valuable help from the foreman, Dionysios Androutsakis, who administered first aid to the poorly preserved bones and badly corroded bronzes, as they were uncovered.

[81] The Expedition is indebted to Mr. E. Vayenas for his permission to excavate in his *aloni.*

depth and with a flat rounded base, lay bottom upwards against an oval shaped pithos that was leaning over towards the south. Both seemed to be in fairly good condition. Later, the blade of a sword—or rapier, as it turned out to be—appeared alongside the pithos with its tip pointing up at the heavens. The blade had been bent round a full 90 degrees but its extremity touched neither the cauldron nor the pithos (Fig. 198). It was later found that the pithos was sunk in a shallow pit and this became known as Pit 1.

Meanwhile work proceeded in the main, original trench. A constant stream of miscellaneous objects continued to issue from the soil; large numbers of flint arrowheads, some also of obsidian, and most of them unbroken; an increasing number of beads of all sizes, of which the greater part was of glass paste; and a terracotta button of biconical form. At about the center of the trench, if one excludes the extension, and at a depth of ca. 0.65 m. the middle part of a skeleton was uncovered (Fig. 200). Between its legs there was a flint arrowhead with its point facing south. A circular bronze mirror lay in the area of the pelvis; it was in poor condition. Immediately above it (to the south of it) was a bronze awl with an ivory handle. Above that again, but more to the southeast, was a figurine of Φ type lying face down on the right breast of the dead. The painted decoration on the object was just visible; its head lay to the north. To the west of the mirror (and on the left side of the skeleton) was a short dagger or knife with spatulate blade; beyond that was an undecorated little askos [33] of gray fabric lying upside down. Of course, this account of the burial is written with hindsight. All these details were not immediately apparent at the time. Nor was it clear till later that this skeleton had been laid in an oblong pit, which came to be known as Pit 2.

But there was more to come from this unexpectedly rich trench. After the fallen stones at the east end of it had been taken up, there appeared the lower part of a pithos protruding from the north side of the trench. It was evident that the jar lay on its side and it seemed to be in good condition and unbroken. Up against it, to the east of it, the point of a rapier was directed skywards. Like the other one already referred to, it was bent out of true. Shortly afterwards, on the opposite side of the trench and at about the same level, part of another bronze cauldron started to emerge. It was of a different kind to the one previously described. Its shape was conical with a narrow base and it had a vertically offset rim. The cauldron was lying on its side with its mouth tilted towards the northeast. Unfortunately, it was not in good state of preservation. Nearby and to the west of it was another pithos, this time standing upright but in very fragmentary condition. The soil around cauldron and pithos was found to be *stereo*. Both, it was verified later, had been placed in a pit (Pit 3).[82] A large amber bead, broken, was found in the vicinity. At this stage a depth of ca. 0.50 m. had been reached but miscellaneous objects, at one time so profuse, had come to a stop. The level at which this was noticeable was ca. 0.30 m. below the surface.

(a) Introduction of the grid

It had already become apparent that instead of excavating in the upper levels of a tholos we were working close to its presumed foundations, although the small size of these and the lack of any sign of them at the other end of the trench remained unexplained. Shortly before this was realized and in view of the many objects that were coming out of the trench, it was decided to introduce a grid system. The grid consisted of squares of one meter and the original trench (Trench A = A on the grid) was used as its base (Fig. 328). The latter obviously occupied the center of the tomb and it was clear that the diameter of the supposed tholos could not be much more than 5 m.[83] Therefore the squares in the grid in Trench A were limited to six and the numbering of them was from east to west.[84] When it became necessary to extend the excavation, a northerly direction was chosen. A trench 2 m. x 2.20 m. was opened to the north of Trench A and near its eastern extremity. It was called Trench L (Fig. 199). It was subdivided into four squares of the grid: B.1, B.2 in the south, C.1, C.2 in the north. The extra length of 0.20 m. in the west-east axis fell across the wall of the circle and beyond it (Fig. 328).

In Trench L the line of the original foundation course continued, forming the arc of a circle. There was the usual disarray of fallen stones. Very soon a dagger with a spatulate blade was uncovered in the southeast part of the trench. It lay horizontally in a north-south axis, the hilt end towards the south (Fig. 201). The tip was missing but was found later. At a level of ca. 0.20 m.-0.25 m. below the surface two clay alabastra [1, 4] and a one-handled jar [3] were revealed (Fig. 202). For their exact position see plan (Fig. 329). All except one were complete, though broken. They were decorated in the style of Late Helladic II and Late Helladic II-III. A flint arrowhead was found in the mouth of the one-handled jar but this was probably fortuitous. At this same level there were once again numerous miscellaneous objects but confined entirely

[82] Pit 3 (SE) to be exact. There were several pits in close proximity in this part of the tomb. They have been treated as one complex and designated individually by the points of the compass.

[83] It was actually ca. 5.50 m. as previously stated.

[84] This may appear somewhat perverse, but my

headquarters were situated to the north of the area and I always approached the excavations from that direction. I would have found it confusing if the numbering had been "backwards"—from my point of view.

to stone arrowheads and glass beads except for one which was of amethyst. Just below this level and in the southeast part of the trench the upper part of the pithos appeared (Fig. 203), of which the base lay in Trench A as previously mentioned. The middle part of it was in the balk between the two trenches. It could be seen that it was a tall spouted jar [29] of Cretan type, lying on its side with the spout uppermost. To the east of the jar and between it and the foundations were the hilt ends of two rapiers and the bent blade of a third, the point of which was buried in the ground. They were moderately well-preserved but the rivets were loose and two of them were found in the soil nearby. About nine pieces of ivory lay in the vicinity, too poorly preserved for restoration, but two of the fragments exhibited a section of the socket that received the tang of the weapon and there was no doubt that this had once been an ivory pommel. To the north of the spouted jar, a number of coarse sherds were collected. No identifiable pot or pots could be recognized among these fragments at the time, but from them the potmender was able to make up a jug [5] with cutaway mouth (Fig. 234:24) and a bowl [22] with a high-swung handle (Fig. 234:25). Some of the sherds were found at a depth of ca. 0.40 m., i.e., at a lower level than the majority of the vases from the grave circle. Fragments of a jar of Palace Style were found to the west of the spouted jar. Later, it was established that the complete jar stood there. Trench L was extended a further meter to the north. D.2 of the grid fell within this area. *Stereo* was reached here at ca. 0.35 m. down. The miscellaneous objects from that square were few and of the usual kind except for a stone pestle (Fig. 232:1).

Trench M, 2 m. x 2 m., was started to the west of Trench L and later extended a further meter to the north (Fig. 328). Many fallen stones were found in the surface level. One of them was much larger than the others and measured ca. 0.52 m. x 0.38 m. It lay roughly in the center of the trench. Another 15 vases were uncovered in this area. Except for one pot they were all at levels of 0.20 m.-0.25 m. or 0.25 m.-0.35 m. below the surface. The greater number were alabastra including the angular type. A one-handled jar [19] had the base of a kylix stopping up its mouth, perhaps intended as a lid (Fig. 204). There was also the lower part of a small pithos(?) of coarse red ware that had a base with molded rings or ridges [20] that reminded one of the ringed base of a Minyan goblet (Fig. 205). Other vases (included in the 15) were an elegant spouted jug [8] of Minoan style and decoration (Figs. 206, 234:23, 235:7), a spouted cup [21], a shallow cup [17] with raised handle (Fig. 234:2), which was found on top of one of the alabastra, and an askos [18] (Figs. 234:19, 235:6). The spouted cup was found at ca. 0.42 m. down and very near *stereo* which was confirmed at ca. 0.45 m. The vases were mostly concentrated towards the north end of the circle.

The area proved very rich in small objects, particularly in beads. There were 159 of these, mostly glass paste. About 50 were of the large variety, a few of them exceptionally so. There were 10 amethyst beads and four of carnelian. One of the glass paste beads was a "spacer" of the fluted kind like the one found in Tholos IV (see p. 131), but it was all in pieces. There were many fewer arrowheads (10 of flint and two of obsidian). More interesting finds were: a shanked button of gray steatite (Furumark's type b—Late Helladic III A:1—Figs. 227:7, 230:21)—this and the biconical button were the only ones to be found in this tomb; a lentoid bead seal of mottled agate (Fig. 231:5a, b) and (*CMS* I, No. 294); two slightly concave bronze disks, each punctured at equal intervals with four holes along the circumference; a similar bronze disk but much larger and with no holes when found; and a long bronze rod with a nail-type head at each end, found broken in three pieces but since repaired (Fig. 228:5). The two bronze disks of equal dimensions (0.05 m.) were supplemented by two others found roughly at the same level in the neighboring trench to the west, which was excavated later. They were scale pans and the long rod was the balance staff. Under one of the pans three glass disk beads were recovered.

The extension of Pit 2, which contained the skeleton, was uncovered in the south part of Trench M, while we were digging to *stereo*. The lower part of the legs were now revealed, but it was not possible to excavate them properly as they were in a very friable state; the bone fragments would come away with the soil on the slightest encouragement. The legs seemed to be specially long. In the region of the feet, which were not preserved, a little to the west of where they should have been, another bronze disk, or scale pan, was uncovered. This was decorated with a rosette in repoussé work on its convex surface (Figs. 227:10, 230:7).

Another pit, an entirely new one, was uncovered in Trench M. It occupied the northern sector, had a west-east axis, and part of it lay under the west balk of the trench. It was filled with bones and skulls. It was called Pit 4 and a full description of it will follow later. In another part of the trench fragments of a bone were found at ca. 0.20 m.-0.25 m. below the surface. It was impossible to identify it on account of its condition. It was presumably human and the only bone to be found out of place.

The opening up of Trench N (Fig. 328) to the west of Trench M completed, with its extension, the excavation of the northern half of the area. There were a certain number of fallen stones in this sector, but the line of the foundations of the circle came abruptly to an end halfway in the trench and except for one stone of the second course only the ground course survived. The area to the south in the line of the missing circle was *stereo*. When Trench R was opened to the south of Trench A to investigate and follow up the other end of the circle, only one more stone of the foundations was uncovered (see plan, Fig. 328). Again *stereo* was found beyond. In effect, a little less than half the circle was preserved. Trench N produced few finds. Only two vases were found, both alabastra, of which one with Late Helladic II-III decoration was lodged in the balk dividing Trench M from N. A bronze scale pan appeared at a level of ca. 0.15 m.-0.20 m. below the surface and another was uncovered at roughly the same level when the balk was taken down. These were the two scale pans referred to previously. Altogether then four were found in close proximity. (It should be noted that the scale pan discovered near the feet of the skeleton was at a much lower level.) Other finds from Trench N were a cylindrical bead of glass paste carved in the form of a spiral coil (Fig. 232:7), two small paste beads, and three flint arrowheads.

(b) The sections

Sufficient of the north half of the circle had been excavated to allow sections to be drawn. One of the principal of these (Section II — Fig. 331) and the most instructive, was on a north-south axis. The most striking feature here is the white layer that passes almost the whole way across the section from south to north. It suffers an interruption over Pit 4 and a strip that represents its continuation is bent down to the north edge of the pit. There are also two vertical white layers, though one is rather nebulous, to the south of the pit. One alabastron is shown *in situ* on the same level as, or just above, the white layer. A considerable number, if not the majority, of the vases were on this same level. The horizontal white layer fades out as it approaches the south side of the pit. It is mixed with, and replaced by, a much darker layer. In fact, on the other side of the balk (west side)[85] only this dark layer could be seen, but the white layer showed up clearly on that side further to the south. Section I (Fig. 330), which is 2 m. further over to the east does not show this white layer at all. In its place there is a black layer that does not, however, extend for any great distance. Section III (Fig. 332) is along the west-east axis of the circle. Except for the white layer that can be discerned in, and is confined to, the west part of the section, there is no horizontal stratification at all. Instead there are vertical strata shown by a slight variation in the color of the soil at the east end and what was the white layer is here dispersed around and above the spouted jar. The few stones that can

[85] No section drawn of that side of the balk.

be seen above the pit in which the skeleton lay suggest that there was a fair accumulation of earth over the body; and the comparatively undisturbed state of the finds on and around the skeleton would bear this out. Section IV (Fig. 333) is also along the west-east axis of the grave circle and represents the situation a further meter to the south. The white layer is now restricted in length, firstly by the cutting of Pit 1 in the west and secondly by the excavation of Pit 2 (the pit with the skeleton) in the east. There is slightly darker earth over the skeleton, which reaches up vertically to the surface and this seems to indicate the outline of the trench dug for the deposition of the deceased.

It seems fairly evident that this white layer represents the floor or basic level of the original grave circle. It is best preserved in Section II, a line that passes through the northwest sector of the burial ground, an area that was undisturbed except for the digging of Pit 4; and this is one of the earliest pits in the grave circle, for it contained the gold diadem with Shaft Grave antecedents and some of the pottery placed over the filled-in pit belonged to Late Helladic I. Moreover, Section IV shows that the white layer was cut by the early Grave Pit 1. In the very disturbed east sector, where Pit 3 is situated, only traces of the white layer are to be found. It is true that this layer is absent in the north part of Section I (northeast sector), but it is just here that a small number of the vases were unearthed at a lower level than elsewhere in the grave circle (see pp. 138f.).

The corresponding trenches to L, M, N in the north were Trenches R, S, T in the south (see plan, Fig. 328). Trench R was the only one to produce any finds and these were few. There were fragments of a bowl [23] of coarse red ware in square E.2; these lay just under the surface. A kylix [24] in pieces was found close by (Fig. 234:9) and an amethyst bead-seal of amygdaloid form further to the south (Fig. 231:6a, b = *CMS* I, No. 299). Finally, the pointed end of a bronze pin in moderate condition was discovered in cleaning the south face of the balk between Trench R and Trench A. Apart from fallen stones in the middle and north parts of the area and a few sherds just below the surface, nothing was found in Trench S. Trench T was completely sterile. Sections V and VI, made of the west and east sides of Trench S respectively, are consequently not very informative (Figs. 334, 335). Prominent areas of whitish soil were noticeable in both sections and these are probably related to the white layer observed in the other part of the grave circle. If uninformative in other respects, the sections serve to show the slope of the *stereo* downwards from north to south. This is particularly noticeable in the case of Section VI. The comparative sterility of Trenches R, S, and T demonstrated that all the principal finds were concentrated in the north half of the circle.

(c) The grave pits

The major part of the excavation was now completed and a start was made on removing the remaining balks. The head of the skeleton in Pit 2 was uncovered. The skull, which was facing east, was found to be in fairly good condition and the teeth in the upper jaw appeared to be sound and all present. Dr. Angel later diagnosed the skull as that of a young man. A small bronze bowl in a very friable state was uncovered to the west of the skull (Fig. 207), and a large white glass bead, a little more than half preserved, was retrieved near the left collarbone; its diameter was ca. 0.0165 m. These were the last of the many objects to be found that were associated with this burial. It was clear that the skeleton was supine (Fig. 208) but the bones were badly decomposed and it was only with difficulty that the position of the left arm could be determined. This was extended downwards with the forearm resting across the pelvis; the hand, of which a few phalanges remained, may have held the mirror. The right arm was extended to its full length alongside the body. On the left breast of the skeleton was part of the skull of another individual and a few bones, presumably belonging to this skull, were scattered over the central part of the skeleton (Fig. 207). They did not articulate with the skull in any way, nor could it be said what part of the anatomy they represented because of their ruined state. It was not possible, according to Dr. Angel, to say with any certainty whether this skull was that of a man or a woman. The circumstances of the second interment remain a mystery.[86]

Attention was now directed to Pit 3, which contained the cauldron of conical form and the pithos alongside it (Fig. 209). To the west of this complex were a large number of bones and fragments of skulls. It was a bone pit ca. 0.85 m. wide and 2.25 m. long. In the north it adjoined the Palace Style jar (see Fig. 210 and p. 138) so that in effect this pit, the Palace Style jar, the spouted jar to the east of it, and the cauldron and pithos to the south were all contained in one large pit, but the levels within this pit varied greatly. The position of the bones and skulls in this pit were sketched and photographed before removal and each one was numbered for later identification but the functional extremities of the bones had decomposed to such an extent that they were useless for diagnosis. Ten skull fragments were recovered.

The excavation of the area of the cauldron and pithos was full of interest. A weapon with a strange handle could be seen protruding from the lower rim of the former (Fig. 212). The handle was in the shape of a thick bar of round section that tapered towards its end, which was bent over into a ring. On extraction

[86] Professor Blegen, however, has drawn my attention to the circumstances of the burial of the queen in the Royal Tomb of Dendra. Her skeleton was laid in the same grave as the king and on top of his skeleton (*RT,Dendra,* 16).

it proved to be a short sword of a type found in the Shaft Graves excavated by Schliemann (Grave Circle A). Other weapons and a whetstone lay underneath or alongside. They were, in the order of their removal: a long slender knife with a flanged hilt, of which the edge was scalloped; a long whetstone, square in section; a dagger with a laurel-leaf blade; a short slender dagger or knife; a dagger with a blade of triangular form (for descriptions, see catalogue). The soil in which these objects were found was much darker than the earth that filled the rest of the cauldron. It was black and sandy, and may represent the remains of scabbards or the material in which the weapons were wrapped. Just to the north of the cauldron and approximately at its depth the broken point of a bronze pin was found; close by it three large beads, one of amethyst and two of amber; and a large shaped piece of amber that may have been a talisman. Another large bead was found just inside the cauldron (see p. 162). At the level at which the cauldron lay and in between it and the pithos four rapiers were uncovered, their points directed towards the northeast (Fig. 211). They were of a well-known type made familiar by the many examples unearthed in the Shaft Graves. Their layout was somewhat haphazard, blade overlapping blade in two cases. Two of the rapiers had ivory pommels but they had weathered so badly that their shapes were difficult to determine. One was found close to the hilt of one of the weapons, the other had rolled some distance away (Fig. 211). The earth round the blades of the rapiers was especially dark and here again this discolored soil may represent perished scabbards. A few centimeters above the rapiers two flint arrowheads and several fragments of boar's tusks were discovered. An almost complete boar's tusk, but in pieces, was found in cleaning up round the swords. These tusks were very fragmentary and there cannot have been more than five or six of them. The complete one had no perforation. Of the other fragments, two were pierced with one hole each and one with two holes. Other finds with the rapiers were an ivory pin, the point of a bone(?) pin, an obsidian arrowhead, another talisman(?) of amber, a large amber bead and fragments of another, and a spacer bead. This was also of amber; it was rectangular in shape and pierced with three string-holes (see p. 162). Another bronze pin, almost complete and with a nail-type head, was located near one of the pommels. A small carnelian bead and a flint arrowhead were found in sifting.

The pithos [28] was the next to be excavated. Its mouth was closed by a circular stone which had broken in two. The largest piece was still in position and the other fragment was found in the earth. The pithos was complete but had crumbled to about a third of its height. When the lid was removed, the pithos was found to contain a burial. As before, each layer of bones was sketched and photographed, and the bones numbered prior to removal, but all to no purpose because they were in such a bad state. They were in great disorder and it would appear that there had been complete dismemberment before the remains were placed within the pithos; for instance, a large fragment of the skull was found in the top layer of bones and a jawbone in the fifth layer. A bronze knife occupied a central position in the top layer of bones (Figs. 213, 230:10). In the next layer to be removed there were further skull fragments, but whether these were part of the same skull referred to above or belonged to another individual was not certain. A bronze pin with a disk head, like the one found with the rapiers, was recovered from the fourth layer. Two similar pins appeared in the fifth layer together with a third which may have been pointed at both ends; it was poorly preserved. These may have been used for pinning the shroud. In two cases a bone was adhering to the pin; one of these bones was either a phalange or a knuckle bone. In the final clearing of the pithos a large boar's tusk, complete but in three pieces, was retrieved; it was pierced with two holes set closely together. But the most interesting find, located near the base of the pithos, was part of a silver vessel in a very fragmentary state. It appears to have been a shallow cup of very thin ware and is decorated with a repoussé design (Figs. 225:4, 227:11). When the last sherds of the pithos were gathered up, fragments of an amber bead were found underneath.

The Palace Style jar [30] was set in a small pit made to receive it, the depth of which was ca. 1 m. down from the surface. Near its base but some centimeters higher was a shallow cup [31] turned upside down (Fig. 210). This lay between the jar and the bone pit and it was not clear to which it belonged; but as no other pottery was found associated with the bones it probably goes with the jar. The latter had collapsed but was found to be complete. On restoration it proved to be a very fine example of its kind (Fig. 233:4a-c) and that it was highly prized in ancient times was demonstrated by the fact that it had been repaired; seven bits of lead were recovered and several of the sherds were pierced with holes. In gathering up the fragments of the vase, we were surprised to find that it too had been used for a burial jar. The bones indeed were few but at the bottom of the jar the skull was so firmly wedged that it could only be extracted in the laboratory (Fig. 214). Although the impression received was that the deceased had been buried head downwards, the mouth of the Palace Style jar would scarcely be wide enough to permit the introduction of the complete corpse.

The spouted jar [29] in the northeast corner of this extensive pit also contained a burial. The mouth of this vessel was closed by a large thin slab roughly square in plan; one of its edges was slightly curved out of the true. As the jar was lying on its side the slab was in a vertical position and it did not completely cover the wide opening. It seems that the pithos was placed purposely on its side, for, had it toppled over, the lid would not be likely to have retained its position, and the jar was intact, although it had cracked with age. The burial inside the vessel was not found in the same confusion as in the other two jars. The bones seemed to be roughly in the position that one would expect to find with a crouched or squat burial. The head lay at the base of the jar and faced northwards. The corpse may have been trussed up in order to fit it into such a confined space; at least, that was the impression given by the appearance of the skeleton (Fig. 215). The only find within the jar was a small deep cup [32] painted with a tortoise-shell pattern popular in Late Helladic I and II (Figs. 215, 234:1). The removal of the sherds of the pithos helped to clarify the relationship between the rapiers referred to on page 138. These were all located between the jar and the side of the pit to the east. The blades of all of them were bent, two of them as much as 90 degrees (Figs. 215, 229:12, 14, 15). It could perhaps be said of the one that was least bent that it was the result of pressure from the curved side of the pit, but not of the others. The haft end of one rapier, the least bent, projected originally ca. 0.12 m. beyond the rim of the pithos in a northerly direction; its blade lay against and along the wall of the pit. The hilt end of a second one lay ca. 0.08 m. to the south of the rim and its point was directed towards the sky as mentioned previously. The third rapier pointed in the opposite direction: the hilt end was ca. 0.40 m. to the south of, and below, the upper rim, and the blade curved over near the rim to point downwards.[87] The removal of the spouted jar also revealed a dagger and a knife lying against the wall of the pit, and nearby two ivory pommels belonging to two of the rapiers (Fig. 216). The form of the pommels was no longer recognizable because of the bad state of the ivory. The knife and dagger lay close together with their points to the north. The knife was long and slender and of the same type as the one found in the cauldron; like the other its hilt was flanged and scalloped (Fig. 229:10). The dagger was much shorter. It had a broad butt and rounded point (Fig. 229:17). One of the pommels lay just to the north of the knife and dagger and the other to the south. From their position they seem to have fallen from the tangs of the second and third rapiers respectively. Some other ivory fragments appear to have belonged to the pommel of the third rapier as they were found close to it. The pommel of the first rapier was not recovered but it is probably represented by the nine fragments of ivory found earlier in the vicinity (see p. 138).

---

[87] See Fig. 203 for position of rapiers in relation to the jar before its removal.

With the removal of the spouted jar and accompanying weapons the excavation of this large multiple pit (Pit 3) was completed.[88] No beads or arrowheads were found in this last operation. There were a few small objects that could be related to the bone pit alongside the Palace Style jar, though none of them were found when removing the bones. The following finds were made when destroying balks, part of which covered the northern sector of the bone pit: four glass and two amethyst beads, and one flint arrowhead. These may or may not have had any connection with the pit, but the following were found near *stereo* in its close neighborhood: six glass and two amethyst beads, two flint arrowheads and one of obsidian.

Pit 1, in which the flat- to round-bottomed cauldron lay leaning against a pithos (the first to be found, see pp. 135f.), was comparatively shallow. It may have been artificially created by us in our attempt to find *stereo*. Here as elsewhere in this region the hardpan is extraordinarily soft and it is often difficult to distinguish it from worked soil. The cauldron was found to be in reasonably good condition. It contained waterlaid soil, clearly discernible in the form of stratification, and some laminated fragments that might possibly be ivory; but the soil at the bottom of the cauldron was quite different, it was dark and sandy. The pithos [27] was complete but cracked throughout all its frame. It had no lid. This jar too contained a burial that was badly disturbed, but the bones did not appear to be so divorced from one another as in the case of the pithos with the conical-shaped cauldron, and the disarray could perhaps be attributed to the action of rain and waterborne soil. Moreover, the mouth of this pithos was wider than the others (0.25 m.) and a trussed body could conceivably have been introduced into the jar.[89] The skull was in the upper layer of bones (Fig. 217). Mixed with the latter were fragments of three ivory pins and bits of bronze wire. Sometimes this wire was found attached to pieces of silver, soldered, as it were, along the edge and suggesting a hinge. Several fragments of silver, decorated with a repoussé pattern, formed parts of four half-diadems of a type

[88] Levels taken in relation to floor of grave circle, southeast of Pit 3 near wall, which is treated as zero (measurements to the nearest centimeter):

Depth of spouted jar emplacement. Pit 3 (NE). 0.10 m.
Palace Style jar emplacement. Pit 3 (N). 0.68 m.
Floor of bone pit. Pit 3 (NW). 0.47 m.
Floor of bone pit. Pit 3 (SW). 0.60 m.
Cauldron emplacement. Pit 3 (SE). 0.69 m.
Pithos emplacement. Pit 3 (SE). 0.90 m.
Depth of Pit 2 near feet of skeleton. 0.41 m.
Emplacement of pithos in Pit 1. 0.44 m.

Depth of Pit 4. 0.51 m.
Southeast corner of Trench R. 0.00 m.
Southwest corner of Trench T. Plus 0.03 m.
Surface level to north of grave circle. Plus 0.50 m.
Surface level to south of grave circle. Minus 0.29 m.
Surface level to west of grave circle. Plus 0.28 m.
Surface level to east of grave circle. Minus 0.29 m.

[89] Small jars for adult burials were sometimes used in Crete, and Seager suggests that probably the collarbones and hipbones were intentionally broken to insert the burial (*Pachyammos*, 12).

known from the Shaft Graves of Grave Circle A (Figs. 225:6, 227:8). Another find among the bones was a plaque of ivory ca. 0.042 m. broad and ca. 0.005 m. thick. It had lost its outline through weathering, but was pierced centrally with a round hole and it may have been the section of a pommel (see Fig. 225:3). At the bottom of the jar was another mysterious object. It was shaped like a quoit and around it was wrapped gold leaf (Figs. 218, 225:2). Many fragments of the gold had come away and revealed the inner core. Of whatever substance this may once have consisted (perhaps wadding), it had now turned to earth. The gold leaf was impressed with a design that can be reconstructed in part and the same pattern was probably continued throughout (Fig. 227:9). The "quoit" may possibly have been a wreath or garland. After the removal of the pithos, the bent rapier was retrieved. Underneath it lay a knife, the hilt end of which had previously been visible near the blade of the sword. It was of the long, slender, laneolate type like the one found in the other cauldron and with the spouted jar.

The existence of another pit was mentioned on pages 135, 139. This was Pit 4, approximately 1.70 m. long, 0.64 m. wide, and 0.35 m. deep. Roughly almond-shaped, it was situated in the north part of the area, near the foundations of the circular enclosure and away from the other burials. The mortal remains of some five individuals had been crammed into this pit. Bones and skulls were all mixed together without any semblance of the relationship they had borne to one another in life (Fig. 219). No sherds, beads, or arrowheads came from this pit, but it produced six knives and/or daggers, a whetstone, and—surprisingly—a gold diadem. The diadem was represented by four crumpled pieces of gold foil found in different parts of the pit (two fragments visible in Fig. 219). When straightened out and put together they were found to be decorated with a repoussé and pointillé design that bore a strong resemblance to the great "diadems" from the Shaft Graves in Grave Circle A, only this one was on a much smaller scale (Figs. 225:1, 230:15). Except for one dagger, which was found right at the bottom of the pit, all the other weapons came from the top layer of bones. Two of them had broad butts and ogival to rounded points. They were not unlike the short dagger found with the spouted jar. The dagger found in the lowest level was of this variety but it had a more pronounced point. There were two knives with lanceolate blades and flanged, scalloped hilts; a type now well-known from this grave circle. One of them was of the long, slender type; the other short. One knife or dagger resembled the broken one found inside the cauldron. The hone, unlike the one found in that vessel, was round in section. It tapered at both ends and had a hole for suspension (for description, see p. 167).

[147]

(d) Extended exploration

In 1958 a further investigation was made southwest of the grave circle excavated in the previous year. A trench, 1 m. by 14 m., and with north-south axis was dug at the southern end of the spur referred to on page 155, suggested as a possible site for a dromos. From certain surface indications it was thought that there might be a small tholos in the vicinity. This test was to prove a disappointment but it led to certain negative findings. The foundations of a rectangular building ca. 2.50 m. by 4.25 m. were uncovered, but only three sides of this construction were relatively well preserved (Fig. 336). The long axis was northwest-southeast. The wall least well preserved was on the northeast side. No foundations were more than one course deep except for the short cross walls. These were found to have up to three courses in places (Figs. 223, 224). The ruined foundations on the northeast side of the building were ca. 0.30 m. higher than those on the southwest. Both to the north and south of this structure *stereo* was soon found. It is doubtful whether this building had any connection with the grave circle which lay ca. 15 m. to the north, as nearly all the potsherds found in this test were Late Helladic III B. About a further 4 m. to the south a few stones that might have been the foundation course of a wall were uncovered. These were at an even lower level than the rectangular building, because the spur slopes steadily downward to the south as has been previously mentioned. If so little of these later buildings has survived with the weathering away of this strip of land, it is not so surprising that half the foundation course of the grave circle, a much earlier building, should have disappeared.

Discussion

The excavation of the site was now completed. So far as can be judged, the burials within it had remained intact from the time they had been deposited (Figs. 220, 221, 222). The professional tomb robber had not penetrated and such disturbance as had taken place was confined to the upper levels and was the unconscious interference of people living in our times. One could not ask for more. Yet many problems remained. What had happened to the rest of the circle? Why were these unplundered grave pits so lacking in gold vessels and rich tomb furniture? What was the significance of the pithos burials and the bent rapiers? To which burial belonged the many vases that in style of decoration varied from the beginning of Late Helladic I to the transitional Late Helladic II-III period? There were minor problems also.

The latest interment was almost certainly the extended burial in Pit 2, located in the very center of the circle. Section IV (Fig. 333) shows the excavation of this pit and seems to indicate that the burial was subsequently covered with earth, and perhaps a layer of stones laid over it. The fragment of skull and sporadic bones scattered haphazardly over the "torso" of the skeleton must have come from an earlier burial to be in such a condition. Perhaps they had been buried previously in this very spot in the center of the grave circle and were reinterred on top of the newly deceased because of some intimate connection between the two.[90] The absence of bead-seals on the dead man is difficult to explain. Only two were found in the whole excavation and in the top level, where the majority of small finds were uncovered. They could not have been transported from the skeleton to the position in which they were found through later disturbance, because the burial was at a much lower level. To whom then did they belong? The same problem arises over the beads. There was a great number of them, over 200, and they were nearly all of glass paste. These are commonly associated with the later Mycenaean Period and it would be permissible therefore to attribute them to the latest burial, namely, the skeleton in Pit 2. Or were they the property of what has been presumed to be the previous burial, whose exiguous remains were scattered over the corpse in that pit? One could then say that the beads from the disintegrated necklaces were largely purloined by subsequent mourners and the many beads that would get overlooked or lost in the soil would be dispersed at a much later period, when modern activities disturbed the upper earth. Only one bead was found near the collarbone of the skeleton, but its position, I think, was fortuitous.

Neither the equipment nor the pottery found with the skeleton could provide any close date as to its burial. There was only one pot, an undecorated askos. Stylistically the latest pottery in the rest of the tomb does not go beyond Late Helladic II-III. The latest object in the tomb is the shank button of steatite. According to Furumark this is the earliest type of stone button and he puts it in Late Helladic III A:1. Apart from this object and five undecorated vases that are not closely datable, none of the rest of the pottery is later than Late Helladic II-III and some of it is much earlier. Stylistically the earliest are the two pithoi with the cauldrons. They were both decorated but the paint has largely worn off. The pithos [27] from Pit 1 has suffered most in this respect, but diagonal crosses can still be made out underneath the handles; the upper part of the jar appears to be monochrome (Fig. 233:1). The patterns on the other pithos [28] are better preserved. They show a zone of linked crosshatched diamonds and a zone of diagonal lines alternating backwards and forwards. This decoration is in white on a dark background (Fig. 233:2). It is typical of late Middle Helladic painted wares, and the pithoi are therefore to be attributed to the Middle

[90] See footnote 86, p. 142.

Helladic-Late Helladic transitional period. The spouted jar [29] (Fig. 233:5a, b) is probably only a little later. It is decorated with the Ripple pattern (*MP*, Motive 78:1, p. 422 fig. 73) of Late Helladic I and II and the small deep cup [32] found inside the jar has the same pattern (Fig. 234:1). But what is most remarkable about this jar is its Minoan form both in shape and decoration. The trickle pattern is highly characteristic. I do not think that any jar of this type has so far been discovered on the Greek mainland. Its inspiration, if not its origin, is Minoan.

The Palace Style jar [30] (Fig. 233:4a-c) was the latest of the pithos burials. The use of these handsome vases for that purpose was previously unknown, unless it be that the many examples of this kind of jar found in the Kakovatos tholos tomb were put to similar use. These were all completely smashed but the report speaks of a quantity of bones scattered around the tomb.[91] One of the most striking features of this grave circle is the pithos burials, a custom foreign to Greece at this period, although isolated examples are known from Middle Helladic times.[92] The practice was widespread in Crete and one is inclined to attribute its introduction into southwestern Greece to Minoan influence. There seems to have been no definite rule as to the method of pithos burial in this grave circle. There was a squat burial in the spouted jar and the same may also be true of the burial in the Pit 1 pithos. The body in the other pithos, perhaps the earliest of the pithoi, was almost certainly dismembered, and the same treatment was used in the Palace Style jar burial. This funerary practice was discontinued in Late Helladic II, perhaps towards the end of it, because the Palace Style jar had been repaired and it may (but not necessarily) have been in use by the family for some time.

Among the earlier vases found distributed around the area but mostly in the northern sector are the two angular alabastra [13] (Fig. 234:21), [16] (Figs. 234:10, 235:2), the cup with running spirals [7] (Fig. 234:7), the one-handled jar [3]

---

[91] *AM* xxxiv (1909), 325.

[92] I append a list of sites where Middle Helladic pithos burials have been noted; it is not claimed to be complete: Aphidna (*AM* xxi [1896], 391ff.); Thorikos (*EphArch* 1895, 228ff.); Aegina (*op.cit.*, 248); *Asine*, 116 and 121; Tiryns and Amorgos (*EphArch* 1898, 210); Lerna (*Hesperia* xxiv [1955], 28 and xxvi [1957], 148); Argos (*BCH* xxx [1906], 10-11; 79 [1955], 312-313; 83 [1959], 770-771); Berbati (*AA* li [1936], 139-140); *Korakou*, 100-101; Zerelia and Orchomenos (Wace & Thompson, *Prehistoric Thessaly*, 161 and 196); Asea (Holmberg, *Asea*, 24); Amyklaion (*BSA* 55

[1960], 76; Olympia (Dörpfeld, *Alt-Olympia*, 94-95); Malthi (*SME* 206-207); Myrsinokhori-Routsi (*Praktika* 1953, 250); and more recently Pappoulia (*Deltion* 16 [1960], 113); Koukirikos (*Praktika* 1964, 92-93). But nearly all these burials, with the exception of the last two mentioned sites in Messenia, are of children; sometimes the description is a "youngish person" (*Asine*, 116). Excluded from this list are the numerous pithos burials, many of them adult, from the "R" graves at Levkas, which are apparently Early Helladic (Dörpfeld, *Alt-Ithaka*, 221 and table on p. 249).

painted with the racket motive (Figs. 234:11, 235:5), the askos [18] decorated with circles (Figs. 234:19, 235:6), and the goblet [24] (Fig. 234:9). But having said this, we are no nearer a solution as to which burials the vases are to be attributed. All that can be said is that the Late Helladic II-III vases could have belonged to the skeleton burial and/or its predecessor, and that some of the earlier pots may have been associated originally with interments that were later gathered up and thrown into pits dug for them. Only the cup near the base of the Palace Style jar can with all probability be attributed to that burial. I have not suggested that any of the vases belonged to the other three pithos burials—though this is possible—because the latter seem to have been complete self-contained units; and when one remembers that the total number of smaller vases was about 25 and that the estimated burials were 27, there was scarcely a vase per burial.

The best equipped of the pithos burials was the one with four rapiers. These and the cauldron have Shaft Grave prototypes, though rapiers were still thought of as serviceable in war as late as Late Helladic II-III. Two of the rapiers had ivory pommels. The cauldron contained a short sword, four daggers and/or knives of different kinds, and a whetstone. This was a real warrior's grave. Several boar's-tusk fragments, some of them worked, were found among the rapiers and one in the pithos but not enough to equip a helmet of this type. Many pieces may have perished in the soil but it was noticeable that two of the best-preserved tusks had not been cut into oblong units as is usual in the case of the adornment of these helmets. They were complete tusks, point and all. One was pierced with two holes, very prominent to the eye; the other, the less complete, had no holes at all, though there may have been some on a missing fragment. On the other hand, the perforations in the tusk fragments from Tholos IV were made so as not to be seen when fitted. If it were not for the fact that the best-preserved example is pierced with two holes in the central part of the tusk, one would suggest that they were attached in series to the helmet as shown on the warriors that decorate the spout of a small faience jug from the Third Shaft Grave (*Schachtgräber*, 61, fig. 16). This was the only burial with which beads were closely associated and these were of amber, but they were few. There were certainly not enough of them to make up a necklace and one of the beads was a spacer. The majority of them may have perished, but the surviving specimens were in quite good condition. It would not be surprising if they were filched on the occasion of a subsequent funeral. Two ivory pins, both broken, and a very damaged silver cup(?) were found inside the pithos. They would not be worth the taking.

[151]

Both the spouted jar and Pit 1 pithos burials had one thing in common. Their rapiers had been purposely bent, three of them through an angle of 90 degrees. The reason for this is obscure, but it quite possibly may have had ritual significance. I do not think any other examples are known of this practice. The cauldron from Pit 1 also has a Shaft Grave prototype (see pp. 156f.). Only a rapier and a knife accompanied this burial but the pithos contained fragments of a silver headdress (see p. 156) and a gilded garland(?) at its base. The spouted jar, on the other hand, contained only a terracotta cup, probably of Late Helladic I date. The other funerary furniture, as stated, consisted of three rapiers, a dagger, and a knife. These swords also had ivory pommels.

The pommels from all three pithos burials seem to have been of the same kind. Unfortunately, with one exception the surfaces have perished and some of them are almost amorphous. Still, what is left of them suggests a flattened spherical shape. This is the form of the best-preserved example which was found ca. 0.30 m. away from the hilt of the rapier lying nearest to the conical cauldron. It had evidently become detached and rolled a little distance away. It would appear therefore that this pit was not filled in on the deposition of the body in the pithos. The same is true of the spouted jar burial. There two of the pommels had dropped off the hilts and fallen by the daggers that were placed low down by the side of the jar. The third pommel, on the other hand, must have become detached at a later date. Fragments of it were found ca. 0.70 m. away to the west of the jar at ca. 0.10 m.-0.15 m. above *stereo*.[93]

Of the four pithos burials discussed the Palace Style jar is the latest. The spouted jar on stylistic grounds is the next latest. It is difficult to decide between the two other pithoi with Middle Helladic style decoration, but perhaps the one with the bent rapier may be the later of the two as it shares this peculiar custom with the spouted jar burial. At least three of the tomb groups associated with the pithoi are contemporary with the earlier Shaft Graves of Grave Circle A and it is a familiar fact that the latter were rich in gold and silver vessels but that the pots found with them were few. It is indeed remarkable that no pottery was found with the two pithoi, presumed to be the earliest in our grave circle. Most of the vases were concentrated in the northern part of the area away from the pithos burials and, as has been stated, the pottery was of different periods. It is difficult to believe that any of these vases could be associated with the earliest burials. If they did belong, they would surely have been put with the rest of the tomb furniture in the grave pit. The implication is that the missing vessels, essen-

[93] If the pits were filled in, one can only attribute the subsequent position of these pommels to burrowing animals.

tial to the needs of the dead, were of precious metals and that these have vanished. It may be that the vision of so much finery displayed in the open pit was too much of a temptation to the relations present on a later funerary occasion. And it is perhaps significant that the one gold object that has survived almost complete from the tomb was the gold diadem found torn and crumpled up into four separate pieces in Pit 4. Its damaged state had detracted from its value.

Pit 4 was the only one of the two bone pits to contain any miscellaneous objects. Apart from the diadem these were all weapons, roughly in the ratio of one per person (skull). The other pit, long and comparatively shallow, lay alongside and to the west of the Palace Style jar and the other pithos to the south; it was devoid of all finds. The pits are presumably later than the three early pithos burials, but they could also be partly contemporary as other funerary practices may have been in vogue at the same time. The presence of both Mycenaean and Minoan elements in the same tomb suggests that a few of the dead may have been "naturalized" Minoans who preferred the style of burial customary in their homeland. The vases are all Mycenaean but a Minoan style jug [8] (Figs. 234:23, 235:7) and the cup [32] (Fig. 234:1) found in the spouted jar could be Minoan imports.

It is the absence of a dromos and of any vault that led us finally to believe that these graves were not enclosed within a tholos as originally thought. The present interpretation of a grave circle is based on analogies with other constructions of this nature that have been found in Greece. Roughly in chronological order these are the "S" graves in Levkas (W. Dörpfeld, *Alt-Ithaka*, 207ff. — early Middle Helladic); [94] Koukirikos, Messenia (*Praktika* 1964, 92-93 — Middle Helladic); Pappoulia, Messenia (*Deltion* 16 [1960], 113 — Middle Helladic); Grave Circles B and A at Mycenae — Middle Helladic-Late Helladic; the "Kyklos" at Peristeria, Messenia (*Deltion* 21 B1 [1966], 167 — Middle Helladic-Late Helladic); Samikon, Elis (*Deltion* 20 A [1965], 6-40 — Middle-Late Helladic); and Makrysia, Elis (*Deltion* 23 A [1968], 284-292.[95] But with the exception of Samikon and Makrysia all of these grave circles are very much larger than ours. Grave Circles A and B have a diameter of ca. 28 m. (Mylonas, *Ancient Mycenae*, 130), the "S"

---

[94] The "R" graves (*ibid.*, 217-249), generally thought to be Early Helladic, are excluded from this list. Similarly, I have not included other grave circles that have yielded little information to date and appear in several cases to be late. For a recent discussion of grave circles see Professor Hammond's article "Tumulus-burial in Albania, the Grave Circles of Mycenae and the Indo-Europeans" (*BSA* 62 [1967], 77-105).

[95] This grave circle was discovered only in February 1968. It is not very far from the one at Samikon. Only about a third of the circle remains. Its diameter is estimated to be 4.70 m. The wall, roughly built of flattish stones, consists of five or six courses and stands to a height of 0.60 m. Its width is 0.45 m. (*ibid.*, 284 and pl. 121). Only one cist grave was found, but associated with it were about 20 vases of Late Helladic I date (*ibid.*, pls. 124-127).

Grave Circle 12.10 m.; the walls are correspondingly thicker and higher. Adult pithos burials were found at Koukirikos and Pappoulia, but in all the others there were cist burials or shaft graves. At Samikon, one of the latest in the series, the graves were partly cut in the rock and there were covering slabs. This grave circle offers the closest parallels to the one at Pylos. Its size is identical and the circle is incomplete. The width of the wall was 0.50 m., its height in places 0.60 m. Moreover, some of the pottery is very similar. In both cases there is Middle Helladic or Middle Helladic-Late Helladic pottery but the grave circle at Samikon had a longer life and was still being used in Late Helladic III B. On the other hand, it contained no pithos burials and, although there were pit graves, many of them had slab covers. None such were found at Pylos.

However, the original interpretation of this site as a tholos should not be lightly dismissed. Both at Samikon and Pylos there was a tumulus over the graves, which was removed in modern times to make an *aloni*. At Pylos, if the evidence of the owner's family is to be credited, a great many stones were dug up in the course of this operation. These supplied building material for the construction of a storage and tool hut to the north of the site and there was sufficient left over to build a terrace wall. There could therefore have been enough stones to provide a dome over the graves. Although the foundation courses cannot have been more than 0.60 m. wide, this would have been a small tholos with a diameter just over half that of Tholos IV where the thickness of the wall is estimated at ca. 1 m. The weight of the superstructure would have been correspondingly less and the same kind of small stones were used in both constructions. It can be argued that the objects in the tomb suffered less damage than could be expected on the collapse of the vault, but the vault would not have been more than 5 m. high and many of the pots in the center of the area were badly broken and dispersed. The pithos with the conical cauldron and the Palace Style jar were crushed to a third of their height. The spouted jar, on the other hand, and the other pithos in the west sector escaped unscathed, but these were situated near the wall of the circle and would have had the protection of the vault, if there was one. The skeleton in the center of the area was protected by a mound of earth with a covering of stones (fallen?) as is shown in Sections III and IV (Figs. 332, 333, see pp. 140f.). The theory of a grave circle, adopted in this report, leaves some awkward questions unanswered. For instance, the evidence seems to show that both the spouted jar and cauldron burials in Pit 3 were left open (see p. 152). Moreover, much of the pottery was distributed widely, dispersed, and at about the same level. It was very far from being of the same date and must therefore have been deposited at different periods. This implies that there was open space within the circle to move about in. How would this be possible if there was a mound over the grave circle that had to be dug into every time there was a new interment? Even if one were to think in terms of little tumuli over the grave pits within the temenos, there would have been only two such, before the burial of the extended skeleton (the last interment), i.e., Pits 1 and 3; and the latter would include three burials of different periods. There would be, and was, a vast amount of unused space and yet 27 individuals found their resting place in this grave circle. The only answer that suggests itself in this dilemma is that the walls of the circle were sufficiently high, perhaps 1.50 m., to permit movement within the circumscribed area and that they supported a roofing of horizontal beams, a feat that should not have proved impossible with a maximum span of 5.50 m. to be bridged. The walls could be buttressed with ramps of earth on the outside. In effect, such a construction would present the aspect of a truncated tholos. And perhaps, after the last interment in the early part of Late Helladic III A when the place of burial was officially closed, a mound would have been raised over the grave circle. In the course of time the roof would cave in damaging exposed objects in the center of the area.

One of the reasons why the theory of a tholos of the traditional type has had to be abandoned is the complete lack of evidence of any chamber doorway, for which much larger stones would be required,[96] and of any dromos. The position of the latter could only be on the side of the "open" semicircle and more specifically to the south. Here the high ground slopes down gently towards the south in the form of a spur. To explain the disappearance of the dromos one would have to suppose that it had been eroded away over the centuries under the recurring action of winter rains. Although the local rock, a kind of marl, which is not very much harder than compressed earth, is easily and rapidly worn away, too great a mass of earth is involved for this to be a likely explanation.[97] But undoubtedly this phenomenon of erosion ensured the immunity of the grave circle from tomb robbers. The burial ground ceased to be used about the beginning of Late Helladic III A, that is, at a time when Mycenaean civilization was in its full vigor and its ascendancy was to continue for another 150 to 200 years. It is unlikely that there would be any attempt to rob the tomb during that flourishing period; but it was perhaps during that time and shortly after the last

---

[96] But the larger stones would certainly be selected for the building of tool hut and terrace wall (see above).

[97] There is always the possibility that there never was a dromos. Cf. the small tholoi in Euboea (Papavasileiou, Περὶ τῶν ἐν Εὐβοία ἀρχαίων τάφων, 33, fig. 22, α — Oxylithos; p. 48, fig. 34, β — Belousia). But these had very thick walls and a

massive doorway. The Analipsis tholos, on the border of Arcadia and Laconia, had a doorway but no dromos (*Praktika* 1954, 274). On the other hand, a grave circle at Koukounara, Messenia (*Ergon* 1959, 118), which cannot be dated with certainty, contained three very small tholoi that had no door at all! Consequently, a dromos was superfluous.

interment that the mound caved in. With the passage of decades it would lose its characteristic shape and cease to be a landmark. The existence of the grave circle would be forgotten. By the twentieth century the mound had shrunk to a fraction of its former size and when what was left of it was removed to create a modern *aloni,* only the upper levels would have suffered some disturbance. The deeper sunk pits and their contents escaped unscathed. In this manner the burials survived intact from the closing of the tomb in the early fourteenth century until it was reopened for excavation at the present day. The site has now been filled in and it has once more become an *aloni.*

W. D. T.

OBJECTS FOUND
(Figs. 327-329)

Pit 1

GOLD LEAF

Wreath? (CM. 2006-11, Figs. 225:2, 227:9): fragments embossed with recurrent pattern. As found, fragments wrapped round core of earth (CM. 2011) shaped like a quoit. Reconstruction of pattern based on best-preserved piece (CM. 2009): l. 0.052 m.; max. w. 0.0185 m. Design apparently confined to upper surface only. Not possible to estimate diameter of "wreath" as it had broken apart in the soil.

Pattern seems based on foliate band decoration of cross pieces on gold ornament from Shaft Grave III (*Schachtgräber,* pl. XVI:15, 17, 19).

Tiny pieces (CM. 2017) probably belonging to the above.

SILVER

Ornaments (CM. 2004, Figs. 225:6, 227:8), 4 restored from many fragments: l. ca. 0.24 m., max. w. ca. 0.07 m. Gold examples in shaft graves of Grave Circle A, which they resemble, are pointed (*Schachtgräber,* pl. XIV:5). Edges reinforced with bronze wire as shown by a few fragments found with bronze adhering. Same technique used on shaft grave examples (*ibid.,* p. 44:5). Design, stamped in dots, is same on all four ornaments apparently representing stylized palm trees, one on top of another and di-

minishing in size. On each side of palm trees a triangle. No parallel to treatment of the palm in this way known to me. Use of the ornaments is uncertain. Karo suggests that those in the shaft graves were adapted to a crown with points directed upwards (*ibid.,* 183).

Small pieces (CM. 2012) belonging to ornaments, CM. 2004.

BRONZE

Cauldron (CM. 2199, Fig. 228:3a, b): restored h. without handle 0.162 m.; h. with handle 0.225 m.; d. rim 0.377 m.; d. ca. 0.40 m.; th. 0.003 m.; w. (inner—of one handle) 0.075 m.; th. handle 0.011 m.; l. of "hands" 0.068 m.; distance between hands 0.085 m. Almost complete; pieces of body missing; bottom much dented. Shallow vessel with rounded bottom and incurving rim. Two handles, round in section, placed vertically, riveted to vessel just below rim. Terminals of handles shaped like human hands with extended fingers (Fig. 228:3b) held together (w. hand ca. 0.03 m.; w. fingers ca. 0.015 m.). One rivet passes through hand and a second between second and third fingers at their base.

Several cauldrons of exactly this form were found in the shaft graves, one having same kind of handle attachment, though fingers of hand are not incised (*Schacht-gräber*, pl. CLIX, bottom right).

Rapier (CM. 2186, Fig. 229:13): l. from shoulder 0.68 m.; w. 0.036 m.; th. blade ca. 0.002 m.; th. with midrib ca. 0.01 m. Fair condition; most of tang missing. Blade bent at angle of 90°. One rivet originally attached to end of tang but has since become detached. Midrib angular in section and on each side of it are two or possibly three grooved lines. Probably decorated, since at tang end traces of what appears to be stylized palm leaf in silver. Shoulders of blade rounded, i.e., this is Type A rapier (*Schachtgräber*, 97, fig. 31 and pl. LXXIII:434, 399, 417, 414). Two large and one small rivet belonging to this rapier were found separately:

a (CM. 2005): l. 0.026 m.; d. shaft 0.0048 m.; d. head 0.011 m. Shaft roughly square in section, head convex.

b (CM. 2005): l. 0.026 m.; d. shaft 0.0045 m.; d. head 0.01 m. Section of shaft irregular hexagon, head convex.

c (CM. 2013): l. 0.0135 m.; d. shaft 0.004 m.; d. head 0.0065 m. Shaft round to square in section, head convex. Small rivet would be fixed to blade just below shoulder.

For further details concerning rapiers see below (p. 163).

Knife (CM. 2192, Fig. 229:11): l. 0.325 m.; w. blade 0.028 m.; th. blade 0.004 m.; l. hilt 0.11 m.; d. hilt 0.013 m. Almost complete; fair condition. Tip and part of blade missing. Narrow blade, slightly wider at center and tapering to point. Hilt consists of central partition in axis of blade (of which it is an extension) with flanges on each side, that have been folded over to grip the two hilt plates. The latter of wood, some fragments of this material are still *in situ*. Edges of flanges scalloped and V-shaped notch cut out of base of partition.

This type of knife is fairly common, and its context seems to be invariably Late Helladic I or II. Vertical flanges, cf. *Schacht-*gräber, pl. XCVI:923 from Shaft Grave VI; *BSA* XXV (1921-23), 291, fig. 51 from Cyclopean tomb. Flanges folded over, cf. *Schachtgräber*, pl. XCVII:450 from Shaft Grave IV (according to text). Flanges with scalloped edge and folded over, cf. *ibid.*, pl. CII:458 from Shaft Grave IV; *EphArch* 1889, pl. 8:9 from Vapheio tholos tomb; *Praktika* 1964, pl. 94:3 from Kephalovryson, Messenia.

Pins (CM. 2001β), fragments.

IVORY

Pin (CM. 2001α): l. pres. 0.065 m.; d. 0.006 m.; d. head 0.012 m.; th. head 0.008 m. Fair condition. Incomplete: upper part of pin, round in section, with mushroom type of head. Suggestion of vertical incisions on head.

Pin (CM. 2003, Fig. 225:5): l. pres. 0.116 m.; d. 0.006 m.; d. head 0.005 m. Fair condition. Almost complete but point missing. Head merely indicated by slight swelling ending in flat surface.

Fragment of pommel? (CM. 2002, Fig. 225:3): d. 0.038 m.; d. hole 0.02 m.; th. 0.004 m.-0.008 m. Fair condition. Probably section of pommel of spherical form. Hole would be part of socket for tang.

POTTERY

Pithos [27] (CM. 1600, Fig. 233:1): h. 0.49 m.; h. rim 0.066 m.; d. rim 0.31 m.; d. 0.42 m.; d. base 0.135 m.; h. to bottom of handle 0.375 m.; th. handle 0.03 m. Restored; complete but for a few fragments. Oval shape with flat base. Wide mouth. Two round loop-handles, uptilted. Pink to red clay containing sherd or pebbly grits, fired soft to medium. Firing uneven so that surface shows red blotches in places. Decoration almost entirely effaced, but upper part of vase from just below handle to bottom of rim appears to have been covered with red wash. Traces of band of irregular St. Andrew crosses between two parallel lines below one handle and to right of it. Paint black, appears to be matt.

Handleless undecorated jars used for burial at Asine (*Asine*, 281, fig. 193:8, 9, 10) resemble in shape the pithos from our grave circle but their period is Middle Helladic II. Nearer the date of our pithos but only approximating the shape are storage jars from *Mochlos* (fig. 51, facing p. 88) and *Pachyammos* (pl. 1:3; pl. v, right, pl. xvi: xiv-c). These are jar burials of Middle Minoan III. A closer parallel but of larger size is a pithos from Olympia used for a child burial (Dörpfeld, *Alt-Olympia* I [1935], 94, fig. 15). Rim sherd of a pithos from a grave shaft at Lerna may have belonged to the same type of jar decorated in white on red-brown paint with a pattern similar to that from Pylos grave circle but above handle instead of below (*Hesperia* xxiv [1955], pl. 17:e).

Pit 2 (Figs. 327-329)

BRONZE

Knife (CM. 2027α, Fig. 230:9): l. 0.233 m.; w. 0.016 m.-0.043 m.; th. blade 0.0085 m.; l. rivets 0.017 m.; d. rivet 0.004 m. Complete; fair condition. No differentiation between hilt and blade; both cast as one piece. Blade expands to rounded end, greatest breadth being near tip. End of hilt has V-shaped notch. Three rivets in row in long axis still in position. At third rivet there was visible originally a curved line, an arc, open towards the tip of knife; this probably marked limit of hafting.

An almost identical knife from the Vapheio tomb (*EphArch* 1889, pl. 8:7) is a little smaller and has no notch in hilt. A single-edged knife with similar hafting comes from a chamber tomb at Dendra; blade different but appears to have notch in hilt, although it is described "as broken off at both ends" (*NT, Dendra*, 44, fig. 48:3, 45, no. 11). Cf. also notched hilt of knife from the Heraeum (*Prosymna*, fig. 263:7).

Awl with ivory handle (CM. 2027b, Fig. 230:8): l. over-all 0.19 m.; th. awl 0.006 m.; l. handle 0.073 m.; w. handle 0.014 m.-0.022 m. Fair condition. Awl square in section and slightly curved; found in that state. Ivory handle not well preserved; half of lower half and part of upper half missing. Round in section and wider at broken end. This presumably would allow a better grip. Cf. almost identical handle of ivory from Menidi tholos (*KG*, pl. ix:19) and an awl handle of bone in Tomb 533 at Mycenae (*ChT*, 119, no. 8a).

Mirror (CM. 2026, Fig. 228:4): d. 0.146 m.; th. ca. 0.003 m. Fair condition; part of rim missing. Two holes, 0.017 m. apart, near edge of rim indicate where handle was fixed. Cf. *RT, Dendra*, pl. xxxiii:1 and 2; There are many examples from other sites.

Bowl (CM. 2028, reconstruction Fig. 227:3): complete but in many fragments and not restorable (Fig. 228:2). Approximate measurements when found: h. 0.06 m.; d. 0.11 m.-0.13 m.; d. base 0.05 m.; h. handles above rim 0.013 m.; w. handles 0.017 m. Handles round in section, base concave. Fragment of silver bowl with handle attached may have been part of a similar vase (*Schachtgräber*, 155, fig. 74, top, left). Cf. also bronze bowl of slightly larger diameter (*ibid.*, 156, fig. 75).

Scale pan (CM. 2025, Figs. 227:10, 230:7): d. 0.055 m., th. ca. 0.0015 m. In good condition; almost complete. Parts of rim missing. Slightly concave. Embossed on convex side with twelve-leaf rosette. Three suspension holes (and probably a fourth broken away) at equidistant intervals along edge (cf. CM. 2066, 2072, 2076, p. 168). Elaborately decorated scale pans of gold were found in the shaft graves (*Schachtgräber*, pl. xxxiv: 81, 82). They presumably had symbolic significance and were not intended for everyday use.

FLINT

Arrowhead (CM. 2023): l. pres. 0.017 m.; w. 0.0093 m.; th. 0.0023 m. Point missing. Type vi (see p. 127 and Fig. 226). Found between legs of skeleton.

PASTE

White bead (CM. 2029): d. 0.0165 m.; th. 0.01 m.; d. hole ca. 0.005 m. Two fragments, mended. Found by left collarbone of skeleton.

TERRACOTTA

Female figurine (CM. 2024, Fig. 232:5a-c) [98]: h. 0.112 m.; w. 0.0503 m.; w. head 0.025 m.; th. head 0.0233 m.; th. below arms 0.027 m.; w. stem 0.026 m.; th. stem 0.022 m.; d. base 0.037 m.-0.0395 m. Good condition. Birdlike head with pellet eyes. Suggestion of ears. Breasts and arms molded, the latter away from body so that light shines through. Slight swelling of body above "hands. Thick stem with splaying base, hollowed out underneath. Fairly well levigated and well-fired clay; surface polished where preserved. Black-brown to brown, lustrous paint, worn away in many places. Head, breasts, and pellet eyes originally solidly painted. Most of paint has worn off arms so that it is not possible to say whether they were treated in same manner. Rest of body decorated with broad to narrow, vertically wavy lines; these are best preserved on back. Suggestion of slanting sash below hands but in front part of body only. May be one of earliest-known figurines, since no pottery later than early Late Helladic III A (Furumark's III A:1) came from our grave circle.

POTTERY

Askos [33] (CM. 1583, Fig. 234:20): h. 0.086 m.; d. 0.081 m.; d. base 0.025 m. Found with skeleton. Complete; spout mended. Flattened piriform shape, flat base. Tapering, conical spout with offset rounded rim. Vertical loop-handle on top of vase in axis of spout. Handle round in section (no exact parallel in *MP*, cf. Type 195, pp. 32, 41, 44, 67, figs. 6, 11, 12, 20). Light gray clay reminiscent of Minyan ware, fired medium to soft. Undecorated. Askoi have long tradition but when undecorated are difficult to date.

Pit 3 (SE) (Figs. 327-329)

SILVER

Cup?, fragment (CM. 2048, Figs. 225:4, 231:7, bottom left): l. 0.0355 m., w. 0.029 m. Small part preserved; very fragile condition. Metal as thin as gold leaf. A reconstruction of the design has been attempted (Fig. 227:11): the pattern seems to have consisted of central circle enclosed within two concentric series of smaller circles. Center piece (estimated d. 0.0185 m.) marked out by little engraved dashes giving effect of repoussé. Within the circle six arcs arching inward from the circumference. Outside center motive a ring of eight circles (d. 0.0115 m.) outlined in same technique but with central part embossed. Outer ring composed of 15 similar smaller circles (d. 0.0083 m.). Professor Lang suggests that this may be base of shallow cup; if so, one must suppose that the metal was originally very much stronger than it is now. So little is preserved that it is impossible to produce parallels, though many examples in gold of embossed circles are known from the shaft graves.

Fragments, apparently undecorated, that may be part of the above fragment. All were found within the pithos.

BRONZE

Rapiers, four almost complete in fair condition (Fig. 229:1-4): fragments missing from each blade. Only a small part of tang preserved in each instance but most of rivets have survived. Three large rivets usually in tang in axis of blade; two smaller fixed near edge of blade just below shoulder, one on each side. Shoulders rounded. Midrib, split down middle in nearly every case, angular in section with exception of No. 2 (CM. 2189) which appears to be rounded. Two or three longitudinal grooves incised on each side of midribs, but oxidized condition of bronze renders them barely visible. Blade of CM. 2198 shows traces of design in silver no longer recognizable.

[98] E. French, "The Development of Mycenaean Terracotta Figurines." *BSA* LXVI (1971) 101-187, p. 109.

No. 1 (CM. 2188): l. from shoulder 0.825 m.; w. 0.052 m. One large rivet in tang and two small rivets in blade preserved. The two missing from tang (CM. 2064) recovered separately. Shafts of all three rectangular in section with average measurements of 0.0065 m. x 0.005 m. (Fig. 231:7). Rivet in tang has l. 0.019 m., two loose rivets l. 0.0225 m. and 0.025 m. respectively. Heads slightly domed.

No. 2 (CM. 2189): l. from shoulder 0.722 m.; w. 0.05 m. One large rivet in tang (l. 0.016 m.) and one small rivet in blade preserved. Other small rivet is fixed to broken-off fragment of blade. Large rivet round in section.

No. 3 (CM. 2196), the best preserved: l. from shoulder 0.702 m.; w. 0.05 m.; w. near point 0.016 m.; th. blade 0.0035 m.; th. with midribs 0.0175 m.; one large rivet in tang (l. 0.017 m.; rectangular shaft 0.0075 m. x 0.0055 m.) and one small rivet in blade (l. 0.012 m.; d. head 0.0065 m.) are still in position. The small loose rivet (CM. 2103) measures: l. 0.0135 m.; d. shaft (round to square in section) ca. 0.004 m.; d. head (more or less flat) ca. 0.0065 m. Rivet heads are coated with silver.

No. 4 (CM. 2198): l. from shoulder 0.687 m.; w. 0.048 m.; th. blade 0.004 m.; th. with midribs 0.026 m. One large rivet (l. 0.018 m.; w. shaft-square 0.006 m.) still in position in tang. Two small rivets in blade also preserved.

Pin (CM. 2050A, Fig. 230:11): l. 0.115 m.; th. 0.002 m.; d. head 0.011 m. Found with rapiers. Good condition. Complete; point has been reattached. Disk head. Shaft projects slightly through disk.

Pins (CM. 2051, Fig. 230:12-14): three restored, complete. Similar to CM. 2050A. Found in pithos with fourth and fifth layers of bones. Probably pins of shrouds. Dimensions: (a) l. ca. 0.115 m. (bent); th. 0.002 m.; d. head 0.013 m. (b) l. 0.108 m.; th. 0.002 m.; d. head 0.013 m. (c) l. 0.106 m.; th. 0.002 m.; d. head 0.012 m.

Pin? (CM. 2082): l. pres. 0.127 m.; th. ca. 0.004 m. Found ca. 0.23 m. down to south of cauldron. Rectangular in section. Tapering at both ends. An implement?

Pin? (CM. 2082, Fig. 230:17): l. pres. 0.112 m.; th. 0.0018 m. On level with cauldron. Broken but restored.

Pin (CM. 2047, Fig. 231:7): l. pres. 0.072 m.; th. 0.002 m. In pithos with fifth layer of bones. Good condition. Point preserved. Probably had disk head like CM. 2050A, 2051.

Disk heads of pins (CM. 2048, 2054, Fig. 231:7): Found with silver fragment CM. 2048 at bottom of pithos. Badly corroded. May belong to headless pins described above.

Knife (CM. 2056, Fig. 230:10): l. 0.205 m.; w. 0.011 m.-0.015 m.; th. 0.0035 m.; l. rivets 0.014 m.; d. rivets 0.0025 m. Second layer of bones in pithos. Restored, complete. No differentiation between haft and blade. Four rivets in a row in axis of blade; three in position, end one missing. Shape well represented in tombs at Heraeum (*Prosymna*, figs. 262:1; 377:6; cf. also fig. 503:2).

Cauldron (CM. 2366, Fig. 228:1a-c): h. 0.36 m.; h. with handle 0.396 m.; d. 0.352 m. x 0.43 m.; d. base 0.155 m. x 0.18 m.; h. rim 0.03 m.; th. rim 0.003 m.; h. base 0.03 m.; w. handle 0.008 m.; th. handle 0.004 m. Fair condition. Almost complete; several pieces of body and base missing. Shape of body basically conical with bulging shoulder below vertical rim. Body made of two metal plates: (i) from base to middle of belly; (ii) from middle to rim, riveted together. Edge of rim thickened or rolled. Torus base. Narrow ribbon handles, rectangular in section, set vertically on upper edge of rim. The ends of each handle are split into two plates that grip rim one on each side and are riveted to rim on both sides. Rim itself apparently made separately of two pieces riveted to one another and to a vertical flange on upper part of vessel. A great number of rivets were used in this operation. Cf. three cauldrons of same shape from shaft graves, two illustrated (*Schachtgräber,* pl. CLX). The technique of riveting rim to body and handles to rim the same, but bodies of shaft grave examples are made of several plates riveted together, because of their greater size.

Fragments (CM. 2038), belonging to cauldron, not used in its restoration.

Short sword or "machete" (CM. 2197, Fig. 229:5): l. 0.525 m.; w. 0.038 m.; th. 0.0145 m.; d. ring 0.031 m. Inside cauldron. Fair condition; corroded, parts of blade missing. Shape that of very large knife with rounded, tapering handle, end of which is curled over into a ring. Much like Central American machete. Three very similar weapons, called *Schlachtmesser* by Karo, illustrated in *Schachtgräber,* pl. XCVII:445, 447, 443, come from Shaft Grave IV (*ibid.,* 103-104) and are somewhat longer than our example. All have unique feature of a terminal ring.

Knife (CM. 2195, Fig. 229:6): l. 0.347 m.; l. hilt 0.11 m.; d. hilt 0.015 m.; w. blade 0.023 m.; th. blade 0.006 m. Inside cauldron. Fair condition, almost complete. Tip missing. One rivet and part of wooden hilt preserved. Type is exactly similar to one described on p. 157, but blade narrower.

Dagger (CM. 2194, Fig. 229:7): l. without end rivet 0.171 m.; w. 0.07 m.; w. butt 0.035 m. Inside cauldron. Repaired. Almost complete; parts of blade missing. Leaf-shaped blade with rounded to pointed tip. Outline of blade rounder and butt end narrower when found (0.015 m.), the three transverse rivets were not visible,[99] and there was no room for them. Only end rivet, larger than others, seen. This immediately behind central transverse rivet.

When uncovered, its form, laurel leaf shape, bore some resemblance to a dagger from the Heraeum (*Prosymna,* fig. 299:2). It may be that when it was cleaned three additional rivet holes, or the outline of them, were revealed and in that case it has been

correctly restored. Its present shape relates it to the broad-based daggers, of which several examples were found in this tomb and are described below.

Short dagger or knife (CM. 2191, Fig. 229: 9): l. 0.21 m.; w. 0.015 m.; th. blade 0.004 m.; l. hilt 0.085 m.; w. hilt 0.01 m.; th. hilt 0.005 m. Inside cauldron. Fair condition. Slender blade slightly wider at center. Hilt consists of central partition with parallel flanges on each side. These are not folded over as in the other knives, nor are they scalloped. Hilt end has V-shaped notch. For vertical flange see examples quoted under CM. 2192 (p. 157).

Fragment, knife or short dagger (CM. 2193, Fig. 229:8): l. without end rivet 0.096 m.; w. 0.033 m.; th. blade 0.003 m. Transverse row of three small rivets;[100] behind middle one a larger rivet (l. 0.014 m., d. head 0.012 m.). Inside cauldron. Small weapon; poorly preserved, exact shape uncertain. Possibly like knife with ivory handle from Shaft Grave II (*Schachtgräber,* pl. LXXII:216, center). Arrangement of rivets similar (*ibid.,* p. 70:216a). Cf. also triangular dagger from the Heraeum (*Prosymna,* fig. 283:1) and one from Mycenae (*ChT,* pl. XXIX:17—same hafting as knife from Shaft Grave).

STONE

Hone (CM. 2102, Fig. 232:2): l. 0.165 m.; w. 0.018 m.; d. hole 0.008 m. Inside cauldron. Complete; fair condition. Rather soft, dark gray schist? Surface flakes easily. Square in section with rounded corners. One end pierced for suspension. Several whetstones of similar type are known from shaft graves (*Schachtgräber,* pl. CII:512 from Grave IV; p. 163, fig. 79:930 from Grave VI; p. 149, numbers 860 and 861 from Grave V). Cf. also *NT, Dendra,* 46, fig. 49:2. Dimensions vary; some larger, some smaller than our example.

Amethyst bead (CM. 2043β, Fig. 232:6): d. 0.0095 m.; d. hole 0.0015 m. Found a few

---

[99] They are silver-capped and belong to rapiers.

[100] They are silver-capped and belong to rapiers.

centimeters above rapiers. Intact. Spherical.

Flint arrowheads (CM. 2043ϵ, Fig. 232:6):
(a) l. 0.035 m.; w. 0.011 m.; th. 0.0033 m.;
(b) l. 0.028 m.; w. 0.01 m.; th. 0.003 m.
Found a few centimeters above rapiers.
Type VI (Fig. 226). Light yellow flint. Beautifully worked on both faces.

Obsidian arrowhead (CM. 2055δ, Fig. 231:7):
l. 0.025 m.; w. 0.011 m.; th. 0.0033 m.
Found a few centimeters above rapiers.
Intact. Type VI; thicker than usual.

AMBER

Spacer bead (CM. 2040, Figs. 227:2, 231:7):
l. ca. 0.026 m.; w. 0.0195 m.; th. ca. 0.005
m. Found among rapiers. Complete in four
fragments, broken along string-holes. Not
restored. Originally oblong, pierced with
three parallel holes in the short axis. Similar beads found in Fourth Shaft Grave
(*Schachtgräber*, pl. LVII:513). (For discussion
of amber spacer beads in general see above,
p. 128).

Spherical beads, 2 complete: found a few
centimeters above rapiers in fairly good
condition.
(a) CM. 2040, Fig. 231:7: d. 0.0215 m.;
th. 0.019 m.; d. hole 0.003 m. Broken
in two. Repaired?
(b) CM. 2043β, Fig. 232:6: d. 0.0127 m.;
th. 0.011 m.; d. hole ca. 0.0035 m.

Flattened spherical bead (CM. 2040, Fig.
231:7): d. 0.02 m.; th. 0.0145 m.; d. hole
ca. 0.003 m. Just inside cauldron. Complete; fair condition.

Drum bead (CM. 2043β, Fig. 232:6): d.
0.0145 m.-0.016 m., th. 0.01 m.-0.012 m.;
d. hole 0.005 m. A few centimeters above
rapiers. Complete; fair condition. Irregular
form.

Fragments (CM. 2047): two pieces of large
bead (largest: h. 0.014 m.; w. 0.0125 m.)
found under pithos. Fairly good condition.
Two other fragments (not measurable),
perhaps from bead, found among rapiers.

Two pieces, apparently not beads, possibly
talismans. Almost complete. Crackly surface, very friable.

CM. 2043β, Figs. 227:5, 232:6: l. 0.023 m.;
w. 0.018 m.; th. 0.009 m. A few centimeters above rapiers. Partly damaged.
Resembles an oval bead.

CM. 2055α, Fig. 231:7: l. 0.0315 m.;
w. 0.0185 m.; th. 0.0115 m. Among rapiers. Irregular shape.

IVORY

Pommel (CM. 2050, Fig. 231:4): h. 0.043 m.;
d. 0.05 m.-0.055 m.; d. socket ca. 0.015 m.;
depth socket for tang ca. 0.006 m.; drill-hole (d. 0.004 m.) for side locking pin.
Complete; good condition. Flattened spherical and slightly irregular in shape. Apparently made in two pieces, the smaller
upper section having different veining
from that of lower part, and the axes of
the veining are at right angles to one another. Pommel undecorated. Best-preserved example of those found in this tomb.
Not attached to any of the four rapiers but
had rolled a little distance away. No exact
parallel to the shape, as far as I have been
able to discover. Several examples of ivory
pommels are known from the shaft graves.
One from Fourth Shaft Grave somewhat
similar (*Schachtgräber*, pl. LXXVI:485).

Pommel (CM. 2051α, Fig. 231:2): th. 0.05
m.-0.073 m. At head of rapier CM. 2196
or CM. 2198. Fairly solid although badly
worn. Original shape cannot be exactly
determined, but probably similar to CM.
2050.

Pin, two fragments (CM. 2049, Fig. 231:7):
(a) l. 0.045 m.; th. 0.005 m.; (b) l. 0.027 m.;
th. 0.005 m. Found with rapiers. Fair condition, point missing.

BOAR'S TUSKS

Three, almost complete (Fig. 231:7); two of
them mended.

CM. 2057: l. pres. 0.088 m.; w. 0.0125 m.;
th. 0.004 m. Found at bottom of pithos.
Good condition; repaired from three
pieces. Best-preserved example. Two
holes, drilled close together in middle
of tusk in long axis.

CM. 2040, three fragments: total l. pres.

ca. 0.082 m.; w. 0.016 m.; th. 0.0045 m. Outside pithos among rapiers. Tip and many small pieces missing. No drill holes traceable. It would have been about same size as tusk CM. 2057.

CM. 2055γ, three joining fragments: l. 0.043 m.; w. 0.013 m.; th. 0.0035 m. A few centimeters above rapiers. Smaller than two preceding. One pierced hole.

Two fragments (CM. 2043γ, Fig. 232:6): (a) repaired from two pieces l. 0.022 m.; w. ca. 0.015 m.; th. 0.003 m. (b) l. 0.017 m.; w. 0.016 m.; th. 0.003 m. Both found a few centimeters above rapiers. Fair condition. Each pierced with three holes, two parallel near straight-cut edge and one at other end of the break.

Fragments (a) and (b) are the only pieces that have sawn edges and may therefore have been used on a helmet. The three pointed examples described above are all pierced for attachment but may have been used for other purposes, unless they were terminals of the cheek pieces of the helmet (*ChT*, pl. XXXVIII).

Fragment (CM. 2040, Fig. 231:7): l. 0.02 m.; w. 0.0125 m.; th. 0.003 m. Found among rapiers.

BONE

Pin, point only (CM. 2055β, Fig. 231:7): l. pres. 0.026 m.; d. 0.005 m. Found a few centimeters above rapiers. Repaired, possibly ivory.

POTTERY

Pithos [28] (CM. 1601, Fig. 233:2): h. 0.625 m.; d. mouth 0.318 m.; d. neck 0.268 m.; d. 0.472 m.; d. base 0.146 m.; w. rim 0.028 m.; l. handle ca. 0.145 m.; min. w. handle 0.042 m.; min. th. handle 0.021 m. Almost complete, repaired. Ovoid shape tapering to narrow, flat base. Wide mouth with sharply offset rim. Two horizontal strap handles, slightly channeled, placed just above greatest diameter. Grayish-white clay rather soft-fired, containing grits and small pebbles. Jar covered with black paint fairly well preserved on lower part. Deco-ration, white on dark, very worn, confined to shoulder zone, consists of three bands or zones separated from one another by broad bands of white. In upper zone a group of diagonal lines alternating with group slanting in opposite direction; mid-dle zone series of crosshatched diamonds; lower zone groups of diagonal lines in series, all sloping in same direction. Deco-ration typically Middle Helladic.

Shape recalls jar from Phaistos (*PM* II, i, 205, fig. 116) and fine example from Argo-lis (*Asine*, color pl. 1), but both are earlier — Middle Minoan II and Middle Helladic II respectively. Closest analogy is pithos of Middle Helladic III from Lerna. Shape not so elegant. It is in fact very bulbous and has an extra handle (or pair of han-dles?) below rim, but decoration is in same tradition (*Hesperia* XXIX [1960], pl. 70:k). Cf. also very large pithos of Middle Hel-ladic III from Eleusis with extremely nar-row base; the mouth unfortunately is missing (*Eleusis*, 100, fig. 81).

Pit 3 (NE) (Figs. 327-329)

BRONZE

Rapiers, three (CM. 2182, CM. 2183, CM. 2184, Fig. 229:12, 14, 15). Fair condition; one broken, all bent, two at angle of ca. 90°. Identical in form with those found in Pit 3 (SE). All have angular midribs flanked by two or more parallel grooved lines. All rapiers from this grave circle are of Type A. Type B not represented (see *Schachtgräber*, 97-98).

Rapier (CM. 2182, Fig. 229:15): l. from shoulder 0.768 m.; max. w. 0.045 m. May have had some decoration, no longer vis-ible. Three rivets in tang when found, but most of tang having perished, rivets came loose. Their dimensions and character-istics differ slightly: CM. 2055ε, Fig. 231:7, round shafts and convex heads. (a) l. 0.0242 m.; d. shaft 0.0075 m.; d. head 0.0115 m. (b) l. 0.023 m.; d. shaft 0.0073 m.; d. head 0.012 m. CM. 2036, Fig. 231:9 (c) l. 0.021 m.; w. shaft 0.0058 m.-0.0075 m.; d. head 0.011 m. Shaft rectangular in section, heads flat. Apparently the end rivet, i.e., the one near tip of tang. Of the two smaller rivets in blade below shoulder, one had become detached, its shape distorted (CM. 2058α): l. 0.01 m.-0.013 m.; w. shaft 0.0035 m.-0.0052 m.; d. head 0.008 m. Rectangular in section, flat head. The remaining rivet, still fixed in blade, appears to be round in section.

Rapier (CM. 2183, Fig. 229:14): l. from shoulder 0.756 m.; w. 0.031 m.; th. blade 0.002 m.; th. blade with midribs 0.0105 m. Best preserved. Originally had three rivets in tang but only one can be allotted to it with certainty (CM. 2058α): l. 0.0235 m.; w. shaft 0.004 m.-0.008 m.; d. head ca. 0.012 m. Shaft rectangular in section, heads more flat than convex. The two small rivets just below shoulder not preserved.

Decoration: running spirals in silver on each face of midrib. Pattern identical with that on rapier of same type from Fifth Shaft Grave (*Schachtgräber*, pl. LXXXII:727).

Rapier (CM. 2184, Fig. 229:12): l. from shoulder pres. 0.475 m.; w. 0.041 m. The point (CM. 2187, Fig. 229:16), l. pres. 0.23 m.; w. 0.021 m., broken in two pieces, found still adhering to fracture. Originally had three large rivets; one, attached when it was lifted, probably that incorrectly shown with rapier CM. 2182 in Fig. 229:15. The other two found loose in the soil near spouted jar: CM. 2058α: (a) l. 0.0202 m.; d. 0.0082 m.; d. head ca. 0.011 m.; shaft round, head flat. (b) l. 0.021 m.; w. shaft 0.0043 m.-0.007 m.; d. head ca. 0.011 m.; shaft rectangular in section, head convex. The two smaller rivets in blade are missing.

Decoration: four grooved lines on each side of midrib extending up blade to shoulder where each group splays or curves to right and left. Outermost grooved line decorated with series of stylized leaves, Furumark's "Foliate Band" (*MP*, Motive 64:6, p. 397 fig. 69). See also rim and handle decoration on bronze bowl from Knos-

sos (*PM* II, ii, 639, figs. 403, 404). Design poorly preserved but apparently carried out in silver.

Knife (CM. 2190, Fig. 229:10): l. 0.387 m.; w. 0.037 m.; th. 0.003 m.; l. hilt 0.11 m.; d. hilt 0.02 m. Complete; good condition. Longest knife of this type found in our grave circle. Hilt has central partition with scalloped flanges folded over exactly as in previous examples (pp. 157, 161). No notch at base.

Dagger (CM. 2185, Fig. 229:17): l. 0.18 m.; max. w. 0.051 m.; w. hilt end 0.035 m.; th. blade 0.003 m. Fair condition; almost complete. Bits of blade and one rivet missing. Broad hilt end with three rivets in a transverse row. When found, a larger rivet immediately behind central one of the three. Blade expands to slightly greater width than hilt end and finishes in rounded tip.

Daggers of this type are well-known in Argolis, all apparently of Late Helladic I or Late Helladic II (*Prosymna*, 332ff., Class b and figs. 604, 606; *NT, Dendra*, 44, Fig. 48:2; *Schachtgräber*, pl. LXXII:224 left, p. 71: 224c "*rasiermesser*" from Grave II; p. 140, fig. 57, unnumbered, from Grave V; pl. XCIX:482 from Grave IV. The last-named although badly preserved shows fourth rivet behind the other three as was found in our example.

I V O R Y

Pommel (CM. 2052, Fig. 231:1): h. 0.052 m.; d. pres. 0.053 m.-0.085 m. Shapeless but in fair condition.

Pommel (CM. 2053, Fig. 231:3): h. 0.042 m.; w. 0.059 m.-0.065 m. Shapeless; fair condition. Originally probably flattened spherical.

Fragment (CM. 2045). Possibly part of a third pommel or may belong to CM. 2053.

Ten fragments (CM. 2037) that may have belonged to CM. 2045. Not possible to reconstruct shape from these pieces. Two show sections of a socket suitable for tang of rapier.

POTTERY

Spouted jar [29] (CM. 1602, Fig. 233:5a, b): h. 0.615 m.; d. 0.437 m.; d. at 0.27 m. above floor, where there is a slight bulge, 0.405 m.; d. base 0.17 m.; d. rim 0.445 m.; w. rim 0.036 m.; h. or th. rim 0.025 m.; h. spout 0.085 m.; outer w. spout 0.046 m.; l. spout 0.075 m.; min. th. handle 0.022 m. Repaired; complete but for rear vertical handle. Tall conical jar of uneven profile. Slight bulge in body about two-fifths up from base. Slightly projecting flat-topped rim. Immediately below, short cylindrical spout. Opposite, at back of jar, originally a vertical loop-handle. Two round, uptilted loop-handles equidistant between spout and rear handle slightly lower than spout. Flat base. Very coarse whitish clay, red in parts, containing pebbly grits. Reddish-pink surface covered with white wash on which rather worn red to black paint. Decoration Ripple Pattern (*MP*, Motive 78:1, p. 422 fig. 73) in three zones separated by very broad bands of solid paint; one band below rim and above upper zone, another band below third zone, narrower band just above base. Pattern finishes ca. 0.18 m. above base, but paint was allowed to trickle onto undecorated surface. Not certain whether ripple pattern applied before or after zonal bands were painted. Paint on rim and handles largely worn off, but inside of jar painted to depth of 0.12 m. Pattern, according to Furumark, is confined to Late Helladic I.

No parallel to this jar on mainland known to me but type well-known in Crete during Middle Minoan III and Late Minoan I. Very fine Middle Minoan III example, but without spout, found near Knossos (*PM* I, 585, fig. 428). The excavator, Hatzidakis, says "the vessel lay with its mouth to the West. The head of the skeleton was at the bottom, and the knees were drawn up level with the mouth" (*Deltion* 4 [1918], 61, pl. 6 facing 64; *PM* I, 584, note 2). This is an exact description of our jar burial ex-

cept that its mouth faced north. Another concurrence is that only a single object, a Vapheio cup, was found with each jar (*PM* I, 584; *Deltion* 4 [1918], 58, fig. 5). Also in region of Knossos Hatzidakis uncovered similar pithos burial. Shape of jar the same but vessel apparently undecorated. It lay on its side in a pit supported by stones and a stone slab covered the mouth as in the case of our jar (*ibid.*, 59, fig. 6). In East Crete (Middle Minoan III–Late Minoan I) the bodies of adult burials had been trussed up (*Pachyammos*, 11, 12), the pithoi turned upside down (*Sphoungaras*, pl. XI). The jars, similar to type from our grave circle, are undecorated (*ibid.*, 65, fig. 36; *Pachyammos*, pl. VII: middle; pl. XVII:XIV-b, band decoration only) but on other types of pithoi the trickle or drip pattern was common (*ibid.*, pls. V and XVI). Ripple pattern is used on lower half of magnificently painted spouted jar from Mochlos of Late Minoan I (*Mochlos*, pl. XI). Sufficient has been said to demonstrate the close relation between the Cretan form of burial and that found in our grave circle and this also extends to type of jar used and to certain aspects of its decoration, but as Mr. Mervyn Popham has pointed out to me, execution is far superior on the Minoan decorated examples. It is probable therefore that this spouted jar was produced on mainland but destined for someone who was familiar with, and desirous of, Minoan style of interment. Consequently, it is not unlikely that he was of Cretan origin.

Deep cup [32] (CM. 1580, Fig. 234:1): h. 0.059 m.; h. with handle 0.061 m.; d. rim 0.077 m. in handle axis, at right angles 0.085 m.; d. base 0.038 m. Inside spouted jar. Intact except for crack. Shape (*MP*, Type 221, p. 53 fig. 15) uneven particularly in relation to circumference. Flat to round handle slightly raised above rim. Base of handle has swelling. Raised, flat base with torus molding. Rather soft clay fired pink. Red, slightly lustrous paint.

Decoration: Ripple Pattern (*MP*, Motive 78:1, p. 422 fig. 73) with thick band above and below design. Lower band passes just below base of handle. Underside of cup painted as well as torus base. Handle painted inside and out. Inside of cup appears to be painted, a Minoan feature, although it also occurs occasionally on mainland. Its position inside spouted jar may account for better preservation of paint and color, which on other vases exposed to the soil, is usually black and very worn.

Pit 3 (N) (Figs. 327-329)

LEAD

Rivets (CM. 2013), seven used in repair of Palace Style jar. Largest: l. 0.059 m.; th. 0.005 m.

POTTERY

Palace Style jar [30] (CM. 1586, Figs. 233: 4a-c): h. 0.703 m.; d. rim 0.323 m.; w. rim 0.04 m.; d. 0.50 m.; d. base 0.13 m. Almost complete, repaired. Shape *MP*, Type 15, p. 22 fig. 3. Horizontal projecting rim. Slightly concave neck with pronounced ridge at its base. Three grooved horizontal handles set almost vertically high up on shoulder. Flat base with torus molding. Coarse buff clay containing many grits. Black to red lustrous paint on off-white slip. Main decoration based on "Sacral Ivy" (*MP*, Motive 12, pp. 270f. figs. 35, 36) with filling motives Rosette (*MP*, Motive 17:5, p. 281 fig. 40) but ranging from nine to eleven petals, Rock Pattern II (*MP*, Motive 33:19, p. 327 fig. 55), and a generous number of large dots. At top and at bottom of decorated area Rock Pattern II (*MP*, Motive 33:10, 18, p. 327 fig. 55) is used. Rim, neck, and handles painted solid as well as extensive area at base. In shape and decoration this jar, according to Furumark's criteria, is Late Helladic II A.

Many vases of this type were found at Kakovatos and throughout the tombs a considerable quantity of bones (*AM* XXXIV [1909], 325). The jars were broken and scattered over the chambers but could be reconstructed. They may have been used for burials. The decoration on our jar resembles that on several of the Kakovatos Palace Style jars (*ibid.*, pls. XX, XXI, XXII:1). A large sherd (*ibid.*, pl. XXIV:7) shows the same type of ivy-leaf and this rendering likewise appears on a jug from Shaft Grave I (*Schachtgräber*, pl. CLXIX:199). Cf. also decoration on Palace Style jar from Traganes tholos tomb (*EphArch* 1914, pl. 2:1).

Shallow cup [31] (CM. 1582, Fig. 234:22): h. 0.031 m.; h. with handle 0.054 m.; d. 0.11 m.; d. base 0.038 m. Complete, repaired. Found beside Palace Style jar. Shape *MP*, Type 237, p. 48 fig. 13, Late Helladic I-II. Horizontal lip with central ridge, convex and tilted slightly downward. Ring-type handle raised above rim but away from it. Handle attached to upper and under surface of lip with lumps of clay. Raised, slightly concave base. Light yellow clay, medium-fired. Very worn black paint. Outside of cup undecorated; inside appears to be painted with bands but may be solidly coated. Rim and handle painted.

Pit 4 (Figs. 327-329)

GOLD

Diadem (CM. 2100, Figs. 225:1, 230:15): l. 0.26 m.; w. 0.028 m.; th. ca. 0.0002 m. Put together from four fragments. Almost complete; two bits missing. Fair condition. Diadem in form of elongated olive leaf, punctured at both ends with hole for attachment. Repoussé and pointillé work. Design consists of row of five "suns," largest in center, and toward each end two smaller suns to conform with tapering shape. Each sun has an embossed center outlined by a double circle of tiny, engraved dashes. Outer circumference of the "suns" is outlined by another circle of dashes. Pointillé dots follow all around edge of diadem and lines of pointillé dots in long axis fill end sections of diadem (four at one end, five at the other). This ornament is much smaller than the diadems from the shaft graves, which range in length from 0.303 m. (*Schachtgräber,* pl. XVII:37) to 0.65 m. (*ibid.,* pl. XIV:3). No exact parallel in pattern but arrangement of suns on the great diadem (*loc. cit.*) similar and technique of No. 286 (*ibid.,* pl. XXXVIII) comes nearest to that of our example. Cf. also diadem found by Prof. Marinatos at Peristeria, which is very similar in design (*Praktika,* 1965, pl. 134:2; *Deltion* 21 B1 [1966], pl. 171α).

BRONZE

Knife (CM. 2089, Fig. 230:6): l. pres. 0.333 m.; w. 0.028 m.; l. hilt 0.078 m.; d. hilt 0.017 m.; th. blade 0.006 m. Almost complete, tip missing. Fair condition. Hilt has central partition in axis of blade with scalloped flanges on each side that are folded over. Same type as daggers CM. 2192, 2195, 2190 (see pp. 157, 161, 164) but has three small rivets (l. 0.014 m.; d. 0.004 m.) in haft; no notch at hafting end.

Knife or short dagger (CM. 2089, Figs. 227:4, 230:5): l. 0.204 m.; w. blade 0.02 m.; l. hilt 0.07 m.; w. hilt 0.011 m.; th. blade 0.003 m. Almost complete, point missing. Good condition. A smaller version of the above. Flanges are scalloped though not folded over.[101] No rivets and no notch at end. Small part of original wooden hilt preserved on one side. This weapon also related to dagger described on p. 161 (CM. 2191).

Knife (CM. 2088, Fig. 230:4): l. 0.118 m.; w. hilt end 0.016 m.; th. blade 0.005 m. Complete, repaired, fair condition. Slightly curved blade. Two rivets, only one preserved, in axis of blade. Bears remarkable likeness to knife blade from Shaft Grave II (*Schachtgräber,* pl. LXXII:216, lower), but hafting is different. Cf. CM. 2193, p. 161.

Short dagger (CM. 2088, Fig. 230:2): l. without rivet 0.147 m.; w. estimated 0.035 m.; th. blade 0.003 m. Almost complete; pieces of blade missing. Repaired, fair condition. Broad hafting end of blade with three rivets, central one missing, in transverse row and an end rivet larger than others behind missing rivet. Slightly curved blade ending in rounded tip. Shape similar to CM. 2185 on p. 164.

Short dagger (CM. 2088, Fig. 230:1): l. pres. 0.127 m.; max. w. 0.034 m.; th. blade 0.0025 m.; l. rivets 0.008 m.; d. rivets 0.0035 m. Almost complete; tip and parts of blade missing. Broad, straight hafting end. Three small rivets in transverse row. No end rivet found. Straight-sided blade tapering toward tip. Similar to preceding.

Short dagger (CM. 2090, Fig. 230:3): l. without end rivet 0.168 m.; w. 0.04 m.; w. hafting end 0.035 m.; th. blade 0.0025 m.; l. rivets 0.009 m.; d. rivets 0.0045 m. Almost complete; a few pieces missing from blade. Three rivets in transverse row at hafting end. Another rivet immediately behind middle one of the three. Straight-sided blade tapering to rounded tip. Shape that of the two preceding.

Small rivet (CM. 2087): l. 0.0115 m.; d. shaft 0.0035 m.; d. head 0.005 m. Complete. Rivet recovered loose, belonging to one of above weapons.

STONE

Hone (CM. 2091, Fig. 232:3): l. ca. 0.20 m.; d. max. ca. 0.036 m.; d. one end ca. 0.015 m.; d. end with hole ca. 0.01 m.; d. hole ca. 0.008 m. Almost complete; pieces missing from surface. Good condition. Dark gray schist(?), powdery and friable surface. Rounded in section tapering at both ends but not to a point. Ends flat with rounded edges. Hole for suspension at one end. Cf. example from Fifth Shaft Grave (*Schachtgräber,* 149, no. 459) and *Deltion* 18 B1 [1963] pl. 122γ: from Tholos 2, Peristeria (a small specimen).

Cannot be definitely related to any specific pit grave (Fig. 329)

BRONZE

Knife (CM. 2099, Fig. 230:18): l. pres. 0.188 m.; w. 0.045 m.; w. hafting end estimated

---

[101] Cf. similar hilt of weapon from Vlachopoulos, Messenia (*Praktika* 1964, pl. 94:3, top).

0.028 m.; th. blade 0.0055 m.; l. middle rivet 0.012 m.; d. middle rivet 0.007 m. Almost complete, repaired. Fairly good condition. Pieces from blade, hafting end, and possibly two rivets missing. Straight end with three rivets in a row parallel to it (one missing). Blade expands slightly and reaches maximum width near rounded tip. Shape approximates to broad-ended daggers described above but this appears to be a knife (corroded but apparently has only one cutting edge). Although butt of blade is broader and hafting is different, I think it is related to knife found with skeleton (CM. 2027α, p. 158).

Two small rivets (CM. 2031, Fig. 231:9): (a) l. 0.0125 m.; d. shaft 0.005 m.; d. head 0.0075 m. (b) l. 0.0093 m.; d. shaft 0.0075 m.; d. head 0.0085 m. Complete but distorted. Good condition. One belongs to the knife above and has bits of metal base adhering. Source of other uncertain.

Balance beam (CM. 2076, Fig. 228:5): l. 0.368 m.; d. shaft 0.006 m.; d. head 0.011 m. Complete, repaired. Good condition. Modern hooks and string have been added and two scale pans, found in excavation, attached to demonstrate its use. Three complete balances found in Third Shaft Grave (*Schachtgräber*, 53, fig. 13; pl. XXXIV: 81 and 82) are of gold with pans elaborately decorated.

Five scale pans: three only partly complete. Fair condition.

CM. 2076 (Fig. 228:5): two, with diameters of 0.0775 m. and 0.07 m. respectively, used for demonstration. Concave, pierced with four holes each and undecorated.

CM. 2066 (Fig. 230:20): d. 0.05 m., th. 0.0015 m. Badly preserved with only two suspension holes.

CM. 2072 (Fig. 230:16) lacks most of rim. Embossed with a twelve-leaf rosette, a companion piece to the one found with the skeleton (CM. 2025, p. 158). The circle surrounding center of rosette is prominent.

CM. 2067 (Fig. 230:19): d. ca. 0.08 m. Badly preserved. Large pieces have come away. Two holes for suspension can be recognized. Embossed with eight-petaled rosette. Circle surrounding center of flower (d. 0.024 m.) very prominent.

These pans, distributed in north part of the grave circle, may originally have been in neighborhood of skeleton and become dispersed by later agricultural activity. Scale pans are frequently found in Late Helladic tombs. Apart from the decorated gold pans from shaft graves referred to above, cf. plain bronze examples from Mycenae, Prosymna, Dendra, Vapheio, etc. (*ChT*, pl. XXIX:20 and p. 190, note 5; *Prosymna*, fig. 215:6, 7; fig. 543:5. These three are all Late Helladic I [*ibid.*, 351-2]; *NT, Dendra*, 72, fig. 86, and p. 73; *EphArch* 1889, pl. 8:4).

Pin (CM. 2083 or 2082?): l. ca. 0.127 m.; th. ca. 0.004 m. Fair condition. Partly preserved; had a point and no head when found. May belong to pithos burial in Pit 3 (SE) where several pins were uncovered. Found in same area at a higher level.

STONE

Pestle (CM. 2085, Fig. 232:1): l. 0.0565 m.; d. 0.0405 m.-0.0425 m. Complete but chipped at base. Cleaned. Coarse-grained stone, light gray in color. Roughly conical shape with rounded top and slight carination toward broad base worn smooth from use. Pestles are very common but seldom illustrated. For shape cf. *SME*, pl. XXVIII:E, last in row.

Shanked button or whorl (CM. 2065, Figs. 227:7, 230:21): h. 0.0155 m.; d. top 0.008 m.; d. broad end 0.0255 m., small end 0.008 m.; d. hole 0.004 m. Complete but slightly chipped at base. Furumark type b (*MPChron*. 89, fig. 2). Dark blue to gray steatite spotted with white. Broad end slightly concave. Type rare. Furumark gives only one example of type b in his table (*ibid.*, 90) and that from tholos tomb at Dendra. He dates it to Late Helladic III A:1.

Lentoid seal (NM. 8532, Fig. 231:5a, b = *CMS* I, No. 294): d. 0.0243 m.; th. 0.001 m.-0.01 m.; d. hole 0.0025 m. Good condition. Mottled red agate? with greenish-brown, white, and black veins. Two opposite sides of "lens" are flattened (max. w. 0.0045 m.) and are pierced for suspension. Very vivid scene of man spearing wild boar between the eyes, aided by fierce dog visible behind his legs. Man naked except for belt and boar's tusk helmet; not clear whether this plumed or not. Forepart of boar with particular accentuation of bristles is deeply engraved and there is special emphasis on juxtaposed heads of boar and dog and on their prominent eyes. Scene skillfully arranged to fill the circle.

Amygdaloid seal (NM. 8531, Fig. 231:6a, b = *CMS* I, No. 299 [102]): l. 0.0148 m.; w. ca. 0.005 m.-0.0123 m.; th. 0.0085 m.; d. hole ca. 0.002 m. Fair condition. Dark violet amethyst. Ends of seal flattened and string-hole passes through long axis. Basically an abstract design. Main feature a double wavy line, which on other seals is variously interpreted as composite bow or snake. Engraved on lower half of seal in long axis, but just off center.[103] Within big, central loop two vertical lines that may possibly represent tree; suggestions of foliage to right and left of these lines. Under each of two lesser loops a stylized plant and between them, at bottom of seal, a few slanting and opposed lines that look like gabled roof of house. Above double wavy line a series of parallel, horizontal lines, upper of which contain frieze of double zigzags.

Amethyst beads: 17 spherical. One chipped and one cracked. Fifteen are of consistent color; one, the largest, is dark violet and one light violet. Diameters vary: one 0.005 m.; six 0.006 m.; eight 0.007 m.; one 0.01 m.; one 0.012 m. Two flattened spherical, both with d. 0.006 m. and th. 0.004 m.

Carnelian beads: five spherical, d. 0.004 m. One flattened spherical, d. 0.009 m.; th. 0.006 m. One gadrooned (CM. 2095, Figs. 227:1, 232:7): d. 0.013 m.; th. 0.006 m.; d. hole 0.0015 m. Flattened spherical shape with gadrooned border. Both sides incised with groups of rays (about three to a group) like spokes of a wheel.

Flint arrowheads (Figs. 230:22, 231:8, 9), 60 of which 38 intact, six almost complete, 11 without point, five points only and four butts only. Color of flint in nearly all cases dark brown, but 10 banded examples, i.e., bands of yellow alternating with dark brown. Three yellow, two light brown, one translucent light brown, one red, and one cinnamon color. All are of Type VI (see Fig. 226 and p. 127) with exception of one that has rounded to pointed butt (CM. 2069, Fig. 232:4); [104] the latter is also banded. Point of some arrowheads very narrow and tapering. Great variety in length (one 0.019 m.; one 0.021 m.; one 0.022 m.; three 0.023 m.; two 0.024 m.; one 0.025 m.; one 0.026 m.; one 0.028 m.; three 0.029 m.; four 0.03 m.; four 0.031 m.; two 0.032 m.; six 0.033 m.; two 0.034 m.; three 0.035 m.; three 0.036 m.; two 0.038 m.; two 0.039 m.; two 0.04 m.). Apparently longer type was preferred.

Obsidian arrowheads, 11 of which six are intact. Four have broken points and of one point only survives. All are of Type VI except for one (CM. 2018, Fig. 231:8) that has a rounded butt similar to flint example above.[105] There is a certain variation in color: one is translucent black, one translucent light blue, one partly translucent

---

[102] Included with seal-stones from Palace of Nestor (*CMS* I, p. 333).

[103] I have interpreted the design the other way up to that illustrated in *CMS* I, p. 338, on account of the direction of the "plant" growth.

[104] This is perhaps a variation of Type I (Fig. 226).

[105] This is perhaps a variation of Type I (Fig. 226).

with a greenish hue, one greenish-black, the rest are opaque. Best preserved have one each of following lengths: 0.021 m.; 0.022 m.; 0.026 m.; 0.027 m.; 0.029 m.; 0.031 m.

PASTE

Spacer bead (CM. 2096). About half preserved, in eight pieces. Not measurable. Form recognizable; same type as beads found in Tholos IV (see p. 131) and also at Mycenae (*ChT*, 66, 5c). Greenish-blue on outside, yellow inside.

Beads, 184 (Figs. 231:8, 9; 232:4). Some well preserved, others in fragments and not measurable; but the above estimate is conservative. Measurable and/or well-preserved beads number 154 and can be divided into the following categories:

(a) 137 spherical with diameters as follows:

beads	diameter	beads	diameter
3	0.004 m.	2	0.012 m.
55	0.005 m.	4	0.013 m.
37	0.006 m.	4	0.014 m.
8	0.009 m.	3	0.015 m.
16	0.010 m.	2	0.016 m.
2	0.011 m.	1	0.019 m.

By far greater number small (Fig. 231:8, 9). There are no beads with diameters of 0.007 m. and 0.008 m.

(b) Eight flattened spherical (one, d. 0.0055 m.; two, d. 0.0075 m.; one, d. 0.009 m.; two, d. 0.0105 m.; one, d. 0.011 m.; one, d. 0.0145 m.).

(c) Three drum beads (two with d. 0.005 m.; one with d. 0.0055 m.). Blue paste.

(d) Four disk beads of blue paste (CM. 2063, Fig. 232:4, CM. 2080).

    (i) d. 0.008 m., th. 0.003 m., d. hole 0.003 m.

    (ii) d. 0.0085 m., th. 0.003 m., d. hole 0.0033 m.

    (iii) d. 0.0085 m., th. 0.0013 m., d. hole 0.004 m.

    (iv) d. 0.010 m., th. 0.0015 m., d. hole 0.0033 m.

(e) Melon bead (CM. 2062α): d. 0.0078 m.; th. 0.0062 m.; d. hole ca. 0.002 m. Dark rainbow color. Alternate vertical ribs and flutes. Cf. *Prosymna*, fig. 199:3 and *NT, Dendra* 85, fig. 95:1.

(f) Spiral bead (CM. 2093, Fig. 232:7): l. ca. 0.0205 m.; d. ca. 0.008 m.; d. hole ca. 0.005 m. Fragile, therefore earth not removed. Ends of spiral missing. Bead resembles a spring under tension, i.e., gap between each spiral. Color green and yellow. Not many examples of this kind of bead known: one of paste from Menidi has solid appearance unlike our example (*KG*, pl. v:7); two of faience from Dendra tholos (*RT, Dendra*, 30, no. 21). Another from same tomb is of agate (*ibid.*, 30, no. 12 and pl. xxv:2). Cf. also two gold spiral beads from Knossos (*PM* IV, ii, pl. xxxiv, facing p. 963).

Without exception all small beads, those with diameter of 0.006 m. or less, are blue or light blue. As a rule large beads have dark rainbow color; exceptions are: yellow inside, green out (7); yellow (2); blue-green (2); very light blue (1). Flattened spherical beads are dark rainbow with exception of one small (d. 0.0055 m.) that is blue and a very large one (d. 0.0155 m.) that is yellow inside and green outside. Only two white paste beads, and one found with the skeleton presumed to be the latest burial in the grave circle.

TERRACOTTA

Button or whorl (CM. 2019, Fig. 227:6): h. pres. 0.0215 m.; d. 0.024 m.; d. broad end 0.017 m., small end estimated 0.009 m.; d. hole 0.005 m. Piece of small end missing. Biconical shape. Furumark's type a 2 (*MPChron.* 89, fig. 2), but one cone larger than other and form is nearer to Middle Helladic type. Coarse, black clay with dirty yellow-brown patch. Dark gray core. Type well-known and almost invariably found in Late Helladic I-II context (*Prosymna*, 313). At the Heraeum there were 31 examples corresponding to our type (*ibid.*). Several are illustrated (*ibid.*, figs. 107:3; 142:12; 215:3). Cf. also *ChT*, pl. xxxv:35 middle.

Whorl? (CM. 2097): max. d. ca. 0.035 m. Two joining fragments make three-quarters of circle with an inner diameter of ca. 0.011 m. Terracotta colored core. White encrustation on outside. Friable surface.

UNKNOWN SUBSTANCE

Fragment with one straight side (CM. 2097): l. 0.027 m.; w. 0.0205 m.; th. 0.003 m. Pierced with hole near broken edge.

POTTERY

Shallow cup or saucer [2] (CM. 1598, Figs. 234:3, 235:1): h. 0.029 m.; h. with handle 0.058 m.; d. 0.124 m.; d. base 0.039 m. About three-fifths preserved; restored from fragments collected near northwest corner of Pit 3. Small part of rim, large parts of body and base missing. Horizontal lip with central ridge, slightly convex. Ring handle (w. 0.015 m.) raised above rim and attached to inner and outer part of it, showing a protuberance below rim. Slightly raised, countersunk base (*MP*, Type 237, p. 48 fig. 13). Late Helladic II. Light yellow, rather soft-fired clay. Black, worn paint. Outside decoration: "Sacral Ivy" (*MP*, Motive 12:23, p. 271 fig. 36) combined with Crocus (*MP*, Motive 10:1, p. 261 fig. 33) or Palm I (*MP*, Motive 14:k, p. 277 fig. 38) repeated four times. Inside of cup painted monochrome. Rim and handle painted. Vase in shape and decoration almost identical with one found at Mycenae (*ChT*, pl. II:7). Cf. also *Praktika* 1963, pl. 164:2 (246), a cup from A. Elia-Ithorias, Aetolia, and *Prosymna*, fig. 345:987, right (alabastron).

Immediately to north of spouted jar (Fig. 329)

Jug with cutaway mouth [5] (CM. 1604, Fig. 234:24): h. 0.27 m.; d. mouth 0.093 m.; d. 0.20 m.; d. base 0.072 m.; w. handle 0.034 m. Less than half preserved. Restored. Shape *MP*, Type 131 or 132, p. 22 fig. 3. Strap handle. Flat base (restored).

Yellow-white clay, soft- to medium-fired. Faint traces of paint; possibly linear decoration. Exact position uncertain, but coarse sherds probably belonging to this jug found in area to north of spouted jar. Because so few fragments recovered, shape uncertain. Closest analogies in jugs from Chalcis (*BSA* XLVII [1952], pl. 24:481) and Korakou (*Korakou*, 50, figs. 67, 66:2). But perhaps better parallels for the shape as restored are the undecorated Middle Helladic jug with cutaway mouth from the Heraeum (*Prosymna*, fig. 75:1202) and another Middle Helladic jug with sloping mouth from Lerna (*Hesperia* XXIV [1955], pl. 12:c). Cf. also jug from Kephalovrison, Messenia (*Praktika* 1964, pl. 94:2, left). Two jugs from Samikon seem to be of this kind (*Deltion* 20 A [1965], pl. 6β, γ).

Bowl with high-swung handle [22] (CM. 1595, Fig. 234:25): h. 0.149 m.; h. with handle 0.195 m.; d. 0.20 m.; d. base 0.063 m. About half complete. Restored. No exact parallel in Furumark's shapes (cf. *MP*, Type 279, p. 48 fig. 13). Ovoid, conical form. Offset rim. High-swung handle rectangular in section. Rather coarse dark blue clay, fired to metallic blue-gray surface with patches of brilliant red. Undecorated. Obviously vessel intended for domestic use and such pottery rarely attains the distinction of publication. I know of no parallel, but it probably has a long tradition carrying on unchanged into later periods.

Isolated vases (Fig. 329)

Alabastron [1] (CM. 1599, Fig. 234:18): h. pres. 0.031 m.; d. 0.096 m.; d. mouth pres. 0.036 m. Complete except for rim, which has been restored. Found in southwest corner of C.2. Shape (*MP*, Type 82, p. 41 fig. 11). Yellow clay, soft-fired. Black to brown paint, much faded. Pattern not clear; apparently a lily on its side, a much simplified version of Lily (*MP*, Motive 9:15, p. 258 fig. 32). Cf. also *Prosymna*, fig. 688. Composition of the design apparently similar to that on askos from Melos (*Phylakopi*, 136, fig. 109). Under each handle Rock Pattern (*MP*, Motive 32:5, p. 323 fig. 54) with two parallel rows of dots added. On base two groups of concentric circles. Neck painted inside and out. Handles solidly painted. Late Helladic II.

Cup [7] (CM. 1585, Fig. 234:7): h. 0.09 m.; d. rim 0.127 m.; d. base 0.042 m. Restored from pieces found in north central part of grave circle. About four-fifths complete. Shape *MP*, Type 211, p. 48 fig. 13. Soft-fired, light yellow powdery clay. Black, worn paint. Decoration: Running Spirals (*MP*, Motive 46:29, p. 353 fig. 59) with three bands below design. Rim painted inside and out. Handle decorated with diagonal strokes. Late Helladic I-II.

Near boundary wall (NE) (Fig. 329)

One-handled jar [3] (CM. 1587, Figs. 234:11, 235:5): h. 0.086 m.; d. 0.11 m.; d. mouth 0.08 m.; d. base 0.046 m. Complete but restored. Shape *MP*, Type 87, p. 41 fig. 11. Pink to light brown clay, medium to soft-fired, slightly powdery. Red to brown, very slightly lustrous paint. Decoration: racket pattern in series, similar to Hatched Loop (*MP*, Motive 63:3, p. 397 fig. 69). Two thick bands below pattern. Band at base. Handle decorated with diagonal stripes or blobs and vertical band on underside. Rim and neck painted inside and out. Late Helladic I-II. No fewer than seven of these jars, painted with same pattern, found in Samikon grave circle; there dated to Late Helladic I (*Deltion* 20 A [1965,], pl. 9:ζ and pl. 10); and two others from neighboring Makrysia (*Deltion* 23 A [1968], 127).

Alabastron [4] (CM. 1594, Fig. 234:15): h. 0.092 m.; d. 0.183 m.; d. mouth 0.104 m. About four-fifths preserved. Restored. Shape *MP*, Type 81, p. 41 fig. 11. Light yellow clay, soft-fired and powdery. Black and brown, worn paint. Decoration based on Rock Pattern I (*MP*, Motive 32:8, p. 323 fig. 54). Two bands below design.

Wheel pattern (*MP*, Motive 68:2, p. 403 fig. 70) on base. Rim and neck painted inside and out. Handles solidly painted. Late Helladic II-III A:1.

Near wall (N) (Fig. 329)

Pedestaled dish? [11] (CM. 1603, Fig. 233:3), fragment comprising stem and a very small part of body: h. pres. 0.07 m.; d. base 0.06 m. Shape *MP*, Type 307, p. 65 fig. 18. Flat base of bowl with slight depression surrounded by a ring. Pedestal hollow expanding slightly toward base. Rather soft-fired, pink to light brown clay. Very faded red paint. Decoration: four medium bands evenly spaced, starting from base. Fragmentary bit of design on bowl undecipherable. Apparently solidly painted inside.

From what little is left of this pot nearest parallel is non-Mycenaean vase found at Mycenae (*ChT*, pl. XLII:9) which Wace, while not accepting it as Minoan, thought might have come from one of the islands (*ibid.*, 80). Several examples of similar type vase found at Melos (*Phylakopi*, 138, fig. 110; pl. XXVII:1 B) but these have torus molding at foot of pedestal, which also has flat base. A Minyan bowl from same site has hollow pedestal, which is broken (*ibid.*, 154, fig. 137); it has been restored with shape similar to our fragment. The pedestaled dish is well-known in Crete (Knossos, *BSA* 62 [1967], pl. 76:f; *Gournia*, pl. II:74; *Palaikastro*, 61, fig. 49; 66, fig. 53:25 — described as *kalathos* on p. 70; *Mallia Maisons* I, pl. XLVIII, top left). All these vases have torus moldings at base of pedestal with exception of those from Knossos and Mallia (the latter has hole in bottom of dish). There are also the "stalked jars," which have the same kind of pedestals as the last-mentioned, i.e., no torus molding, but these are closed vessels (*Palaikastro*, 71, fig. 56). On mainland, apart from vase found at Mycenae, a related type from tholos of Koryphasion, not far from our grave circle (*Hesperia* XXIII [1954], pl. 38:b). Only pedestal is preserved, described as a "broad open vessel in Early Mycenaean fabric" (*ibid.*, p. 161). Perhaps our example represents mainland version of Cretan vase.

One-handled jar [19] (CM. 1627, Fig. 234:8): h. 0.106 m.; d. rim 0.073 m.; d. neck 0.051 m.; d. 0.136 m.; d. base 0.05 m. Restored. Almost complete; large part of rim and piece of handle missing. Wide flaring lip. Flat, vertical handle, 0.016 m. wide, tapering to small blob. Flat base. Shape *MP*, Type 87, p. 41 fig. 11. Whitish-yellow clay with very slight green tinge. Medium-fired. Worn black paint. Decoration recalls Ogival Canopy (*MP*, Motive 13:3, p. 275 fig. 37) but is difficult to decipher. Design with supporting thick band stops just above bottom of handle. Three bands at base. Rim and neck painted. Late Helladic II. Covered with stopper (CM. 1628).

Kylix base (CM. 1628): d. 0.056 m. Fragment used as cover for one-handled jar (CM. 1627) above (Figs. 204, 205). Slightly concave. Pink-buff clay, rather soft biscuit. Yellow slip?

Beaked jug [8] (CM. 1579, Figs. 234:23, 235:7): h. 0.28 m.; d. 0.20 m.; d. base 0.07 m. Restored; three-quarters preserved; parts of rim and body missing. Shape *MP*, Type 141, p. 606. Cut-away mouth. Ridge at bottom of neck. Ridge along handle, ending in knob below its base. Brownish-yellow clay, soft-fired and powdery. Red, brown, and black paint, rather faded. Very elaborate decoration. Shoulder painted with Foliate Band (*MP*, Motive 64:7, p. 397 fig. 69) in two tiers; on neck motive reversed in two tiers; again used on the spout. Pendant (*MP*, Motive 38:6, p. 333 fig. 56) decorates middle part of vase on three faces but not under handle. This motive presented in a triangular composition: one pendant occupies apex of triangle and is enclosed within a "tent" of dots; two pendants fill the other corners of triangle and are joined together by Rock

Pattern 1 (*MP*, Motive 32:5, p. 323 fig. 54) reversed; from this last-mentioned motive issues variation of "Seaweed" (*MP*, Motive 30:2, p. 323 fig. 54). Handle, painted with form of "Adder Mark" (*MP*, Motive 69:1, p. 403 fig. 70) on both sides of the ridge and outlined on each side by stripe or band which continues onto and around spout of jug. Lower part of vase decorated with Arcade Pattern (*MP*, Motive 66:2, p. 403 fig. 70) and band at base. Inside mouth painted. Late Helladic II.

This type of jug well-known in Crete. Cf. several examples from Mallia [106] (*Mallia Maisons* II, pl. XVI:1-4 and frontispiece) and others (*Gournia*, pl. VIII:16, 17; and *Praktika* 1962, pl. 159:2 from Zakro). Cf. also jug from Hagia Triada (H. Th. Bossert, *The Art of Ancient Crete*, London [1937], fig. 357). A jug from Samikon has rather similar decoration and is of the same kind (*Deltion* 20 A [1965], pl. 7). The "pendant" decoration is a prominent feature on a "pithoid amphora" from Knossos (*PM* II, ii, 427, fig. 248). On mainland fine example from Mycenae (*ChT*, pl. III:2) has same arcade pattern.

Alabastron [25] (CM. 1593, Fig. 234:4): h. 0.055 m.; d. 0.108 m.; d. mouth 0.051 m. Restored. Almost complete; part of rim and some pieces of body missing. Shape *MP*, Type 82, p. 41 fig. 11. Yellow clay, rather soft-fired. Very worn black paint. Decoration: "Sacral Ivy" (*MP*, Motive 12:24, 25, p. 271 fig. 36). Cf. *ChT*, pl. XXVII:8. Band below design. Base apparently painted with two groups of concentric circles. Rim, neck, and handles painted inside and out. Late Helladic II.

Alabastron [26] (CM. 1590, Fig. 234:13): h. 0.088 m.; d. 0.16 m.; d. mouth 0.099 m. Restored. Almost complete; few pieces of body missing. Shape *MP*, Type 82 or 84, p. 41 fig. 11. Light yellow clay, soft-fired and powdery. Black to brown very faded paint. Decoration: Rock Pattern 1 (*MP*,

---

[106] I am indebted to Mr. Mervyn Popham for the Mallia references.

Motive 32:8 or 24, p. 323 fig. 54). Rim and handles painted. Five-spoke wheel on bottom (cf. *MP*, Motive 68:2, p. 403 fig. 70). Late Helladic II-III A:1.

Group over Pit 4 (E) (Fig. 329)

Alabastron [14] (CM. 1584, Fig. 234:12): h. pres. 0.053 m.; d. 0.145 m. Complete except for rim, neck, and handles. Shape *MP*, Type 82, p. 41 fig. 11. Pink to brown-buff clay, medium to soft biscuit. Surface much worn, paint nearly gone. Body apparently decorated with Lily (*MP*, Motive 9:2, p. 258 fig. 32) and base with "Wheel" (*MP*, Motive 68:2, p. 403 fig. 70) but this is not certain. Late Helladic II.

Askos, small [18] (CM. 1588, Figs. 234:19, 235:6): h. 0.068 m.; d. 0.081 m.; d. base 0.03 m. Restored. Almost complete; parts of body missing. Cf. *MP*, Type 195, p. 41 fig. 11, p. 617. Pink, rather soft biscuit. Black to ruddy brown paint, much worn. Decoration: Circles (*MP*, Motive 41:2, p. 343 fig. 57) with row of dots above and below instead of lines. Two stripes below design and at greatest diameter of vase. Handle and spout painted inside and out. Late Helladic I-II.

Cup with raised handle [17] (CM. 1630, Fig. 234:2): h. 0.045 m.; h. with restored handle 0.08 m.; d. 0.115 m.; d. base 0.045 m. Repaired from many pieces. Scattered pieces of rim, bowl, base, and large part of handle missing. Shape *MP*, Type 218 or 219, p. 48 fig. 13. Everted lip, flat base, flattened handle (w. 0.016 m.). Spring of handle on rim and body shows that it was raised, but neither angle nor shape certain. Rather coarse, red clay, soft-fired. Undecorated. Late Helladic II. The fragments of this cup found on top of CM. 1581.

Angular alabastron [16] (CM. 1581, Figs. 234:10, 235:2): h. 0.076 m.; d. 0.122 m.; d. mouth 0.083 m. Complete but mended. Shape *MP*, Type 91, p. 44 fig. 12. Pinkish-white clay. Soft and powdery biscuit. Red to brown paint, very faded. Decoration of shoulder based on Hatched Loop (*MP*, Motive 63:6, p. 397 fig. 69), but only one "racket" is used in each panel and this is straight-sided, exactly as on alabastron from the Heraeum (*Prosymna*, fig. 667). Vertical face decorated with variation of Foliate Band (*MP*, Motive 64:3, p. 397 fig. 69), base with filled circle surrounded by two concentric circles. Band at base of neck with row of dots underneath. Handles and rim painted inside and out. Late Helladic I-II.

Alabastron [15] (CM. 1589, Fig. 234:17): h. 0.049 m.; d. 0.086 m.; d. mouth 0.049 m. Restored. Almost complete; pieces of neck and body missing. Shape *MP*, Type 83, p. 41 fig. 11. Pinkish-yellow clay. Soft and powdery biscuit. Very worn black paint. Design apparently Rock Pattern 1 (*MP*, Motive 32:5, p. 323 fig. 54) with row of dots following contour of the undulations, and a line below pattern. In one panel, cluster of dots making oblong shape on its side can be recognized (cf. *Prosymna*, figs. 667, 709; *BSA* XLVII [1952], pl. 17:472 G from Chalkis; *Praktika* 1963, pl. 165:2 [251] from A. Elia-Ithoria, Aetolia). Underside of our vase painted with "Wheel" (*MP*, Motive 68:2, p. 403 fig. 70). Late Helladic II-III A:1.

Spouted cup, miniature [21] (No museum number—vase misplaced): h. 0.025 m.; h. with handle 0.042 m.; d. 0.079 m.; d. base 0.034 m. Restored. Almost complete. Shape *MP*, Type 253, p. 48 fig. 13. Handle rises vertically above rim as a loop. Greenish-yellow clay, soft-fired and powdery. Paint very faded. Inside of cup apparently decorated with a series of Crosses (*MP*, Motive 54:4, p. 373 fig. 65); outside with Grass or Reed (*MP*, Motive 16:5, p. 281 fig. 40). Design in both cases is very indistinct. Rim and handle painted. Late Helladic I-II.

Small pithos [20] (not registered, Fig. 233:6): h. pres. 0.285 m.; d. base 0.184 m. Part of base and lower half of body only preserved. Partly restored from sherds found scattered over wide area. Base flat with squared torus molding. Above this thick stem of vessel has two molded "rings" which recall those on Minyan goblets. "Rings" have ridged or angular profile. Lower half of body spreads out but its shape cannot be determined. Coarse red clay containing many pot grits. Red paint, no longer lustrous. Traces of band decoration but only one band is preserved about middle of the vase. Late Helladic I-II? For ring decoration on stem cf. *Eutresis*, 136, fig. 183:5 and *AJA* XL (1936), 418, fig. 3, top right, from Eleusis.

Group over Pit 4 (W) (Fig. 329)

Alabastron [6] (CM. 1591, Figs. 234:14, 235:4): h. 0.08 m.; d. 0.17 m.; d. mouth 0.107 m. Restored. About three-quarters complete; parts of neck and body missing. Found a little to south of Pit 4 (W). Shape *MP*, Type 81, p. 41 fig. 11. Light yellow clay, soft and powdery biscuit. Faded black and red paint. Decoration: very similar to Hatched Loop (*MP*, Motive 63:6, p. 397 fig. 69).[107] Fill motive, pendant from band at base of neck (visible in Fig. 235:4) combination of stylized rock and seaweed (Trefoil Rock-work, *MP*, Motive 29:5, p. 315 fig. 53) and "Seaweed," *MP*, Motive 30:1, p. 323 fig. 54). Thick band supports main design. Rim, neck, and handles painted inside and out. Late Helladic I-II.

Angular alabastron [13] (CM. 1629, Fig. 234:21): h. 0.055 m.; d. mouth 0.05 m.; d. neck 0.035 m.; d. body 0.09 m.; d. base 0.086 m. Restored. Almost complete; large piece of rim and small piece from base missing. Shape *MP*, Type 92, p. 44 fig. 12. Pronounced splaying neck. Flat base. White-yellow clay, medium-fired. Very worn, black-brown paint. Design on shoulder apparently consists of dots; five rows of dots on vertical face—Variegated Stone Patterns (*MP*, Motive 76:1, p. 422

fig. 73). Base decorated with "Wheel" (*MP*, Motive 68:2, p. 403 fig. 70). Rim, neck, and handles painted. Late Helladic II.

Alabastron [10] (CM. 1592, Figs. 234:16, 235:3): h. 0.049 m.; d. 0.142 m.; d. mouth 0.072 m. Restored. About four-fifths complete; parts of rim and body missing. Shape *MP*, Type 84, p. 41 fig. 11). Dark yellow clay, fired rather soft. Black to brown paint, worn in places. Decoration: "Sacral Ivy" (*MP*, Motive 12:27, p. 271 fig. 36) repeated twice in each panel. Rock Pattern I (*MP*, Motive 32:5, p. 323 fig. 54) used as base of pattern. Over one handle and under another, fill element consisting of half Trefoil Rock-work (*MP*, Motive 29:15, p. 315 fig. 53); attached to base of another handle an ivy leaf, of which the stalk appears under yet another handle. On base "Wheel" (*MP*, Motive 68:2, p. 403 fig. 70) but with five spokes. Rim, neck, and handles painted; rim also painted on inside. Late Helladic III A:1. This is the only vase that can definitely be placed later than the others on stylistic grounds.

Group in southeast part of grave circle (Fig. 329)

Bowl with high-swung handle [23] (CM. 1596, Fig. 234:5): h. 0.103 m.; h. with handle 0.152 m.; d. rim 0.14 m.; d. base 0.05 m. Restored. Almost complete; pieces from body missing. Furumark has no exact parallel. Everted rim. Ovoid body. Handle round in section. Rounded flat base. Coarse red ware containing small pebbly grits. Fired hard to medium. Undecorated. This appears to be domestic ware and cannot be dated.

Kylix [24] (CM. 1597, Fig. 234:9): h. 0.086 m.; d. rim 0.11 m.; d. body 0.103 m.; d. base 0.057 m. Restored. About four-fifths complete; pieces of rim, handle, body, and base missing. Shape *MP*, Type 254, p. 60

[107] Cf. *Prosymna*, fig. 667; also two alabastra from Samikon (*Deltion* 20 A [1965], pl. 12:δ, ε), an alabastron from Makrysia (*Deltion* 23 A [1968], pl.

124:δ), and a one-handled jar from Kephalovryson (*Praktika*, 1964, pl. 94:4).

fig. 16. Sharply everted rim. Thin flat handle (not certain that it has been correctly restored; it may have been high-swung (cf. *MP*, Type 270, p. 60 fig. 16). Concave base with small circular depression. Very fine ware, though roughly finished inside. Pink clay, soft to medium biscuit. Undecorated. Late Helladic I-II. Among many other early unpainted kylikes cf. *ChT*, pl. xxxiv:17; *Eleusis*, 109, fig. 85, middle and fig. 86, right; *Korakou*, 57, fig. 78, but none have the same elegant lines as our example.

W. D. T.

CHAMBER TOMBS

During the campaign of 1956 a search was made for the cemetery which one would expect to find near the Mycenaean settlement below the palace. Several areas northeast of the palace were explored first and 17 trial trenches dug with the kind permission of the owners of the properties, Mr. Charalambopoulos and Mr. Paraskevopoulos. There was little trace of human habitation, a few sherds, an occasional flake of obsidian or flint, and no trace of burials. In one area (Trenches H, M, and N) on the property of Mr. Paraskevopoulos, approximately 350 m. from the palace, quantities of sherds, mostly Middle Helladic, including pieces of Mattpainted Ware, were found, but the removal of a stump some years before had destroyed any walls or stratification that may have existed. This deposit does indicate, however, that there was an establishment of some kind on this hill before the end of the Middle Helladic Period.

On the western and lower extension of the ridge upon which the palace stood, 30 trial trenches were opened, here too with the generous consent of the owner of the land, Mr. Tsakalis. On the northwest side of the hill, in an area otherwise unexplored, a pit grave (E-3, Fig. 301) was excavated in 1956 under the supervision of W. P. Donovan. It seems likely that this was not an isolated grave and that chamber tombs might well be found on this slope.

W. P. D.

Grave E-3
(Plan, Fig. 337)

Grave E-3 was discovered on a terrace of the olive grove on the northwest side of the Tsakalis hill. It is a simple pit oriented approximately from east to west, 0.48 m. wide, 1.66 m. long at the bottom, and the floor was reached at a depth of 0.85 m. Over the east end of the grave was a group of stones, one of which (h. 0.43 m.; w. 0.19 m.; th. 0.10 m.) might have been a marker. Beneath these stones a cup with painted decoration (CM. 1515) had been placed upside down and near it was a carnelian bead (CM. 2155).

Beneath this modest monument two persons had been interred in a simple pit.

There was no lining or floor except the clay itself. The two skeletons were found, one lying directly above the other, with the skulls toward the east; each had been placed in an extended position on its back with arms at the sides and hands over the pelvis. The remains of the upper burial were those of an adult male, the lower of an adult female.[1]

The only objects buried with the two were four small decorated alabastra placed at the west end of the pit above the feet of the upper skeleton.

The character of this grave and the paucity of its contents suggest that it belonged to people of a lower station than those buried in the chamber tombs; it is puzzling that no other similar graves have been found in this cemetery. The fact that all objects were placed above the second body and the absence of any detectable sign that the tomb had been reopened may indicate that the two bodies had been placed in the grave at the same time. If this hypothesis is true, one is led to speculate about the disease or accident that could have brought about the simultaneous deaths of these two people.

Within general limits the date of the grave can be established from the pottery. All the vases seem to belong to Late Helladic III A:2, or perhaps III B.

OBJECTS FOUND

STONE

Carnelian bead (CM. 2155): d. 0.016 m.; th. 0.006 m. From stones above grave. Flattened, spherical.

POTTERY

Cup (CM. 1515, Fig. 236:3): h. 0.065 m.; d. rim 0.128; d. 0.125 m.; d. base 0.043. From stones above grave. Buff clay; surface badly worn. One flat, vertical handle. Traces of solid band of lustrous brown-black paint on upper surface of handle, rim.

Alabastron (CM. 1516, Fig. 236:4): h. 0.045 m.; d. rim 0.049 m.; d. 0.102 m. Greenish-buff clay; surface badly worn. Lustrous brown-black paint. Squat, globular body; three vertical round handles on shoulder (*MP*, Type 84, p. 41 fig. 11). Two horizontal

[1] J. Lawrence Angel, Curator-in-Charge, Division of Physical Anthropology, The Smithsonian Institution, has described these remains in a letter dated July 5, 1966, as follows:

"*1 Py* is a medium size male, stature about 165-167 cm. with thick and robust long bones, much flattening of the upper femur shaft (platymeric index 69.5) and no obvious arthritis; probably 25-30 years old; skull short ovoid ('Alpine') . . . probably a squarish face, average jaw and mouth, and excellent slightly worn teeth (only one developed caries). Length 171, Breadth 140, Height 117, Forehead br. 96?, Palate 57 x 62?, Chin 32, Jowl br. 93, angle 108°.

"*2 Py* is a female, about 25, not tall (stature 148-150 cm.) robust, with definite upper femur flattening (index 73.8) and also really bowed and narrow tibia shaft (index 59.4); definite arthritic erosion of the sterno-clavicular joint; the skull is large, long and low with wide forehead and fairly robust, probably squarish face—robust Mediterranean or 'Basic White' like a great many Mycenaeans (also Early Bronze); teeth are average, slightly worn, with seven lost in life (two being recently lost with abscesses), all of these molars, and one carious molar (eight 'lesions' in all). Length 188, Breadth 140, Height 114, Forehead br. 99, Cheek br. (120), Palate 49 x 61, Chin ht. 32?, Jowl br. (93)."

lines below rim, one around body; above this line and below handles continuous rock pattern (*MP,* Motive 32:5, p. 323 fig. 54, Late Helladic III A-III B).

Alabastron (CM. 1517, Fig. 236:1): h. 0.055 m.; d. rim 0.06 m.; d. 0.125 m. Greenish-buff clay; surface poorly preserved. Lacks pieces from rim, one handle. In shape, paint, decoration very similar to CM. 1516. Continuous rock pattern very thick, covering lower portion of shoulder.

Alabastron (CM. 1518, Fig. 236:5): h. 0.05 m.; d. 0.102 m. Red clay; original surface entirely destroyed. Lacks rim. In shape similar to CM. 1516, 1517. Design cannot be made out.

Alabastron (CM. 1519, Fig. 236:2): h. 0.04 m.; d. rim 0.042 m.; d. 0.083 m. Greenish-buff clay; lustrous red paint. Similar to preceding three in shape. Rim, handles solidly painted; two horizontal lines under rim, one around middle of body; two wavy lines on shoulder connect handles (*MP,* Motive 53: 11, p. 373 fig. 65, Late Helladic III A:2).

W. P. D.

Trial Trenches

In trenches dug in other parts of the hill some fragments of Late Helladic pottery and bits of flint, chert, and obsidian were found. One complete alabastron and a flint arrowhead rested on the south slope, near dromoi of the chamber tombs, in trenches AG and AL.

Higher on the hill, in an area where Mr. Tsakalis had reported finding walls (Trenches T, U, and V), many Late Helladic sherds, including the stems of 316 kylikes, bits of painted plaster, and small stones were found, but it was impossible to trace the line of a single wall. Either the debris came from a building that had collapsed down the hillside, or the building had been so thoroughly destroyed that not even its foundations survived. The appearance of the debris suggests that an earthquake may have been responsible; no trace of burning was noted.

In addition to sherds, a bronze pin, a steatite seal with a quadruped incised, and the head of a terracotta female figurine were found among the stones in Trenches T, U, and V.

OBJECTS FOUND

BRONZE

Pin (CM. 2158, Fig. 236:17): l. 0.055 m.; d. 0.0018 m. From Trench U. Now bent; pin, circular in section, tapers towards point.

STONE

Lentoid seal of black steatite (CM. 2156, Fig. 236:19): l. 0.015 m.; th. 0.005 m. From Trench V. Lacks upper portion of front surface, upper half of rear. Quadruped in profile moves to left; head, chest missing. Cf. *CMS* v.

Arrowhead (CM. 2163, Fig. 236:20): l. 0.021 m.; w. 0.016 m.; th. 0.003 m. From Trench AL. Reddish flint. Sides form convex curves towards point; one deeply concave curve, unbroken by tang, between barbs. Cf. *Prosymna,* fig. 441:9.

TERRACOTTA

Head of female figurine (CM. 2162, Fig. 236:21): h. 0.029 m. From Trench U. Pale buff clay; surface very worn. Triangular head broken off at base of neck; of the type represented by CM. 2164, 2170a, 2170b below (pp. 182f., 189).

POTTERY

Alabastron (CM. 1520, Fig. 236:6): h. 0.087 m.; d. rim 0.088 m.; d. 0.168 m. From Trench AG. Greenish-buff clay; surface badly worn. Lustrous brown paint. Lacks several small pieces from side, bottom. Squat, globular body; three horizontal round handles on shoulder (*MP*, Type 84, p. 41 fig. 11). Inside of rim, handles solidly coated; two horizontal lines below rim, one below handles above which continuous rock pattern (*MP*, Motive 32:5, p. 323 fig. 54. Late Helladic III A-III B).

W. P. D.

Most thoroughly examined was the south slope of the hill and here traces of 13 dromoi have been noted (Fig. 301). Eight of these have been excavated, E-1, E-2, E-4, E-6 in 1956 and 1957, E-8, E-9, E-10 in 1966 under the supervision of W. P. Donovan, and K-1 in 1957 under the direction of Lord William Taylour (pp. 208ff.). Of this number six were true chamber tombs; E-1 and E-2 had never been completed.

The presence of ledges of soft limestone to serve as roofs for the chambers makes the selection of this slope as a site for a cemetery by the Mycenaean inhabitants understandable.[2] All the chamber tombs so far found are on this slope and all have dromoi oriented roughly from south to north. Today the upper terraces of the hill are covered with olive trees, while those below are occupied by vineyards. Most of the dromoi were cut in yellowish clay, or in the stone at the edge of a terrace where olive cultivation gives way to viniculture and where the outcropping of rock is clearly evident. Tomb K-1, however, is lower and ca. 100 m. to the west of the others.

Dromos E-1

The easternmost trace of the cemetery is a dromos found beside a path leading up the hill, ca. 77 m. from the modern road. The dromos was cut in the soft limestone. Its walls slope inwards slightly as they rise (a batter of almost 0.08 m. in a rise of 1 m.). The floor descending northward is 1.17 m. wide. No doorway or chamber could be found, however, and the Mycenaean builders must have abandoned their work 3.50 m. from the south end of the dromos

[2] Mr. T. C. Buschbach, Illinois State Geological Survey, reports on this stone as follows: "X-rays show the sample to be almost pure calcium carbonate, $CaCO_3$ (limestone). Insoluble residue consists of a little silt and fine quartz sand. The rock contains a few microfossils, Foraminifera. Due to the great deposits of travertine in Greece and Jugoslavia, most people would refer to this as travertine. Two other terms could be applied, agaric mineral or marl. The regional setting and geologic history would have to be better understood to choose decisively among the three names. Porous limestone is a general term that would also fit."

when they failed to find a ledge of rock to form the roof of a chamber.[3] The earth filling the dromos yielded scanty sherds, mostly coarse ware.

Dromos E-2

This dromos was cut in limestone about 10 m. west of E-1. Its walls slope inward, but the batter is much more pronounced than that of E-1 (almost 0.20 m. in 1 m.). At the floor, 2 m. below the present ground surface, the dromos is 1.50 m. wide at its northern end. The floor slopes downward irregularly for 9 m., but again there is no chamber or doorway at the end. Evidently the builders stopped work here for the same reason that they did in E-1. A rough stone slab (h. 0.50 m.; w. 0.30 m.; th. 0.08 m.) was found close to the surface at the inner end of the dromos. With its position and dimensions it resembles the stone markers found in the dromoi of some chamber tombs, but its function here is not clear. Recovered from the fill of this dromos was one basket of sherds, including stems of nine kylikes, and one terracotta whorl (CM. 2159, Fig. 236:18: h. 0.0185 m.; d. 0.026 m.; bright orange clay; worn surface; biconical).

Tomb E-4
(Plan and Section, Fig. 338)

The dromos of this tomb is 9.50 m. west of Dromos E-2 in the scarp of the lowest terrace of the Tsakalis olive grove. Since it extends into the vineyard below, the dromos was only partially cleared, from 2.50 m. south of the door to the chamber. The sides of the dromos have a slight inward batter (0.08 m. in a rise of 1 m.). The floor slopes down to the door where it is 3 m. below modern ground level. A strip of earth was left undug along the east side during the early stages of excavation so that the stratification of the fill might be studied. In this scarp were traces of at least two reopenings of the tomb. When this earth was removed two empty niches in the eastern wall of the dromos were revealed. One, 1.30 m. from the door, is 0.30 m. wide, 0.70 m. high, and 0.27 m. deep; the other, 0.40 m. south of the first, is 0.57 m. wide, 0.47 m. high, and 0.30 m. deep. Both niches are about 1 m. above the floor. In addition to fragments of pottery, two carnelian and two paste beads (CM. 2167) were found in the earth that filled the dromos.

---

[3] A similar dromos was noted at the Argive Heraeum (*Prosymna*, 231, Tomb XXXIX), but interments were made at the end of the dromos. Tsountas found three dromoi at Mycenae without chambers (*EphArch* 1888, 123); there the hardness of the rock, rather than the lack of it, seemed responsible for the abandonment of the dromoi.

The doorway, measuring at the bottom 0.90 m. wide and 1 m. deep from front to back, is preserved to its full height of 1.67 m. (Fig. 237). The jambs were cut in clay, but the lintel, as well as the roof of the chamber, were formed by the ledge of limestone. The width of the doorway diminishes very slightly toward the top.

The wall blocking the doorway, preserved to a height of 1 m., was carelessly built of irregular stones. The upper part had fallen into the dromos where the stones were encountered as far as 0.80 m. from the door. It is possible that the partial collapse of the roof of the chamber caused the upper stones of this wall to be pushed into the dromos. Inside the chamber to the west several more stones were found which probably had been left there on an occasion when the tomb had been reopened and had not been reused. The undisturbed lower portion of the wall extended to the full depth of the opening. Several beads were found among these stones (CM. 2166).

The chamber was entirely filled with pieces of limestone and clay; but as the ledge was preserved over the southern half of the tomb, the debris came from the collapse of the roof in the northern half. It proved necessary to excavate the chamber partially from above.

The chamber is roughly oval, 3.30 m. from north to south and 5.20 m. from east to west. Two pits are cut in the floor, one in the western half (A) and one in the eastern (B). Pit A is rectangular, 1.50 m. long from north to south, 0.60 m. wide from east to west, and 0.90 m. deep, except at the northern end where the clay was dug to a depth of only 0.50 m. forming a ledge 0.50 m. wide.

Pit B, much more irregularly shaped, occupies almost the entire eastern half of the chamber. It is 0.60 m. deep at its southwestern corner and its floor slopes up towards the north. It is 2.50 m. long from north to south, its northern edge coinciding with the north wall of the chamber, and 2.10 m. wide. The pit is divided longitudinally about 0.80 m. from its eastern edge by a crude wall made of irregular pieces of stone.

The skeletal remains were in a much damaged state of preservation and were badly scattered as a result of the collapse of part of the roof. No complete skeleton was found and only two skulls could definitely be recognized, one at the southern end of Pit A and the other at the northern end of Pit B. Scattered bones were found from 0.40 m. to 0.50 m. above the floor at the north edge of the chamber opposite the entrance. All the other bone fragments came from or above Pit B, some from east of the wall. In the absence of crania, it was impossible to determine accurately how many interments there had been, but the size of the chamber, the pits, and especially the division of one of them (for the wall seems to have separated the remains of two burials at least) indicate that there were more than two.[4]

Pit A contained only a terracotta female figurine (CM. 2164) in addition to the bones of the child. In Pit B were several beads at its southern end and at least six vases, five of which could be mended. The oldest seems to be an alabastron (CM. 1621) found under the wall. Next in order were three vases from the north end of the pit (CM. 1620 [1], 1535 [2], 1538 [3]). The last vase from Pit B, a cup (CM. 1536 [4]), found above the pit, was filled with gray ash. Presumably the latest objects in the tomb were those recovered from the floor along the west side, namely a steatite button (CM. 2168) and three vases (CM. 1521 [5], 1522 [6], 1537 [7]). The earth from the chamber was sifted, producing a number of beads of carnelian and paste (CM. 2166), as well as a crystal pendant which could not be connected with any specific burial.

The datable vases from Pit B belong to Late Helladic III A:1, whereas those from the floor of the chamber can be assigned to Late Helladic III A:2 l-III B. The tomb seems, thus, to have been first made by the middle of Late Helladic III A and to have continued in use possibly as late as Late Helladic III B.

OBJECTS FOUND

Dromos

STONE

Carnelian beads (CM. 2167, Fig. 236:16): nine spherical ranging in diameter from 0.007 m. to 0.01 m.

PASTE

Beads (CM. 2167, Fig. 236:16): three spherical, light blue, d. 0.0085 m.; one grooved, brown d. 0.007 m.

Chamber

STONE

Carnelian beads (CM. 2166, Fig. 236:16): 11 spherical ranging in diameter from 0.0075 m. to 0.01 m.; one cylindrical, l. 0.015 m.; d. 0.0085 m. Sifting.

Steatite button (CM. 2168, Fig. 236:16): h. 0.005 m.; d. 0.018 m. Pit A. Short cone of smooth greenish steatite; several fragments.

Crystal pendant (CM. 2166, Fig. 236:16): d. 0.021 m.; th. 0.008 m. Sifting. Perhaps central bead of necklace; translucent.

PASTE

Beads (CM. 2166, Fig. 236:16): nine spherical, dark blue, ranging in diameter from 0.0055 m. to 0.008 m.; one and one half light blue spherical, d. 0.008 m. Sifting.

TERRACOTTA

Female figurine (CM. 2164, Fig. 236:15a, b): h. 0.138 m.; d. stem 0.038 m. Pit A. Pale buff clay; front surface worn; red to brown

---

[4] Dr. Angel describes these skeletal remains as follows: "*3 Py* (Pit A) is the fragmentary remains of a child, about 12. *3a Py,* bones A B C D E includes a partial femur with large ball joint (49 mm)

suggesting a short and powerful man, perhaps 30-35 years old; the skull remains are too broken to tell much; teeth wear is average."

lustrous paint. Crude triangular head, disk-shaped body, cylindrical stem. Eyes, breasts represented by small, flattened pellets of clay; both arms bent with hands resting on body just below breasts. Back of head solidly coated; back covered with vertical lines; stem with horizontal bands to suggest garments. (Cf. *Prosymna*, fig. 611:417, 420, arms in slightly different position.)

Chamber: west side

POTTERY

Stirrup-vase [5] (CM. 1521, Fig. 236:13): h. 0.098 m.; d. 0.098 m.; d. base 0.031 m. Buff clay; lustrous red paint. Globular body, slightly raised base (*MP*, Type 171, pp. 30f. figs. 5, 6). Upper surface of handles solidly painted; top of false spout, line around edge with solid circle in center. Multiple stem and tongue on shoulder (*MP*, Motive 19:23, p. 299 fig. 47, Late Helladic III A:2 l).

Two-handled jug [6] (CM. 1522, Fig. 236: 11a, b): h. 0.085 m.; d. rim 0.028 m.; d. neck 0.015 m.; d. 0.068 m.; d. base 0.026 m. Buff clay; surface flaking; lustrous red paint. Tall, narrow neck; two flat handles from shoulder to high on neck; spreading rim; small raised base (*MP*, Form 49, Type 190, p. 616). Handles solidly painted; horizontal lines on body, base, top of neck, inner and outer surface of rim. Parallel chevrons or zigzag lines (*MP*, Motive 58 or 61, p. 383 fig. 67) on neck; "U" pattern in shoulder zone (*MP*, Motive 45:6, p. 345 fig. 58). Late Helladic III A:2-III B.

Alabastron [7] (CM. 1537, Fig. 236:8): h. 0.05 m.; d. rim 0.046 m.; d. 0.092 m. Buff clay; surface badly worn. Lustrous red paint. In shape similar to CM. 1516-1519 from Pit Grave E-3 (pp. 177f.). Handles, neck solidly coated; lines on rim, body; decoration on shoulder no longer visible.

Chamber: Pit B

Cup [2] (CM. 1535, Fig. 236:9): h. cup 0.036

m.; h. with handle 0.057 m.; d. rim 0.096 m. Coarse red clay completely covered with worn brown paint. Lacks one small chip from rim. Flat vertical handle rising high above rim and ending low on body; flat base.

Cup [4] (CM. 1536, Fig. 236:10): h. cup 0.034 m.; h. with handle 0.052 m.; d. rim 0.092 m.; d. base 0.033 m. Pinkish clay covered with thick coat of lustrous red paint. Narrow spreading rim, flat vertical ring handle rising from rim and terminating below it; flat base (*MP*, Type 238, p. 53 fig. 15, Late Helladic III A:1).

Beaked jug [3] (CM. 1538, Fig. 236:14a, b): h. 0.31 m.; d. neck 0.038 m.; d. 0.249 m.; d. base 0.092 m. Pale buff clay; surface worn. Worn red-brown paint. Complete except for small fragments. Sloping, ridged handle from rim to shoulder. Extension of handle on shoulder is vertically pierced. Short tapering beak; ledge molding at base of neck; base slightly spreading (*MP*, Type 144, p. 30 fig. 5). Bottom of body, outer surface of handle, ledge molding, tip of beak, neck (with one horizontal line above) solidly coated. Not visible in illustration: two groups of two wavy lines depend from handle; small quirks encircle shoulder below molding (*MP*, Motive 48:5, p. 360 fig. 61). Three groups of three large linked spirals cover most of body (*MP*, Motive 22:16, "Curtailed Argonauts," p. 307 fig. 50, Late Helladic III A:1).

Kylix [1] (CM. 1620, Fig. 236:12): h. 0.137 m.; h. stem 0.035 m.; d. 0.157 m.; d. base 0.057 m. Buff clay; undecorated; body warped. Two flat, vertical handles; bottom concave with hollow (*MP*, Type 264, p. 60 fig. 16, Late Helladic III A:1-2).

Alabastron (CM. 1621, Fig. 236:7): h. 0.056 m.; d. rim 0.058 m.; d. 0.122 m. From under wall in Pit B. Greenish-buff clay; undecorated. Lacks parts of rim, body, bottom, one handle. In shape similar to CM. 1516-1519, 1537, above.

W. P. D.

Tomb E-6
(Plan and Section, Fig. 339)

The dromos of this tomb was exposed about 65 m. west of Tomb E-4 on the same terrace. As the dromos descends toward the north, it was cut through hard, yellowish clay. Oriented from south-southeast to north-northwest, it is 8.50 m. long, 0.70 m. wide at the floor at its outer end, broadening to 1.28 m. before the door. The slope of the floor is uneven, being much steeper in the outer section; at the entrance to the chamber the floor is 4.30 m. below modern ground level. The irregularly cut walls have a pronounced inward inclination (0.12 m. in each 1 m. of rise), so that at the inner end the dromos is barely 0.40 m. wide at the top.

High in the earth filling of the dromos, close to the entrance, stood a trapezoidal stone slab[5] set upright on its narrow end, presumably to serve as a marker. Below the marker a mass of irregular stones rested on the earth fill which blocked the inner 0.80 m. of the dromos to a depth of 0.60 m. Stones in a similar position were frequently encountered in the dromoi of tombs at the Argive Heraeum, where they were explained as being perhaps material left over in the several rebuildings of the closing wall.[6] When the chamber of Tomb E-6 was cleared, however, a second doorway and chamber appeared, evidently laid out above the predecessors after a partial collapse of the roof of the chamber. These stones were perhaps part of the wall of this upper doorway. Among them were recovered the pieces of a kylix (CM. 1559); this was possibly the last vase connected with this tomb, broken and buried as the upper door was closed after the final burial.[7] Below the stones a terracotta button (CM. 2173) was found.

A study of the stratification visible in the scarp which was left along the east wall of the dromos showed a clear line of division corresponding to the later floor of the dromos in use at the time the upper door was built. Beneath this line there were indications that the lower part of the dromos had been reopened at least five times.

The lower doorway, its jambs cut in clay, is 0.95 m. wide at the bottom, narrowing to 0.70 m. at the top, 1.57 m. above the threshold. The depth of the opening from front to back is 0.90 m. The lintel was partially constructed of a large block of stone, supplementing the rocky ledge. The block spanning the entrance (1.12 m.) is 0.40 m. wide and 0.30 m. thick. The wall closing the doorway filled the entire depth of the opening and, at the bottom, projected slightly into the dromos (Fig. 238). It was built of unworked stones, small in the upper

---

[5] 0.37 m. long, 0.40 m. wide at broad end, 0.17 m. wide at narrow end, 0.07 m. thick.

[6] *Prosymna*, 236.

[7] Apparently a common Mycenaean practice, e.g., *Prosymna*, 237-238.

courses and large in the lower. It was completely preserved and the uppermost stones were tightly wedged under the lintel.

The sides of the dromos formed the jambs of the very irregularly shaped upper doorway and the same block partially served also as its threshold. The lintel, approximately 1.38 m. above the block, was a ledge of limestone which marked the inner end of the dromos. The stone wall which blocked this door was much less regular than the lower one and may even have extended 0.80 m. out into the dromos.

The chamber itself is roughly rectangular, 2.30 m. from south to north and 3.86 m. from east to west. The doorway is not on axis but east of it. The walls were cut in clay and still preserve the marks of the tools of the builders. The original roof, that is to say the rocky ledge, had at some time subsequently collapsed. Before the roof had completely given way the chamber had filled with clay and pieces of stone and at no level was the fill free from sherds. The chamber had to be excavated from above.

The last period in the use of the tomb was represented by three burials (A, B, and C), the skulls of which were encountered 2.35 m. above the floor of the chamber.[8] Associated with them were three vases, two kylikes (CM. 1539), one of which was too fragmentary to mend, and a jug with cutaway spout (CM. 1622); this pottery serves to date the burials to Late Helladic III A:2, or, more probably, III B.

The next earlier interment (D) lay 0.80 m. above the floor in the southwestern corner of the chamber. It was not clear whether or not this was the last burial through the lower door, or the first through the upper. It may be that the family owning this tomb, when they saw the chamber filled to such a depth, sealed the door after this burial and made a new entrance above for the next one. Near the skull were recovered 15 and one-half beads of gold and nine of ivory from the same necklace (CM. 2177, 2178), as well as nine ivory triangles and two disks, probably inlays (CM. 2176). The only vase was a sidespouted jug with basket-handle (CM. 1558) which lay upside down slightly above, and north of the skull.

That the chamber had begun to fill with debris early in the history of its use was indicated by the fact that a still earlier interment (E) rested 0.45 m. above the floor (Figs. 239, 339). This was seemingly the best-preserved skeleton from the tomb (although the bones disintegrated when they were removed); of the bones

[8] These are the only skeletal remains from this tomb that Dr. Angel could interpret, the others being too poorly preserved. He writes as follows: "From Tomb E-6 there are only real scraps: *28* *Py*, Skull A, is a female(?) about 16 years old; *29, Py*, Skull B, is a young adult female; and *30 Py*, Skull C, is a child about 10 years old."

that came to light at a higher level only the crania were readily identifiable. The skeleton, carefully wrapped in some thick red material, traces of which were spread over the skull, along the sides, and under the feet, had been laid on its back with the head supported on two flat stones. The arms were placed at the sides with the hands over the pelvis. The body lay, just inside the door, in the eastern side of the chamber with the head to the north. Beside the left shin had been placed three bronze weapons, a sword (CM. 2204), a cleaver (CM. 2206), and a spear point (CM. 2207); a dagger of bronze lay beside the right leg (CM. 2205). Two pithoid jars (CM. 1540 [1], 1541 [2]) had been set upright against the wall of the chamber beyond the feet. One was filled with bits of bone, sherds, and ash. Both indicate a date of Late Helladic III A:2 for this burial.

Three other interments representing approximately the same phase in the history of the use of the tomb had been made on the floor of the western side of the chamber. The westernmost (F) lay in the extended position with the head toward the north (Fig. 241). A bronze mirror (CM. 2202) lying beside the skull, with three vases (CM. 1544 [3], 1545 [4], 1546 [5]), one to the right, two to the left, all belong probably to Late Helladic III A:2.

The small size and the fragileness of the bones indicate that the other two skeletons belonged to children. Each was placed with the head toward the south. The southern one (G), its head close to the wall of the chamber, was accompanied by a bronze mirror (CM. 2203) lying on the skull beneath which were some bits of ivory. A great number of small segmented beads, as well as some larger ellipsoid and spherical beads of paste, were salvaged from among the ribs (CM. 2171).

Associated with the burial of the other child (I) were two terracotta figurines (CM. 2170a, 2170b) and many spherical paste beads (CM. 2174). Six vases, including two very small alabastra and a miniature jug, lay close to these two skeletons (CM. 1547 [6], 1548 [7], 1549 [8], 1550 [9], 1551 [10], 1557 [11]).

When skeleton E was removed, in the eastern side of the chamber, another burial (H) appeared directly beneath it on the floor with its skull pointing toward the south (Fig. 240). It, too, was stretched out with the arms at the sides and hands over the pelvis. A bronze dagger (CM. 2201) was found beside the left knee and a knife of the same material (CM. 2200) a few centimeters from the left hip. A pithoid jar (CM. 1552 [12]) had been left by the head and three vases by the right leg (CM. 1553 [13], 1554 [14], 1555 [15]). They may all be dated to Late Helladic III A:1, or, perhaps, Late Helladic III A:2e.

A shallow depression in the northeastern corner of the chamber contained two more skulls (J, K), together with a few bones. Presumably these remains were the earliest in the tomb. The only objects associated with them were two spherical carnelian beads (CM. 2180).

Three vases could not be connected with a specific burial. Two stood on the floor of the chamber close to the north wall (CM. 1542 [16], 1543 [17]). The other (CM. 1556 [18]), since it was just inside the door where clear traces of a small fire were visible on the floor, may have been left there after a funeral ceremony.[9] The late date of the vase (Late Helladic III A:2) would correspond with the presumed date of interment E.

The following sequence of events may be suggested: Tomb E-6 was built late in Late Helladic III A:1, or early in III A:2. Almost at once clay began to accumulate on the floor as the result of seepage. The Mycenaean family continued, however, to bury their dead here until, near the end of Late Helladic III A:2, a partial collapse of the roof nearly filled the chamber. Unwilling to abandon the tomb, they cut a new door and chamber directly above the old. Here the final burials were made in Late Helladic III B, bringing the total number to at least 11.

O B J E C T S   F O U N D

Dromos

STONE

Steatite button (CM. 2173, Fig. 242): h. 0.009 m.; d. 0.017 m. Short cone; dark gray, polished.

TERRACOTTA

Button (CM. 2173, Fig. 242): h. 0.003 m.; d. 0.0155 m. From beneath stones. Dark buff clay; surface worn. Short cone. Cf. *Prosymna*, fig. 602:1.

POTTERY

Kylix (CM. 1559, Fig. 244:8): h. 0.14 m.; d. 0.138 m.; d. base 0.063 m. From stones. Green clay; undecorated. Slightly spreading rim from which two flat handles descend to body. Late Helladic III A-III B.

Doorway

POTTERY

Beaked jug [18] (CM. 1556, Fig. 244:21): h. 0.32 m.; h. neck 0.10 m.; d. neck 0.041 m.;

d. 0.23 m.; d. base 0.084 m. Pale buff clay; lustrous red-brown paint. Lacks a few small pieces. Globular body with narrow neck ending in short beak spout; one vertical ridged handle looping from rim to shoulder, where ridge continues for short distance; torus base. Upper face of handle, base solidly coated; line above base, three around belly, two on neck, two on underside of spout; band along inner and outer edge of rim and spout. Upper half of body decorated with four connecting figures, each made up of two parallel curving lines connected by cross strokes (cf. *MP*, Motive 33:II:8, p. 327 fig. 55); this zone is set off from neck by wavy border line (cf. *MP*, Motive 42:7, 8, p. 343 fig. 57). Possibly Late Helladic III A:2.

Chamber

GOLD

Beads (CM. 2178, Fig. 243:1): 15 whole and one half; l. 0.011 m.; w. 0.011 m.; th.

---

[9] A fire may have been necessary to fumigate the chamber when one interment followed another closely. (Similar traces in the tombs at the Argive Heraeum, *Prosymna*, 250.)

0.003 m. Burial D. Made of two sheets of gold leaf fastened together, upper face bearing ivy pattern in repoussé technique. Two parallel string-holes. Probably strung with ivory beads (CM. 2177, below). Cf. *ChT*, 27, fig. 12:42 (paste); *RT,Dendra*, pl. XVIII:2 (gold and paste); *Asine*, 387, fig. 251 (gold).

BRONZE

Knife (CM. 2200, Fig. 243:10): l. 0.20 m.; l. handle 0.072 m.; w. blade 0.017 m.; d. handle 0.008 m. Burial H. Handle solid bronze; terminates in knob (d. 0.011 m.). Blade slit to receive some material which would have served as actual cutting edge. Cf. Evans, "The Prehistoric Tombs of Knossos," *Archaeologia* 59 (1905), 415, fig. 19.

Dagger (CM. 2201, Fig. 243:9): w. blade 0.055 m.; w. hilt 0.03 m. Burial H. Lacks tip of blade. Blade broad, leaf-shaped. Two rivets for attachment of handle preserved. Cf. *Prosymna*, fig. 158.

Mirror (CM. 2202, Fig. 243:11): d. 0.115 m. Burial F. One rivet hole for attachment of handle 0.005 m. from edge of mirror; traces of a second.

Mirror (CM. 2203, Fig. 243:7): d. 0.109 m. Burial G. Two rivet holes 0.013 m. apart, 0.007 m. from edge by which handle was attached.

Cruciform sword (CM. 2204, Fig. 243:5): l. 0.633 m.; l. hilt 0.118 m.; w. blade at heel 0.039 m.; w. guard 0.067 m.; w. tang 0.02 m.; w. flange 0.007 m. Burial E. Blade reinforced on each face by rounded midrib which tapers toward point. Hilt flanged up to pommel (missing). Handle of wood some traces of which visible when sword found. Wood attached by means of three large, flat-headed rivets on tang, which terminates in prong for pommel, and four small rivets on guard, two on each side of midrib. Cf. Evans, "The Prehistoric Tombs of Knossos," *Archaeologia* 59 (1905), pl. XCI, fig. 109, 55a, 42a.

Dagger (CM. 2205, Fig. 243:6): l. 0.387 m.; w. blade 0.058 m.; l. hilt 0.107 m.; w. hilt 0.023 m.; w. pommel 0.057 m. Burial E. Blade broad, narrowing gradually to end where edges curve sharply to rather blunt tip. Hilt, which ends in broad, rounded pommel, edged by flange running 0.025 m. onto blade. Within flanged area, traces of wooden handle attached with seven rivets, three evenly spaced along hilt, two on each shoulder. Cf. *Prosymna*, figs. 377:1, 198; *RT,Dendra*, pl. XXXIII:4; *NT,Dendra*, fig. 35:1.

Cleaver (CM. 2206, Fig. 243:12): l. 0.248 m.; w. blade 0.049 m.; l. tang 0.066 m.; w. tang 0.015 m. Burial E. Slightly curved tang has three rivets for attachment of wooden handle. Back edge of cleaver (0.003 m. thick) formed in double curve, convex handle, concave back. Convex cutting edge now uneven, perhaps as result of corrosion. Cf. *Prosymna*, fig. 512:4, p. 348 no. 4; *Eph-Arch* 1888, pl. IX:18.

Spear point (CM. 2207, Fig. 243:8): l. 0.359 m.; l. blade 0.229 m.; w. blade 0.052 m.; d. socket 0.02 m. Burial E. Broad, flat midrib (0.008 m.) along axis from socket to tip. Rib bears simple decoration of two raised lines, one on each side, which continue on socket. At outer end of socket, a nail hole to fasten spear point to wooden haft. Cf. *Prosymna*, fig. 510.

STONE

Carnelian beads (CM. 2180, Fig. 242): 2 spherical, d. 0.008 m.; 0.011 m. Depression in northeast corner of chamber.

IVORY

Disks, triangles (CM. 2176, Fig. 242): two flat disks (d. 0.009 m.; th. 0.0035 m.); nine flat triangles (w. 0.03 m.; h. 0.03 m.; th. 0.0035 m.) which have one straight, two concave sides. Burial D. Probably inlaid in wood.

Leaf-shaped beads (CM. 2177, Fig. 243:1): nine pieces with same dimensions (l. 0.011 m.; w. 0.011 m.; th. 0.003 m.) and design (sacral ivy leaves) as gold beads (CM. 2178, above). Burial D.

PASTE

Beads (CM. 2171, Fig. 243:2): three types: 15 spherical (d. 0.006 m. to 0.014 m.), 13 ellipsoid (l. 0.014 m.; d. 0.0075 m.), segmented, of which great number found. Burial G.

Beads (CM. 2174, Fig. 242): eight spherical (d. 0.006 m. to 0.014 m.). Burial I.

TERRACOTTA

Female figurine (CM. 2170a, Fig. 243:3a-c): h. 0.115 m.; w. across disk 0.032 m. Burial I. Pale buff clay; red to brown lustrous paint. Same type as CM. 2164 from Tomb E-4 (pp. 182f.), although arms, hands not so distinctly modeled here, left resting on chest, right on abdomen. Dots of paint on eyes which are also outlined with paint; top, rear of head solidly coated; wavy vertical lines on both disk and stem.

Female figurine (CM. 2170b, Fig. 243:4a-c): h. 0.102 m.; w. across disk 0.032 m. Burial I. Greenish-buff clay; dark brown lustrous paint. Same type as CM. 2170a except breasts are not shown and both arms bent in same fashion, hands on chest. Decorated in same manner as preceding, but horizontal replace vertical lines on stem.

Whorl or button (CM. 2173, Fig. 242): h. 0.019 m.; d. 0.017 m. Above burial F. Red clay; smooth surface. Short cone.

POTTERY

Kylix (CM. 1539, Fig. 244:9): h. 0.103 m.; h. stem 0.025 m.; d. 0.116 m.; d. base 0.063 m. Burial B. Pale buff clay; undecorated. Lacks small chip from rim. Small, one-handled; slightly spreading rim; angular profile. Above angle sides vertical, or slightly concave; below sides narrow to short stem. Flat vertical handle from rim to slightly below angle; convex base with conical depression on under side (*PN* I, Shape 27, pp. 366f. *MP*, Type 267, p. 61 fig. 17, Late Helladic III B).

Pithoid jar [1] (CM. 1540, Fig. 244:20): h. 0.30 m.; d. rim 0.118 m.; d. 0.218 m.; d. base 0.08 m. Burial E. Pale buff clay; lustrous red-brown paint. Below horizontally

spreading rim concave sides of neck meet convex sides of body; lower, almost straight sides narrow gradually toward spreading torus base. Three flat vertical handles on shoulder (*PN* I, Shape 52, pp. 386f.; *MP*, Type 31, p. 589). Base, neck, handles solidly painted; horizontal lines above base, below neck, below shoulder, on upper surface of rim. In three panels on shoulder, between handles, curve-stemmed spirals (*MP*, Motive 49:10, p. 363 fig. 62) with hatching in curve of stems; parallel chevrons (*MP*, Motive 58:15, p. 383 fig. 67) and multiple stem and tongue patterns (*MP*, Motive 19:15, p. 299 fig. 47) as filling ornaments. Late Helladic III A:2-2 l.

Pithoid jar [2] (CM. 1541, Fig. 244:5): h. 0.175 m.; d. rim 0.099 m.; d. 0.148 m.; d. base 0.056 m. Burial E. Pale buff clay; lustrous paint varying from red to dark brown. Lacks one handle, several small pieces from body. Handles round and horizontal, neck low and wide, base spreading (*PN* I, Shape 51, p. 386; *MP*, Type 44, p. 23 fig. 4). Neck, base, handles solidly coated; horizontal lines above base, around body. Shoulder, upper part of body completely cross-hatched (*MP*, Motive 57:2 "diaper net," p. 383 fig. 67, Late Helladic III A:1-III C:1).

Angular alabastron [16] (CM. 1542, Fig. 244:14): h. 0.13 m.; d. rim 0.10 m.; d. 0.176 m. North wall. Pale buff clay; worn brown-black paint. Lacks several small pieces. Angular profile; sides of body and shoulder slightly convex, neck pronouncedly concave. Broad, horizontal, slightly beveled rim; three round horizontal handles on shoulder; flat bottom (*PN* I, Shape 64, p. 402; *MP*, Type 93, p. 44 fig. 12). Handles, neck solidly coated. Lower part of body encircled by broad horizontal bands and lines; shoulder solidly cross-hatched. Late Helladic III A:1-2.

Three-handled conical bowl [17] (CM. 1543, Fig. 244:3): h. 0.095 m.; d. 0.165 m.; d. base 0.045 m. North wall. Pale buff clay; worn red-brown paint. Lacks part of one handle. Spreading base with underside hollowed; above, straight sides widen only to curve in slightly below narrow spreading rim. Three small, round handles rise vertically from top of rim. Shape not found in *MP*. Handles, interior and exterior of base, exterior of rim solidly coated. Group of three horizontal lines midway up on exterior of body; between them and rim a single wavy line (*MP*, Motive 53:17, p. 373 fig. 65). Transverse lines on upper surface of rim and five groups of three wavy lines arranged vertically between horizontal lines on inside of bowl.

Alabastron [3] (CM. 1544, Fig. 244:17): h. 0.07 m.; d. rim 0.067 m.; d. 0.133 m. Burial F. Yellow-buff clay; lustrous red-brown paint. Lacks small pieces. Bottom slightly convex; sides form continuous convex curves to very low neck; three small round horizontal handles on shoulder (*MP*, Type 84, p. 41 fig. 11). Handles, neck inside and out solidly painted. Bottom decorated with concentric circles, three close to center, two to edge; two broad lines around body above which three groups of three concentric semicircles on shoulder (*MP*, Motive 43:6, p. 343 fig. 57, Late Helladic III A:2 l).

Three-handled conical bowl [4] (CM. 1545, Fig. 244:2): h. 0.092 m.; d. 0.157 m.; d. base 0.045 m. Burial F. Pale buff clay; lustrous paint ranging from red to brown. Shape identical with that of CM. 1543, above, as is decoration of interior. Exterior similar except that wavy line replaced on upper part of body by series of spirals with short, curving stems (*MP*, Motive 49:19, p. 363 fig. 62 where stems have small subsidiary spirals, stems are at left, and are attached to base line). Late Helladic III A-III B.

Alabastron [5] (CM. 1546, Fig. 244:18): h. 0.05 m.; d. rim 0.05 m.; d. 0.143 m. Burial F. Yellowish-buff clay; thick brown-black paint. Very squat body with curving sides; spreading rim slightly rounded; three horizontal round handles high on shoulder

(*MP*, Type 84, p. 41 fig. 11). Handles, neck, rim solidly painted; broad horizontal band below shoulder from which irregular triangles ascend between handles (*MP*, Motive 32:1:5, "rock," p. 323 fig. 54). Late Helladic III A-III B.

Miniature jug [6] (CM. 1547, Fig. 244:15a, b): h. 0.10 m.; d. rim 0.041 m.; d. 0.086 m.; d. base 0.03 m. Burials G, I. Yellowish-buff clay; lustrous red paint. Flat bottom; slightly convex sides spread to maximum diameter narrowing above in convex curve to base of neck; moderately high slightly concave neck rising to out-turned rim from which round vertical handle descends to shoulder; two small, round horizontal handles at greatest diameter (no exact parallel found in *MP*). Horizontal handles, inner and outer surface of rim solidly painted; lines at bottom of neck, on vertical handles, below horizontal handles. Three groups of parallel chevrons arranged vertically on shoulder (*MP*, Motive 58:8, p. 383 fig. 67, Late Helladic III A-III B).

Side-spouted jug with basket-handle [7] (CM. 1548, Fig. 244:11a, b): h. 0.116 m.; h. without handle 0.097 m.; d. rim 0.044 m.; d. 0.08 m.; d. base 0.025 m. Burials G, I. Buff clay; red paint. Flat bottom; globular body; neck with concave sides; slightly spreading rim; flat basket-handle; tubular, tapering spout (*MP*, Type 159-161, pp. 30f. figs. 5, 6). Rim, neck, spout solidly coated; transverse strokes on basket-handle; three horizontal lines encircle body below spout. Shoulder decorated with two wavy lines below pendant rock pattern (related to *MP*, Motive 32:1:5, p. 323 fig. 54). Late Helladic III A-III B.

Miniature alabastron [8] (CM. 1549, Fig. 292:6): h. 0.035 m.; d. rim 0.03 m.; d. 0.058 m. Burials G, I. Yellowish-buff clay; very worn brown paint. Lacks large piece from rim. Squat body with steeply sloping shoulders below horizontal beveled rim; three horizontal, round handles. (Exact parallel not found in *MP*.) Handles, neck, rim solidly coated; four concentric circles on flat bottom; wide band below angle above which runs continuous rock pattern (*MP*, Motive 32:1:5, p. 323 fig. 54). Late Helladic III A-III B.

Miniature alabastron [9] (CM. 1550, Fig. 244:19): h. 0.037 m.; d. rim 0.028 m.; d. 0.067 m. Burials G, I. Pinkish-buff clay; worn red paint. In shape like the preceding (CM. 1549) except rim not beveled and neck more clearly articulated. Decoration similar to that on CM. 1549.

Three-handled conical bowl [10] (CM. 1551, Fig. 244:4a-c): h. 0.095 m.; d. 0.17 m.; d. base 0.048 m. Burials G, I. Pale buff clay; red-brown paint. Shape identical with that of CM. 1543, 1545, above. Decoration very similar to that on CM. 1543. Line around inside of bowl, at bottom, has short strokes, resembling rising petals or rays. On exterior, quirks take place of wavy lines found on CM. 1543 (*MP*, Motive 48:5, p. 360 fig. 61). Late Helladic III.

Pithoid jar [12] (CM. 1552, Fig. 244:6): h. 0.215 m.; d. rim 0.105 m.; d. 0.17 m.; d. base 0.066 m. Burial H. Yellowish-buff clay; red-brown paint. Shape very similar to that of CM. 1541, but neck slightly taller and shoulder narrower, proportionally. Handles, base, neck solidly painted; lines on flat rim, above base, low on body, below shoulder. On shoulder two groups of two wavy lines intertwine around vessel (*MP*, Motive 33:11:6 or 11, p. 327 fig. 55). Late Helladic III A:1-2: filling ornament of triangles which have one convex side and two concave sides (*MP*, Motive 11, p. 265).

Amphoroid jug [13] (CM. 1553, Fig. 244:13): h. 0.283 m.; h. neck 0.068 m.; d. neck 0.028 m.; d. 0.174 m.; d. base 0.07 m. Burial H. Pale buff clay; undecorated. Lacks small fragments. Narrow neck with concave sides terminating in short beaked spout above and in plastic ridge below; two sloping round handles extending from just below rim to shoulder; upper part of body has curved sides straightening and narrowing sharply toward spreading base (*MP*,

Type 150, pp. 22, 23 figs. 3, 4). Late Helladic III A:1-2e.

Pithoid jar [14] (CM. 1554, Fig. 244:7): h. 0.243 m.; d. rim 0.107 m.; d. 0.185 m.; d. base 0.07 m. Burial H. Pale greenish clay; worn brown-black paint. Lacks small bits. In shape similar to CM. 1540, although sides of neck are more nearly straight. Neck, rim, handles, base solidly coated; groups of horizontal lines above base and around belly. In each of three panels formed by handles on shoulder two running spirals connected by a tangent, right-hand spiral ending with curved stem (*MP*, Motive 49, p. 363 fig. 62). Late Helladic III A:1-2.

Cup [15] (CM. 1555, Fig. 244:16): h. including handle 0.086 m.; h. to rim 0.055 m.; d. 0.13 m.; d. base 0.044 m. Burial H. Bright orange clay; undecorated. Lacks one small fragment. Above flat base convex sides turning in slightly to spreading rim. One high flat handle rises from rim to terminate on body at greatest diameter (*MP*, Type 236, p. 49 fig. 14).

Three-handled bowl [11] (CM. 1557, Fig. 244:1): h. 0.062 m.; d. 0.134 m.; d. base 0.04 m. Burials G, I. Orange-buff clay; red paint. Lacks small chips. Shape similar to that of conical bowls (CM. 1543, 1545, 1551, above); three small handles on rim, but sides are doubly curved, convex above, concave below; raised flat base. Broad bands around base, over handles, around rim both inside and out. Transverse lines on edge of rim; two horizontal lines in two groups on inside of bowl; on exterior, one line above base and three higher on body; above is one wavy line (cf. *MP*, Motive 53:30, p. 373 fig. 65).

Side-spouted jug with basket-handle (CM. 1558, Fig. 244:10): h. with handle 0.158 m.; h. to rim 0.114 m.; d. rim 0.052 m.; d. 0.093 m.; d. base 0.034 m. Burial D. Orange-buff clay; exterior entirely coated with lustrous red paint. Lacks spout. Shape similar to that of CM. 1548, but sides of neck more concave, spreading sides of body more nearly straight above flat bottom, handle round rather than flat in section. Late Helladic III A-III B.

One-handled jug with cutaway spout (CM. 1622, Fig. 244:12): h. with spout 0.237 m.; h. without spout 0.225 m.; d. neck 0.057 m.; d. 0.222 m.; d. base 0.10 m. Burials A-C. Buff clay; traces of worn black paint. Lacks parts of spout, body. Sides spread rapidly from raised base in slightly convex

curves before arching in to base of neck the walls of which are concave. Broad flattened handle arches from rim to shoulder (*MP*, Type 136, p. 31 fig. 6, Late Helladic III A:2 l-III B). Decorated with broad horizontal bands, one just above base, two or three at mid-height, one narrower at bottom of neck. Traces of paint on handle and along rim.

W. P. D.

Tomb E-8
(Plan and Section, Fig. 340)

The largest dromos in this cemetery is that of E-8 which lies ca. 16 m. west of Tomb E-6 (Fig. 301).[10] It runs from south to north and is 7 m. long. The floor slopes downward unevenly toward the north where it is 2.90 m. below modern ground level. The width of the dromos at the floor varies from 1.36 m. at the south to 1.67 m. at the north. The dromos was cut through the ledge of limestone with its walls nearly vertical, limestone above and clay below (Fig. 245). The Mycenaean builders constructed niches in both the east and west sides (Fig. 246). That on the east is 0.85 m. high, 2.40 m. long, and the bottom of the niche is 0.45 m. above the floor of the dromos 1.60 m. south of the doorway into the chamber. The niche in the west side (Fig. 247) 1 m. south of the doorway is 2.70 m. long, 0.65 m. above the floor, and is 0.90 m. high. Both niches are about 0.20 m. deep. The walls were made of undressed stones, many of them broken from the ledge itself, laid in irregular courses. In addition to sherds, 12 beads of paste (CM. 2900) were found in the earth filling the dromos. The potsherds represented almost every phase of the Late Helladic Period (from I to III C:1e).[11]

A stone slab which may have been a marker stood, not in the dromos, but above the chamber itself (0.50 m. long, 0.30 m. wide, and 0.075 m. thick).

The doorway, cut in clay, provided an opening 0.87 m. wide. About 0.85 m. above the floor, however, the east jamb was cut away and the width of the open-

---

[10] Traces of another, unexcavated tomb, E-7, were noted in 1957 midway between E-6 and E-8.

[11] There were five examples of early spirals (*MP*, Motive 46:9, 11, 12, 29, p. 353 fig. 59, Late Helladic I-III A:1), two of simple running spirals (*MP*, Motive 46:54, p. 357 fig. 60, Late Helladic III A:2-III C:1 e). Other patterns include ripple, Motive 78, p. 422 fig. 73, Late Helladic I-II A;

diaper net, Motive 57:2, p. 383 fig. 67, Late Helladic III A:1-III C:1; curved stripes, Motive 67:5, 6, p. 403 fig. 70, Late Helladic I-III A:2; continuous rock pattern, Motive 32:1:5, p. 323 fig. 54, Late Helladic I-III B; a pattern which closely resembles Motive 70:1, p. 403 fig. 70, Late Helladic II A-III B.

ing increased to 1.25 m. The total height of the doorway is 1.95 m. and its depth from south to north 1 m. The opening was entirely filled with irregular stones some of which spread 0.40 m. into the dromos and others up to 0.80 m. into the chamber itself (Fig. 246). The lintel was the ledge of limestone, which was so crumbling that it had to be cut away when the stones below had been removed during the course of the excavation. The traces of stratification in the earth filling the dromos, as well as the appearance of the opening and of the stone packing, suggest that originally the doorway was narrow (0.85 m.) and high, but that after the tomb had begun to fill with debris, the doorway was rebuilt and made much wider (1.25 m.) and less high (ca. 1.10 m.).

The chamber, oval-shaped in plan, measures 3.50 m. from south to north and 3.75 m. from east to west. The chamber was enlarged to the east by a niche 0.67 m. deep. The chamber was filled with earth and bits of stone which made it necessary to excavate from above.

In the center of the chamber lay the remains of three skeletons, probably the last burials (Fig. 248). The final one seems to have been C, laid on its back directly inside the door 0.25 m. above the floor; the skull, which had completely decayed, would have been to the south. A broken jug with a side spout (CM. 2889 [1]) rested between the knees. The next to last (G) was also on its back with the skull, almost in the center of the chamber, 0.30 m. above the floor. G lay from southeast to northwest. The bones of the third (H) seem to have been pushed aside to make room for G; at any rate they were uncovered 0.55 m. above the floor, a little to the south and west of the skull of G, and from their disorder obviously not in their original position.

An alabastron (CM. 2862) stood near skull G and may be dated to Late Helladic III A:2. Two jugs were found near, but seemingly unrelated to, G; one (CM. 2888 [2]) lay against the north wall of the chamber and the other (CM. 2895 [3]) at an angle west of the skeleton.

Four skulls at the western edge of the chamber (A, D, F, and J), 0.80 m. above the floor, probably were from late burials. The upper two (A and D) were badly smashed, whereas J, upside down beneath them, was intact. Their position establishes the depth of the accumulated sediment and debris in this part of the chamber toward the end of the use of the tomb. Between these skulls and the doorway, 1.15 m. above the floor, were four broken vases (CM. 2859 [4], 2860 [5], 2874 [6], and 2875 [7]). It was impossible to determine to which burial these vessels belonged, but their date, Late Helladic III A-III B, shows that they were among the last items deposited.

Traces of earlier interments which had been pushed aside also existed along the east wall of the chamber about the same height above the floor. Remains of

[193]

two skulls (B and E) were recognized; near B were two pots (CM. 2876 [8] and 2877 [9]), which may be dated between Late Helladic III A and III C:1 e. Between B and E two badly smashed vases were recovered (CM. 2879-2880) of the same period.

Remains of at least nine skeletons were uncovered above the floor of the tomb. The final interments were made in the center after the bones and vessels of earlier ones had been pushed up on the east and west sides of the chamber. The ceramic evidence indicates that the tomb continued to be used until the end of Late Helladic III B, or perhaps the beginning of III C.

The leg bones of two skeletons lay, undisturbed, on the floor of the chamber. L, the skull of which would have been close to the door, was stretched out from south to north in the west side of the tomb; the other, K, from west to east along the north side. Both had been laid on their backs. No objects could be associated with these skeletons, although possibly a small goblet (CM. 2896) found under G close to the north wall and assignable to Late Helladic II B may have belonged with them.

Twelve vases, almost all broken (CM. 2861 [10], 2864 [11], 2865 [12], 2866 [13], 2867 [14], 2885 [15], 2886 [not shown on plan], 2887 [16], 2890 [17], 2893 [18], 2897 [19], 2898 [20]), were scattered over the floor in the south and eastern sections of the tomb and with them were two bronze daggers. The earth around the daggers showed clear traces of the decayed material of their scabbards and a bright orange pigment which was presumably from their decoration. Most of these vases may be dated to Late Helladic II A and B; a few are transitional to Late Helladic III A:1. The spread of dating suggests that this group includes vessels from several interments; one pot contained human teeth (CM. 2898 [20]). The position of the pots, blocking the approach to the niche in the east wall, indicates that they were placed here after that niche had been closed.

Also on the floor of the chamber, toward the northeast, were fragments of human bones (I) and five vases (CM. 2863 [21], 2868 [22], 2869 [23], 2891 [24], 2892 [25]), nearly all smashed. It is worth noting that a piece of one of them (CM. 2891 [24]) was found near the door. The condition of the bones, the very small size of the first three pots, and the quantity of paste beads suggest that this was the burial of a child. More than a dozen beads were recognized, but many disintegrated as they were removed. The pottery may be dated from Late Helladic II to III A.

The niche in the east wall, 2.01 m. from south to north, 0.60 m. high, and from 0.47 m. to 0.67 m. deep, was found undisturbed, blocked by a wall of irregular pieces of limestone. The stones were laid roughly in courses and the face of the wall recedes eastward as it rises. The niche contained the remains of a skeleton

(O) lying on its back with the skull to the south. Near the skull lay a jug (CM. 2871 [26]) on its side and, beside the right femur, an alabastron (CM. 2872 [27]). A large terracotta whorl completed the list of burial offerings. A conical cup (CM. 2878 [28]) lying upside down outside the niche at the foot of the wall is reminiscent of the kylikes so frequently found at the entrances to tombs. This burial took place early in the history of the use of the tomb. The pottery is not later than Late Helladic II B and may well be earlier; the alabastron (CM. 2872 [27]) is very similar to some from Prosymna which were attributed to Late Helladic I.[12]

Two pits had been dug in the clay floor. Pit 1 (at the west side of the chamber), 1.24 m. long, 0.59 m. wide, and 0.48 m. deep, contained bones of one skeleton (P) in extended position with the skull to the south. Three very small vases had been placed near the feet (CM. 2873 [29], 2881 [30], 2884 [31]); the pit also produced two paste beads and a terracotta whorl. Since the contents had not been disturbed, this was a primary burial. The pottery was judged to belong to Late Helladic II.

Pit 2, along the northwest edge of the chamber, measured 1.15 m. long, 0.51 m. wide, and 0.37 m. deep. The great number of bones and the two fragmentary skulls (M and N) made clear that the pit contained secondary interments after the tomb had become crowded. At the east end of the pit were four vases (CM. 2870 [32], 2882 [33], 2883 [34], 2894 [35]) which may be assigned to Late Helladic II or III A. The pit also contained a bronze knife (CM. 2914) and a terracotta button. The neatness of the disposition of these objects and bones suggests that they were moved with a measure of reverence by those who transferred them to their new resting place: it was in marked contrast to the chaotic state of many of the deposits on the floor of the tomb itself.

The ceramic evidence establishes the fact that Tomb E-8 was used for a longer period than any other as yet cleared in this cemetery. Its use began in Late Helladic II A, if not earlier, and continued until the end of Late Helladic III B. It also seems clear that the burial practices remained essentially the same throughout this time; except for the changing fashions of pottery, no differences can be seen between the early interments and the most recent ones.

OBJECTS FOUND

Dromos

PASTE

Beads (CM. 2900, Fig. 250:19): d. from 0.0055 m. to 0.018 m. 11, spherical or flattened spherical.

Chamber: above floor

POTTERY

Alabastron [4] (CM. 2859, Fig. 249:12): h. 0.09 m.; d. rim 0.078 m.; d. 0.12 m.; d. base 0.10 m. Western area 1.15 m. above

---

[12] *Prosymna*, figs. 654, 667.

floor. Greenish clay; thin brown-black paint. Lacks one of three loop-handles, chips from bottom. Wide, relatively tall neck, spreading rim. Shape similar to *MP*, Type 84, p. 41 fig. 11, Late Helladic III A:1. Neck, rim, handles solidly coated; two horizontal lines below neck, three below shoulder. Traces of continuous rock pattern on shoulder.

One-handled jug [5] (CM. 2860, Fig. 249:16): h. 0.24 m.; d. rim 0.083 m.; d. 0.172 m.; d. base 0.054 m. Western area, 1.15 m. above floor. Greenish clay; worn brown-black paint. Shape resembles *MP*, Type 120, pp. 30f. figs. 5, 6, Late Helladic III A:2 e-III B. Three broad bands just above broadest diameter, one high on shoulder, one around base of neck, one on underside of rim, one on top of rim. Band around each end of oval, vertical handle and three transverse stripes on its outer surface.

Angular alabastron (CM. 2862, Fig. 249:4): h. 0.075 m.; d. rim 0.051 m.; d. 0.089 m.; d. base 0.085 m. Near skull G. Pale green clay; brown paint. Lacks part of rim, neck, one piece from shoulder. Flat bottom, straight sides, sloping shoulder, horizontally spreading rim. Solidly coated neck, handle. Three pairs of horizontal lines on body; single line on upper surface of rim. Multiple stem and tongue on shoulder (*MP*, Motive 19:11 or 17, p. 299 fig. 47, Late Helladic III A:2).

Side-spouted jug with basket-handle [6] (CM. 2874, Fig. 249:9): h. 0.237 m.; d. rim 0.099 m.; d. 0.1585 m.; d. base 0.73 m. Western area, 1.15 m. above floor. Orange clay; coarse fabric, thick walls. Undecorated. Trumpet-shaped spout. (Similar to *MP*, Type 159, p. 30 fig. 5.) Late Helladic III.

Stirrup-vase [7] (CM. 2875, Fig. 249:11): h. 0.208 m.; d. 0.169 m.; d. base 0.068 m. Western area, 1.15 above floor. Pale buff clay; slipped surface. Lustrous, dark brown paint. Lacks few chips from body. Broad, spreading pedestal-base; body bulging upwards; triple handles (*MP*, Type 165 or 167, "advanced piriform," pp. 22f. figs.

3, 4, Late Helladic III A:1, III B). Foot solidly coated. Six broad parallel horizontal bands around body. In space between third and fourth bands, five fine parallel lines; between fourth and fifth, concentric semicircles running around vessel (*MP*, Motive 43:13, p. 343 fig. 57, Late Helladic III B); between fifth and sixth, six fine lines. On top, in handle zone, two groups of parallel arcs in each quadrant (*MP*, Multiple stem and tongue, Motive 19:28, p. 299 fig. 47, Late Helladic III A:2 l). Circle motive (*MP*, 41:14, p. 343 fig. 57, Late Helladic III A-III B) on top of disk of false neck.

Stirrup-vase [8] (CM. 2876, Fig. 249:13): h. 0.09 m.; d. 0.132 m.; d. base 0.055 m. Near skull B. Green clay; worn thin brown-black paint. Lacks one handle, spout, one-third of body. Shape close to *MP*, Type 178, 179, or 180, pp. 30f. figs. 5, 6. Late Helladic III A:2 e-III B. Band around base, two sets of two horizontal bands framing five thin lines on body and on shoulder. On top, groups of parallel chevrons with apices toward center (*MP*, Motive 58:15, or 17, p. 383 fig. 67, Late Helladic III A:2-III C:1 e). Circle motive on disk of false neck.

Alabastron [9] (CM. 2877, Fig. 249:1): h. 0.067 m.; d. rim 0.078 m.; d. 0.147 m. Near skull B. Buff clay; soft; worn red-brown paint. Lacks pieces from body, bottom, rim. Squat body, spreading rim (*MP*, Type 82 or 84, p. 41 fig. 11). Neck, rim, handles solidly painted; concentric circles on bottom (two at center, three at edge). Three large ivy leaves each on triple curving stem on shoulder (*MP*, Motive 12:c or d, 21, pp. 270f. figs. 35, 36, Late Helladic II B-III A:1).

Kylix (CM. 2879, fragments): h. not preserved; d. ca. 0.17 m. Between skulls B and E. Green clay; smooth surface. Lacks all but portion of rim, one handle, part of base. Body would have been large, deep bowl (*MP*, Type 274, p. 61 fig. 17, Late Helladic III B).

Alabastron (CM. 2880, Fig. 249:14): h. 0.07

m.; d. rim 0.052 m.; d. 0.096 m. Between skulls B and E. Pale green clay; worn brown-black paint. Lacks one-third of rim, body, one of three handles. Rounded bottom and body; neck curves outward slightly, but rim does not spread (*MP*, Type 85, p. 41 fig. 11). Neck, rim solidly coated. Two lines below shoulder, two below neck. Continuous rock pattern forms main decoration (*MP*, Motive 32:5, p. 323 fig. 54, Late Helladic I-III B).

Jug with cutaway neck [2] (CM. 2888, Fig. 249:20): h. to top of handle 0.26 m.; h. to rim 0.236 m.; d. neck 0.078 m.; d. 0.19 m.; d. base 0.07 m. Near skull G. Buff clay; undecorated. Lacks few small pieces. Larger version of CM. 2871.

Side-spouted jug with basket-handle [1] (CM. 2889, Fig. 249:7): h. to top of handle 0.244 m.; h. to rim 0.189 m.; d. rim 0.104 m.; d. 0.159 m.; d. base 0.075 m. With burial C. Orange-red clay; rather coarse fabric. Lacks several small pieces. Basket-handle round in section; cylindrical spout rises high on shoulder at steep angle (*MP*, Type 159, p. 30 fig. 5).

One-handled jug [3] (CM. 2895, Fig. 249:28): h. 0.152 m.; d. rim 0.093 m.; d. 0.138 m.; d. base 0.052 m. West of skull G. Greenish-buff clay; traces of pattern in dark brown paint. Lacks few small pieces. Small, almost piriform jug; flat bottom; concave neck spreading to plain rim; oval handle from rim to greatest diameter (*MP*, Type 109, p. 35 fig. 7, Late Helladic III A). Band on rim, inside and out; two broad parallel zigzag lines on neck and shoulder. Traces of horizontal bands below greatest diameter. Spots of color on handle possibly from diagonal stripes.

Chamber: on floor

B R O N Z E

Dagger (CM. 2912, Fig. 250:17): l. pres. 0.21 m.; w. 0.0475 m.; thickness (max.) 0.006 m. Southeast area. Without tang, broad blade lacking tip. Three rivets for attachment of handle. Edges taper gradually to

point, but not uniformly straight; slightly concave near heel.

Knife (CM. 2913, Fig. 250:18): l. 0.20 m.; w. 0.024 m.; w. tang 0.02 m.; th. upper edge 0.0085 m. Southeast area. Thin metal, poorly preserved. Short tang with two rivets. Blade leaf-shaped; edges form continuous convex curves from tang to point.

P A S T E

Beads (CM. 2901, Fig. 250:19): 18 spherical or flattened spherical. D. from 0.0055 m. to 0.018 m. Near Burial I.

P O T T E R Y

Jug with cutaway neck [10] (CM. 2861, Fig. 249:10): h. 0.252 m.; d. neck 0.05 m.; d. 0.172 m.; d. base 0.07 m. Southeastern area. Buff clay; smoothed surface; red-brown paint. Ridge at base of neck, slightly spreading base. Ridged handle. (*MP*, Type 132, p. 22 fig. 3, Late Helladic II B-III A:1.) Neck and upper surface of handle solidly coated. Broad band around bottom, two pairs of bands low on body. Two wavy bands around middle of body; sacral ivy on single line stems on shoulder (*MP*, Motive 12:c or d, p. 270 fig. 35, Late Helladic II B-III A:1).

Diminutive pithoid jar [21] (CM. 2863, Fig. 249:15): h. 0.053 m.; d. rim 0.034 m.; d. 0.049 m.; d. base 0.03 m. Northeast area. Buff clay; solidly coated with red-brown paint. Lacks one of two small round horizontal handles on shoulder. Flat bottom; sides slightly concave toward base (*MP*, Type 33, p. 44 fig. 12).

Jug with cutaway neck [11] (CM. 2864, Fig. 249:17): h. 0.137 m.; d. rim 0.048 m.; d. 0.119 m.; d. base 0.047 m. Southeast area. Buff clay; rough surface. Slightly concave bottom; flat, vertical handle (*MP*, Type 135, p. 35 fig. 7, Late Helladic III A). Undecorated.

Alabastron [12] (CM. 2865, Figs. 249:3, 250:13): h. 0.061 m.; d. rim 0.088 m.; d. 0.163 m. Southeast area. Buff clay; hard, smooth surface. Lustrous brown-black paint. Very squat body (*MP*, Type 82, p. 41 fig. 11, Late Helladic II B). Neck, rim, handles solidly coated. Wheel pattern on bottom (*MP*, Motive 68:2, p. 403 fig. 70, Late Helladic II A-III A:1). Between handles three lilies with V-shaped stamens with anthers (*MP*, Motive 9:f or i; 12 or 13, p. 258 fig. 32, Late Helladic II B-III A:1).

Alabastron [13] (CM. 2866, Fig. 249:5): h. 0.085 m.; d. rim 0.096 m.; d. 0.175 m. Southeast area. Pale buff clay; smooth surface; lustrous, very dark brown paint. Lacks few small pieces from rim, body. Similar in shape to, although not as squat as, CM. 2865 (*MP*, Type 82 or 84, p. 41 fig. 11, Late Helladic II B-III A:1). Neck, rim, handles solidly painted. Two circles at center, two at edge of bottom connected in wheel pattern. Continuous rock pattern on shoulder with dots along edge of design; also two rows of dots below neck (*MP*, Motive 32:1:19, p. 323 fig. 54, Late Helladic II B).

Side-spouted jug with basket-handle [14] (CM. 2867, Fig. 249:8): h. 0.09 m.; d. rim 0.057 m.; d. 0.091 m.; d. base 0.04 m. Southeast area. Dark buff clay; rather rough undecorated surface; basket-handle restored. Spout is cylindrical, slightly concave, with spreading rim (*MP*, Form 45, Type 163, p. 610, Late Helladic III A:2-III B).

Alabastron [22] (CM. 2868, Figs. 249:6, 250:11): h. 0.043 m.; d. rim 0.043 m.; d. 0.082 m.; d. base 0.0655 m. Northeast area. Buff clay; smooth surface; brown paint. Lacks chip from rim. Squat; flat bottom, sloping shoulders, spreading, broad rim. Neck, rim, handles solidly coated. On shoulder three sacral ivy plants on triple stems, separated by handles (*MP*, Motive 12:d, 25, pp. 270f. figs. 35, 36, Late Helladic II B-III A:1). Wheel pattern on bottom: two small concentric circles at center from which radiate four double wavy spokes (*MP*, Motive 68:2, p. 403 fig. 70. Late Helladic II A-III A:1).

Alabastron [23] (CM. 2869, Figs. 249:2, 250:12): h. 0.0385 m.; d. rim 0.0385 m.; d. 0.064 m.; d. base 0.064 m. Northeast

area. Similar to CM. 2868 in clay, paint, shape. Handles, neck, rim solidly coated; two concentric circles at center, two at edge of bottom. Three palm flowers on shoulder (*MP*, Motive 14:13, p. 277 fig. 38, Late Helladic II B).

Conical handleless cup [28] (CM. 2878, Fig. 249:24): h. 0.045 m.; d. 0.099 m.; d. base 0.04 m. Outside niche in east wall. Pale buff clay. No decoration. Slightly raised base above which walls curve outward (*PN* I, Shape 11, pp. 359f.; *MP*, Type 204, p. 53 fig. 15).

Alabastron [15] (CM. 2885, Figs. 249:22, 250:15): h. ca. 0.04 m.; d. rim 0.044 m.; d. 0.079 m. Southeast area. Green clay; worn brown-black paint. Lacks most of rim. Three pairs of concentric circles on bottom. Handles, neck solidly painted. Continuous rock pattern on shoulder with wavy line above; in spaces between handles pattern which seems to resemble papyrus or lily (*MP*, Motives 9 or 11, pp. 258, 261 figs. 32, 33). Possibly Late Helladic II.

Shallow cup with high handle [not numbered on plan; with 15 and 16] (CM. 2886, Fig. 249:29): h. to top of handle 0.109 m.; h. to rim 0.05 m.; d. 0.1165 m. Southeast area. Pinkish-buff clay, very soft; red-brown paint. Lacks one or two small pieces. Rounded bottom, slightly spreading rim, flat handle rising from rim in high loop swinging to low on body (similar to *MP*, Type 236, p. 48 fig. 13). Four broad horizontal lines on lower part of body; transverse lines on handle. Inner and outer surface of rim solidly coated. Below rim, simple running spiral (*MP*, Motive 46:33, p. 353 fig. 59, Late Helladic II B).

Cup with flat ring-handle [16] (CM. 2887, Fig. 249:27): h. 0.074 m.; d. 0.146 m.; d. base 0.046 m. Southeast area. Buff clay; slipped; red to dark brown paint. Lacks one small piece from body. Raised base concave underneath; curving walls; spreading rim; very small ring-handle circling from rim to midpoint on body where its attachment extends down side of body

(*MP*, Type 211 medium, p. 48 fig. 13, Late Helladic II A). Interior, top of handle, broad zone around base solidly coated. Two lines low on body. Running spiral in zone bordered above by rim and below by the two lines (*MP*, Motive 46:12, p. 353 fig. 59, Late Helladic I-II A).

Conical rhyton [17] (CM. 2890, Fig. 249:26): h. 0.244 m.; d. rim 0.102 m. Southeast area. Buff clay; slipped surface. Paint varies from orange-red to brown; worn in places. Shape is that of *MP*, Type 199, p. 67 fig. 20, but handle does not rise above rim. Tip, outer surface of handle, inner and outer surface of rim solidly coated. In tall zone between are six palm trees (*MP*, Motive 14:2, top, type b, p. 277 fig. 38); from above depends arched rock pattern (*MP*, Motive 33:II:2, p. 327 fig. 55). Fill ornaments; crosses (*MP*, Motive 54:4, p. 373 fig. 65); isolated waves (*MP*, Motive 33:II:19, p. 327 fig. 55); rosettes (*MP*, Motive 27:6, "Sea Anemone," p. 315 fig. 53); two short wavy vertical lines. Late Helladic II A.

Cylindrical cup with flat handle [24] (CM. 2891, Fig. 249:21): h. 0.093 m.; d. rim 0.1075 m.; d. base 0.054 m. Northeast area. Buff clay. Red-brown paint. Lacks one-half of body and handle. Flat bottom above which sides rise vertically to rib (0.04 m. above bottom) then splay outward to rim. Vapheio shape (*MP*, Type 224, p. 53 fig. 15). Band of paint around bottom, at base of body, around rib, on inner and outer surface of rim. Exterior of handle solidly coated. In two zones on exterior, vertical ripple pattern (*MP*, Motive 78:1 or 2, p. 422 fig. 73, Late Helladic I).

Cylindrical cup with flat handle [25] (CM. 2892, Fig. 249:19): h. 0.101 m.; d. rim 0.115 m.; d. base 0.059 m. Northeast area. Buff clay. Brown paint. Lacks only few chips. Slightly taller, larger version of CM. 2891. Decoration essentially the same. Late Helladic I.

Alabastron [18] (CM. 2893, Figs. 249:23, 250:14): h. 0.074 m.; d. rim 0.091 m.; d.

0.183 m. Southeast area. Pinkish-buff clay. Worn red-brown paint. Lacks a few chips. Squat body; low, spreading neck; three round handles set horizontally on shoulder (*MP*, Type 82, p. 41 fig. 11, Late Helladic II B). Wheel pattern on bottom; two small concentric circles in middle from which radiate four double wavy spokes (*MP*, Motive 68:2, p. 403 fig. 70, Late Helladic II A-III A). Neck, handles solidly coated. Two horizontal lines on body; continuous rock pattern on shoulder extending up to row of dots around band at bottom of neck (*MP*, Motive 32:I:22, p. 323 fig. 54, Late Helladic II B).

Stemmed, two-handled goblet (CM. 2896, Fig. 250:9): h. 0.091 m.; d. stem 0.015 m.; d. 0.13 m.; d. base 0.051 m. Under Burial G. Buff clay. Worn red-brown paint. Lacks few chips. Edge of base vertical, upper surface slopes up to stem. Body has rounded sides, spreading rim. Flat handles from rim to widest part of body (*MP*, Type 263 or 264, p. 60 fig. 16, Late Helladic II B-III A). Rim, inside and out, handles, stem and foot (except for reserved stripe at base of stem and top of foot) solidly coated. Three horizontal lines below greatest diameter. In upper zone four running spirals on each side, with four lines in each spiral (*MP*, Motive 46:51 or 52, p. 357 fig. 60, Late Helladic I-II A or III A:1-III B).

One-handled bowl [19] (CM. 2897, Fig. 249:18): h. 0.055 m.; d. 0.154 m.; d. base 0.04 m. Southeast area. Buff clay; surface coated solidly with mat red wash. Badly warped. Lacks handle and pieces from body. Bottom flattened; flaring sides which round in at shoulder; narrow, spreading rim. Handle probably rose from rim to considerable height; terminated low on body; flat.

Stirrup-vase [20] (CM. 2898, Fig. 249:25): h. 0.222 m.; d. 0.252 m.; d. spout 0.038 m.; d. disk 0.044 m.; d. base 0.09 m. Southeast area. Buff clay; lustrous slip. Worn, streaky brown paint. Lacks few small pieces. Body squat, almost globular; disk concave on top; concave vertical spout, rim about same height as top of disk; flat handle, between other two, opposite spout (*MP*, Type 169, p. 30 fig. 5, Late Helladic II A). False neck, spout solidly coated. At bottom, two broad horizontal bands enclosing two narrower; above, three horizontal zones bordered below and above by two narrow bands. Each zone contains running pattern of sacral ivy leaves (*MP*, Motive 12:7, p. 270 fig. 35) alternately pointing up and down, each leaf joined to next by S-curved line (no stems), and large dot on either side of point of leaf. On top, irregular bands of linked quirks ending in dot (*MP*, Motive 48:5, p. 360 fig. 61). Three handles striped horizontally.

Chamber: niche

T E R R A C O T T A

Whorl (no CM number): h. 0.018 m.; d. 0.024 m. Short cone.

P O T T E R Y

Jug with cutaway neck [26] (CM. 2871, Fig. 250:7): h. 0.165 m.; d. rim 0.064 m.; d. 0.124 m.; d. base 0.04 m. Buff clay; coarse surface. Undecorated. Shape similar to that of CM. 2864, but more conical; flat handle rising high above rim before descending almost vertically to shoulder.

Angular alabastron [27] (CM. 2872, Fig. 250:6a, b): h. 0.063 m.; d. rim 0.065 m.; d. 0.092 m.; d. base 0.05 m. Buff clay; smooth surface. Red-brown paint, worn in places. Straight sides spread from flat bottom to angle above which sides rise vertically until, after second angle, they narrow to neck. Two flattened horizontal handles on shoulder (*MP*, Types 89, 93, p. 44 fig. 12). Solidly coated rim, neck, handles; broad band around lower angle, two parallel bands on vertical sides. Two crosshatched loops on shoulder; two small loops, not hatched, depend from neck as filling ornament (*MP,* Motive 63, p. 397 fig. 69, Late Helladic I-III A).

Chamber: Pit 1

P A S T E

Beads (CM. 2901, Fig. 250:19): two spherical. D. 0.007, 0.012 m.

T E R R A C O T T A

Whorl (CM. 2899, not illustrated): d. 0.026 m.; h. 0.02 m.

P O T T E R Y

Alabastron [29] (CM. 2873, Fig. 250:2a, b): h. 0.039 m.; d. rim 0.039 m.; d. 0.067 m.; d. base 0.065 m. Pale buff clay. Red-brown paint. Flat bottom, sloping shoulders. Pairs of concentric circles on bottom. Three sacral ivy leaves on shoulder; two dots on either side of point of each leaf (*MP*, Motive 12:c, p. 270 fig. 35, and 12:23, p. 271 fig. 36, Late Helladic II A-II B). Three filling ornaments of dot surrounded by circle of dots.

Squat jar with vertical ring-handle [30] (CM. 2881, Fig. 250:1): h. 0.059 m.; d. rim 0.043 m.; d. neck 0.03 m.; d. 0.073 m.; d. base 0.029 m. Dark buff clay; dark brown paint. In shape similar to *MP*, Type 87, p. 41 fig. 11, Late Helladic II-III A:2. Neck, rim solidly coated; transverse oblique lines on handle. Band just above base, two below shoulder. Simple running spiral on shoulder (reverse of *MP*, Motive 46:33, p. 353 fig. 59, Late Helladic II B).

Stemmed goblet with high handle [31] (CM. 2884, Fig. 250:3): h. 0.086 m.; d. 0.092 m.; d. stem 0.0195 m.; d. base 0.035 m. Pale buff to ivory clay; paint varies from red to brown. Spreading base, short stem, deep bowl narrowing sharply to stem, spreading rim, flat handle rises above rim and terminates low, below greatest diameter of body (*MP*, Type 270, p. 60 fig. 16, Late Helladic II A). Base, stem, top of handle, inner and outer side of rim solidly coated. Body decorated with slanting, curved stripes (*MP*, Motive 78:3, p. 422 fig. 73, Ripple Pattern, Late Helladic II A).

[200]

Chamber: Pit 2

BRONZE

Knife (CM. 2914, Fig. 250:16): l. 0.215 m.; l. handle 0.043 m. Cutting edge, concave; blunt edge (0.002 m. thick), convex. Handle is extension of convex curving edge with six holes for rivets in two groups of three, one near blade, one near end of handle.

TERRACOTTA

Button (CM. 2901a, not illustrated): h. 0.01 m.; d. 0.013 m. Short cone.

POTTERY

Squat jar with vertical ring-handle [32] (CM. 2870, Fig. 250:10): h. 0.081 m.; d. rim 0.049 m.; d. 0.092 m.; d. base 0.032 m. Buff clay. Dark brown paint. Flat handle rises from shoulder, swinging down to greatest diameter (*MP*, Type 87, p. 41 fig. 11, Late Helladic II-III A:2). Top of handle, inside of rim, exterior of rim, neck solidly coated. Row of dots below neck. Four horizontal lines around lower part of body. On shoulder pattern made as if from two bands of continuous rock pattern (*MP*, Motive 32:1:5, p. 323 fig. 54) arranged back to back.

Shallow cup with high-swung handle [33] (CM. 2882, Fig. 250:4): h. to top of handle 0.067 m.; h. to rim 0.038 m.; d. 0.109 m.; d. base 0.039 m. Orange-buff clay. No decoration. Raised base, curving walls, spreading rim. Flat handle rises obliquely from rim, terminates below it. *MP* has no precise parallel.

Shallow cup with ring-handle [34] (CM. 2883, Fig. 250:5): h. to top of handle 0.047 m.; h. rim 0.025 m.; d. 0.107 m.; d. base 0.034 m. Pale buff clay. No decoration. Differs from CM. 2882 in base, in less spreading rim, in shape of handle. No exact parallel found in *MP*.

Angular alabastron [35] (CM. 2894, Fig. 250:8a, b): h. 0.068 m.; d. rim 0.06 m.; d. 0.10 m. Buff clay. Streaky brown paint. Lacks few chips. Flat bottom, straight sides, sloping shoulder, low neck, splaying lip. Bottom decorated with wheel pattern and four spokes (*MP*, Motive 68:2, p. 403 fig. 70, but with solid center, Late Helladic II A-III A:1). Neck, handles, rim coated solidly. Two rows of short dashes between bordering horizontal lines on sides; narrow rock pattern at bottom of shoulder; between handles, palm motive with two sprays above each spiral (*MP*, Motive 14:11, p. 277 fig. 38, Late Helladic II B).

W. P. D.

Tomb E-9
(Plan and Section, Fig. 341)

Toward the west, parallel to the dromos of E-8 and only 8 m. distant, was exposed the dromos of Tomb E-9 (Fig. 251). It is shorter and narrower than that of Tomb E-8 (5.85 m. long, ranging from 0.71 m. to 1.20 m. wide at the floor, and from 0.82 m. to 1.03 m. broad at the top). The sides of the dromos were cut through hard earth and rock with a slight inward inclination. Above and just south of the doorway, a large stone (0.90 m. long, 0.38 m. wide, 0.26 m. thick) which seemingly had fallen toward the east from an upright position, had perhaps marked the tomb.

A row of flat stones, 1.45 m. above the floor, spanned the doorway where once there must have been a lintel (Fig. 251). Since these stones were but a few centimeters below the modern surface, either this tomb was very close to the surface, or, more probably, erosion near the end of the ridge where it is located has removed much of the earth over it. The doorway is 0.85 m. wide and 0.65 m. deep from front to back. The jambs of clay are not equal (Fig. 252), that on the west jutting out into the dromos 0.35 m., whereas that on the east extends merely 0.05 m. The wall of stones, which had originally filled the opening, was preserved only to a height of 0.50 m. above the floor (Fig. 253). In front, upside down, was a kylix (CM. 2832) whose shape suggests a date of Late Helladic III B. Above the stones earth filling the doorway contained several large fragments of a pithos.

Since the roof had collapsed, it was necessary to excavate the chamber from above. The earth above the tomb was nowhere free from sherds and, when the level of the stones above the doorway was reached, many flat stones were encountered extending from the doorway to the north and northeast for ca. 2.40 m. (Fig. 254). The width of the area covered by the stones was slightly larger than that of the dromos itself. The presence of these stones and the disturbed earth above them indicate that the chamber had been opened from above and had been carefully closed.

After the stones were removed, it soon became possible to trace the walls of the chamber. It is almost circular — 2.72 m. from south to north and 2.68 m. from east to west (Fig. 255). Stones from the packing of the doorway became visible 0.50 m. above the floor extending into the chamber almost 1 m.

The first traces of the contents of the tomb were encountered 0.40 m. above the floor. The last interment, A (Fig. 256), the only undisturbed skeleton in the tomb, lay inside the doorway with the skull to the northwest and feet toward the southeast. The body had been laid on its back in the usual position. The bones of the right leg rested on top of stones from the doorway (Fig. 256); therefore this burial was made after the chamber had begun to fill and after the stone packing had fallen in. It seems reasonable to suppose that the gravediggers, finding the tomb already partially filled, dug down from above the chamber to form a pit grave, placed A in it, and covered this grave with a layer of flat stones which took the place of the original roof of the chamber.

Near skull A lay a black lentoid seal of steatite (CM. 2902) and, near the left leg, a broken kylix (CM. 2837 [1]) of Late Helladic III B. Another kylix (CM. 2836 [2]) lay on its side near the east wall of the chamber; it seems to belong to Late Helladic III A:2 l. Three other vessels (CM. 2833 [3], 2834 [4], 2835 [5]), also on their sides, appeared among many fragments of bones near the north edge of the tomb at the same level. All belong to Late Helladic III, the stirrup-jar to III A and the two jugs either to III A:2 or to III B. These pots and bones represent remains of earlier interments pushed aside during the burial of A.

Two other vessels, together with bones, were found near the west wall of the chamber (CM. 2838 [6], 2839 [7]). Several beads of paste and one of steatite (CM. 2903-2905) and quantities of snail shells were recovered from the earth that filled the chamber at this level.

Directly beneath the small jug (CM. 2834 [4]) and east of Burial A were the nearly complete remains of another skeleton (B) lying on the right side, with the skull toward the north and the sharply bent legs to the south (Fig. 256). This is the only example that has yet been found in the cemetery of a burial in the contracted position.

At the lowest level almost the entire chamber was divided into three pits (Figs. 257, 341). Pit 1 was the largest, 2.20 m. long from south to north. It seems to have been dug in two stages; at any rate there were two sections, one running obliquely toward the northeast and the other reaching the north edge of the chamber. The shape of the pit might thus be described as a letter V with the apex near the doorway. Each branch is 0.60 m. wide and 0.40 m. deep.

Pit 2 is more regular, rectangular in plan, 0.65 m. long, 0.35 m. wide, and 0.15 m. deep (Fig. 258). Close to the east wall of the tomb it almost intersects the northeast branch of Pit 1. Pit 3, rectangular in plan (0.98 m. long, 0.47 m. wide, and 0.48 m. deep), occupies the western part of the chamber (Fig. 259).

One small alabastron (CM. 2840 [8]) lay upside down on the floor between Pits 1 and 3; it is Late Helladic III A:1. All other pottery was found in Pits 1 and 2, together with bits of bone and a few paste beads; all these items were poorly preserved and the bones and beads especially crumbled as they were removed.

Three pots stood near the north end of the western section of Pit 1 (CM. 2841 [9], 2842 [10], 2843 [11]), all perhaps assignable to Late Helladic II B-III A:1. Near the junction of the two branches was a shallow cup (CM. 2844 [12]) on its side. Most of the vases lay on the slope between Pits 1 and 2 (CM. 2847 [13] and 2850 [14]) or in Pit 1 just below (Fig. 258): a kylix and jar (CM. 2845 [15], 2846 [16]) on their sides, mouth to mouth, with three small vases (CM. 2848, 2849, and 2853) inside them. None of these vessels can be dated with precision but all may tentatively be assigned to Late Helladic III A.

Pit 2, in addition to bones, contained two terracotta female figurines (CM. 2906, 2907), one lacking the bottom of her skirt, and three pots (CM. 2851 [17], 2852 [18], and 2855 [19]) attributable to Late Helladic III A. It was possible to restore, at least partially, two vessels from sherds, some found in Pit 1, the others in Pit 2 (CM. 2854 and 2856). Both pits apparently are nearly contemporaneous, Pit 2 small and relatively full, Pit 1 large and containing little.

Pit 3 produced only a button (CM. 2905a) and some small pieces of bone. What had become of its original contents, if any, could not be determined.

Tomb E-9, like most of those cleared in this cemetery, with the exception of Tomb E-8, seems to have been in use from early Late Helladic III to late III B. Unless the tomb had been plundered by marauders mainly in antiquity, it probably belonged to a family of relatively modest means.

OBJECTS FOUND

Dromos

POTTERY

One-handled angular kylix (CM. 2832, Fig. 260:2): h. 0.118 m.; d. stem 0.025 m.; d. 0.113 m.; d. base 0.07 m. Gray-brown clay; smoothed surface, undecorated. One-third of rim and body missing. (*PN* I, Shape 27, pp. 366f.; *MP*, Type 267, p. 61 fig. 17, Late Helladic III B).

Chamber

STONE

Lentoid seal of black steatite (CM. 2902, Fig. 260:28a, b): d. 0.017 m. Near Skull A. Quadruped, an ox or bull with horns, in profile moving to left, head turned back. A bird(?) perched on right horn.

Steatite bead (CM. 2905b, Fig. 260:27): l. 0.018 m.; d. 0.01 m. Earth filling chamber. Oval with diagonal incisions.

PASTE

Beads. Earth filling chamber. Five spherical (CM. 2903, Fig. 260:27): d. from 0.007 m. to 0.015 m. Two fluted (CM. 2904, Fig. 260:27): d. 0.01 m. and 0.019 m. One amygdaloid (CM. 2904, Fig. 260:27): w. 0.011 m.; th. 0.004 m.

POTTERY

Jug with cutaway neck [3] (CM. 2833, Fig. 260:9): h. 0.208 m.; d. rim 0.095 m.; d. neck 0.079 m.; d. 0.164 m.; d. base 0.057 m. North area. Pale green clay; smoothed

surface, undecorated. Rounded rim, cutaway section very slight; flat handle from rim to shoulder. Somewhat like *MP*, Type 135, p. 35 fig. 7, Late Helladic III A.

Side-spouted jug with basket-handle [4] (CM. 2834, Fig. 260:18): h. 0.12 m.; h. to rim 0.095 m.; d. rim 0.048 m.; d. neck 0.035 m.; d. 0.09 m.; d. base 0.04 m. North area. Pale buff clay; red-brown, powdery paint. Spout tapers to tip (*MP*, Type 159, p. 30 fig. 5, Late Helladic III A:1). Neck, handle, spout solidly painted; two lines below neck, two around body. Continuous rock pattern on shoulder (*MP*, Motive 32:1:5, p. 323 fig. 54, Late Helladic I-III B).

Stirrup-vase [5] (CM. 2835, Fig. 260:17): h. 0.087 m.; d. 0.085 m.; d. base 0.031 m. North area. Lustrous buff surface; bright red paint. Lacks small piece from bottom. Slightly raised base, handles round in section (*MP*, Type 171 or 173, pp. 30f. figs. 5, 6). Tops of handles, base of neck and spout, exterior of rim solidly coated. Three pairs of horizontal bands enclosing two or three thin lines spaced over lower part of body. Main pattern on shoulder resembles *MP*, Motive 18 (Flower) p. 293 fig. 45, Motive 19:13 or 18 (Multiple stem and tongue) p. 299 fig. 47, or Motive 25:9 (Bivalve shell) p. 315 fig. 53, Late Helladic III A.

One-handled angular kylix (CM. 2836, Fig. 260:10): h. 0.113 m.; d. stem 0.022 m.; d. 0.111 m.; d. base 0.063 m. Near east wall. Pinkish-buff clay; undecorated. Lacks small piece from body; vessel warped. Shape similar to CM. 2832 (*PN* I, Shape 27, pp. 366f.; *MP*, Type 267, p. 61 fig. 17, Late Helladic III A:2 l).

One-handled angular kylix [1] (CM. 2837, Fig. 260:8): d. 0.118 m.; d. stem 0.021 m.; d. 0.10 m.; d. base 0.064 m. Near Skull A. Pale green clay; undecorated. Lacks half of bowl and rim. Similar to CM. 2832 and 2836 (Late Helladic III B).

Conical cup [6] (CM. 2838, Fig. 260:1): h. 0.05 m.; d. 0.125 m.; d. base 0.038 m. Near west wall. Orange clay; smoothed surface, undecorated. Shape similar to *PN* I, Shape 11, pp. 359f.; *MP*, Type 204, p. 53 fig. 15, Late Helladic I-III B.

Beaked jug [7] (CM. 2839, Fig. 260:15): h. 0.078 m.; d. neck 0.013 m.; d. 0.067 m.; d. base 0.029 m. Near west wall. Buff clay; entire body, except for underside of base, solidly coated with lustrous paint; color varies from bright red to brown. Slightly raised base, globular body, narrow neck; short, horizontal beak-spout. Flat handle, rim to shoulder (no exact parallel in *MP*).

Angular alabastron [8] (CM. 2840, Fig. 260:16): h. 0.057 m.; d. rim 0.046 m.; d. neck 0.034 m.; d. 0.08 m. Near west wall. Pale green clay; thin, brown paint. Lacks piece of rim. Slightly convex bottom, straight sides, sloping shoulders, spreading rim (*MP*, Type 93, p. 44 fig. 12, Late Helladic III A:1). Neck, rim, handles solidly coated. Two horizontal bands and two lines around body. Shoulder zone cross-hatched below two lines (*MP*, Motive 57:2, Diaper Net, p. 383 fig. 67, Late Helladic III A:1-III C:1).

Short-stemmed goblet [13] (CM. 2847, Fig. 260:22): h. 0.101 m.; d. rim 0.11 m.; d. stem 0.025 m.; d. 0.112 m.; d. base 0.058 m. Between Pits 1 and 2. Buff clay; smoothed surface, undecorated. Lacks one small piece from body and one from base. Rim slightly offset; body curves toward conical base, concave underneath. Flat handle rises slightly above rim and swings

down to attachment just below greatest diameter.

Kylix with two high handles [14] (CM. 2850, Fig. 260:14): h. 0.093 m.; h. to rim 0.065 m.; d. 0.07 m.; d. stem 0.019 m.; d. base 0.043 m. Between Pits 1 and 2. Buff clay; undecorated surface discolored. Lacks portion of rim and one handle. Conical base, hollow underneath; short stem; S-curve in upper part of body. Two flat, high-swung handles. Related to *MP*, Type 270, 271, or 272, p. 60 fig. 16, Late Helladic I-III A:2 e.

Chamber: Pit 1

POTTERY

Small pithoid jar [9] (CM. 2841, Fig. 260:12): h. 0.084 m.; d. rim 0.053 m.; d. 0.083 m.; d. base 0.0425. Ivory clay; dark brown-black paint. Lacks one of three round horizontal handles and greater part of spreading rim. (*MP*, Type 28 or 44, pp. 22f. figs. 3, 4, Late Helladic II B-III A:2 e). Rim, neck, handles solidly coated. Lower part of body, horizontal bands separated by groups of three lines. Uppermost band is continuous rock pattern out of which spring ivy plants on curving double stems (*MP*, Motive 12:23-27, Sacral Ivy, p. 271 fig. 36, Late Helladic II B-III A:1).

Alabastron [10] (CM. 2842, Fig. 260:20): h. 0.079 m.; d. rim 0.10 m.; d. 0.184 m. Hard, lustrous buff surface; thick orange-red paint. Only one or two tiny chips missing. Rim, three handles solidly painted. Two concentric circles in center of flat bottom from which five pairs of wavy spokes radiate to two outer circles (cf. *MP*, Motive 68:2, Wheel, p. 403 fig. 70, Late Helladic II A-III A:1). Like CM. 2893 from Tomb E-8, with five spokes instead of four. Continuous rock pattern at greatest diameter, above which two types of flowers on double wavy stems (*MP*, Motive 12:23, 24, Sacral Ivy, p. 271 fig. 36, Late Helladic II B, and Motive 14:14, Palm, p. 277 fig. 38, Late Helladic II B). Row of dots and rosettes made of dots circle shoulder below neck.

Alabastron [11] (CM. 2843, Fig. 260:13): h. 0.04 m.; d. rim 0.045 m.; d. 0.073 m. Ivory clay; very worn brown-black paint. Sloping shoulders, narrow neck, wide-spreading rim. Two groups of two concentric circles on bottom. Rim, neck, handles solidly coated. On body, between handles, triple chevrons related to *MP*, Motive 19:15, p. 299 fig. 47, or Motive 58:1, p. 383 fig. 67, with traces of a flower above.

Shallow one-handled cup [12] (CM. 2844, Fig. 260:11): h. 0.04 m.; d. 0.11 m.; d. base 0.038 m. Coarse, orange fabric. Undecorated. Flat bottom, rounded body, spreading rim. Lacks most of flat, high-swung handle. Cf. *PN* I, Shape 14, p. 361, figs. 355, 356.

One-handled kylix [15] (CM. 2845, Fig. 260:24): h. 0.13 m.; d. 0.133 m.; d. stem 0.0185 m.; d. base 0.061 m. Buff clay completely coated with thick orange-red paint. One or two chips missing. Deep bowl, slight angle in upper portion; one handle. Somewhat similar to *PN* I, Shape 27, p. 366f., figs. 359, 360, but not as angular, and stem more slender.

Pithoid jar [16] (CM. 2846, Fig. 260:23): h. 0.163 m.; d. rim 0.096 m.; d. 0.133 m.; d. base 0.052 m. Greenish clay; brown paint. Lower part of body conical; three horizontal round handles on shoulder, wide neck, short spreading rim (*MP*, Types 44, 45, p. 23 fig. 4). Three broad horizontal bands around middle of body; single band above foot and below neck. Handles, neck, lowest portion of body solidly coated.

Alabastron (CM. 2848, Fig. 260:21): h. 0.039 m.; d. rim 0.041 m.; d. 0.079 m. Found in kylix, CM. 2845. Ivory clay; red-brown paint. Sloping shoulders, narrow, short neck, broad horizontal rim. Rim, neck, three handles solidly coated. Continuous rock pattern below handles (*MP*, Motive 32:1:5, p. 323 fig. 54, Late Helladic I-III B). Two concentric circles in center of flat bottom.

Alabastron (CM. 2849, Fig. 260:19): h. 0.046 m.; d. rim 0.042 m.; d. 0.077 m. Found in kylix, CM. 2845. Ivory clay; brown paint. Shoulders more rounded and rim not so flat as CM. 2848. Rim, neck, handles solidly coated. Two bands on body; rising above the upper in each space between handles a large single rock unit.

Miniature jug (CM. 2853, Fig. 260:3): h. 0.05 m.; d. rim 0.028 m.; d. 0.067 m.; d. base 0.023 m. In CM. 2846. Orange clay; worn red paint. Lacks parts of rim, handle, and, probably, tubular spout. Solidly coated on exterior.

One-handled cup (CM. 2854, Fig. 260:5): h. 0.061 m.; d. 0.089 m.; d. base 0.032 m. Restored from sherds, Pits 1 and 2. Ivory clay; smoothed surface; thick brown-black paint. Lacks one-third of rim and body. Slightly raised base concave underneath. Sides spread sharply to angle low on body, then more gradually to rim. One flat handle from rim to middle of body (*PN* I, Shape 17, p. 362; *MP*, Type 230, p. 53 fig. 15, Late Helladic III A:2-III B). Rim, inside and out, and upper surface of handle solidly coated. Two horizontal bands around base. At angle continuous rock pattern from which, on triple curving stems, sacral ivy pattern (*MP*, Motive 12:27, p. 271 fig. 36, Late Helladic III A:1).

Angular alabastron (CM. 2856, Fig. 260:7): d. rim 0.062 m. Fragments of bottom, shoulder, and rim from Pits 1 and 2. (Cf. *PN* I, Shape 64, p. 402f.; *MP*, Type 94, p. 44 fig. 12.) Pale buff clay; red-brown paint. Hatched loops on shoulder; between each pair an irregular loop depends from solidly painted neck (*MP*, Motive 63, p. 397 fig. 69, Late Helladic III A:2).

Chamber: Pit 2

T E R R A C O T T A

Female figurine (CM. 2906, Fig. 260:25): h. 0.118 m.; w. across back 0.052 m.; d. skirt 0.045 m.; d. base 0.044 m. Orange-buff clay; red paint. Pellets for eyes and breasts.

Arms bent at elbows with hands below breasts. Two horizontal bands around bottom of skirt; vertical wavy lines above on one side. Horizontal wavy band above breasts. Breasts, arms, eyes solidly painted; eyes outlined in red. Top and back of head solidly coated.

Female figurine (CM. 2907, Fig. 260:26): h. 0.093 m.; w. across back 0.05 m.; d. waist 0.024 m. Clay orange-buff; lustrous red paint. Lacks bottom and most of skirt. Breasts indicated by pellets, eyes merely painted. Arms very short, folded at elbows, hands under breasts. Fingers painted in splayed position (8 on right hand, 9 on left). Bands around waist, neck, and on shoulders; wavy vertical lines cover head and face, back, and from waist down in front. Breasts, arms, top of head solidly coated.

P O T T E R Y [13]

Kylix with two high handles [17] (CM. 2851, Fig. 260:6): h. to rim 0.047 m.; d. 0.069 m.;

d. stem 0.016 m.; d. base 0.031 m. Pale buff clay; undecorated. Lacks both handles. Shape similar to CM. 2850 except walls form continuous simple curve from stem to slightly spreading rim.

Handleless conical cup [18] (CM. 2852, Fig. 260:4): h. 0.035 m.; d. 0.069 m.; d. base 0.021 m. Orange clay; flaking lustrous red paint. One chip missing from rim. Flat bottom, conical body (*PN* I, Shape 11, pp. 359f., *MP*, Type 204, p. 53 fig. 15, Late Helladic I-III B). Interior only solidly painted.

Handleless conical cup [19] (CM. 2855, not illustrated): h. 0.045 m.; d. estimated 0.125 m. Buff clay. Undecorated. Lacks two-thirds of body and rim. In shape similar to CM. 2852.

Chamber: Pit 3

S T O N E

Button (CM. 2905a, Fig. 260:27): h. 0.01 m.; d. 0.015 m. Short cone; brown stone.

W. P. D.

Tomb E-10
(Plan and Section, Fig. 342)

Another dromos, E-10, was found 8 m. west of Tomb E-9. Since the same interval of 8 m. separated E-9 from E-8, some organization in the placement of the tombs, at least in the western part of the cemetery, is indicated. There is a similar regularity in the orientation of these three dromoi, all exactly parallel from south to north.

During the preliminary stages of excavation this dromos seemed perfectly normal, 4.42 m. long with its sides cut through the limestone ledge and into the clay beneath (Fig. 261). The dromos was 0.76 m. wide at the floor, but, as a result of the irregular inclination of the walls, it was from 0.48 m. to 0.64 m. wide at the top. As in dromoi E-1 and E-2, however, no chamber seems to have been built at its north end. Once again the explanation seems to be that at this point there was no ledge of rock to form a roof for such a tomb.[14]

---

[13] CM. 2854 and 2856 are listed under Pit 1, but fragments of both were also found in Pit 2.

[14] The irregular appearance of the north end of the dromos shown on the plan (Fig. 342) pre-

sumably does not reflect the activity of the builders, but our attempt to ascertain that, in fact, no chamber had been dug.

In the floor of the dromos, 0.55 m. from its southern end, a pit had been dug ca. 2 m. long from south to north (Fig. 262). The bottom of the pit was reached at 1 m. below the presumed level of the original sloping floor of the dromos. A niche had been hollowed out from the pit into the west wall in a place where the limestone was thickest and could possibly provide a roof (Fig. 264). The niche has a height of 1.30 m. and a depth of 1 m. from east to west.

The niche was set off from the pit by a wall ca. 0.60 m. high made of irregular pieces of the same limestone as the ledge (Fig. 263). The stones had been laid flat in irregular courses. Behind them lay a single skeleton with the skull in the northwest corner of the niche. Although the bones were very poorly preserved, it seems clear that the body had been placed on its back with the feet toward the south. Beside the remains, close to the center of the niche, two small vases were found lying on their sides (CM. 2857 [2], 2858 [1]). These were the only contents of the tomb.

It seems clear that a real chamber tomb had been planned. When it was discovered that the rock formation rendered that impossible, a substitute chamber was made to the west beneath the limestone ledge through which the dromos had been cut. This substitute was used, however, only once—sometime during the period Late Helladic III A:2-III B, the date indicated by the pottery.

O B J E C T S   F O U N D

POTTERY

Stirrup-vase [2] (CM. 2857, Fig. 265:2): h. 0.08 m.; d. 0.077 m.; d. base 0.028 m. Pale buff clay; brown-black paint. Lacks part of spout. Surface worn and flaking. Slightly raised base (*MP*, Type 171, pp. 30f. figs. 5, 6, Late Helladic III A:2-III C:1). Concentric circles on disk, handles solidly painted, thick and thin horizontal bands above base, low on body, and below shoulder. Multiple stem and tongue on shoulder (*MP*, Motive 19:25, p. 299 fig. 47, Late Helladic III A:2-III B).

Flask [1] (CM. 2858, Fig. 265:1): h. 0.079 m.; d. rim 0.026 m.; d. neck 0.016 m.; d. 0.068 m.; d. base 0.032 m. Greenish clay; thin brown-black paint. Lacks part of rim. Surface worn and flaking. Globular body, flat bottom (*MP*, Type 190-192, p. 31 fig. 6, Late Helladic III A:2-III B). Flaring rim solidly coated inside and out as are handles. Two horizontal bands around base of neck and three lower on body. Parallel chevrons or triangles on shoulder (*MP*, Motives 58, p. 383 fig. 67 or 61A:1, p. 391 fig. 68, Late Helladic III C:1-2).

W. P. D.

Tomb K-1
(Plans and Sections, Figs. 343-346)

This chamber tomb is situated in an olive grove belonging to Aristomenos Kontos, to whom we owe grateful thanks for permission to excavate on his property. The tomb is less than half a kilometer from the Palace of Nestor and to the west of it (Fig. 301). It lies on the southern flank of a spur that runs parallel to, and to the northwest of, the road that goes from Chora to modern Pylos (Navarino). The gaping dromos, usually in deep shadow in summer except at midday, can be seen quite clearly from the road. Excavation was started on July 16, 1957, and was completed in eight days. Three to four men were employed.

The dromos has a south-north axis (5° east of north). It is 6.60 m. long and about 1.25 m. wide. One has to step down about 0.50 m. into the passage which follows a level course for about 3 m. and then slopes down gradually to the entrance of the tomb (Figs. 343, 345). The sides of the dromos are inclined inwards so that in front of the doorway its width at the top is only 0.53 m. A pit, 1.90 m. x 0.53 m., and ca. 0.70 m. deep was uncovered at the very entrance of the dromos. Nothing was found in it except a few almost disintegrated bones, some teeth, fragments of a skull, and parts of a kylix that came from the upper levels and from the northeast corner of the pit. Very little in the way of pottery was found in the dromos and none complete, a few kylix fragments and parts of an alabastron. A tiny fragment of bronze and a small piece of carbon were also recovered. A preliminary longitudinal trench was dug in the dromos leaving enough earth against the eastern side to show the stratification (Fig. 346). The most notable feature in this section is the gravelly texture of the filling in the northern and lower end. There are also two small dark patches (free from gravel), one in front of the doorway and one near the entrance. These disturbances were no doubt caused by frequent reopenings of the dromos. The upper part of the section is fairly consistent in texture. Its color is a little lighter than that of the lower part. Near the entrance the earth is much whiter and this appears to be disintegrated rock. Here too there was some indication that the dromos had not been excavated to its full depth when it was reopened.

The doorway, cut in the rock, was 1.85 m. high and 0.77 m. broad at the base. Its sides had a slight batter so that the width near the top, which was rounded, was only 0.64 m. An irregularly built wall, in which stones of all sizes and shapes had been used, closed the entrance (Fig. 266). So haphazard was the construction that one stone projected quite a distance from the façade into the dromos. Just in front of the wall was placed a crude stone marker, 0.43 m. high and about 0.12 m. thick; at its base were fragments of a kylix (Fig. 267). The stone was presumably set up after the first burial, for, although the blocking wall would have been taken down on several occasions to admit later burials, the general custom seems to have been only to dismantle sufficient of the upper part of the wall to allow access to the tomb; the lower part would remain covered with earth. When removed in the course of the excavation the wall was found to have an average thickness of 1 m., measuring 1.04 m. at the east end and 0.82 m. at the west. The doorway splays outward toward the chamber where it acquires a width of just over 1 m. The western door jamb measures 1.24 m. from front to back, the eastern 1 m. The jambs show definite tool marks made probably by a bronze adze, the impressions indicating very clearly the central ridge of the tool and longitudinal striations on each side of it (Fig. 268). Similar marks were found on the walls of the chamber. Some marks resembling graffiti high up on the west door jamb were, however, probably made by animal claws (mice, rats, etc.). The soffit of the doorway slopes up slightly to coincide with the level of the tomb ceiling, and in like manner there is a slight downward inclination of the "threshold" to the floor.

The chamber, which does not follow exactly the axis of the dromos (Fig. 343), is roughly square in plan (2.63 m. from north to south and 2.68 m. from west to east) with blunt right angles; the curvature is more pronounced in the northwest and northeast corners. The existing height is 2.16 m., but part of the roof had collapsed, leaving debris ca. 0.30 m. thick covering the floor of the chamber. A clump of rock in the northwest corner either was not cut away when the tomb was originally made or had fallen from above and solidified against the walls of the chamber. The rock, in which the tomb was cut, differs from that in the dromos, being softer, with claylike texture, easy to cut. The entire west part of the chamber was occupied by earlier discarded burials and the pottery that belonged to them. As can be seen from Figures 269, 270, 344, these were disposed of in a summary and unceremonious manner. Two adult skulls and one of a child indicate that at least three burials were represented and the total number of vases accompanying them was 14. Two of these [18, 19] were later discovered up against, and partly embedded in, the west wall of the tomb. They may have belonged to an earlier interment that had been laid out in this part of the chamber before it came to be used as a charnel area. Nearly all the pots were intact and those vases that were broken probably suffered from occasional falls from the disintegrating roof. This was not the case, however, with one vase, a kylix [6], the stem of which lay in the southwest corner of the tomb whereas fragments of the bowl were found resting on top of a three-handled jar [9] in the northwest corner. They looked as if they had been placed there purposely. A stone, which had probably fallen from the blocking wall, occupied the southeast corner.

An extended burial had lain in the east part of the chamber but except for the skull and the leg bones very little of the skeleton was left. The skull, apparently that of a woman, lay to the south in a decayed state. The leg bones were stretched in a northwesterly direction. Four pots were distributed over the lower part of the skeleton: a large jug [14] on its side in the region of the pelvis;

the base of a "feeding bottle" [15] between the knees—the upper part of it beside the legs to the east; a three-handled jar [16] between the shin-bones; and a stirrup-jar [17] to the east of the right shin bone (Fig. 271). Four flattish stones, but of no particular shape, appear to have been placed of set purpose round the skeleton; two were at the head and two on either side of the feet (Figs. 271, 344). This was evidently the last interment in the tomb as the associated pottery indicated. It was not the latest type of Late Helladic III B but later than any of the vases collected in the west part of the chamber. One other burial remains to be described, a small pit 0.50 m. by 0.30 m. and only 0.15 m. deep in the center of the tomb, its axis running north-south. Into this pit had been compressed the skull and bones of an adult(?). The skull was placed at the bottom facing south, and the bones were neatly arranged around and above it (Fig. 272). Nothing accompanied this burial. Miscellaneous small objects from the tomb were few and except for an ivory roundel (Fig. 273:3), which was picked up among the debris of disintegrated rock that had fallen from the roof, they were confined to the west part of the chamber. The most important of these were eight "lily" beads of glass paste (Fig. 273:2a, b) found in sifting. Other finds were two minute beads of uncertain material, flakes of flint, a pellet of bronze, a bit of carbon, and some red coloring matter.

This tomb had the good fortune to escape the attentions of the plunderer and is a classic example of a Mycenaean chamber tomb. In accordance with custom the last interment was laid out extended in the chamber or deposited in a pit.

The tomb yielded five stirrup-jars, five three-handled jars, five jugs, one angular alabastron, one kylix, and one "feeding bottle." There were five burials in the tomb. One is tempted to allot a stirrup-jar, a three-handled jar, and a jug to each burial; and certainly the last interment was accompanied by all three of these vases.

The pots from this burial are clearly the latest and are Late Helladic III B; the stirrup-jar is III B:1.[14a] The rest of the vases are earlier in style. Both in shape and design they belong to Late Helladic III A. The two vases found against the west wall of the tomb, which it has been suggested might be earlier, afford little information as to their date, but they could be Late Helladic III A:1. On the stylistic criteria of the vases it can be said that the tomb was begun in III A and continued in use in III B.

[14a] I am very grateful to Mrs. Elizabeth French for this information.

Dromos

POTTERY

Alabastron. Two body fragments only (Fig. 273:12a, b).

(a) h. pres. 0.04 m.; w. 0.092 m.

(b) h. pres. 0.037 m.; w. 0.061 m.

Shape, *MP*, Type 84?, p. 41 fig. 15. Profile from bottom of neck to start of base of pot preserved. Pink clay, hard-fired. Reddish-brown, lustrous paint on white slip. Lower part of vase decorated with continuous Rock Pattern (*MP*, Motive 32:5, p. 323 fig. 54). Rest of design fragmentary, based on Rock Pattern II (*MP*, Motive 33:16 or 21, p. 327 fig. 55). Thick band at neck, two medium bands preserved below design. Good fabric. Late Helladic III A.

Angular kylix (CM. 1605, Fig. 273:11): h. 0.106 m.; d. rim estimated 0.11 m.; d. base 0.062 m. In front of blocking wall. About two-fifths preserved, including profile. Restored. Most of rim, all of handle, and part of bowl missing. Shape, *MP*, Type 267, pp. 6of. figs. 16, 17. Slightly everted rim. Underside of base slightly concave with small depression bearing spiral-shaped clay button. Light brown-buff clay, fired hard to medium, containing white grits. Undecorated. Late Helladic III.

Kylix (CM. 1606, Fig. 273:10): h. pres. 0.10 m., h. restored 0.148 m.; d. 0.129 m.; w. handle 0.014 m. In pit. Restored. Bowl only partly preserved. Shape, *MP*, Type 265, p. 61 fig. 17 but shape of bowl is Type 272, p. 60 fig. 16. Very slightly everted rim. Hard- to medium-fired, light brown clay, burnt pink in two places on one side. Same side also shows impressions of soil. Unsmoothed outer surface showing three ridges. Undecorated. Late Helladic III A.

[15] *RT, Dendra*, 29, C:4 and pl. XXVII. Cf. also *AM* XXXIV (1909), 295, fig. 12:2 — a lapis lazuli bead from Kakovatos, and *EphArch* 1887, pl.

Chamber

IVORY

Roundel in form of rosette (CM. 2117, Fig. 273:3): d. 0.021 m.; th. 0.002 m. Chipped and worn in parts, but mostly in good condition. Rosette executed in relief. Petals are in deepest relief emphasized by hollows cut in tips of each of them. Back of roundel has striations, probably to act as purchase for inlay work. Roundels usually reproduced in gold foil, less frequently in glass paste; in ivory less common. Cf. examples from Heraeum (*Prosymna*, fig. 446:14, fig. 417:8; fig. 242:12). Last mentioned offers best parallel. Cf. also fragmentary specimen from Kakovatos (*AM* XXXIV [1909], pl. XIV:15).

PASTE

Eight spacer beads (CM. 2118, Fig. 273:2a, b), of which six in reasonably good condition: h. 0.014 m.; w. 0.0095 m.; th. 0.0035 m.; w. upper string-hole 0.006 m.; w. lower string-hole 0.0038 m.; d. string-holes 0.001 m. Original color of beads probably yellow, but glaze has worn off in most cases. Several now white. Shape that of stylized lily in relief with corrugated cylinder above, containing upper string-hole (Fig. 273:2b), and tiny rosette beneath concealing lower string-hole. One bead lacks lower string-hole, another lacks both. These beads probably used as spacers for a double necklace of much smaller beads. Stylized lily is frequent motive in jewelry and inlay work. In former commonly used as pendant bead, seldom as spacer. What appear to be three spacer beads, almost identical to our type but in gold, were found in the Dendra tholos.[15]

Two red beads (CM. 2118, Fig. 273:1): d. 0.0022 m.; th. 0.0013 m. Minute, red. Not

13:15 — bone bead from Mycenae. Neither of last two are spacers.

certain that they are paste. These could be beads used with spacers above.

POTTERY

Chamber: west side

Stirrup-jar [7] (CM. 1562, Fig. 274:5a, b): h. 0.102 m.; d. 0.145 m.; d. base 0.075 m. Intact. Shape, *MP*, Type 180, p. 31 fig. 6. Pseudo-ring base. Medium-fired pink-buff clay with buff slip. Red lustrous paint. Shoulder decoration: Multiple Stem (*MP*, Motive 19:31, p. 299 fig. 47). Just above greatest diameter a zone of quirks (*MP*, Motive 48:5, p. 360 fig. 61) separated from shoulder pattern by zonal band of stripes. Two more zonal bands complete decoration, one below subsidiary design, one at base. Top of false spout flat, painted with solid disk surrounded by circular band. Handles solidly painted; thick band surrounds bottoms of false neck and spout, rim of which outlined in paint.

Stirrup-jar [2] (CM. 1563, Fig. 274:3a, b): h. 0.098 m.; d. 0.116 m.; d. base 0.05 m. Broken on one side but restored. Shape, *MP*, Type 179, pp. 31, 44 figs. 6, 12. Ring-base. Buff clay with white buff slip. Black and brown lustrous paint. Shoulder decoration: one side painted with Whorl-shell (*MP*, Motive 23:5, p. 311 fig. 51) three times and slanting. "Sea Anemone" (*MP*, Motive 27:18, p. 315 fig. 53) is used in each "spandrel." Zonal band of stripes below design and another farther down. Single medium band at base. Top of false spout flat, painted with solid disk within two circles. Handles solidly painted except for small reserved triangle near false spout, which has thick band at base, as also spout painted with irregular band round rim.

Stirrup-jar [3] (CM. 1564, Fig. 274:2a, b): h. 0.093 m.; d. 0.12 m.; d. base 0.047 m. Intact. Shape *MP,* Type 180, p. 31 fig. 6. Ring-base. Medium-fired buff clay with white buff slip. Black to brown lustrous paint, but worn. Shoulder decoration: Mycenaean III Flower (*MP*, Motive 18:92,

p. 293 fig. 45). Zonal band decoration similar to that of CM. 1563. Top of false spout flat, painted with solid disk within circle. Handle decoration same as on CM. 1563. False spout and spout linked by thick band. Irregular band around rim of spout.

Stirrup-jar [4] (CM. 1565, Fig. 274:1a, b): h. 0.111 m.; d. 0.103 m.; d. base 0.035 m. Intact but surface worn. Shape, *MP*, Type 171, pp. 30, 31 figs. 5, 6. Ring-base. Pink clay fired soft to medium. Red, worn but lustrous paint. Shoulder decoration: Multiple Stem (*MP*, Motive 19:17, p. 299 fig. 47). Three zonal bands of stripes, evenly spaced, between design and base. Disk of false spout flat, painted with concentric circles. Handle decoration as on CM. 1563. Thick band surrounds bottoms of false spout and spout. Bands overlap. Irregular band around rim of spout.

Three-handled jar [8] (CM. 1566, Fig. 273:9): h. 0.188 m.; d. mouth 0.114 m.; d. 0.157 m.; d. base 0.062 m. Almost complete, restored. Shape *MP,* Type 45, p. 23 fig. 4. Round, uptilted loop-handles. Pseudo-ring-base; part of base misshapen. Grayish-yellow clay, rather soft-fired. Black to brown lustrous paint, much worn in places. Shoulder decoration: Diaper Net (*MP*, Motive 57:2, p. 383 fig. 67) bounded by medium bands (one above, three below). Two medium bands on lower part of body. Thick band at base with medium one above. Neck and handles solidly painted, rim inside and out.

Three-handled jar [9] (CM. 1576, Fig. 273:7): h. 0.252 m.; d. mouth 0.127 m.; d. 0.191 m.; d. base 0.068 m. Intact. Shape, *MP*, Type 39, p. 23 fig. 4. Beveled rim. Round, uptilted loop-handles. Convex base, concave underneath with kylix type hollow. Medium-fired buff to pink clay. Very slightly lustrous brown to black paint. Thick to medium band decoration only: two below handles, two low on body, one above base which is solidly painted as are neck and handles. Trickle of paint from one handle. Inside of rim painted.

Angular alabastron [5] (CM. 1568, Fig. 273:6): h. 0.116 m.; d. mouth 0.105 m.; d. 0.152 m. Intact. Shape, *MP*, Type 94, p. 44 fig. 12. Slightly beveled rim. Three round loop-handles, set almost vertically. Medium-fired buff clay with off-white slip. Light to dark brown lustrous paint. Shoulder decoration: Foliate Band (*MP*, Motive 64:21, p. 397 fig. 69) but slanting. Thick and medium band below design. Medium and thick band near base. Neck and handles solidly painted, rim inside and out.

Kylix [6] (CM. 1570, Fig. 274:12): h. 0.168 m.; d. 0.162 m.-0.168 m.; d. base 0.093 m. Broken but restored. Shape, *MP*, Type 257, p. 61 fig. 17, but with horizontal loop-handles.[16] Slightly offset and fairly rounded rim. Concave base with hollow. Medium-fired buff clay. Black to brown lustrous but faded paint. Off-white slip. Decoration Whorl-shell (*MP*, Motive 23:6, p. 311 fig. 51) slanting and a variation of Palm II (*MP*, Motive 15:15 right, p. 279 fig. 39) on its side. Trefoil Rock-work (*MP*, Motive 29:10, p. 315 fig. 53) used as a filling motive. Design fairly well preserved on one face, but much faded on other. Three to four thin stripes below design. Series of zonal bands on stem. Thin and medium stripes on base. Lip painted inside and out. On bottom of bowl concentric circles.

Beaked jug [12] (CM. 1573, Fig. 274:9): h. 0.289 m.; d. 0.22 m.; d. base 0.095 m. Intact. Shape, *MP*, Type 145, p. 31 fig. 6. Slight ridge at bottom of neck. Pseudo-ring-base. Medium-fired buff clay. White slip. Reddish-brown to dark brown lustrous paint. Thick band decoration only: one band on neck, one at bottom of neck, three

below handle, one above base, and one on base. Two loops encircle spout, rim of which outlined. Borders of handle painted and band around bottom of it.

Beaked jug [10] (CM. 1578, Fig. 274:7): h. 0.295 m.; d. 0.237 m.; d. base 0.087 m. Broken but restored. Shape, *MP*, Type 145, p. 31 fig. 6. Slight ridge on handle and at bottom of neck. False ring-base. Buff clay with pink outer surface, rather soft-fired. Band decoration only: one at bottom of neck, three below handle, one at base. Rim outlined with paint. Edges of handle painted; band encircles its lower part.

Jug with cutaway neck [11] (CM. 1574, Fig. 274:11): h. 0.322 m.; d. rim 0.077 m.; d. 0.227 m.; d. base 0.083 m. Intact. Shape, *MP*, Form 34, Type 133, p. 605; body Type 133, p. 23 fig. 4. No ridge at neck but slight bulge where neck joins body. Almost a torus type of base. Pseudo-ring-base. Medium-fired buff clay with white slip. Black to brown lustrous paint. Decoration: Curved Stripes (*MP*, Motive 67:10, p. 403 fig. 70) but with very thick stripe and no subsidiary stripes. Band on outer rim. Surface of rim painted with series of blobs; band lower down inside neck. Band round neck and at bottom of neck. Solid area around base of vase. Edges of handle painted. Cf. three jugs of same type with identical stripe decoration from Messenia (*EphArch* 1914, 112, figs. 23, 24—two from Traganes; *Praktika* 1964, pl. 95:β from Vlakhopoulos).

Jug [13] (CM. 1575, Fig. 274:10): h. 0.338 m.; d. mouth 0.11 m.; d. 0.281 m.; d. base 0.12 m. Intact. Shape, *MP*, Type 120, pp. 30, 31 figs. 5, 6. Splaying neck; no ridge at its base. Plain rim. Handle flattened in section. Flat base. Medium-fired buff clay

---

[16] It should be noted that the horizontal handles of this example are unusual on a vessel of this profile. The handles are those typical of a stemmed bowl (*MP*, Type 305, p. 65 fig. 18) while the profile and decoration are those of a kylix (*MP*, Type

266, pp. 60, 61 figs. 16, 17). The rare use of horizontal handles is paralleled by earlier material (Late Helladic III A:1) from the Lower Town of Pylos. Information kindly provided by Mrs. Elizabeth French.

with off-white slip. Black, slightly lustrous paint, red in one spot where burnt in firing. Band decoration only: four below handle, one on rim, and one at base of neck. Band encircles handle where it joins neck and another where it joins body. Outer surface of handle has vertical wavy band.

Chamber: up against west wall

Three-handled jar [18] (CM. 1567, Fig. 273:4): h. 0.155 m.; d. mouth 0.096 m.; d. 0.136 m.; d. base 0.06 m. Intact. Shape, *MP,* Form 7, Type 50, p. 592. Beveled rim. Round loop-handles set almost vertically. Base has torus molding and broad ring-base. Medium-fired, greenish-buff clay. Undecorated. Compare *ChT,* pl. XIX:4.

Three-handled jar [19] (CM. 1571, Fig. 273:8): h. 0.211 m.; d. mouth 0.112 m.; d. 0.172 m.; d. base 0.069 m. Intact. Shape, *MP,* Type 40, p. 23 fig. 4. Beveled rim. Vertical loop-handles, round to flattened in section. Ring-base. Medium-fired buff to pink clay with off-white slip. Red to dark brown slightly lustrous paint. Decoration: broad wavy band in each panel. Surface of rim painted. Broad band on neck. Two medium stripes above handles. Three thick bands below them. Solid uneven area of paint at base. Handles painted with vertical band. Simple pattern, but in more elegant form, is matched on alabastra (*NT, Dendra,* 93, fig. 104:1; *Prosymna,* fig. 712).

Chamber: east side

Stirrup-jar [17] (CM. 1561, Fig. 274:6a, b): h. 0.128 m.; d. 0.126 m.; d. base 0.053 m. Intact except for chip on base. Shape, *MP,* Type 171, pp. 30, 31 figs. 5, 6. Slightly concave disk on false spout. Concave base. Pink to buff clay with slip(?). Black to brown lustrous paint. Shoulder decoration: Mycenaean III Flower (*MP,* Motive 18:71, p. 293 fig. 45). Subsidiary decoration on body: Wavy Line (*MP,* Motive 53:31, p. 373 fig. 65). Zonal band and line decoration between main and subsidiary designs. Similar zonal band below latter and again at base. Disk of false spout decorated with close spiral with solid center. Rim of spout outlined with paint. Bottoms of false neck and of spout linked by thick band. Underside of base painted with concentric circles.

Three-handled jar [16] (CM. 1569, Fig. 273:5): h. 0.137 m.; d. mouth 0.091 m.; d. 0.122 m.; d. base 0.057 m. Intact except for chips of base and rim. Shape, *MP,* Type 49, p. 23 fig. 4. Beveled rim. Rather angular profile with no differentiation for neck. Vertical handles. Ring-base. Medium-fired greenish-buff clay with patches of pink where overfired. Black lustrous paint. Same shoulder decoration in each panel: "triglyph" of vertical stripes, on each side of which is double line pendant from neck and ending in an outward curl. Two broad bands below design and another at base. Rim and neck solidly painted inside and out, handles on outside, and loop band passes round each handle. For shape compare *Prosymna,* fig. 115:278. I have not been able to find a parallel for the design.

Jug [14] (CM. 1572, Fig. 274:8): h. 0.283 m.; d. mouth 0.104 m.; d. base 0.098 m. Intact. Shape, *MP,* Type 109, p. 35 fig. 7. Slightly overhanging rim cut away at handle. Handle round to flattened in section. Flat base. Rather coarse, medium-fired pink to orange clay. Undecorated.

Side-spouted necked jug with basket-handle [15] (CM. 1577, Fig. 274:4): h. with handle 0.20 m.; h. without handle 0.155 m.; d. 0.14 m.; d. base 0.085 m. Almost complete, restored. Shape, *MP,* Type 161, p. 31 fig. 6; Shape 41, *PN* I, pp. 378, 379 figs. 369, 370. Ovoid body with rather short neck which is not differentiated. Flat base. Handle round in section. Very coarse, reddish-brown clay, medium-fired. Undecorated.

W. D. T.

DISCOVERIES
OUTSIDE THE CITADEL

DISCOVERIES OUTSIDE THE CITADEL

THROUGH many annual campaigns of our excavation on the Englianos Hill we constantly used the highway back and forth between our house in the village of Chora and the Palace of Nestor. We also frequently drove down to the Bay of Navarino and to the modern town of Pylos. Along the way, north and south and on each side of the road, we were often tempted to stop to see if we might detect a knoll or tumulus — possibly of a tomb — or a heap of stones or a ruin, perhaps of an ancient structure. In 1958 and 1959 we determined to investigate several spots that we thought might be worth sounding.

Lord William Taylour generously undertook the task of probing into three different places. The first attempt, kindly allowed by the owner, in the threshing floor of Mr. Deriziotis, revealed the remnants of stone walls of the Early Helladic Period, long before Mycenaean times. With a similar permit from the Kokkevis family, nearly three kilometers south of Englianos, on a short steep slope, the second effort found a chamber tomb that had been partly plundered but still yielded gold beads, a bronze vessel and mirror, and pottery of Mycenaean III B and C. The third find, just a little below the second, was exposed, showing the half of a small stone-built tholos that had been sliced in two on the very edge of the road. Several interesting articles that had been undisturbed since 1895, when the road was made, were only recovered in 1958. The tholos belonged to the Protogeometric Period.

All the objects retrieved from the three areas that were excavated were duly described and recorded by Lord William and deposited in the Museum at Chora.

C. W. B.

AN EARLY HELLADIC SITE
(Plans and Sections, Figs. 347-350)

A line of stones, showing up on the surface of an *aloni*, the property of Evstathios Deriziotis, led us to expect the existence of a tholos at this spot. With the kind permission of the owner an excavation was made, which started on July 7, 1958, and was completed on July 16. Three workmen were employed. The site is about 500 m. southwest of the Palace of Nestor and on a terrace leveled on a spur of a hill that slopes down in the direction of the island of Sphakteria (Fig. 301). A bearing on the palace from the site gives an angle of approximately 43°.

A trench, 1 m. by 7 m., was laid across the line, or rather the arc of stones, for a slight curve in the line was noticeable. It was soon realized, however, that these stones had no connection with a tholos because there was only one course to the wall, which was laid on earth. Within the area of the *aloni* were the partial structural remains of a Bronze Age settlement that was probably transitional between Early and Middle Helladic. One cannot be more specific than that, for the pottery evidence was very scant and so much of it was made up of coarse ware.

It was not possible to recover much of the plan of the settlement. There is little depth of soil in the area and even within the confines of the *aloni*, which is at a slightly higher level than the surrounding terrain, the rock was not far below the surface. On an average it was found at a depth of 0.40 m.-0.45 m., in one exceptional case at 0.95 m., and occasionally at 0.20 m.-0.25 m. There was, moreover, evidence of modern intrusions not only in the form of surface disturbance but in the shape of trenches dug for young vines; these frequently cut through earlier walls. In spite of these unpromising circumstances some coherent picture seemed to emerge during the course of the excavation. Plan I (Fig. 347) gives a record of the surviving walls. Groups of pithos sherds, some of which represent hearths, are also indicated and the intrusive vine trenches are marked. Plan II (Fig. 348) is a schematic version of Plan I. Only the walls are reproduced and the missing sections of them sketched in. This plan serves to emphasize that there are two apsidal, or maybe circular, buildings, one superimposed on the other; and this was borne out by the excavation. The line of stones that was visible from the start, and which was the occasion of this exploratory sounding, is referred to on the plan as Wall M (Fig. 275). Its continuation could be traced—with gaps—in a southwesterly and southerly direction. This wall is of one course only and seldom far below the surface. At one point it passes over the curving Wall B, which is consistently at a lower level, that is, 0.30 m.-0.35 m. below the surface. Wall B ties up with Wall A, also at a lower level. This is a straight aligned wall with a west-northwest east-southeast axis, which is terminated abruptly by a vine trench to the east (Fig. 276); it probably joined up again with Wall B after the latter had completed its semicircular curve farther toward the east. At this eastern end of the excavation we are unfortunately on the edge of the *aloni* and little is preserved. Possibly the solitary upright stone shown on the plan represents the extension of Wall B southwards.

The excavation yielded a fair amount of pottery but more than 90 percent of it was coarse ware and of this the greater part consisted of pithos fragments; indeed these were an outstanding feature of the site. Small groups of pithos sherds were revealed only a few centimeters below the surface. Much larger groups were uncovered in the lower levels (0.35 m.-0.45 m. deep) and these, it was clear, were laid out with some care. Two groups that are situated to the south of Wall A (Plan I, Fig. 347) were almost certainly used as hearths. They are roughly square in plan but the central part is bare of sherds; the enclosed earth is burnt red (Fig. 277). Another large group of pithos sherds was found against the south flank of Wall B in the north part of the area. When these were taken up, a second and more extensive layer was discovered immediately underneath. There were several other patches of pithos fragments, laid out in a kind of mosaic, which were uncovered in the space bounded by Wall A in the south and Wall B in the north. One of these was associated with a very small area of pebble floor (Plan 1, Fig. 347 and Fig. 278)[1] against the north flank of Wall A. It is more likely therefore that these isolated patches of neatly arranged pithos fragments represent some kind of flooring to the habitation.[2] It should be emphasized that this "floor" and the hearths are all about the same level and are clearly associated with the lower building. Similar phenomena probably persisted in the later building, represented by Wall M, and mention has already been made of groups of pithos sherds found in the upper levels, but being so near the surface they have obviously suffered from modern disturbance and can no longer give a coherent plan.

The walls of both periods are built of the same kind of stone, a soft limestone called by the workmen *poros*, though it was certainly not of the quality of *poros* limestone found in the outer wall of the Palace of Nestor and also at Mycenae where it is associated with monumental constructions. The width of Wall B, the curved wall of the earlier building, averaged 0.45 m.-0.50 m. Exceptionally, its width near the east end of the *aloni* was 0.60 m. Wall A, which if complete would probably be the "chord" of the "arc" Wall B, is somewhat narrower with a width varying from 0.30 m. to 0.40 m. No definitive measurements can be given for Wall M, the only surviving wall of the later building, as it is so badly preserved. It was the first wall to be discovered, being the original line of stones across which the first trench was laid. Here its width was only 0.30 m., but such traces of it as were picked up later to the west and southwest seemed to indicate a width of 0.50 m. There is little that can be said about the construction of the walls in either period. Only one course survives of the upper building and barely two of the lower one. The stones used were not large. Several of them are small slabs such as were commonly employed in the construction of Tholos IV and the grave circle. It is probable that the superstructure was of mudbrick; fragments of this material were found in the west part of the excavation.

Although there was very little depth of soil, it was thought worthwhile to record two sections in that part of the area that seemed to offer most information. These both represent north-south sections in the central part of the site

---

[1] One of the sherds in this group seems purposely to have been fixed upright, and this was not an isolated instance.

[2] Cf. *Eutresis* 23 and p. 22 fig. 21.

as viewed from the east. Section I (Figs. 349, 348) cuts through Wall A and a small part of Wall B. Immediately to the south of Wall A are the two hearths; their relationship to Wall A seems quite clear. It should be noted that the hearths are associated with the lightest colored soil, which is not easily distinguished from *stereo* or the natural soft rock; the hearths were indeed laid on the rock. A similar irregular-shaped stratum of light-colored soil can be seen between Walls A and B. Adjoining and to the south of this patch, the earth is darker; it is possible that we have here—though it is not certain—a foundation trench for Wall A. Elsewhere in the section variations in the color of soil were not well defined. Broadly speaking, the darkest soil is to be found to the south of Wall A and above the area of the hearths. This perhaps represents a layer of occupational debris. The layer above it, which is slightly lighter in color, is in effect topsoil; it would also correspond to the habitation level connected with Wall M. The outlines left by the intrusive trenches dug for vines, initiated in modern times, need no comment.

Section II (Figs. 350, 348), about 1 m. further to the east, includes Wall A and the small bit of pebble floor with pithos sherds to the north of it; it stops just short of Wall M. This section could profitably have been extended farther north to include Wall M but the balk, which could have provided this record, had unfortunately to be taken down at an early stage before the record was made. To the south of Wall A the same dark layer, noted in Section I, can be observed in this section also, though it is not continuous and the layer of lighter soil underneath has greater depth, but this is probably because it includes a proportion of the natural rock that has been dug away; here as elsewhere in this district the rock is very soft and difficult to distinguish from undug soil. Wall A was almost certainly built on the rock.

In conclusion, this small excavation, circumscribed both in extent and in depth, has revealed two buildings of different periods, both of which have curved walls. As these walls are only partially preserved it is impossible to say whether they belong to apsidal houses, such as are quite common in the Middle Helladic period, or to a circular structure. On the present site more is preserved of the earlier house than the later one and a case could be made out for a circular building with a wall (Wall A) dividing it into two equal halves. The north half may have been used as a storeroom, the south half as a living room. Communication between the two would be by a doorway in the east part of Wall A—there was no evidence of a threshold in the surviving west part. The finds from the excavation were few. Some of these were of a type associated with Early Helladic culture and there were definite Early Helladic traits in the pottery, but some of the pottery was black Minyan. It is for that reason that a transitional date between Early and Middle Helladic is suggested for these two habitations.

OBJECTS FOUND

STONE

Saddle quern. Volcanic stone. Very small piece picked up from surface.

Shaft-hole axe, fragment (CM. 2112, Fig. 279:16): h. 0.059 m.; l. pres. 0.061 m.; w. 0.018 m.-0.026 m.; d. hole estimated 0.02 m. Found in upper levels. Light green, speckled stone, very hard. Shaft-hole shows clear signs of use of drill. For shaft-hole axes cf. *Eutresis,* 207, fig. 278:7, 8 (Middle Helladic) and *SME,* 345, fig. 73.

Five pounders or grinders (CM. 2111). Very hard stone, dark blue and purple. Roughly cubical in shape with rounded corners. Three are large with diameters of 0.075 m. to 0.09 m. Dimensions of one smaller: 0.046 m. x 0.042 m. x 0.039 m. (Fig. 279:15). Last-named found in upper level, other four in lowest levels. Such primitive artifacts frequently found on prehistoric sites. Cf. *Zygouries,* 200, fig. 188.

Three whorls? of slate (Fig. 279:10-12). Disk-shaped, pierced centrally. Hole made by drilling from both sides; hence each surface has conical depression. Dimensions:

(10) CM. 2106: d. 0.049 m.; d. inner hole 0.005 m.; d. outer hole 0.01 m.; th. 0.0068 m.-0.0075 m. Gray slate.

(11) CM. 2106: d. 0.0405 m.-0.044 m.; d. inner hole 0.0065 m.; d. outer hole 0.01 m.; th. 0.0073 m. Grayish-brown slate.

(12) CM. 2108: l. 0.0435 m.; w. 0.0385 m.; d. hole 0.0035 m.; th. 0.008 m. Dark gray slate. Roughly square. Unfinished, hole never having been completed; drill only penetrated fifth of thickness. Found in lowest level. The other two are from surface levels. Cf. whorl found in Tholos IV (NM. 7952, p. 126).

Flint blade (CM. 2104, Fig. 279:7): l. 0.0385 m.; w. 0.024 m.; th. 0.0045 m. White and gray. Serrated cutting edge; flake struck from flint core.

Flint saw, two fragments, dark brown: (Fig. 279:4, 8).

(4) CM. 2105: l. 0.032 m.; w. 0.02 m.; th. 0.008 m. Flake from core with secondary working along one edge, found in surface level.

(8) CM. 2108: l. 0.035 m.; w. 0.02 m.; th. 0.0065 m. Triangular shape. Has primary working on both faces and secondary working along one edge (base of triangle). From one of lower levels.

Flint saws seem to belong to all periods of Bronze Age. Cf. *Zygouries,* 198, fig. 187 (flint—Early Helladic); *Eutresis,* 205, fig. 276:3, 5, 7, 8, 9 (flint and obsidian—Early Helladic); 208, fig. 280:7, 8 (flint—Middle Helladic) and *PN* I, fig. 315:13; fig. 322: 9-13 (flint—Late Helladic).

Several splinters of flint (CM. 2107, Fig. 279:1) and of obsidian (CM. 2105, Fig. 279:2) from all levels.

BONE

A few fragments of bone, very much weathered, found against southern flank of Wall A and some to northwest of it, i.e. outside house.

BOAR'S TUSK

Boar's tusk, fragment (CM. 2107, Fig. 279:3): l. 0.0485 m.; w. 0.0105 m.; th. 0.0073 m. Very small piece; unworked. Apparently from an upper level.

TERRACOTTA

Spool (CM. 2110, Fig. 279:14): l. 0.0375 m.; d. 0.017 m.-0.021 m. From surface level. Yellow clay covered with off-white wash? Cf. *Zygouries,* 190, fig. 179:4, 5.

Pot base pierced centrally with hole (CM. 2104, Fig. 279:6): d. 0.032 m.-0.033 m.; th. ca. 0.009 m. From surface level. Base concave. On inner surface central part shows a depression of ca. 0.002 m. in depth and 0.02 m. in diameter.

Conical "button" (CM. 2109, Fig. 279:13a-b): h. 0.031 m.; d. 0.042 m. Found in lowest level. Black to dark brown core with many grits; red outer surface. "Button" pierced transversally with hole. Shape recalls Early Helladic buttons of conical form but this one pierced transversally instead of vertically, and sides are concave instead of convex.

POTTERY

Spherical vase. Fragments only. Not made up. Black, gray core. Pinkish-mauve surface. From lowest levels.

Multiple handle, fragments only. Not made up. Reddish-brown ware with black (painted) surface. From lowest levels.

Vertical handle (CM. 2104, Fig. 279:5): h. pres. 0.042 m.-0.062 m.; w. 0.03 m.; th. 0.008 m. Found in upper level. Four sticks of clay pressed together. Coarse dark brown clay with many grits, hard-fired. Outer surface burnt red with black finish (paint?). Underside of handle smoothed, presenting flat surface. Similar handles found at *Eutresis* (113, fig. 150:3, 4 — Early Helladic) and at Tiryns (K. Müller, *Tiryns* IV [1938], pl. xx:3). Cf. also triple handle on jug from Lerna, though sticks of clay

not in same axis (*Hesperia* XXV [1956], pl. 40:d — Middle Helladic).

Handle (CM. 2113, Fig. 279:9): l. pres. 0.0895 m.; w. 0.016 m.-0.048 m.; th. 0.01 m. Grip-handle (of cooking pot?) pierced at one end for suspension when not in use. Repaired. Handle rectangular to square in section. One end elliptical, pierced with hole. Soft-fired clay with gray core, grayish-yellow surface.

Although a considerable amount of pottery was gathered up in this excavation, the bulk of it consisted of pithoi and coarse ware: fine wares were practically negligible. No vases could be put together. The pithos sherds, fitted together like a jigsaw puzzle, were either used as the foundation for a hearth or as flooring (or so it would seem). They formed the bulk of the pottery. Many of the rims were decorated with finger and nail impressions and in a variety of designs. In the surface levels there were a few modern sherds, no doubt to be associated with the digging of the vineyard trenches. There was one kylix stem, apparently Mycenaean. Otherwise, all the sherds insofar as they were datable were either Middle or Early Helladic. There was a certain amount of black Minyan of local manufacture in the upper levels, but it also occurred occasionally in the lower strata. Coarse red and black ware appeared in all levels. Incised ware (not often found) seemed to be confined largely to the upper ones.

W. D. T.

CHAMBER TOMB K-2
(Plan and Sections, Figs. 351-354)

About 17 m. to the east of the Protogeometric tholos on higher ground and in an olive grove (the property of John Kokkevis), is Chamber Tomb K-2 (Fig. 300). The hill in which it lies has been terraced and it is situated on the second terrace above the road. Attention was drawn to this spot by evidence of a clandestine excavation that had recently taken place. The potential tomb robbers knew enough about Mycenaean chamber tombs to recognize the entrance of a dromos, that is, the vertical cut in the rock revealed by subsidence of the soil filling the cutting. They had tunneled in the dromos, but fortunately to no great depth before their work was discovered.

The dromos and doorway were cleared at the end of the 1958 excavation season. The task took six days and four to five men were employed. One of them was used for sifting. The dromos and doorway were then filled in. In the season of 1959 the chamber was excavated. It was already clear from the previous year's work that the roof of the tomb had collapsed and the overlying soil and fallen rock had to be removed before the floor of the chamber was reached. It took nine days to clear the tomb. Three to four men were used in the early stages and six men towards the end. I had unfortunately to leave before the work was completed and the final operation, which took a day, was carried out under the supervision of Professor Lang.

The entrance to the tomb faces due west. The dromos is 4.30 m. long and slopes down with a very uneven surface toward the doorway. At its west (outer) end it is 0.75 m. broad at floor level. At a higher level the width narrows to 0.56 m., showing that the walls inclined inwards. As it approaches the tomb, the dromos widens out until it attains a width of 1.25 m. in front of the doorway. The latter was filled with a blocking wall (Fig. 280), which was preserved to a height of 1.56 m. This may represent the original height of the door. The width of the doorway was 0.75 m. at the dromos end and 0.90 m. at the entrance to the chamber. The door jambs were not uniform. The northern one measured 0.84 m. at its base but 1 m. higher the width was only 0.70 m. The corresponding measurements for the southern jamb were 0.95 m. at the floor and 0.80 m. higher up. Hence both door jambs had a batter in the west-east axis. This was more noticeable at the outer end and can be seen in the section of the dromos (Fig. 353). The blocking wall not only filled the doorway but extended a short distance into the dromos and partly overlapped the door jambs; or this appears to have been the original arrangement of a structure that had obviously been rebuilt many times. Only the bottom courses to a height of 0.30 m. remained of the original construction (Fig. 281). These courses were firmly laid to a thickness of 0.95 m. Higher up, the wall was loosely built and its thickness varied from 1 m. to 1.10 m. except near the top where it was much narrower (0.60 m.-0.070 m.), but no doubt many stones had fallen from the upper courses. When the wall was dismantled, the stones were found to be of all shapes and sizes. The largest was roughly 0.72 m. x 0.32 m. x 0.18 m. and triangular in shape.

That the dromos was not cleared to *stereo* on the frequent occasions when the tomb was reopened was indicated by the finding of stones above floor level in the passageway. These presumably came from the blocking wall. Three other stones were found in the entrance to the dromos. Although the section (Fig.

353) is not as informative as it might be, there is a clear indication of one reopening of the tomb where the darkest soil descends abruptly towards the doorway and stops at a level of 0.30 m. above *stereo,* that is, at the top course of the undisturbed foundations of the blocking wall. Another partial clearance of the dromos is perhaps shown by the V-shaped dip in the lighter soil overlying the dark earth. No pit was found in the dromos but there was a fair amount of pottery, of which the significant pieces were Late Helladic III C. A small fragment of an iron pin was found in sifting on the last day of the excavation (1958 campaign). The most notable find was part of a Late Helladic III C krater depicting a stag hunt(?) (Fig. 289a-e). Several of the sherds of this vase turned up in the earth thrown out by the would-be tomb robbers and it is to be feared that they may have made off with some of the best pieces.

As the chamber had to be dug from above (Fig. 282) and owing to the extreme difficulty of distinguishing the soft rock from excavated soil, the dimensions of the tomb could not be established with absolute certainty (Fig. 351). The chamber was roughly rectangular in plan and measured approximately 4.50 m.-4.60 m. from west to east and 3.30 m.-3.40 m. from north to south. There was no means of gauging its height, but the floor of the tomb was about 3.10 m. below the ground surface. The contents appeared to be undisturbed. The first objects to be found were a group of pots in the center of the tomb (Groups I and Ia — Figs. 283, 352). They consisted of a two-handled jar [1], a narrow-necked jug [2], a pedestaled bowl [6], a stirrup-jar [4], and a squat jug [7]; they are decorated in the style midway between Late Helladic III B and III C, but stylistically the two-handled jar is definitely III C. About 0.10 m. to the east of the squat jug was a bronze arrowhead with the point facing west. All the vases except the pedestaled bowl were intact and the base of this was found close by. Associated with these vases was a very poorly preserved skeleton of a child (Figs. 284, 352). The bones were all mixed up but the general layout had a west-east axis with the skull at the east. The remains had been placed in a pit. Not far removed to the northwest from this assemblage was another child's skeleton (Group II) in an even worse state of preservation, a mass of friable bones among which not even the skull was recognizable. This skeleton also lay with a west-east axis but apparently above the existing floor of the chamber. It may therefore be one of the last burials in the tomb. The only vase found with it was a Late Helladic III C cup [3] that lay just to the west of it (Fig. 293:3a, b). To the north of this burial was another group of pots (Group III), which seem to have been associated with a dismembered skeleton further to the west in the northwest part of the tomb. They were an angular alabastron [8], a composite vase [5] consisting of three alabastra, a conical krater [9], a narrow-necked jug [10], and a squat jug [11]—all Late

Helladic III C (Fig. 287). A lentoid sealstone was found between the vases and the skeleton. Whether by accident or design, two stones lay over the bones of the skeleton; but as this burial was close to the doorway these stones — and there were two more nearby — were most probably left over from the frequent building and dismantling of the blocking wall. On the other hand, other stones were found scattered all over the tomb and far from the doorway. They mostly had flat upper surfaces but were too thick to be described as slabs. When these pots from the north area of the tomb were taken up, further excavation revealed more scattered bones together with two skulls, and among this agglomeration two jugs [13, 15] and a plain cup [14] (Group v — Figs. 286, 354). One of the jugs [13] had linear decoration, the other [15] was plain. It is not certain that this interment was laid in a pit. It is more likely that it was just covered over with earth and the vases of the later burial (Group III) placed over it.

In the southwest corner of the chamber a large shallow bronze bowl with three handles, rectangular in plan, was uncovered. Not only was the shape of the handles unusual but they were made of twisted bronze, torque fashion. The bowl was finely decorated with repoussé and engraved designs. Immediately to the east was a pit containing three skulls and a mass of bones (Group IV — Figs. 285, 288, 352). No pottery was found with them except some fragments of a kylix [12] and a few sherds. But this interment was laid over an earlier one that contained four skulls with accompanying bones in disarray (Group VI — Fig. 354). With these was an almost complete vase, an undecorated three-handled jar [17] (Fig. 292:1), also fragments of two kylikes and two stirrup-jars [19, 20] (to right on plan). The latter were painted with Late Helladic III B designs and one of the stirrup-jars could be partly restored. A silver ring found in sifting could have belonged to either of these two groups and the same may be said of the bronze bowl, though I should be inclined to assign it to one of the later burials. In the northeast area of the chamber, and close to what must have been the wall of the tomb, two isolated vases were found (Group VII — Fig. 354). They were a small squat stirrup-jar [22] and an angular alabastron [21]. They were in the same axis as Group I but apparently not associated with it, as their style of decoration (Late Helladic III B) is earlier. In between the two collections of vases was a bronze mirror, which, lying ca. 0.40 m. to the east of the two-handled jar, is more probably to be associated with Group I. Finally, in the easternmost part of the chamber four complete vases came to light on the last day: a four-handled jar [26], a large narrow-necked jug [23], and two angular alabastra [24, 25] (Group VIII — Fig. 352). They were all decorated in an advanced Late Helladic III C style. A skull and a few fragments of small bones had previously been discovered in this area but they lay ca. 0.80 m. away from the nearest vase. However, as no other mortal remains were found in the vicinity of these pots, the skull is presumably to be associated with them. Other finds belonging to this group were a bronze sickle(?) just to the west of the large jug, a tiny fragment of burnt ivory(?) near the skull, and a collection of 26 gold beads that lay ca. 0.40 m. to the south of one of the alabastra. There was also a steatite button or whorl.

Altogether there were 13 burials (based on the skulls) in this tomb and 26 vases, including the three fragmentary kylikes. It is obvious that some of the dead were buried without pots or that some were removed later. One would have expected to find traces of them in the dromos, but apart from sherds there were only four or five fragmentary vases. The tomb was in use during the last half of Late Helladic III B and the whole of Late Helladic III C. The latest interment was undoubtedly the one against the east wall of the chamber (Group VIII) and the next latest the child burial with the cup (Group II). The latter would have been preceded by the disturbed skeleton which was accompanied by five vases (Group III). This pottery, it will be remembered, lay directly above two scattered skeletons that were buried with three pots (Group V). As these had no pattern they are not closely datable. The earliest interment would appear to be the second layer of skulls and bones in the south part of the chamber with which fragments of five pots were found, all of Late Helladic III B (Group VI). There is no means of dating the upper layer of skeletons (Group IV), but the kylix base found with them was not later than Late Helladic III B. There remains the pit burial in the center of the tomb (Group I). Five vases were closely associated with it and they were late Late Helladic III B or III C, so this must be one of the earlier interments (on account of its III B affinities). The two isolated pots in the northeast part of the tomb (Group VII) remain a mystery; there was no burial near them. The suggested sequence of burials above is, of course, based on the stylistic analysis of the pottery. It may not, therefore, be altogether valid. For greater clarity two plans are given of the tomb (Figs. 352, 354). The second plan shows the interments of Groups V and VI which lie below Groups III and IV respectively; and Group VII. Also included is the skeleton of Group III which is obscured in the first plan by stones laid over it. (The numbering of the groups is in the order in which the burials came to light.)

W. D. T.

Dromos

BRONZE

Two shapeless fragments (CM. 2143, Fig. 291:9, 10). Found in front of blocking wall near its bottom.

OBSIDIAN

Arrowhead (CM. 2153, Fig. 291:8): l. 0.013 m.; w. pres. ca. 0.009 m.; th. 0.0022 m. One barb chipped, the other missing. Miter shape, form of notch at butt not preserved. Secondary working on both faces.

POTTERY

Krater (CM. 1999, Fig. 289:a-e): h.0.24 m.; d. mouth ca. 0.33 m.; d. body ca. 0.31 m. Restored. About one-third preserved; half of rim, large parts of body missing. Shape, *MP*, Type 282, p. 49 fig. 14. Flat, horizontal rim, two round loop-handles, uptilted (not twisted as appears in Fig. 289d). Torus ring-base. Light buff, well-fired clay with green tinge. Black-brown, fairly lustrous paint. Pictorial design difficult to interpret. To left of handle a stag. To right of handle and facing stag a lion(?)[3] pursued by two dogs. Immediately behind them stands (or kneels?) a huntsman wearing a helmet that appears to be identical with those worn by warriors on "Warrior Vase."[4] No break in continuity of scene from stag to huntsman, but on other face of krater all that is preserved, apart from stag, is rear quarters of strange animal (dog?) under opposite handle (Fig. 289:e). Thick band at rim, three below design, one above base and on base itself. Handles painted with uneven brush work splashed round stumps. Inside of krater is monochrome. Late Helladic III C.

Kylix, fragment (CM. 2668, Fig. 290:1a, b). Restored: h. 0.205 m.; d. ca. 0.22 m.; w. handle 0.015 m. Two-thirds of bowl, most of handle, stem and base missing. Shape, *MP*, Type 275, p. 61 fig. 17. Straight-sided bowl. Handle rectangular in section, slightly grooved. Light brown-buff clay, fired hard to medium. Brown to black slightly lustrous paint. Close style decoration: on largest fragment Paneled Patterns (*MP*, Motive 75:30, p. 414 fig. 72) repeated twice with Zigzag (*MP*, Motive 61:18, p. 383 fig. 67) shown vertically to left of it; on left of this "metope" design are pendant loops from rim, on right of it part of spiral; on smaller fragment (opposite side of vase) same "metope" design used but with Motive 61:18 this time on right; a small part of spiral(?) can be seen further to right. Inside of bowl and outside of handle painted. Below pattern a series of circling lines and stripes (stripe, two lines, stripe, three lines). A stripe crosses lower half of design part way but this may be a mistake. Late Helladic III C.

Krater 1. About a sixth preserved including most of profile (Fig. 290:2a): h. pres. 0.275 m.; d. body estimated 0.35 m.; d. base 0.147 m. Shape, *MP*, Type 10, p. 65 fig. 18. Parts of rim (two pieces described below), both handles, most of body, and about a third of base missing. Pedestal made separately from body. Torus base; underside concave in form of truncated cone. Yellow-buff to pink hard-fired clay. Off-white slip? Dark brown to black paint is very slightly lustrous. Close style decoration based on Paneled Patterns (*MP*, Motive 75:17, p. 414 fig. 72) but more elaborate. Closely serried band decoration below design (three medium, one very thick, three medium). Solidly painted base. Inside vessel over-all monochrome. Late Helladic III C.

---

[3] Cf. the lion depicted on a krater fragment from Lefkandi (M. R. Popham and L. H. Sackett, *Excavations at Lefkandi, Euboea 1964-66* (London, 1968), 21, fig. 46 and *AR* 1965-66, 11, fig. 19).

[4] *Crete and Mycenae*, pl. 233.

Four other pieces seem to belong to this krater (Fig. 290:2b). Two are from rim with flat, horizontal lip: (i) h. pres. 0.057 m.; w. 0.195 m. (ii) h. pres. 0.054 m.; w. 0.10 m. Rim reproduces same panel design with further elaboration: vertical form of Zigzag (MP, Motive 61:18, p. 383 fig. 67) in center and on each side, and adjoining, is motive referred to above (MP, Motive 75:17, p. 414 fig. 72). Rim painted; band above design. Other two pieces are from body: (iii) h. 0.122 m., w. 0.115 m., shows same pattern as rim (shown attached to rim but does not join). (iv) h. 0.095 m., w. 0.125 m., has very little of design but reproduces some of band decoration below. All four pieces are painted on inside.

Krater 2. Four sherds including small part of rim and base (Fig. 290:3a-c).

(3a) Rim: h. pres. 0.135 m.; w. ca. 0.195 m.
(3b) h. 0.084 m.; w. 0.09 m.
(3c) h. 0.101 m.; w. 0.093 m.
(3d) (not illustrated) Base: h. pres. ca. 0.14 m.; w. ca. 0.17 m.

Hard-fired, yellow-buff clay. Off-white slip with slight green tinge. Dark brown to black paint, very slightly lustrous. (3a) very small part of rim, lip flat, horizontal. Largest piece has panel design, which has no close parallel. Resembles Elaborate Triangle (MP, Motive 71:h, p. 411 fig. 71); from that motive one must eliminate all lines, straight and curved, except for one curved line on each side of central element; these two lines are attached to the latter by hatching. To right and left of central motive, but some distance from it, is "triglyph" border like Joining Semicircles (MP, Motive 42:9, p. 343 fig. 57). Rim painted, band below. A thick line and a medium band is preserved below the design.

(3b) and (3c) from body (Fig. 290:3b, c); apparently represent birds. Not certain that they belong to this krater.[4a] (3b) rear part of bird and two curved lines to right; (3c) seems to show tail of one bird and part

of another; (3d) (not illustrated) preserves small part of base with band and thick line decoration above. All above sherds painted on inside.

Krater 3. Part of rim only preserved (Fig. 290:4). Shape, MP, 282(?), p. 49 fig. 14. Flat, horizontal lip. Slightly flaring rim with ridge at base of rim band decoration. Yellow-buff biscuit with pink outer surface, fired medium to hard. Dirty yellow slip. Red to brown very faded paint apparently matt. What is preserved of design shows most of one goat facing front part of second goat with "tree of life" in between, from which they are eating. Surface of lip painted with six strokes in white on dark. Inside of vase over-all monochrome. Late Helladic III C.

Chamber

GOLD

Spherical beads, 26 (CM. 2149, Fig. 291:12): average d. 0.0022 m., largest 0.0032 m. Similar beads found in chamber tomb at Mycenae displayed in National Museum of Athens. (NM. 9007).

SILVER

Ring (CM. 2147, Fig. 291:7): bezel, l. 0.027 m., w. 0.019 m.; ring, l. pres. 0.012 m., w. 0.005 m. Found in sifting. Bezel and small part of ring preserved. Very corroded.

BRONZE

Shallow three-handled vessel (CM. 2912, Fig. 291:1a-e): h. 0.095 m.; d. 0.287 m.-0.293 m.; l. handle 0.107 m.; w. 0.13 m. About two-thirds preserved. Fair condition after treatment. Restored. Parts of rim, pieces of body missing. Vessel in very poor state when taken up, original dimensions and profile of bowl not certain. May have been rounded, possibly with a slight carination, 0.045 m. below rim. Approximate dimensions of vessel when found: inner d. 0.23 m.; w. rim 0.028 m.; depth of bowl 0.08

[4a] But the decoration on the lower right hand corner of 3a may represent the tail of a bird.

m. Rim offset horizontally from bowl. Each handle is square in plan, consisting of two bronze rods twisted round one another in torque fashion. Ends riveted to rim. Arrangement of handles round bowl roughly symmetrical. One badly bent out of the horizontal, which was the original axis of all three handles.

Center of bowl decorated with six-leaf rosette, hammered out from back. Rest of bowl has pointillé decoration, interrupted by three undecorated bands or circles spaced between rosette and rim. Owing to wear, much of pointillé decoration has worn through and shows light. Design hammered out on rim from underside is unusual (see reconstruction in Fig. 291:1b). Consists of elongated, double-lined S spirals in series that follow one another round rim. From terminals of each S issues short ribbon-shaped appendage. S spirals occasionally reversed thus reproducing antithetic pattern, but no consistency about this. In one part of rim artist has miscalculated and series does not join up properly. Rim pattern throughout executed in hammered-dot-technique.

No Mycenaean parallel to this vessel either in shape[5] or in style of decoration. Rosette is about the only Mycenaean element in design. When he saw this bowl, Dr. Buchholz pointed out to me that the torque handles and the rim pattern are strongly reminiscent of Central European, in particular of Urnenfelder, workmanship; on his advice I wrote to Professor Müller-Karpe, who confirmed this opinion and gave me useful references on the subject.[6] But it is difficult to recognize this as Urnenfelder work or even a close connection with that culture on account of the chronological aspect. Earliest examples of duck motif, which rim decoration resembles, are not known before tenth century. The bronze vessel is not closely associated with any burial but cannot be later than latest pottery in tomb and dromos, which contain vases with advanced Late Helladic III C decoration. There is a gap of 100 to 150 years. Although resemblance with duck motif is striking, S spiral has long Mycenaean tradition. Even appendage to S spiral finds prototype in shaft graves though form is different.[7] Both S spiral and plain spiral frequently have some attachment throughout whole of Mycenaean period.[8] The inner rim decoration on a deep conical bowl (*MP*, Type 291, p. 53 fig. 15) from Langada, Cos, shows a curious affinity to design under discussion. The motif, repeated several times, is a spiral, to which is attached a duck's head on a long neck (*Annuario* XLIII-XLIV [1965-66], 120, fig. 101) or so it has been interpreted by the excavator: "una testa dal becco simile a quello delle anitre" (*ibid.*). Date, Late Helladic III C (late). Torque technique used in Central Europe and Near East from an

---

[5] A shattered, *shallow* bronze vessel from the Heraeum, impossible to reconstruct (*Prosymna*, 353), had depth of 0.10 m. and diameter of 0.35 m., but handles of Cypriot type.

[6] I should like to express my gratitude to these two scholars for their helpful advice and suggestions.

[7] *Schachtgräber*, pl. XIII, border of great gold diadem; same anomaly in arrangement of spirals, some following one another, others antithetic. Compare also S spirals *ibid.*, pl. LXXV:276 on the gold pommel covers; pl. LXXXIV:634 and 723 on gold hilt; and particularly design on pl. LXVII:271,

not unlike a duck's head.

[8] Compare double spiral, i.e., elaborate S spiral, with fill motifs on Late Helladic II jug (*Korakou*, pl. V); the treatment of the argonaut on Late Helladic III A three-handled jars from Ialysos (*Annuario* VI-VII [1926], 203, fig. 126; 213, fig. 136); arrangement of S spirals with fill motifs on larnax from Knossos (Evans, "The Prehistoric Tombs of Knossos," *Archaeologia* 59 [1905], pp. 480, 481, fig. 102a); the spirals with spurs on a silver goblet (*NT,Dendra*, pl. VI:2) and similar motif on ivory fragment from Palace of Nestor — Late Helladic III B? (*PN* I, fig. 284:1).

early date. Examples are known from Crete.[9] I think it unnecessary therefore to associate this bronze vessel with Urnenfelder culture, though it may have been produced under foreign influence.

Arrowhead (CM. 2146, Fig. 291:2): l. 0.093 m.; w. 0.015 m.; l. stem 0.024 m.; d. stem 0.003 m. Complete; much corroded. Shape of olive leaf with stem. Cf. similar arrowhead from chamber tomb at Thebes (*Deltion* 3 [1917], 188, fig. 134:6), and one from Ialysos (*Annuario* VI-VII [1926], 220, fig. 142:4787).

Sickle? (CM. 2151, Fig. 291:13): l. 0.122 m.; w. 0.025 m. Fragment, broken at both ends, very corroded. Blade pierced with hole at one end for hafting. Curved and tapers slightly at both ends; edge (not preserved) on inner curve of blade. Probably sickle, like one in Tiryns Treasure, though latter is iron (*AM* LV [1930], 136, fig. 6). If a knife, cf. *Annuario* VI-VII, 149, fig. 70, right (from Ialysos).

Bronze strip, folded (CM. 2154, Fig. 291:11). Perhaps part of above. Found in sifting.

STONE

Lentoid seal of black haematite (NM. 8535 = *CMS* I, No. 295): d. 0.018 m.-0.019 m.; th. 0.0085 m. More convex on one face than on other. No flattening of sides or rim for transverse perforation bored through seal from one side only. Close to smaller hole on other side, another bore-hole started but very little penetration made. Apparently original intention was to bore seal from both sides but was abandoned. Design worn or incomplete. What appears to be stag is shown standing with head turned back. One long antler, engraved near edge of seal, is shown. It seems to be separated from the root (of antler). Middle part of animal's body scarcely indicated.

Button or whorl (CM. 2152, Fig. 291:3): h.

0.017 m.; d. small end 0.01 m.; d. large end 0.024 m.; d. hole 0.0035 m. Complete. Furumark type a 1 (*MPChron*, 89, fig. 2). Mottled dark green steatite. Broad end badly chipped.

Miniature bead (CM. 2154, Fig. 291:4). Sifting.

IVORY?

Very small fragment (CM. 2148, Fig. 291:5): ca. 0.008 m. x ca. 0.005 m. Possibly burnt ivory. Incised with a few lines.

Pin, four fragments: longest piece l. ca. 0.022 m.; d. ca. 0.004 m. Neither head nor point preserved. Vertical striations or flutes on each piece, probably due to weathering.

POTTERY

Group I (Center of tomb—child burial)

Pedestaled bowl [6] (CM. 1750, Fig. 292:10): h. 0.091 m.; d. rim 0.112 m.; d. base 0.051 m. Almost complete. Restored. Pieces of rim missing. Shape, *MP*, Type 305 or 306, p. 65 fig. 18. Flaring rim. Underside of pedestal base has usual circular depression as on kylikes. Yellow-buff, medium to hard biscuit. Red to dark brown paint without luster. Decoration based on Antithetic Spiral (*MP*, Motive 50:9, p. 363 fig. 62) but without "triglyph." Arms of loop attached to one another by tielines and a fill element, Trefoil Rock-work (*MP*, Motive 29:10, p. 315 fig. 53) is placed in each loop. Below design, used on both sides of vase, is line between two bands. Thin band on rim. Base painted solidly. Handles decorated with three strokes of brush. Inside of vase is monochrome coat. Late Helladic III B-C.

Narrow necked jug [2] (CM. 1746, Fig. 293:9): h. 0.132 m.; d. mouth 0.037 m.; d. 0.134 m.; d. base 0.042 m. Almost intact. Shape, *MP*, Type 123, p. 31 fig. 6. Flaring rim lacking fragment. Flattened handle from neck to shoulder. Almost biconical body. Raised ring-base. Medium to hard-

---

[9] Evans, "The Prehistoric Tombs of Knossos," *Archaeologia* 59 [1905], 541, fig. 129. "Hooked pin of spirally twisted gold," l. 0.115 m. from the Royal Tomb, Isopata. Evans says "bronze pins of similar type have been found on other Cretan sites" and gives names of sites in footnote d (*loc. cit.*).

fired, white-buff clay. Self slip? Brown, slightly lustrous paint. Main design round zone just above widest diameter of vase based on lozenge and spiral in alternation. Lozenge is either crosshatched or has filling of arcs in two opposite angles. Spiral issues from one corner of lozenge and touches corner of next one. This composition repeated five times round vase, but one lozenge has extra spiral. Shoulder decoration consists of series of five triangles, three or four being inscribed within each triangle. Cf. *MP*, Motive 61A:1 (Triangle), p. 391 fig. 68. Upper and lower registers divided from one another by three narrow bands; this band decoration is repeated under lower design. Handle painted with vertical, wavy band and thick band encircles its base. Rim and bottom of neck also have bands. Late Helladic III C.

Stirrup-jar [4] (CM. 1748, Fig. 293:6a, b): h. 0.122 m.; d. 0.12 m.; d. base 0.047 m. Intact. Broken spout mended. Shape, *MP*, Type 176, p. 31 fig. 6. Flat disk. Rounded to beveled rim of spout. Base concave and slightly conical. Brown-buff, well-fired clay. Self slip. Dark brown, slightly lustrous paint. Vase decorated with Scale Pattern (*MP*, Motive 70:7, p. 403 fig. 70), which covers most of jar including disk; rather careless execution. Handles painted with horizontal strokes and rim of spout with dots. Thin band links spout and false neck. Late Helladic III B-C.

Squat jug [7] (CM. 1751, Fig. 292:14): h. 0.084 m.; d. mouth 0.041 m.; d. 0.081 m.; d. base 0.035 m. Shape, *MP*, Type 114, p. 31 fig. 6. Intact. Biconical to spherical body. Fairly broad splaying neck. Mouth has very slight beak. Round, vertical handle from rim to shoulder. Slightly conical, raised base, concave on underside. Pink, well-fired biscuit, yellow slip; red, slightly lustrous paint. Shoulder decoration: Wavy Line (*MP*, Motive 53:25, p. 373 fig. 65); band at base of neck, three at widest diameter of jug, one on base; thick band on

underside of base, an irregular band round bottom of handle, painted with seven horizontal strokes. Thick band on inside of rim. Late Helladic III B-C.

Group Ia (Center of tomb)

Amphora [1] (CM. 1745, Figs. 292:16, 293:4): h. 0.277 m.; d. neck 0.084 m.; d. 0.258 m.; d. base 0.092 m. Almost complete. Restored. Small part of rim and several pieces from the body missing. Shape, *MP*, Type 70, p. 596. Flattened ovoid body. Flaring neck. Molded rim, concave on inside. Two flattened, vertical handles joining neck and shoulder. Handles slanted toward neck. Torus, flat base. Well-fired, pink biscuit covered with buff slip. Dark brown, very slightly lustrous paint. Vase solidly coated except for shoulder decoration, reserved band just above greatest diameter, and lower part of jar. Shoulder decoration on one side Parallel Chevrons (*MP*, Motive 58:28, p. 383 fig. 67) with, on each side, motive based on Isolated Semicircles (*MP*, Motive 43:4, p. 343 fig. 57). Other side has similar decoration but flanking motive is Motive 43:h, p. 345 fig. 58. Handles solidly painted on outside with encircling band at base. Dots used on rim and inside of neck painted. Late Helladic III C. This vase stylistically is later than Group I and may not belong to it, but in that case it is an isolated vase unconnected with any burial.

Group II (Northwest—child burial)

Cup [3] (CM. 1747, Fig. 293:3a, b): h. 0.078 m.; d. 0.124 m.; d. base 0.039 m.; w. handle 0.013 m. Almost complete. Restored. Pieces of rim missing, base chipped. Shape, *MP*, Type 216, p. 49 fig. 14. Flaring rim. Roundish vertical handle. High, rounded conical base, hollow on underside with rough "button" in center. Yellow-buff clay except at base where pink. Fired hard to medium. Red to brown, lusterless paint. Outside of cup is undecorated; inside painted with filled circle at center surrounded by band. Two bands further up in bowl and two more at rim. Upper part of handle painted on outside. Late Helladic III C.

Group III (North—with dismembered skeleton)

Deep conical bowl [9] (CM. 1766, Figs. 292:9, 293:5): h. 0.119 m.; d. rim 0.237 m.; d. base 0.10 m. Intact but chipped. Shape, *MP*, Type 291, p. 53 fig. 15. Sides of bowl are concave, lower part expanding slightly. Flat rim, slightly beveled outwards; two horizontal, round loop-handles just beneath rim; flat base. Pink, well-fired clay with yellow slip. Red, very slightly lustrous paint, overpainted in white on rim and inside of bowl. Outside decoration: Wavy Line (*MP*, Motive 53:20, p. 373 fig. 65) between handles with thick band above reaching rim and four horizontal lines in two pairs below. Lower part of vessel painted solid, except for small strip at base. Outside handles solidly painted. Large blobs of paint disfigure outer surface of vase. Inside of bowl is coated over-all except for bottom, decorated with filled circle surrounded by thick ring. Inside decoration in white consists of Zigzag (*MP*, Motive 61:18, p. 383 fig. 67) bordered by two thin bands above and below. Pattern incomplete in one place and does not join up, potter having failed to mark out his triangles beforehand! Thin band below rim, upper surface of which painted with five groups of 10 to 13 strokes, also in white. Late Helladic III C.

Narrow necked jug [10] (CM. 1753, Fig. 292:2): h. 0.10 m.; d. 0.10 m.; d. mouth 0.042 m.; d. base 0.044 m. Almost complete. Restored. Bit of rim and handle, pieces of body missing. Shape, *MP*, Type 123, p. 31 fig. 6. Small version of CM. 1746 above, similar in shape. Flat vertical handle joins neck just below rim. Ring-base. Underside of jug slightly concave. Soft to medium-fired, pink clay. Dirty white slip. Red to dark brown paint without luster. Shoul-

der decoration: Isolated Semicircles (*MP*, Motive 43:h, p. 345 fig. 58) with same motive reversed, and on smaller scale, in interstices. Pattern bordered by stripe above and below. Zonal band of two lines between two stripes just underneath. One stripe on lower part of jug. Solid area at bottom overlapping ring-base. Handle painted on outside with thick circle round its base. Upper part of neck painted inside and out. Late Helladic III C.

Squat jug [11] (CM. 1754, Fig. 292:13): h. 0.085 m.; d. mouth 0.048 m.; d. 0.081 m.; d. base 0.033 m. Almost complete. Restored. Two pieces of rim missing. Shape (*MP*, Type 114, p. 31 fig. 6) and decoration very similar to CM. 1751 above. Roundish oblong, vertical handle. Raised base; underside slightly concave, has a small "button" in center. Yellow-buff biscuit, fired hard to medium. Red-brown, slightly lustrous paint. Decoration: Wavy Line (*MP*, Motive 53:25, p. 373 fig. 65) on shoulder. Three bands below design. Thick band at base of neck. Band encircles rim. Back of handle painted. Late Helladic III C.

Composite vase [5] (CM. 1749, Fig. 293:7): h. three vases 0.082 m.; h. complete with handle 0.147 m.; w. 0.122 m.; d. base of one vase 0.06 m. Almost complete. Restored. Piece of rim of one vase missing. Shape, *MP*, Type 96, p. 44 fig. 12, triple handleless jars comprising Type 330, p. 642. Three angular alabastra, flaring necks, beveled rims, attached to one another in horizontal axis. Three flattish clay strips rise from junction points of vases joining together in apex surmounted by clay ring. Each vase has triangular-shaped leg holding up whole composition. Greenish-yellow clay, fairly hard-fired. Black, non-lustrous paint, much worn in places, covers the entire complex except underside of vases. Inside of necks painted. Late Helladic III C.

Angular alabastron [8] (CM. 1752, Fig. 292:3):

h. 0.075 m.; d. mouth 0.058 m.; d. 0.082 m.; d. base 0.08 m. Almost complete. Restored. Pieces of rim and body missing. Shape, *MP*, Type 96, p. 44 fig. 12. Flaring neck. Outward beveled lip. Two round loop-handles, practically vertical, almost angular at apex. Flattened slightly convex base. Medium-fired, yellow-buff clay. Self slip? Dark brown paint without luster. Shoulder decoration Quirk (*MP*, Motive 48:18, p. 360 fig. 61) on both sides of jar. Thick band below design, on vertical face, and base. Bottom of vase bears three concentric circles. Handles painted; also neck inside and out. Late Helladic III C.

Group IV (Southwest — with scattered skeleton and bronze bowl)

Kylix fragments [12]. Too small to make up. No dating possible.

Group V (North — Lower layer with dismembered skeletons)

Broad necked jug [13] (CM. 1755, Fig. 293: 11): h. 0.136 m.; d. mouth 0.053 m.; d. 0.107 m.; d. base 0.042 m. Intact. Shape, *MP*, Type 110, p. 35 fig. 7. Biconical body. Slightly flaring rim; thick flattened vertical handle from rim to shoulder; flat base. Medium-fired, yellow-buff clay. Brown, worn paint. Band decoration only: three bands round greatest girth, one at base of neck. Two blobs of paint on handle. Late Helladic III B.

Cup, small [14]. Not seen in the museum. It was a small plain cup of dark brown to black clay.

Broad necked jug [15] (CM. 1756, Fig. 293: 10): h. 0.135 m.; d. mouth estimated 0.058 m.; d. 0.114 m.; d. base 0.04 m. Almost complete. Restored. Large piece from rim and neck missing. Shape, *MP,* Type 109, p. 35 fig. 7. Similar shape to CM. 1755 above. Body more spherical, handle joins body at slightly lower level. Flat base. Medium to hard-fired, greenish-white clay.

Undecorated. Late Helladic III B-C.

Group VI (Southwest — Lower layer with dismembered skeletons)

Three-handled jar [17] (CM. 1757, Fig. 292: 1): h. estimated 0.134 m.; d. 0.106 m.; d. base 0.048 m. Restored: whole neck and rim missing. Shape, *MP*, Type 48, p. 44 fig. 12. Piriform with constriction towards base. Three horizontal round, loop-handles, uptilted. Pseudo-ring-base, underside markedly hollow. Pink-brown, hard-fired biscuit. Undecorated. Late Helladic III B.

Stirrup-jar [19] (CM. 1758, Figs. 292:5, 293:1): h. pres. 0.04 m.; w. max. span 0.08 m. Upper part only and most of one handle preserved. Exact shape unknown. Brown biscuit with pink tinge, fired hard to medium. Pink-buff slip. Black to brown paint no longer lustrous. Design: "Sea Anemone" (*MP*, Motive 27:17, p. 315 fig. 53) with many fewer dots. Part of zonal band below design. False top painted with two concentric circles. Two oblique bars on surviving handle. Bases of spout and false neck linked with band. Late Helladic III B?

Stirrup-jar [20] (CM. 1759, Figs. 292:12, 293:2): h. pres. 0.082 m.; d. 0.09 m. About two-thirds complete. Restored. Base and parts of body missing. Shape, *MP*, Type 171 or 173, p. 31 fig. 6. False top has slight mound. Pink-brown clay. Yellow-buff slip. Dark brown to reddish-brown paint, most of luster gone. Shoulder decoration: Mycenaean III Flower (*MP*, Motive 18:109, p. 293 fig. 45), with dots instead of dashes. Typical zonal band decoration: upper and lower bands separated by two horizontal stripes. Part of third zonal band preserved at base. Handles painted except for reversed triangle near false top. Rim of spout painted, thick band at its base. Smaller band encircles false neck. Late Helladic III B.

Kylix fragments. Pieces of two but no restoration was possible. Apparently Late Helladic III B.

Group VII (Northeast — no burial)

Angular alabastron [21] (CM. 1760, Fig. 292:8): h. 0.12 m.; d. rim 0.095 m.; d. 0.162 m. Complete but chipped in many places. Shape, *MP,* Type 94 or 96, p. 44 fig. 12. Concave neck, outward beveled rim, three round loop-handles, almost vertical. Slightly convex base. Yellow-buff biscuit with slight green tinge, fired soft to medium. Self slip. Faded brown paint. Shoulder decoration: Foliate Band (*MP,* Motive 64:21, p. 397 fig. 69) with inscribed triangles under handles. Above pattern narrow band and six circling lines reaching neck, painted solid. Line decoration used on beveled rim (very indistinct). Inside of neck painted. Decorative scheme for body decoration consists of band with line above and below, used on shoulder, half way down, and on base. Two groups of concentric circles on bottom of vase. Late Helladic III B.

Stirrup-jar [22] (CM. 1761, Fig. 292:11): h. 0.087 m.; d. 0.129 m.; d. base 0.057 m. Complete but many cracks and badly chipped. Restored. Shape, *MP,* Type 180, p. 31 fig. 6. Disk on false neck slightly convex. Ring-base. Rather soft-fired, pink biscuit. Whitish-yellow slip. Red to brown very worn paint. Shoulder design: based on Mycenaean III Flower (*MP,* Motive 18:139, p. 293 fig. 45). Typical zonal band below pattern. Another zonal band on and below greatest diameter. On disk solid center surrounded by two circles. Back of handles painted, reserved triangle near disk. Careless band round rim and base of spout. Another band round base of false neck. Late Helladic III B.

Group VIII (East)

Large narrow-necked jug [23] (CM. 1762, Fig. 292:7): h. 0.212 m.; d. mouth 0.063 m.; d. 0.196 m.; d. base 0.087 m. Almost complete. Restored. Two pieces from body missing; base chipped. Shape, *MP,* Type 120, p. 31 fig. 6. Ovoid to spherical body. Narrow neck with flaring rim. Flat, vertical handle from below rim to shoulder. Raised flat base. Light brown-buff clay, medium-fired. Self slip? Black to brown, non-lustrous paint. Shoulder design: Joining Semicircles (*MP,* Motive 42:21, p. 343 fig. 57) in four groups; two have flat top (i.e., no apex). Three bands below design, three on lower part of body, one at base, one at bottom of neck, one just below rim, one on rim, overlapping slightly onto top of lip. Handle painted outside with reserved triangle at top. Late Helladic III C.

Angular alabastron [24] (CM. 1763, Fig. 292:4): h. 0.063 m.; d. mouth 0.048 m.; d. 0.083 m.; d. base 0.083 m. Almost complete. Restored. Part of rim missing; body chipped and cracked. Shape appears to be unique; does not correspond with any in Furumark's catalogue (cf. *MP,* Type 96, p. 44 fig. 12). Flaring rim with rounded edge, very high shoulder with correspondingly low, vertical body. Two flat loop-handles, uptilted. Flat base. Pink-buff biscuit, medium-fired. Self slip. Red to brown paint. Band decoration only: three lines between two bands on lower part; two circling lines on shoulder below solid coating covering neck and upper part of shoulder. Handles painted on outside. Late Helladic III C.

Angular alabastron [25] (CM. 1764, Fig. 293:8): h. 0.106 m.; d. mouth 0.086 m.; d. 0.128 m.; d. base 0.125 m. Almost complete; restored. Several bits of rim missing, body cracked. Shape, *MP,* Type 96, p. 44 fig. 12. Flaring neck, two handles, roundish in section, set almost vertically. Flat base with beveled edge. Pink clay with white grits, fired medium to hard. White slip. Red non-lustrous paint. Shoulder decoration: three crosshatched triangles bordered by dots on each panel between handles. A circling line round top of shoulder touches apex of each triangle. Vertical face of vase, neck, inside of rim, and handles solidly painted. Late Helladic III C. Compare decoration on sherds from Dymaion Wall (*Praktika* 1964, pl. 65:β).

Amphora [26] (CM. 1765, Fig. 292:15): h. 0.334 m.; d. rim 0.123 m.; d. 0.323 m.; d. base 0.107 m. Almost complete. Restored. Part of rim and pieces of body missing. Shape, *MP*, Type 58, p. 36 fig. 8. Ovoid to spherical body. Concave neck, outward beveled lip. Two round loop-handles, up-tilted, on middle of body; two lugs, pierced horizontally, on upper part of shoulder with axis at right angles to handles. Raised, flat base. Pink, medium-fired biscuit. Pink-ish-yellow slip? Red to dark brown paint without luster. Shoulder decoration same as that on preceding vase, CM. 1764, but on larger scale. Reversed Isolated Semi-circles (*MP*, Motive 43:j, p. 345 fig. 58) inserted in intervening space between two triangles in two cases. Band decoration: three bands below design, one on lower part of body, and one at base of neck. Brushwork painting of handles. Lugs and neck, inside and out, painted. Late Helladic III C. Compare similar amphora from Tra-ganes (*EphArch,* 1914, 106, fig. 9).

W. D. T.

PROTOGEOMETRIC THOLOS
(Plan and Section, Figs. 355-356)

This small tholos is about three kilometers (two miles by road) south of the palace and on the main road from Chora to modern Pylos (Navarino) (Fig. 300). The road descends from Ano Englianos and after a steep fall in three hairpin bends it turns south on level ground. About 100 m. further on and on the left as one travels to Pylos (i.e., on the east side of the road) the remnants of this tholos are visible in the steep cutting for the road. It lies almost opposite a soli-tary olive tree. Approximately 5 m. to the north of the tomb the number 436 is painted on the rock (the number of the road?). The village of Koryphasion is about one kilometer down the road.

Today the tomb looks like the ruined apse of a small chapel (Fig. 294), but when it was discovered it formed part of the embankment and it was only with difficulty that its outline could be discerned among the thick undergrowth (Fig. 295). Cleaning of the face of the cutting showed up the section and it was liter-ally a section, for the tomb had been sliced vertically in two, when the modern road was built in 1894-95. This half tholos and a chamber tomb (pp. 224ff.) lie within the property of Mr. John Kokkevis, and I should like to express my sincere thanks to him for allowing us to work in his olive grove.

The excavation of the tholos took only three and a half days, but the sifting of the soil required a couple of days more. Two men were employed. There was no dromos; this had presumably been cut away in the making of the new road. Nor was there any evidence of a doorway. A little over half the tholos had been preserved to a height of ca. 1.20 m. The lower courses had been laid vertically up to a height of ca. 0.50 m. Above this level the succeeding courses started to overlap one another very slightly inducing the barely perceptible curve of the vault. At ca. 0.95 m. above *stereo* the curvature began to be more pronounced and each successive course projected beyond the one below to an increasing extent. At first the overhang was only 0.03 m.; for the next two courses it was 0.04 m. each and for the following two 0.07 m. each. These measurements were taken for the five uppermost courses which were the only ones accessible for that purpose. From such small data it is difficult to arrive at an accurate estimate of the height of the dome but, if one allows for an average projection of 0.07 m. and an average thickness of 0.06 m. for each stone, it would take nine courses more to reach the level of the capping stone. On that basis the height of the tholos would be ca. 1.75 m. The diameter of the tomb could be more easily determined at 2.35 m. The tholos seems to have been built of one thickness of stones only. These varied much in size. They were seldom more than 0.30 m.-0.35 m. in length and this measurement represents the thickness of the wall; one of the longest was 0.40 m. The width did not as a rule exceed 0.25 m. The stones were usually flat and their thickness also varied a great deal. Sometimes it was as much as 0.12 m.-0.14 m. and stones with this dimension seem to have been used mostly for the lower part of the wall. But a great many of the stones had a thickness of 0.06 m.-0.08 m. and these often appear in the upper part of the vault. The largest of all had the following dimensions: 0.52 m. x 0.38 m. x 0.15 m. It may have been the capping stone.

The tholos was excavated from the top downwards in two separate operations, the south quadrant being dug first (Figs. 296, 355). In this manner a section was given of the north half of the tomb (Figs. 297, 356). This shows some fallen stones of varying thickness. Most of them are of the thinner type but one large stone lies almost on the floor of the tomb. Because of its greater size it may have fallen from the doorway. The top layer or stratum occupies about a third of the section. It is the darkest of all and represents the latest fill after the collapse of the tomb. The roots of vegetation and rotted organic matter have no doubt contributed to its color. The layer below is light brown. It takes up about half the section and is earlier fill. Below that comes a dark grayish-brown stratum. This is the area of the burial and it rests on the lowest stratum of all, the floor of the tholos, which is of a light grayish-brown color. This layer is thickest near the wall and tapers towards the center of the tomb.

The burial or burials had been thoroughly disturbed, but I do not think the modern builders of the road can be blamed for this. It is true that the only skull found was near the center of the tomb and consequently part of the skeleton may have been quarried away in engineering activity, but other bones, though few, were found scattered about in the surviving part of the chamber and they included the fragment of a skull; whether this was part of another skull is not certain. A small shallow pit against the east wall, ca. 0.65 m. x 0.20 m., was investigated (Fig. 355). It was only 0.08 m.-0.10 m. deep and contained nothing. Six vases came from this tomb: two amphorae, two small deep bowls or cups of Granary style, one lekythos, and one cup. The fragments of the amphorae and the lekythos were found scattered over the northeast quadrant of the tholos. These vases could only partly be made up. No doubt the missing pieces were in that part of the chamber that had been dug away. One deep bowl was found near the east wall of the tomb, the other lay against the southeast wall, and the one-handled cup next to, and on the east side of, the skull. Small objects from the tholos were few, in bad condition, and of poor quality. Nothing was found in its place and it would appear that the tomb had been rifled. Recovered were fragments of the blade of an iron knife, of the shaft of an iron pin, of the spherical head of another (coated with bronze and in a very corroded state), a plain bronze ring, a stone bead, and two buttons or spindle whorls (one of terracotta and one of steatite).

The pottery recovered from the tholos is of the Protogeometric Period and there appears to be nothing earlier. The two deep bowls, or rather two-handled cups, are indeed painted in the Granary style; they are monochrome inside and out except for a reserved band between the handles. This style, however, carried on into the later period. The continuity of the Mycenaean into the Protogeometric is exemplified not only in the pottery but in the architecture, and perhaps in dress (the buttons of Mycenaean form). In architecture it was evident that the science of the tholos building had not been forgotten in this part of Greece, though the size of the tomb is now much reduced. This small Protogeometric tomb was until recently unique in this area, but in 1967 another tholos was discovered at Karpophora, Messenia (*AAA* 2 [1968], 205-9). Its height is 1.22 m. and the diameter varies from 1.70 m. to 1.90 m. If one excludes the rather doubtful tholoi with Geometric vases in Achaia (*Opuscula Atheniensia* V [1965], 101—P. Åström), there are no other tholoi of this period on the mainland except in Messenia and again in Thessaly, where there is a considerable number. It is hard to think of any connection, though traditionally these two distant regions were related; the Neleids came to Pylos from Iolkos in Thessaly. But there are also several vaulted tombs of this period in East Crete (V. Desborough, *The Last Mycenaeans*, 187 and 268)—though the foundations are square—and strong connections with Crete have already been noted in a much earlier period in the case of the Grave Circle.[10]

---

[10] I am greatly indebted to Mr. Desborough for his comments on my account of this tomb and for many useful suggestions he has made.

OBJECTS FOUND

BRONZE

Ring (CM. 2125, Fig. 298:5): outer d. 0.023 m.; w. 0.005 m.; th. 0.0025 m. Corroded and in four fragments. Plain, like wedding ring.

IRON

Pin with bronze-covered head, fragment (CM. 2127, Fig. 298:2): l. pres. 0.0325 m.; d. head 0.013 m.; d. shaft ca. 0.005 m. Shaft much corroded. A metal disk at the end corresponding to "fins" or "collars" on Geometric pins disintegrated when pin was taken up. Head once spherical.

Long pin (CM. 2130, Fig. 298:7): l. as found ca. 0.29 m.-0.30 m.; d. 0.0085 m.-0.01 m. In pieces, very corroded. Two pieces found by skull probably belong to pin head above.

Long pin in fragments (CM. 2123, Fig. 298: 9): *In situ* length measured ca. 0.24 m. Corroded. From north quadrant of tomb.

Two knives (CM. 2136, Fig. 298:1): fragments only, much corroded; broken up since original measurements taken (a) l. pres. 0.127 m., w. 0.032 m.; (b) l. pres. 0.082 m., w. 0.023 m. Fragment (b) still retains rivet, plain pin with d. ca. 0.0025 m. H. of rivet above hilt: ca. 0.002 m.

Blade (CM. 2132, Fig. 298:3): fragment perhaps belonging to one of above.

STONE

Button or whorl (CM. 2134, Fig. 298:8): h. 0.0155 m.; d. broad end 0.0245 m.; d. small end 0.009 m.; d. hole 0.0055 m. Chipped. Furumark type a 1 (*MPChron*, 89, fig. 2). Mottled purple steatite. Asymmetrical work.

Large bead (CM. 2137, Fig. 298:6): h.0.0135 m.; d. 0.027 m.; d. hole 0.005 m. Upper and lower surfaces pitted. Roughly shaped like drum. Mottled purple steatite(?) harder than CM. 2134 above.

A few bits of obsidian and flint.

SHELL

Fragments of mother-of-pearl, perhaps for decorating haft of knife or dagger.

TERRACOTTA

Button or whorl (CM. 2126, Fig. 298:4): h. 0.021 m.; d. broad end 0.0305 m.; d. small end 0.01 m.; d. hole 0.006 m. Complete. Form same as CM. 2134 above. Broad end of button concave. Reddish clay burnt black on one side with purple patches. Coarse ware containing pebbly grits.

POTTERY

Two-handled cup or small bowl (CM. 1657, Fig. 298:13): h. 0.073 m.; d. rim 0.075 m.; d. base 0.037 m. Pieces from rim, bowl, and base missing; restored. Spherical body. Flaring lip. Two round loop-handles, up-tilted. Raised, conical slightly convex base, small "button" on inside of bottom. Pink to yellow-buff clay, lighter on outside (slip?); medium-fired. Faded brown to black paint, not lustrous; covering over-all inside and out, except for reserved band in handle zone and another on inner side of lip.

One-handled cup (CM. 1658, Fig. 298:10): h. 0.097 m.; d. 0.095 m.; d. rim 0.075 m.; d. base 0.041 m. Pieces missing from rim and bowl. Restored. Flat, vertical handle attached to rim. Offset lip. Ovoid body. High, conical, slightly flaring base markedly hollow on underside. Light brown clay, rather soft-fired; faded paintwork, mostly red outside, black inside. Paint over-all inside and out except for reserved band with cross-hatching below the rim.

Two-handled cup or small bowl (CM. 1659, Fig. 298:12): h. 0.069 m.; d. rim 0.082 m.; d. 0.089 m.; d. base 0.042 m. Almost all rim, part of body, and one handle missing. Restored. Similar in shape to CM. 1657 but more biconical. Round loop-handles, up-tilted. Everted lip. Ring base with concave outer profile. Greenish-yellow clay, soft-fired. Very faded black paint, not lustrous. Decoration: same as CM. 1657 above.

Lekythos (CM. 1660, Fig. 298:11): h. pres. 0.083 m.; h. with handle 0.098 m.; d. neck-restored-0.025 m.; d. 0.09 m.; d. base 0.043 m. Rim, neck, part of handle, and part of body missing. Restored. Biconical body. Conical base, concave underneath. Reddish-pink to buff clay, medium-fired. Brown slip? Reddish-brown to dark brown paint, somewhat faded but slightly lustrous. Decoration: four groups of inscribed triangles in shoulder zone above three thin to medium bands. Lower half of vase painted solid. Handle (not restored) oblong in section, painted with horizontal bars.

Amphora (CM. 1661, Fig. 298:15): h. 037 m.; d. rim 0.142 m.; d. neck 0.092 m.; d. 0.267 m.; d. base 0.122 m. Small pieces of rim, neck, handles, and large part of body missing. Restored. Squared and projecting horizontal lip slightly hollowed on inside. Two flat, vertical handles, 0.03 m. wide, from upper part of neck to top of shoulder. Narrow plastic band on neck decorated with diagonal incisions. Conical ring base. Underside convex. Soft-fired, orange clay, rather powdery. Pink slip? Red to black paint, much worn, perhaps slightly lustrous. Shoulder decoration: one panel with cross-hatched diamond between compass-drawn circles (or spirals?); the other panel has similar decoration but with vertical cross-hatched oblong in place of diamond. Below design three narrower between two broad bands, followed by two narrow and one

thick band lower down. Lower part of vase apparently coated over-all. Rim seems painted outside only. Handle (only one preserved) painted with horizontal bars, vertical sides also painted. Decoration of neck: one medium band above and below plastic ridge; two stripes at level of top of handles; one band at base of neck.

Amphora (CM. 1662, Fig. 298:14): h. 0.35 m.; d. rim 0.146 m.; d. 0.35 m.; d. base 0.113 m. About half preserved. Large parts of body, rim, and handles missing. Restored. Spherical body. Concave neck with splaying rim. Flat, horizontal lip. Two uptilted loop-handles, round in section, placed just above maximum diameter of jar; two lugs in axis at right angles to the above, set high on shoulder. Conical ring base; underside slightly convex. Whitish-yellow clay with very slight green tinge. Black, very worn paint. Design mostly obliterated. Traces of wavy line between two stripes in handle zone. Horizontal zigzag line between thick bands recognizable on part of neck. Other side of neck might have had wavy line high up, but this doubtful; in any case no room for zigzag pattern. Rest of jar seems painted over-all. Handles and base painted.

The following comments on the pottery have been supplied to me by Mr. Vincent Desborough on the basis of photographs and descriptions submitted to him: [11]

"I appreciate that you cannot tell how many burials there were, but I think one would have to assume that the vases are a single group. That being the case, they should fall within the Protogeometric period, on the basis of CM. 1661 (Fig. 298:15), and I doubt whether the date is much earlier than ca. 950 B.C. The most helpful vase is probably CM. 1658 (Fig. 298:10), as it is clearly related to a characteristic shape of the West Peloponnese, Ithaca, and Aetolia, current at the end of the tenth century and during the ninth (for a good discussion, see J. N. Coldstream, *Greek Geometric Pottery* [London, 1968], 221ff.), and it is of great interest that a similar vase should now have been found in Messenia.

[11] Once more I am indebted to Mr. Desborough and I have to thank him for his kind permission to publish this information.

"What, however, of the other vases? CM. 1662 is surprisingly close in shape to an amphora from Ancient Elis (*Ergon* 1961, 188, fig. 191). CM. 1657 and CM. 1659 surely go back for their eventual origin to the Granary Class—do they reflect the survival of a local tradition? I do not think one can tell, since as yet there is so little other material.

"Assuming that this is a single group—and it looks as though it could be— there seems to me to be three points of particular stylistic interest. There is the influence of the Athenian Protogeometric style (now clear from Karpophora, *AAA* 2, 205ff., and Antheia [Thouria], *Deltion* 20 B² [1965] 207, pl. 215:α-γ), there is the link with the West Peloponnese, and there is the suggestion of the survival of a local tradition going back to latest Mycenaean times."

W. D. T.

INDEX OF REFERENCES TO ILLUSTRATIONS

Pages

1. Northeast Gateway and Circuit Wall. From North. 1960 .... 4, 5, 7
2. Stone Steps in Gateway, Lateral Walls, and Water Channel. From Northeast. 1959 .... 4, 5
3. Circuit Wall to Northwest of Gateway. From North by East. 1959 6
4. Northeast Gateway, Tholos Tomb IV Beyond Hollow. From South. 1960... 4
5. Pavement of Tile Fragments of Medieval Building. From North. 1959..... 6
6. Dilapidated Arc of Stones in Front of Northeast Wall. From Northeast. 1959 7
7. Trench W 2: Fallen Stones. From North. 1959..................... 8
8. Trench W 4: Fallen Stones North of Wall. From North. 1959 8
9. Trench W 6: Transverse Wall. From South. 1959.................. 8
10. Trench W 6: Fall of Stones in Upper Part. From Northwest. 1959 8
11. Trench W 8: Wall on Northwest Slope. From North. 1959.................... 9
12. Trench W 9: Transverse Wall. From Southwest. 1963.......................... 9
13. Trench W 13: Wall. From West. 1961.................... 10
14. Trench W 12: Pot against Wall. From North. 1962.................... 10
15. Trench W 15: Wall. From West by North. 1961 11
16. Trench W 17: Northwest of West Corner of Palace. From North by East. 1961 11
17. Trench W 19: Section of Circuit Wall. From Southeast. 1964 12
18. Trench W 19: Pavement of Stones. From North. 1964 12
19. Trench W 19: Circuit Wall. From Northeast. 1964.................... 12
20. Trench W 19: Stucco Pavement. From Northwest. 1960 12
21. Trench W 19: Circuit Wall, Outside Face. From Southwest by West. 1964... 12
22. Trench W 20: Early Wall Laid on or against Foundation of Building X. From Southwest. 1965 12
23. Trench W 20: Foundation of South Wall of Building X. From South by West. 1965....................... 13
24. Trench W 20: Stratification in Deposit against Face of Circuit Wall. From South by West. 1964....................... 13
25. Trench W 21: Two Crumbling Walls in South Corner. From East. 1965... 14
26. Trench W 21: Space between Walls in South Corner. From Northwest. 1965....................... 14
27. Trench W 21: Northeast Face of Northeastern Wall. From Northwest. 1965....................... 14
28. Trench W 21: Southern Wall. From East. 1965..................... 14
29. Trench W 28: Wall. From Northwest. 1959..................... 15
30. Trench W 30: Column Base. From West. 1962.................... 15
31. Trench W 32: Stones. From Southeast. 1962.................... 15
32. Trench W 33: Stones. From Northwest. 1962.................... 15
33. Trench W 33: Scattered Stones. From East. 1962 15
34. Trench W 34: Stones in Black Earth. From Southeast. 1962................... 16
35. Trench W 35: From Southeast. 1962 17
36. Trench W 36: From Southeast. 1962 17
37. Trench W 38: Belvedere. From Southeast. 1965.................... 17, 22, 23

Pages

38. Trench W 39: From Southeast. 1959 17
39. Trench W 45: From Northeast. 1959 .... 5, 17
40. Trench W 46: From Northeast. 1959 17
41. View of Pylos, Navarino, Sphacteria from Belvedere. 1960 18
42. Belvedere Area: From Southeast. 1960 18
43. Belvedere Area: From North. 1959 .... 19, 20
44. Belvedere Area: Kiln. From West. 1965 19
45. Belvedere Area: Kiln. From North. 1965 19
46. Platform at Northern Part of Belvedere Area. From North. 1965 20
47. Belvedere Area: Street and Walls. From North. 1959 .... 20, 21
48. Belvedere Area: General View. From Northwest. 1959 21
49. Belvedere Area: Street Showing Ends of Walls J and H. From South. 1965 .... 21, 22
50. Belvedere Area: Drain across Rectangular Area. From West. 1965 22
51. Belvedere Area: Drain in Steep Bank. From East. 1965 22
52. Trench S 10: From Southeast. 1962 25
53. Trench S 12: From Southeast. 1962 25
54. Trench IV: Eastern End. From West. 1939 26
55. Trench III: Eastern End. From West. 1939 26
56. Trench E 3: Cross Wall and Corner. From Southeast. 1965 26
57. Trench MY 1: Black Deposit. From West. 1958 26
58. Trench P 13: Foundations North of Wine Magazine. From Northwest. 1964 28
59. Water Channel North of Wine Magazine. From Southeast. 1964 29
60. Walls and Stucco Pavements Southeast of Wine Magazine. From South. 1958 29
61. Remains of an Open Court of Pre-palatial Era. From Northeast. 1958 30
62. Column Base in Pre-palatial Court. From West. 1958 30
63. Foundations of Buildings Demolished for Erection of Wine Magazine. From West. 1958 30
64. Early Wall under Southeast End of Vestibule (104). From Northwest. 1958 32
65. Sounding under Corridor 26: Group of Pithoi. From Northeast. 1960 32
66. Substantial Wall under Corridor 26. From Southwest. 1960 32
67. Trench outside Room 24 behind Main Building. From Northwest. 1955 ... 33
68. Earlier Wall under Room 21. From South. 1960 34
69. Broad Wall below Northwest Wall of Room 65. From West. 1962 37
70. Earlier Wall under Room 74. From Southwest. 1964 38
71. Sounding (64-6) under Room of Late Palace Phase. From West. 1964 38
72. Wall under Corridor 61. From West. 1964 39
73. Sounding (64-17) against Section 10 of Southwest Wall of Southwestern Building. From West. 1964 40
74. Building X: Southwest Part. From East by South. 1961 40
75. Building X: Foundation of Northwest Corner. From West. 1964 40
76. Scarp Showing Stratification in South Corner. From Southeast. 1963 41
77. Southern Corner: Pots Lying on Floorlike Earth. From Northwest. 1965 ... 41
78. Circular Building and House Beyond. From Southeast. 1958 43

Pages

79. Area behind Main Building: Walls from Northeast. 1962...................... 44
80. Stratification on South Side of Trench 7 in Area behind Main Building. From East. 1962 45
81. Building X: South Wall. From Southeast. 1961............................ 50
82. Broken Pottery Scattered in South Corner. From East and Above. 1962...... 50
83. Trench LT I: From North. 1959... 52
84. Trench LT I: From South. 1959... 54
85. Trench LT I: Remnants of Table of Offerings. From South. 1959........... 54
86. Trench LT II: From East. 1959... 57
87. Trench LT III: Walls and Fallen Stones. From Northwest. 1959.............. 57
88. Trench LT IV: Walls and Pithos Appearing. From Northwest. 1959 59
89. Trench LT IV: Wall of Last Period and Large Pithos. From North. 1959... 60
90. Trench LT V: Remnant of Wall. From South. 1959........................ 61
91. Trench AA I, below Southeast Slope. From Southeast. 1960 61
92. Trench AA II: Southeast End of Trench. From Northwest. 1960............ 62
93. Trench across *Aloni* of G. Petropoulos. From South. 1959.................... 63
94. Trench across *Aloni* of G. Petropoulos: Early Walls. From North. 1959...... 63
95. Trench Crossing Northeast Hollow: Deposit of Stones. From Northwest. 1968 64
96. Trench Crossing Northeast Hollow: Deposit of Stones. From Northwest. 1968 65
97. Trench Crossing Northeast Hollow: Final Cleaning, Sections 3, 4, 5. From Southeast. 1968 65
98. Trench Crossing Northeast Hollow: Sections 3, 4, 5. From Southeast. 1968 65
99. Transverse Trench across Hollow: Deposit of Stones. From Southwest. 1969 66
100. Transverse Trench across Hollow: Deposits of Stones. From Northeast. 1969 66
101. Transverse Trench across Hollow: Deep Sections. From Southwest. 1969... 66
102. Transverse Trench across Hollow: Deep Sections. From Southwest. 1969... 66
103. Figurine and Pots from Transverse Trench across Hollow. 1969............
    1-3: 66   4-6: 67   7-9: 66
104. Miscellaneous Objects: Nos. 1-8 from Petropoulos *Aloni*; Nos. 9, 10 Trench MY 1; Nos. 11-20 Northeast Gateway; No. 21 Trench W 28.................
    1-8: 64   11-20: 7, 8   21 *
    9-10: 27
105. Miscellaneous Objects: No. 1 Trench W 32; Nos. 2, 3 Trench W 31; No. 4 Northeast Gateway...
    1-3: 16   4: 8
106. Miscellaneous Objects: Nos. 1-5 Trench W 9; No. 6 Trench W 10; Nos. 8-14 Trench W 16; Nos. 7, 15-17 South Corner.................................
    1: 9, 49   7: 42   12: 50
    2: 49   8: 50   13, 14: 49
    3-5: 9, 49   9-11: 49   15-17: 42
    6: 49

* Not mentioned in text.

107. Miscellaneous Objects: No. 1 Trench W 33; No. 2 Trench S 12; Nos. 3-7 Trench CK 8 Extension III; No. 8 Trench W 31; Nos. 9, 10 CK 24; No. 11 Trench W 36 ....

    1: 16   7: 27   9, 10 *

    2: 25   8: 16   11: 17

    3-6: 27

108. Fragments: Diadem of Gold from Trench W 31 (reconstruction by Piet de Jong) 16

109. Miscellaneous Objects from Belvedere Area (W 38)............................. 24

110. Miscellaneous Objects: Nos. 1-6, 15 Section W 19; Nos. 8-10 Section W 20; Nos. 11, 13, 14 under Room 74; No. 12 Trench P 13.........................

    1-6: 51   11: 38   13, 14: 38

    7 *   12: 28 n. 10   15: 51

    8-10: 51

111. Seal Stone of Jasper Found on Surface of Southwestern Slope by Mrs. C. S. Lamy. 1963 37

112. Miscellaneous Objects from Area Northeast and Southeast of Wine Magazine 31

113. Miscellaneous Objects from Trench W 16..

    1-5: 50   6: 49

114. Miscellaneous Objects from Exploratory Trenches Northwest of Main Building (W 14)..

    1-8: 46   9-16: 47

115. Miscellaneous Objects: Nos. 1-12 Trench LT IV; Nos. 13-15 Trench LT V; No. 16 Trench LT I...

    1-12: 60   13-15: 61   16: 57

116. Miscellaneous Objects from Trench LT III..

    1: 59   8: 58   13-15: 59

    2: 58   9, 10: 59   16, 17: 58

    3-7: 59   11, 12: 58

117. Seal Stone of Steatite from Trench LT III.. 58

118. Lentoid Seal of Ivory from Trench LT III 59

119. Sherds from Northeast Gateway (W 1). Late Helladic I and II................ 6, 7, 8

120. Sherds from Northeast Gateway (W 1). Late Helladic I and II................ 6, 7, 8

121. Sherds from Late Intrusion Northwest of Gateway: Nos. 1-7 Plain Ribbed Ware; Nos. 8-18 Glazed Ware.. 6

122. Sherds from Trench W 5 8

123. Sherds from Trench W 6 (Nos. 1-16) and Area between CK 8 and CK 19 (Nos. 17-27).. 9

124. Sherds from Trench W 9, Pit at End of Corridor Northeast of Wine Magazine 31

125. Sherds from Trench W 9, Pit at End of Corridor Northeast of Wine Magazine 9, 31

126. Sherds from Trench W 9 (Nos. 1-4, 7, 8) and Trench W 10 (Nos. 5, 6, 9-12)... 9, 10

127. Sherds from Trench W 16 11

* Not mentioned in text.

Pages

128. Sherds from Areas W 19 and W 20 .... 12, 13
129. Sherds from Areas W 19 and W 20 13
130. Sherds from Areas W 19 and W 20 13
131. Sherds from Belvedere Area (W 38) 22, 24
132. Sherds from Belvedere Area (W 38) 22, 24
133. Middle Helladic Jug from Trench CK 8 Extension III 28
134. Middle Helladic Sherds from Trench CK 8 Extension III 27
135. Sherds from under Corridor 26 33
136. Sherds from Pit under Corridor 25 (Stratum 2, Nos. 1-5; Stratum 3, Nos. 6-12; Stratum 4, Nos. 13-18) 33
137. Sherds from Pit under Corridor 25 (Stratum 5, Nos. 1-5; Stratum 6, Nos. 6-15; Stratum 7, Nos. 16-20) 33
138. Sherds from Pit under Corridor 25 (Stratum 8, Nos. 1-8; Stratum 9, Nos. 9-14; Stratum 10, Nos. 15-18) 33
139. Sherds from under Hall 65 36
140. Sherds from Trench 64-1 12
141. Sherds from under Hall 65 36
142. Sherds from Trench 64-6 39
143. Pots from South Corner; Sherds and Impressions Left by Them, from Trench W 28 ....

      1-14: 42   15, 16: 15

144. Sherds from Area Northeast and Southeast of Wine Magazine 30
145. Sherds from Trench Northwest of Room 24 34
146. Sherds from Northwest of Palace 43
147. Sherds from Northwest of Palace 43
148. Pots from Areas Northwest of Palace (W 14 and W 12) ....

      1-16: 47   17, 18 *   19-21: 49

149. Sherds from Area Northwest of Palace (W 14) 45
150. Sherds from Area W 14 Northwest of Palace 45
151. Sherds from Section W 21, The South Corner 51
152. Sherds from Section W 21, The South Corner 51
153. Fragment of Conical Rhyton from Trench LT I 56
154. Sherds from Trench LT III 58
155. Pots from Section W 21, The South Corner (Nos. 1-10) and Trench LT I (Nos. 11-18) ....

      1-10: 52   14: 54   18: 55
      11-13: 55   15-17: 56

156. Sherds from Trench LT III 58
157. Sherds from Trench LT III 58
158. Sherds from Trenches AA I and AA II 62
159. Sherds from Trench across *Aloni* of G. Petropoulos 63
160. Storehouse Built over Tholos III. From South. 1939 73
161. Doorway of Tholos III: Roof of New Storeroom in Background. 1939 73
162. Tholos III: Fallen Lintel Block as Found. From Inside Chamber. 1939 74
163. Tholos III: Fallen Lintel Block as Left after Excavation. From North. 1939 74

* Not mentioned in text.

Pages

164. Tholos III: Remnants of Upper Wall Closing Doorway. From Southwest. 1939 75

165. Tholos III: Remains of Early Wall Closing Doorway. From Southeast. 1966 75

166. Tholos III: Fairly Large Stones in Lower Courses of Tholos Wall. From East, Inside. 1939 76

167. Tholos III: Bones and Stones in Central Pit. From Northeast. 1939 77

168. Tholos III: Stones and Human Bones in Disorder in Large Pit. From Northeast. 1939 77

169. Tholos III: Miscellaneous Objects of Gold, Bronze, and Stone (drawings by E. Gillieron) ....

1-3: 83	8, 9: 82	16, 17: 84
4, 5: 81	10: 82, 83	18, 19: 82
6: 81, 83	11-14: 84	20: 84
7: 82, 83	15: 82	

170. Tholos III: Fragments of Ivory (drawings by E. Gillieron)....................

1: 86	4-6: 86	8: 86
2: 85	7: 85	9: 85
3: 84		

171. Tholos III: Miscellaneous Objects of Glass Paste...............................

1, 2: 87	5: 88	9: 90
3: 88	6: 87	10, 11: 89
4: 87	7, 8: 88	12: 90

172. Tholos III: Beads of Glass Paste ....

1: 89	5, 6: 89	11: 92
2: 91	7, 8: 90	12: 91
3: 90	9: 92	13: 90-92
4 *	10: 91	14: 90, 91

173. Tholos III: Pots..

1-5: 92	9, 10: 82	11-13: 93
6-8: 93		

174. Tholos III: Pots and Fragments of Pots...

1: 93	2-7: 94

175. Tholos IV: Broken Lintel Block as Seen before Excavations Started. From Southwest. 1953 95

176. Tholos IV: Doorway and Blocking Wall. From Southwest. 1953 .... 95, 96

177. Tholos IV: Removal of Blocking Wall. From Southwest. 1953 .... 96, 101

178. Tholos IV: Curve of Vault, Doorway, and Lower Part of Blocking Wall. From South and Above. 1953 96

179. Tholos IV: Inner Face of Blocking Wall from Northeast, Inside Chamber. 1953 .... 96, 100

180. Tholos IV: Curved Pit Parallel to Northwestern Wall of Chamber. From Southwest. 1953 97

181. Tholos IV: Stone Cist against Southeastern Wall of Chamber. From North. 1953 .... 97, 105

* Not mentioned in text.

Pages

182. Tholos IV: Blocking Wall and Southeastern Door Jamb. From South and
Above. 1953.. 100

183. Tholos IV: Course of Squared Blocks in Partly Dismantled Blocking Wall.
From Northwest and Above. 1953.. 100

184. Tholos IV: Earth under Large Stones in Outer Face of Blocking Wall. From
South. 1953.. 100

185. Tholos IV: Coping Stones Found in Chamber. 1953......................... 104

186. Tholos IV: Doorway and Chamber, Stone Cist at Left, Curving Pit at
Right. From Northeast by North. 1953.................................. 97

187. Tholos IV: Chamber with Stone Cist. From West and Above. 1953........... 97

188. Tholos IV: Doorway and Chamber with Curving Pit at Right. 1953......... 97, 98

189. Tholos IV as Restored. From South. 1960................................. 98

190. Tholos IV: Miscellaneous Objects of Gold ....

1: 117	10: 115	16: 115
2, 3: 111, 112, 118	11: 116	17: 119
4, 5: 116	12: 115	18, 19: 118
6: 114	13: 116	20: 88, 114
7: 113	14: 118	21: 118
8: 115	15: 116	22: 119
9: 120		

191. Tholos IV: Miscellaneous Objects of Gold (drawings by H. A. Shelley
based on sketches by W. D. Taylour, except for Nos. 2, 4, 14, 15a by M.
Rawson) ....

1: 111	9: 119	12-14: 116
2: 113	10: 118	15, 16: 119
3-6: 115	11: 117	17: 119
7, 8: 116		

192. Tholos IV: Miscellaneous Objects of Gold (drawings by Piet de Jong)........

1-7: 117	8, 9: 113

193. Tholos IV: Seal Stone and Impressions (drawings by Piet de Jong)............ 124

194. Tholos IV: Miscellaneous Objects of Bronze, Stone, Amber, Ivory, Paste,
and Terracotta ....

1: 112	24: 126	47: 129
2-5: 123	25: 125	48, 49: 128
6: 121	26 *	50: 133
7: 123	27-32: 130	51: 132
8, 9: 127	33: 127	52: 126
10: 113, 127	34: 126	53 *
11-13: 127	35-39: 125	54: 126
14, 15: 125	40: 110	55: 131
16: 133	41: 130	56 *
17: 127	42: 129	57: 126
18: 126	43: 129 n. 71	58 *
19: 125	44, 45: 129	59-61: 126
20: 131	46: 128	62 *
21-23: 125		

* Not mentioned in text.

Pages

195. Tholos IV: Miscellaneous Objects of Bronze, Stone, Amber, Ivory, and
Paste (drawings by H. A. Shelley based on sketches by W. D. Taylour)......

1: 120	11, 12: 123	18: 128
2: 118	13: 127	19: 133
3, 4: 121	14: 111	20: 111
5: 122	15: 112	21: 131
6-9: 125	16: 129	22: 129
10: 126	17: 130	

196. Tholos IV: Amphora, Fragment of Jug, and Sherds ....

1: 105, 133	3: 105, 112, 134	5: 111
2: 105, 111	4: 105, 133	6: 134

197. Grave Circle, Trench A. From East. 1957... 135
198. Grave Circle, Pit 1: Cauldron, Pithos, and Rapier. From West. 1957......... 136
199. Grave Circle, Trench L. From North-Northeast. 1957........................... 137
200. Grave Circle, Pit 2: Remains of Skeleton and Accompanying Objects.
From North. 1957.. 136
201. Grave Circle, Trench L: Curving Wall, Dagger, and Other Objects. From
North. 1957.. 137
202. Grave Circle, Trench L: One-handled Jar and Fragments of Alabastra.
From South. 1957.. 137
203. Grave Circle: Spouted Jar Found in Balk between Trenches A and L. From
South. 1957 .... 138, 145 n. 87
204. Grave Circle, Trench M: Balance Staff and Alabastron with Base of Kylix
in its Mouth. From South. 1957.. 138
205. Grave Circle: Pottery in Trench M. From Southeast. 1957..................... 138
206. Grave Circle, Trench M: Shoulder of Spouted Jug of Minoan Style and
Decoration, *in situ*. From North. 1957 138
207. Grave Circle, Pit 2: Upper Half of Skeleton with Bronze Bowl to Right of
Skull. Remains of Another Burial, Center. From North. 1957 142
208. Grave Circle, Pit 2: Skeleton. From East. 1957 142
209. Grave Circle, Pit 3: Cauldron and Pithos. From East. 1957................... 142
210. Grave Circle, Pit 3: Bone Pit and Palace Style Jar. From West. 1957........... 142, 144
211. Grave Circle, Pit 3: Cauldron, Pithos, and Rapiers. Ivory Pommel, Loose, to
Right. From Northwest. 1957 143
212. Grave Circle, Pit 3: Cauldron with Handle of Short Sword Protruding.
From South. 1957.. 142
213. Grave Circle, Pit 3: Pithos. Bronze Knife among Bones. From Northwest.
1957 144
214. Grave Circle, Pit 3: Skull Wedged into Base of Palace Style Jar. From East.
1957 144
215. Grave Circle, Pit 3: Spouted Jar with Trussed Burial. From North. 1957... 145
216. Grave Circle, Pit 3 (NE) after Removal of Spouted Jar Showing Rapiers,
Knife, Dagger, and Ivory Pommel. From West. 1957 145
217. Grave Circle, Pit 1: Skull and Bones in Pithos, Cauldron to North. From
South. 1957 146
218. Grave Circle, Pit 1: Gold Wreath at Bottom of Pithos. From North and
Above. 1957.. 147

219. Grave Circle, Pit 4: Skulls, Bones, Daggers, Hone (left), Two Fragments of Gold (top, left and bottom, right). From West. 1957 147

220. Grave Circle from Southwest. 1957 148

221. Grave Circle from East-Southeast. 1957 148

222. Grave Circle from North. 1957 148

223. Exploratory Trenches Southwest of Grave Circle. From Southeast. 1958 ... 148

224. Exploratory Trenches Southwest of Grave Circle. From South of West. 1958 148

225. Grave Circle: Miscellaneous Objects of Gold (Nos. 1-2), Silver (Nos. 4, 6), and Ivory (Nos. 3, 5) ....

    1: 16, 147, 166   3: 147, 157   5: 157
    2: 147, 156   4: 144, 159   6: 147, 156

226. Typical Arrowheads of Flint and Obsidian from Tholos IV ....

    Type   I: 127, 169 n. 104, n. 105   Type IV: 127
    Type II: 127   Type V: 127
    Type III: 113, 127   Type VI: 127, 158, 162, 169

227. Grave Circle: Miscellaneous Objects of Gold (9), Silver (8, 11), Bronze (3, 4, 10), Stone (1, 7), Amber (2, 5), and Terracotta (6) (drawings by H. A. Shelley [Nos. 1-7] and A. C. Evans [Nos. 8-11] based on sketches by W. D. Taylour) ....

    1: 169   5: 162   8, 9: 147, 156
    2: 162   6: 170   10: 139, 158
    3: 121, 158   7: 139, 168   11: 144, 159
    4: 167

228. Grave Circle: Miscellaneous Objects of Bronze ....

    1: 160   3: 156   5: 139, 168
    2: 121, 158   4: 158

229. Grave Circle: Swords, Rapiers, and Daggers of Bronze ....

    1-4: 159, 160   11: 157   14, 15: 145, 163, 164
    5-9: 161   12: 145, 163, 164   16: 164
    10: 145, 164   13: 157   17: 145, 164

230. Grave Circle: Miscellaneous Objects ....

    1-6: 167   11-14: 160   18: 167
    7: 139, 158   15: 147, 166   19, 20: 168
    8, 9: 158   16: 168   21: 139, 168
    10: 144, 160   17: 160   22: 169

231. Grave Circle: Miscellaneous Objects (drawings by Piet de Jong) ....

    1: 164   4: 162   7: 159, 160-163
    2: 162   5: 139, 169   8: 169, 170
    3: 164   6: 141, 169   9: 163, 168-170

232. Grave Circle: Miscellaneous Objects ....

    1: 138, 168   4: 169, 170   6: 161-163
    2: 161   5: 159   7: 140, 169, 170
    3: 167

233. Grave Circle: Burial Jars (Nos. 1, 2, 4, 5), Bases of Other Pots (Nos. 3, 6)

    1: 149, 157   3: 172   5: 150, 165
    2: 149, 163   4: 144, 150, 166   6: 174

234. Grave Circle: Pots (except No. 6 found in Tomb K-1) ....

      1: 145, 150, 153, 165   10: 150, 174   18: 171
      2: 138, 174   11: 151, 172   19: 138, 151, 174
      3: 171   12: 174   20: 159
      4: 173   13: 173   21: 150, 175
      5: 175   14: 175   22: 166
      6: 212   15: 172   23: 138, 153, 173
      7: 150, 172   16: 175   24: 138, 171
      8: 173   17: 174   25: 138, 171
      9: 141, 151, 175

235. Grave Circle: Pots (water colors by Piet de Jong) ....

      1: 171   4: 175   6: 138, 151, 174
      2: 150, 174   5: 151, 172   7: 138, 153, 173
      3: 175

236. Pots and Miscellaneous Objects: Trial Trenches Nos. 6, 17, 19-21; Dromos E-2 No. 18; Grave E-3 Nos. 1-5; Tomb E-4 Nos. 7-16 (water colors by Piet de Jong) ....

      1, 2: 178   7-14: 183   17: 178, 180
      3, 4: 177   15: 182   18: 180
      5: 178   16: 182   19-21: 178
      6: 179

237. Tomb E-4: Dromos and Doorway. From South. 1956 181
238. Tomb E-6: Doorway and Blocking Wall. From South-Southeast. 1957 184
239. Tomb E-6: Burial E and Pots in Eastern Side of Chamber. From North-Northwest. 1957 185
240. Tomb E-6: Burial H and Pots. From Southwest. 1957 186
241. Tomb E-6: Burials F, G, and I. From North-Northeast. 1957 186
242. Tomb E-6: Miscellaneous Objects 187-189
243. Tomb E-6: Miscellaneous Objects ....

      1: 187, 188   2-4: 189   5-12: 188

244. Tomb E-6: Pots (water colors by Piet de Jong).........................

      1: 191   9: 189   15: 190
      2: 190   10: 191   16: 191
      3: 189   11: 190   17, 18: 190
      4: 191   12: 192   19: 191
      5: 189   13: 191   20: 189
      6, 7: 191   14: 189   21: 187
      8: 187

245. Tomb E-8: Dromos. From North End, above Doorway. 1966 192
246. Tomb E-8: Doorway and Blocking Wall; Walled Niches on Each Side of Dromos. From South. 1966 .... 192, 193
247. Tomb E-8: Doorway and Blocking Wall, Niche in West Wall. From South. 1966 192
248. Tomb E-8: Burials and Pots in Chamber. From East and Above. 1966 193
249. Tomb E-8: Pots ....

      1: 196   11: 196   21: 199
      2: 198   12: 195   22: 198

3: 197   13, 14: 196   23: 199
4: 196   15: 197   24: 198
5, 6: 198   16: 196   25, 26: 199
7: 197   17: 197   27: 198
8: 198   18, 19: 199   28: 197
9: 196   20: 197   29: 198
10: 197

250. Tomb E-8: Pots and Miscellaneous Objects ....

1-3: 200   10: 201   15: 198
4, 5: 201   11, 12: 198   16: 201
6, 7: 200   13: 197   17, 18: 197
8: 201   14: 199   19: 195, 197, 200
9: 199

251. Tomb E-9: Dromos and Blocking Wall. From South. 1966 201
252. Tomb E-9: Dromos and Doorway. From South. 1966 202
253. Tomb E-9: Dromos and Blocking Wall. From South. 1966 202
254. Tomb E-9: Dromos and Stones Above Doorway. From Southwest. 1966 ... 202
255. Tomb E-9: Blocking Wall in Doorway. From Northeast and Above. 1966 ... 202
256. Tomb E-9: Two Skeletons (A, B) on East Side of Chamber. From West.
     1966 .... 202, 203
257. Tomb E-9: Pits in Chamber (Pit 3 at Left, Pit 1 Center and Right). From
     Above. 1966 203
258. Tomb E-9: Group of Pots between Pits 1 and 2. From West. 1966 203
259. Tomb E-9: Pits in Chamber (Pit 3 at Left). From Southwest. 1966 203
260. Tomb E-9: Pots and Miscellaneous Objects ....

1: 205   9, 10: 204   20: 205
2: 204   11: 206   21: 206
3: 206   12: 205   22: 205
4: 207   13: 206   23-25: 206
5: 206   14-16: 205   26: 207
6: 207   17, 18: 204   27: 204, 207
7: 206   19: 206   28: 204
8: 205

261. Tomb E-10: Dromos. From South. 1966 207
262. Tomb E-10: Stones over Pit in West Side of Dromos. From Northeast.
     1966 208
263. Tomb E-10: Stones in West Side of Dromos. From Northeast. 1966 208
264. Tomb E-10: Niche in West Wall of Dromos. From North-Northeast. 1966... 208
265. Tomb E-10: Pots. 208
266. Tomb K-1: Doorway and Blocking Wall. From South. 1957 209
267. Tomb K-1: Stone Marker and Fragment of Kylix in Front of Blocking
     Wall. From South. 1957 209
268. Tomb K-1: Adze Tool Marks on Eastern Jamb of Doorway. 1957 210
269. Tomb K-1: Pottery and Bones in Southwestern Corner of Chamber. From
     East. 1957 210
270. Tomb K-1: Pottery, Bones, and Skull Lying in Northwestern Corner of
     Chamber. From East. 1957 210

Pages

271. Tomb K-1: Pottery and Bones in Northeast Corner of Chamber. From West. 1957.. 211

272. Tomb K-1: Small Pit Burial in Chamber in Front of Doorway. From North. 1957 211

273. Tomb K-1: Miscellaneous Objects of Ivory (No. 3) and Paste (Nos. 1, 2); Pots (Nos. 4-11) and Sherds (No. 12a, b) (drawing by H. A. Shelley based on sketch by W. D. Taylour)...

1: 212	5: 215	8: 215
2, 3: 211, 212	6: 214	9: 213
4: 215	7: 213	10-12: 212

274. Tomb K-1: Pots..

1-3: 213	6: 215	8: 215
4: 215	7: 214	9-12: 214
5: 213		

275. Early Walls under *Aloni* on Deriziotis Property. From Southeast. 1958...... 220

276. Early Walls under *Aloni* on Deriziotis Property. General View from Northwest. 1958.. 220

277. Early Hearths under *Aloni* on Deriziotis Property. From Southwest. 1958... 221

278. Pebble Floor and Pithos Fragments under *Aloni* on Deriziotis Property. From North and Above. 1958.. 221

279. Miscellaneous Objects Found with Early Walls under *Aloni* on Deriziotis Property (drawing by H. A. Shelley based on sketch by W. D. Taylour)......

1-4: 223	9: 224	13: 224
5, 6: 224	10-12: 223	14-16: 223
7, 8: 223		

280. Chamber Tomb K-2: Blocking Wall Filling Doorway. From West. 1958...... 225

281. Tomb K-2: Lower Courses of Original Blocking Wall. From West. 1958..... 225

282. Tomb K-2: Excavation of Chamber from Above. From Northeast. 1959... 226

283. Tomb K-2: Pots in Center of Chamber (Groups I and Ia). From South. 1959 226

284. Tomb K-2, Center of Chamber: Skeleton of Child. From West. 1959......... 226

285. Tomb K-2, Southwestern Part of Chamber: Bronze Vessel on Edge of Bone Pit. From East. 1959.. 227

286. Tomb K-2, North Part of Chamber: Two Jugs with Lower Burial. From South. 1959 227

287. Tomb K-2, North Part of Chamber: Pots and Skeleton of Child in Foreground. From South. 1959.. 227

288. Tomb K-2, South Part of Chamber: Bone Pit (continuing Fig. 285). From East. 1959 227

289. Tomb K-2: Fragmentary Krater with Hunting Scene from Dromos (drawing by Piet de Jong) 226, 229

290. Tomb K-2: Sherds of Kylix and Kraters from Dromos ....

1: 229	2: 229, 230	3, 4: 230

291. Tomb K-2: Bronze Vessel and Miscellaneous Objects from Chamber (drawings by A. C. Evans)...

1: 230, 231	7: 230	12: 230

Pages

2-5: 232   8-10: 229   13: 232
6 *   11: 232

292. Tomb K-2: Pots from Chamber (No. 6 from Tomb E-6).....................

    1: 227, 235   7, 8: 236   13: 234
    2, 3: 234   9: 234   14: 233
    4: 236   10: 232   15: 237
    5: 235   11: 236   16: 233
    6: 190   12: 235

293. Tomb K-2: Pots from Chamber ....

    1, 2: 235   5: 234   8: 236
    3: 226, 233   6: 233   9: 232
    4: 233   7: 234   10, 11: 235

294. Protogeometric Tholos Tomb after Excavation. From West. 1958   237
295. Protogeometric Tholos Tomb before Excavation. From West. 1958   237
296. Protogeometric Tholos Tomb: Southern Quadrant Cleared. From West. 1958   238
297. Protogeometric Tholos Tomb: Fragment of Skull and Pots on Floor in Southern Quadrant. From Southwest. 1958   238
298. Protogeometric Tholos Tomb: Miscellaneous Objects and Pots ....

    1-9: 240   11-13: 240   14, 15: 241
    10: 240, 241

MAPS, PLANS, AND SECTIONS

Pages

299. Sketch Map of Southwestern Peloponnesos (drawn by W. B. Dinsmoor, Jr.)...   vii
300. Sketch Map of Western Messenia (drawn by W. B. Dinsmoor, Jr.)............   vii, 224, 237
301. Palace Site and Surrounding Area (surveyed and drawn by J. Fant and J. W. Shaw)... 61, 63, 64, 72, 73, 95, 134, 176, 179, 192, 208, 219
302. Plan of Site. 1960 (surveyed, measured, and drawn by J. Travlos, adapted by J. W. Shaw)... 4, 5, 8-18, 25-28, 36, 37, 41, 43, 48, 50
303. Palace of Nestor, Key Plan (drawn by J. Travlos)................................. 29, 32-38, 40, 43, 52
304. Northeast Gate (drawn by G. Papathanasopoulos, adapted by J. W. Shaw)   4, 5
305. Detail of Northeast Gate (adapted by A. C. Evans and J. W. Shaw from sketch by M. Rawson)   7
306. Southwestern Area of Hill (drawn by G. Papathanasopoulos, adapted by J. W. Shaw)... 12, 13, 38-41, 50
307. Plan of Belvedere Area (drawn by G. Papathanasopoulos, adapted by J. W. Shaw)... 17-20, 22, 23

* Not mentioned in text.

	Pages
308. Plan of Kiln (adapted by A. C. Evans)..	19
309. Area between Wine Magazine and Northeastern Building (measured and drawn by J. Travlos, adapted by J. W. Shaw)......................................	26, 29, 30
310. Walls Northeast of Propylon (drawn by M. Rawson, adapted by H. Athanasiades)..	35
311. Area Northwest of Palace (drawn by G. Papathanasopoulos 1958, adapted by W. G. Kittredge and J. W. Shaw)..	10, 44
312. Plan of Palace and Trenches in Lower Town (measured and drawn by D. R. Theocharis 1959, additions by G. Papathanasopoulos)....................	52, 57
313. Trench LT I: Section (measured and drawn by G. Papathanasopoulos)......	53, 57
314. Trench LT I: Plan (measured and drawn by G. Papathanasopoulos).........	53, 54, 57
315. Trench LT II: Plan (measured and drawn by G. Papathanasopoulos).........	57
316. Trench LT III: Plan (measured and drawn by G. Papathanasopoulos)......	57
317. Trench LT IV: Plan (measured and drawn by G. Papathanasopoulos)......	59
318. Trench LT V: Plan (measured and drawn by G. Papathanasopoulos).........	61
319. Tholos III: Plan (drawn by L. T. Lands based on measurements taken by C. W. Blegen)...	73, 75, 77, 79
320. Tholos III: Section (drawn by L. T. Lands based on measurements taken by C. W. Blegen)..	73
321-326. Tholos IV: Plans and Sections (drawn by D. R. Theocharis, adapted by H. A. Shelley)	
321. Plan and Section of Lintel Looking Northeast	95, 96
322. Plan Showing Northeastern and Southwestern Sectors...........................	95, 96, 102
323. Plan of Chamber Showing Pits...	95, 97, 105
324. Section of Dromos Looking Northwest	95, 98, 101
325. Section of Inner Doorway Looking Northwest..	95, 99
326. Section of Chamber Looking Southwest..	95, 102, 103, 109
327, 329. Grave Circle: Plans I and III (drawn by W. D. Taylour, adapted by H. A. Shelley)	
327. Plan I: Burial Pits	134, 156, 158, 159, 163, 166
328, 330-336. Grave Circle: Plan II and Sections (drawn by W. D. Taylour, adapted by H. A. Shelley)	
328. Plan II, Showing Trenches and Position of Sections	134, 137-141, 156, 158, 159, 163, 166
329. Plan III: Distribution of Objects..	134, 137, 156, 158, 159, 163, 166, 167, 171, 172, 174, 175
330. Section I, Looking West...	134, 140
331. Section II, Looking West..	134, 140
332. Section III, Looking South	134, 140, 154
333. Section IV, Looking South	134, 141, 148, 154
334. Section V, Looking West..	134, 141
335. Section VI, Looking West...	134, 141
336. Plan of Walls Southwest of Grave Circle (drawn by W. D. Taylour, adapted by H. A. Shelley)..	148

Pages

337. Grave E-3: Plan (drawn by W. P. Donovan, adapted by W. E. Wolfley)...... 176

338. Tomb E-4: Plan and Section (drawn by W. P. Donovan, adapted by W. E. Wolfley)... 180

339. Tomb E-6: Plans and Section (drawn by W. P. Donovan, adapted by W. E. Wolfley)... 184, 185

340. Tomb E-8: Plans and Section (drawn by W. P. Donovan, adapted by W. E. Wolfley)... 192

341. Tomb E-9: Plans and Section (drawn by W. P. Donovan, adapted by W. E. Wolfley)... 201, 203

342. Tomb E-10: Plan and Section (drawn by W. P. Donovan, adapted by W. E. Wolfley)... 207, 207 n. 14

343-346. Tomb K-1: Plans and Sections (drawn by W. D. Taylour and J. Benson [Fig. 344], adapted by H. A. Shelley)

343. Plan of Dromos and Chamber.. 208-210

344. Plan of Chamber Showing Location of Pots and Bones........................ 208, 210, 211

345. Longitudinal Section of Dromos and Chamber.................................. 208, 209

346. Section of Dromos, Looking East.. 208, 209

347-350. Excavation under *Aloni* on Deriziotis Property (drawn by W. D. Taylour, adapted by H. A. Shelley)

347. Early Walls: Plan I.. 219-221

348. Plan II: Showing Presumed Line of Walls and Position of Sections.......... 219, 220, 222

349. Section I, Looking West.. 219, 222

350. Section II, Looking West... 219, 222

351-354. Tomb K-2: Plans and Section (drawn by W. D. Taylour, adapted by H. A. Shelley)

351. Plan of Dromos and Chamber.. 224, 226

352. Plan I of Chamber, Upper Burials.. 224, 226-228

353. Section of Dromos, Looking South 224-226

354. Plan II of Chamber, Lower Burials... 224, 227, 228

355. Protogeometric Tholos: Plan (drawn by W. D. Taylour, adapted by H. A. Shelley) 237-239

356. Protogeometric Tholos: Section Looking North (drawn by W. D. Taylour, adapted by H. A. Shelley).. 237, 238

INDEX

adze, tool marks of 210
Aegina 150 n. 92
Aetolia 241, A. Elia-Ithorias 171, 174
alabaster see STONE OBJECTS, VARIE-
TIES OF STONE USED
alabastron 94, 137, 138, 150, 171,
172, 173, 174, 175, 177, 178, 179,
183, 189, 190, 191, 193, 195, 196,
197, 198, 199, 200, 201, 203, 205,
206, 211, 212, 214, 226, 227, 235,
236 see POTTERY, shapes
Alaca Höyük 115
Alexiou, St. 91
aloni xii, 47, 63, 64, 67, 71, 95, 110,
135, 154, 219, 220
Alpheios River 72
amber imported from Baltic
throughout Mycenaean period
129; objects made of: beads 87,
102, 104, 111, 137, 143, 144, 151,
carinated 129, cylindrical 129,
drum 162, flattened spherical 105,
128, 162, lozenge 129, oval 162,
spacer 105, 128, 143, 162, spherical 162; talismans 129, 143, 162
American School of Classical Studies
at Athens x, 80
amethyst see STONE OBJECTS, VARIE-
TIES OF STONE USED
Amorgos 150 n. 92
amphora 67, 105, 133, 134, 233, 237,
239, 241 see POTTERY, shapes
amphoriskos 67 see POTTERY, shapes
Amyklaion 150 n. 92
Analipsis Tholos 155 n. 97
Anastasopoulos, Andreas viii, 47, 61
Androutsakis, Dionysios x, 95 n. 29,
96 n. 32, 135
Angel, J. Lawrence 107, 135, 142,
177 n. 1, 182 n. 4, 185 n. 8
animal: bones 23, 27, 30, 32, 33, 34,
38, 43, 76, 79, 103; pot, fragments
of 94
animal pot 94
Antheia (Thouria) 242
Antonopoulos, Nikos viii, 47, 52
Aphidna 150 n. 92
apsidal building 220
aqueduct 4, 5, 24, 26, 27
Arcadia 155 n. 97
areas of excavation
   Northeast and Southeast of Wine
      Magazine 29-31
   Northwest of Main Building 43-47
   Northwest of Aqueduct (III, IV,
      CK 8, 18, 19, BB) 27-29
   Northern Quarter 63-64
   Northeastern Quarter 64-68

Southeast of Palace and Aqueduct
   (E-3) 24-27
under palace of Mycenaean III B:
   Room 7 3, 35, 36; Room 18 34;
   Room 20 34; Room 21 34, 43;
   Room 22 34, 43; Room 23 43;
   Room 24 33, 43; Room 27 10,
   32; Room 32 32; Room 55 35;
   Room 56 35; Room 57 35; Room
   60 40; Room 62 39; Room 74
   37, 38, 50; Room 100 25; Room
   104 32; Corridor 25 33, 43; Cor-
   ridor 26 32; Corridor 61 39;
   Corridor 70 37; Court 63 39;
   Hall 65 12, 36
outside Room 65 50, 52; Room 98
   26
northwest of: Room 82 43, 44;
   Rooms 83-87 43; Building 103
   5, 30
Building X 40, 41
Southern Quarter 41, 42
Southwest of Grave Circle 148
Trial Trenches 176-178: 64-1 12;
   64-5 40; 64-6 38; 64-17 40;
   B 58 36; LT I 52; LT II 57; LT
   III 57; LT IV 59; LT V 60;
   MY 1 26; P-13 28; R-62 37;
   S-3-12 25; W 1 4, 8, 17, 18; W
   2-W 5 8; W 6 8, 9, 27; W 7-W 8
   9; W 9 9, 49; W 10 9, 10, 49;
   W 11 9, 10; W 12 10, 49; W 13
   10; W 14 10, 11, 18, 43; W 15
   11; W 16 11, 49; W 17 11; W 18
   11, 18; W 19 11, 12, 13, 18, 50;
   W 20 13, 18, 50; W 21 13, 18,
   41; W 22 14; W 23 14; W 25 14;
   W 26 14; W 27 14, 15; W 28 14,
   15; W 29 14, 15; W 30 15; W 31
   15-16; W 32 15, 16; W 33 15,
   16; W 34 16; W 35 16, 17;
   W 36 16, 17; W 37 17; W 38 17,
   18-24; W 39-W 47 5, 17; AAI
   61; AAII 62
Argive Heraeum 83, 88, 90, 91, 92,
   112, 158, 160, 161, 170, 171, 174,
   180 n. 3, 184, 187 n. 9, 212
Argolis 73, 84, 85, 88, 90, 164
Argos 28, 85, 88, 94, 150 n. 92
arrowhead see STONE OBJECTS, BRONZE
   OBJECTS
arthritic erosion of sterno-clavicular
   joint (Skeleton 2 Py Grave E-3)
   177 n. 1
Asea 150 n. 92
ashes 54
ashlar blocks 36
ashy burnt matter 38

Asine 83, 85, 90, 91, 112, 158, 163
askos 136, 138, 151, 159, 174 see
   POTTERY, shapes
Aström, P. 239
Athanasiades, Hero ix
Athenian Agora 80
awl see BONE OBJECTS, BRONZE OB-
   JECTS

basin 42, 52 see POTTERY, shapes
baugrube, evidence of outside Room
   24 34
bead, fossilized twig 126, snail 12, see
   also AMBER, BRONZE, IVORY, PASTE,
   STONE OBJECTS
bead seal 149, see STONE OBJECTS
beaker 56 see POTTERY, shapes
Beck, Curt W. 129
"beehive" tombs 71; see Tholoi
Belvedere area (W 38) ix, 18-24, 26
bench or shelf 62
Bennett, Emmett L., Jr. x
Berbati 150 n. 92
Berlin Museum 85
black earth 38, 77; layer with Geometric sherds 26, 27
black-glazed see POTTERY, fabrics and
   wares
Blegen, Anne H. x
Blegen, Carl W. 13, 41, 52, 64, 95 n.
   29, 107 n. 36, 142 n. 86
Blegen, Mrs. Carl W. vii, x, xi, 11,
   36, 41, 50, 71, 72, 73, 80, 90
blocking wall, of tombs 75, 98, 112,
   181, 184, 202, 209, 225
blocks of poros 3, 4, 12, 13, 22, 33,
   38, 39, 77
boar's tusk 144, 162, 223, fragments
   of 143, 151, 162, pierced with
   holes 163; helmet 131, 163, 169;
   slices cut from 87, 130
BONE OBJECTS
   awl 24; needle 50; pendant 50;
      pin 64, 113, 131, 143, 163;
      spacer 131
   bones 75, 76, 77, 78, 81, 82, 102,
      103, 142, 147, 181, 203, 210, 223
      see also animal bones, skeletal re-
      mains
Boudouroglou, Miss 81
Bouga, stream called 48
Boulter, Cedric G. xi
Boulter, Mrs. Cedric G. xi
bowl 42, 47, 66, 83, 92, 138, 141,
   171, 175, 189, 190, 191, 199, 226,
   232, 234, 239 see POTTERY, shapes
Bradeen, Mrs. Donald W. xi

bronze: bits, chunks, fragments, pieces, scraps of 58, 60, 74, 76, 78, 82, 84, 102, 103, 124, 229

BRONZE OBJECTS
    arrowhead 24, 75, 100, 104, 112, 123, 124, 226, 232
    awl point 46, 49; with ivory handle 136, 158
    balance beam or staff 139, 168
    beads 121
    bowl 142, 158, 227, 230, 231
    cauldron 135, 136, 142, 146, 152, 156, 160
    cleaver 186, 188
    coils 111, 122
    coin with Geometric pottery 63
    dagger 105, 111, 122, 143, 145, 147, 152, 161, 164, 167, 186, 188, 194, 197; broad blade 188; curved blade 167; leaf-shaped blade 143, 161, 188; spatulate blade 136, 137; straight-sided blade 167; blade of triangular form 143; *see also* knife, rapier, sword
    disk 139 *see also* scale pan
    javelin point 9
    knife 122, 143, 144, 145, 147, 152, 157, 158, 160, 161, 164, 167, 186, 188, 195, 197, 201; tang of 58; *see also* dagger
    mirror 136, 142, 158, 186, 188, 227
    nail 27
    pin 7, 38, 49, 75, 82, 121, 141, 143, 144, 160, 168, 178
    pinhead crooked 49, disk 144, 160, nail type 143, pointed 144, spherical 240
    rapier 136, 138, 143, 145, 147, 151, 152, 157, 159, 163, 164; decoration on 164; points bent up 136, 143, 147, purposely 152; *see also* swords
    ring 104, 120, 239, 240
    rivet 102, 104, 105, 122, 157, 158, 159, 160, 163, 164, 167, 168, 188; shaft rectangular in section, heads flat 164; round in section, heads convex 163, flat 164
    rivet-head 82, 84, 160; domed 122, gilded 84, 122, silver-plated 122, 160
    rod 139
    scale pans 139, 140, 158, 168
    sickle 228
    spearhead 123, base ring? 123
    spearpoint 186, 188
    strip 7, flat 37; folded 232
    studs, decorated 121
    sword 84, 110, 122, 136, 143, 161, 186, 188; cruciform 188; short with ring 143, 161; or machete 161

tang, flanged 84
vessel: shallow three-handled 230, 231, 232; base of 122; handles of, flat in section 46, loop 121; round in section 46, 121, scroll 122; leg of 121; rim of 122
weapons 79
wire 146; ends flattened 60; gilded 103; silver-plated 122; twisted 112
Buchholz, H. G. 231
Buck, Robert J. x, 28
Building X 12, 13, 40, 50
Building 103, area northwest of 5, 30
bull or ox 76, 79
burial markers, stone 184, 192, 201, 209, 211, 227
burial vaults 72
burials 144, 146, 148, 150, 151, 185, 186, 187, 191, 192, 193, 195, 202, 210, 211, 228, 238; pithos 135, 144, 150, 154; of child 194
Buschbach, T. C. 179 n. 2
button 9, 37, 139 *see* STONE OBJECTS, TERRACOTTA OBJECTS

Camp, John, II x, 64, 65
carbon 102, 103, 110
carbonized deposit 26
carnelian beads *see* STONE OBJECTS
Caskey, John L. ix, x
cemetery of chamber tombs 72; search for in 1956 176
central Europe 128, 231
Chalandriane 16
Chalcis 171, 174
chalice 93
chamber of tomb 72, 96, 181, 183, 184, 185, 187, 193, 195, 200, 201, 202, 204, 205, 206, 207, 210, 212, 225, 226; objects from 80, 83, 182, 197
chamber tombs ix, 72, 176, 219, 224; discovery of 72, 176, 179; Tomb E-4 xii, 179, 180-183; Tomb E-6 xii, 179, 184-192; Tomb E-7 192 n. 10; Tomb E-8 xii, 192-201; Tomb E-9 xii, 179, 201-207; Tomb E-10 xii, 179, 207-208; Tomb K-1 xii, 179, 208-215; Tomb K-2 224-237
Charalambopoulos, Nikos viii, 176
Charalambropoulos, Nikolaos 73
Chora 219, 237; museum of viii, 7, 46 n. 16, 95; people of x
Cincinnati, University of. Archaeological Expedition vii, viii, ix; Classics Fund vii
circuit wall 3, 8-18, 40
circular flat stone, NE of Main Building 30
circular building, Early Helladic 220, 222

cist, burials 154; of stone 97, 105
cistern, built over Tholos III 73, 76, 80
classical *see* POTTERY, *fabrics and wares*
clay, dromoi cut in 179
CLAY OBJECTS
    bowl 24, disk 49
Coldstream, J. N. 241
colonnade 40
column 23, 30, base 15, 30, 36, 40
composite vase 226, 234 *see* POTTERY, *shapes*
corridor, dog-leg 30; Corridor 25 33, 43; Corridor 26 32; Corridor 61 39; Corridor 70 37
Coulton, James 130 n. 74
court northwest of Building 103 30; Court 3 26; Court 42 4, 26; Court 58 40; Court 63 39; Court 88 26
Crete 37, 71, 85, 86, 89, 90, 91, 92, 146 n. 89, 150, 165, 173, 239
crude brick 15, 19, 26, 41, 45, 61, 62
cult scene, on signet ring 113
cup 42, 47, 51, 52, 54, 55, 62, 66, 83, 92, 134, 138, 144, 145, 150, 160, 165, 166, 171, 172, 174, 177, 183, 191, 195, 198, 199, 201, 205, 206, 207, 226, 227, 233, 234, 235, 239, 240 *see* POTTERY, *shapes*
curved walls 222

de Jong, Piet vii, ix, x
de Teran, F. Callentes 132 n. 76
Dendra 87, 88, 90, 91, 128, 142, 158, 168, 170, 212
deposit above stones 67; in lowest layer 53; of ashy gray earth 36; of disintegrated brick 41; of ruins and rubbish 43; of very black earth 63
Deriziotis, Eustathis viii, 73, 219
Desborough, Vincent 239, 239 n. 10, 241, 241 n. 11
diadem *see* GOLD OBJECTS
Dinsmoor, Wm. B., Jr. ix
Donovan, William P. ix, x, xi, xii, 72, 179
Donovan, Mrs. William P. x
door jambs 74, 95, 181, 184, 185, 202, 210, 225
doorway 61, 72, 74, 75, 79, 80, 82, 95, 181, 184, 185, 192, 201, 209, 210, 225
Dörpfeld, Wilhelm 28, 40
drain 4, 5, 9, 12, 17, 19, 22, 23, 44
drawings vii, ix
dromos 68, 72, 73, 80, 81, 95, 100, 107, 110, 179, 180, 180 n. 3, 182, 184, 187, 192, 195, 201, 204, 207, 209, 212, 225, 229; Dromos E-1 179-180; Dromos E-2 180
dump, outside southern corner 41

Early Helladic period, walls and pottery of xii, 219, 220, 221, 222, 224
Early Helladic pottery in south, central and North Greece 28
Early Mycenaean *see* POTTERY, *fabrics and wares*
earthquake 34, 74 n. 4, 76, 78, 80, 108, 178
Egypto-Syrian pots 94
Eleusis 163, 175
Elis, Ancient 242
Englianos hill viii, 3, 18, 24, 25, 48, 62, 64, 65, 67, 68, 72, 73, 77, 134; Ano Englianos 237
Enkomi 114
erosion 5, 6, 67
Euboea 155 n. 97
Eutresis 49, 224
Evans, Angela C. ix
Evans, Sir Arthur 83, 85, 188
exedra 7, 23

faience *see* PASTE OBJECTS
Fant, Jesse E. ix
feeding bottle 211
fire: damage, destruction caused by 3, 34, 38, 50; evidence of 53, 54, 57, 58, 60, 77, 78, 187 n. 9
flask 208 *see* POTTERY, *shapes*
flint *see* STONE OBJECTS, VARIETIES OF STONE USED
floors 22, 32, 39, 50, 63, 77, 79, 97, 104, 141; of earth 23, 32, 36, 58; of flat stones 62; of pebbles 35, 54; of stucco 12, 29, 30, 34, 35, 39, 61
foundation 12, 18, 40, 41, 53, 148
Frantz, Alison ix, 6 n. 3, 80
French, David x, 32
French, Elizabeth 159 n. 98, 211 n. 14a, 214 n. 16
frescoes 51, 86
funeral ceremony 187, monuments 71
Furtwaengler, A. 85

gateway 3, 4
gems 78
Geometric *see* POTTERY, *fabrics and wares*
Gillieron, E. ix
glass, medieval 6
glass paste *see* paste
Gliatas, Nikolaos viii, 72, 73, 76
goblet 151, 199, 200, 205 *see* POTTERY, *shapes*
GOLD OBJECTS
  beads 75, 83, 185, 187, 228; amygdaloid 81; biconical 116; cylindrical 83; drum 104, 106, 109, 115; figure eight shield 83, 114; seal 104; signet 113, 114; spacer 106, 114, 115; spherical 82, 230; tubular with spirals 115

bead mounting 116
diadem 16, 141, 147, 153, 166
disk 81, 82, 83, 118
earring 104, 116
foil 119, 120
fragments 76, 106
fringe 106, 120
inlay 74, 118, 119
leaf, pieces of 75, 81, 84, 102, 103, 106, 108, 110, 120, 147
ornaments: bird 117; butterfly 111, 117; owl 106, 117; shield 83
pendant: jug or ewer 83; leaf-shaped 83, 104, 105, 109, 115, 116; shield 104, 114
pin mounting 116
plate, fragments of 117
ring, with heart-shaped bezel 113; signet 105, 113
rivet 118
rosette 75, 81, 82, 83, 100, 102, 104, 106, 111, 112, 118, 119
roundel 118, 119
sequin 118
strip 84, 120
stud 118
wire inlays 81, 84; gold-plated 120
wreath 147, 152, 156
Granary style pottery 239, 242
Grave Circle xi, 71, 72, 73, 134-176, 221: date of 148; description 134; doorway and dromos, lack of 154; excavation 135; extended exploration 148; grave pits 142; grid, use of 137; objects found 156
Grave Circles A and B at Mycenae 72, 152, 153
Grave E-3 xii, 176-178, 183
grave markers *see* burial markers, stone
grave robbers 78
Greek Archaeological Service vii, viii, 33
griffin 104

habitation debris 43
Hachmann, R. 128, 128 n. 70
Hagia Triada 173
Hall 64 37
Hall 65 12, 36, 37
Hammond, N. G. L. 153 n. 94
Hatzidakis, J. 165
Haussoullier, B. 86
hearth 36, 220, 222
Hellenic-American Archaeological Expedition 72
Hellenistic *see* POTTERY, *fabrics and wares*
helmet, boar's tusk 151, 163
Hendrickson, Eiler, Jr. x, 65
Higgins, R. A. 116
Hill, Bert Hodge 80
Hill, Mrs. Bert Hodge 73

Holmberg, E. J. 28
Hope, Rosemary x
houses 10, 11, 19, 23, 26, 29, 40, 41, 44, 48, 62
Hubbe, Rolf x, 33
Hughes-Brock, Helen 113, 121, 126, 132
hydria or amphora 134

Ialysos 85, 232
Iolkos 85, 239
IRON OBJECTS
  knife 239, 240; nail 14; pin 226, 239, 240
Ithaca 241
ivory, carved decoration 62, 79, 86: bull 54; half rosettes back to back 85, 86; head of sphinx 86; lion 86; longitudinal grooves and ridges 86; nautiluses, double 84; single 85; panels of spirals 85, 86; rosettes 86, 212; sacral ivy leaves on leaf-shaped beads 188; wings or feathers 62
IVORY OBJECTS
  bead cylindrical 130, leaf-shaped 188; chest or box, fragments of 85, 86, 102, 110, 130; chunk 50; disk 86, 185, 188; finial 130; fragments 60, 62, 76, 79, 85, 86, 99, 113, 138, 145, 164, 228, 232; handle of awl 136, 158; inlay 86; pin 86, 143, 146, 151, 157, 162, 232; plaque 84, 130, 147; pommel 138, 143, 145, 151, 152, 157, 162, 164; roundel 211, 212; seal, lentoid 59; shield 129; triangle 185, 188

jasper, sealstone of 37
jar 49, 105, 137, 138, 142, 144, 150, 152, 165, 166, 172, 173, 200, 201, 211, 213, 215, 226, 227, 235 *see* POTTERY, *shapes*
javelin point *see* BRONZE OBJECTS
jug 28, 42, 47, 49, 52, 105, 112, 133, 134, 138, 171, 173, 183, 185, 187, 190, 191, 192, 193, 196, 197, 198, 200, 204, 205, 206, 210, 211, 214, 215, 226, 227, 232, 233, 234, 235, 236 *see* POTTERY, *shapes*

Kakovatos 117, 118, 122, 126, 128, 129, 133, 150, 166, 212, 212 n. 15
Kallipolitis, B. viii, 81
Karo, G. 127, 156, 161
Karouzos, Christos viii, 95 n. 29
Karpophora, Messenia 239, 242
Kato Englianos 71, 72, 77
Kephalovrison, Messenia 72, 128, 171, 175 n. 107
kiln 19
Kittredge, Caryl F. x, 10, 15, 16, 17, 25, 27, 48

Kittredge, William G. x, 10, 43, 45, 46
Knossos 85, 86, 90, 91, 164, 165, 172, 173
Kokkevis, Ioannis and family viii, 73, 81, 219, 224, 237
Konsola, Mrs. Dora 81
Konstantopoulos, Kosta ix
Kontogeorges, Triandaphyllos 81
Kontos, Aristomenos viii, 73, 208
Korakou 150 n. 92, 171
Koryphasion 107, 133, 172, 237
Koşay, H. S. 115 n. 46
Koukirikos, Messenia 150 n. 92, 153, 154
Koukounara, Messenia 155 n. 97
Kourouniotis, Konstantinos vii, 71, 77 n. 7, 85
krater 52, 226, 229, 230 see POTTERY, *shapes*
krater-bowl 67, 93 see POTTERY, *shapes*
kylix 47, 55, 56, 66, 67, 82, 83, 92, 93, 138, 141, 173, 175, 178, 180, 183, 184, 187, 189, 196, 202, 204, 205, 206, 207, 211, 212, 214, 227, 229, 235 see POTTERY, *shapes*
Kypraiou, Mrs. 81

Lachish 132
Laconia 155 n. 97
Lake, Wiltshire 128
Lakkithra, Kephallenia 115
Lamy, Mrs. Charles S. 37
Lands, Lewey T. ix, 73
Lang, Mabel ix, x, xi, 10, 53 n. 17, 159, 225
Langada, Cos 231
Langsam, Walter C. xi
Langsam, Mrs. Walter C. xi
Late Helladic I, II, III, Late Mycenaean see POTTERY, *fabrics and wares*
lead glaze on medieval pottery 6
LEAD OBJECTS
    disk 31, 58, 82; rivet 49, 166; wire 84
Lefkandi 229 n. 3
lekythos 239, 240, 241
Lempese, Miss A. 81
Lerna 63, 127, 150 n. 92, 158, 171, 224
Levkas 150 n. 92, 153
libations 67
limestone rock 76, 179, 181, 207; walls of rough, unworked 5, 221
Linear A 94
Linear B viii, 53, 94
Loeschcke, G. 85
lower town 3, 10, 13, 41, 47-68

Main Building viii, 4, 9, 10, 14, 18, 24, 25, 26, 30, 32, 33, 34, 36, 43, 46

Makrysia, Elis 153, 172, 175 n. 107
Mallia 117, 172, 173, 173 n. 106
Malthi 76, 150 n. 92
Mari, Palace of 115
Marinatos, Spyridon vii, viii, 95, 167
marl 155
Matarrubilla Dolmen 132
Mattpainted see POTTERY, *fabrics and wares*
Matzaka, Mrs. Antonia T. x
Mavraganis, Andreas 80, 81, 86
Mavroudia 72
McCredie, James x
McDonald, William A. x, 4 n. 1, 9, 10, 11, 14, 17, 18, 26, 48, 95 n. 29
Megiddo 132
Melos 122, 123
Menidi 83, 85, 86, 87, 89, 94, 111, 125, 130, 158, 170
Merhart, G. V. 128 n. 70
Mesopotamia 132
Messenia vii, viii, 28, 67, 71, 77, 80, 214, 239, 241
mica, clay containing 36
Middle Helladic see POTTERY, *fabrics and wares*
Midea 83, 91
Milojcic, V. 128, 128 n. 68
Minyan see POTTERY, *fabrics and wares*
Mochlos 158, 165
mold, for beads and ornaments 85, 88, 90, 91
mudbrick 221
mug or tankard 134
Müller-Karpe, H. 231
Mycenae, comparative material from 24, 56, 78, 83, 85, 86, 87, 88, 89, 90, 91, 92, 94, 107, 111, 112, 113, 115, 116, 118, 123, 126, 127, 128, 129, 130, 131, 132, 143, 147, 151, 154, 156, 157, 158, 161, 162, 164, 166, 168, 171, 173, 221 see also Grave Circles A and B
Mycenaean I, II, III see POTTERY, *fabrics and wares*
Mylonas, George E. x, 28, 37, 128 n. 68
Myrsinokhori-Routsi 150 n. 92

National Museum, Athens viii, ix, 80, 81, 87 n. 20, n. 21, 88 n. 22, 89 n. 23, 90 n. 24, n. 25, n. 26, 91 n. 27, n. 28
Navarino 209; bay of 18, 134, 219
Neleids 239
Neolithic in south, central, and north Greece 28
niches, in wall of tombs 193, 194; of dromos 180, 192, 208
Northeast Gateway ix, 4, 8, 17, 18, 27
Northeastern Building 25
northeastern quarter 64
northern quarter 63

northwestern scarp 48
Nuzi 132

obsidian see STONE OBJECTS, VARIE-TIES OF STONE USED
olive oil press 6
Olympia viii, 28, 150 n. 92, 158
Orchomenos 150 n. 92
Oxylithos 155 n. 97

Pachyammos 158, 165
Palace of Nestor vii, 3, 18, 79, 83, 95, 123, 208, 219, 221
Palace Workshop 25, 26, 29
Palaikastro 172
Panagopoulos, Charalambos x
Papathanasopoulos, George viii, ix, x, 10, 11, 32, 38, 43, 46, 48, 50, 52, 53, 57, 81
Pappoulia, Messenia 150 n. 92, 153, 154
Paraskevopoulos, Demetrios viii, 73, 176
paste (glasspaste, faience) 79, 82, 87
PASTE OBJECTS
    beads: 74, 76, 77, 79, 85, 87, 89, 102, 105, 136, 138, 139, 140, 142, 146, 149, 170, 180, 195, 212; fragments of 131; amygda-loid 92, 133, 204; cylindrical 90, 132, 140; disk-shaped 91, 139, 170; floral 89, 90, 211; leaf-shaped 82, 90, 91; spacer 104, 131, 139, 170, 212; spherical 82, 91, 92, 131, 132, 170, 182, 186, 189, 195, 197, 200, 204; tubular 90; various shapes 82, 89, 90, 91, 92, 159, 170
    button 111; disk 100, 113; jewel 133; ornaments 85, 87; shield 88; plaque 79, 85, 87, 88; rosette 88; strip or inlay 59, 89; talis-man 133
pavement 12, 35; earlier 35
Pedley, John x, 11, 13, 28, 38, 40
Peloponnesos 48, 67, 71, 77, 107, 241
Peristeria, Messenia 116, 117, 120, 120 n. 56, 153, 167
Petropoulos, George viii, 47, 48, 63, 64
Phaistos 85, 89, 90, 91, 111, 163
photographers ix
Piggott, S. 128 n. 70
pit, outside Room 24 33
pit-graves xi, 71, 176
pithoid jar 42, 93, 186, 189, 191, 197, 205, 206 see POTTERY, *shapes*
pithos 94, 136, 138, 142, 143, 146, 149, 157, 163, 174 see POTTERY, *shapes*
plaster, painted 9, 10, 15, 29, 34, 48, 178; preserved on floor 62, on walls 61, 62

pointillé design 147
Popham, Mervyn 165, 173 n. 124,
229 n. 3
portico 30
pottery, catalogues 8, 24, 28, 42, 47,
49, 51, 52, 54-57, 62, 66-67, 82-83,
92-95, 111, 112, 113, 133-134,
157-158, 159, 163, 165-166, 171-
176, 177-178, 179, 183, 187, 189-
192, 195-201, 204-206, 207, 208,
212, 213-215, 224, 229-230, 232-
237, 240-241
POTTERY, *decoration*
motives, impressed: finger and
nail impressions 224
motives, incised 9, 13, 25, 28, 33,
62, 224, 241; inscribed 241;
signs 94
motives, painted:
all over coating 52, 93
bands 42, 49, 52, 55, 56, 67, 93,
94, 133, 134, 196, 206, 214,
215, 229, 235, 237, 241
chevrons 28
circle 151, 196; compass drawn
241; concentric 56, 208, 215,
235
crosses 157
diagonal lines 55, 56, 149, 163
diamond, crosshatched 241
double axes 94
flower with large bulb 67
goat 230
hunting scene 206, 229
linear patterns 93, 105, 227
racket 151
spiral 94, 134
stripes 49, 52
tortoise-shell 105, 145
trickle 150
triglyph 215
wavy line 55
wheel pattern 94
zigzag 56, 93, 197, 241
motives, painted:
Furumark's represented
Motive 9: f or i, 2, 15 (lily) 171,
174, 198
Motive 10: 1 (crocus) 171
Motive 11: 54 (papyrus) 55, 191
Motive 12: c or d, 7, 23, 24, 25,
26, 27 ("sacral ivy") 55, 83,
166, 171, 173, 175, 196, 197,
198, 199, 200, 205, 206
Motive 13: 3 (ogival canopy) 173
Motive 14: 2, k, 11, 13 (palm I)
171, 198, 199, 201
Motive 15: 15 (palm II) 214
Motive 16: 5 (grass or reed) 56,
174
Motive 17: 5 (rosette) 166
Motive 18: 71, 92, 109, 139
(Mycenaean III flower) 204,
213, 215, 235, 236

Motive 19: 1, 11, 13, 15, 17, 23,
25, 31 (multiple stem and
tongue pattern) 55, 56, 183,
189, 196, 204, 206, 208, 213
Motive 22: 15, 16 (curtailed
argonaut) 55, 183
Motive 23: 5, 6 (whorl-shell) 213,
214
Motive 25: 9 ("bivalve shell") 204
Motive 27: 6, 17, 18 ("sea anemone") 199, 213, 235
Motive 29: 5, 10, 15 (trefoil
rock-work) 175, 214, 232
Motive 30: 1, 2 ("seaweed") 173,
175
Motive 32: 5, 8, 19, 22, 24 (rock
pattern I) 172, 173, 174, 175,
178, 179, 190, 197, 198, 199,
201, 204, 206, 212
Motive 33: 2, 6, 8, 10, 11, 16, 19,
21 (rock pattern II) 166, 187,
191, 199, 212
Motive 35: 4 (double axe) 94
Motive 38: 6 (pendant) 173
Motive 41: 2, 14 (circles) 174,
196
Motive 42: 7, 8, 9, 21 (joining
semicircles) 187, 230, 236
Motive 43: h, j, 4, 6, 13 (isolated semicircles) 190, 196,
233, 234, 237
Motive 45: 6 (U-pattern) 183
Motive 46: 9, 12, 29, 33, 51, 52,
54 (running spiral) 56, 172,
190, 192 n. 11, 199, 200
Motive 48: 5, 18 (quirk) 183,
191, 200, 213, 235
Motive 49: 10, 19 (curved-stem
spiral) 189, 190, 191
Motive 50: 9 (antithetic spiral
pattern) 232
Motive 53: 11, 17, 20, 25, 30, 31
(wavy line) 55, 178, 190, 191,
215, 233, 234
Motive 54: 4 (cross) 174, 199
Motive 57: 2 (diaper net) 189,
192 n. 11, 205, 213
Motive 58: 1, 8, 15, 17, 28
(parallel chevrons) 183, 189,
190, 196, 206, 208, 233
Motive 61: 18 (zigzag) 56, 229,
230, 234
Motive 61 A: 1 (triangle) 233
Motive 62: 10 (tricurved arch)
118 n. 52
Motive 63: 3, 6 (hatched loop)
172, 174, 175, 206
Motive 64: 3, 7, 21, 25 (foliate
band) 119 n. 53, 173, 174,
214, 236
Motive 66: 2 (arcade pattern)
173
Motive 67: 5, 6, 10 (curved
stripes) 192 n. 11, 214

Motive 68: 1, 2 (wheel) 94, 172,
174, 175, 198, 199, 201, 205
Motive 69: 1 ("adder mark") 173
Motive 70: 1, 7 (scale pattern)
192 n. 11, 233
Motive 71: h (elaborate triangle) 229
Motive 75: 17, 30 (paneled patterns) 229, 230
Motive 76: 1 (variegated stone
patterns) 175
Motive 77 (stipple pattern) 55
Motive 78: 1, 2, 3 (ripple pattern) 134, 150, 192 n. 11, 199,
200
Furumark's on various shapes
alabastron Motive 9: f, i, 2, 12,
13, 15 lily: 171, 174, 198;
Motive 12: c, d, 12: 23, 24,
25, 27 "sacral ivy" 115, 173,
196, 198, 200, 205; Motive
14: 11, 13 palm I 198, 201;
Motive 19: 11, 15, 17 multiple stem and tongue 196,
206; Motive 29: 5, 15 trefoil rock-work 175; Motive
30: 1 "seaweed" 175; Mo-
tive 32: 5 rock pattern I
172, 173, 174, 175, 178,
179, 190, 197; Motive 32: 8,
19, 21, 22, 24 rock pattern I
172, 173, 198, 199; Motive
33: 16 or 21 rock pattern II
212; Motive 35: 4 double
axe 94; Motive 43: 6 con-
centric semicircles 190; Motive 48: 18 quirk 235;
Motive 53: 11 wavy lines
178; Motive 57: 2 diaper
net 205; Motive 58: triple
chevrons 206; Motive 63: 6
hatched loop 174, 175, 206;
Motive 64: 3, 21 foliate
spray 174, 236; Motive 68:
1, 2 wheel 94, 172, 174, 175,
198, 199, 201, 205; Motive
76 stone patterns 175
amphora Motive 43: 4, h, j
isolated semicircles 233, 237
askos Motive 41: 2 circles 174
beaker Motive 19: 1 multiple
stem and tongue 56; Mo-
tive 46: 54 running spiral
56; Motive 61 zigzag 56
bowl, deep conical Motive 53:
20 wavy line 234; Motive
61: 18 zigzag 234; pedes-
taled Motive 29: 10 trefoil
rock-work 232; Motive 50:
9 antithetic spiral pattern
252; three-handled conical
Motive 48: 5 quirks 191;
Motive 49: 19 curve-
stemmed spiral 190; Motive

POTTERY, *decoration,* Furumark's on various shapes, bowl (*cont.*)

    53: 17, 30 wavy line 190, 191

cup, bell-shaped Motive 77 stipple pattern 55; cylindrical Motive 78: 1 or 2 ripple pattern 199; deep Motive 78: 1 ripple pattern 166; one low handle Motive 77 stipple 55, Motive 46: 12, 29 running spiral 172, 199, Motive 12: 27 "sacral ivy" 206; one high handle Motive 22: 15 curtailed argonaut 55, Motive 46: 33 running spiral 198; shallow or saucer Motive 10: 1 crocus 171, Motive 12: 23 "sacral ivy" 171, Motive 14: k 171; spouted Motive 16: 5 grass or reed 174, Motive 54: 4 cross 174

flask Motive 58 parallel chevrons 208

goblet, one high handle Motive 78: 3 200; two low handles Motive 46: 51 or 52 running spirals 199

jar, one-handled Motive 13: 3 ogival canopy 173, Motive 63: 3 hatched loop 172; Palace Style Motive 12 "sacral ivy" 166, Motive 17: 5 rosette 166, Motive 33: 10, 19; rock pattern II 166; spouted Motive 78: 1 ripple pattern 165; squat Motive 32: 5 rock pattern I 201, Motive 46: 33 running spiral 200; three-handled jar Motive 57: 2 diaper net 213

jug, beaked Motive 22: 16 curtailed argonaut 183, Motive 30: 2 "seaweed" 173, Motive 32: 5 rock pattern I 173, Motive 33: 8 rock pattern I 187, Motive 38: 6 pendant 173, Motive 64: 7 foliate band 173, Motive 66: 2 arcade pattern 173, Motive 42: 7, 8 joining semicircles 187, Motive 48: 5 quirks 183, Motive 69: 1 adder mark 173; cutaway neck Motive 12 c or d "sacral ivy" 197, Motive 67: 10 curved stripes 214; narrow-necked Motive 42: 21 joining semicircles 236, Motive 43: h isolated semicircles 234, Motive 61 A: 1 triangle 233; one-handled

Motive 78: 1 ripple pattern 134; side-spouted Motive 32: 5 rock pattern I 190, 204; squat Motive 53: 25 wavy line 233, 234; three-handled Motive 58: 8 parallel chevrons 190; two-handled Motive 58 or 61 parallel chevrons 183, Motive 45: 6 U-pattern 183

krater Motive 42: 9 joining semicircles 230, Motive 61: 18 zigzag 230, Motive 71: h elaborate triangle 230, Motive 75: 17 paneled patterns 229, 230

kylix Motive 11: 54 papyrus 55, Motive 12: 27 "sacral ivy" 55, Motive 15: 15 palm II 214, Motive 19: 1 multiple stem and tongue 55, Motive 23: 6 whorl-shell 214, Motive 29: 10 trefoil rock-work 214, Motive 53: 20 wavy line 55, Motive 61: 18 zigzag 229; Motive 75: 30 paneled patterns 229

pithoid jar Motive 11 papyrus 191, Motive 12: 23-27 "sacral ivy" 205, Motive 19: 15 multiple stem and tongue pattern 189, Motive 33: 6 or 11 rock pattern II 191, Motive 49: 10 curved stem spiral 189, 191, Motive 57: 2 diaper net 189, Motive 58: 15 parallel chevrons 189

rhyton Motive 14: 2, top, type b palm I 199, Motive 16 grass or reed 56, Motive 27: 6 "sea anemone" 199, Motive 33: 2, 19 rock pattern II 199

stirrup-jar (-vase) Motive 12: 7 "sacral ivy" 199, Motive 18: 71, 92, 109, 139 Mycenaean III flower 204, 213, 215, 235, 236, Motive 19: 13, 17, 23, 25, 31 multiple stem and tongue pattern 183, 204, 208, 213, Motive 23: 5 whorl-shell 213, Motive 25: 9 "bivalve shell" 204, Motive 27: 17, 18 "sea anemone" 213, 235, Motive 41: 14 circles 196, Motive 43: 13 isolated semicircles 196, Motive 48: 5 quirk 200, 213, Motive 53: 31 wavy line 215, Motive 58: 15 or 17 parallel chevrons 196, Motive 70: 7 scale pattern 233

motives, plastic
    band on neck 241
    ledge molding 183
    molded head of deer 95
    raised ridge at junction of neck and body 42
    raised ring between neck and shoulder 93
    ridge at base of neck 191, 197; on handle 183, 191
    rope bands bearing transverse gashes 36

POTTERY, *fabrics and wares*
black-glazed, classical 26; Geometric 63

coarse 9, 25, 33, 45, 76, 111, 112, 113, 134, 141, 224; semi- 111, 113

domestic 175

Early Helladic xii, 28, 222, 224

Early Mycenaean 7, 9, 11, 20, 22, 23, 24, 25, 32, 33, 37, 40, 57, 71, 72 *see also* Late Helladic I, Late Helladic II

Geometric 6, 27, 61, 62, 63

glazed, of medieval times 6

Granary style 239, 242

Hellenistic 6, 67

Late Helladic I 3, 6, 7, 8, 9, 11, 13, 18, 29, 31, 31 n. 12, 33, 34, 36, 43, 45, 46, 58, 134, 141, 148 *see also* Early Mycenaean

Late Helladic I or II *see also* Early Mycenaean

Late Helladic II 3, 7, 8, 9, 13, 36, 43, 45, 46, 58, 61, 75, 79, 83, 166 *see also* Early Mycenaean

Late Helladic II-III 140, 149

Late Helladic III, undecorated 106

Late Helladic III A 11, 43, 46, 155, 193, 203 *see also* Mycenaean III A

Late Helladic III A-III B 179, 182

Late Helladic III B 7, 10, 13, 43, 46, 62, 111, 148, 204, 228, 232, 235, 236, coarse ware 112 *see also* Mycenaean III B

Late Helladic III B-III C 226, 228, 233

Late Helladic III C 226, 229, 233, 234, 235 *see also* Mycenaean III C

Late Mycenaean 10, 11, 32, 33 *see also* Late Helladic III A, III B, III C

Mattpainted 6, 9, 13, 25, 31 n. 12, 33, 34, 43, 45, 49, 53, 58, 111

Middle Bronze Age 32

Middle Helladic 9, 10, 11, 13, 16, 26, 27, 29, 32, 33, 40, 46, 48, 49, 63, 107, 111, 112, 134, 224; coarse 9, 45; decoration 152; in south, central, and north

POTTERY, *fabrics and wares,* Middle Helladic (*cont.*)

   Greece: incised 9; late 46; layer at Eutresis 49; *see also* Matt-painted and Minyan

Middle Helladic III at Lerna 163

Minoan imports 153

Minyan 13, 25, 43, 53, 111, 159, 175; Argive 33, 45, 62; black 34, 223, 224; gray 25, 33, 34

monochrome 105

Mycenaean 10, 48, 53, 62, 63, 67, 111, 113

Mycenaean I 45

Mycenaean I-II 53

Mycenaean II 45

Mycenaean III, plain 22

Mycenaean III A 31, 32, 36, 39, 41, 45, 50, 51, 52, 53, 54, 57, 58, 60, 61, 65, 79 *see also* Late Helladic III A

Mycenaean III A-III B 54

Mycenaean III B 15, 17, 26, 29, 36, 38, 39, 40, 41, 45, 61, 65, 79, 82, 83, 93 *see also* Late Helladic III B

Mycenaean III C 93 *see also* Late Helladic III C

Neolithic in south, central, and north Greece 28

plain 82

Protogeometric 237, 241, 242

ribbed 6

transitional between Early and Middle Helladic 220, between Middle Helladic and Late Helladic 105, 107

POTTERY, *shapes*

alabastron 45, 113, 137, 172, 175, 177, 178, 183, 193, 195, 203; angular 138, 150, 174, 175, 189, 196, 200, 201, 205, 206, 211, 214, 226, 227, 235, 236; high 94; miniature 190, 191; squat 171, 197, 198, 199, 212; *see* Shape 64, *MP* Types 81, 82, 83, 84, 85, 87, 89, 91, 92, 93, 94; POTTERY, *decoration, MP* Motives on

amphora 67, 105, 133, 134, 233, 237, 239, 241; ovoid 133; *see* Shape 47, *MP,* Types 58, 70; POTTERY, *decoration, MP* Motives on

amphoriskos 67 *see* Shape 47

animal pot, fragments 94

askos 136, 138, 151, 159, 174 *see MP,* Type 195; POTTERY, *decoration, MP* Motives on

basin 42, 52 *see* Shape 1, *MP,* Type 295

beaker 56 *see MP,* Type 225; POTTERY, *decoration, MP* Motives on

bowl: conical, deep 234, three-handled 189, 190, 191; deep 239; miniature 66; one-handled 199, high-swung 138, 171, 175; pedestaled 226, 232; rounded, shallow, angular 92, spouted 42, two pinched-out handles 47; small 83, *see* Shapes 4, 7, *MP* Types 279, 291, 295, 305 or 306, 307; POTTERY, *decoration, MP* Motives on

chalice or handleless goblet 93-94

composite vase 226, 234 *see MP,* Types 96, 330

cup: bell-shaped 47; conical (handleless) 42, 47, 51, 52, 54, 83, 92, 195, 198, 205, 207; cylindrical 199; deep 145, 160; flaring 55; Geometric 62; one-handled 66, 166, 206, 240, flat vertical 177, high swung 55, 183, 191, 198, 205, low 55, ring 201; pedestal cup or saucer 52, 171; plain 226, 227; shallow 145; small 235; spouted 138; two-handled 239, 240; Vapheio 113, 165; *see* Shapes 11, 12, 17, 19; *MP* Types 220, 221, 222, 224, 225, 230, 231, 236, 237, 238, 241, 253; POTTERY, *decoration, MP* Motives on

feeding-bottle 211 *see* side-spouted jug with basket handles

flask 208 *see MP,* Types 190-192; POTTERY, *decoration, MP* Motives on

goblet: short stemmed 151, 205, with high handle 200; stemmed, two-handled 199 *see MP,* Types 263 or 264, 270; POTTERY, *decoration, MP* Motives on

jar: four-handled 227; one-handled 137, 138, 150, 172, 173; "Palace Style" 79, 105, 138, 142, 144, 150, 152, 166; squat with vertical ring handle 200, 201; tall spouted (Cretan type) 138, 144, 150, 152, 165; three-handled 211, 213, 215, 227, 235; two-handled 226, two horizontal 49; wide mouthed 49 *see MP* Types 15, 39, 40, 45, 48, 49, 50; POTTERY, *decoration, MP* Motives on

jug: 105, 133, 211, amphoroid 191; beaked 173, 183, 187, 205, 214, 215; bridge-spouted, broad-necked 227, 235; cutaway mouth 138, 171, 192, neck 197, 200, 204, 214, spout 192; large 210; miniature 190, 206; narrow-necked 226, 227, 232, 234, 236, spouted 42, two-handled 183; one-handled 47, 196, 197; side-spouted with basket handle 185, 191, 193, 196, 197, 198, 204; small spherical 112; spouted Minoan style 138, small two-handled 52; squat one-handled 28, 226, 233, 234; three-handled 49, *see* Shape 41, *MP,* Types 103, 109, 110, 114, 120, 122, 123, 126, 131, 132, 133, 135, 136, 141, 144, 145, 150, 151, 159, 160, 161, 163; POTTERY, *decoration, MP* Motives on

krater 52, 226, 229, 230; conical 226; stemmed, with two handles 52; *see* Shape 63, *MP,* Types 8, 10, 282; POTTERY, *decoration, MP* Motives on

krater-bowl 67, 93 *see* Shape 60, *MP* Type 284

kylix 30, 53, 56, 68, 82, 113, 138, 141, 173, 175, 178, 180, 183, 184, 187, 189, 196, 202, 211, 227, 229, 235: angular 83, 212, one-handled 47, 92, 204, 205, 212, small 66; diminutive 66; high-stemmed, small 55; horizontal loop handles 214, ribbon handles 55; large 93; one-handled 206; small 47; two-handled 67, 92, 93, high 47, 56, 207; *see* Shapes 26, 27, 29b, 29c, 30c, *MP* Types 254, 257, 259, 264, 265, 266, 267, 270, 271, 272, 274, 275; POTTERY, *decoration, MP* Motives on

lekythos 239, 240-241

mug 56, 134

pithoid jar 186, 189, 191, 206: diminutive 197; small 42, 205; three-handled on pedestal 93 *see* Shapes 51, 52, 53, *MP,* Types 28, 35, 42, 44, 45, 49; POTTERY, *decoration, MP* Motives on

pithos 32, 35, 36, 60, 76, 79, 136, 142, 143, 146, 149, 157; Middle Helladic decoration on 163; oval-shaped 136; ovoid 163; pointed bottom 94; small 138, two-handled 94, with molded rings 174; *see MP,* Type 13a

rhyton, conical 56, 199 *see MP,* Type 199; POTTERY, *decoration, MP* Motives on

scoop 82, 93 *see also* Shape 66, *MP,* Type 311

stirrup-jar (-vase): 196, 199, 200, 204, 208, 213, 215, 233, 235, 236; disk concave 199, flat 213, 233; globular body on slightly raised base 183; small with pedestal base 94; spreading pedestal base triple handles 196; squat 227; *see MP,* Types 165 or 167, 167, 169, 171 or 173, 176,

POTTERY, *shapes*, stirrup-jar (-vase) (*cont.*)
178, 179, 180, 182; POTTERY, *decoration, MP* Motives on tankard or mug 134
urnlike cup 94

POTTERY, *shapes*
Furumark's Types (*MP*)
Type 8 (deep krater with two vertical handles) 52
Type 10 (deep krater with two vertical handles, stemmed, semiglobular) 229
Type 13a (pithos, pointed base) 94
Type 15 (pithoid jar) 166
Type 28 (small pithoid jar) 42, 205
Type 35 (pithoid jar) 93
Type 37 (pithoid jar) 93
Type 39 (three-handled pithoid jar) 213
Type 40 (three-handled pithoid jar) 215
Type 44 (small pithoid jar) 189, 205, 206
Type 45 (small pithoid jar) 206, 213
Type 48 (three-handled pithoid jar) 235
Type 49 (three-handled pithoid jar) 215
Type 50 (three-handled pithoid jar) 215
Type 58 (large, late, III C, storage jar) 237
Type 70 (amphora, handles from below rim) 233
Type 81 (squat jar with curved profile—alabastron-shaped) 172, 175
Type 82 (alabastron-shaped) 171, 173, 174, 196, 197, 198, 199
Type 83 (alabastron-shaped) 174
Type 84 (alabastron-shaped) 173, 175, 177, 179, 190, 195, 198, 212
Type 85 (alabastron-shaped) 94, 196, 197
Type 87 (squat jar with one vertical ring-handle) 172, 173, 200, 201
Type 89 (squat jar with angular profile) 200
Type 91 (squat jar with angular profile) 174
Type 92 (squat jar with angular profile) 175
Type 93 (squat jar with angular profile) 200, 205
Type 94 (squat jar with angular profile) 206, 214, 236
Type 96 (squat jar with angular profile) 235, 236
Type 103 (bridge-spouted jug) 133
Type 109 (globular wide-necked jug) 215, 235
Type 110 (globular wide-necked jug) 235
Type 114 (small squat globular jug) 233, 234
Type 120 (narrow-necked jug, handle from below rim) 196, 214, 236
Type 123 (narrow-necked jug, handle from below rim) 232, 234
Type 126 (handmade miniature) 112
Type 131 or 132 (tall jug with cut-away neck) 171
Type 133 (tall jug with cut-away neck) 214
Type 135 (small early jug with cut-away neck) 197, 204
Type 136 (globular jug with cut-away neck) 192
Type 141 (tall beaked jug) 173
Type 144 (low beaked jug) 42, 183
Type 145 (low beaked jug) 214
Type 150, 151 (amphoroid beaked jug) 52, 191
Type 159-161 (side-spouted necked jar with basket handle) 190, 196, 204, 215
Type 163 (side-spouted necked jar with basket handle; small, handmade) 198
Type 165 or 167 (tall false-necked jar; three handles) 196
Type 169 (globular false-necked jar) 199
Type 171 (globular false-necked jar) 183, 208, 213, 215
Type 171 or 173 (globular false-necked jar) 204, 235
Type 176 (globular false-necked jar, Eastern type) 233
Type 178 (squat false-necked jar) 196
Type 179 (biconical false-necked jar) 196, 213
Type 180 (squat, perked-up false-necked jar) 196, 213, 236
Type 182 (conical false-necked jar) 94
Type 190-192 (globular flask, horizontal type; two-handled) 183, 208
Type 195 (based askos) 159, 174
Type 199 (conical rhyton) 56, 199
Type 204 (handleless conical cup) 42, 47, 51, 52, 54, 92, 198, 205
Type 211 (semiglobular cup "teacup") 172, 198
Type 216 (bell-shaped cup) 233
Type 218 or 219 (shallow semiglobular cup with raised base, flat handle) 55, 174
Type 220 (shallow semiglobular cup with one handle) 47, 66, 92
Type 221 (straight-sided cup) 165
Type 222 (domestic shallow cup) 66
Type 224 (cylindrical cup) 199
Type 225 (cylindrical cup) 56
Type 230 (conical cup, flat or flattened handle from rim to side) 55, 206
Type 231 (conical cup, splaying sides, flattened handle, rim to side) 47, 55
Type 236 (semiglobular cup with raised handle) 191, 198
Type 237 (shallow cup with ring-handle) 166, 171
Type 238 (shallow cup with ring-handle) 183
Type 241 (shallow cup with one or two raised handles) 55
Type 253 (spouted cup: raised handle at 90° to open horizontal spout) 42, 174
Type 254 (stemmed cup, kylix: two flat handles, short stem) 175
Type 257 (stemmed cup, two handles forming U loops) 214
Type 259 (stemmed cup, Rhodo-Mycenaean type) 56, 93
Type 263 (stemmed cup with deep bowl, two handles) 199
Type 264 (stemmed cup with deep conical bowl, two flat handles) 183, 199
Type 265 (stemmed cup height greater than diameter) 212
Type 266 (shallow, high stemmed cup with high handles) 55, 214 n. 16
Type 267 (low-stemmed, one-handled angular cup) 47, 66, 92, 189, 204, 205, 212
Type 270 (low-stemmed cup, one or two flat high handles) 175, 200, 205
Type 271 (low-stemmed cup, one or two high handles) 205
Type 272 (low-stemmed cup, one or two high handles) 56, 205, 212

POTTERY, *shapes*, Furumark's Types (*MP*) (*cont.*)

Type 274 (stemmed cup; conical bowl, two low handles) 93, 196

Type 275 (stemmed cup; conical bowl, two low handles) 229

Type 279 (deep rounded bowl with horizontal handles) 171

Type 282 (large, deep, rounded bowl, two handles) 229, 230

Type 284 (small, deep, rounded bowl with horizontal handles) 67, 93

Type 291 (deep conical bowl) 234

Type 295 (shallow bowl with flat horizontal handle) 42, 47, 55, 92

Type 305 (small, deep, stemmed bowl with horizontal handles) 214 n. 16, 232

Type 306 (small high stemmed bowl with horizontal handles) 232

Type 307 (conical handleless stemmed bowl, II A) 172

Type 311 (ladle or brazier with supporting handle) 42, 82, 93

Pylos classification (*PN* I pp. 235-418)

Shape 1 (basin with pinched-out handles) 42, 52

Shape 4 (bowl) 47, 92

Shape 7 (bowl with bridged spout) 42

Shape 11 (conical cup) 39 n. 13, 42, 47, 51, 52, 54, 83, 92, 195, 198, 205, 207

Shape 12 ("teacup") 47, 55, 66, 92

Shape 17 (cup: bell-shaped) 47, 55

Shape 19 (cup: two high handles, ring base) 55

Shape 26 (kylix: diminutive, two high straddle handles) 66

Shape 27 (kylix: small, angular one low handle) 47, 66, 92, 204, 206

Shape 29b (kylix: small, high stem, two flattened handles) 93

Shape 29c (kylix: "standard size," mostly high stem, two handles) 56, 67, 93

Shape 30c (kylix: deep conical bowl, stem of medium height, two high handles) 56

Shape 41 (jug: basket handle, tubular spout) 215

Shape 47 (amphora: small narrow neck, pedestal base, two vertical handles) 67

Shape 50 (jar: very large; three handles, two horizontal, one vertical) 49

Shape 51 (jar: pithoid, small, three horizontal handles, wide mouth, pedestal base) 42

Shape 52 (jar: pithoid, small; three vertical handles, wide mouth) 93

Shape 53 (jar: pithoid, pedestal foot; three vertical handles, narrow neck) 93

Shape 60 (krater-bowl "deep bowl": small; two horizontal handles) 67, 93

Shape 63 (pedestaled krater: high; two flat vertical handles from rim to side) 52

Shape 66 (ladle or scoop) 42, 82, 93

Propylon 36

Prosymna 92, 116, 132, 168, 195

Protogeometric 237

Protogeometric Tholos *see* Tholos

Pseira 112

rabbet 75

Ramp 91 25

Rawson, Marion x, xi, 4 n. 1, 8, 10, 11, 14, 17, 18, 25, 26, 29, 32, 37, 48, 52, 61, 63, 95 n. 29

rebate carried across front of lintel 75

reopenings of tomb 180

repoussé decoration 106, 139, 144, 147, 166, 227

rhyton 56, 199 *see* POTTERY, *shapes*

Richter, G. M. A. 20 n. 7

roadway, stone paved 4

Robinson, Henry S. x

rooms 39, 61, 62; of Palace: Room 7 3, 35, 36; Room 18 34; Room 20 34; Room 21 34, 43; Room 22 34, 43; Room 23 43; Room 24 33, 43; Room 27 9, 10, 32; Room 32 26, 32; Room 55 35; Room 56 35; Room 57 35; Room 60 40; Room 62 39; Room 65 50, 52; Room 74 37, 38, 50; Room 82 43, 44; Room 83 43; Room 84 43; Room 85 43; Room 86 43; Room 87 43; Room 98 26; Room 100 25; Room 104 32

rosette, decorative motif 139, 168; of gold and ivory 83

roundels 212 *see also* GOLD OBJECTS, IVORY OBJECTS

Rowe, Grace xi

rubble, heap of 41

Rutkowski, B. 113 n. 43

Sackett, L. H. 229 n. 3

Samikon, Elis 72, 153, 154, 171, 172, 173, 175 n. 107

Sandars, N. K. 128 n. 70

Saraphis, Emile ix

scabbards, traces of 143, 194

Schliemann, Heinrich 88, 90, 143

scoop 82, 93 *see* POTTERY, *shapes*

Seager 146 n. 89

sealstone *see* STONE OBJECTS

Semple, William T. vii

Semple, Mrs. William T. vii

sepulcher, royal 79

sepulchral rites 67

shaft grave, in Tholos III 77

Shaw, Joseph W. ix

shelf or bench 77

shell 8, 203, 240

Shelley, H. A. ix

SILVER OBJECTS

cup 151, 159; diadem 146; fragments 78, 79, 84, 120; headdress 152; ornaments 156; ring 120, 127, 230; vessel 144; wire 37

skeletal remains: skeletons 135, 136, 139, 142, 145, 177, 177 n. 1, 181, 182 n. 4, 186, 193, 194, 195, 202, 203, 208, 211, 226, 228, 233; skulls 74, 75, 77, 79, 102, 107, 142, 144, 146, 181, 185 n. 8, 186, 193, 194, 210, 211, 227, 238 *see also* bones

Smith, Peter x, 9, 10, 11, 14, 29, 30, 41, 48

Smith, Watson x

southeastern quarter 61

southern corner 41

Southwestern Building 11, 12, 37, 38, 39

southwestern quarter 52, scarp 50

Spata 83, 85, 86, 87, 88, 89, 90, 91

Sphakteria 134, 219

Sphoungaras 165

Stairway 69 37

Starr, R. F. S. 132 n. 78

steps 4, 7, 37

stereo 4, 6, 11, 13, 14, 15, 16, 17, 20, 23, 25, 26, 27, 28, 30, 31, 32, 33, 34, 35, 36, 38, 43, 45, 53, 58, 59, 61, 62, 65, 66, 67, 77, 95, 103, 105, 109, 138, 140, 141, 146, 148, 225; cutting in 6, 10, 23, 25, 26, 27, 35, 41, 65; kiln sunk in 19; stone slab fitted into 23; walls founded on 9, 15, 20, 21, 22, 23, 32, 37, 44, 53, 54, 61

stirrup-jar (-vase) 82, 94, 183, 196, 199, 200, 204, 208, 211, 213, 215, 226, 227, 233, 235, 236 *see* POTTERY, *shapes*

STONE OBJECTS, VARIETIES OF STONE USED

agate, seal 139, 169

STONE OBJECTS, VARIETIES OF STONE USED (*cont.*)

alabaster, pommel of sword 102, 127

amethyst, beads 102, 103, 138, 139, 143, 146: amygdaloid 124, 141, 169; carinated 125; cod-faced 125; drum 125; lozenge 125; oval 125; flattened spherical 125, 169; pear-shaped 125, 126; pentagonal 125; scarab 125; spherical 82, 125, 161, 169; tubular 125

carnelian, beads 74, 76, 79, 139, 143, 180: amygdaloid 82; annular 84; flattened spherical 169, 177; fluted 82; gadrooned 169; quatrefoil 126; spherical 24, 57, 82, 84, 182, 187, 188

crystal: fragments 84; pendant 182

flint: arrowheads 7, 16, 24, 25, 28 n. 10, 31, 32, 37, 42, 46, 49, 51, 60, 102, 104, 113, 127, 135, 136, 137, 139, 140, 143, 146, 158, 162, 169, 178, types of 127; blade 7, 24, 25, 27, 31, 47, 49, 51, 223; chips, flakes, fragments, pieces 23, 25, 27, 58, 74, 82, 84, 240; petal-shaped point 24, 42; saw 223

gypsum: plaque 84

haematite: seal 105, 227, 232

jasper: seal 37, 84; whetstone 84

Lacedemonian stone: rhyton, fragments of 24

lapis lazuli: seal 104, 124

limestone: grinder 84; pommel 126; whorl 126

marble, fragment 51; lamp 98, 111; pommel 58

obsidian: arrowhead 7, 9, 27, 46, 51, 82, 102, 127, 136, 143, 146, 162, 169, 229; blade 27, 31, 47; flake 82, 113, 128; fragment 23, 27, 74

sandstone: disk 24

schist: hone or whetstone 143, 147, 161, 167; whorl 126

serpentine: celt 127; lamp (Cretan) 112

slate: disk 223

steatite: beads 126, 204, 239, 240; button or whorl 24, 31, 37, 38, 46, 49, 60, 84, 113, 139, 149, 168, 182, 187, 228, 232, 239, 240; disk 126; seal 58, 178, 202, 204

unidentified stone: axe 223; bead 126, 232; blade 51; button 27, 46, 59, 207; celt 31, 47, 61, 102, 127; cup 27; disk 8, 16, 49; pestle 7, 49, 138, 168; pounder

223; saddle quern 223; seal 46; whetstone 31

stone, used to cover pithos 60, 143, 144 *see also* burial markers

stratification 12, 13, 30, 33, 43, 45, 58, 61, 73, 184, 193, 209

street 19, 21

substructures, in W 14 45

sword pommel *see* IVORY OBJECTS, STONE OBJECTS

Syria 94

table of offerings 54

Talcott, Lucy 6 n. 3

tankard or mug 134

Taylour, William D. ix, x, xi, xii, 16, 71, 72, 76, 179

TERRACOTTA OBJECTS

bowl 64

button 8, 31, 59, 60, 61, 136, 170, 187, 195, 201, 224, 239, 240

disk 8, 64, 111, 224

figurine: animal 31, 47; female 38, 42, 58, 59, 60, 66, 136, 159, 178, 182, 186, 189, 203, 206, 207

loomweight 8, 16

spool 223

whorl 27, 47, 50, 59, 61, 75, 82, 171, 195, 200; biconical 24, 31, 47, 50, 51, 59, 60, 92, 133, 180; conical 24, superposed on cylinder 31; flattened spherical 64; short cone 189, 200

Thebes 88, 125, 232

Theocharis, Demetrios R. ix, x

Thessaly 71, 239

tholoi, discovery of by Kourouniotes 71

Tholos II 77 n. 7

Tholos III vii, xi, 71, 72, 73-95: blocking wall 74, 75; chamber 74, 75, 76, 77, 78, 80, 81; date of 79; doorway 73, 74, 75, 79, 80, 81; dromos 73, 74, 75, 76, 80, 81; holes in floor 78; interments 75, 77, 79; lintel 74, 78; objects from dromos 81, doorway 82, chamber 83; pits 77; traces of fire 78; vaulting 78

Tholos IV viii, ix, xi, 4, 67, 68, 76, 77 n. 7, 95-134, 221: blocking wall 96, 98, 99, 108, 112; chamber (tholos) 96, 97, 107, 113; curving pit 97, 104, 105, 107, 108, 109; date of 108; doorway 95, 96, 111; dromos 95, 100, 107, 110; excavation 98, 101; floor 106; lintel 71, 95, 99; objects found 102, 103, 104, 105, 106, 110-134; pits 97, 104, 105; stone cist 97, 108, 109; vault 96, 97, 104

Tholos V 71, *see* Grave Circle

Protogeometric Tholos xii, 72, 219, 237-242

Thorikos 150 n. 92

tomb *see* Grave Circle, THOLOI, chamber tomb

threshing floor 71, 73, 219

Throne Room 36

tiles, roofing 6, 63

Tiryns 150 n. 92, 224, 232

tool marks, on door jambs 210

toreutics, Mycenaean 114

torque technique, Central Europe and Near East 231

Touloupa, Mrs. 81

tower-like structure, flanked Northeast Gateway 18

Traganes 166, 214, 237

Travlos, John ix

trenches 3, 5, 8, 11, 17 *see also* areas of excavation

Troy vii, 40, 111

Tsakalis, Panagiotis viii, 73, 176, 178, 180

Tsakonas family viii, 64

Tsaritsane 94

Tsountas, C. 16, 83, 85, 86, 87, 88, 89, 90, 91, 111, 113, 180 n. 3

Tufnell, O. 132 n. 79

tumulus at Samikon 154, over Tholos IV 67, 68

Urnenfelder 231

urnlike cup 94

Valmin 28, 76

Vanderpool, Eugene x, 33

Vapheio 83, 111, 117, 119, 121, 122, 158, 168

Vayenas, Evstathis viii, 71, 72, 135

Vlachopoulos, Messenia 167 n. 101, 214

Volimidia 95

Vollgraff, C. W. 28, 85, 88

Volos 88, 120

Wace, A. J. B. 56, 83, 85, 86, 87, 88, 91, 172

walls, bordered gateway 4, 56; built of field stones 39, 40, 63, of large squared blocks 3; contemporary with Room 82 44; circuit, defensive 3, search for 8, 9, 10, 11, 12, 13; exterior of Southwestern Building 38, 39, 40, 50; in AA I 61, AA II 62; in Belvedere Area 17, 18, 20, 21, 22, 23; in Early Helladic site 222; in exploratory trenches 8, 9, 10, 11, 12, 13; in Trenches LT I 53, 54, 57, LT II 57, LT III 57, LT IV 59, LT V 61; in W 14 43, 44; Mycenaean along northwestern scarp 48; northeast of Main Building 30; of earlier palace 36, Hall 64 37, houses 11;

walls (*cont.*)
 under Corridor 26 32; under
 Court 63 39; under Petropoulos
 aloni 63; under Vestibule of Wine
 Magazine 32
Warren, Peter 111 n. 39, 113
"Warrior Vase" 229
warrior's grave 151
water channel 4, 5, 6, 17, 19, 20, 21,
 22, 29, 44
watercolors ix
Wessex, England 105
whetstone *see* STONE OBJECTS
Wine Magazine 9, 10, 28, 29, 30, 32
Wolfley, Edward L., Jr. xi
Wolfley, Wilma E. ix
wood, fragments of 110, 157, 161,
 167, 188
wooden bridge carried water 5
Woodward, Jeannette xi

Yalouris, Nikolaos viii, 72, 81
Yalouris, Mrs. Nikolaos viii

Zafer Papoura cemetery 85, 90, 119
Zakro 173
Zerelia 150 n. 92

1. Northeast Gateway and Circuit Wall. From North. 1960

2. Stone Steps in Gateway, Lateral Walls,
and Water Channel. From Northeast. 1959

3. Circuit Wall to Northwest of Gateway.
From North by East. 1959

4. Northeast Gateway, Tholos Tomb IV Beyond Hollow.
From South. 1960

5. Pavement of Tile Fragments of Medieval Building. From North. 1959

6. Dilapidated Arc of Stones in Front of Northeast Wall. From Northeast. 1959

7. Trench W 2: Fallen Stones. From North. 1959

8. Trench W 4: Fallen Stones North of Wall. From North. 1959

9. Trench W 6: Transverse Wall. From South. 1959

10. Trench W 6: Fall of Stones in Upper Part. From Northwest. 1959

11. Trench W 8: Wall on Northwest Slope.
From North. 1959

12. Trench W 9: Transverse Wall.
From Southwest. 1963

13. Trench W 13: Wall. From West. 1961

14. Trench W 12: Pot against Wall.
From North. 1962

15. Trench W 15: Wall. From West by North. 1961

16. Trench W 17: Northwest of West Corner of Palace.
From North by East. 1961

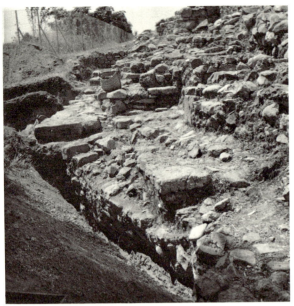

17. Trench W 19: Section of Circuit Wall.
From Southeast. 1964

18. Trench W 19: Pavement of Stones.
From North. 1964

19. Trench W 19: Circuit Wall.
From Northeast. 1964

20. Trench W 19: Stucco Pavement.
From Northwest. 1960

21. Trench W 19: Circuit Wall, Outside Face.
From Southwest by West. 1964

22. Trench W 20: Early Wall Laid on or against
Foundation of Building X. From Southwest. 1965

23. Trench W 20: Foundation of South Wall of
Building X. From South by West. 1965

24. Trench W 20: Stratification in Deposit against
Face of Circuit Wall. From South by West. 1964

25. Trench W 21: Two Crumbling Walls in South Corner.
From East. 1965

26. Trench W 21: Space between Walls in South Corner.
From Northwest. 1965

27. Trench W 21: Northeast Face of Northeastern Wall.
From Northwest. 1965

28. Trench W 21: Southern Wall.
From East. 1965

29. Trench W 28: Wall. From Northwest. 1959

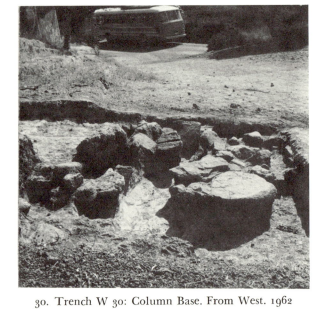

30. Trench W 30: Column Base. From West. 1962

31. Trench W 32: Stones. From Southeast. 1962

32. Trench W 33: Stones. From Northwest. 1962

33. Trench W 33: Scattered Stones.
From East. 1962

34. Trench W 34: Stones in Black Earth.
From Southeast. 1962

35. Trench W 35. From Southeast. 1962

36. Trench W 36. From Southeast. 1962

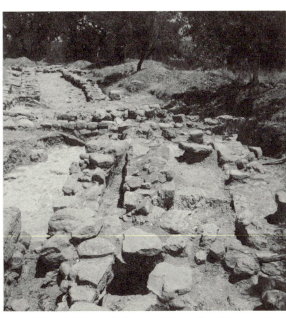

37. Trench W 38: Belvedere. From Southeast. 1965

38. Trench W 39. From Southeast. 1959

39. Trench W 45. From Northeast. 1959

40. Trench W 46. From Northwest. 1959

41. View of Pylos, Navarino, Sphacteria from Belvedere. 1960

42. Belvedere Area. From Southeast. 1960

43. Belvedere Area. From North. 1959

44. Belvedere Area: Kiln. From West. 1965

45. Belvedere Area: Kiln. From North. 1965

46. Platform at Northern Part of Belvedere Area.
From North. 1965

47. Belvedere Area: Street and Walls.
From North. 1959

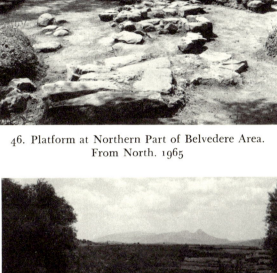

48. Belevedere Area: General View.
From Northwest. 1959

49. Belvedere Area: Street Showing Ends of
Walls J and H. From South. 1965

50. Belvedere Area: Drain across Rectangular Area.
From West. 1965

51. Belvedere Area: Drain in Steep Bank.
From East. 1965

52. Trench S 10. From Southeast. 1962

53. Trench S 12. From Southeast. 1962

54. Trench IV: Eastern End. From West. 1939

55. Trench III: Eastern End. From West. 1939

56. Trench E 3: Cross Wall and Corner.
From Southeast. 1965

57. Trench MY 1: Black Deposit.
From West. 1958

58. Trench P 13: Foundations North of Wine Magazine.
From Northwest. 1964

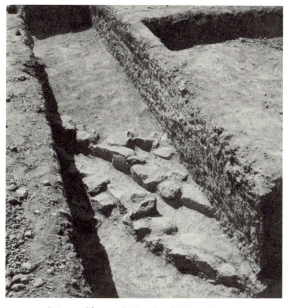

59. Water Channel North of Wine Magazine.
From Southeast. 1964

60. Walls and Stucco Pavements Southeast of
Wine Magazine. From South. 1958

61. Remains of an Open Court of Pre-palatial Era.
From Northeast. 1958

62. Column Base in Pre-palatial Court.
From West. 1958

63. Foundations of Buildings Demolished for Erection
of Wine Magazine. From West. 1958

64. Early Wall under Southeast End of Vestibule (104). From Northwest. 1958

65. Sounding under Corridor 26: Group of Pithoi. From Northeast. 1960

66. Substantial Wall under Corridor 26. From Southwest. 1960

67. Trench outside Room 24 behind Main Building. From Northwest. 1955

68. Earlier Wall under Room 21. From South. 1960

69. Broad Wall below Northwest Wall of Room 65. From West. 1962

70. Earlier Wall under Room 74.
From Southwest. 1964

71. Sounding (64-6) under Room of Late Palace
Phase. From West. 1964

72. Wall under Corridor 61. From West. 1964

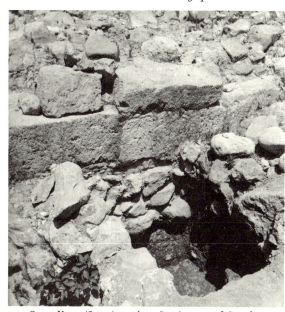

73. Sounding (64-17) against Section 10 of Southwest
Wall of Southwestern Building. From West. 1964

74. Building X: Southwest Part.
From East by South. 1961

75. Building X: Foundation of Northwest Corner.
From West. 1964

76. Scarp Showing Stratification in South Corner.
From Southeast. 1963

77. Southern Corner: Pots Lying on Floorlike Earth.
From Northwest. 1965

78. Circular Building and House Beyond.
From Southeast. 1958

79. Area behind Main Building:
Walls from Northeast. 1962

80. Stratification on South Side of Trench 7
in Area behind Main Building. From East. 1962

81. Building X: South Wall. From Southeast. 1961

82. Broken Pottery Scattered in South Corner.
From East and Above. 1962

83. Trench LT I. From North. 1959

84. Trench LT I. From South. 1959

85. Trench LT I: Remnants of Table of Offerings.
From South. 1959

86. Trench LT II. From East. 1959

87. Trench LT III: Walls and Fallen Stones.
From Northwest. 1959

88. Trench LT IV: Walls and Pithos Appearing.
From Northwest. 1959

89. Trench LT IV: Wall of Last Period and Large
Pithos. From North. 1959

90. Trench LT V: Remnant of Wall.
From South. 1959

91. Trench AA I, below Southeast Slope.
From Southeast. 1960

92. Trench AA II: Southeast End of Trench.
From Northwest. 1960

93. Trench across *Aloni* of G. Petropoulos.
From South. 1959

94. Trench across *Aloni* of G. Petropoulos:
Early Walls. From North. 1959

95. Trench Crossing Northeast Hollow: Deposit
of Stones. From Northwest. 1968

96. Trench Crossing Northeast Hollow:
Deposit of Stones.
From Northwest. 1968

97. Trench Crossing Northeast Hollow:
Final Cleaning, Sections 3, 4, 5.
From Southeast. 1968

98. Trench Crossing Northeast Hollow:
Sections 3, 4, 5.
From Southeast. 1968

99. Transverse Trench across Hollow: Deposit of Stones. From Southwest. 1969

100. Transverse Trench across Hollow: Deposits of Stones. From Northeast. 1969

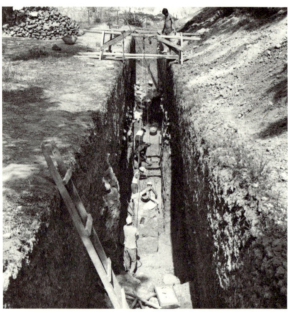

101. Transverse Trench across Hollow: Deep Sections. From Southwest. 1969

102. Transverse Trench across Hollow: Deep Sections. From Southwest. 1969

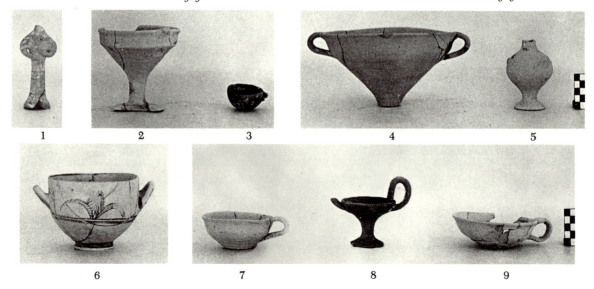

103. Figurine and Pots from Transverse Trench across Hollow. 1969

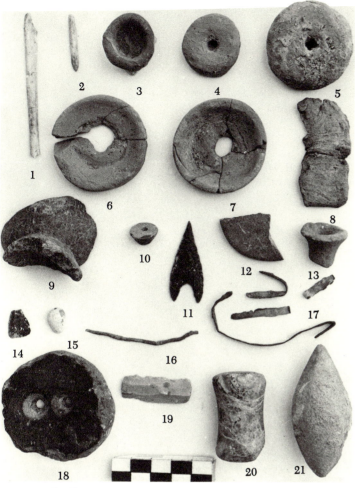

104. Miscellaneous Objects: Nos. 1-8 from Petropoulos *Aloni*;
Nos. 9, 10 Trench MY 1; Nos. 11-20 Northeast Gateway;
No. 21 Trench W 28

105. Miscellaneous Objects: No. 1 Trench W 32;
Nos. 2, 3 Trench W 31; No. 4 Northeast Gateway

107. Miscellaneous Objects: No. 1 Trench W 33;
No. 2 Trench S 12; Nos. 3-7 Trench CK 8
Extension III; No. 8 Trench W 31; Nos. 9, 10 CK 24;
No. 11 Trench W 36

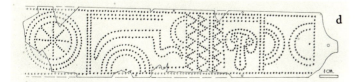

106. Miscellaneous Objects: Nos. 1-5 Trench W 9; No. 6 Trench
W 10; Nos. 8-14 Trench W 16; Nos. 7, 15-17 South Corner

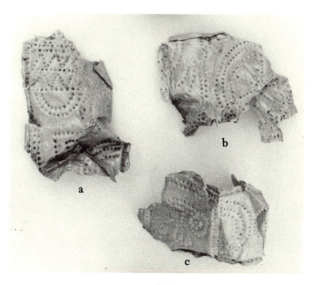

108. Fragments: Diadem of Gold from Trench W 31 (reconstruction by Piet de Jong)

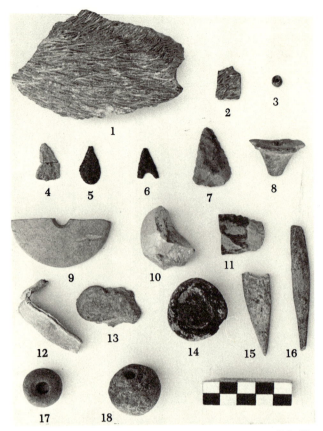

109. Miscellaneous Objects from Belvedere Area (W 38)

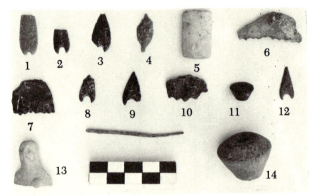

110. Miscellaneous Objects: Nos. 1-6, 15 Section W 19;
Nos. 8-10 Section W 20; Nos. 11, 13, 14
under Room 74; No. 12 Trench P 13

112. Miscellaneous Objects from Area
Northeast and Southeast of Wine Magazine

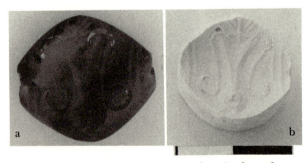

111. Seal Stone of Jasper Found on Surface of
Southwestern Slope by Mrs. C. S. Lamy. 1963

113. Miscellaneous Objects from Trench W 16

114. Miscellaneous Objects from Exploratory Trenches
Northwest of Main Building (W 14)

115. Miscellaneous Objects: Nos. 1-12 Trench LT IV;
Nos. 13-15 Trench LT V; No. 16 Trench LT I

116. Miscellaneous Objects from Trench LT III

117. Seal Stone of Steatite from Trench LT III

118. Lentoid Seal of Ivory from Trench LT III

119. Sherds from Northeast Gateway (W 1).
Late Helladic I and II

120. Sherds from Northeast Gateway (W 1).
Late Helladic I and II

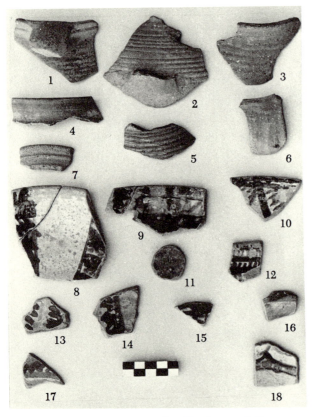

121. Sherds from Late Intrusion Northwest of Gateway:
Nos. 1-7 Plain Ribbed Ware; Nos. 8-18 Glazed Ware

122. Sherds from Trench W 5

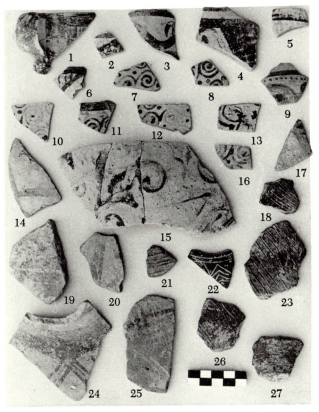

123. Sherds from Trench W 6 (Nos. 1-16) and Area between CK 8 and CK 19 (Nos. 17-27)

124. Sherds from Trench W 9, Pit at End of Corridor Northeast of Wine Magazine

125. Sherds from Trench W 9, Pit at End of Corridor Northeast of Wine Magazine

126. Sherds from Trench W 9 (Nos. 1-4, 7, 8) and Trench W 10 (Nos. 5, 6, 9-12)

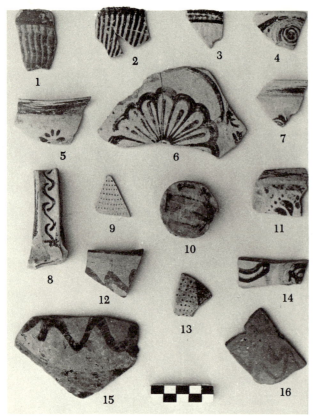

127. Sherds from Trench W 16

128. Sherds from Areas W 19 and W 20

129. Sherds from Areas W 19 and W 20

130. Sherds from Areas W 19 and W 20

131. Sherds from Belvedere Area (W 38)

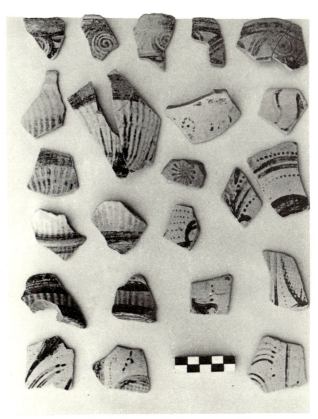

132. Sherds from Belvedere Area (W 38)

133. Middle Helladic Jug from
Trench CK 8 Extension III

134. Middle Helladic Sherds from Trench CK 8 Extension III

135. Sherds from under Corridor 26

136. Sherds from Pit under Corridor 25 (Stratum 2, Nos. 1-5; Stratum 3, Nos. 6-12; Stratum 4, Nos. 13-18)

137. Sherds from Pit under Corridor 25 (Stratum 5, Nos. 1-5; Stratum 6, Nos. 6-15; Stratum 7, Nos. 16-20)

138. Sherds from Pit under Corridor 25 (Stratum 8, Nos. 1-8; Stratum 9, Nos. 9-14; Stratum 10, Nos. 15-18)

139. Sherds from under Hall 65

140. Sherds from Trench 64-1

141. Sherds from under Hall 65

142. Sherds from Trench 64-6

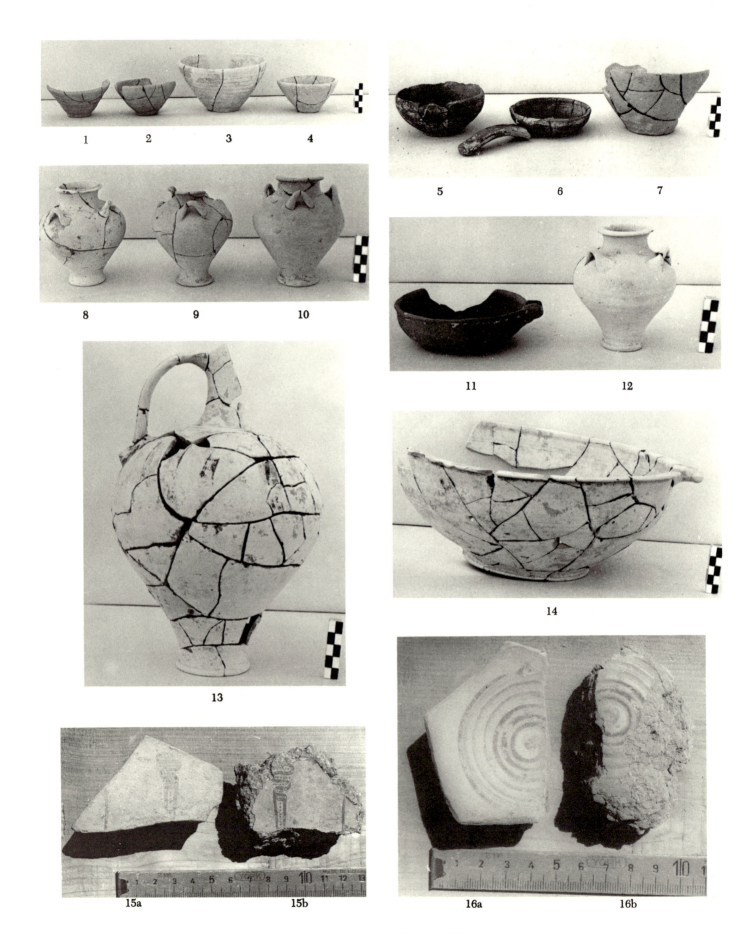

143. Pots from South Corner; Sherds and Impressions
Left by Them, from Trench W 28

144. Sherds from Area Northeast and Southeast
of Wine Magazine

145. Sherds from Trench Northwest of Room 24

146. Sherds from Northwest of Palace

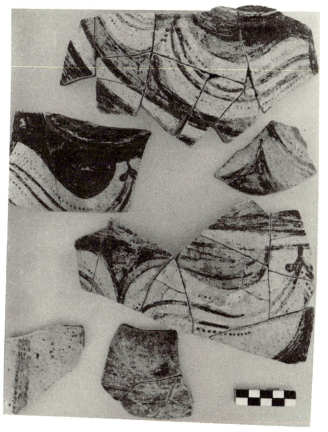

147. Sherds from Northwest of Palace

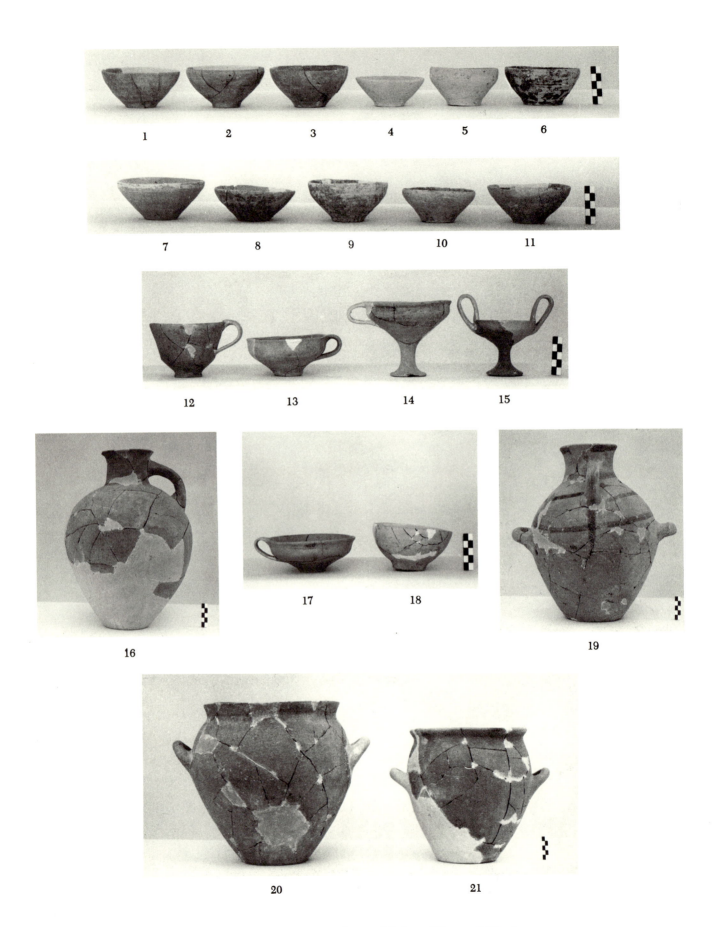

148. Pots from Areas Northwest of Palace (W 14 and W 12)

Group III

Group IV

Group V

Group V

Group VI

149. Sherds from Area Northwest of Palace (W 14)

150. Sherds from Area W 14
Northwest of Palace

151. Sherds from Section W 21,
The South Corner

153. Fragment of Conical
Rhyton from Trench LT I

152. Sherds from Section W 21, The South Corner

154. Sherds from Trench LT III

155. Pots from Section W 21, The South Corner (Nos. 1-10) and Trench LT I (Nos. 11-18)

156. Sherds from Trench LT III

157. Sherds from Trench LT III

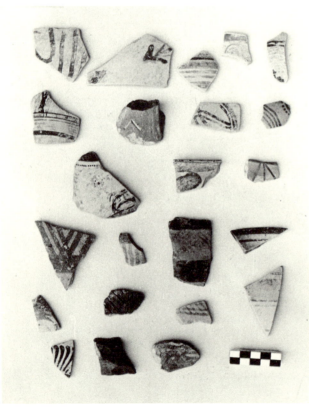

158. Sherds from Trenches AA I and AA II

159. Sherds from Trench across *Aloni* of G. Petropoulos

160. Storehouse Built over Tholos III.
From South. 1939

161. Doorway of Tholos III: Roof of New Storeroom
in Background. 1939

162. Tholos III: Fallen Lintel Block as Found.
From inside Chamber. 1939

163. Tholos III: Fallen Lintel Block as Left
after Excavation. From North. 1939

164. Tholos III: Remnants of Upper Wall Closing
Doorway. From Southwest. 1939

165. Tholos III: Remains of Early Wall Closing
Doorway. From Southeast. 1966

166. Tholos III: Fairly Large Stones in Lower
Courses of Tholos Wall. From East, Inside. 1939

167. Tholos III: Bones and Stones in Central Pit.
From Northeast. 1939

168. Tholos III: Stones and Human Bones in Disorder
in Large Pit. From Northeast. 1939

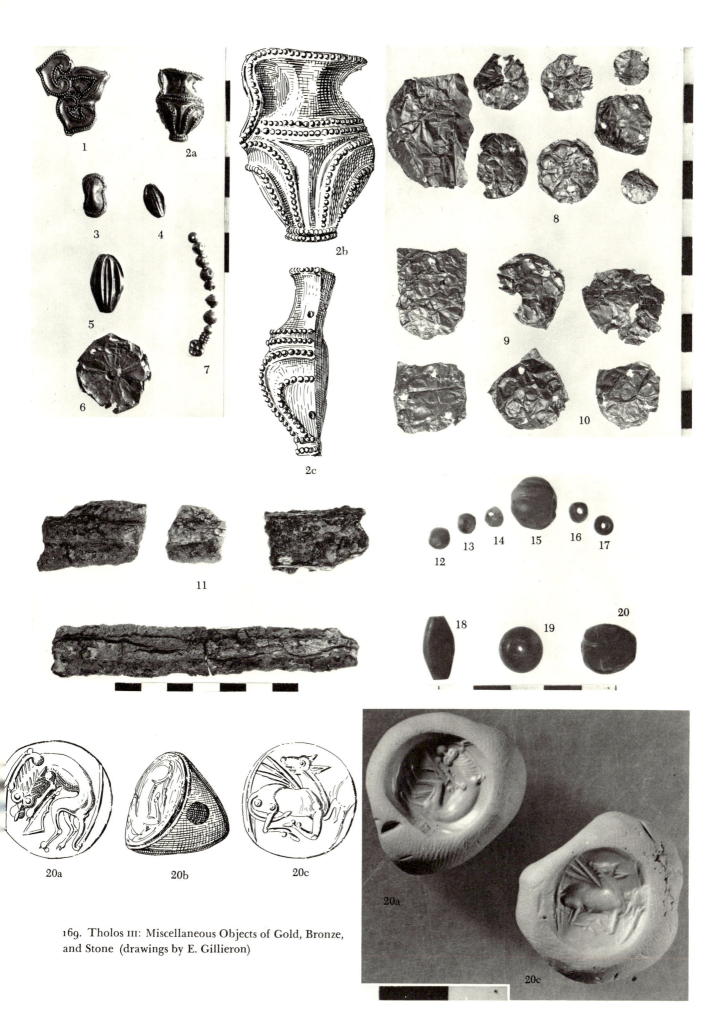

169. Tholos III: Miscellaneous Objects of Gold, Bronze, and Stone (drawings by E. Gillieron)

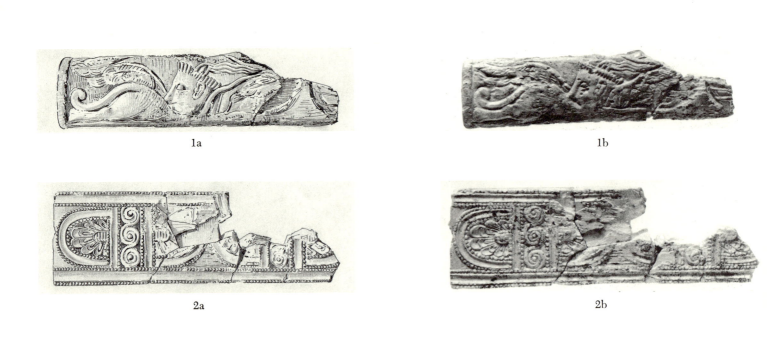

1a

1b

2a

2b

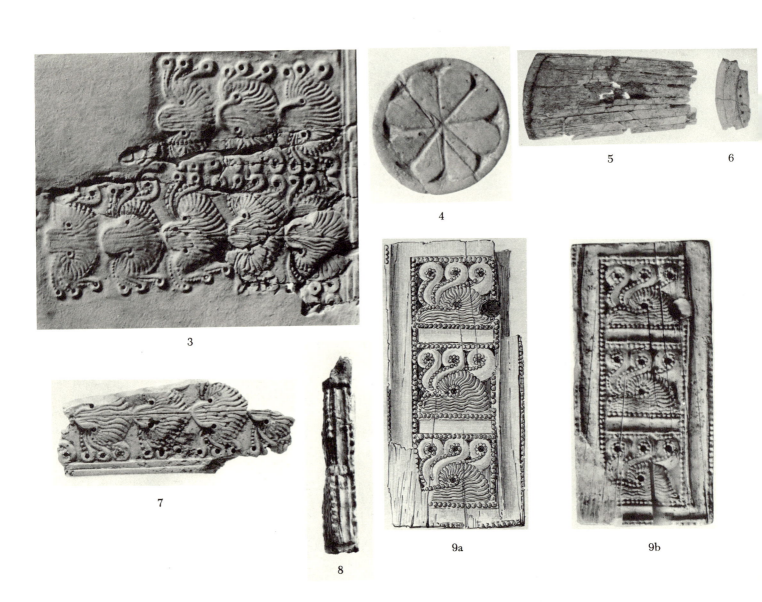

3

4

5

6

7

8

9a

9b

170. Tholos III: Fragments of Ivory (drawings by E. Gillieron)

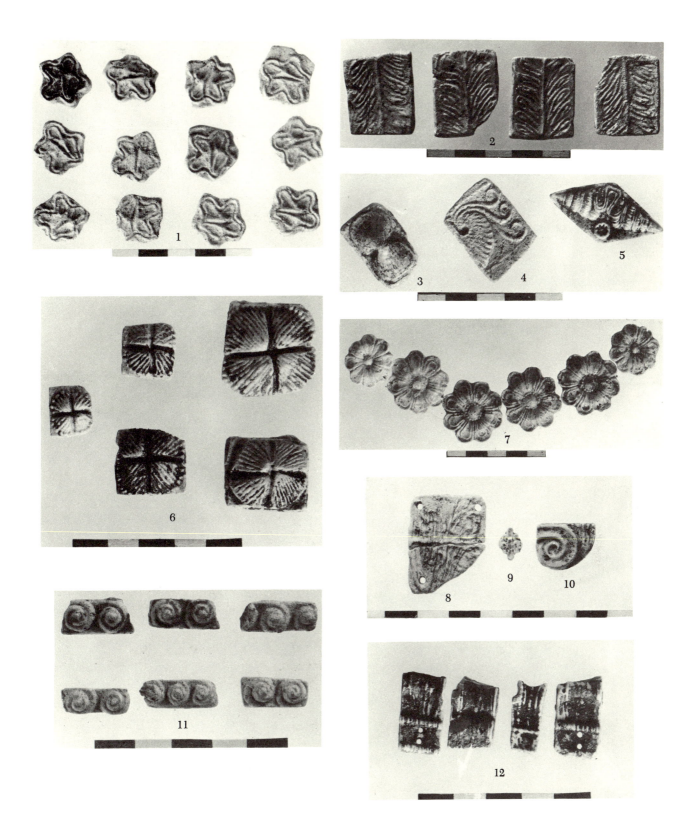

171. Tholos III: Miscellaneous Objects of Glass Paste

172. Tholos III: Beads of Glass Paste

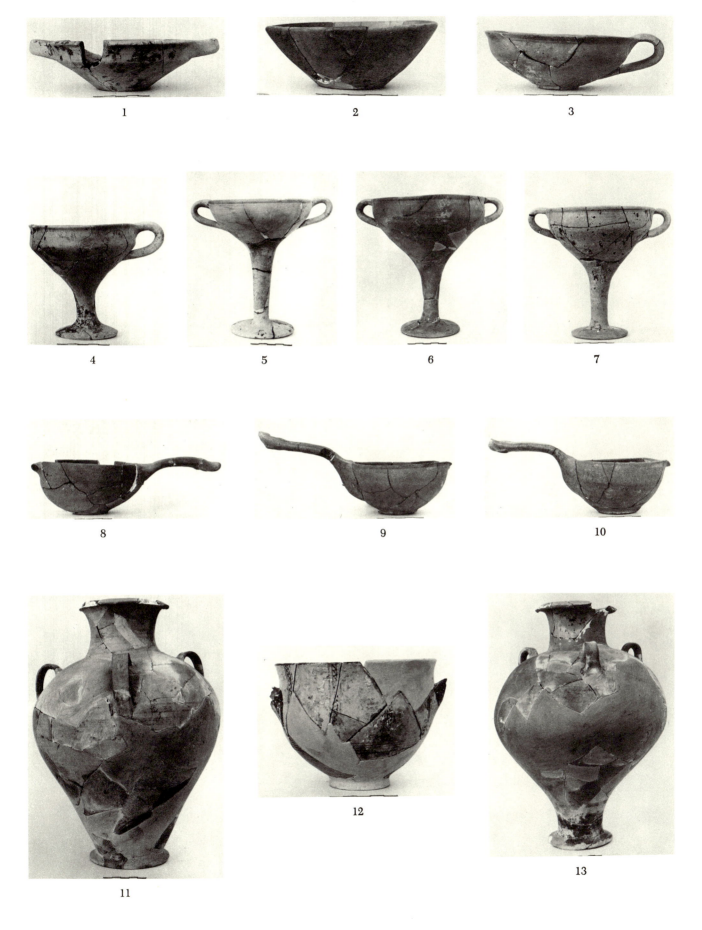

1   2   3

4   5   6   7

8   9   10

12

13

11

173. Tholos III: Pots

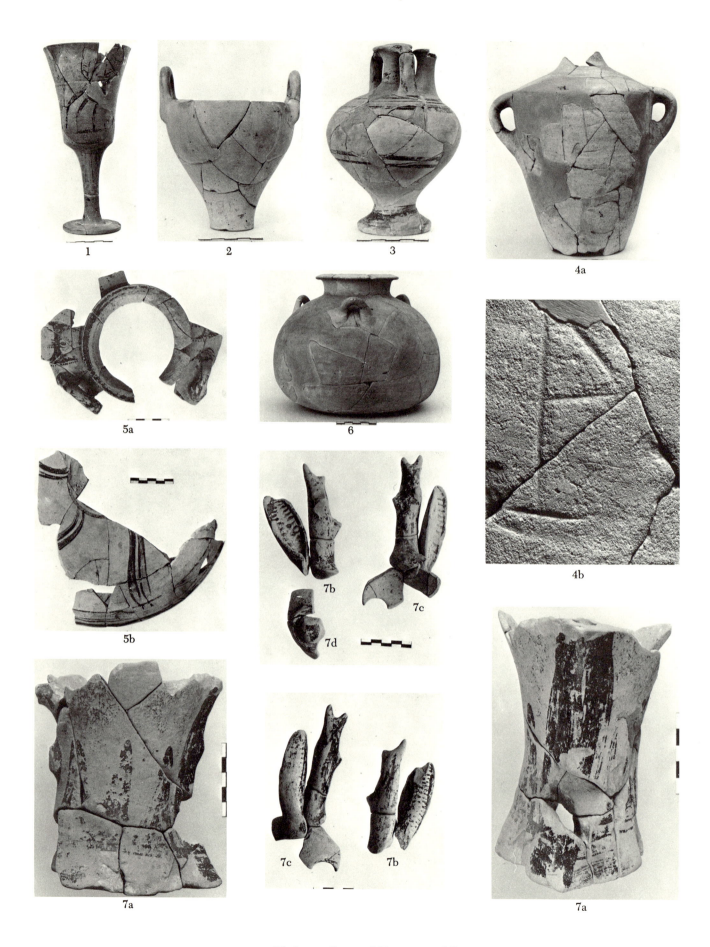

1   2   3

4a

5a   6

4b

5b

7b

7c

7d

7a

7c   7b

7a

174. Tholos III: Pots and Fragments of Pots

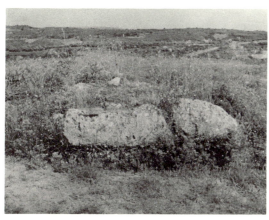

175. Tholos IV: Broken Lintel Block as Seen before Excavations Started. From Southwest. 1953

176. Tholos IV: Doorway and Blocking Wall. From Southwest. 1953

177. Tholos IV: Removal of Blocking Wall. From Southwest. 1953

178. Tholos IV: Curve of Vault, Doorway, and Lower Part of Blocking Wall. From South and Above. 1953

179. Tholos IV: Inner Face of Blocking Wall from Northeast, Inside Chamber. 1953

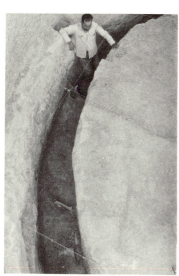

180. Tholos IV: Curved Pit Parallel to Northwestern Wall of Chamber. From Southwest. 1953

181. Tholos IV: Stone Cist against Southeastern Wall of Chamber. From North. 1953

182. Tholos IV: Blocking Wall and Southeastern Door Jamb. From South and Above. 1953

183. Tholos IV: Course of
Squared Blocks in Partly
Dismantled Blocking Wall. From
Northwest and Above. 1953

184. Tholos IV: Earth under
Large Stones in Outer Face of
Blocking Wall.
From South. 1953

185. Tholos IV: Coping Stones Found
in Chamber. 1953

187. Tholos IV: Chamber with Stone Cist.
From West and Above. 1953

186. Tholos IV: Doorway and Chamber, Stone Cist at Left,
Curving Pit at Right. From Northeast by North. 1953

188. Tholos IV: Doorway and Chamber with
Curving Pit at Right. 1953

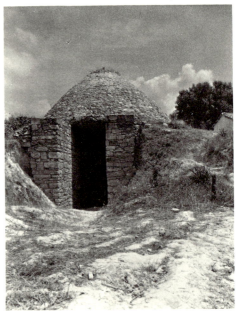

189. Tholos IV as Restored.
From South. 1960

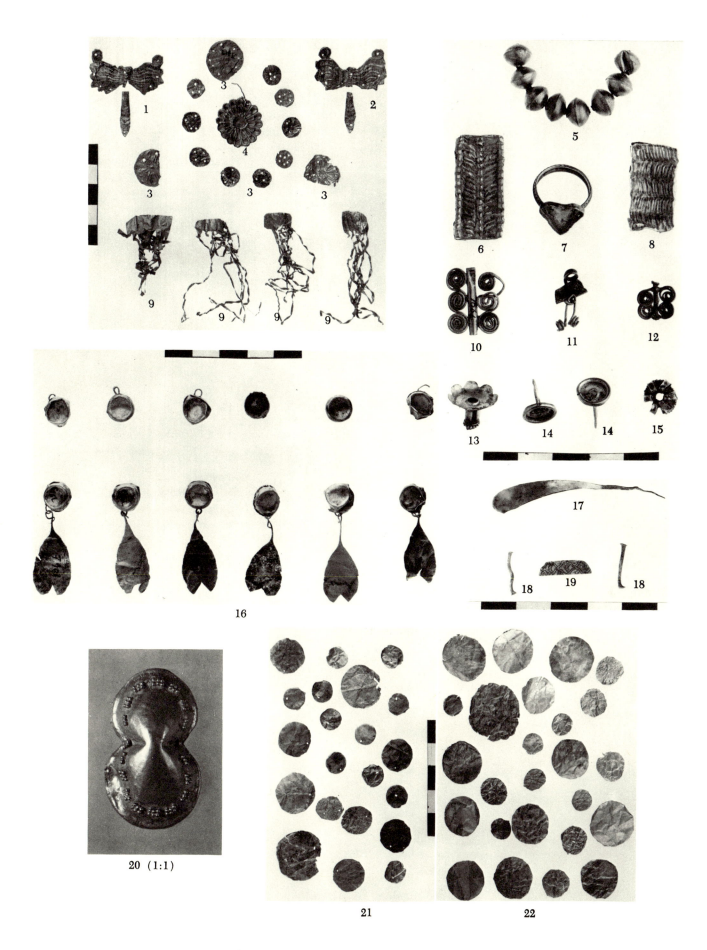

190. Tholos IV: Miscellaneous Objects of Gold

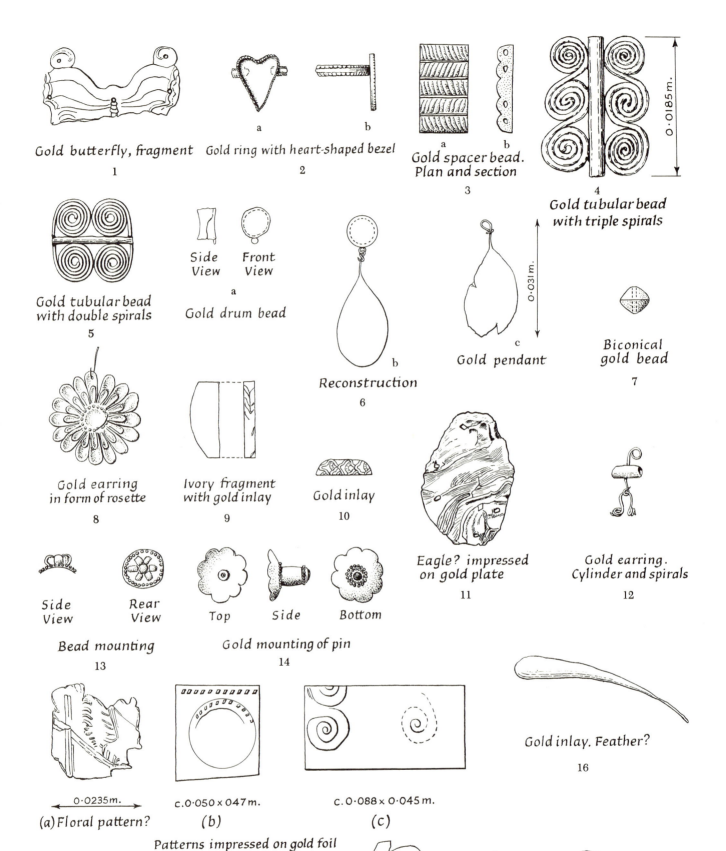

Gold butterfly, fragment
1

Gold ring with heart-shaped bezel
2

Gold spacer bead.
Plan and section
3

Gold tubular bead
with triple spirals
4

Gold tubular bead
with double spirals
5

Side View   Front View

Gold drum bead

Reconstruction
6

Gold pendant

Biconical
gold bead
7

Gold earring
in form of rosette
8

Ivory fragment
with gold inlay
9

Gold inlay
10

Eagle? impressed
on gold plate
11

Gold earring.
Cylinder and spirals
12

Side View   Rear View

Bead mounting
13

Top   Side   Bottom

Gold mounting of pin
14

Gold inlay. Feather?
16

0·0235m.

(a) Floral pattern?

c.0·050 × 047 m.

(b)

c. 0·088 × 0·045 m.

(c)

Patterns impressed on gold foil
15

a   b   c   d

Patterns cut out in gold foil
17

191. Tholos IV: Miscellaneous Objects of Gold (drawings by H. A. Shelley,
based on sketches by W. D. Taylour, except for Nos. 2, 4, 14, 15a by M. Rawson)

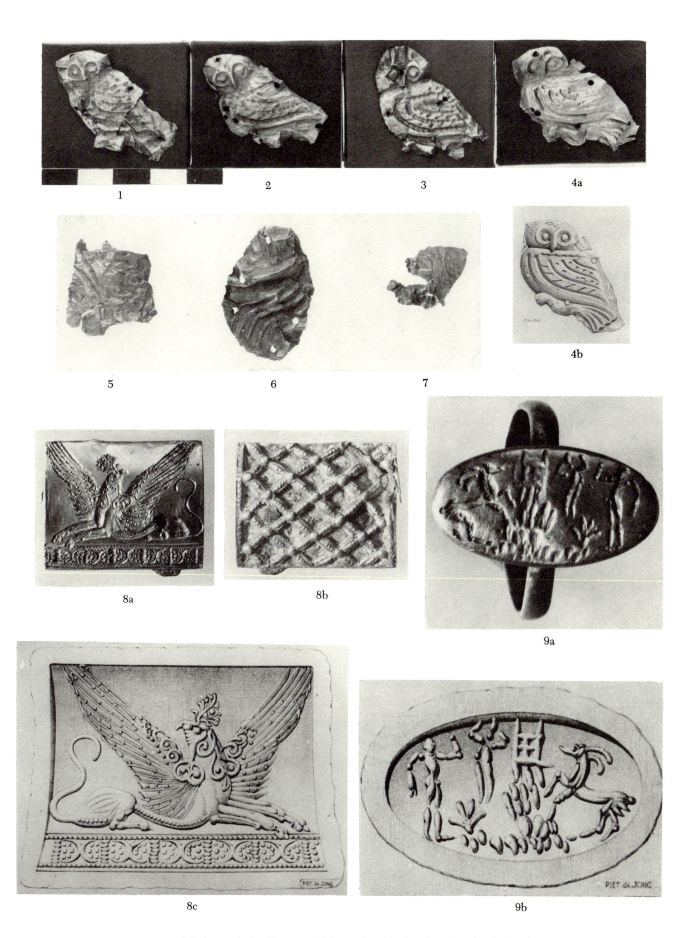

1 2 3 4a

5 6 7 4b

8a 8b 9a

8c 9b

192. Tholos IV: Miscellaneous Objects of Gold (drawings by Piet de Jong)

1a

2a

2b

1b

1c

4a

3a

3b

4b

193. Tholos IV: Seal Stone and Impressions (drawings by Piet de Jong)

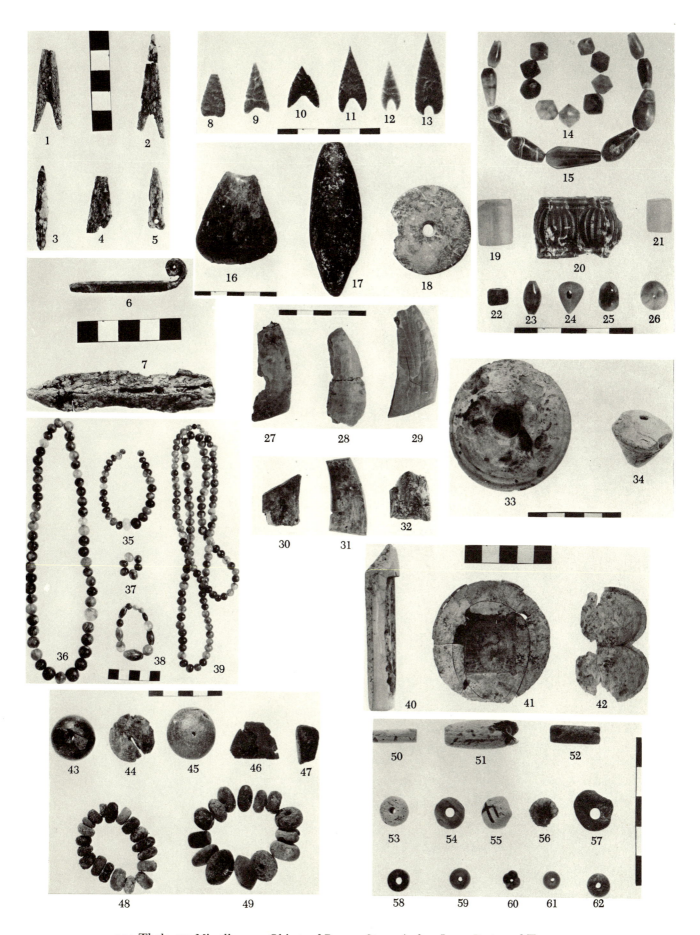

194. Tholos IV: Miscellaneous Objects of Bronze, Stone, Amber, Ivory, Paste, and Terracotta

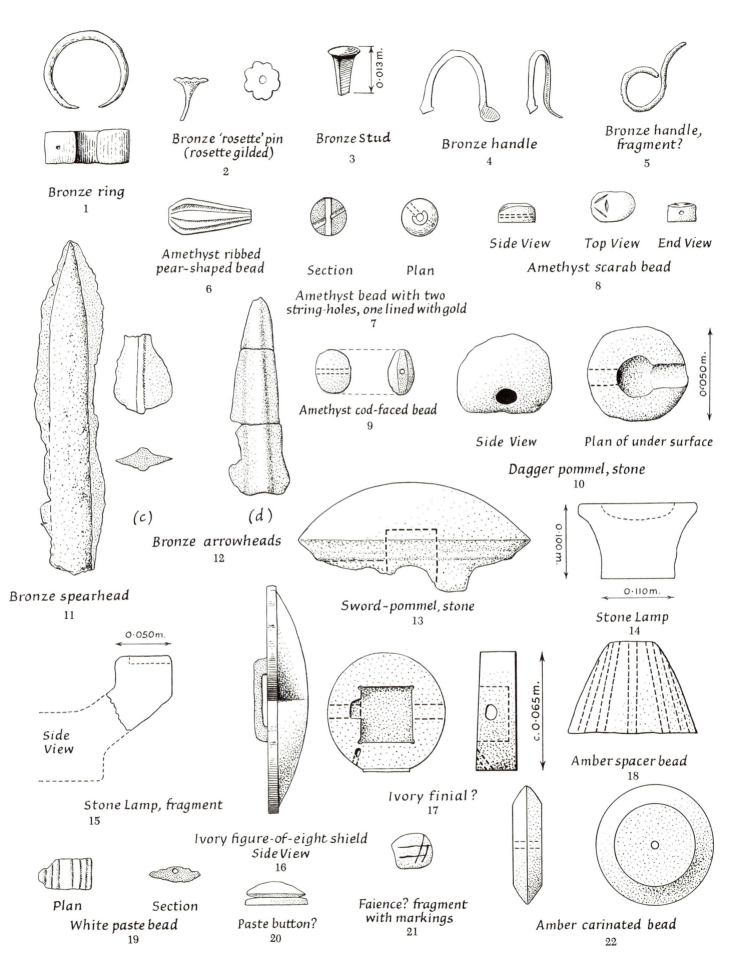

Bronze ring
1

Bronze 'rosette' pin
(rosette gilded)
2

Bronze Stud
3

Bronze handle
4

Bronze handle,
fragment?
5

Amethyst ribbed
pear-shaped bead
6

Section   Plan

Amethyst bead with two
string-holes, one lined with gold
7

Side View   Top View   End View

Amethyst scarab bead
8

Amethyst cod-faced bead
9

Side View   Plan of under surface

Dagger pommel, stone
10

(c)   (d)

Bronze arrowheads
12

Sword-pommel, stone
13

Stone Lamp
14

Bronze spearhead
11

Side
View

Stone Lamp, fragment
15

Ivory figure-of-eight shield
Side View
16

Ivory finial?
17

Amber spacer bead
18

Plan   Section

White paste bead
19

Paste button?
20

Faience? fragment
with markings
21

Amber carinated bead
22

195. Tholos IV: Miscellaneous Objects of Bronze, Stone, Amber, Ivory, and Paste
(drawings by H. A. Shelley based on sketches by W. D. Taylour)

196. Tholos iv: Amphora, Fragment of Jug, and Sherds

197. Grave Circle, Trench A.
From East. 1957

198. Grave Circle, Pit 1: Cauldron, Pithos,
and Rapier. From West. 1957

200. Grave Circle, Pit 2: Remains of Skeleton
and Accompanying Objects. From North. 1957

199. Grave Circle, Trench L.
From North-Northeast. 1957

201. Grave Circle, Trench L: Curving
Wall, Dagger, and Other Objects.
From North. 1957

202. Grave Circle, Trench L:
One-handled Jar and Fragments of
Alabastra. From South. 1957

203. Grave Circle: Spouted Jar
Found in Balk between Trenches A
and L. From South. 1957

204. Grave Circle, Trench M: Balance Staff and Alabastron with Base of Kylix in its Mouth. From South. 1957

205. Grave Circle: Pottery in Trench M. From Southeast. 1957

206. Grave Circle, Trench M: Shoulder of Spouted Jug of Minoan Style and Decoration *in situ*. From North. 1957

208. Grave Circle, Pit 2: Skeleton. From East. 1957

207. Grave Circle, Pit 2: Upper Half of Skeleton with Bronze Bowl to Right of Skull. Remains of Another Burial, Center. From North. 1957

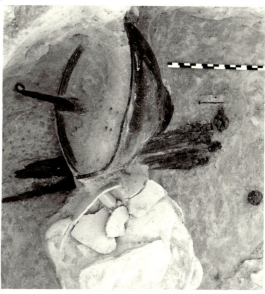

209. Grave Circle, Pit 3: Cauldron and Pithos. From East. 1957

210. Grave Circle, Pit 3: Bone Pit and Palace Style Jar. From West. 1957

211. Grave Circle, Pit 3: Cauldron, Pithos, and Rapiers. Ivory Pommel, Loose, to Right. From Northwest. 1957

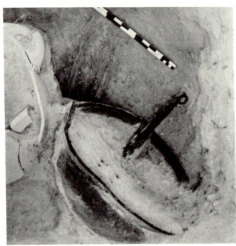

212. Grave Circle, Pit 3: Cauldron with Handle
of Short Sword Protruding. From South. 1957

213. Grave Circle, Pit 3: Pithos. Bronze
Knife among Bones. From Northwest. 1957

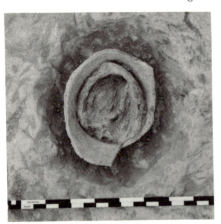

214. Grave Circle, Pit 3: Skull
Wedged into Base of Palace Style
Jar. From East. 1957

215. Grave Circle, Pit 3: Spouted Jar
with Trussed Burial. From North. 1957

216. Grave Circle, Pit 3 (NE) after
Removal of Spouted Jar Showing
Rapiers, Knife, Dagger, and Ivory
Pommel. From West. 1957

217. Grave Circle, Pit 1: Skull
and Bones in Pithos, Cauldron
to North. From South. 1957

218. Grave Circle, Pit 1: Gold Wreath
at Bottom of Pithos.
From North and Above. 1957

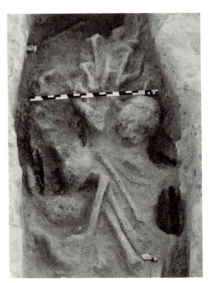

219. Grave Circle, Pit 4: Skulls,
Bones, Daggers, Hone (left), Two
Fragments of Gold (top, left and
bottom, right). From West. 1957

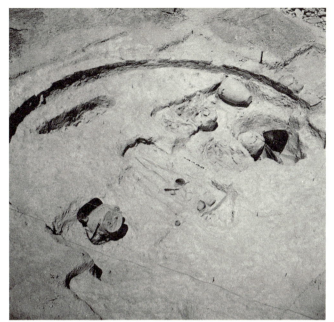

220. Grave Circle from
Southwest. 1957

221. Grave Circle from
East-Southeast. 1957

222. Grave Circle from
North. 1957

223. Exploratory Trenches Southwest of Grave Circle.
From Southeast. 1958

224. Exploratory Trenches Southwest of Grave Circle.
From South of West. 1958

1

2   2

2

2   2

2   3

5

4

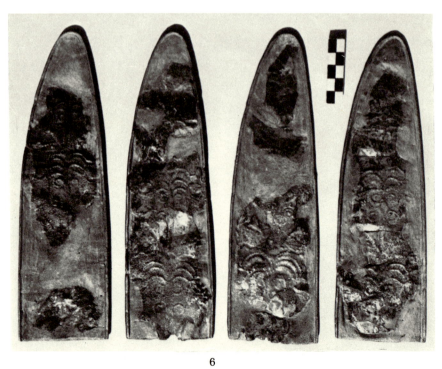

6

225. Grave Circle: Miscellaneous Objects of Gold (Nos. 1-2), Silver (Nos. 4, 6), and Ivory (Nos. 3, 5)

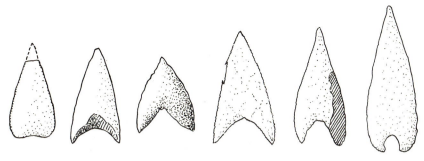

Type I   Type II   Type III   Type IV   Type V   Type VI

226. Typical Arrowheads of Flint and Obsidian from Tholos IV

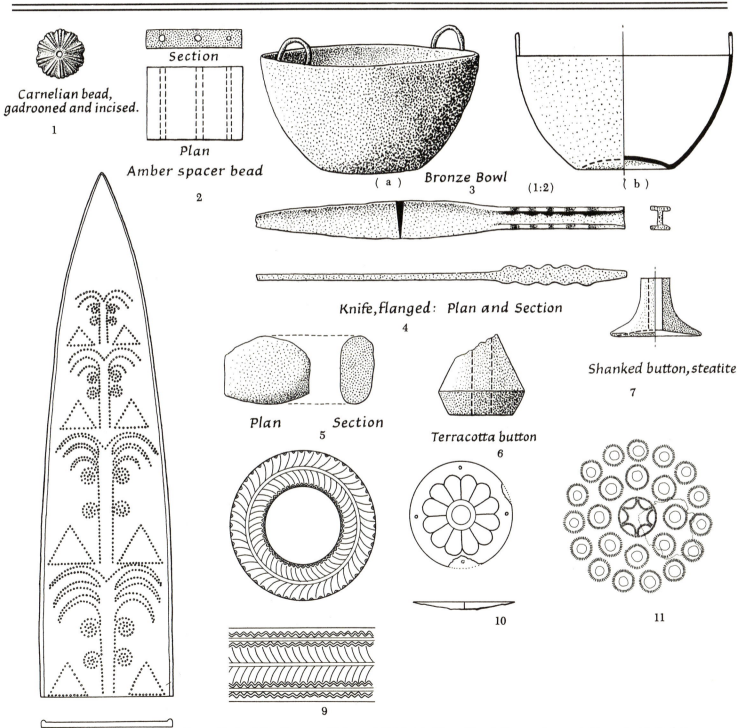

Carnelian bead,
gadrooned and incised.
1

Section

Plan

Amber spacer bead
2

Bronze Bowl
(a)   3   (1:2)   (b)

Knife, flanged: Plan and Section
4

Plan   Section
5

Terracotta button
6

Shanked button, steatite
7

8

9

10

11

227. Grave Circle: Miscellaneous Objects of Gold (9), Silver (8, 11), Bronze (3, 4, 10), Stone (1, 7), Amber
(2, 5), and Terracotta (6) (drawings by H. A. Shelley [Nos. 1-7] and A. C. Evans [Nos. 8-11]
based on sketches by W. D. Taylour)

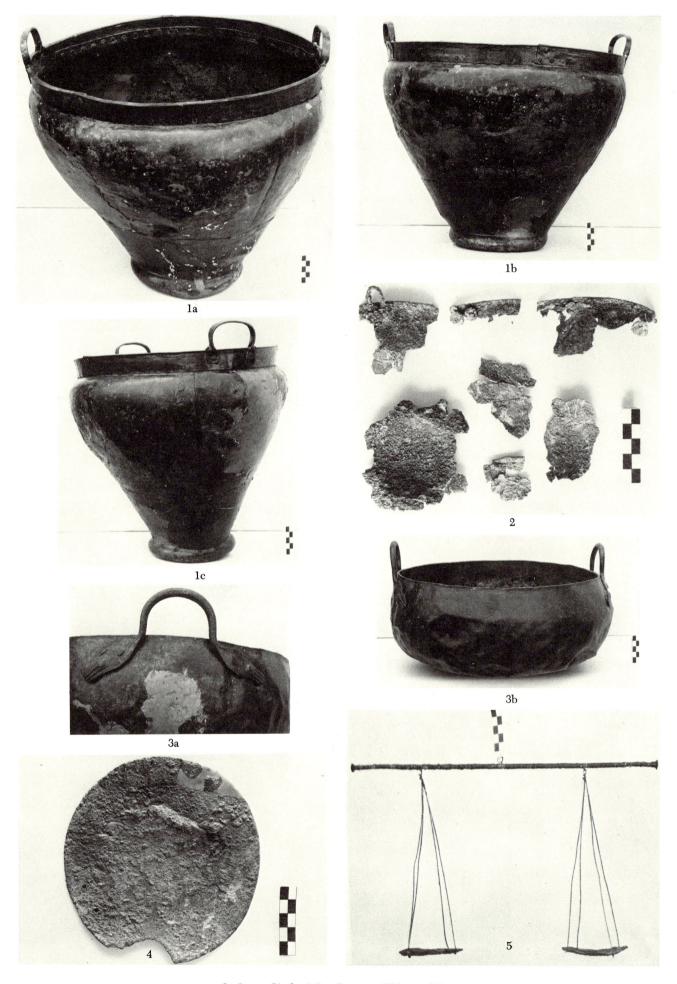

1a

1b

1c

2

3a

3b

4

5

228. Grave Circle: Miscellaneous Objects of Bronze

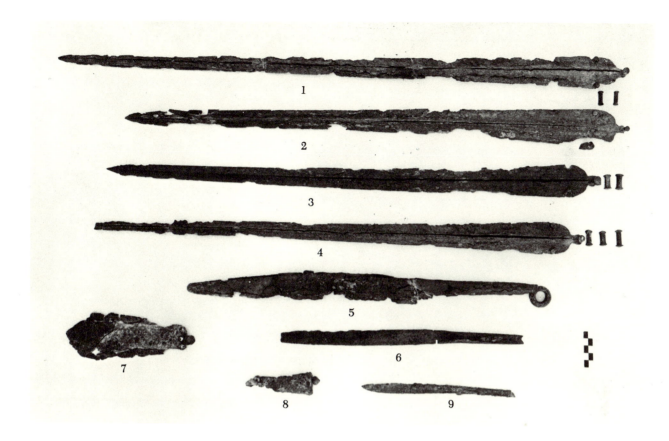

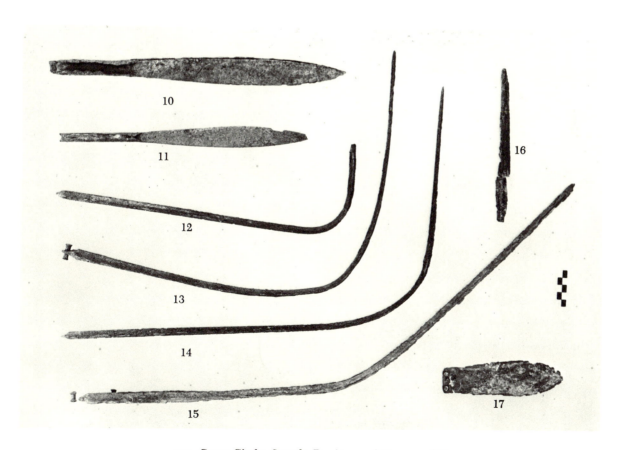

229. Grave Circle: Swords, Rapiers, and Daggers of Bronze

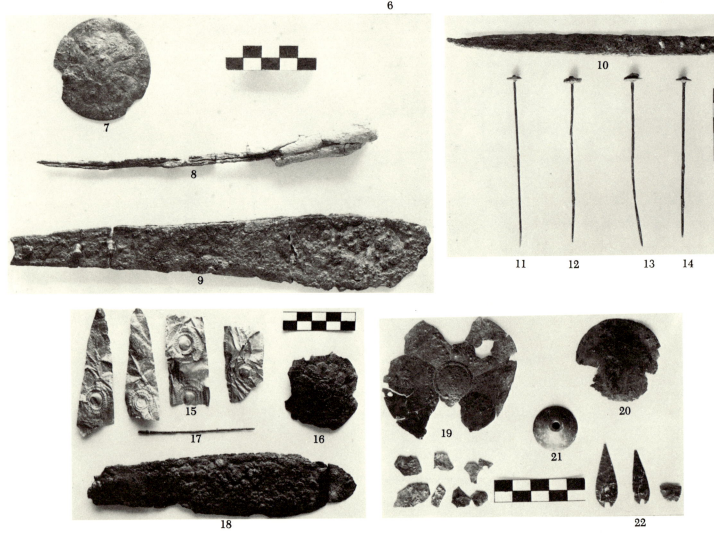

230. Grave Circle: Miscellaneous Objects

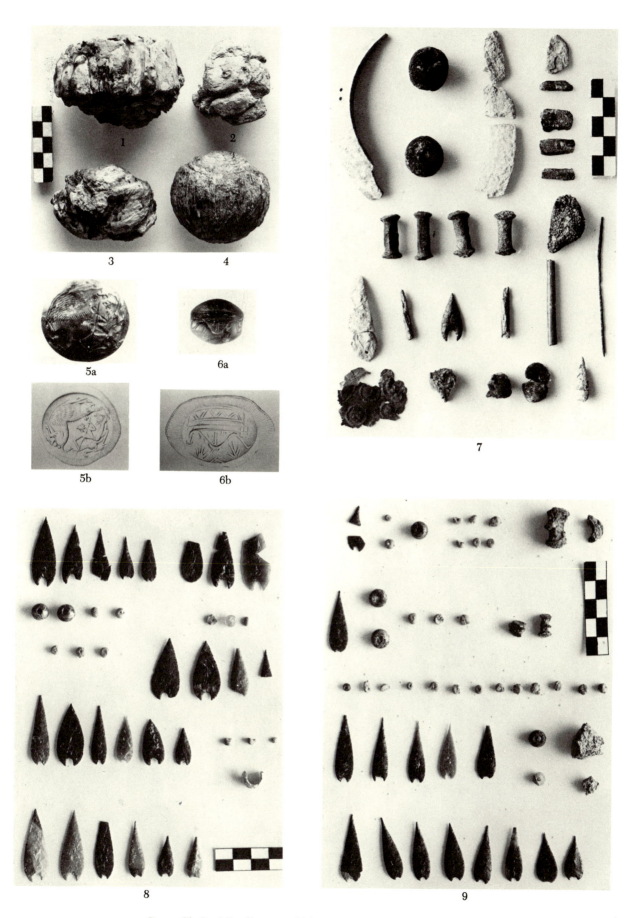

231. Grave Circle: Miscellaneous Objects (drawings by Piet de Jong)

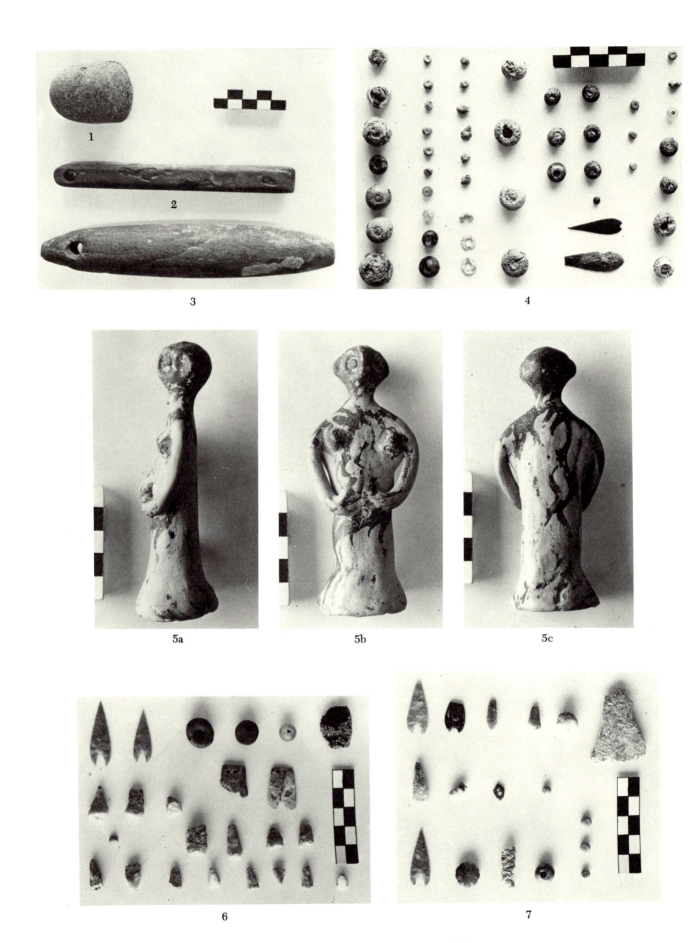

1

2

3

4

5a   5b   5c

6   7

232. Grave Circle: Miscellaneous Objects

1   2   3

4a   4b   4c

5a   5b   6

233. Grave Circle: Burial Jars (Nos. 1, 2, 4, 5) and Bases of Other Pots (Nos. 3, 6)

234. Grave Circle: Pots (except No. 6 found in Tomb K-1)

235. Grave Circle: Pots (water colors by Piet de Jong)

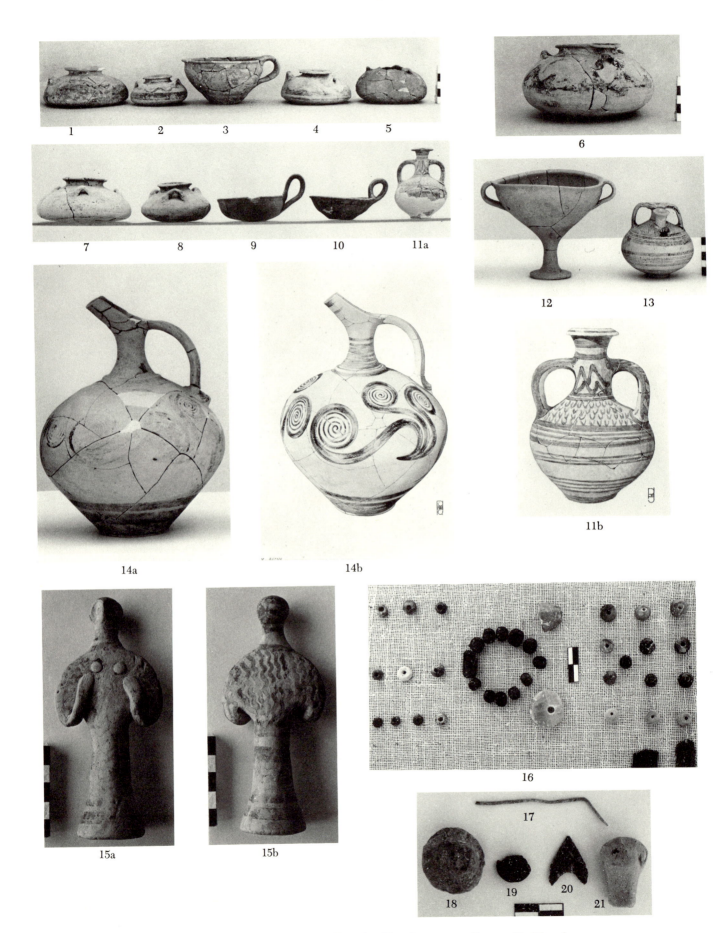

236. Pots and Miscellaneous Objects: Trial Trenches Nos. 6, 17, 19-21; Dromos E-2 No. 18;
Grave E-3 Nos. 1-5; Tomb E-4 Nos. 7-16 (water colors by Piet de Jong)

237. Tomb E-4: Dromos and Doorway. From South. 1956

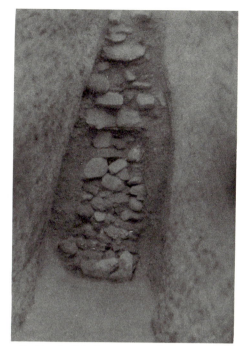

238. Tomb E-6: Doorway and Blocking Wall.
From South-Southeast. 1957

239. Tomb E-6: Burial E and Pots in Eastern Side of Chamber.
From North-Northwest. 1957

240. Tomb E-6: Burial H and Pots. From Southwest. 1957

241. Tomb E-6: Burials F, G, and I.
From North-Northeast. 1957

242. Tomb E-6: Miscellaneous Objects

243. Tomb E-6: Miscellaneous Objects

244. Tomb E-6: Pots (water colors by Piet de Jong)

245. Tomb E-8: Dromos. From North End, above Doorway. 1966

246. Tomb E-8: Doorway and Blocking Wall; Walled Niches on Each Side of Dromos. From South. 1966

247. Tomb E-8: Doorway and Blocking Wall, Niche in West Wall. From South. 1966

248. Tomb E-8: Burials and Pots in Chamber. From East and Above. 1966

1 2 3

4 5 6

7 8 9

10 11

12 13 14 15

16 17 18

19 20 21

22 23 24

25 26 27 28 29

249. Tomb E-8: Pots

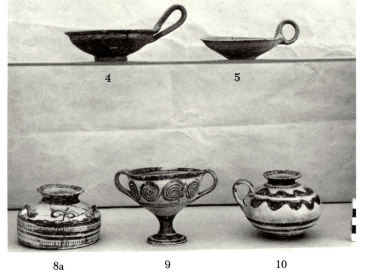

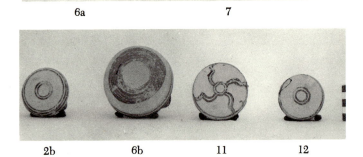

1 2a 3

6a 7

4 5

8a 9 10

16

17

18

2b 6b 11 12

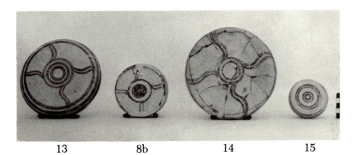

13 8b 14 15

250. Tomb E-8: Pots and Miscellaneous Objects

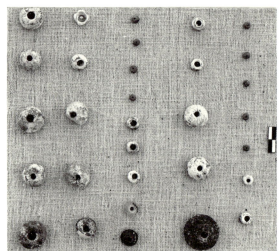

19

251. Tomb E-9: Dromos and Blocking Wall. From South. 1966

252. Tomb E-9: Dromos and Doorway. From South. 1966

253. Tomb E-9: Dromos and Blocking Wall. From South. 1966

254. Tomb E-9: Dromos and Stones Above Doorway. From Southwest. 1966

255. Tomb E-9: Blocking Wall in Doorway. From Northeast and Above. 1966

256. Tomb E-9: Two Skeletons (A, B) on East Side of Chamber. From West. 1966

257. Tomb E-9: Pits in Chamber (Pit 3 at Left, Pit 1 Center and Right). From Above. 1966

258. Tomb E-9: Group of Pots between Pits 1 and 2. From West. 1966

259. Tomb E-9: Pits in Chamber (Pit 3 at Left). From Southwest. 1966

260. Tomb E-9: Pots and Miscellaneous Objects

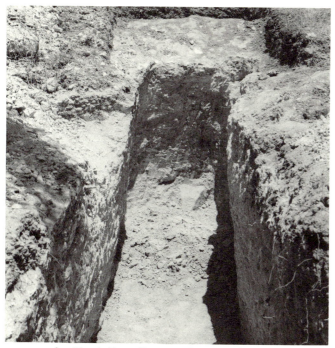

261. Tomb E-10: Dromos. From South. 1966

262. Tomb E-10: Stones over Pit in West Side of Dromos. From Northeast. 1966

263. Tomb E-10: Stones in West Side of Dromos. From Northeast. 1966

264. Tomb E-10: Niche in West Wall of Dromos. From North-Northeast. 1966

265. Tomb E-10: Pots

267. Tomb K-1: Stone Marker and Fragment of Kylix in Front of Blocking Wall. From South. 1957

268. Tomb K-1: Adze Tool Marks on Eastern Jamb of Doorway. 1957

266. Tomb K-1: Doorway and Blocking Wall. From South. 1957

269. Tomb K-1: Pottery and Bones in Southwestern Corner of Chamber. From East. 1957

270. Tomb K-1: Pottery, Bones, and Skull Lying in Northwestern Corner of Chamber. From East. 1957

271. Tomb K-1: Pottery and Bones in Northeast Corner of Chamber. From West. 1957

272. Tomb K-1: Small Pit Burial in Chamber in Front of Doorway. From North. 1957

Plan   Section

Lily Bead

273. Tomb K-1: Miscellaneous Objects of Ivory (No. 3) and Paste (Nos. 1, 2); Pots (Nos. 4-11) and Sherds (No. 12a, b) (drawing by H. A. Shelley based on sketch by W. D. Taylour)

1a   2a   3a

4   5a   6a

7   8   9   10   11

12   3b   5b   2b   6b   1b

274. Tomb K-1: Pots

275. Early Walls under *Aloni* on Deriziotis Property. From Southeast. 1958

276. Early Walls under *Aloni* on Deriziotis Property. General View from Northwest. 1958

277. Early Hearths under *Aloni* on Deriziotis Property. From Southwest. 1958

278. Pebble Floor and Pithos Fragments under *Aloni* on Deriziotis Property. From North and Above. 1958

13b *EH Button*

279. Miscellaneous Objects Found with Early Walls under *Aloni* on Deriziotis Property
(drawing by H. A. Shelley based on sketch by W. D. Taylour)

280. Chamber Tomb K-2: Blocking
Wall Filling Doorway.
From West. 1958

281. Tomb K-2: Lower Courses of
Original Blocking Wall.
From West. 1958

282. Tomb K-2: Excavation of Chamber from
Above. From Northeast. 1959

283. Tomb K-2: Pots in Center of
Chamber (Groups I and Ia).
From South. 1959

284. Tomb K-2, Center of Chamber:
Skeleton of Child.
From West. 1959

285. Tomb K-2, Southwestern Part of Chamber:
Bronze Vessel on Edge of Bone Pit.
From East. 1959

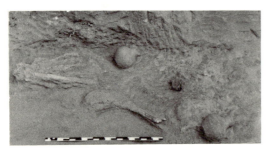

286. Tomb K-2, North Part of Chamber: Two
Jugs with Lower Burial. From South. 1959

288. Tomb K-2, South Part of Chamber:
Bone Pit (continuing Fig. 285).
From East. 1959

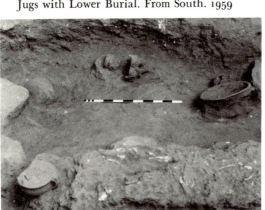

287. Tomb K-2, North Part of Chamber: Pots and
Skeleton of Child in Foreground. From South. 1959

289. Tomb K-2: Fragmentary Krater with Hunting Scene from Dromos (drawing by Piet de Jong)

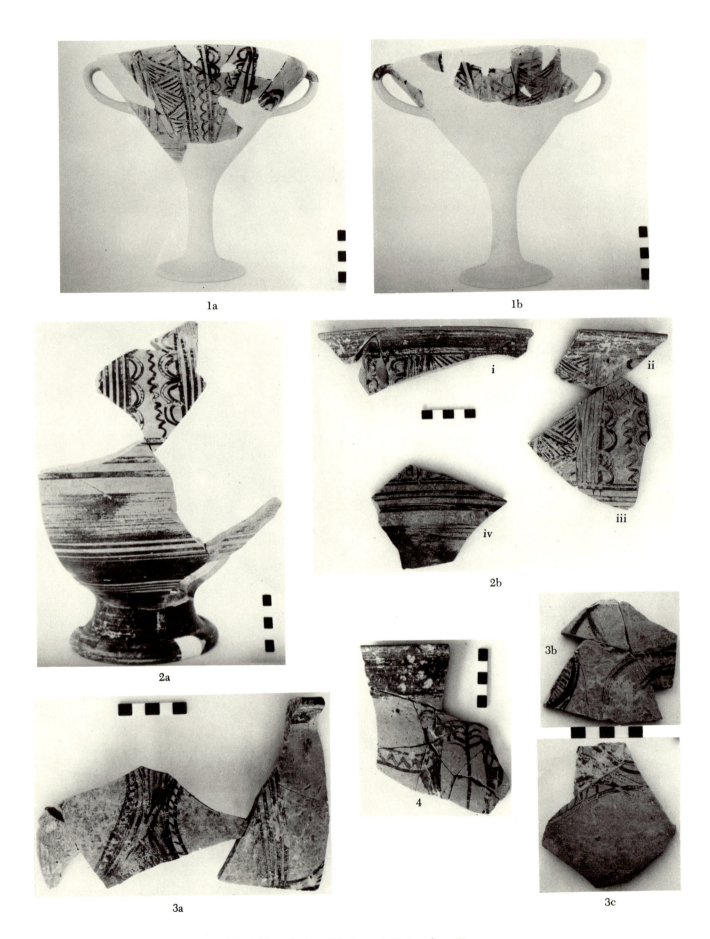

1a

1b

2a

2b

i

ii

iii

iv

3a

4

3b

3c

290. Tomb K-2: Sherds of Kylix and Kraters from Dromos

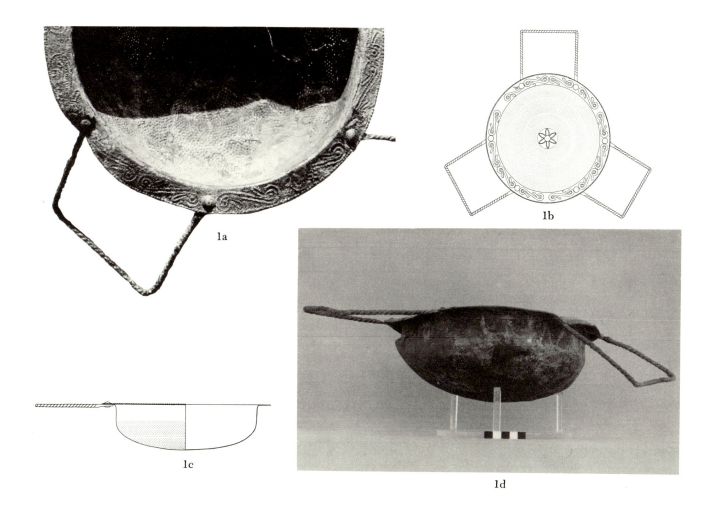

1a

1b

1c

1d

1e

291. Tomb K-2: Bronze Vessel and Miscellaneous Objects from Chamber (drawings by A. C. Evans)

292. Tomb K-2: Pots from Chamber (No. 6 from Tomb E-6)

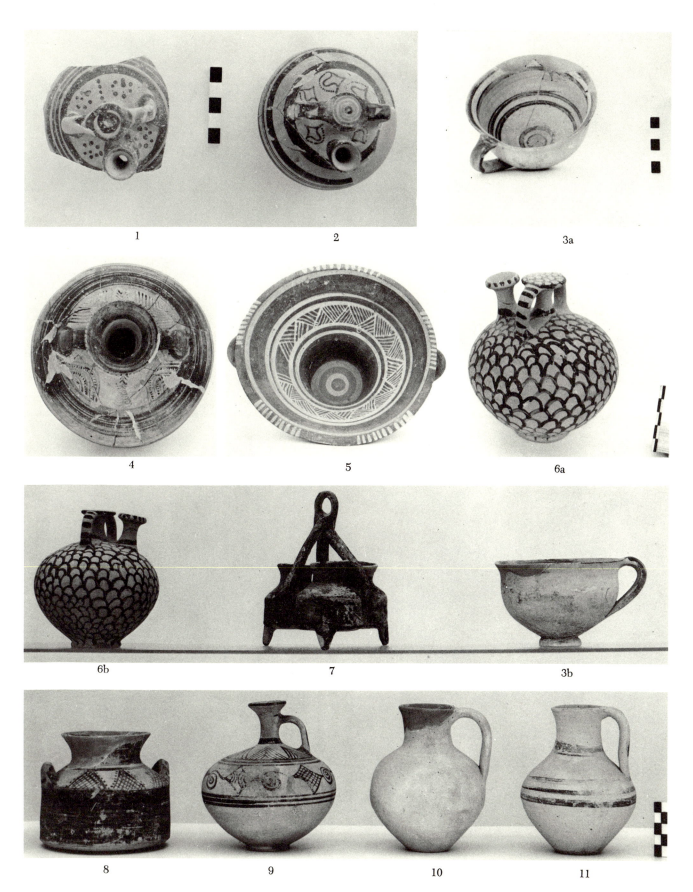

1 2 3a

4 5 6a

6b 7 3b

8 9 10 11

293. Tomb K-2: Pots from Chamber

294. Protogeometric Tholos Tomb after Excavation. From West. 1958

295. Protogeometric Tholos Tomb before Excavation.
From West. 1958

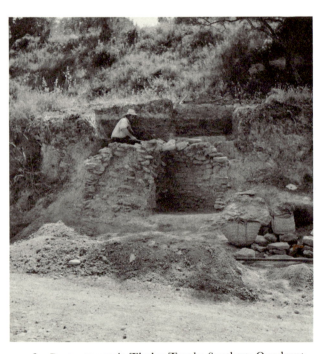

296. Protogeometric Tholos Tomb: Southern Quadrant
Cleared. From West. 1958

297. Protogeometric Tholos Tomb: Fragment of Skull
and Pots on Floor in Southern Quadrant.
From Southwest. 1958

298. Protogeometric Tholos Tomb: Miscellaneous Objects and Pots

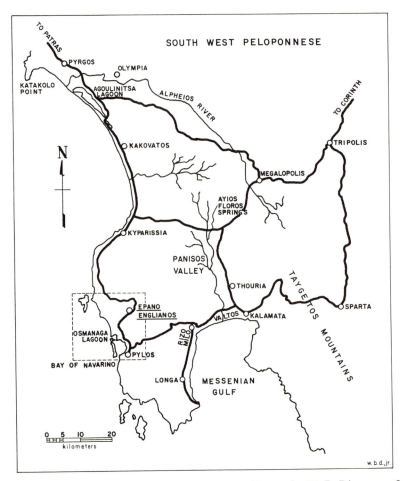

299. Sketch Map of Southwestern Peloponnesos (Drawn by W. B. Dinsmoor, Jr.)

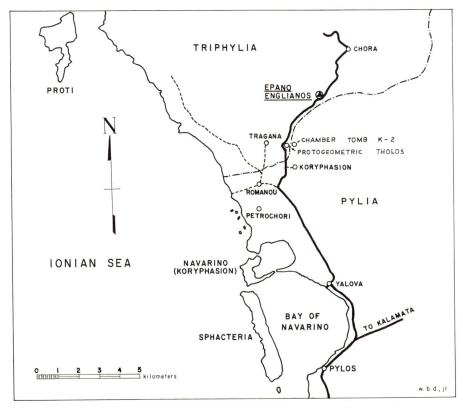

300. Sketch Map of Western Messenia (drawn by W. B. Dinsmoor, Jr.)

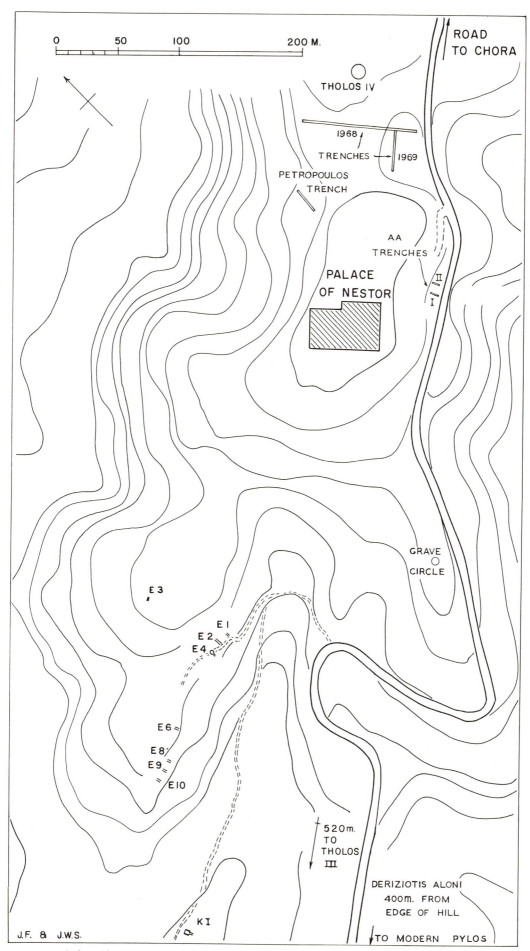

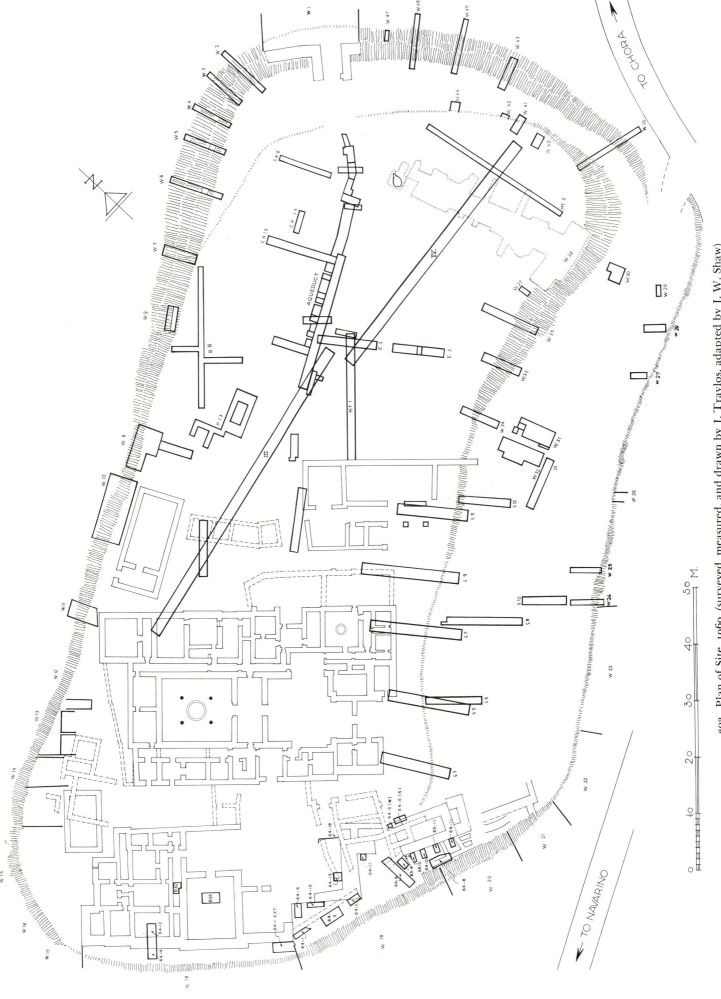

302. Plan of Site. 1960 (surveyed, measured, and drawn by J. Travlos, adapted by J. W. Shaw)

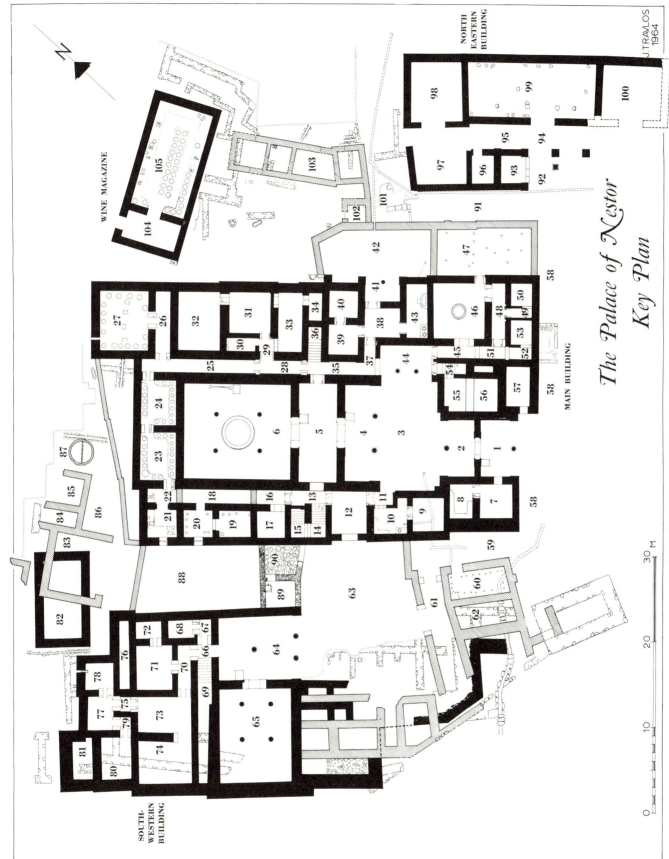

N

NORTH
EASTERN
BUILDING

98

99

100

97

95

94

96

93

92

91

101

102

42

47

58

J. TRAVLOS
1964

WINE MAGAZINE

105

104

103

27

26

32

31

30

29

28

25

24

23

22

21

20

19

18

17

16

15

14

13

12

11

10

9

8

7

41

34

40

33

36

39

35

37

38

43

44

45

46

48

49

50

51

52

53

54

55

56

57

58

6

5

4

3

2

1

58

59

60

61

62

63

64

65

66

67

68

69

70

71

72

73

74

75

76

77

78

79

80

81

82

83

84

85

86

87

88

89

90

MAIN BUILDING

The Palace of Nestor
Key Plan

SOUTH-
WESTERN
BUILDING

0   10   20   30 M.

303. Palace of Nestor, Key Plan (drawn by J. Travlos)

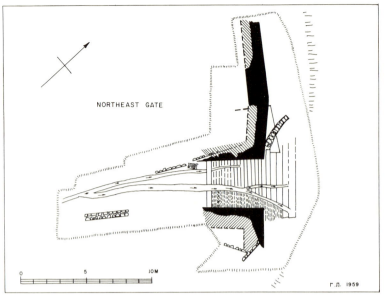

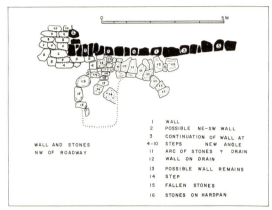

305. Detail of Northeast Gate (adapted by
A. C. Evans and J. W. Shaw
from sketch by M. Rawson)

304. Northeast Gate (drawn by G. Papathanasopoulos,
adapted by J. W. Shaw)

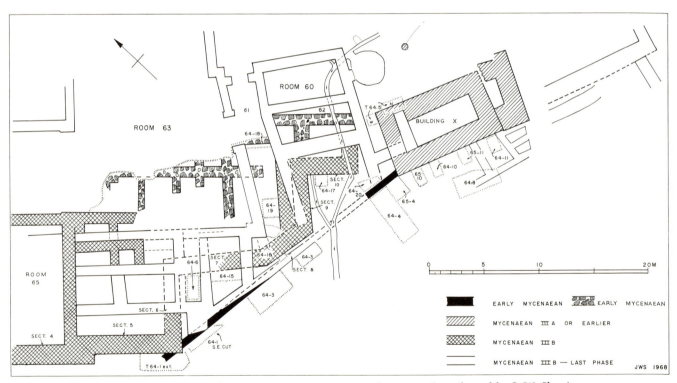

306. Southwestern Area of Hill (drawn by G. Papathanasopoulos, adapted by J. W. Shaw)

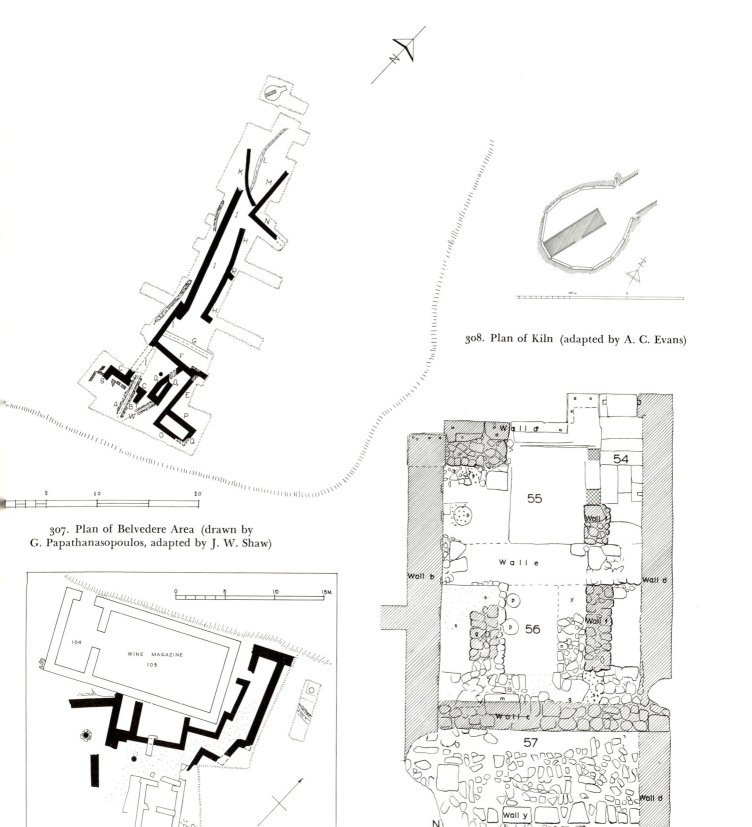

307. Plan of Belvedere Area (drawn by
G. Papathanasopoulos, adapted by J. W. Shaw)

308. Plan of Kiln (adapted by A. C. Evans)

310. Walls Northeast of Propylon
(drawn by M. Rawson, adapted by H. Athanasiades)

309. Area between Wine Magazine and Northeastern Building
(measured and drawn by J. Travlos, adapted by J. W. Shaw)

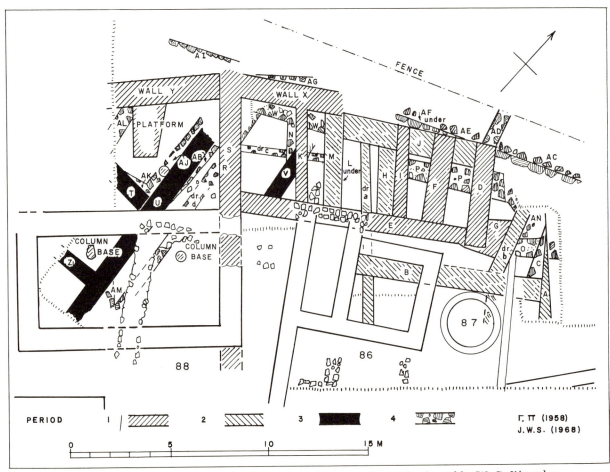

311. Area Northwest of Palace (drawn by G. Papathanasopoulos 1958, adapted by W. G. Kittredge and J. W. Shaw)

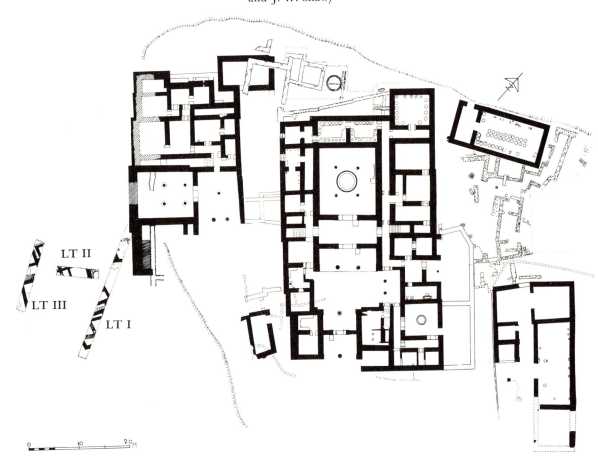

312. Plan of Palace and Trenches in Lower Town (measured and drawn by D. R. Theocharis 1959, additions by G. Papathanasopoulos)

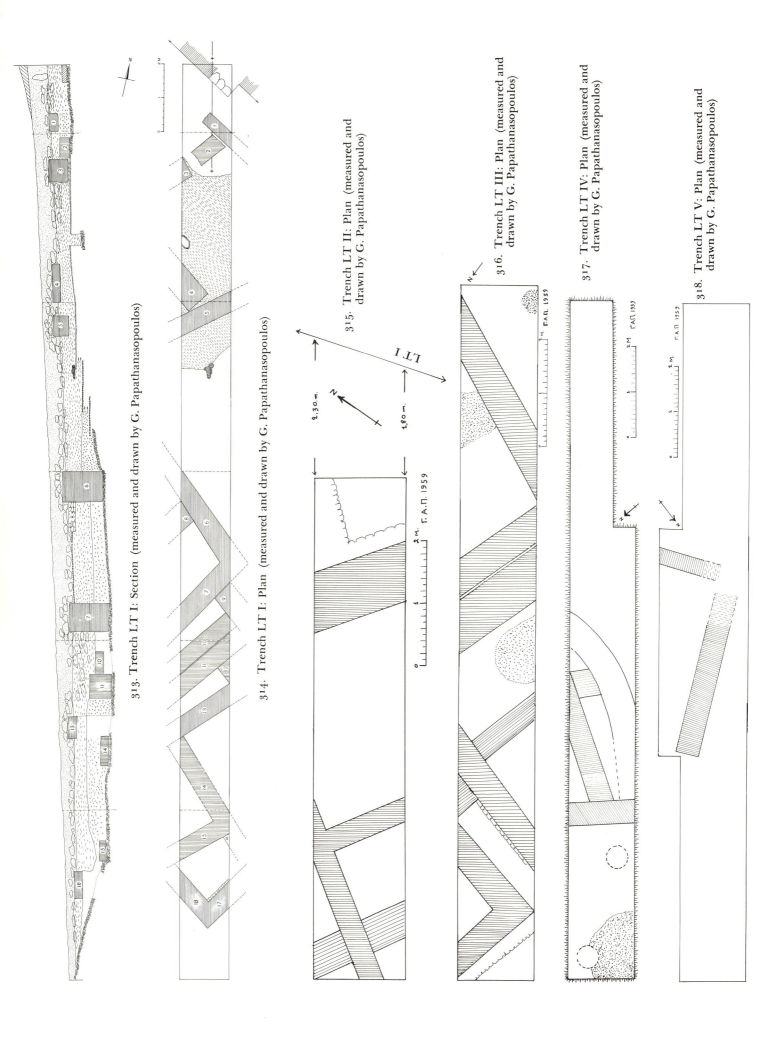

313. Trench LT I: Section (measured and drawn by G. Papathanasopoulos)

314. Trench LT I: Plan (measured and drawn by G. Papathanasopoulos)

315. Trench LT II: Plan (measured and drawn by G. Papathanasopoulos)

316. Trench LT III: Plan (measured and drawn by G. Papathanasopoulos)

317. Trench LT IV: Plan (measured and drawn by G. Papathanasopoulos)

318. Trench LT V: Plan (measured and drawn by G. Papathanasopoulos)

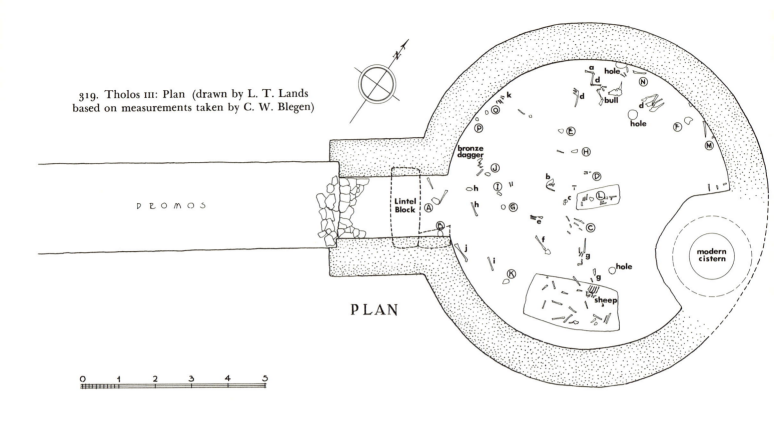

319. Tholos III: Plan (drawn by L. T. Lands based on measurements taken by C. W. Blegen)

DROMOS

Lintel Block

bronze dagger

bull

hole

hole

hole

hole

hole

modern cistern

sheep

PLAN

0 1 2 3 4 5

STRATIFIED DEPOSIT

SECTION

320. Tholos III: Section (drawn by L. T. Lands based on measurements taken by C. W. Blegen)

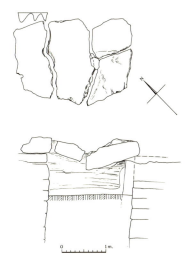

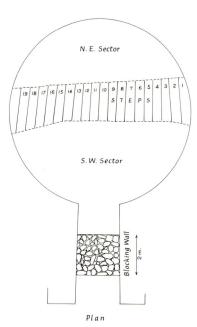

321. Plan and Section of Lintel Looking Northeast

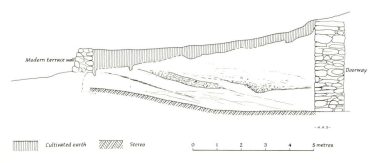

Modern terrace wall

Doorway

||||| Cultivated earth   Stereo   0 1 2 3 4 5 metres

324. Section of Dromos Looking Northwest

322. Plan Showing Northeastern and Southwestern Sectors

N. E. Sector

19 18 17 16 15 14 13 12 11 10 9 8 7 6 5 4 3 2 1
S T E P S

S. W. Sector

Blocking Wall

2 m.

Plan

(Looking NW)   0 1 2 m.   ----- Line of tholos wall   ///// Blocking wall

325. Section of Inner Doorway Looking Northwest

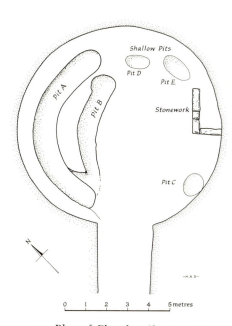

Shallow Pits

Pit D   Pit E

Pit A   Pit B   Stonework

Pit C

N   0 1 2 3 4 5 metres

323. Plan of Chamber Showing Pits

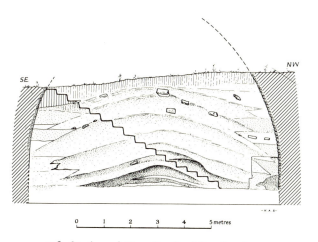

SE   NW

0 1 2 3 4 5 metres

326. Section of Chamber Looking Southwest

321-326. Tholos IV: Plans and Sections (drawn by D. R. Theocharis, adapted by H. A. Shelley)

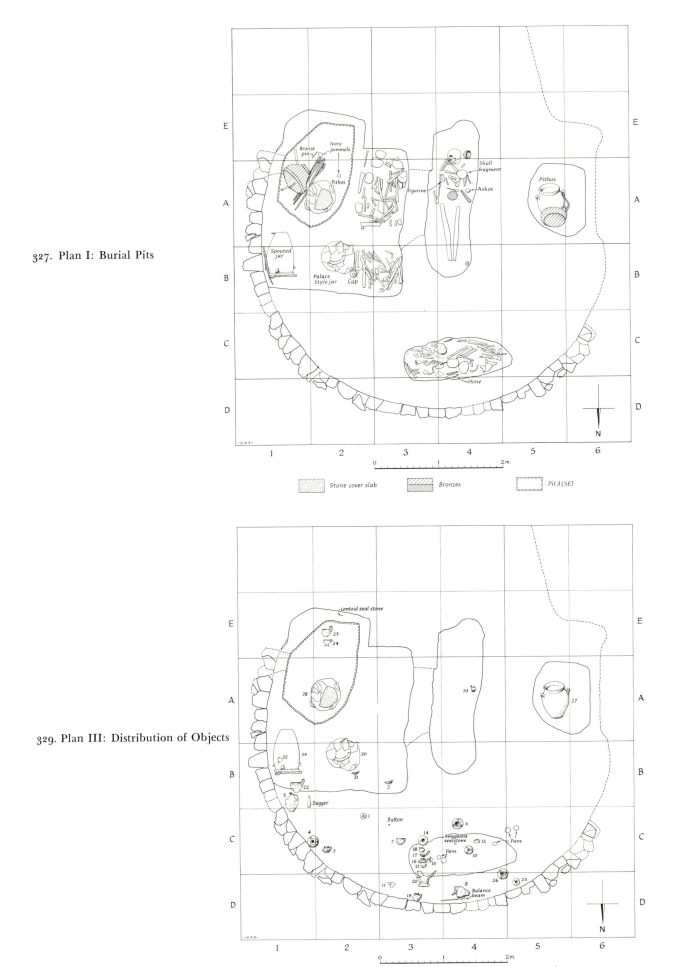

327. Plan I: Burial Pits

329. Plan III: Distribution of Objects

327, 329. Grave Circle: Plans I and III (drawn by W. D. Taylour, adapted by H. A. Shelley)

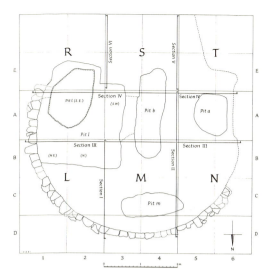

328. Plan II, Showing Trenches and
Position of Sections

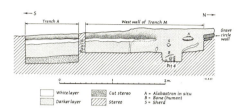

330. Section I, Looking West

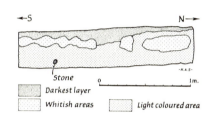

331. Section II. Looking West

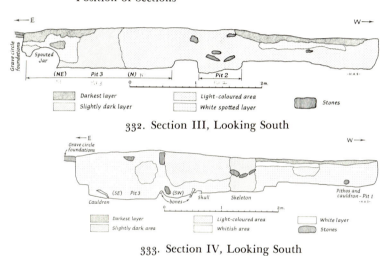

332. Section III, Looking South

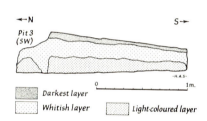

334. Section V, Looking West

333. Section IV, Looking South

335. Section VI, Looking West

328, 330-335. Grave Circle: Plan II and Sections (drawn by W. D. Taylour, adapted by H. A. Shelley)

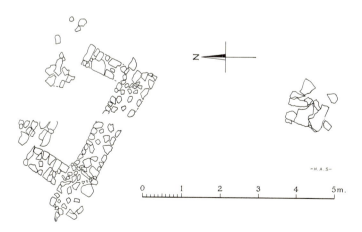

336. Plan of Walls Southwest of Grave Circle
(drawn by W. D. Taylour, adapted by H. A. Shelley)

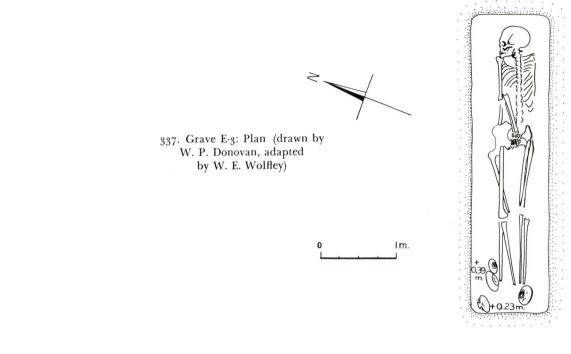

337. Grave E-3: Plan (drawn by
W. P. Donovan, adapted
by W. E. Wolfley)

N

0   1m.

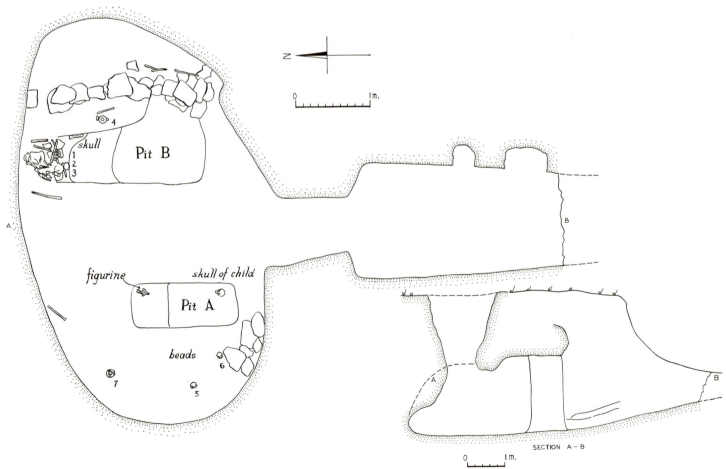

N

0   1m.

skull

Pit B

4

1
2
3

figurine   skull of child

Pit A

beads

6

7   5

A

B

B

SECTION A – B

0   1m.

338. Tomb E-4: Plan and Section (drawn by W. P. Donovan, adapted by W. E. Wolfley)

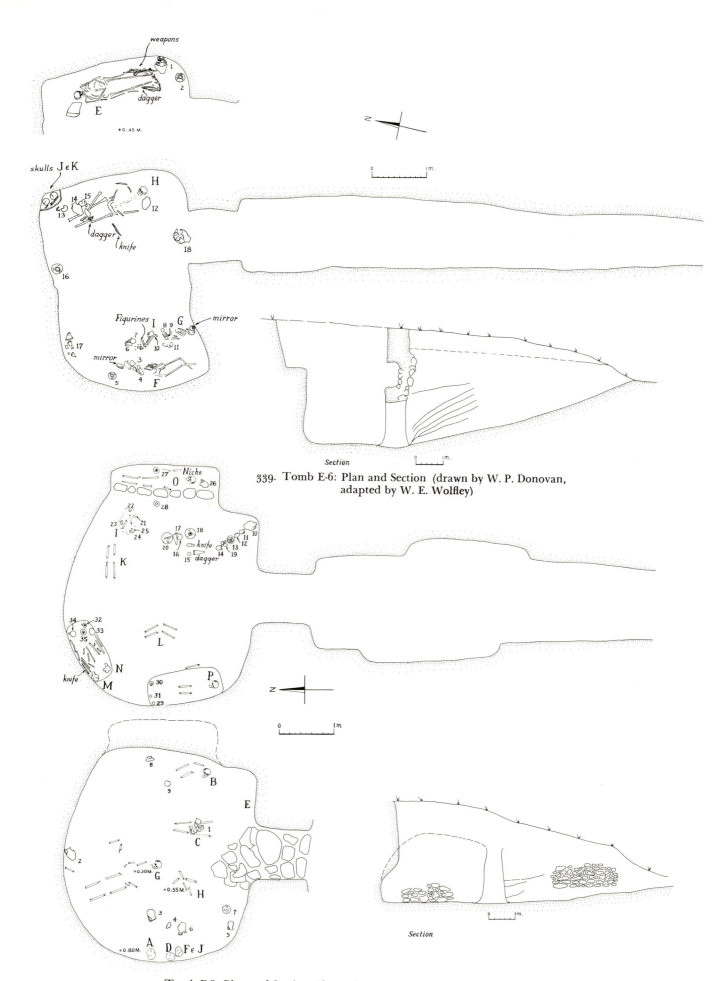

339. Tomb E-6: Plan and Section (drawn by W. P. Donovan, adapted by W. E. Wolfley)

340. Tomb E-8: Plan and Section (drawn by W. P. Donovan, adapted by W. E. Wolfley)

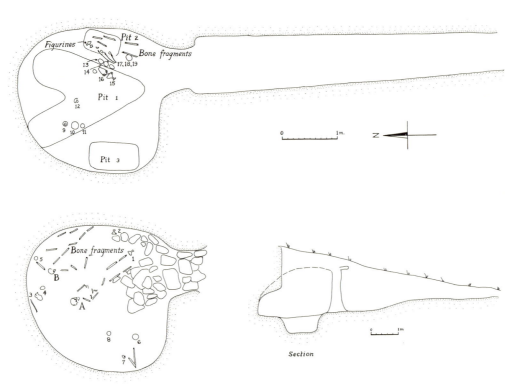

341. Tomb E-9: Plan and Section (drawn by W. P. Donovan, adapted by W. E. Wolfley)

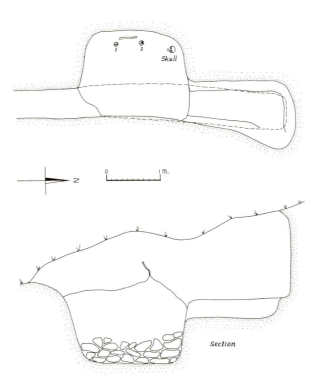

342. Tomb E-10: Plan and Section (drawn by W. P. Donovan, adapted by W. E. Wolfley)

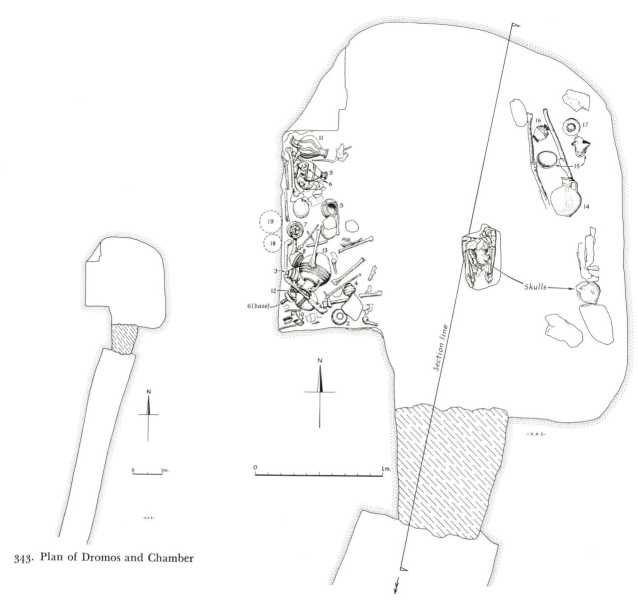

343. Plan of Dromos and Chamber

344. Plan of Chamber Showing Location
of Pots and Bones

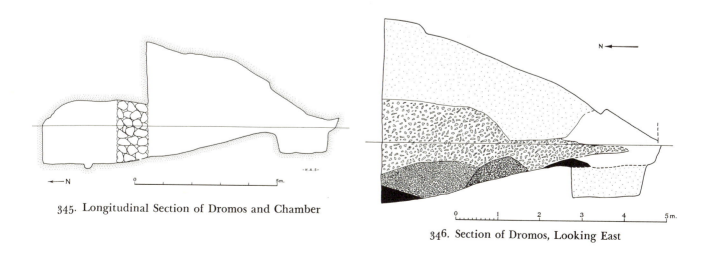

345. Longitudinal Section of Dromos and Chamber

346. Section of Dromos, Looking East

343-346. Tomb K-1: Plans and Sections (drawn by W. D. Taylour and J. Benson [Fig. 344],
adapted by H. A. Shelley)

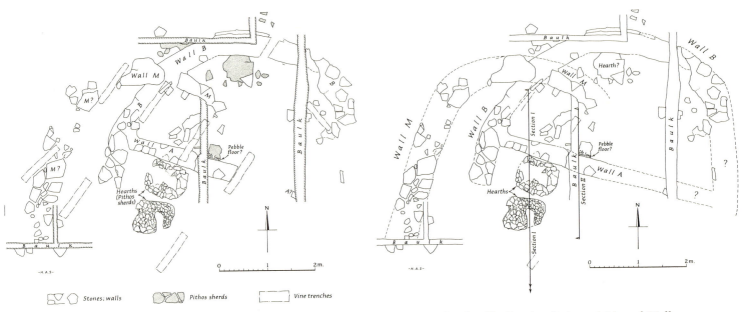

347. Early Walls: Plan I

348. Plan II: Showing Presumed Line of Walls and Position of Sections

Stones; walls   Pithos sherds   Vine trenches

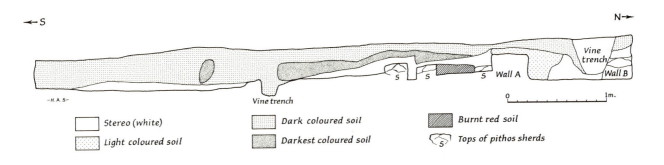

Stereo (white)   Dark coloured soil   Burnt red soil

Light coloured soil   Darkest coloured soil   Tops of pithos sherds

349. Section I, Looking West

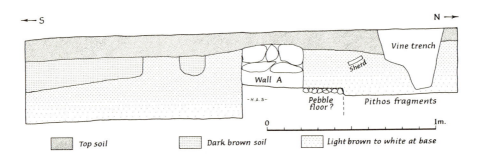

Top soil   Dark brown soil   Light brown to white at base

350. Section II, Looking West

347-350. Excavations under *Aloni* on Deriziotis Property (drawn by W. D. Taylour, adapted by H. A. Shelley)

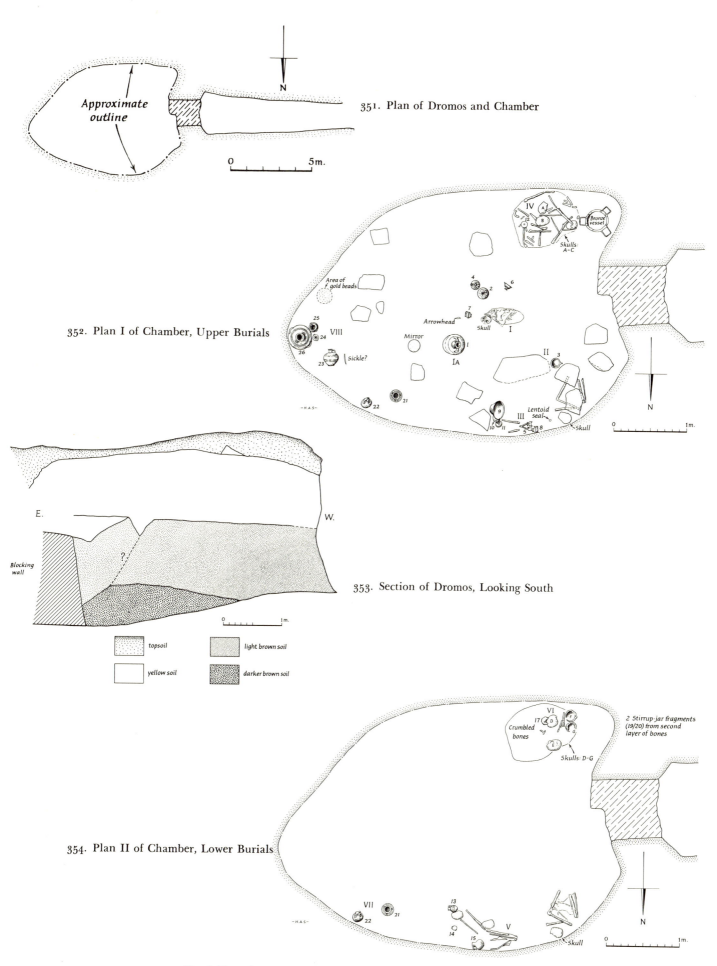

351. Plan of Dromos and Chamber

352. Plan I of Chamber, Upper Burials

353. Section of Dromos, Looking South

topsoil

yellow soil

light brown soil

darker brown soil

354. Plan II of Chamber, Lower Burials

351-354. Tomb K-2: Plans and Section (drawn by W. D. Taylour, adapted by H. A. Shelley)

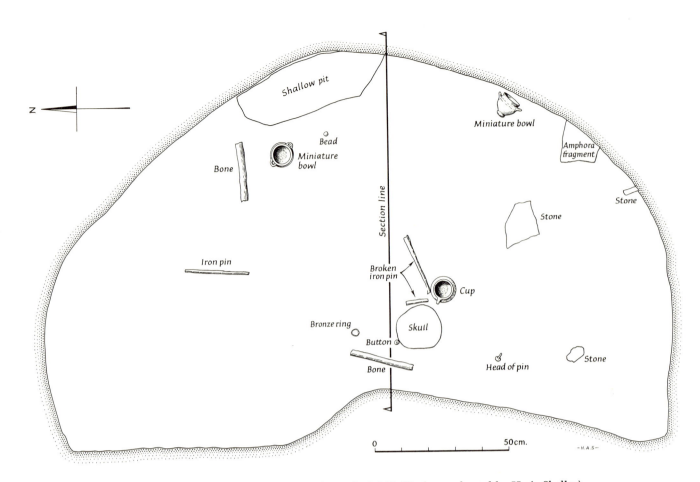

355. Protogeometric Tholos: Plan (drawn by W. D. Taylour, adapted by H. A. Shelley)

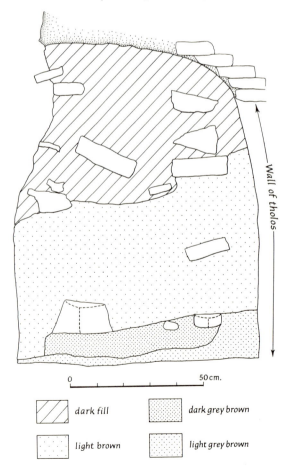

| | dark fill | | dark grey brown |
| | light brown | | light grey brown |

356. Protogeometric Tholos: Section Looking North (drawn by W. D. Taylour, adapted by H. A. Shelley)